Lecture Notes in Computer Science 14908

Founding Editors

Gerhard Goos
Juris Hartmanis

AF166326

The series Lecture Notes in Computer Science (LNCS), including its subseries Lecture Notes in Artificial Intelligence (LNAI) and Lecture Notes in Bioinformatics (LNBI), has established itself as a medium for the publication of new developments in computer science and information technology research, teaching, and education.

LNCS enjoys close cooperation with the computer science R & D community, the series counts many renowned academics among its volume editors and paper authors, and collaborates with prestigious societies. Its mission is to serve this international community by providing an invaluable service, mainly focused on the publication of conference and workshop proceedings and postproceedings. LNCS commenced publication in 1973.

Arunesh Sinha · Jie Fu · Quanyan Zhu ·
Tao Zhang

Editors

Decision and Game Theory for Security

15th International Conference, GameSec 2024
New York City, NY, USA, October 16–18, 2024
Proceedings

Springer

Editors
Arunesh Sinha 🆔
Rutgers University
New Brunswick, NJ, USA

Quanyan Zhu 🆔
New York University
Brooklyn, NY, USA

Jie Fu 🆔
University of Florida
Gainesville, FL, USA

Tao Zhang 🆔
Washington University in St. Louis
St. Louis, MO, USA

ISSN 0302-9743   ISSN 1611-3349 (electronic)
Lecture Notes in Computer Science
ISBN 978-3-031-74834-9   ISBN 978-3-031-74835-6 (eBook)
https://doi.org/10.1007/978-3-031-74835-6

This Springer imprint is published by the registered company Springer Nature Switzerland AG
The registered company address is: Gewerbestrasse 11, 6330 Cham, Switzerland

If disposing of this product, please recycle the paper.

Preface

The rapidly evolving information technologies have benefited society in many ways. These technologies range from ubiquitous communication to the rise of Artificial Intelligence (AI) tools. Indeed, these technologies have become essential for individuals, communities, businesses, and society in general. However, the same technologies present risks originating from malicious actors. There are two facets to such risk (1) the technologies are themselves vulnerable to attacks, and (2) sometimes the technologies enable attackers to conduct attacks with ease. Addressing such risk is a significant challenge.

First, the notion of perfect (or nearly perfect) security has proven to be unachievable in the real world. Indeed, the attack surface is so large in real-world systems that securing all parts is nearly impossible. Further, clever adversaries employ sophisticated schemes to exploit weaknesses in any cyber-system. This motivates the notion of minimizing risk rather than eliminating risk. Game theory is an apt tool for such analysis.

Modern game theory provides a framework to reason about an adversary (and a defender) in terms of cost, observability, and other strategic considerations. It allows reasoning from a control, mechanism design, incentive analysis, economics, or AI perspective. Recent advances in AI and machine learning have also led to interesting work at the intersection of AI and game theory, with various works focusing on game models of security of AI and various AI tools used in strategic reasoning.

Since its first edition in 2010, GameSec has attracted novel, high-quality theoretical and practical contributions. This year also continued the tradition. Over the years, GameSec has expanded its focus from traditional game theory to modern game theory with influences from various research communities including AI, control, economics, behavioral science, and more. The conference program included 15 full and two extended abstract papers as well as one presentation-only work. Reviews were conducted on 27 submitted papers, of which two were invited papers. Reviews were single-blind, and submissions received two reviews on average. The selected papers were geographically diverse, with many international and transcontinental authorship teams.

GameSec 2024 featured two keynote speakers who explored future research directions at the intersection of Game theory/AI and cybersecurity. David Nicol from the University of Illinois at Urbana-Champaign addressed emerging cybersecurity challenges and discussed how new AI tools and theoretical frameworks can help mitigate these threats. Cleotilde Gonzalez from Carnegie Mellon University highlighted the pivotal role of human behavior in cybersecurity, emphasizing the need to model and understand human vulnerabilities. These vulnerabilities are crucial to securing increasingly complex networks and systems, as they introduce new layers of risk that expand the attack surface. Addressing these open challenges requires innovative theoretical modeling and design methods, and calls for the active engagement of the next generation of researchers.

The themes of the conference this year were broad and encompassed work in the areas of systems security, security economics, equilibrium and control computation. network and privacy, adversarial machine learning, and cyber-physical systems. Each area took on critical challenges including the detection/mitigation problems associated with several specific attacks on cyber systems, exploring the economics of cyber extortion and bitcoin mining and the impact of generative AI on content creation, fundamental results in multi-player game equilibrium computation as well as in robust control and equilibrium computation in a game model of logistics, novel usages of strategic deception, games played on networks and game analysis of anonymous messaging, adversarial machine learning focusing on aspects of membership inference attacks, and work in cyber-physical systems focusing on anomaly detection and advanced persistent threats.

Overall, the conference presented many novel contributions and directly impacted the consideration of security in a wide range of settings, including generative AI, adversarial machine learning, cyber extortion, automated pen testing and defense, bitcoin, advanced persistent threats (APT), cyber-physical systems, deception, and logistics.

We would like to thank Springer for its continued support of the GameSec conference and for publishing the proceedings as part of their Lecture Notes in Computer Science (LNCS) series. We hope that not only security researchers but also practitioners and policy makers will benefit from this edition.

October 2024

Arunesh Sinha
Jie Fu
Quanyan Zhu
Tao Zhang

Organization

General Chair

Quanyan Zhu   New York University, USA

Technical Program Committee Chairs

Arunesh Sinha   Rutgers University, USA
Jie Fu   University of Florida, USA

Publication Chair

Tao Zhang   Washington University in St. Louis, USA

Publicity Chair

Luyao Zhang   Duke Kunshan University, China

Web Chair

Ya-Ting Yang   New York University, USA

Steering Committee

Tansu Alpcan   University of Melbourne, Australia
John S. Baras   University of Maryland, USA
Tamer Başar   University of Illinois at Urbana-Champaign, USA
Anthony Ephremides University of Maryland, USA
Radha Poovendran   University of Washington, USA
Milind Tambe   Harvard University, USA

Advisory Committee

Fei Fang	Carnegie Mellon University, USA
Tiffany Bao	Arizona State University, USA
Branislav Bošanský	Czech Technical University in Prague, Czech Republic
Stefan Rass	Johannes Kepler University Linz, Austria
Manos Panaousis	University of Greenwich, UK
Quanyan Zhu	New York University, USA
Yezekael Hayel	Avignon University, France

Program Committee

Habtamu Abie	Norwegian Computing Centre, Norway
Palvi Aggarwal	Carnegie Mellon University, USA
Bo An	Nanyang Technological University, Singapore
Konstantin Avrachenkov	Inria, France
Carlos Barreto	KTH, Sweden
Abderrahim Benslimane	Université d'Avignon, France
Sanjay Bhattacherjee	University of Kent, UK
Siddhant Bhambri	Arizona State University, USA
Shaunak Bopardikar	Michigan State University, USA
Svetlana Boudko	NR, Russia
Andrew Clark	WPI, USA
Andrew Cullen	University of Melbourne, Australia
Edward Cranford	Carnegie Mellon University, USA
Francesco De Pellegrini	Avignon University, France
Andrey Garnaev	Rutgers University, USA
Jens Grossklags	Technical University of Munich, Germany
Robert Gutzwiller	Arizona State University, USA
Ashish Ranjan Hota	Indian Institute of Technology Kharagpur, India
Ahmed Hemida	Army Research Lab, USA
Karel Horák	Czech Technical University in Prague, Czech Republic
Murat Kantarcioglu	University of Texas at Dallas, USA
Christopher Kiekintveld	University of Texas at El Paso, USA
Abdellatif Kobbane	ENSIAS, Mohammed V University in Rabat, Morocco
Henger Li	Tulane University, USA
Christian Lebiere	Carnegie Mellon University, USA
Yee Wei Law	University of South Australia, Australia

Spiros Mancoridis	Drexel University, USA
Katerina Mitrokotsa	Chalmers University of Technology, Sweden
Shana Moothedath	Iowa State University, USA
Parinaz Naghizadeh	Ohio State University, USA
Stefan Rass	Johannes Kepler University Linz, Austria
Alexandre Reiffers	IMT, France
Palash Sarkar	Indian Statistical Institute, India
Jayneel Vora	University of California, Davis, USA
Tomàš Votroubek	Czech Technical University in Prague, Czech Republic
Yevgeniy Vorobeychik	Washington University in St. Louis, USA
Zizhan Zheng	Tulane University, USA
Quanyan Zhu	New York University, USA
Jun Zhuang	SUNY Buffalo, USA

Sponsors

New York University
Springer

Invited Talks

Learning Provably Trustworthy Control in Nonlinear Dynamical Systems

Junlin Wu [iD] and Yevgeniy Vorobeychik [iD]

Washington University in St. Louis, St. Louis, MO, 63130 USA

Learning a trustworthy controller for autonomous systems is a central issue in modern autonomy. Here, we overview our recent work that aims to develop methods for learning provably trustworthy controllers from two perspectives: *stability* and *safety*.

Learning Provably Stable Controllers [11]: Traditionally, guaranteeing stability in autonomous systems involves finding a Lyapunov function and an associated control policy. While this approach is well-established for linear systems, it presents significant challenges for nonlinear systems [7, 8]. Existing methods often use neural networks to represent Lyapunov functions but typically focus on continuous-time systems or specific classes of nonlinear dynamics [1, 4, 5, 13]. We developed a novel approach for learning neural Lyapunov control that is applicable to a broad class of *discrete-time nonlinear* systems. Our approach incorporates three innovative components: 1) a novel mixed-integer linear programming approach that verifies discrete-time Lyapunov stability conditions by leveraging their specific structure; 2) a new method for computing verified sublevel sets to enhance the precision of stability assessments; and 3) a heuristic gradient-based method for quickly identifying counterexamples, significantly speeding up training. Our experiments demonstrate that our approach significantly outperforms state-of-the-art baselines.

Learning Provably Safe Controllers [12]: Next, we delve into the problem of learning provably safe controllers for nonlinear neural network dynamics [3, 6, 10]. We developed a novel approach for learning controllers that can be verified to be safe in the sense of finite-horizon reachability proofs, while maximizing overall performance. Our approach builds on safe reinforcement learning [2, 9] and consists of three key parts. The first is a novel curriculum learning scheme that iteratively increases the verified safe horizon. Second, we leverage the iterative nature of gradient-based learning for incremental verification, reusing information from prior verification runs. Third, we learn multiple verified initialstate-dependent controllers, an idea that is especially valuable for more complex domains where learning a single universal verified safe controller is extremely challenging. Our experiments on five safe control problems demonstrate that our trained controllers can achieve verified safety over horizons that are as much as an order of magnitude longer than state-of-the-art baselines, while maintaining high reward, as well as a perfect safety record over entire episodes.

Keywords: Trustworthy AI · Learning Provably Safe Control

References

1. Abate, A., Ahmed, D., Giacobbe, M., Peruffo, A.: Formal synthesis of lyapunov neural networks. IEEE Control Syst. Lett. **5**(3), 773–778 (2020)
2. Achiam, J., Held, D., Tamar, A., Abbeel, P.: Constrained policy optimization. In: International Conference on Machine Learning, pp. 22–31. PMLR (2017)
3. Bastani, O., Pu, Y., Solar-Lezama, A.: Verifiable reinforcement learning via policy extraction. In: Advances in Neural Information Processing Systems, vol. 31 (2018)
4. Chang, Y.C., Roohi, N., Gao, S.: Neural lyapunov control. In: Neural Information Processing Systems (2019)
5. Dai, H., Landry, B., Yang, L., Pavone, M., Tedrake, R.: Lyapunov-stable neuralnetwork control. In: Robotics: Science and Systems (RSS) (2021)
6. Ivanov, R., Weimer, J., Alur, R., Pappas, G.J., Lee, I.: Verisig: verifying safety properties of hybrid systems with neural network controllers. In: Proceedings of the 22nd ACM International Conference on Hybrid Systems: Computation and Control, pp. 169–178 (2019)
7. Khalil, H.K.: Nonlinear Control, vol. 406. Pearson, New York (2015)
8. Lavaei, R., Bridgeman, L.J.: Systematic, lyapunov-based, safe and stabilizing controller synthesis for constrained nonlinear systems. IEEE Trans. Autom. Control (2023)
9. Stooke, A., Achiam, J., Abbeel, P.: Responsive safety in reinforcement learning by pid lagrangian methods. In: International Conference on Machine Learning, pp. 9133–9143. PMLR (2020)
10. Wei, T., Liu, C.: Safe control with neural network dynamic models. In: Learning for Dynamics and Control Conference, pp. 739–750. PMLR (2022)
11. Wu, J., Clark, A., Kantaros, Y., Vorobeychik, Y.: Neural lyapunov control for discrete-time systems. In: Advances in Neural Information Processing Systems, vol. 36, pp. 2939–2955 (2023)
12. Wu, J., Zhang, H., Vorobeychik, Y.: Verified safe reinforcement learning for neural network dynamic models. arXiv preprint arXiv:2405.15994 (2024)
13. Zhou, R., Quartz, T., De Sterck, H., Liu, J.: Neural lyapunov control of unknown nonlinear systems with stability guarantees. In: Neural Information Processing Systems (2022)

Bayesian Defense Against Membership Inference Attacks in Sharing Genomic Summary Statistics

Tao Zhang and Yevgeniy Vorobeychik

Washington University in St. Louis, St. Louis, MO, 63130 USA
{taoz,yvorobeychik}@wustl.edu

The rapid advancement in genomic sequencing and the widespread availability of online genomic data-sharing services have led to increased accessibility of large genomic datasets. These datasets are essential for distinguishing clinically significant genomic variations. However, sharing even summary statistics of these data poses substantial privacy risks, particularly due to membership inference attacks (MIAs), which can re-identify individuals within these datasets. Existing defenses against MIAs, such as likelihood ratio test (LRT) based methods, often assume non-adaptive attacks, which limits their effectiveness. We propose a Bayesian game-theoretic framework that models the interaction between an attacker, who aims to perform MIA, and a defender, who seeks to protect the membership privacy of the dataset. Our first contribution introduces a bounded-rational Bayesian attacker model, which we show to be more powerful than traditional LRT-based models. This attacker induces greater privacy loss for the defender, who is modeled as a von Neumann-Morgenstern (vNM) decision-maker. We demonstrate that this holds true even when the attacker has a non-informative prior, making the defense against such Bayesian attacks particularly challenging. We analytically compare the Bayesian attacks with arbitrary subjective priors to the Neyman-Pearson optimal LRT attacks under the Gaussian mechanisms. Our results show that under certain conditions, Bayesian attacks can lead to a higher worst-case privacy loss for the defender than LRT attacks, thus emphasizing the need for stronger defense mechanisms.

To address this challenge, we propose a method for approximating Bayes-Nash equilibria of the game, where the defender's and attacker's strategies are represented by deep neural networks. The defender's strategy is modeled as a neural network generator that perturbs summary statistics, while the attacker's strategy is modeled as a neural network classifier that performs membership inference. Our experiments on genomic datasets demonstrate that our game-theoretic framework significantly outperforms state-of-the-art methods [1, 2, 3, 4] in both attacking and defending, providing a more robust solution for privacy-preserving genomic data sharing. We offer a novel and robust framework for optimizing the privacy-utility tradeoff in genomic data sharing, paving the way for more secure and effective methods of data sharing in sensitive domains.

Keywords: Privacy-Utility Tradeoff · Genomic Data Sharing · Membership Inference Attacks · Bayesian Game Theory · Privacy · Deep Learning

References

1. Sankararaman, S., Obozinski, G., Jordan, M.I., Halperin, E.: Genomic privacy and limits of individual detection in a pool. Nat. Genet. **41**(9), 965–967 (2009)
2. Shringarpure, S.S., Bustamante, C.D.: Privacy risks from genomic data-sharing beacons. Am. J. Hum. Genet. **97**(5), 631–646 (2015)
3. Venkatesaramani, R., Wan, Z., Malin, B.A., Vorobeychik, Y.: Defending against membership inference attacks on beacon services. arXiv preprint arXiv:2112.13301 (2021)
4. Venkatesaramani, R., Wan, Z., Malin, B.A., Vorobeychik, Y.: Enabling trade-offs in privacy and utility in genomic data beacons and summary statistics. Genome Res. gr–277674 (2023)

Contents

Network and Privacy

Adversarial Machine Learning

Cyber-Physical Systems

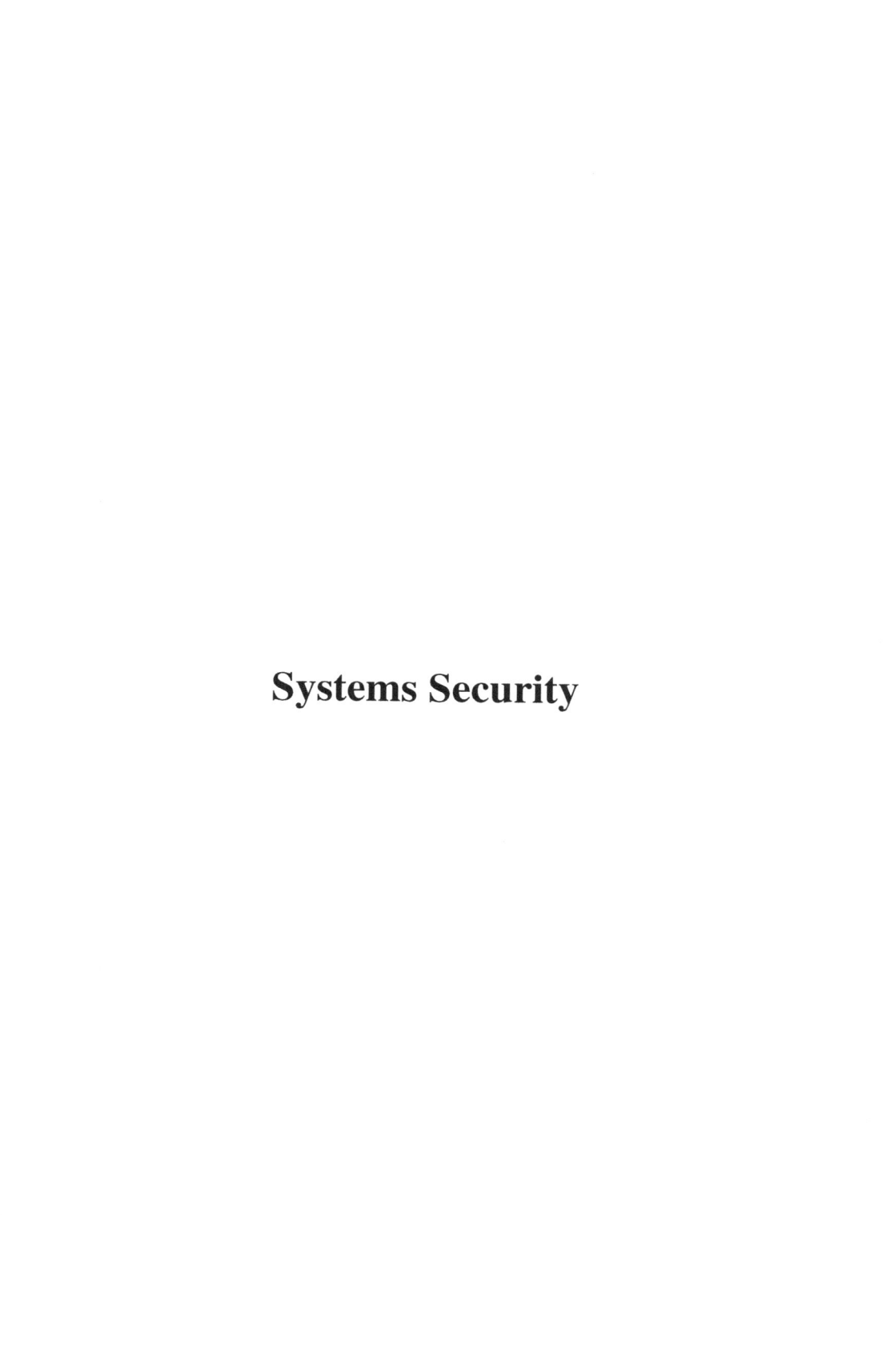

Systems Security

Intrusion Tolerance as a Two-Level Game

Kim Hammar$^{(\boxtimes)}$ and Rolf Stadler

KTH Royal Institute of Technology, Stockholm, Sweden
{kimham,stadler}@kth.se

Abstract. We formulate intrusion tolerance for a system with service replicas as a two-level game: a local game models intrusion recovery and a global game models replication control. For both games, we prove the existence of equilibria and show that the best responses have a threshold structure, which enables efficient computation of strategies. State-of-the-art intrusion-tolerant systems can be understood as instantiations of our game with heuristic control strategies. Our analysis shows the conditions under which such heuristics can be significantly improved through game-theoretic reasoning. This reasoning allows us to derive the optimal control strategies and evaluate them against 10 types of network intrusions on a testbed. The testbed results demonstrate that our game-theoretic strategies can significantly improve service availability and reduce the operational cost of state-of-the-art intrusion-tolerant systems. In addition, our game strategies can ensure any chosen level of service availability and time-to-recovery, bridging the gap between theoretical and operational performance.

Keywords: Cybersecurity · network security · intrusion tolerance · BFT · game theory · optimal control · reliability theory

1 Introduction

As our reliance on online services grows, there is increasing demand for reliable systems that provide service without disruption. Traditionally, the main causes of disruption in networked systems have been hardware failure and power outages. While tolerance against these types of failures is important, a growing source of disruptions is network intrusion.

We call a system *intrusion-tolerant* if it provides *correct service* while intrusions occur [6]. The common approach to building an intrusion-tolerant system is to replicate the system across a set of *nodes*, which allows *compromised* and *crashed* nodes to be substituted by *healthy* nodes. This approach to intrusion tolerance includes three main building blocks: (*i*) a protocol for service replication that tolerates a subset of compromised and crashed nodes; (*ii*) a replication strategy that adjusts the replication factor; and (*iii*) a recovery strategy that determines when to recover potentially compromised nodes [6].

Replication protocols that satisfy the condition in (*i*) are called *Byzantine fault-tolerant* (BFT) and have been studied extensively (see survey [7]). Few prior works have studied (*ii*) and (*iii*). Current intrusion-tolerant systems typically

A. Sinha et al. (Eds.): GameSec 2024, LNCS 14908, pp. 3–23, 2025.
https://doi.org/10.1007/978-3-031-74835-6_1

use a fixed replication factor and rely on inefficient recovery strategies, such as periodic recovery, heuristic rule-based recovery, or manual recovery by system administrators [7].

In this paper, we address the above limitations and present a game-theoretic model that allows us to characterize optimal recovery and replication strategies for intrusion-tolerant systems. (This paper builds on our earlier *control-theoretic* work on intrusion tolerance [15].) Our model assumes a set of nodes that collectively offer a service to a client population (see Fig. 1.a). This service is also accessible to an attacker who attempts to compromise nodes. Each node is segmented into two domains: an application domain, which runs a service replica, and a privileged domain, which runs security and control functions (see Fig. 1.b). The replicas are coordinated through a replication protocol that guarantees correct service if no more than f nodes are compromised or crashed simultaneously. To prevent the number of compromised and crashed nodes from exceeding f, the system employs automatic control techniques to determine when to recover service replicas and when to add or evict nodes.

We formulate the scenario described above as a game with two levels: local and global. The local game involves *node controllers* that independently perform intrusion recovery, and the global game involves a *system controller* that manages the replication factor (see Fig. 1.a). Both games are modeled as stochastic zero-sum games and incorporate safety constraints. We prove the existence of constrained perfect Bayesian and Markov equilibria in the local and global games, respectively. We also derive a threshold structure of the best responses, which enables efficient computation of strategies. To assess the performance of the equilibrium strategies, we evaluate them against 10 types of network intrusions on a testbed. The results show that the equilibrium strategies can significantly improve service availability and reduce the operational cost of state-of-the-art intrusion-tolerant systems. Moreover, the equilibrium strategies provide guarantees that ensure a chosen level of service availability and time-to-recovery.

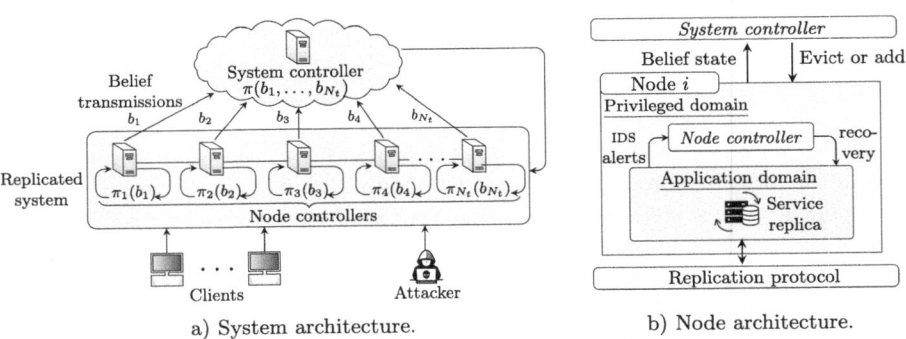

a) System architecture.   b) Node architecture.

Fig. 1. Node controllers with strategies $\pi_1, \ldots, \pi_{N_t}$ compute belief states $b_1, \ldots, b_{N_t}$ and make local recovery decisions; a global system controller with strategy π receives belief states and manages the replication factor N_t.

Our contributions can be summarized as follows:

1. We present a novel formulation of intrusion tolerance as a two-level game. The local game models intrusion recovery, and the global game models replication control. We derive control strategies that are optimal against a dynamic attacker and for which we provide theoretical guarantees.
2. We prove the existence of equilibria and that the best responses have a threshold structure. Based on these insights, we design efficient algorithms for computing the best responses.
3. We evaluate the equilibrium strategies in an emulation environment where we run 10 types of network intrusions. The results show that the equilibrium strategies can improve service availability and reduce the operational cost of state-of-the-art intrusion-tolerant systems.

2   Background on Intrusion-Tolerant Systems

The common approach to building an intrusion-tolerant service is based on *redundancy*, whereby the service is provided by a set of replicas. Through such redundancy, compromised and crashed replicas can be substituted by healthy replicas as long as they can coordinate their service responses. This coordination problem is known as the *consensus problem*, which can be solved under synchrony and failure assumptions [5]. The main synchrony options are (i) the *synchronous model*, which mandates an upper bound on the communication delay between nodes; (ii) the *partially synchronous model*, which warrants an upper bound but allows for periods of instability where the bound is violated; and (iii) the *asynchronous model*, where no bound exists [5]. Similarly, the main failure options are (i) the *crash-stop failure model*, where nodes fail by crashing; (ii) the *Byzantine failure model*, where nodes fail arbitrarily; and (iii) the *hybrid failure model*, where nodes fail arbitrarily but are equipped with trusted components that fail by crashing [24].

Theorem 1 (Solvability of the consensus problem).

1. *Consensus is not solvable in the asynchronous model.*
2. *Consensus is solvable in the partially synchronous model with N nodes and at most $\frac{N-1}{2}$ crash-stop failures, $\frac{N-1}{3}$ Byzantine failures, and $\frac{N-1}{2}$ hybrid failures.*
3. *Consensus is solvable in the synchronous model with N nodes and at most $N-1$ crash-stop failures, $\frac{N-1}{2}$ Byzantine failures, and $\frac{N-1}{2}$ hybrid failures.*

Theorem 1 summarizes several decades of research; hence, the proofs are scattered across the literature. A reference to a proof of each statement can be found in the supplementary material [16, App. M]. This theorem provides the basis for designing an intrusion-tolerant system and indicates the number of nodes required to tolerate f compromised nodes. However, the theorem does not provide guidance on the likelihood that the threshold f will be exceeded. Quantifying this likelihood is the objective of *reliability theory*.

The reliability of a system is defined as the probability that the system performs its task under the operating conditions encountered [4]. If $T^{(\mathrm{F})}$ is a random variable representing the time to failure (e.g., compromise), then the reliability function can be defined as $R(t) \triangleq \mathbb{P}[T^{(\mathrm{F})} > t]$ and the mean time to failure (MTTF) is $\mathbb{E}[T^{(\mathrm{F})}]$. In the context of intrusion tolerance, we also consider the metrics *average time-to-recovery* $T^{(\mathrm{R})}$, *average availability* $T^{(\mathrm{A})}$, and *frequency of recovery* $F^{(\mathrm{R})}$.

3 System Model

We consider a (distributed) system with $N_t \geq 2f + 1$ *nodes* connected through an authenticated network. (In an authenticated network, nodes can verify each other's digital signatures [5, §2.4.6].) Each node is segmented into two domains: an application domain, which runs a *service replica*, and a privileged domain, which runs security and control functions (see Fig. 1.b). The replicas are coordinated through a *reconfigurable* consensus protocol (e.g., reconfigurable MINBFT [24, §4.2]). (A reconfigurable consensus protocol allows dynamic addition and removal of nodes from the system [7, §8.6].) This protocol guarantees *correct service* if no more than f nodes are compromised or crashed simultaneously.

Definition 1 (Correct service). *The system provides correct service if the healthy replicas satisfy the following properties:*

Each request is eventually executed.	(Liveness)
Each executed request was sent by a client.	(Validity)
Each replica executes the same request sequence.	(Safety)

To maintain correct service when intrusions occur, the system can take three types of control actions: (i) recover a compromised service replica, e.g., by replacing the virtual machine where the replica executes; (ii) evict a crashed node from the system; and (iii) add a new node. The RECOVER action is taken by a node controller on the local level, and the system controller takes the EVICT and ADD actions on the global level (see Fig. 1.a).

Proposition 1. *The system provides correct service if*

An attacker can not forge digital signatures.	(P1.A)
An attacker can not access the privileged domains.	(P1.B)
Network links are authenticated and reliable [5, p. 42].	(P1.C)
At most k nodes recover simultaneously.	(P1.D)
At most f nodes are compromised or crashed simultaneously.	(P1.E)
$N_t \geq 2f + 1 + k.$	(P1.F)
The system is partially synchronous [5, §2.5.3].	(P1.G)

Proof. (P1.A)–(P1.C) imply the hybrid failure model [24]. (P1.D)–(P1.F) state that at least $f + 1 + k$ nodes are healthy. These properties together with the tolerance threshold $f = \frac{N_t - 1 - k}{2}$ of the consensus protocol (e.g., MINBFT [24, §4.2]) imply (Safety) (Theorem 1, [24, Thms. 1–2]). Next, it follows from (P1.G) that the healthy nodes will eventually agree on the response to any service request, which allows to circumvent FLP [9, Thm. 1] and achieve (Liveness). Finally, (Validity) is ensured by the consensus protocol. □

Assumptions (P1.A), (P1.C), (P1.D), (P1.G) imply that the system uses standard cryptographic mechanisms and network equipment. Similarly, (P1.E)–(P1.F) can always be met by tuning f and N_t. The strongest assumption is (P1.B), which implies that the controllers are securely separated from the service replicas. This separation can be realized in several ways. One option is to use a secure coprocessor to execute the privileged domain (e.g., IBM 4758). Another option is to implement the privileged domain using dedicated hardware modules, such as a smart card or an FPGA [7]. A third option, which does not require special hardware, is to use a security kernel to run the privileged domain [24]. A fourth option, used in [7], is to separate the application domain from the privileged domain using a secure virtualization layer.

Proposition 1 implies that, to guarantee correct service (Definition 1), the controllers must ensure (in expectation) that: a) the number of compromised and crashed nodes is at most f, which is achieved by recovery; and b) the number of nodes satisfies $N_t \geq 2f + 1 + k$, which is achieved by replacing crashed nodes. In the following section, we model the problem of meeting these two constraints while minimizing operational cost as a game with a local and a global level. On the local level, node controllers minimize cost while meeting a), and on the global level, the system controller minimizes cost while meeting b). At the same time, an attacker aims to maximize the cost of the system.

Remark 1 (Extension of Proposition 1). By appropriate use of cryptographic methods, the system can provide confidentiality in addition to (Safety), (Liveness), and (Validity). See the supplementary material [16, App. N].

4   Modeling Intrusion Tolerance as a Two-Level Game

Our game-theoretic model is based on the following assumptions.

Assumption 1. *The probability that the system controller crashes is negligible.*

Assumption 2. *Compromise and crash events are statistically independent across nodes.*

Assumption 3. *(P1.D) is enforced by the system implementation.*

Assumption 4. *The attacker has access to the controllers' observations.*

Assumption 1 can be satisfied by deploying the system controller on a crash-tolerant system, e.g., a RAFT-based system. Assumption 2 means that we can analyze and solve each local game independently. This assumption can be satisfied in practice by distributing the nodes geographically and employing software diversification [12]. Assumption 3 can be met through proper implementation design. Lastly, Assumption 4 holds for insider attacks and reflects that it is generally not known what information is available to the attacker.

Notation. Random variables are denoted by upper-case letters (e.g., X) and their values by lower-case (e.g., x). $\mathbb{P}$ is a probability measure. (Since we focus on countable sample spaces, the construction of the underlying probability space is standard.) The expectation of ϕ with respect to X is written as $\mathbb{E}_X[\phi]$. (As the sample spaces are countable, no question of the existence of $\mathbb{E}_X[\phi]$ will arise.) When ϕ includes many random variables that depend on π, we simply write $\mathbb{E}_\pi[\phi]$. $x \sim \phi$ means that x is sampled from ϕ. We use $\mathbb{P}[x]$ as a shorthand for $\mathbb{P}[X = x]$. Calligraphy letters (e.g., $\mathcal{V}$) represent sets. The set of probability distributions over $\mathcal{V}$ is written as $\Delta(\mathcal{V})$. $\mathbb{1}_\phi$ is the indicator function. A table with notations is available in the supplementary material [16, Table. 1].

4.1 The Local Intrusion Recovery Game

The local game involves two players: a node controller that aims to minimize operational cost by performing intrusion recovery and an attacker that aims to maximize that cost. The attacker can perform two actions to achieve its goal: (i) compromise the node's service replica; and (ii) trigger excess recoveries by the deliberate generation of false intrusion alarms.

Let $\mathcal{N}_t \triangleq \{1, 2, \ldots, N_t\}$ be the set of nodes and $\pi_{i,t}^{(C)}$ the corresponding *behavior control strategy* at time t [20, Def. 5]. Controller i takes one of two actions $a_{i,t}^{(C)}$: (R)ecover or (W)ait. Similarly, the attacker follows a *behavior strategy* $\pi_{i,t}^{(A)}$ and takes one of two actions $a_{i,t}^{(A)}$: (A)ttack or (F)alse alarm.

Node i has state $s_{i,t} \in \mathcal{S}_N$ with three values: $\emptyset$ if it is crashed, $\mathbb{C}$ if it is compromised, and $\mathbb{H}$ if it is healthy (see Fig. 2.a). The evolution of $s_{i,t}$ can be written as $s_{i,t+1} \sim f_{N,i}(\cdot \mid s_{i,t}, a_{i,t}^{(C)}, a_{i,t}^{(A)})$, where $f_{N,i}$ is defined as

$$f_{N,i}(\emptyset \mid \emptyset, \cdot, \cdot) \triangleq 1 \tag{1a}$$

$$f_{N,i}(\emptyset \mid \mathbb{H}, \cdot, \cdot) \triangleq f_{N,i}(\emptyset \mid \mathbb{C}, \cdot, \cdot) \triangleq p_{C,i} \tag{1b}$$

$$f_{N,i}(\mathbb{H} \mid \mathbb{H}, \mathsf{W}, \mathsf{A}) \triangleq (1 - p_{A,i})(1 - p_{C,i}) \tag{1c}$$

$$f_{N,i}(\mathbb{H} \mid \mathbb{H}, \cdot, \mathsf{F}) \triangleq f_{N,i}(\mathbb{H} \mid \mathbb{C}, \mathsf{R}, \cdot) \triangleq f_{N,i}(\mathbb{C} \mid \mathbb{C}, \mathsf{W}, \cdot) \triangleq (1 - p_{C,i}) \tag{1d}$$

$$f_{N,i}(\mathbb{C} \mid \mathbb{H}, \cdot, \mathsf{A}) \triangleq (1 - p_{C,i})p_{A,i}. \tag{1e}$$

$p_{A,i} \in (0, 1)$ is the probability that an attack on node i is successful and $p_{C,i} \in (0, 1)$ is the probability that the node crashes during the time interval $[t, t + 1]$. These parameters can be set based on domain knowledge or be obtained through system measurements. In fact, companies such as Google, Meta, and IBM have documented procedures for estimating such parameters, see e.g., [10].

(1a)–(1b) capture the transitions to the crashed state $\emptyset$, which is absorbing. (A crashed node can be restarted and appears as a new node in our model.) Next, (1c)–(1d) define the transitions to the healthy state $\mathbb{H}$ after the controller takes action R. Lastly, (1e) captures the transition to the compromised state $\mathbb{C}$ when an intrusion occurs. All other transitions have probability 0. It follows from (1) that the number of time-steps until a node fails (crash or compromise) is geometrically distributed, see Fig. 2.b.

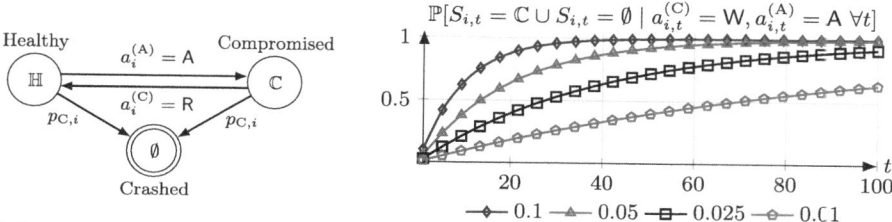

a) State transition diagram of node i (1).   b) Failure (crash or compromise) probability.

Fig. 2. a) disks represent states, arrows represent state transitions, labels indicate probabilities and conditions for state transition, self-transitions are not shown; b) the probability that a node is compromised ($\mathbb{C}$) or crashed ($\emptyset$) by time-step t if no recoveries occur; the curves relate to values of $\min[p_{A,i} + p_{C,i}, 1]$.

Observability. The attacker has complete observability in the sense that it knows the state $s_{i,t}$, the controller's action $a_{i,t}^{(C)}$, and the controller's observation. In contrast, the controller has a restricted view. It only has access to an observation $o_{i,t} \in \mathcal{O}$, which is based on the number of IDS alerts received during the time interval $[t-1, t]$ ($\mathcal{O}$ is finite). Consequently, the *information feedback* for the controller and the attacker at time t are

$$\mathbf{i}_{i,t}^{(C)} \triangleq (o_{i,t},) \quad \text{and} \quad \mathbf{i}_{i,t}^{(A)} \triangleq (s_{i,t}, a_{i,t-1}^{(C)}, o_{i,t}), \quad \text{where } o_{i,t} \sim z_i(\cdot \mid a_{i,t-1}^{(A)}). \quad (2)$$

Remark 2. While we focus on the IDS alert metric in this paper, alternative sources for metrics can be used. A comparison between different metrics is available in the supplementary material [16, App. L].

Both the controller and the attacker have *perfect recall* [20, Def. 7], which means that they remember their respective history $\mathbf{h}_{i,t}^{(j)} \triangleq (\mathbf{b}_{i,1}, (a_{i,l-1}^{(j)}, \mathbf{i}_{i,l}^{(j)})_{l=2,\ldots,t})$, where $j \in \{C, A\}$. Based on this history, the controller computes the *belief state*

$$\mathbf{b}_{i,t}(s_i) \triangleq \mathbb{P}[S_{i,t} = s_i \mid \mathbf{h}_{i,t}^{(C)}] \stackrel{(a)}{=} \frac{\sum_{a_{i,t-1}^{(A)}} z_i(o_{i,t} \mid a_{i,t-1}^{(A)}) \mathbb{P}[s_i \mid a_{i,t-1}^{(C)}, \mathbf{h}_{i,t-1}^{(C)}, \pi_{i,t}^{(A)}]}{\mathbb{P}[o_{i,t} \mid a_{i,t-1}^{(C)}, \mathbf{h}_{i,t-1}^{(C)}, \pi_{i,t}^{(A)}]} \quad (3)$$

$$\stackrel{(b)}{=} \frac{\sum_{s_{i,t-1}} \sum_{a_{i,t-1}^{(A)}} z_i(o_{i,t} \mid a_{i,t-1}^{(A)}) \pi_{i,t}^{(A)}(a_{i,t-1}^{(A)}) b_{i,t-1}(s_{i,t-1}) f_{N,i}(s_i \mid s_{i,t-1}, a_{i,t-1}^{(C)}, a_{i,t-1}^{(A)})}{\sum_{\hat{s}_i, s_i'} \sum_{a_{i,t-1}^{(A)}} z_i(o_{i,t} \mid a_{i,t-1}^{(A)}) \pi_{i,t}^{(A)}(a_{i,t-1}^{(A)}) f_{N,i}(s_i' \mid \hat{s}_i, a_{i,t-1}^{(C)}, a_{i,t-1}^{(A)}) b_{i,t-1}(\hat{s}_i)},$$

where (a) is an expansion of the conditional probability using Bayes' rule and (b) follows from the Markov properties of $f_{N,i}$ (1) and z_i (2) [17, Eq. 11].

Since $b_{i,t} \triangleq \mathbf{b}_{i,t}(\mathbb{C})$ (3) is a sufficient statistic for $s_{i,t}$ [19], we can define $\pi_{i,t}^{(C)}$ as a function $[0,1] \to \Delta(\{\mathsf{W},\mathsf{R}\})$. Similarly, since the attacker has complete observability, it can also compute $b_{i,t}$, and hence we can define $\pi_{i,t}^{(A)}$ as a function $\mathcal{S}_N \times [0,1] \to \Delta(\{\mathsf{A},\mathsf{F}\})$ [17]. (Strategies can be time-dependent, as indicated by the subscript t.)

Proposition 2. *Let $X_{i,t}$ represent the number of recoveries of node i that occurred by time t and define $T_{i,\emptyset} \triangleq \inf_t[s_{i,t} = \emptyset]$. If $(\pi_i^{(C)}, \pi^{(A)})$ are stationary and $\pi_i^{(C)}(\mathsf{R} \mid b) > 0$ for all b, then $(X_{i,t})_{t=1,\dots,T_{i,\emptyset}}$ is a renewal process.*

Proof. To establish that $(X_{i,t})_{t=1,\dots,T_{i,\emptyset}}$ is a renewal process we need to show that a) the times between recoveries are independent and identically distributed (i.i.d); and b) $(X_{i,t})_{t=1,\dots,T_{i,\emptyset}}$ are not all zero with probability 1 [4, Ch. 3.2]. a) follows from the stationarity assumption and the Markov properties of $(\pi^{(C)}, \pi^{(A)})$ and $f_{N,i}$ (1). b) follows from the assumption that $\pi^{(C)}(\mathsf{R} \mid b) > 0$ for all b. □

Controller Objective. When selecting the strategy $\pi_{i,t}^{(C)}$, the controller balances two conflicting goals: minimize the average time-to-recovery $T_i^{(R)}$ and minimize the frequency of recovery $F_i^{(R)}$. The weight $\eta > 1$ controls the trade-off between these two objectives, which leads to the cost

$$J_i \triangleq T_\emptyset(\eta T_i^{(R)} + F_i^{(R)}) = \sum_{t=1}^{T_\emptyset} \eta s_{i,t}(1 - a_{i,t}^{(C)}) + a_{i,t}^{(C)} = \sum_{t=1}^{T_\emptyset} c_N(s_{i,t}, a_{i,t}^{(C)}), \quad (4)$$

where $T_\emptyset \triangleq \inf_t[s_{i,t} = \emptyset]$, c_N is the cost function, and $(\mathbb{H}, \mathbb{C}, \mathsf{W}, \mathsf{R}) \triangleq (0, 1, 0, 1)$.

The objective in (4) corresponds to the cumulative cost optimality criterion [19]. The following lemma establishes a relationship between (4) and the discounted optimality criterion. It is key for our subsequent analysis.

Lemma 1.

$$\mathbb{E}_{\mathbf{H}_{i,T_\emptyset}^{(A)}, T_\emptyset}[J_i] = \mathbb{E}_{\mathbf{H}_{i,T_\emptyset}^{(A)}}\left[\sum_{t=1}^{\infty} \gamma^{t-1} c_N(S_{i,t}, A_{i,t}^{(C)})\right] \quad \text{where } \gamma \triangleq (1 - p_{C,i}).$$

Proof. For ease of notation, let $C_t \triangleq c_N(S_{i,t}, A_{i,t}^{(C)})$. Then

$$\mathbb{E}_{\mathbf{H}_{i,T_\emptyset}^{(A)}, T_\emptyset}[J_i] = \mathbb{E}_{\mathbf{H}_{i,T_\emptyset}^{(A)}}\left[\sum_{T_\emptyset=1}^{\infty} \sum_{t=1}^{T_\emptyset} \mathbb{P}[T_\emptyset] C_t\right] \stackrel{(a)}{=} \mathbb{E}_{\mathbf{H}_{i,T_\emptyset}^{(A)}}\left[\sum_{t=1}^{\infty} \sum_{T_\emptyset=t}^{\infty} \mathbb{P}[T_\emptyset] C_t\right]$$

$$= \mathbb{E}_{\mathbf{H}_{i,T_\emptyset}^{(A)}}\left[\sum_{t=1}^{\infty} \sum_{T_\emptyset=t}^{\infty} p_{C,i}(1 - p_{C,i})^{T_\emptyset-1} C_t\right] = \mathbb{E}_{\mathbf{H}_{i,T_\emptyset}^{(A)}}\left[\sum_{t=1}^{\infty} C_t(1 - \gamma) \sum_{T_\emptyset=t}^{\infty} \gamma^{T_\emptyset-1}\right]$$

$$= \mathbb{E}_{\mathbf{H}_{i,T_{\emptyset}}^{(A)}} \left[\sum_{t=1}^{\infty} C_t (1-\gamma)\gamma^{t-1} \sum_{T_{\emptyset}=1}^{\infty} \gamma^{T_{\emptyset}} \right] \overset{(b)}{=} \mathbb{E}_{\mathbf{H}_{i,T_{\emptyset}}^{(A)}} \left[\sum_{t=1}^{\infty} \gamma^{t-1} C_t \right].$$

In (a) we use the fact that $\sum_{T_{\emptyset}=1}^{\infty} \sum_{t=1}^{T_{\emptyset}} \varphi(t, T_{\emptyset})$ is an infinite sum with constraints $1 \leq t \leq T_{\emptyset} \leq \infty$, which is equivalent to $\sum_{t=1}^{\infty} \sum_{T_{\emptyset}=t}^{\infty} \varphi(t, T_{\emptyset})$. In (b) we use the fact that $\sum_{T_{\emptyset}=1}^{\infty} \gamma^{T_{\emptyset}} = (1-\gamma)^{-1}$ is a convergent geometric series. $\square$

Based on Lemma 1, we model intrusion recovery as a *zero-sum game* where the controller and the attacker aim to minimize and maximize J_i (4), respectively.

Game 1 (Local Intrusion Recovery Game.)

$$\underset{\pi_{i,t}^{(C)}}{\text{minimize}} \ \underset{\pi_{i,t}^{(A)}}{\text{maximize}} \quad \mathbb{E}_{(\pi_{i,t}^{(C)}, \pi_{i,t}^{(A)})} \left[J_i \mid b_{i,1} = 0 \right] \tag{5a}$$

$$\textit{subject to} \quad \tau_k - \tau_{k-1} \leq \Delta_{\text{R}}, \tau_k \triangleq \inf_{t > \tau_{k-1}} [a_{i,t}^{(C)} = \text{R}] \qquad \forall i, k \tag{5b}$$

$$s_{i,t+1} \sim f_{\text{N},i}(\cdot \mid s_{i,t}, a_{i,t}^{(C)}, a_{i,t}^{(A)}) \qquad \forall t \tag{5c}$$

$$o_{i,t+1} \sim z_i(\cdot \mid a_{i,t}^{(A)}) \qquad \forall t \tag{5d}$$

$$a_{i,t}^{(C)} \sim \pi_{i,t}^{(C)}(\cdot \mid b_{i,t}), \quad a_{i,t}^{(A)} \sim \pi_{i,t}^{(A)}(\cdot \mid b_{i,t}, s_{i,t}) \quad \forall t, \tag{5e}$$

where $t = 1, 2, \ldots$; $k = 0, 1, \ldots$; $\tau_0 \triangleq 0$; $b_{i,1}$ defines the initial state distribution; (5b) is a bounded-time-to-recovery (BTR) constraint; (5c) is the dynamics constraint; (5d) captures the observations; and (5e) captures the actions.

Remark 3. Throughout this paper, we write $\min \max$ (5a) instead of $\inf \sup$ as the optimization problems we consider have solutions (see Theorems 2–4 below).

Remark 4. We choose to minimize the expected cost (5a) to model the preferences of the controllers. This approach is justified by the fact that the preference relations of the controllers satisfy the von Neumann-Morgenstern axioms [22, p. 26], as we show in the supplementary material [16, App. Q].

Remark 5. The BTR constraint (5b) with $\Delta_{\text{R}} < \infty$ ensures that undetectable intrusions are eventually recovered. It also implies that the optimal recovery strategy may be time-dependent.

Remark 6. Game 1 is a partially observed stochastic game with one-sided partial observability [17, Def. 3.1].

Equilibrium Analysis. We say that a control strategy $\tilde{\pi}_{i,t}^{(C)}$ in Game 1 is a *best response* against an attacker strategy $\pi_{i,t}^{(A)}$ if it minimizes (5). Similarly, we say that an attacker strategy $\pi_{i,t}^{(A)}$ is a best response against $\pi_{i,t}^{(C)}$ if it maximizes (5). When both the controller and the attacker play best response, their strategy pair is a *Nash equilibrium* (NE) $\boldsymbol{\pi}_i^{\star} = (\pi_{i,t}^{(C),\star}, \pi_{i,t}^{(A),\star})$. Such an equilibrium, together with the belief operator in (3), can also form a stronger equilibrium, namely a *perfect Bayesian equilibrium* (PBE) [16, Def. 2].

Theorem 2 (Equilibrium and best response in Game 1).

(A) For each strategy pair $\boldsymbol{\pi}_i$ in Game 1, there exists a pair of best responses.
(B) Game 1 has a perfect Bayesian equilibrium (PBE).
(C) If $s_{i,t} = \mathbb{H} \iff b_{i,t} = 0$, then Game 1 has a unique pure PBE.
(D) The average equilibrium cost in Game 1 is not larger than 1.

Proof. By definition, the best response problems in Game 1 correspond to finite Partially Observable Markov Decision Processes (POMDPs). Lemma 1 implies that these POMDPs can be formulated with the discounted cost optimality criterion. Claim (A) thus follows from [19, Thms. 7.6.1-7.6.2]. The proof is based on Banach's fixed-point theorem. We omit it here as it is standard.

We prove (B) using the same approach as in [17, Prop. A.1]. Consider a modified version of Game 1 where the time horizon $T_{\emptyset} = T < \infty$ is fixed, and the optimality criterion is the discounted objective in Lemma 1. Since this game has a finite horizon, it can be represented in extensive form [16, App. G]. Consequently, it has a value [21, Thm. 4.3, Thm. 4.6]. Denote this value by v_T and let $(\pi_{i,t}^{(C),T}, \pi_{i,t}^{(A),T})$ be the corresponding NE. Next, let $\pi_{i,t}^{(C),T\infty}$ be an infinite-horizon extension of $\pi_{i,t}^{(C),T}$ where the controller follows strategy $\pi_{i,t}^{(C),T}$ for the first T time-steps and then follows an arbitrary strategy in the rest of the game. Define $\underline{c} \triangleq \min c_N(\cdot)$ and $\bar{c} \triangleq \max c_N(\cdot)$ (4). It follows from Lemma 1 that the cost incurred by $\pi_{i,t}^{(C),T\infty}$ is at most $\bar{v}_T \triangleq v_T + \sum_{t=T+1}^{\infty} \gamma^{t-1}\bar{c} = v_T + \gamma^T \frac{\bar{c}}{1-\gamma}$ and at least $\underline{v}_T \triangleq v_T + \gamma^T \frac{\underline{c}}{1-\gamma}$. Since $\gamma^T \to 0$ as $T \to \infty$, the bounds $[\underline{v}_T, \bar{v}_T]$ converge to a single value, denoted v_∞. Let $v^\star = \inf_{\pi_{i,t}^{(C)}} \sup_{\pi_{i,t}^{(A)}} [J_i]$. By definition, $\underline{v}_T \leq v^\star \leq \bar{v}_T$. Hence, $v_\infty = v^\star$ is the value of Game 1. Consequently, any *reachable* subgame of Game 1 has a NE. Since the proof of this claim is independent of $b_{i,1}$ (5a), we can obtain a PBE by combining the NEs of all reachable subgames with those of the unreachable subgames [13, Thm. 2] and (3).

We prove (C) by construction. It follows from (4) that if $s_{i,t} = \mathbb{H} \iff b_{i,t} = 0$, then the control strategy $\tilde{\pi}_{i,t}^{(C)}(b) = \mathsf{R} \iff b \neq 0$ is strictly dominating [11, Def. 1.1]. Given this control strategy, it follows from (4) that the strategy $\tilde{\pi}_{i,t}^{(A)}(s,b) = \mathsf{A}\forall s,b$ is strictly dominating for the attacker. Hence, $(\tilde{\pi}_{i,t}^{(C)}, \tilde{\pi}_{i,t}^{(A)})$ is the unique pure PBE.

Lastly, to see why (D) holds, consider the control strategy that always recovers, i.e., $\pi_{i,t}^{(C)}(\mathsf{R} \mid \cdot) = 1$. It follows from (4) that the average cost incurred by this strategy against any attacker strategy is 1. $\qquad\square$

Theorem 2 guarantees the existence of a strategy pair $\boldsymbol{\pi}_i^\star$ that solves (5). Such a pair can be computed using the HSVI algorithm [17, Alg. 3], see Fig. 3.a. The theorem also establishes that when one player's strategy is fixed, a best response for the opponent exists. Such a strategy can be computed using standard solution algorithms for POMDPs. Figure 3.b shows the expected cost for a best response $\tilde{\pi}_{i,t}^{(C)}$. We note that $\tilde{\pi}_{i,t}^{(C)}$ has a threshold structure, as stated below.

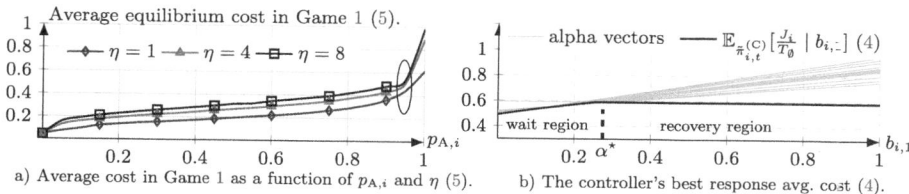

a) Average cost in Game 1 as a function of $p_{A,i}$ and η (5).   b) The controller's best response avg. cost (4).

Fig. 3. a) the ellipse indicates the place where the equilibrium strategy for the defender is to almost always recover; b) the dashed red lines indicate alpha-vectors [19]: hyperparameters are listed in [16, App. E]. (Color figure online)

Theorem 3 (Threshold structure of best responses in Game 1).
For any $\pi_{i,t}^{(A)}$ in Game 1, there exists a best response $\tilde{\pi}_{i,t}^{(C)}$ that satisfies

$$\tilde{\pi}_{i,t}^{(C)}(b_{i,t}) = \mathsf{R} \iff b_{i,t} \geq \alpha_{i,t}^{\star} \quad \forall t \quad \text{where the threshold } \alpha_{i,t}^{\star} \in [0,1]. \quad (6)$$

Corollary 1. *The thresholds satisfy $\alpha_{i,t+1}^{\star} \geq \alpha_{i,t}^{\star}$ for $t \in [\tau_k, \tau_{k+1}]$. As $\Delta_\mathrm{R} \to \infty$, all thresholds converge to $\alpha_i^{\star}$, which is time-independent.*

Theorem 3 states that there exists a best response for the controller that performs recovery when the belief (3) exceeds a threshold (6). Further, Corollary 1 states that the threshold increases until the next periodic recovery. When there are no periodic recoveries (i.e., when $\Delta_\mathrm{R} = \infty$), the threshold is independent of time.

We prove Theorem 3 and Corollary 1 by showing that the region of the belief space where recovery is a best response is a connected interval $[\alpha^{\star}, 1]$. To show this property, we leverage optimal stopping theory and the concavity of $\mathbb{E}_{\tilde{\pi}_{i,t}^{(C)}}[J_i | b_{i,1}]$ (4). We provide detailed proof in the supplementary material [16, App. B].

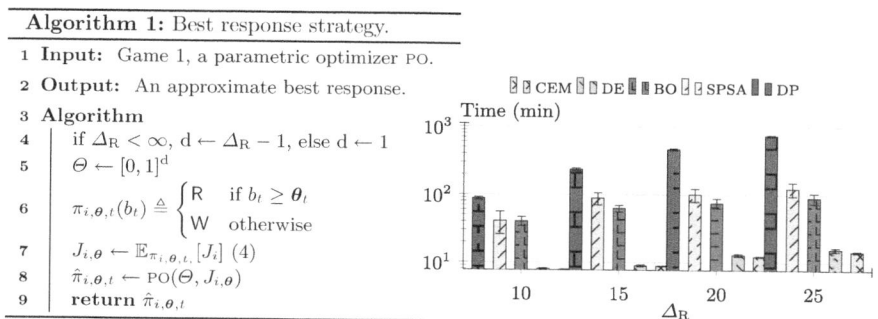

Fig. 4. Algorithm for computing a best response control strategy in Game 1 (left); mean compute time of Algorithm 1 for different values of Δ_R and different parametric optimizers: SPSA, BO, CEM, and DE, as well as a dynamic programming baseline (DP) (right); the error bars indicate the 95% confidence interval based on 20 measurements; hyperparameters are available in [16, App. E].

Numerical Evaluation. Computing a best response is equivalent to solving a POMDP, which generally is PSPACE-hard [23, Thm. 6]. However, Theorem 3 and Corollary 1 imply that we can parameterize $\tilde{\pi}_{i,t}^{(C)}$ with a finite number of thresholds. Given such parametrization, we formulate the best response problem as a parametric optimization problem, which can be solved efficiently with standard optimization algorithms. Algorithm 1 contains the pseudocode of our solution. We observe in Fig. 4.b that our algorithm quickly finds a best response for all Δ_R if we choose the appropriate optimizer. By contrast, dynamic programming (DP) becomes computationally intractable as $\Delta_R \to \infty$.

Figure 5 shows a comparison between the operational cost (4) incurred by the equilibrium strategy in Game 1 and the periodic recovery strategy used in many state-of-the-art intrusion-tolerant systems [7]. We note that the cost of the equilibrium strategy remains consistently lower than the cost of the periodic strategy. However, we also observe that the benefit of the equilibrium strategy reduces when a) the Kullback-Leibler (KL) divergence between $z_i(\cdot \mid F)$ and $z_i(\cdot \mid A)$ (2) decreases (i.e., when the intrusion detection accuracy decreases); and b) when the intrusion cost η (4) becomes very large, in which case it is optimal to always perform recovery.

> **Key insight**
>
> *Game-theoretic recovery strategies* can significantly reduce the operational cost of state-of-the-art intrusion-tolerant systems if an accurate intrusion detection model is available and the cost of recovery is significant. Otherwise, *periodic recovery strategies* can be optimal.

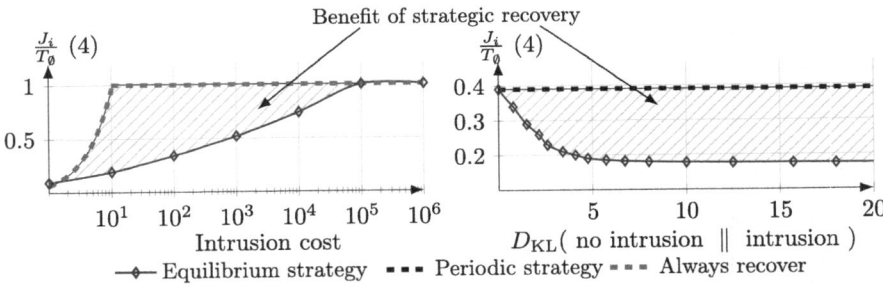

Fig. 5. Comparison between the operational cost incurred by equilibrium and periodic strategies in Game 1 as functions of η (4) and the KL divergence between $z_i(\cdot \mid F)$ and $z_i(\cdot \mid A)$ (2); hyperparameters are listed in [16, App. E].

4.2   The Global Replication Game

The global game involves two players: a *system controller* that adjusts the replication factor N_t in order to maintain service availability and minimize operational cost, and an attacker that aims to maximize that cost. At each time t, the system controller receives the belief states $b_{1,t}, \ldots, b_{N_t,t}$ from the nodes and decides whether or not N_t should be increased (see Fig. 1). Similarly, at each time t, the attacker selects a subset of nodes to attack. A node that fails to send the value of $b_{i,t}$ at time t is considered crashed by the controller, which evicts the node and decrements N_t by 1. (Note that the automatic eviction means that the controller never has to remove a node.)

We define the state of the game to represent the number of healthy nodes as estimated by the controller. The state space thus is $\mathcal{S}_S \triangleq \{0, 1, \ldots, s_{max}\}$ with initial state $s_1 = N_1$. The state evolves as $s_{t+1} \sim f_S(\cdot \mid s_t, a_t^{(C)}, \mathbf{a}_t^{(A)})$, where $a_t^{(C)} \in \{0, 1\}$ is the number of nodes added by the controller at time t, $\mathbf{a}_t^{(A)} \in \{F, A\}^{N_t}$ is the attacker action, and f_S is the transition function, which depends on the local control strategies in Game 1.

System Reliability Analysis. Proposition 1 implies that correct service is guaranteed if $s_t > f$, where f is the tolerance threshold. The MTTF thus equals the mean hitting time of a state where $s_t \leq f$:

$$\mathbb{E}[T^{(F)} \mid S_1 = s_1] = \mathbb{E}_{(S_t)_{t \geq 1}}\left[\inf\{t \geq 1 \mid S_t \leq f\} \mid S_1 = s_1\right].$$

Consider the case where the system controller and the node controllers are passive, i.e., when there are never recoveries or additions of nodes. Then,

$$\mathbb{E}[T^{(F)} \mid S_1 = s_1] = \begin{cases} 0 & \text{if } s_1 \leq f \\ 1 + \sum_{s' \in \mathcal{S}_S} \mathbf{P}_{s_1, s'} \mathbb{E}[T^{(F)} \mid S_1 = s'] & \text{if } s_1 > f, \end{cases}$$

which defines a system of $|\mathcal{S}_S|$ linear equations, one for each state $s \in \mathcal{S}_S$.

The reliability function of the system is $R(t) = \mathbb{P}[T^{(F)} > t] = \mathbb{P}[S_t > f]$. Applying the Chapman-Kolmogorov equation, [19, Eq. 2.12], we have that $R(t) = \sum_{s \in \mathcal{S}_S'} \left(\mathbf{e}_{s_1}^T \mathbf{P}^t\right)_s$, where $\mathbf{e}_{s_1}$ is the s_1-basis vector and $\mathcal{S}_S' \triangleq \{s \mid s > f, s \in \mathcal{S}_S\}$ (see Fig. 6.b).

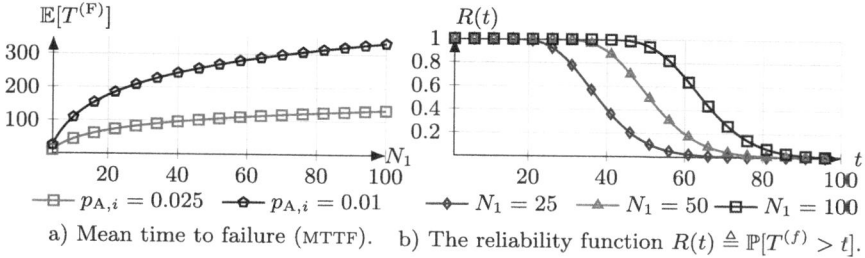

a) Mean time to failure (MTTF).   b) The reliability function $R(t) \triangleq \mathbb{P}[T^{(f)} > t]$.

Fig. 6. The MTTF and the reliability function in Game 2 when all controllers are passive; $T^{(F)}$ is a random variable representing the time when $N_t < 2f + k + 1$ with $f = 3$ and $k = 1$ (Prop. 1); hyperparameters are listed in [16, App. E].

Controller Objective. Increasing the replication factor N_t improves service availability $T^{(\mathrm{A})}$ but increases cost (see Fig. 6.a). The goal of the controller is thus to find the optimal cost-redundancy trade-off, i.e., to minimize

$$J \triangleq \lim_{T \to \infty} \left[\sum_{t=1}^{T} \frac{a_t^{(\mathrm{C})}}{T} \right] \qquad \text{subject to } T^{(\mathrm{A})} \geq \epsilon_{\mathrm{A}}, \qquad (7)$$

where ϵ_{A} is the chosen lower bound on service availability. For example, if $\epsilon_{\mathrm{A}} = 0.999$, then at most 8.4 h of service disruption per year is allowed. Note that the availability constraint can be written in terms of the state s_t as

$$\lim_{T \to \infty} \left[\sum_{t=1}^{T} \frac{\mathbb{1}_{s_t \geq f+1}}{T} \right] \geq \epsilon_{\mathrm{A}}.$$

Remark 7. (7) reflects the fact that the more nodes there are in the system, the lower the throughput of the consensus protocol (see [16, Fig. 15]).

Given (7) and the Markov property of s_t, we define the controller and the attacker strategies as $\pi^{(\mathrm{C})} : \mathcal{S}_{\mathrm{S}} \to \Delta(\{0,1\})$ and $\pi^{(\mathrm{A})} : \mathcal{S}_{\mathrm{S}} \to \Delta(\{\mathsf{F},\mathsf{A}\}^{N_t})$, respectively. (We restrict the strategies to be time-independent, as stationary best responses and equilibria exist; see Theorem 4 below.) Based on these definitions, we model replication control as a *constrained, stochastic zero-sum game.*

Game 2 (Global Replication Game.)

$$\underset{\pi^{(\mathrm{C})}}{\text{minimize}} \; \underset{\pi^{(\mathrm{A})}}{\text{maximize}} \quad \mathbb{E}_{(\pi^{(\mathrm{C})}, \pi^{(\mathrm{A})})} \left[J \mid s_1 = N_1 \right] \qquad (8a)$$

$$\text{subject to} \quad \mathbb{E}_{(\pi^{(\mathrm{C})}, \pi^{(\mathrm{A})})} \left[T^{(\mathrm{A})} \right] \geq \epsilon_{\mathrm{A}} \qquad (8b)$$

$$s_{t+1} \sim f_{\mathrm{S}}(\cdot \mid s_t, a_t^{(\mathrm{C})}, \mathbf{a}_t^{(\mathrm{A})}) \qquad \forall t \qquad (8c)$$

$$a_{t+1}^{(\mathrm{C})} \sim \pi^{(\mathrm{C})}(\cdot \mid s_t), \quad a_{t+1}^{(\mathrm{C})} = 1 \text{ if } s_t \leq f \qquad \forall t \qquad (8d)$$

$$\mathbf{a}_{t+1}^{(\mathrm{A})} \sim \pi^{(\mathrm{A})}(\cdot \mid s_t) \qquad \forall t, \qquad (8e)$$

where (8b) is the availability constraint; (8c) is the dynamics constraint; and (8d)–(8e) capture the actions.

Remark 8. To satisfy (8b) in the presence of network partitions, we use the *primary-partition* model to circumvent the CAP theorem [15, §3.C].

Equilibrium Analysis. When both the controller and the attacker play best response, their strategy pair is a *Nash equilibrium* (NE) $\boldsymbol{\pi}^\star$. Due to the Markov property of the strategies, $\boldsymbol{\pi}^\star$ can also form a stronger equilibrium, namely a *Markov perfect equilibrium* (MPE) [16, Def. 3].

Theorem 4 (Equilibrium and best response in Game 2). *Assuming*

$$f_S(s_{t+1} \mid s_t, a_t^{(C)}, \mathbf{a}_t^{(A)}) > 0 \qquad\qquad \forall s_{t+1}, s_t, a_t^{(C)}, \mathbf{a}_t^{(A)}. \qquad (\text{T4.1})$$

$$\exists \pi^{(C)} \text{ such that } \mathbb{E}_{(\pi^{(C)}, \pi^{(A)})}\left[T^{(A)}\right] \geq \epsilon_A \qquad\qquad \forall \pi^{(A)}. \qquad (\text{T4.2})$$

Then, the following holds.

(A) For each strategy pair $\boldsymbol{\pi}$ in Game 2, a pair of stationary best responses can be obtained through linear programming.

(B) Game 2 has a constrained, stationary Markov perfect equilibrium (MPE).

Assumption (T4.1) implies that Game 2 is *unichain* [2] and (T4.2) implies that the constraint in (8b) is feasible (i.e., a Slater condition [2]). Under these assumptions, Theorem 4 guarantees the existence of an MPE for Game 2. The theorem also establishes that when the strategy of one player is fixed, a best response for the opponent can be computed in polynomial time using linear programming (see Fig. 8) [2, Thm. 4.3]. By contrast, computing an MPE generally means solving a PPAD-complete problem [16, App. H]. Fortunately, upon examination of (8), we find that Game 2 has a special structure that allows efficient computation of equilibria.

Theorem 5 (Threshold structure of best responses in Game 2). *Given (T4.1), (T4.2), any attacker strategy $\pi^{(A)}$, and assuming*

$$\mathbb{E}_{\boldsymbol{\pi}}[S_{t+1}|S_t = s + 1] = \mathbb{E}_{\boldsymbol{\pi}}[S_{t+1}|S_t = s] + 1 \qquad \forall \boldsymbol{\pi}, t \geq 1, \qquad (\text{T5.1})$$

then there exist two strategies $\pi_{\lambda_1}^{(C)}$ and $\pi_{\lambda_2}^{(C)}$ that satisfy

$$\pi_{\lambda_1}^{(C)}(s) = 1 \iff s \leq \beta_1 \quad and \quad \pi_{\lambda_2}^{(C)}(s) = 1 \iff s \leq \beta_2 \quad \forall s \in \mathcal{S}_S, \quad (9)$$

and a best response control strategy $\tilde{\pi}^{(C)}$ that satisfies

$$\tilde{\pi}^{(C)}(s) = \kappa\pi_{\lambda_1}(s) + (1 - \kappa)\pi_{\lambda_2}(s) \qquad\qquad \forall s \in \mathcal{S}_S, \qquad (10)$$

for some $\kappa \in [0,1]$, Lagrange multipliers $\lambda_1, \lambda_2 \geq 0$, and thresholds $\beta_1, \beta_2 \geq f$.

Remark 9. The randomization in (10) is required to ensure that the service availability constraint (8b) is satisfied in expectation [2, Thm. 4.4].

Assumption (T5.1) says that an additional healthy node at time t increases the expected number of healthy nodes at time $t + 1$ by 1. Under this assumption, Theorem 5 states that there exists a best response for the controller that can be written as a mixture of two threshold strategies (see Fig. 7). Such a strategy is (weakly) *decreasing* in the sense that the fewer healthy nodes there are, the more likely it is that the controller will add a node, which is intuitive. This structure means that a (weakly) dominating strategy for the attacker is to minimize the expected number of healthy nodes $\mathbb{E}[S]$ [11, Def. 1.1].

Corollary 2. *Assuming each $\pi^{(C)}$ satisfies (10), then an attacker strategy that minimizes $\mathbb{E}[S]$ is (weakly) dominating [11, Def. 1.1].*

Corollary 2 means that we can obtain an MPE of Game 2 by computing a best response of each player independently. Due to the independence, this computation can be done in polynomial time using the linear program of Theorem 4.

Remark 10. Since Game 1 and Game 2 are zero-sum, every equilibrium leads to the same value [22, Ch. 3], regardless of the strategies employed at equilibrium. Consequently, we do not need to concern ourselves with equilibrium selection.

The proofs of Theorems 4–5 and Cor. 2 involve a combination of techniques from CMDP theory and lattice programming. We defer the rigorous proofs to the supplementary material [16, App. C–D, App. R]. However, for the coherence of our argument, we outline the main steps here. To prove Theorem 4, we start by formulating the problem of computing a best response as a constrained Markov decision process (CMDP). Assumption (T4.1) implies that this CMDP has a unique occupation measure $\rho \in \Delta(\mathcal{S}_S \times \{0, 1\})$ for each stationary π [2]. Since (7) is linear in the occupation measure, the best responses are solutions to certain linear programs. Let $\mathscr{B}_C$ and $\mathscr{B}_A$ be the solution correspondences of these programs. Then $\mathscr{B}(\pi) = \mathscr{B}_C(\pi^{(A)}) \times \mathscr{B}_A(\pi^{(C)})$ satisfies the conditions of Kakutani's fixed point theorem, which means that a constrained MPE exists [3, Thm. 2.1].

To prove Theorem 5, we formulate the best response CMDP for the controller as a discounted MDP through Lagrangian relaxation [2, Thm. 3.7]. Then, leveraging Topkis' theorem, we show that there exists a best response threshold strategy for any nonnegative Lagrange multiplier, discount factor in $[0, 1)$, and attacker strategy. Next, we use the vanishing discount method to establish

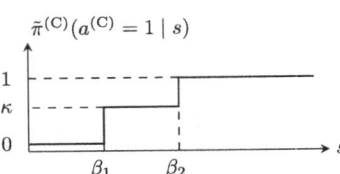

Fig. 7. Illustration of Theorem 5.

that the threshold structure also applies under the average cost optimality criterion (7). Then the proof of Theorem 5 follows from standard results in CMDP theory [2, Thm. 12.7]. Finally, the corollary is obtained by analyzing the Bellman equation induced by Theorem 5.

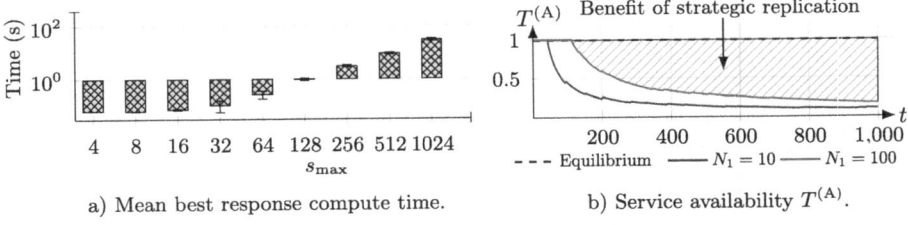

a) Mean best response compute time.   b) Service availability $T^{(A)}$.

Fig. 8. a) compute time to obtain a best response in Game 2 via linear programming; the error bars indicate the 95% confidence interval based on 20 runs; b) availability of the equilibrium strategy and two fixed replication strategies with different numbers of nodes N_1; hyperparameters are listed in [16, App. E].

Numerical Evaluation. Figure 8.a shows the compute time to obtain a best response in Game 2 (Theorem 4). Figure 8.b shows a comparison between the service availability achieved by the equilibrium strategy and the fixed-replication strategy that is used in many state-of-the-art intrusion-tolerant systems [7]. As depicted in the figure, the equilibrium strategy guarantees a high service availability for the system's lifetime. In contrast, the availability of the fixed replication strategy degrades over time.

Key insight

Game-theoretic replication strategies can guarantee a high service availability. By contrast, many state-of-the-art intrusion-tolerant systems are based on *fixed replication strategies*, for which no such guarantee has been given.

---

5   Evaluation of the Game-Theoretic Strategies

To evaluate our game-theoretic control strategies, we implement a proof-of-concept intrusion-tolerant system on a testbed and evaluate it against 10 types of network intrusions. It is a distributed system with 13 nodes, each of which runs a service replica in a Docker container, a node controller, and the SNORT IDS. For details of our implementation and the network intrusions, see [16].

5.1   Baseline Control Strategies

We compare the equilibrium strategies in Game 1 and 2 with those used in state-of-the-art intrusion-tolerant systems, for which we choose three baseline strategies: NO-RECOVERY, PERIODIC and PERIODIC-ADAPTIVE. The first baseline, NO-RECOVERY, does not recover or add any nodes, which corresponds to the strategy used in systems like RAMPART and SECURE-RING. The second baseline, PERIODIC, recovers nodes every Δ_R time-steps but does not add new nodes. This strategy is used in most intrusion-tolerant systems proposed in prior work, including PBFT and VM-FIT [7]. The third baseline, PERIODIC-ADAPTIVE, recovers nodes every Δ_R time-steps and adds a node when $o_{i,t} \geq 2\mathbb{E}[O_{i,t}]$, which approximates the heuristic strategies used in systems such as SITAR, ITSI, and ITUA. We provide a comprehensive review of state-of-the-art intrusion-tolerant systems in the supplementary material [16, App. O].

5.2   Testbed Results

The results are summarized in Fig. 9. The brown bars relate to the equilibrium strategies of Game 1 and 2. The red bars relate to the case where the controllers follow best response strategies against a (different) static attacker. The blue, green, and pink bars relate to the baselines (Sect. 5.1).

The leftmost column in Fig. 9 shows the average availability for different values of Δ_R. We observe that the game-theoretic strategies achieve close to 100% service availability in all of the cases we studied. By contrast, NO-RECOVERY leads to around 0% availability. The availability achieved by PERIODIC and PERIODIC-ADAPTIVE is in-between; they achieve a high availability when Δ_R is small (i.e., when recoveries are frequent) and a low availability when $\Delta_R \to \infty$. We note that increasing N_1 from 3 to 9 doubles the availability achieved by NO-RECOVERY but has a negligible impact on the performance of the other strategies.

The middle column in Fig. 9 shows the average time-to-recovery $T^{(R)}$. We observe that $T^{(R)}$ of the game-theoretic strategies is an order of magnitude smaller than that of PERIODIC and PERIODIC-ADAPTIVE and two orders of magnitude smaller than that of NO-RECOVERY. This result illustrates the benefit of feedback control, which allows the system to react promptly to intrusions.

Finally, the rightmost column in Fig. 9 shows the average frequency of recovery $F^{(R)}$. We note that $F^{(R)}$ of the equilibrium strategy is about the same as PERIODIC and PERIODIC-ADAPTIVE. As expected, $F^{(R)}$ is higher for the best response strategy than the equilibrium strategy. This demonstrates the exploitability of the best response strategy, allowing the attacker to trigger excess recoveries.

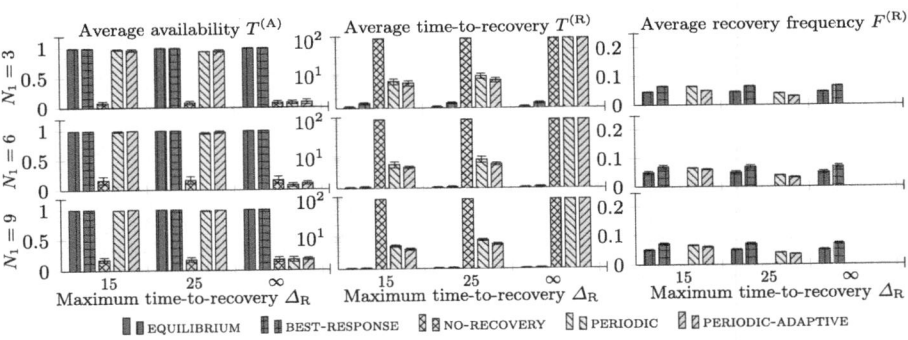

Fig. 9. Comparison between our game-theoretic strategies and the baselines (Sect. 5.1); columns represent performance metrics; x-axes indicate values of Δ_R; rows relate to the number of initial nodes N_1; error bars indicate the 95% confidence interval from evaluations with 20 random seeds.

5.3   Discussion of the Testbed Results and the Theoretical Analysis

The key findings from the evaluation and the analysis are summarized below.

(i) The game-theoretic strategies can achieve a lower time-to-recovery and a higher service availability than the fixed periodic strategies used in state-of-the-art intrusion-tolerant systems (Fig. 9). The BTR constraint (5b) and the availability constraint (8b) provide theoretical guarantees. No such guarantees have been given for the baselines.

(ii) The performance of the game-theoretic strategies depends on the accuracy of the intrusion detection model z_i (2) (see Fig. 5).

(iii) The best response strategies in both Game 1 and Game 2 have threshold properties (Theorem 3–5, Corollary 1), which allow to compute them efficiently (Fig. 4, Fig. 8).

(iv) The benefit of using an adaptive replication strategy as opposed to a fixed strategy is mainly prominent when node crashes are frequent (see Fig. 8.b and cf. the results of PERIODIC and PERIODIC-ADAPTIVE in Fig. 9).

(v) A non-equilibrium strategy is exploitable in the sense that it allows a strategic attacker to trigger excess recoveries (cf. the results of EQUILIBRIUM and BEST-RESPONSE in Fig. 9). However, the increase in operational cost caused by the excess recoveries is relatively small in the scenarios we studied.

6   Related Work

Since the early 2000s, researchers have studied automated security through modeling attacks and response actions on an IT infrastructure as a game between an attacker and a defender (see textbooks [1,26] and survey [25]). The game is modeled in different ways depending on the use case. Examples include: APT games [13,18], honeypot placement games [8], malware games [27], and intrusion response games [14]. While these works have obtained promising results, none of them considers the integration with intrusion-tolerant systems as we do in this paper. Further, a drawback of the existing solutions is that many are inefficient (compared to our threshold-based solutions) and lack safety guarantees. Finally, and most importantly, nearly all of the previous works are limited to simulation environments for evaluation, and it is unclear how their results generalize to practical systems. In contrast, our game-theoretic strategies are useful in practice: they can be integrated with existing intrusion-tolerant systems, they satisfy safety constraints, and they are computationally efficient. (We provide a more detailed review of the related work in the supplementary material [16, App. O].)

7   Conclusion

This paper presents a novel formulation of intrusion tolerance for a system with service replicas as a two-level game: a local game models intrusion recovery and a global game models replication control. We prove the existence of equilibria in both games and derive a threshold structure of the best responses, which enables efficient computation of control strategies. We implement and evaluate the game-theoretic strategies on a testbed and assess their performance against 10 types of network intrusions. The testbed results demonstrate that our game-theoretic strategies can significantly improve service availability and reduce the operational cost of state-of-the-art intrusion-tolerant systems. In addition, our game strategies can meet any chosen level of service availability and time-to-recovery, bridging the gap between theoretical and operational performance.

Acknowledgments. This work has been partially supported by the KTH Center for Cyberdefense and Information Security (CDIS) and by the Wallenberg AI, Autonomous Systems and Software Program (WASP).

References

1. Alpcan, T., Basar, T.: Network Security: A Decision and Game-Theoretic Approach, 1st edn. Cambridge University Press, Cambridge (2010)
2. Altman, E.: Constrained Markov Decision Processes. Chapman and Hall, London (1999)
3. Altman, E., Shwartz, A.: Constrained markov games: nash equilibria. In: Advances in Dynamic Games and Applications, pp. 213–221. Birkhäuser Boston (2000)
4. Barlow, R., Proschan, F., Hunter, L.: Mathematical Theory of Reliability. Classics in Applied Mathematics. SIAM (1996)
5. Cachin, C., Guerraoui, R., Rodrigues, L.: Introduction to Reliable and Secure Distributed Programming, 2nd edn. Springer, Heidelberg (2011). https://doi.org/10.1007/978-3-642-15260-3
6. Deswarte, Y., Blain, L., Fabre, J.C.: Intrusion tolerance in distributed computing systems. In: Proceedings. 1991 IEEE Computer Society Symposium on Research in Security and Privacy, pp. 110–110. IEEE Computer Society (1991)
7. Distler, T.: Byzantine fault-tolerant state-machine replication from a systems perspective. ACM Comput. Surv. **54**(1) (2021)
8. Durkota, K., Lisy, V., Bošansky, B., Kiekintveld, C.: Optimal network security hardening using attack graph games. In: Proceedings of the 24th International Conference on Artificial Intelligence (2015)
9. Fischer, M.J., Lynch, N.A., Paterson, M.S.: Impossibility of distributed consensus with one faulty process. J. ACM **32**(2), 374–382 (1985)
10. Ford, D., et al.: Availability in globally distributed storage systems. In: USENIX Symposium on Operating Systems Design and Implementation (2010)
11. Fudenberg, D., Tirole, J.: Game Theory. MIT Press, Cambridge (1991)
12. Garcia, M., et al.: Os diversity for intrusion tolerance: myth or reality? In: IEEE/IFIP International Conference on Dependable Systems & Networks (2011)
13. Hammar, K., Li, T., Stadler, R., Zhu, Q.: Automated security response through online learning with adaptive conjectures (2024). https://arxiv.org/abs/2402.12499
14. Hammar, K., Stadler, R.: Scalable learning of intrusion response through recursive decomposition. In: Decision and Game Theory for Security (2023)
15. Hammar, K., Stadler, R.: Intrusion tolerance for networked systems through two-level feedback control. In: 2024 54th IEEE/IFIP International Conference on Dependable Systems and Networks (DSN) (2024)
16. Hammar, K., Stadler, R.: Supplementary material for "intrusion tolerance as a two-level game". In: GameSec24 (2024). https://doi.org/10.5281/zenodo.11617815
17. Horák, K., Bošansky, B., Kovařík, V., Kiekintveld, C.: Solving zero-sum one-sided partially observable stochastic games. Artif. Intell. **316**, 103838 (2023)
18. Huang, L., Zhu, Q.: A dynamic games approach to proactive defense strategies against advanced persistent threats in cyber-physical systems. Comput. Secur. **89**, 101660 (2019)
19. Krishnamurthy, V.: Partially Observed Markov Decision Processes: From Filtering to Controlled Sensing. Cambridge University Press, Cambridge (2016)
20. Kuhn, H.W.: Extensive Games and the problem of information. Princeton University Press, Princeton (1953)

21. Myerson, R.B.: Game Theory-Analysis of Conflict. Harvard University Press, Cambridge (1997)
22. von Neumann, J., Morgenstern, O.: Theory of Games and Economic Behavior. Princeton University Press, Princeton (1947)
23. Papadimitriou, C.H., Tsitsiklis, J.N.: The complexity of markov decision processes. Math. Oper. Res. **12**, 441–450 (1987)
24. dos Santos Veronese, G.T.: Intrusion Tolerance in Large Scale Networks. Ph.D. thesis. universidade de Lisboa (2010)
25. Sinha, A., Fang, F., An, B., Kiekintveld, C., Tambe, M.: Stackelberg security games: looking beyond a decade of success. In: International Joint Conferences on Artificial Intelligence Organization (2018). https://doi.org/10.24963/ijcai.2018/775
26. Tambe, M.: Security and Game Theory: Algorithms, Deployed Systems, Lessons Learned, 1st edn. Cambridge University Press, Cambridge (2011)
27. Tsemogne, O., Hayel, Y., Kamhoua, C., Deougoué, G.: Optimizing intrusion detection systems placement against network virus spreading using a partially observable stochastic minimum-threat path game. In: Decision and Game Theory for Security, pp. 274–296 (2023)

MEGA-PT: A Meta-game Framework for Agile Penetration Testing

Yunfei Ge[✉] and Quanyan Zhu

New York University, New York, NY 11201, USA
{yg2047,qz494}@nyu.edu

Abstract. Penetration testing is an essential means of proactive defense in the face of escalating cybersecurity incidents. Traditional manual penetration testing methods are time-consuming, resource-intensive, and prone to human errors. Current trends in automated penetration testing are also impractical, facing significant challenges such as the curse of dimensionality, scalability issues, and lack of adaptability to network changes. To address these issues, we propose MEGA-PT, a meta-game penetration testing framework, featuring micro tactic games for node-level local interactions and a macro strategy process for network-wide attack chains. The micro- and macro-level modeling enables distributed, adaptive, collaborative, and fast penetration testing. MEGA-PT offers agile solutions for various security schemes, including optimal local penetration plans, purple teaming solutions, and risk assessment, providing fundamental principles to guide future automated penetration testing. Our experiments demonstrate the effectiveness and agility of our model by providing improved defense strategies and adaptability to changes at both local and network levels.

Keywords: Penetration Testing · Cyber Security · Meta-Game · Cyber Risk Assessment · Agile Defense

1 Introduction

With the exponential growth of network technologies and the escalating frequency of security incidents, cybersecurity has become a global concern [2,9]. In response to these challenges, penetration testing has emerged as a crucial solution for uncovering system vulnerabilities and assessing network security through authorized ethical attacks [4]. However, traditional manual penetration testing performed by skilled IT professionals has several limitations. It can be time-consuming, resource-intensive, and prone to human error. Relying solely on manual testing often falls short of identifying all vulnerabilities within the system. Thus, there is a need for automation and the integration of advanced threat intelligence into the penetration testing process, enabling a more efficient and scalable approach to enhancing cybersecurity.

Current proposed automated penetration testing methods are increasingly becoming non-standard, complex, and resource-consuming, despite tool advancements. Reinforcement learning (RL) or Markov Decision Process (MDP) based

© The Author(s), under exclusive license to Springer Nature Switzerland AG 2025
A. Sinha et al. (Eds.): GameSec 2024, LNCS 14908, pp. 24–44, 2025.
https://doi.org/10.1007/978-3-031-74835-6_2

methods [3,4] suffer from the curse of dimensionality, as they define the state space as the collection of all known information for each machine on the network. Partially Observable Markov Decision Process (POMDP) methods [8] face scalability issues, making it unfeasible to model and solve for large networks. Additionally, these methods lack adaptability to changes, as they assume the network structure and software configuration remain unchanged to learn the optimal policy. Many proposed models do not follow the Tactics Techniques and Procedures (TTPs) in real cybersecurity practice, relying mainly on hypotheses and simulations, which undermines their transition to praxis. Furthermore, merely identifying vulnerabilities through penetration testing is insufficient; it is crucial to provide defense suggestions and risk analysis based on the testing to enhance overall security.

To address the limitations of current penetration testing methods, we propose a meta-game-based automated penetration testing framework (MEGA-PT). In this framework, the micro tactic game captures the interactions between the defender and attacker at each local node, while the macro strategy process models lateral movement and the attack chain across the entire network. This approach offers several key features: practical implications, as the sequential interactions in each micro tactic game follow the MITRE ATT&CK framework [7] and use extensive-form games to model attack/defense dynamics; distributed penetration testing, with modularized processes at each micro tactic game allowing for parallel computation; and adaptability to changes at both the local and network levels, ensuring efficient testing and scalability.

Our proposed model enables various security schemes, depending on the solution concept selected for the meta-game. This extension of penetration testing goes beyond vulnerability discovery to include defense strategy recommendations and risk analysis. Specifically, the model provides solutions for the following security schemes: optimal local penetration plans under certain defense strategies, purple teaming solutions for enhanced defense suggestions, and risk assessments at equilibrium. Our contributions can be summarized as follows:

1. We propose a meta-security game framework MEGA-PT for automated penetration testing, where micro tactic games at each local node are modeled as extensive-form games, and the macro strategy process is modeled as a Markov decision process.
2. We offer applicable solution concepts for security schemes aimed at vulnerability discovery, defense suggestion, and risk analysis.
3. Our experiments demonstrate the effectiveness of MEGA-PT by providing improved defense strategies and adaptability to changes at both local and network levels.
4. In essence, MEGA-PT establishes fundamental principles to drive the future of automated penetration testing and its practices.

2   Problem Formulation

Penetration testing is an ethical attack aimed at identifying system vulnerabilities, providing defense suggestions, and offering risk assessments. In this context,

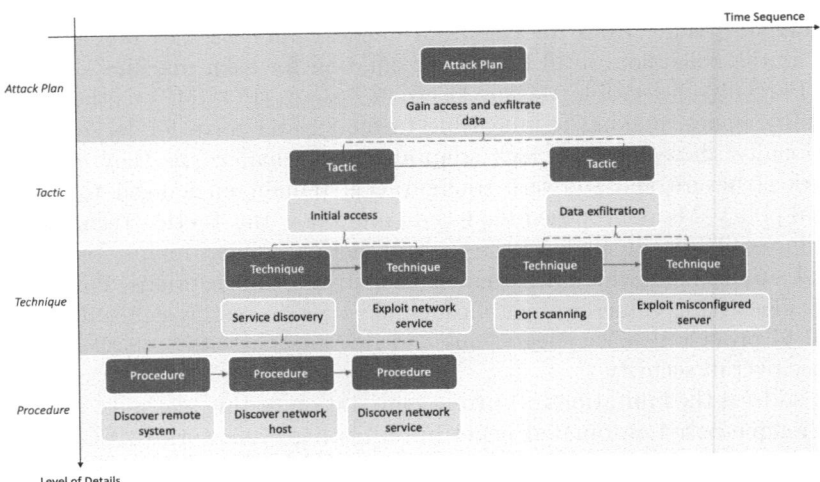

Fig. 1. Attack plan and tactics, techniques, and procedures (TTPs). Depending on the level of detail, each attack plan can be elaborated by a sequence of tactics (from left to right), where each tactic is composed of a sequence of techniques, and each technique can be described by a sequence of procedures.

the term *attacker* refers to the penetration testing agent, while the *defender* represents the system security management engine. To describe attacker behaviors within a security program, Tactics, Techniques, and Procedures (TTPs) are commonly used. Figure 1 illustrates the hierarchy between these terms. For security strategy analysis, we focus on Tactics and Techniques in penetration testing, omitting the detailed Procedures.

To describe interactions in penetration testing using TTPs, we propose a meta-security game over a network graph. The macro strategic game represents strategic attack activities between nodes, while the micro tactic game details tactic-level attack procedures on each local node. Let the directed graph $G = \langle \mathcal{V}, \mathcal{E} \rangle$ represent the target network topology, where $\mathcal{V}$ is a set of nodes (e.g., server, database, device), and $\mathcal{E} \subseteq \mathcal{V} \times \mathcal{V}$ is a set of directed edges representing connections (e.g., SSH, RDP, cloud services) from node u to node v. Self-loops are allowed as they indicate continued exploration of the same node. Let $v^0 \in \mathcal{V}$ be the initial foothold in the system. Figure 2 shows an example of the networked system topology. The penetration tester, as an ethical attacker, aims to explore available information, exploit discovered vulnerabilities, and influence critical assets inside the network.

2.1 Micro Tactic Games

Game-Theoretic Modeling
When an attacker gains access to one node, there are multiple steps involved before he completes the exploration and exploitation process on the node.

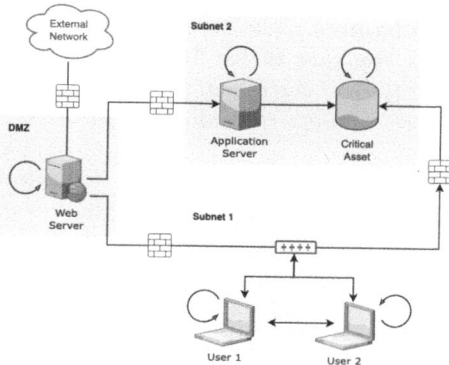

Fig. 2. Illustration of the networked system topology. The system contains 5 nodes (web server, application server, 2 user devices, and critical asset). The penetration testing starts from the web server, which is open to the external network.

To model the sequential moves at each local node, we use the concept of an extensive-form game tree to explicitly and visually represent the sequential moves, possible outcomes, and information available at each decision point in a strategic interaction. Figure 3 illustrates an example of a game tree at the web server. The attacker can choose to perform reconnaissance on hosts and services on the web server and then exploit the host to perform privilege escalation. The defender can choose to accept or deny the access request based on their defense policy. Depending on the privilege levels, the attacker could collect different credentials in the game, leading to various expected tactic outcomes and connecting to different nodes in the network.

Definition 1 (Micro Tactic Game (MTG)). *The Micro Game o_s^t the MEGA-PT is defined by a set of Micro Tactic Games (MTG) $\{\Gamma^v\}_{v\in\mathcal{V}}$ where $\mathcal{V}$ is the set of nodes in the system. Given a node $v \in \mathcal{V}$ in the network, the MTG on node v can be represented by an extensive-form game tuple $\Gamma^v = \langle \mathcal{N} \cup \{c\}, \mathcal{H}^v, P, \{\mathcal{A}_i^v\}_{i\in\mathcal{N}\cup c}, \sigma_c^v, \{u_i^v\}_{i\in\mathcal{N}}, \mathcal{Z}^v \rangle$, where each components represents:*

- **Players** $\mathcal{N} = \{a, d\}$ *There are two main players in the game: the attacker (a) and the defender (d). Additionally, c is the nature that represents the system randomness.*
- **Histories** $\mathcal{H}^v$ *Each vertex in the game tree $h \in \mathcal{H}^v$ corresponds to a unique sequence of actions taken from the beginning of the game.*
- **Turn Function** $P : \mathcal{H}^v \mapsto \mathcal{N} \cup \{c\}$ *The function $P(h)$ determines whose turn it is to make a move at each decision point for a given history vertex h.*
- **Techniques** $\mathcal{A}_i^v$ *$\mathcal{A}_i^v$ is a set of techniques that player i can take. $A(h)$ denote the feasible techniques for player $i = P(h)$ at vertex $h \in \mathcal{H}^v$.*
- **System Randomness** $\sigma_c^v \in \Sigma_c^v$ *Nature's fixed policy σ_c^v specifies the system randomness, which could be related to network traffic load, randomized system configuration, hardware failures, etc.*

- **Tactic Expected Outcomes** $\mathcal{Z}^v$ $\mathcal{Z}^v$ *represents the finite set of possible outcomes for each attack sequence in the MTG. These outcomes correspond to the results observed at the leaf vertices of the game tree, which could be the credentials to user devices, authorized connection to the server, no vulnerability found, etc.*
- **Utilities** $u_i^v : \mathcal{Z}^v \mapsto \mathbb{R}$ *The utility function u_i^v determines the payoff or cost player i receives when reaching a certain outcome.*

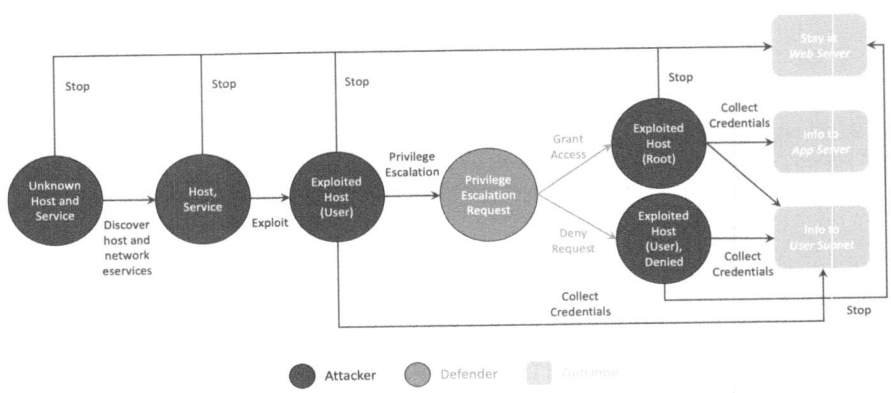

Fig. 3. Micro Tactic Game at the web server. The attacker needs to discover the host and services on the node, requesting privilege escalation to collect the credentials leading to other nodes. The defender could grant or deny the attacker's request depending on the defense strategy. The players' sequence of actions would lead to different expected tactic outcomes.

In the context of TTPs, the attack tactic at the current node corresponds to a sequence of techniques, while the outcomes represent the high-level tactical goals. In this work, we assume that the tactical outcomes are either staying in the current node or leading to another node that can be connected from the current node. Thus, with a slight abuse of notation, we denote $\mathcal{Z}^v = \{u \mid u \in \mathcal{V}, (v, u) \in \mathcal{E}\}$.

Penetration Plans

Before we define tactics or strategies, we need to understand the basis on which players make their decisions. For any strategic player, decisions are made based on the current knowledge of the situation. However, it is sometimes challenging for the player to obtain the complete interaction history due to partial observations. Consequently, there are decision vertices in the game tree that the player cannot distinguish between. In an extensive-form game, this is called an *information set*. In this work, we refer to this information set as a *knowledge set*.

Definition 2 (Knowledge Set). *Given the MTG at node $v \in \mathcal{V}$, a knowledge set $I_i \subseteq \mathcal{H}^v$ of a player i represents a set of decision vertices where the player i has the same available techniques and cannot distinguish between the vertices.*

The concept of knowledge set helps us better describe the decision-making process for both players. Given the MTG at the current node, attackers can construct their tactics in different ways. One approach is to have a sequential plan of techniques from the beginning to the end of the game. This step-by-step pure penetration or defense plan assigns a single technique to each possible knowledge set. Players can also randomize over single-technique plans at each knowledge set, known as a mixed penetration or defense plan.

Definition 3 (Pure Penetration (Defense) Plan). *Consider the MTG defined in Definition 1. Given the MTG Γ^v, a pure penetration or defense plan at node $v \in \mathcal{V}$ for player $i \in \mathcal{N}$ is a mapping $q_i^v : \mathcal{I}_i \mapsto \mathcal{A}_i^v$ that assigns a technique $q_i^v(I_i) \in A(I_i)$ for every knowledge set $I_i \in \mathcal{I}_i$. Denote Q_i^v as the set of all possible pure penetration or defense plans for player $i \in \mathcal{N}$ at this micro game. The pure penetration or defense plan for the entire system is defined as the set $\{q_i^v\}_{v \in \mathcal{V}}$, with $i = a$ means the attacker and $i = d$ means the defender.*

Definition 4 (Mixed Penetration (Defense) Plan). *Consider the MTG defined in Definition 1. Given the MTG Γ^v, a mixed penetration or defense plan at node $v \in \mathcal{V}$ for player $i \in \mathcal{N}$ is a probability distribution over all of player i's pure penetration plans, i.e., $\sigma_i^v \in \Delta(Q_i^v)$. Denote Σ_i^v as the set of all possible mixed penetration or defense plans for player $i \in \mathcal{N}$ at this micro game. The mixed penetration or defense plan for the entire system is defined as the set $\{\sigma_i^v\}_{v \in \mathcal{V}}$, with $i = a$ means the attacker and $i = d$ means the defender.*

The other approach is to focus on each knowledge set instead of defining the step-by-step actions of the entire game. At each knowledge set, a probabilistic distribution is assigned over the feasible techniques. This corresponds to the behavioral strategy in extensive-form games. Instead of planning everything ahead, this policy focuses on the decisions in each knowledge set. In this work, we call it an operational search plan. Denote by $\mathcal{I}_i$ the collection of knowledge sets of player $i \in \mathcal{N}$. By definition, for every knowledge set $I_i \in \mathcal{I}_i$, let $A(I_i)$ be the set of possible actions at I_i. Formally, the definition is given as follows.

Definition 5 (Operational Search Plan). *Given the MTG at node $v \in \mathcal{V}$, an operational search plan for player $i \in \mathcal{N}$ is a function mapping each of his knowledge set to a probability distribution over the set of possible techniques at that knowledge set, given by:*

$$b_i^v : \mathcal{I}_i \mapsto \bigcup_{I_i \in \mathcal{I}_i} \Delta(A(I_i)), \tag{1}$$

such that $b_i^v(I_i) \in \Delta(A(I_i))$ for all $I_i \in \mathcal{I}_i$. Denote B_i^v as the all admissible set of operational search policies of player $i \in \mathcal{N}$ at this MTG.

In this work, we assume that all the players have **perfect recall**; i.e., the player remembers every piece of information that he knows from the past, including his moves, the other player's moves, or chance moves. Under this assumption, we can always find the equivalence between the operational search plan is equivalent to the mixed penetration plans at the MTG of each node.

Theorem 1 (Planning Equivalence). *In every MTG in extensive form, if player $i \in \mathcal{N}$ has perfect recall, then for every mixed penetration plan there exists an equivalent operational search plan, and vice versa.*

Proof. For interested readers, the proof of the theorem follows Kuhn's theorem [1,5] in extensive-form games.

Theorem 1 indicates the equivalence between the mixed penetration plan and the operational search policy. The mixed penetration plan can be reduced to an operational search policy, and conversely, the operational search policy can generate a mixed penetration plan. The mixed penetration plan provides a holistic offline view, assigning a probability to each possible sequence of interactions. In contrast, the operational search policy describes the online decision-making process of the players. The equivalence allows us to choose the appropriate plan for the corresponding security purpose. The theorem, on the one hand, indicates that we can synthesize an operational strategy once we compute or are given a penetration plan. On the other hand, it suggests that a penetration plan or the course of actions of an attacker can be constructed after the penetration testing by obtaining the attacker's strategy at each decision point.

2.2   Security Schemes and Solution Concepts

Depending on the security goals, our framework is able to describe different security schemes and provide corresponding solution concepts.

Optimal Local Penetration Plan

The primary goal of penetration testing is to identify vulnerabilities in the target system. This includes not only surface-level vulnerabilities that can be detected through vulnerability scanning but also deeper vulnerabilities that can only be discovered through a sequence of attack actions. Penetration testing provides a thorough examination of the system, and this type of security scheme is commonly known as red teaming. Red teaming involves simulating a malicious attacker to assess the effectiveness of the current defense policy. In this context, the defender's strategy remains fixed, while the attacker responds optimally to the defense policy. Red teaming aims to determine the optimal local penetration plan $\sigma_a^{v,red}$ that maximizes the attacker's utility, given the defender's strategy and the inherent system randomness in the system. The solution concept for the optimal local penetration plan is defined as follows:

Definition 6 (Optimal Local Penetration Plan). *For the MTG at node $v \in \mathcal{V}$, given the defense strategy σ_d^v and system randomness σ_c^v, the optimal local* *penetration plan is a probability distribution over all attacker's pure penetration plans, i.e., $\sigma_a^v \in \Delta(Q_i^v)$ given by*

$$\sigma_a^{v,red}(\sigma_d^v, \sigma_c^v) \in \arg \max_{\sigma_a^v \in \Sigma_a^v} u_a^v(\sigma_a^v, \sigma_d^v, \sigma_c^v), \qquad (2)$$

where $u_a^v(\sigma_a^v, \sigma_d^v, \sigma_c^v)$ is the expected utility of outcome generated following the plan profile $\Phi^v = (\sigma_a^v, \sigma_d^v, \sigma_c^v)$.

The optimal local penetration plan is an ex-ante strategy where the attacker or penetration tester has complete information about the local node, including defense strategy, possible vulnerabilities, and system randomness. With this information, an optimal pure or mixed penetration plan can be obtained to visualize different attack chains along with their outcomes and probabilities. However, in practice, the attacker or penetration tester may not have complete information. Their penetration plan is developed through learning (e.g., via machine learning or reinforcement learning) without complete prior knowledge about the local node. The practically used penetration plan belongs to the family of operational search plans, which is a mapping from the knowledge set to the probability distribution over the set of possible techniques.

Remark 1 (Optimal v.s. Practical). The practically used penetration plan is equivalent to the optimal local penetration plan when the penetration tester's learning results are perfect. This is possible when the penetration testing agent or attacker, through its learning process, has identified the exact set of actions to take in each state to maximize the expected reward, as if it had known the full model from the beginning. Under these conditions, the practically used penetration plan is identical to the optimal operational search plan. According to Theorem 1, this is thus equivalent to the optimal local attack policy in Definition 6.

The optimal local penetration plan generates useful byproducts that help describe the penetration plan. One such byproduct is the **course of action**, which describes the realized sequence of attack techniques derived from the penetration plan. Another important concept is the **tactic outcome probability**, which represents the total probability of reaching any outcome of the game $z \in \mathcal{Z}^v$. Let $H^z \subset \mathcal{H}$ be the set of leaf vertices with outcome $z \in \mathcal{Z}^v$. Define $L(h^z) = \{(h_1, a_1), (h_2, a_2), \dots\}$ as the sequences of vertices and actions leading to the leaf vertex $h^z \in H^z$. The tactic outcome probability is defined as follows.

Definition 7 (Tactic Outcome Probability). *For the MTG at node $v \in \mathcal{V}$, given the nature's fixed policy (if any) and the plan profile of the attacker and the defender, i.e., $\Phi^v = (\sigma_a^v, \sigma_d^v, \sigma_c^v)$, we define $\tau^v : \mathcal{Z}^v \mapsto [0,1]$ as the tactic outcome probability. We use $\tau^v(z)$ to denote the probability of reaching outcome $z \in \mathcal{Z}^v$ as*

$$\tau^v(z \mid \Phi^v) == \sum_{h^z \in \mathcal{H}^z} \left[\prod_{(h_j, a_j) \in L(h^z)} \sigma_i^v(a_j) \mathbb{1}_{\{P(h_j) = i\}} \right], \qquad (3)$$

where $P(h_j)$ is the turn function and $\sigma_i^v(a_j)$ is the probability that action a_j is chosen by player $i = P(h_j)$.

Purple Teaming Defense Plan

Purple teaming is a collaborative cybersecurity assessment that combines attack and defense strategies to enhance the overall security posture of a system. While red teaming penetration testing predicts the attacker's behavior, purple teaming focuses on improving the defense policy to mitigate potential attacks. This approach corresponds to a Stackelberg game or leader-follower model, where the defender, as the leader, enforces their strategy on the attacker, as the follower. The defender must anticipate the attacker's responses to the defense strategy and optimize the defense policy accordingly, resulting in a bi-level optimization problem. Penetration testing provides credible predictions of the attacker's penetration plan, enabling proactive defense with purple teaming. The solution concept for the purple teaming defense plan is defined as follows:

Definition 8 (Optimal Purple Teaming Defense Plan). *For the MTG at node $v \in \mathcal{V}$, given the system randomness $\sigma_c^v \in$, the optimal purple teaming defense plan includes two parts: $\sigma_d^{v,pur} \in \Sigma_d^v$ is the optimal purple teaming defense plan, which is a probability distribution over all defender's pure defense plans, i.e., $\sigma_d^{v,pur} \in \Delta(Q_d^v)$; $\sigma_a^{v,*} \in \Sigma_a^v$ is the anticipated optimal local penetration plan for the attacker given the defense plan.*

$$\sigma_d^{v,pur}(\sigma_c^v) \in \max_{\sigma_d^v \in \Sigma_d^v} \quad u_d^v(\sigma_a^{v,*}, \sigma_d^v, \sigma_c^v) \tag{4}$$

$$s.t. \quad \sigma_a^{v,*} \in \arg \max_{\sigma_a^v \in \Sigma_a^v} u_a^v(\sigma_a^v, \sigma_d^v, \sigma_c^v). \tag{5}$$

The inner optimization problem aligns with the optimal local penetration plan as defined in Definition 6, aiming to predict the worst-case attacker behavior under the current defense strategy. Penetration testing, utilizing learning techniques, determines the attacker's anticipated response to a given defense strategy. To implement purple teaming defense in practical settings, organizations undergo an iterative process where the defender tests a defense strategy, observes the worst-case attack, and then adjusts the defense to achieve better utility.

Risk Assessment at Equilibrium

Another important venue penetration testing contributes to is the risk assessment of the system. Instead of focusing on individual attack events, a risk assessment would take into account the average or the steady state of the long-term behaviors of the attacker and defender in the long run. The concept of equilibrium in game theory offers a natural way to analyze these steady-state strategic interactions within the system. A Nash Equilibrium (NE) in the MTG provides a solution where no player has an incentive to deviate from their strategy. Formally, the solution concept for risk assessment is defined as follows:

Definition 9 (Nash Equilibrium-Informed Risk Assessment). *For the micro tactic game at node $v \in \mathcal{V}$, given the system randomness $\sigma_c^v \in \Sigma_c^v$, the Nash equilibrium-informed risk assessment is a plan profile $(\sigma_a^{v,*}, \sigma_d^{v,*})$, where $\sigma_a^{v,*}$ is the equilibrium penetration plan for the attacker and $\sigma_d^{v,*}$ is the equilibrium defense plan for the defender. The Nash equilibrium plans satisfy*

$$u_i^v(\sigma_i^{v,*}, \sigma_{-i}^{v,*}) \geq u_i^v(\sigma_i, \sigma_{-i}^{v,*}), \tag{6}$$

for all admissible $\sigma_i^v \in \Sigma_i^v$ and for all $i \in \mathcal{N}$.

To practically solve the game, we consider a refinement of Nash equilibrium in sequential games: Subgame Perfect Nash Equilibrium (SPNE). In addition to satisfying the conditions of Nash equilibrium, SPNE requires that strategies remain in equilibrium at every possible subgame of the overall game. It can be solved using backward induction as the game-theory version of the dynamic programming principles.

Theorem 2. *For every finite micro tactic game at node $v \in \mathcal{V}$ with fixed system randomness $\sigma_v^c \in \Sigma_c^v$, the game with perfect recall has a subgame perfect Nash equilibrium in mixed or operational search penetration/defense plans. The game with perfect information has a subgame perfect Nash equilibrium in pure penetration and defense plans [6].*

Theorem 2 states that we can always find the risk assessment equilibrium in mixed plans or operational search policies, even with imperfect information. Mixed penetration plans provide the probability of the entire attack/defense action sequence occurring, offering a holistic view for analysis purposes. On the other hand, operational search policies focus on what happens in each knowledge set, providing a fine-grained strategy. The equivalence between them allows us to zoom in or out as needed, facilitating flexible and comprehensive analysis.

2.3   Macro Strategic Process

One key component in the MTG is the utility function for each outcome, $u_i^v(z)$, for all $z \in \mathcal{Z}^v$ and $i \in \mathcal{N}$. Utilities represent the payoff or cost of staying or moving to the next node and must be evaluated globally, considering neighboring nodes and their connections. After local exploration and exploitation, the attacker can use obtained credentials or discovered vulnerabilities to move to different nodes, a process known as *lateral movement*. The attacker's movement and the creation of the attack kill chain depend on the network topology and the expected utilities of each node. We model this decision-making process across the network using an MDP, referred to as a Macro Strategic Process (MSP).

MSP Modeling

Definition 10 (Macro Strategic Process (MSP)). *The Macro Strategic Process of the MEGA-PT is defined by an MDP Λ^g. Given the target networked system $\mathcal{G} = \langle \mathcal{V}, \mathcal{E} \rangle$, the MSP for the attacker can be represented by a tuple $\Lambda^g = \langle \mathcal{S}, \mathcal{A}^g, T, R, \gamma \rangle$, where each component represents:*

- **Network Nodes** $\mathcal{S} = \mathcal{V}$: The nodes in the network form the state space. Each node or state $v \in \mathcal{V}$ processes an MTG Γ^v as defined in Definition 1.
- **Connections** $\mathcal{A}^g = \mathcal{E}$: The connections between the nodes are the attacker's action space, which is equivalent to all the directed edges in the network.
- **Transition Success Probability** $T : \mathcal{S} \times \mathcal{A}^g \mapsto \Delta(\mathcal{S})$: This function describes the success rate of the lateral movement attempt between the nodes.
- **Movement Rewards** $R : \mathcal{S} \times \mathcal{A}^g \times \mathcal{S} \mapsto \mathbb{R}$: The immediate reward or penalty for the attacker when trying to laterally move along the edge to the other node.
- **Discounting Factor** $\gamma \in (0, 1]$.

From a global perspective, each node in the network $v \in \mathcal{V}$ can be viewed as a state in the Markov Decision Process. The edges in the network indicate the lateral movement of the attacker within the network. Whether the attack attempt is successful depends on the capability of the attacker. For simplicity, in this work, we assume the transition success probability is defined as follows. For every $s \in \mathcal{V}$ and $a^g \in \mathcal{A}^g$,

$$T(s' \mid s = v, a^g = (v, u)) = \begin{cases} 1 & \text{if } u = v \text{ and } s' = v, \\ c_a & \text{if } u \neq v \text{ and } s' = u, \\ 1 - c_a & \text{if } u \neq v, \text{ and } s' = v, \\ 0 & \text{otherwise.} \end{cases} \tag{7}$$

If the attacker chooses to stay at the same node, the self-loop edge will lead to the same state with probability one. If the attacker chooses to use any outgoing edge and move to another node, the attempt will succeed with probability $c_a \in [0, 1]$, which represents the attacker's capability. If the attempt fails, the attacker will stay at the same node.

The goal of penetration testing is to estimate the potential damage an attacker can inflict by compromising the network and affecting system production. A positive reward is given when the attacker enters a node, with the reward value depending on the node's importance to the system. Conversely, staying at the same node indicates that the attacker either failed to move to another node or that the information obtained from the MTG was insufficient for progression. Therefore, staying at the same node results in a negative penalty for the attacker. The movement reward function is given by the following equation:

$$R(s = v, a^g = (v, u), s') = \begin{cases} M_a & \text{when } s' = v, \\ \bar{V}(v) & \text{when } s' = u, \forall u \in \mathcal{V} \setminus \{v\}. \end{cases} \tag{8}$$

where $M_a \in \mathbb{R}^-$ is a penalty for the attacker staying at the same node without progressing towards the target. $\bar{V} : \mathcal{V} \mapsto \mathbb{R}^+$ is the reward for entering the state. This value depends on the production importance of the node $v \in \mathcal{V}$ to the target system.

Global Attack Strategy

Unlike traditional MDPs, where the attacker can freely choose actions to optimize expected utility, in the realistic penetration testing settings, the attack strategy at the network level depends on explorations at the local nodes. If the attacker does not find any vulnerabilities leading to the next node, they cannot move forward. Therefore, the global attack strategy in the MSP relies on the outcomes of the MTG.

For each MTG Γ^v at node $v \in \mathcal{V}$, the optimal local penetration plans generate the tactic outcome probability as defined in Definition 7. Since the outcome space of the MTG is equivalent to the set of the outgoing edges at node v, i.e., $\mathcal{Z}^v = \{u \mid u \in \mathcal{V}, (v, u) \in \mathcal{E}\}$, we can view the tactic outcome probability $\tau^v(z)$ as the probability that the attacker will choose action $a^g = (v, z)$ for the MSP. Formally, it leads to the following definition.

Definition 11 (Global Attack Strategy). *Consider the MTG defined in Definition 1 and the MSP defined in Definition 10. The global attack strategy in MSP is a mapping from the state space to the global action space, i.e., $\pi^g : \mathcal{S} \mapsto \Delta(\mathcal{A}^g)$. For node $v \in \mathcal{V}$, given the MTG Γ^v and the local plan profile $\Phi^v = (\sigma_c^v, \sigma_a^v, \sigma_d^v)$, the global attack strategy is given by*

$$\pi^g(a^g \mid s) = \pi^g(a^g = (v, z) \mid s = v) = \tau^v(z \mid \Phi^v), \qquad \forall z \in \mathcal{Z}_v, \qquad (9)$$

where $\tau^v(z \mid \Phi^v)$ is the tactic outcome probability as defined in Definition 7.

The global attack strategy in the MTG outlines the cyber kill chain and the sequence of tactics across the entire system. Rather than focusing on the details at each local node, the MSP connects all the nodes in the network, offering a comprehensive risk assessment for the entire system. This holistic approach allows organizations to better understand the interconnections within their network and the cascading effects of vulnerabilities throughout the system.

2.4   Meta Penetration Game and Playbook

Policy evaluation offers a way to estimate the effectiveness of the global attack strategy π^g in terms of expected cumulative utilities. Similar to traditional MDPs, policy evaluation of the global attack strategy computes the value functions using the Bellman equations. For all states $s \in \mathcal{S}$, the value function under π^g is given by

$$V^{\pi^g}(s) = \sum_{a^g \in \mathcal{A}^g} \pi^g(a^g \mid s) \sum_{s' \in \mathcal{V}} T(s' \mid s, a^g) \left[R(s, a^g, s') + \gamma V^{\pi^g}(s') \right]. \qquad (10)$$

The value at each node in the system describes the expected return starting from that node and then acting according to the global attack strategy π^g. For the players at the MTG, the utility of each outcome describes the expected reward of taking that action and moving to the next node in the macro strategy process. Thus, we define the utility functions in the MTG as follows.

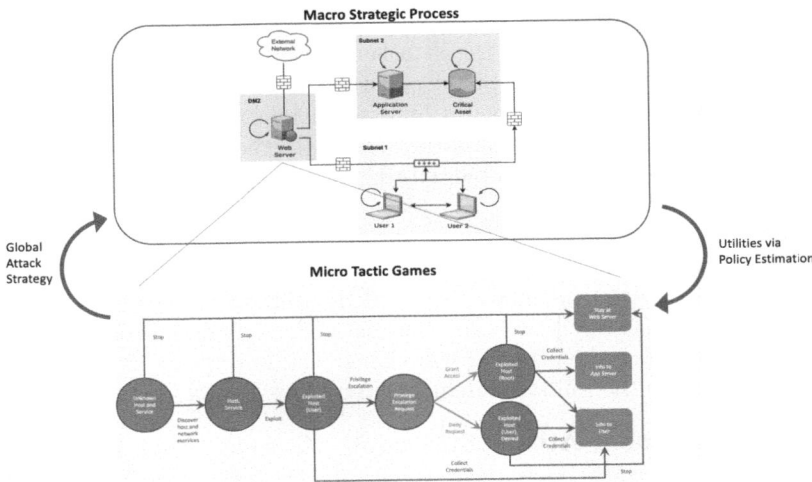

Fig. 4. Relationship between Macro Strategic Process and Micro Tactic Games. The local penetration plans in the micro games affect the global attack strategy, while the policy evaluation at the macro process helps provide the utilities in the micro games.

Definition 12 (MTG Utilities). *Given the global attack strategy $\pi^g \in \Pi^g$, the attacker's utility functions of reaching outcome $z \in \mathcal{Z}^v$ in the MTG at node $v \in \mathcal{V}$ are defined as the*

$$u_a^v(z = u) = \sum_{s' \in \mathcal{V}} T(s' \mid s = v, a^g = (v, u)) \left[R(s, a^g, s') + \gamma V^{\pi^g}(s') \right], \quad (11)$$

where V^{π^g} is the policy evaluation value function in (10). The defender's utility is the opposite of the attacker, i.e., $u_d^v(z) = -u_a^v(z)$ for all $z \in \mathcal{Z}^v$.

Figure 4 illustrates the relationship between the MSP and the MTGs. The MSP defines the global attack strategy, forming an attack kill chain and providing estimated values for each node through policy evaluation under the current strategy. These estimated values represent the expected outcome utilities at each MTG, guiding the formulation of detailed penetration plans at each node. The sequence of attack and defense techniques at the local node influences the global attack strategy in the macro view, emphasizing how lateral movement is determined by exploration and exploitation. This iterative process continues until a meta-solution is reached. Together, the MSP and the MTGs constitute a meta-security game that captures decision-making in penetration testing at both network and node levels.

Definition 13 (Meta-Security Game). *Given the network system graph $\mathcal{G} = \langle \mathcal{V}, \mathcal{E} \rangle$, the meta-security game is composed of two parts: $\Xi = \langle \{\Gamma^v\}_{v \in \mathcal{V}}, \Lambda^g \rangle$, where $\{\Gamma^v\}_{v \in \mathcal{V}}$ is the set of MTGs as defined in Definition 1 and Λ^g is the macro strategy process as defined in Definition 10.*

The MSP and the MTGs are inherently coupled, as the local penetration plans in the MTGS naturally affect the global attack strategy, while the policy evaluation at the MSP helps provide the utilities in the MTGs. Hence, a holistic solution concept is necessary for the proposed meta-security game.

Definition 14 (Meta Penetration Playbook). *Consider the meta-security game* $\Xi = \langle \{\Gamma^v\}_{v \in \mathcal{V}}, \Lambda^g \rangle$ *defined in Definition 13, the meta penetration playbook* $\xi = \langle \{\Phi^v\}_{v \in \mathcal{V}}, \pi^g \rangle$ *is composed of two elements:*

- *Local Penetration profile:* $\Phi^v = (\sigma_a^{v,*}, \sigma_d^{v,*}, \sigma_c^v)$ *constitutes the local penetration plans of all players for the MTG at node* Γ^v *for each* $v \in \mathcal{V}$,
- *Global Attack Strategy:* π^g *is the global attack strategy in the macro strategy process,*

which satisfy two conditions:

- *Policy Dependency: The global attack strategy* π^a *at the macro strategy process depends on the local penetration plans* $\{\Phi^v\}_{v \in \mathcal{V}}$ *as defined in Definition 11,*
- *Value Dependency: For each MTG at node* $v \in \mathcal{V}$, *the utility of each tactic's expected outcome depends on the policy evaluation results of global attack strategy* π^g *according to Definition 12.*

In a global view, a complete cyber attack kill chain comprises a sequence of tactics. The global attack strategy guides how to compose this attack kill chain within the target system. Within each tactic, there is a sequence of techniques. The local penetration profile at each node describes the decision-making process of the players to complete these technique sequences. The policy and value dependencies connect the macro and micro solutions, helping us to form an efficient and consistent meta-penetration playbook for the meta-security game.

3   Computation

To determine the optimal meta-penetration playbook, we propose the following algorithm to find the exact solution. In this section, we use the purple teaming defense as the penetration scheme and solution concept to describe the computational process. For other security schemes, the general structure of the algorithm remains the same, but the method for obtaining the local penetration profile in each MTG differs (line 7 in Algorithm 1).

To analyze the risks of each node and evaluate the effectiveness of the system defense, we define the network risk score as a measurement metric. For each node $v \in \mathcal{V}$ in the system, we are interested in whether the attacker has access to this node, and what is the expected damage he can create. Let $V_{max} \in \mathbb{R}^+$ be the maximum damage that the attacker could cause. Given the meta-security game Ξ and the corresponding meta penetration playbook ξ, the network risk score of node $v \in \mathcal{V}$ is a normalized risk value $Risk(v \mid \xi) \in [0,1]$ given by $V^{\pi^g}(v)/V_{max}$ if $V^{\pi^g}(v)$ is non-negative; otherwise the score is set to 0.

Algorithm 1: Purple Teaming Meta Penetration Playbook Algorithm

---

Input: Meta-security game $\Xi = \langle \{\Gamma^v\}_{v \in \mathcal{V}}, \Lambda^g \rangle$

1 Set the utilities u_i^v in each MTG to arbitrary value;

2 **repeat**

3 | **Micro Penetration Profile Computation:**

4 | For every MTG at $v \in \mathcal{V}$, compute the purple teaming penetration plan profile $\Phi^v = (\sigma_a^{v,*}, \sigma_d^{v,pur}, \sigma_c^v)$;

5 | Compute the attack strategy π^a under $\{\Phi^v\}_{v \in \mathcal{V}}$ using (9) ;

6 | **Macro Attack Strategy Evaluation:**

7 | Compute the value function V^{π^g} of Λ^g using (10);

8 | Update the utilities u_i^v in each MTG Γ^v;

9 **until** *Meta penetration playbook converges*;

Result: Meta penetration playbook $\xi = \langle \{\Phi^v\}_{v \in \mathcal{V}}, \pi^g \rangle$.

Table 1. Movement rewards for the attacker in the network.

Web Server	User Devices	App Server	Critical Asset	Operation Down	Penalty
0	5	20	30	100	-15

4 Case Study

We use the network topology depicted in Fig. 2 as a case study to demonstrate the effectiveness of MEGA-PT. The system consists of 5 nodes, including the web server, two user devices, the application server, and the critical asset. The MTG trees for each node are illustrated in Appendix A. These game trees align with attack scenarios from the MITRE ATT&CK model and can be adjusted to fit specific system structures. We evaluate the performance of our model through numerical experiments conducted in a self-built Python simulator. While the model's applicability extends to practical systems given the network topology and vulnerability trees, the details on how to gather this information are beyond the scope of this paper.

The penetration testing agent acts as an attacker entering the system from the external network, starting at the web server. The goal is to penetrate the system and potentially affect operations at the critical asset. We assume that there is an artificial node in the network representing a successful compromise of operations. Once the attacker reaches this node, the penetration process is considered terminated. In our experiments, we set the parameters as follows: the immediate rewards for entering each node and the penalty are specified in Table 1. The attacker's capability is denoted as $c_a = 0.8$ by default, and we use $\gamma = 0.9$ for the policy evaluation process.

4.1 Optimal Penetration Plan and Purple Teaming

Figure 5 illustrates the value of each node in the network during the meta penetration playbook computation. We consider three types of attackers with differ-

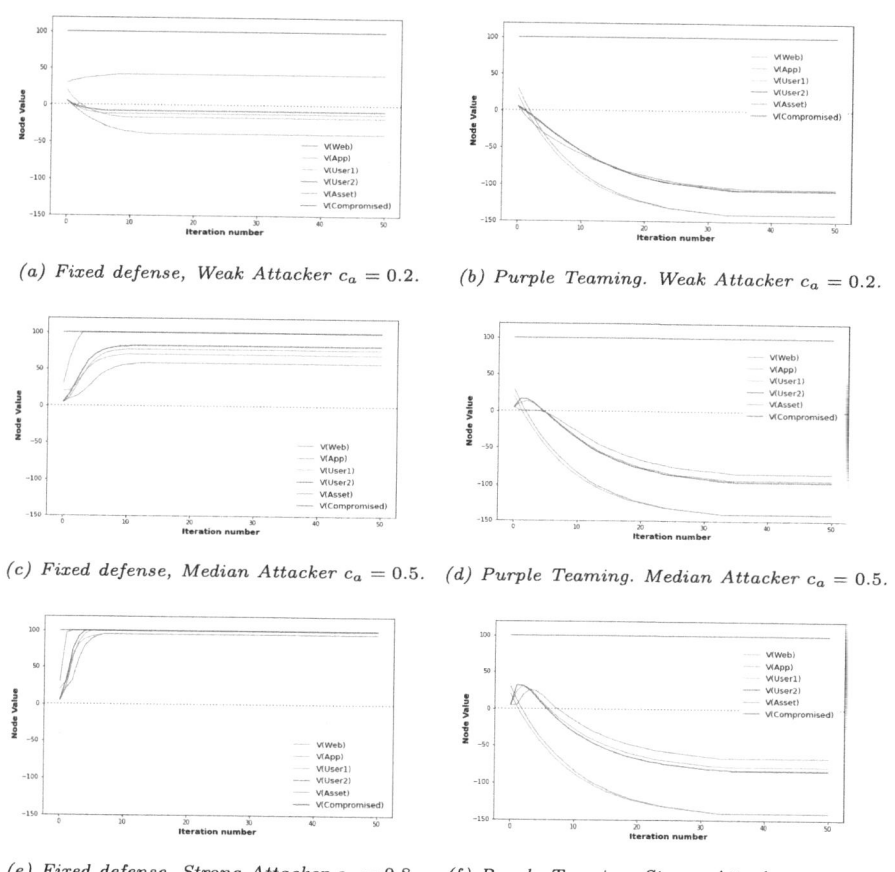

(a) *Fixed defense, Weak Attacker* $c_a = 0.2$.   (b) *Purple Teaming. Weak Attacker* $c_a = 0.2$.

(c) *Fixed defense, Median Attacker* $c_a = 0.5$.   (d) *Purple Teaming. Median Attacker* $c_a = 0.5$.

(e) *Fixed defense, Strong Attacker* $c_a = 0.8$.   (f) *Purple Teaming. Strong Attacker* $c_a = 0.8$.

Fig. 5. Node values under different conditions. The x-axis is the number of iterations and y-axis is the value of the node for the attacker. We consider both fixed defense and purple teaming defense against three types of attackers ($c_a = \{0.2, 0.5, 0.8\}$).

ent capabilities: a weak attacker with $c_a = 0.2$, a median attacker with $c_a = 0.5$, and a strong attacker with $c_a = 0.8$. In the left column, we test the model under a fixed defense strategy. Specifically, at the web server, the probability of the defender granting access is 0.7. At the application server, the probability of the defender enforcing strict authorization policies is 0.3. Finally, at the critical asset, the probability of the defender executing the command is 0.6.

The value of each node represents the expected accumulated reward if the attacker starts penetration from that node. As observed in the figures, when the attacker is weak, even with a fixed defense strategy, no node in the system yields a positive reward. However, as the attacker's capabilities increase, certain states in the system can provide positive rewards. The stronger the attacker, the

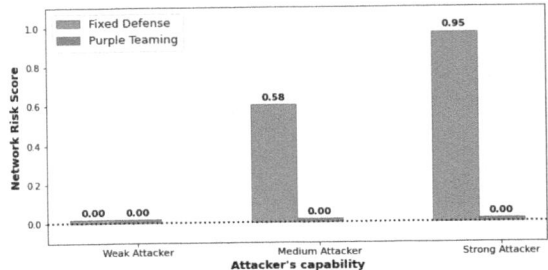

Fig. 6. Network risk score of the web server under different security schemes.

higher the maximum reward achievable. The potential system damage can be mitigated by adopting a purple teaming defense strategy. In Fig. 5, the right column demonstrates that when implementing purple teaming and adjusting the defense plan, scenarios where the attacker previously gained positive rewards turn into negative rewards as the strategy converges. The attacker can only achieve gains when the defense strategy is not yet converged. These results illustrate that our model effectively accommodates varying attacker capabilities, and purple teaming offers enhanced defense capabilities.

Figure 6 shows the network risk score of the web server under different security schemes. We consider $V_{max} = 100$ as the maximum damage the attacker could cause. With a fixed defense, the web server's network risk score increases as the attacker's capability increases. The web server is not risky only when the attacker is weak, and his capability is low ($c_a = 0.2$). With purple teaming defense, the web server is safe against all types of attackers, and the network risk score always remains zero. This indicates that purple teaming defense helps the system find a defense strategy that can reduce the network risk and prevent the system from being compromised.

4.2   Vulnerability Adaptability

We consider a scenario where the MTG changes within the network. In this experiment, we assume a change at the application server where no longer any information can lead to the critical asset. This change might occur if the system encrypts this information or restores the database, preventing the attacker from decrypting or accessing the data related to the critical asset. Consequently, the MTG at the application server changes, with the only outcome being staying at the same node after exploration.

We compute the meta penetration playbook under a fixed defense strategy before and after the local node change:

$$\text{Before: } \xi = \langle \Phi^{web}, \Phi^{app}, \Phi^{user1}, \Phi^{user2}, \Phi^{asset}, \pi^g \rangle;$$
$$\text{After: } \xi' = \langle \Phi^{web}, \Phi^{app,\prime}, \Phi^{user1}, \Phi^{user2}, \Phi^{asset}, \pi^{g,\prime} \rangle$$

Table 2. Global attack strategy π^g before vulnerability change.

	web	app	user	user	asset	final
web	0	0.7	0.3	0	0	0
app	0	0.37	0	0	0.63	0
user	0	0	0	0.5	0.5	0
user	0	0	0.3	0	0.7	0
asset	0	0	0	0	0.4	0.6
final	0	0	0	0	0	1

Table 3. Global attack strategy π^g after vulnerability change.

	web	app	user1	user2	asset	final
web	0	0	1	0	0	0
app	0	1	0	0	0	0
user1	0	0	0.5	0.5	0	0
user2	0	0	0.3	0	0.7	0
asset	0	0	0	0	0.4	0.6
final	0	0	0	0	0	1

It can be noticed that in the meta penetration playbook, the vulnerability change only affects the application server and the global attack strategy, while the other plans remain the same. This indicates that we only need to recompute the MTG at that node while retaining the original structure of the other nodes and updating the global attack policy.

The comparison of global attack strategies before and after this local node change is illustrated in Table 2 and Table 3. Prior to the vulnerability change, the attacker from the web server had a high probability ($\mathrm{Pr} = 0.7$) of transferring to the application server to further attack the system. However, after the change, since there is no longer a connection between the application server and the critical asset, our computed penetration plan adjusts its global attack strategy and no node would transfer to the application server anymore. The attacker would focus solely on the user devices to find any information that could compromise the operation. This result demonstrates that MEGA-PT can effectively adapt to local vulnerability changes.

4.3   Network-Level Scalability

In this scenario, we demonstrate the scalability of MEGA-PT by increasing the number of user devices within the subnet. We assume that all users share the same micro tactic tree, and the outcome leads to other users randomly transferring to another user device in the network with equal probability. Since MEGA-PT is modular, it allows us to compute each micro tactic tree in parallel. This means that if users share the same micro game, we can compute one instance and apply the result to all nodes in the network without recomputation. In contrast, traditional reinforcement learning-based methods treat each node's status in the system as a separate state. As the number of users increases, the state space grows exponentially, resulting in significantly increased computational time.

From a meta penetration playbook point of view, the network-level scale change results in the following change in the playbook:

$$\text{Before: } \xi = \langle \Phi^{web}, \Phi^{app}, \Phi^{user}, \Phi^{asset}, \pi^g \rangle;$$
$$\text{After: } \xi' = \langle \Phi^{web}, \Phi^{app}, \Phi^{user}, \Phi^{user}, \Phi^{user}, \ldots, \Phi^{asset}, \pi^{g,\prime} \rangle$$

Since the user devices are of the same type, each local penetration profile for the user device is the same. The only updated element in the playbook is the global attack strategy as it would consider more nodes in the system.

Figure 7 compares the computational time for finding the optimal strategy between our model and an RL-based model under different numbers of users. In the RL-based model, the state is the aggregation of all related information at each node, such as whether the web server has been discovered or whether the user credential has been found. The transition and reward in the RL-based model follow the same setting, but the state and transition space are enormous. We use Q-learning as the learning method under fixed defense and compare the computational time to find the optimal penetration strategy in the system. It is evident that as the number of users increases, the computational time for the RL-based method increases drastically, whereas our method shows minimal change. These results demonstrate that MEGA-PT scales effectively with large networks containing similar devices, providing robust scalability.

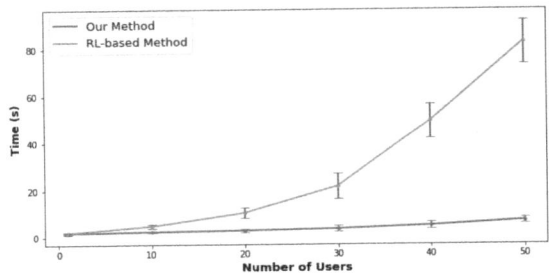

Fig. 7. Scalability comparison between our model and RL-based model.

5   Conclusion

In this work, we propose MEGA-PT, a meta-game agile penetration testing model for automated and effective penetration testing. This model features MTGs for local node interactions and a macro strategy process for network-wide attack chains. It adheres to the TTPs in real cyber security frameworks, allows distributed and modularized penetration testing, and adapts to changes at both local and network levels. Experiments show that using MEGA-PT's purple teaming, the system can find effective defense strategies to reduce the network risk score of each node. Compared to other RL-based automated penetration testing models, MEGA-PT's distributed features enable agile adaptation to both local-level vulnerability changes and network-level topology changes, allowing effective and scalable penetration testing in large network systems.

For future work, we plan to discuss global defense strategies at the macro level and explore partial information in the game. MEGA-PT is promising for extension to different security schemes and can serve as a foundational framework for the next generation of automated penetration testing.

A   Appendix: Micro Tactic Game Trees

(See Figs. 8, 9 and 10)

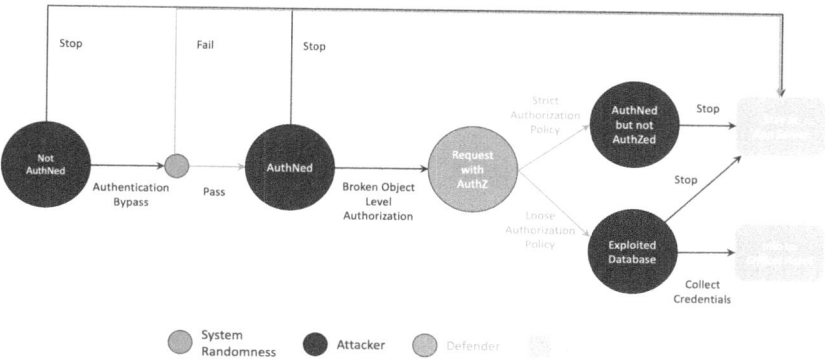

Fig. 8. MTG tree at the application server.

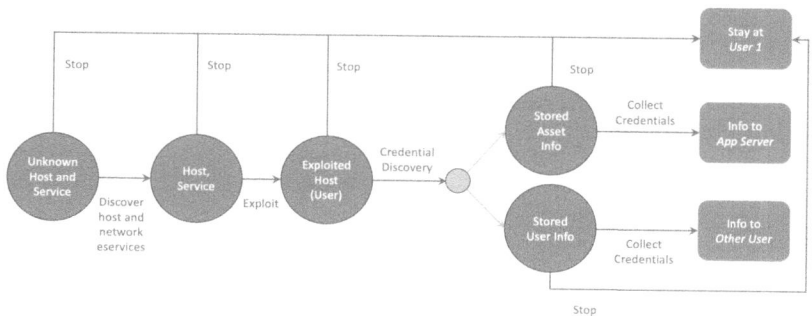

Fig. 9. MTG tree at the user device.

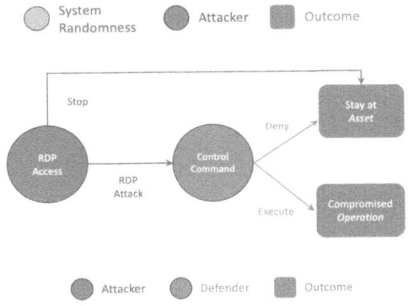

Fig. 10. MTG tree at the critical asset.

References

1. Aumann, R.J.: Mixed and Behavior Strategies in Infinite Extensive Games. Princeton University, Princeton (1961)
2. Ge, Y., Zhu, Q.: Gazeta: Game-theoretic zero-trust authentication for defense against lateral movement in 5G IoT networks. IEEE Trans. Inf. Forensics Secur. (2023)
3. Ghanem, M.C., Chen, T.M.: Reinforcement learning for efficient network penetration testing. Information **11**(1), 6 (2019)
4. Hu, Z., Beuran, R., Tan, Y.: Automated penetration testing using deep reinforcement learning. In: 2020 IEEE European Symposium on Security and Privacy Workshops (EuroS&PW), pp. 2–10. IEEE (2020)
5. Kuhn, H.W.: Extensive games and the problem of information. Contrib. Theory Games **2**(28), 193–216 (1953)
6. Maschler, M., Zamir, S., Solan, E.: Game Theory. Cambridge University Press, Cambridge (2020)
7. MITRE: Mitigations enterprise MITRE ATT&CK (2020). https://attack.mitre.org/mitigations/enterprise/
8. Shmaryahu, D., Shani, G., Hoffmann, J., Steinmetz, M.: Partially observable contingent planning for penetration testing. In: Iwaise: First International Workshop on Artificial Intelligence in Security, vol. 33 (2017)
9. Zhao, Y., Ge, Y., Zhu, Q.: Combating ransomware in internet of things: a games-in-games approach for cross-layer cyber defense and security investment. In: Bošanský, B., Gonzalez, C., Rass, S., Sinha, A. (eds.) GameSec 2021. LNCS, vol. 13061, pp. 208–228. Springer, Cham (2021). https://doi.org/10.1007/978-3-030-90370-1_12

The Price of Pessimism for Automated Defense

Erick Galinkin$^{(\boxtimes)}$ [iD], Emmanouil Pountourakis[iD], and Spiros Mancoridis[iD]

Drexel University, Philadelphia, PA 19104, USA
eg657@drexel.edu

Abstract. The well-worn George Box aphorism "all models are wrong, but some are useful" is particularly salient in the cybersecurity domain, where the assumptions built into a model can have substantial financial or even national security impacts. Computer scientists are often asked to optimize for worst-case outcomes, and since security is largely focused on risk mitigation, preparing for the worst-case scenario appears rational. In this work, we demonstrate that preparing for the worst case rather than the most probable case may yield suboptimal outcomes for learning agents. Through the lens of stochastic Bayesian games, we first explore different attacker knowledge modeling assumptions that impact the usefulness of models to cybersecurity practitioners. By considering different models of attacker knowledge about the state of the game and a defender's hidden information, we find that there is a cost to the defender for optimizing against the worst case.

1   Introduction

Cybersecurity incidents continue to grow in frequency and volume each year, and are estimated to cause $8 billion worth of damage in 2023 [6]. While cybersecurity awareness continues to grow and companies continue to invest in their security functions, the majority of threat response functions are still carried out manually by cybersecurity analysts. As a result, there is a move to automate parts of cyber threat response – something clearly illustrated by the wide availability and marketing of security orchestration, automation, and response (SOAR) systems. These systems, however, are largely rule-based – they take some specific action when some specific criterion is met. This is because SOAR lacks any direct knowledge of the network system it is responsible for helping defend. We instead consider the use of attacker simulation to train defensive agents and aim to answer the question of what assumptions about attacker information should be made to train the most robust defensive agents.

Abstractions of complex systems generally trade accuracy for tractability because there is some use in modeling that system in different scenarios. In cybersecurity, we use modeling to consider potential future states of the system

Funded by the Auerbach Berger Chair in Cybersecurity held by Spiros Mancoridis, at Drexel University.

we are tasked with defending and how different threats and risks [28] may be realized. As an additional constraint in cybersecurity modeling, accuracy and timeliness are constantly in tension. Responding inaccurately to a potentially malicious event that was triggered by benign behavior can have a significant cost, but not responding fast enough to a malicious event can be even more expensive. In the automation of these responses, there is a tendency to optimize for the worst-case. However, as we know from *e.g.* linear programming [16], there are cases where a solution that is worst-case optimal is empirically suboptimal in practice. Our work seeks to understand the "price of pessimism" – that is, the cost to a computer network defender for overestimating the knowledge or capability of an attacker.

While a number of different game types have been used across the security games space [20,30], a small handful comprise the preeminent models used in the space – The Bayesian leader-follower game[1], the stochastic Bayesian game, and the two player zero sum game. When training a learning agent for cyberdefense, decisions about attacker modeling directly impact the policy learned by the defending agent. We concern ourselves primarily with the two Bayesian game variants under differing prior knowledge and observability assumptions where the attacker is an actor who seeks to deploy ransomware across a target network. While the impact of altering a game's state or action space is clear and the implications are well-understood, there are other modeling assumptions that are often made implicitly. These assumptions are critical parts of the game design that impact its usefulness to cybersecurity practitioners. In this work, we make assumptions explicit about the presence of attackers and noise, and consider the impact of assumptions about attacker knowledge.

Our work begins with a presentation of related work in the field of security game theory. We then define the stochastic Bayesian game model and setting we use as an abstraction of attacker-defender interaction on a computer network before presenting a theoretical model of how defender belief about attacker knowledge is liable to influence their behavior. In this manuscript, we are particularly interested in the case we deem most realistic – one where the attacker has limited knowledge of the target network. Our model, being built on partially observable stochastic Bayesian games which have no known general solution concept [14], requires that we develop a decision theory for the players. To overcome the limitations of an attacker to optimize against a particular defender, we introduce the use of the restricted Bayes/Hurwicz criterion [11] for decision making under uncertainty. In order to validate our theoretical findings, we leverage reinforcement learning in a YAWNING-TITAN [5] environment modified to allow attackers and defenders to act as independent learning agents. We leverage the proximal policy optimization reinforcement learning algorithm of Schulman *et al.* [26], an on-policy deep reinforcement learning algorithm with generally good performance that is used in the default implementation of YAWNING-TITAN[2]. We conclude with a discussion of our results and avenues for further work.

---

[1] Also known as the Stackelberg game.
[2] https://github.com/dstl/YAWNING-TITAN/tree/main.

Contributions

This work evaluates the "price of pessimism", a phenomenon wherein the *a priori* assumption about an adversary's knowledge of a system results in a suboptimal response pattern. In particular, this manuscript contributes the following:

1. For reinforcement learning agents in a stochastic Bayesian game, optimizing against a worst-case adversary leads to suboptimal policy convergence.
2. Defending agents trained against attacking agents that learn are also highly capable against algorithmic attackers even when they have not seen those algorithmic attackers during training.
3. An extension of the YAWNING-TITAN [5] reinforcement learning framework for training independent attacking and defending agents
4. A novel use of the Bayes-Hurwicz criterion for parameterizing attacker decision making under uncertainty

2   Related Work

Security game theory is a broad field informed by cybersecurity, decision theory, and game theory. Recent challenges like CAGE [33] have encouraged development of models like CybORG [13] and YAWNING-TITAN [5] that use reinforcement learning to train autonomous agents that defend against cyber attacks. The Ph.D thesis of Campbell [7] also considers a similar problem space to our work and leverages the same game theoretic model. These works address a similar problem space to our work: the development of a defensive agent that disrupts an adversary while minimizing impact to network users. This paper builds on prior work by the authors [14] that uses a simple state and action space for Stochastic Bayesian Games (SBG) as introduced by Albrecht and Ramamoorthy [3]. The partial observability of the proposed SBG relates closely to the work of Tomášek, Bošanský, and Nguyen [32] on one-sided partially observable stochastic games. Their work considers sequential attacks on some target and develops scalable algorithms for solving zero-sum security games in this setting and present algorithms to compute upper and lower value bounds on a subgame. By contrast, our work seeks to understand how the defender's beliefs about the attacker impacts the rewards and outcomes for defenders. Additionally, the aforementioned works and other related works like Khouzani *et al.* [17] and Chatterjee *et al.* [8] consider the attacker as either a deterministic operator or leverage epidemic modeling techniques to describe an attacker's movements through a network. Our work here is unique in the respect that we model the attacker as a learning agent, a phenomenon more in line with real-world attackers.

The work of Thakoor *et al.* [31] and subsequent work by Aggarwal *et al.* [2] informs our point of view on how attackers respond to risk. In this work, we implicitly assume bounded rationality and account for risk and uncertainty within our model. While Thakoor *et al.* and Aggarwal *et al.* use cumulative prospect theory [34] to address deception as a source of uncertainty, we instead consider it one component of a larger overall framework.

A key component of this work is the assumptions about information available to the players. Specifically, the defending player's beliefs about an attacker's knowledge. In the security games context, this dynamic is well-captured by existing literature on deception and counter-deception [24]. Our work extends this research area by exploring this dynamic from a game design perspective concerning beliefs defending players hold about the attackers independent of in-game actions and how that impacts the learning of defensive agents.

3   Modeling Assumptions

Since our work is concerned with modeling assumptions, we aim to make our own assumptions as explicit and general as possible. We extend the state and action space used in prior work [14], but operate under the same assumption that attackers and defenders choose their next action simultaneously at each time step. We maintain, without loss of generality, that there is a single attacker and a single defender present in the game.

3.1   State Space

The state space S of this game consists of a network graph $G = (V, E)$, where each $v \in V$ is a defender-owned computer and each edge $e \in E$ is a tuple indicating a network connection between two nodes $(u, v); u, v \in V$. The state of each machine $v \in V$ is a tuple $(v_p, v_\alpha, v_\delta)$.

- $v_p \in [0, 1]$ is the "vulnerability" of a node: the probability that a basic attack will be successful
- $v_\alpha = \{0, 1\}$ is the "true" state of compromise and is visible only to the attacker
- $v_\delta = \{0, 1\}$ is the defender-visible state of compromise

At each time step, with probability q, an "alert" is generated independent of attacker or defender action that sets $v_\delta = 1$ even if the true compromise state $v_\alpha = 0$, corresponding to a false positive alert. This phenomenon is justified and described in further depth in Sect. 3.4.

3.2   Attackers

The attacker's action space, A_α consists of actions on elements of V subject to visibility constraints. We define a "compromised" node as a node that the attacker has gained access to and thus has $v_\alpha = 1$. An "accessible" node is any node with some edge connecting it to any compromised node. The observable state space of an attacker, S_α consists of all compromised nodes and all accessible nodes. The attacker's action space consists of the following actions, which each incur some cost c:

- Basic Attack: Compromise an accessible $v \in V$ with probability v_p.

- Zero-day Attack: Compromise an accessible $v \in V$ as if $v_p = 1$.
- Move: Move from some compromised $v \in V$ to another compromised $v' \in V$
- Do Nothing: Take no action
- Execute: End the game and realize rewards for all compromised $v \in V$

Attacker types inform what exactly their objectives are and may influence the categories of malware used e.g., coin miner, ransomware, backdoor. Moreover, the attacker's type informs the utility function of the attacker and the cost of each action. For some attacker types, e.g., cybercriminals using ransomware, there is a clear utility: the ransom paid by the victim. However, other attacker types may aim to steal private information that is not be directly convertible to currency. The estimation of these utility functions is thus type-specific, though any compromised machine will confer nonzero utility to the attacker.

For our purposes, we assume that the attacker is a ransomware attacker and aims to compromise as many machines as possible and end the game before the defender can remove them from the system. Assuming unit reward for each node, this means that for a network of size n, the attacker's reward at any time if they take the Execute action or control an attacker-defined percentage of the network is:

$$u_\alpha = \sum_{i=0}^{n} v_{i\alpha} - \sum_{t=0}^{T} c_t$$

where T is the final timestep of the game and c_t is the cost of the action taken at time t. We note that our reward function in Sect. 5 uses a scaling factor for the value of $v_{i\alpha}$ in lieu of unit value, and that this function also holds in cases where each node has a different value.

3.3   Defenders

The defender's action space, A_δ consists of actions on V and E. Although the defender can take only one action at each time step, they may take that action on a set of nodes or edges. The defender's observable space, S_δ consists of the entirety of E and the number of alerts, v_{delta}, for all $v \in V$ at all times. Specifically, the defender may:

- Reduce Vulnerability: For some $v \in V$, slightly decrease the probability that a basic attack will be successful
- Make Node Safe: For some $v \in V$, reduce the probability that a basic attack will be successful to 0.01
- Restore Node: For some $v \in V$, reset the node to its initial, uncompromised state, including the probability that a basic attack will be successful
- Scan: With some probability, detect the true compromised status of each $v \in V$
- Do Nothing: Take no action

The objective of cybersecurity, broadly, is to maintain the confidentiality, availability, and integrity [4] of a system. The defender's utility thus arises from the availability of resources. Each action has some cost c associated with it, where the impact of the action being taken on the availability of that resource on the system dictates c. For example, the Reduce Vulnerability and Make Node Safe actions are very similar, but the Reduce Vulnerability action incurs a much smaller cost under default YAWNING-TITAN settings. The defender's utility u_δ is a fixed-value reward for eliminating the adversary or withstanding the attack minus the sum of all costs associated with the actions taken during the course of the game.

3.4 Presence of Noise

Security detections are not infallible, and some number of both false positives – detections that alert on benign behavior, and false negatives – failures to detect malicious behavior, must be expected. Attackers are incentivized to and have adopted techniques like using cloud infrastructure and software as a service (SaaS) providers to conduct attacks [15] and the use of legitimate executables or "lolbins" for malicious purposes [19]. Attackers seek to blend in, so detection of malicious behavior that is similar to benign behavior is important for defenders. Since there is no way to definitively determine whether or not a program is malicious, these rules and algorithms yield some number of false positive alerts. The empirical rate of these false positive alerts, according to surveys, appears to be somewhere between 20% [27] and 32% [18]. In cases where some number of alerts are not an indicator of actual attack activity, any probabilistic approach to network security must grapple with this noise. The security game setting has modeled this sort of behavior in the realm of deception and counter-deception. Work by Nguyen and Yadav [23] shows that while attacker payoffs are improved by deception, learning defenders can reduce the value of this deception.

Assuming that an attacker's behavior is detected with some probability p, then there is an independent probability of false positives q. Letting p and q characterize two independent Bernoulli processes that may each yield an alert, we can treat the emission of an alert as the joint probability of these two processes. The probability of an alert occurring at all is thus $p + q - pq$, as described in earlier work by the authors [14]. The expected probability that a particular alert is attributable to benign activity is $(1 - p)q$. For simplicity, we assume that p and q are the same across all nodes.

In the absence of the noise assumption, attacker-defender interaction becomes a game of Cops and Robbers on a graph [29] where a defender can eliminate the attacker by finding the "cop number" – the number of nodes required to "surround" the attacker and eliminate all of their access at once – for the subgraph the attacker has explored. This is still an extremely challenging problem, since even without noise, the defender only has a belief about the extremal edges of that subgraph and finding the attacker's possible subgraphs has exponential complexity. As a result, the importance of an assumption about noise relates with assumptions about under what circumstances a defender realizes a reward.

3.5   Presence of Attackers

In non-cooperative game theory, two players are playing a game and each seeks to optimize against some utility function. This comes, of course, with the implicit assumption that both players know they are playing a game. In cybersecurity games, when modeling the beliefs of the defender, we frequently imply that the defender knows an attacker is present *a priori*. In reality, attackers are not always present in our system, and this has a substantial impact on defender expectations. Clearly, any response taken when an attacker is not present incurs a cost and yields no reward.

Let $\mu \in [0,1]$ be the probability that an attacker is present in a system. If our game has alert probability p and no noise – that is, $q = 0$ – then although we know the probability of an alert is μp, the occurrence of an alert allows us to set $\mu = 1$ and the defender can directly pursue the attacker as described in Sect. 3.4. Assuming noise is present in the system, the probability of an alert occurring at any time step is then

$$(1 - \mu)q + \mu(p + q - pq) \tag{1}$$

In this setting, since an attacker may not be present, the probability of a false positive event occurring at any time step is

$$(1 - \mu)q + \mu(1 - p)q$$

4   Attacker Knowledge

As one might predict and as was demonstrated in prior work [14], attacker utility increases monotonically with the knowledge available to them. Knowing the parameters of a simplified game allows defenders to set a threshold of alerts in expectation – that is, if they know the values of p, q, and μ, they can compute the number of alerts that might be expected at time t and shut down any system that has generated more than the threshold number of alerts. However, considering only the value in expectation can lead to poor outcomes for the defender, as even for small values of q, any deviation from expectation can lead to suboptimal outcomes for the defender *e.g.* shutting down systems when no attacker is present. As such, the defender's threshold for taking an action should instead be influenced by the level of deviation from their expectation.

As in Sect. 3.5, our per-node expectation of alerts, conditioned on the presence of an attacker, is $(1 - \mu)q + \mu(p + q - pq)$. The defender establishes some prior μ and at each time step t, observes some number of alerts across the n nodes of the network, where $n = |V|$. The total number of alerts, Al, expected at time t is therefore $nt((1 - \mu)q + \mu(p + q - pq))$, which can be treated as a random sample drawn from a Beta-binomial distribution. Given Al, the defender performs a Bayesian update on μ. The posterior distribution of μ is a beta distribution and so at time t, the defender updates μ as follows:

$$\mu_t = \int_0^1 \frac{\mu_{t-1}^{\alpha-1}(1 - \mu_{t-1})^{\beta-1}}{B(\alpha, \beta)} \tag{2}$$

where $\phi = p + q - pq$ for brevity, B is the beta function, and α, β are empirically derived parameters such that:

$$Al = \frac{\alpha}{\alpha + \beta}$$

$$Var[Al] = \frac{\alpha\beta}{(\alpha + \beta)^2(\alpha + \beta + 1)}$$

This yields the following for deriving α and β from observed alerts:

$$\alpha = \left(\frac{1 - Al}{Var[Al]} - \frac{1}{Al} \right) Al^2$$

$$\beta = \alpha \left(\frac{1}{Al} - 1 \right)$$

Setting $\mu = 0$, the defender should observe, on average, nq alerts at each time step. As the defender observes more than nq alerts at each time step, their confidence that an attacker is present grows. In lieu of simply setting an alert threshold, the defender sets some threshold for μ according to their risk tolerance, which may be calculated given the value of the network compared to costs or given exogenously. Once this empirical posterior estimate of μ is exceeded, remediation action should be taken.

In the full-knowledge scenario, however, the attacker has access to all of the defender's information and can see the threshold for μ. Furthermore, they can directly compute how an action they will take will update μ and choose an action in accordance with that update, subject only to the condition that due to the presence of noise, some triggering event may occur even if they take no action. Thus, just as in prior work [14], the attacker should take the Execute action to end the game and collect the current reward when taking any other action may push μ over the threshold.

4.1   Zero Knowledge

In real-world settings, attackers are unaware of parameters like p and q, so they cannot *ex ante* optimize their actions and must instead seek to achieve their goal by balancing the risk of being caught with the need to achieve their goal. Thus, the "optimistic", from the defender's perspective, zero knowledge setting is the most consequential for generating real security impacts. In the zero knowledge setting, the defender is still armed with full knowledge and chooses some threshold for μ to take an action. However, the attacker does not know any of the parameters of the network and must balance exploration and exploitation given only the state, as each action they take may alert the defender of their presence. Given their limited information, they can use the Restricted Bayes/Hurwicz criterion [11] to choose their action.

Definition 1. *The Restricted Bayes/Hurwicz criterion is a procedure for decision making under uncertainty parameterized by γ and delta defined by:*

$$\gamma\hat{P} + (1-\gamma)[\delta\bar{P}_{x^*} + (1-\delta)\underline{P}_{x^*}] \tag{3}$$

where γ is the decision-maker's confidence in their distribution, δ is the coefficient of pessimism, $\hat{P}$ is the prior distribution over the decision-maker's actions, $\bar{P}_{x^*}$ is the best case probability distribution over actions, and $\underline{P}_{x^*}$ is the worst case probability distribution over actions

The attacker has some initial probability distribution $\hat{P}$ over their actions indicating the probability they will take an action at a given time step given a state. The coefficient of pessimism δ corresponds to the attacker's belief about the value of μ, which we write $\hat{\mu}$. Due to the limited signal available to the attacker, the confidence parameter γ should be monotonically decreasing over time as they observe likely defender actions. For notational simplicity, we set $\delta = 1 - \hat{\mu}$ and write the criterion as follows:

$$\gamma\hat{P} + (1-\gamma)[(1-\hat{\mu})\bar{P}_{x^*} + \hat{\mu}\underline{P}_{x^*}]$$

At the start of the game, the attacker must estimate the probability of an alert occurring when they take an action. The attacker knows that false positive alerts occur and can infer that they need to establish some value that reflects Eq. 1. In the absence of any information about the defender's configuration, the attacker must sample some value $\hat{\phi} \in [0,1]$. The use of the PERT distribution [9], a special case of the Beta distribution, is well-motivated from operations research. We allow the minimum and maximum value in the range $[0,1]$ and set the b parameter of the distribution to the midpoint 0.5. The initial value of $\hat{\mu}$ can be similarly sampled.

When the attacker observes a signal from a defender – that is, when the defender takes some action on an attacker-controlled node, the attacker updates their belief about $\hat{\mu}$, and reduces γ, since they are less confident in their initial distribution over their actions. This update process follows Algorithm 1. In order to conduct this update, the attacker estimated alert generation probability $\hat{\phi}$ is used alongside their estimate of the defender's belief about an attacker's presence, $\hat{\mu}$ since the attacker has no knowledge of the number of alerts and must instead construct a Bayesian estimate $\hat{Al}$ given these parameters.

In the full-knowledge case with thresholding, the best response dynamics are determined exactly by expectation and the parameters of the network [14]. However, this work considers a significantly expanded state space where both attackers and defenders have a richer action space. In both the full-knowledge and zero-knowledge case, the attacker's choice of action depends on the state and any actions observed from the defender. The zero-knowledge case in particular is highly dependent on the establishment of good prior distributions. Prior distributions can be given exogenously or can be learned. In our case, we elect to learn $\hat{P}, \bar{P}, \underline{P}$ via simulation. The results of this simulation are described in Sect. 5.1.

Algorithm 1. Attacker Parameter Update Algorithm

Require: $\hat{\mu} \in [0,1]$, $\hat{\phi} \in [0,1]$
   $k \leftarrow 0$ $\triangleright$ k is the number of observed defender actions
   $\gamma \leftarrow 1$
   $\hat{Al} \leftarrow nt\hat{\mu}\hat{\phi}$
   $Var[\hat{Al}] \leftarrow nt\hat{\mu}\hat{\phi}(1 - \hat{\phi})$
   while not done **do**
      if defender action observed **then**
         $k \leftarrow k + 1$
         $\alpha = \left(\frac{1 - \hat{Al}}{Var[\hat{Al}]} - \frac{1}{\hat{Al}} \right) \hat{Al}^2$
         $\beta = \alpha \left(\frac{1}{\hat{Al}} - 1 \right)$
         $\gamma = \gamma_k / (k + 1)$
         $\hat{\mu} = \int_0^1 \frac{\hat{\mu}_k^{\alpha - 1}(1 - \hat{\mu}_k)^{\beta - 1}}{B(\alpha, \beta)}$

---

5 Empirical Evaluation

Game theoretic proofs about behavior in cybersecurity environments can provide powerful tools for thinking about how attacker-defender interaction occurs in practice. However, they do not always carry over to real-world environments. To gain empirical insight into the way these assumptions manifest in practice, we modify the YAWNING-TITAN (YT) framework [5] to include noise and allow two independent agents – one attacker and one defender – to be trained simultaneously. To do this, we create a new multiagent environment with a single state space where an attacking agent and a defending agent both operate but have their own separate observation and action spaces. This environment extends the functionality of YT by providing the ability to treat the attacking agent as a learner, rather than following a fixed algorithm for determining attacker actions. Moreover, since our zero-knowledge training case involves training both an attacker and a defender with different observation spaces, methods like Multi-Agent DDPG [21] are not suitable, as such methods would disclose hidden information about the environment to each agent. Despite issues of known overfitting to suboptimal policies due to non-stationarity [22], we opt to use two distinct instances of proximal policy optimization (PPO) [26] – one each for the attacker and defender – to train our agents, as this the algorithm generally performs well on a variety of tasks and has been used in prior, related work by others [5].

In this environment, we associate a cost to each attacker and defender action in accordance with those included in YT, and associate a positive reward for the agent that "wins" the episode along with a negative reward for the agent that "loses" the episode. To improve learning, we scale the negative reward for the defender such that they achieve a lesser negative reward for closer failures. Specifically, this scaling factor is the number of timesteps that the game has taken divided by the maximum number of timesteps required for a defender victory. We find that our defensive agent trained to expect the adversary has complete knowledge of the system will make worse decisions by overestimating the adversary when less information is available. For the sake of evaluating defensive agents against a programmatic, non-learning attacker, we adapt YT's NSARed agent [25], based on a description of cyber attack automation, to work within our environment. The implementation of the NSARed agent is purely algorithmic – there is no machine learning component – and defensive agents are not exposed to the agent at training time, making it a stable baseline for comparison. The full code for our training and evaluation implementation is available on GitHub[3].

5.1   Establishment of Priors

The attacker must consider three distributions when playing the game: $\hat{P}, \bar{P}, \underline{P}$. For the "best case" distribution $\bar{P}$, we train an attacking agent against a defender whose only action is to do nothing. For the "worst case" distribution $\underline{P}$, we train an attacking agent against a defender who has access to both attacker and defender observation spaces and thus has full-knowledge of the attacker's moves and the network. The remainder of this subsection describes the training of the model $\hat{P}$ is drawn from.

Our setting assumes an adversary who uses ransomware, where the attacking player "wins" when they control more than 80% of the network. For each training episode, we instantiate a random entrypoint for the attacker on a 50-node network whose edges are randomly generated to ensure the network has 60% connectivity, and that there are no unconnected nodes. We leverage proximal policy optimization (PPO) [26] for our learning agents in two settings:

1. Optimistic (zero-knowledge): The attacking agent can see only the nodes they control and adjacent nodes. They cannot see the vulnerability status of any nodes.
2. Pessimistic (full-knowledge): the attacking agent has access to the same information and observation space as the defending agent.

In accordance with our modeling assumptions, the attacking and defending player simultaneously decide their moves for timestep t from their action space. Each agent is trained in either the optimistic or pessimistic environment for 3000 episodes and evaluated for 500 episodes across randomly generated environments in both the optimistic and pessimistic setting. Based on empirical results from experiments in the environment, the actor learning rate is set to 0.0002 and the critic learning rate is set to 0.0005. Higher learning rates were tried and led to fast convergence to suboptimal policies, as PPO assumes full observability to achieve globally optimal policies and our environment is only partially observable. Values for all hyperparameters and action costs for both players were fixed across all settings and are included in Tables 1 and 2.

Evaluating reinforcement learning findings is notoriously difficult. Therefore, in line with Agarwal et al. [1], we look to more robust measurements that capture the uncertainty in results. Specifically, in addition to standard evaluation

---

[3] https://github.com/erickgalinkin/pop_rocks/.

Table 1. Hyperparameter values for reinforcement learning experiments.

Parameter	Value
Actor Learning Rate	0.0002
Critic Learning Rate	0.0005
Training Epochs	3500
γ	0.99
Update Epochs	5
Batch Size	64
Win Reward	5000
Lose Reward	−100

Table 2. Action costs for attackers and defenders

Attacker	Cost	Defender	Cost
Basic	2	Reduce Vuln	1.5
Zero Day	6	Make Safe	4
Move	0.5	Restore	6
Do Nothing	0	Scan	0.5
Execute	0	Do Nothing	0

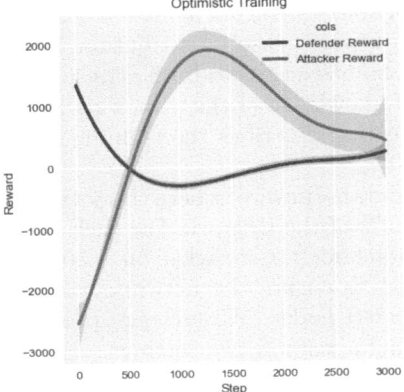

Fig. 1. Training reward curves for attacking and defending agents in the optimistic setting

Fig. 2. Training reward curves for attacking and defending agents in the pessimistic setting

metrics, we consider also score distributions and the interquartile mean across evaluation runs. These metrics help capture the stochasticity in the task and normalize our results. Smoothed training curves in the optimistic setting are shown in Fig. 1; the pessimistic setting is shown in Fig. 2. The average rewards and interquartile mean for evaluation of the defending agents trained in the optimistic and pessimistic settings achieved each of the two evaluation settings are shown in Fig. 3 and Fig. 4. Score distributions are captured in Fig. 5.

We observe in Figs. 1 and 2 that the attacker generally starts out with a poor reward, but learns how to attack the target within 500 epochs. In the optimistic setting, the defender initially starts out with a very high level of reward but once the attacker begins winning more often, they must adapt their strategy, with rewards for both agents converging around epoch 3000. In the pessimistic setting, the defender similarly starts with a reasonably high reward, but the attacker quickly learns how to overcome the defender's strategy. In this setting, the defender does not rebound and instead settles into a local optimum –

minimizing the magnitude of loss rather than continuing to explore for a strategy that eliminates the attacker. Longer runs – up to 10000 training epochs – were attempted, but the pessimistic defender's policy in those cases achieved even worse evaluation results than the defender trained for 3000 epochs. Note that the reward scale for attackers and defenders is not the same and defenders cannot achieve the extreme rewards that attackers do.

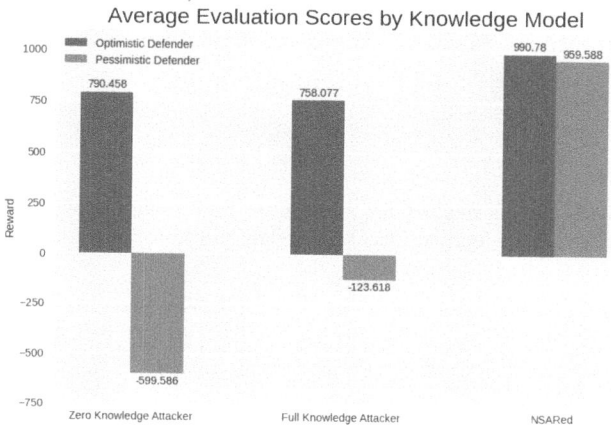

Fig. 3. Average reward for optimistic and pessimistic trained defending agents across 500 evaluation trials against zero knowledge, full knowledge, and NSARed attackers.

What we find from our evaluation is that the defending agent trained in the pessimistic setting performs worse on average than the defending agent trained in the optimistic setting. Across both evaluation settings, the optimistic defender is more robust in general and performs significantly better on average across all settings, as we can observe from Figs. 3 and 4. Note that a negative score implies that the attacker is winning more often than the defender, while a positive score implies that the defender is winning more often. Each defender performs relatively better in the setting they were trained in and experiences less variance, as we can see the relative stability between the mean and interquartile mean for in-domain settings. Interestingly, both optimistic and pessimistic defenders perform well against the NSARed attacker, suggesting that training against learning agents offers substantial benefit over training against more "static" algorithmic attackers.

The score distributions in Fig. 5 demonstrate the impact of the pessimistic defender's convergence. While the optimistic defender has a fairly broad, relatively normal distribution in both settings, the pessimistic defender's probability density is highly concentrated just below zero in domain and widely distributed across highly negative and highly positive out of distribution. This underscores the robustness of the optimistic defender and indicates that in training, the pessimistic defender converges to a policy that expects to achieve a negative reward

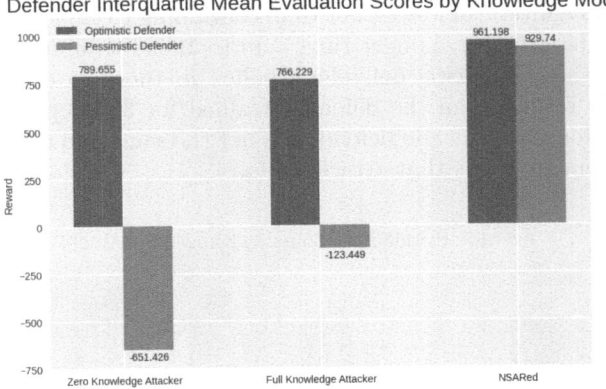

Fig. 4. Interquartile mean reward for optimistic and pessimistic trained defenders across 500 evaluation trials against zero knowledge, full knowledge, and `NSARed` attackers.

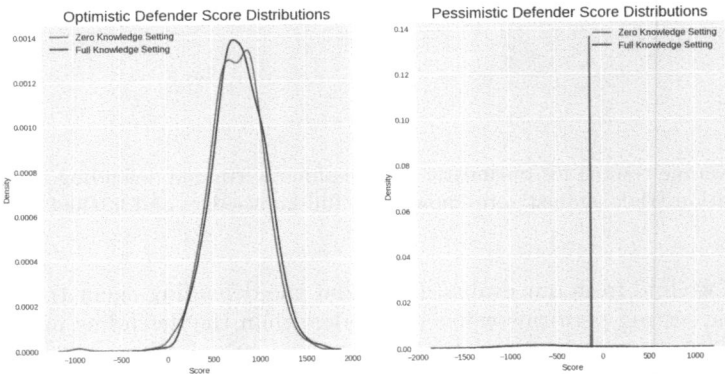

Fig. 5. Score Distributions for optimistic and pessimistic trained defenders across 500 evaluation trials in zero knowledge and full knowledge settings. Note that the scale of x and y axes differ between the subfigures.

and seeks to minimize that negative reward, rather than a policy that expects a positive reward and seeks to maximize it. Since the defender's win condition depends on eliminating the attacker or surviving 500 episodes, this "loss minimization" policy leads to suboptimal performance against learning attackers.

To explain the difference in outcomes and what is learned in training, we can examine the differences in actions taken by the optimistic and pessimistic defenders. We find that the pessimistic defender agent uses the more expensive "restore node" action at a higher frequency than the optimistic agent, while the optimistic agent spends more turns on reducing the vulnerability of nodes and making nodes safe. This is likely an artifact of the attacker in the pessimistic setting having access to significantly more information, requiring a more aggressive response to forestall an attacker win. The distribution of action usage for both agents across all evaluations is shown in Table 3.

Table 3. Percentage of Actions Taken by Defending Agent Across all evaluation episodes, ordered in ascending cost of the action.

Action	Pessimistic	Optimistic	Difference
Do Nothing	0%	1.4%	1.4%
Scan	3.22%	3.19%	0.03%
Reduce Vulnerability	16.1%	20.68%	4.58%
Make Node Safe	38.83%	41.33%	2.5%
Restore Node	41.85%	33.4%	8.45%

In the interest of ensuring our action costs do not have an undue influence on our results, we perform our same reinforcement learning evaluation for our pessimistic setting. We vary two parameters – "connectivity" and "security" – over the range $(0, 1]$, with a floor of 0.000001 to avoid division by zero. To establish the robustness of the model, we multiply the cost of each action by the ratio of connectivity and security such that the importance of security is nearly zero, the cost of actions becomes very high and when the value of connectivity is nearly zero, the cost of actions approaches zero, given fixed security value. We find that there is a nearly linear pattern relating the cost of actions to rewards, but the learned policy remains stable, provided the *relative* costs of actions is fixed and is not degenerate even near extremal values.

5.2 Use of Bayes-Hurwicz Decision Criterion for Attackers

As mentioned in Sect. 4.1, attackers in the real world do not have the luxury of training their priors to convergence against a target and must combine their prior knowledge with what is observed during an attack. Since the attacker is making decisions under uncertainty, some criterion must be used to allow them to do that subject to their own parameters. Using the pretrained, frozen models from Sect. 5.1, we consider how the application of the Restricted Bayes/Hurwicz criterion for the attacker as defined in Eq. 3 impacts the outcomes of the attacking player. Aside from the use of the Restricted Bayes/Hurwicz criterion for the attackers, all of the defender and environmental evaluation settings remain the same.

The attacking agent draws independent prior $\hat{\mu}$ and $\hat{\phi}$ values from PERT distributions in accordance with Algorithm 1 at the start of each round and updates their $\hat{\mu}$ at each timestep if defender activity is observed – that is, if the defender takes an action that removes access to an attacker controlled node. For each evaluation scenario, the relevant trained attacker model – zero knowledge or full knowledge – is used to establish $\hat{P}$, $\bar{P}$, and $\underline{P}$ for the observed state of the game. Specifically, each policy model $\hat{\pi}, \bar{\pi}, \underline{\pi}$ accepts an attacker-observed state S_t and outputs a distribution over the attacker's action space A_α such that $\hat{\pi}(S_t) \sim \hat{P}$, $\bar{\pi}(S_t) \sim \bar{P}$, and $\underline{\pi}(S_t) \sim \underline{P}$. The attacker leverages these model outputs and the values of $\hat{\mu}$, and γ with Eq. 3 to determine their next best action.

Interquartile mean evaluation rewards for the attacker, shown in Fig. 6, illustrate the impact of restricted Bayes/Hurwicz. Against the optimistic defender, the use of restricted Bayes/Hurwicz yields marginally worse performance for the zero-knowledge (in-domain) attacker, but marginally better performance for the full-knowledge (out-of-domain) attacker. Against the pessimistic defender, the pure zero-knowledge attacker performs incredibly well, and using Bayes/Hurwicz

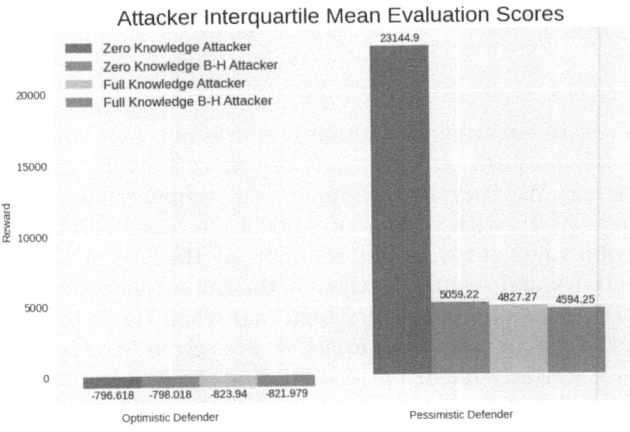

Fig. 6. Interquartile mean reward for attacking players across 500 evaluation trials against both optimistic and pessimistic defenders

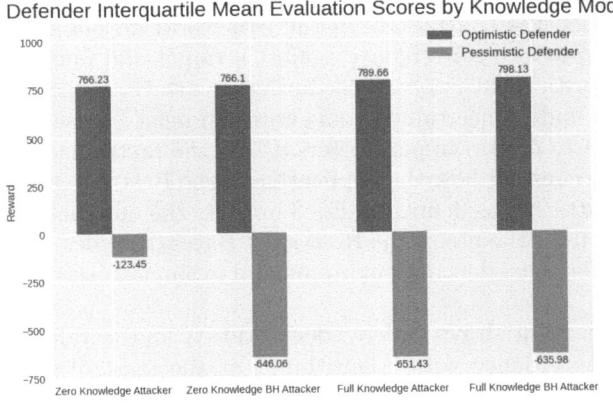

Fig. 7. Interquartile mean reward for optimistic and pessimistic defenders across 500 evaluation trials against all attacker types.

somewhat negatively impacts the attacker's interquartile mean reward While the full-knowledge (in-domain) attacker performs worse overall against the pessimistic defender, the pure strategy is better than using Bayes-Hurwicz, as we would expect (Fig. 8).

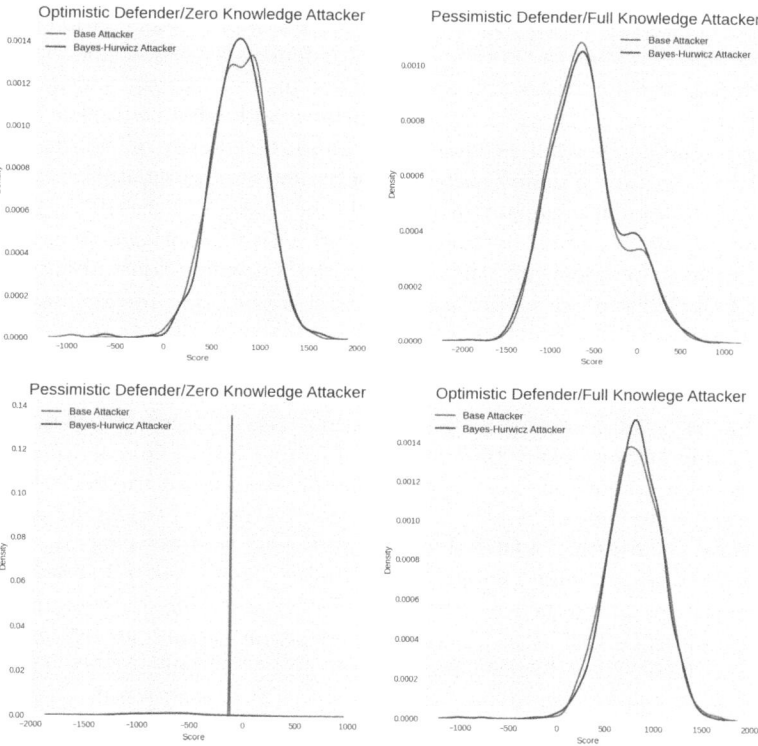

Fig. 8. Score distributions for optimistic and pessimistic defenders against base and restricted Bayes/Hurwicz attackers in full-knowledge and zero-knowledge settings. Note that the scale of x and y axes differ among the subfigures.

Results for defenders against both base attackers and those using restricted Bayes/Hurwicz are shown in Fig. 7, and reflect the information from Fig. 4. The optimistic defender experiences a marginal improvement against the restricted Bayes/Hurwicz attackers in both the zero knowledge and full knowledge case. Meanwhile, the pessimistic defender performs slightly better against the restricted Bayes/Hurwicz attacker in the full knowledge (in-domain) case, but significantly worse against the restricted Bayes/Hurwicz attacker in the zero knowledge (out-of-domain) case.

6   Conclusion and Future Work

The game design assumptions made about an attacker's capabilities and knowledge grow increasingly important as we seek to develop improved mitigation capabilities for cyber defenders. In this work, we have demonstrated a phenomenon we call "the price of pessimism" – the cost incurred by a defender by assuming a more pessimistic view of what an attacker is likely to know. Practically, this suggests that the development of defensive agents necessitates careful consideration of what real-world attackers are likely to know, and model those assumptions correctly. Specifically, assumptions made about attacker knowledge considerably influence what defenders learn and the efficacy of their response. In future work, we aim to define more precisely how environmental factors should be determined and the impact of per-node and subnet variability of true and false positive alert rates on both attacker and defender performance.

Our results demonstrate that a defender's assumptions about *a priori* attacker knowledge of an environment have a measurable impact on how that defender responds to potential intrusions. An assumption that overestimates an attacker's knowledge and the concomitant learned response dynamics from this assumption leads to overreaction to false positives on the part of defending agents, incurring unnecessary costs and leading to poor convergence in reinforcement learning settings. We conclude that future work in this space seeking to have impact on systems in the real world should account for the likely knowledge and learning dynamics of attackers in addition to those of defenders and should aim to more accurately capture the learning behavior of attackers.

In future work, we aim to apply these findings to automated threat response by incorporating human factors, threat modeling, and using more complex simulation frameworks. Although our agents are learning agents, attacks both today and in the foreseeable future are conducted not by pure utility maximizing agents, but by human beings. As a result, we look to incorporate prospect theory [34] in future work similar to how such models have been used to align large language models [12]. We also aim to explore how incorporating threat intelligence information about sequences of attacker actions and how they lead to different outcomes can constrain the defender's action space, allowing for threat-informed defense. Finally, given the restricted node states of the YT reinforcement learning environment, research incorporating threat intelligence may need to leverage a simulation framework more similar to real-world environments, like CybORG [10].

References

1. Agarwal, R., Schwarzer, M., Castro, P.S., Courville, A.C., Bellemare, M.: Deep reinforcement learning at the edge of the statistical precipice. Adv. Neural. Inf. Process. Syst. **34**, 29304–29320 (2021)
2. Aggarwal, P., et al.: Designing effective masking strategies for cyberdefense through human experimentation and cognitive models. Comput. Secur. **117**, 102671 (2022)

3. Albrecht, S.V., Ramamoorthy, S.: A game-theoretic model and best-response learning method for ad hoc coordination in multiagent systems. In: Proceedings of the 2013 International Conference on Autonomous Agents and Multi-agent Systems, pp. 1155–1156 (2013)

4. Anderson, R.: Security Engineering: A Guide to Building Dependable Distributed Systems. John Wiley & Sons, Hoboken (2020)

5. Andrew, A., Spillard, S., Collyer, J., Dhir, N.: Developing optimal causal cyber-defence agents via cyber security simulation. In: Workshop on Machine Learning for Cybersecurity (ML4Cyber) (2022)

6. Brooks, C.: Cybersecurity trends & statistics for 2023; what you need to know (2023). https://www.forbes.com/sites/chuckbrooks/2023/03/05/cybersecurity-trends--statistics-for-2023-more-treachery-and-risk-ahead-as-attack-surface-and-hacker-capabilities-grow/

7. Campbell, R.G.: Autonomous Network Defense Using Multi-Agent Reinforcement Learning and Self-Play. Ph.D. thesis, San Jose State University (2022)

8. Chatterjee, S., Tipireddy, R., Oster, M., Halappanavar, M.: Propagating mixed uncertainties in cyber attacker payoffs : exploration of two-phase monte carlo sampling and probability bounds analysis. In: IEEE International Symposium on Technologies for Homeland Security. IEEE (2016)

9. Clark, C.E.: The pert model for the distribution of an activity time. Oper. Res. **10**(3), 405–406 (1962)

10. Standen, M., et al.: Cyber operations research gym (2022). https://github.com/cage-challenge/CybORG

11. Ellsberg, D.: Risk, Ambiguity and Decision. Routledge, Abingdon (2015)

12. Ethayarajh, K., Xu, W., Muennighoff, N., Jurafsky, D., Kiela, D.: Kto: model alignment as prospect theoretic optimization. arXiv preprint arXiv:2402.01306 (2024)

13. Foley, M., Hicks, C., Highnam, K., Mavroudis, V.: Autonomous network defence using reinforcement learning. In: Proceedings of the 2022 ACM on Asia Conference on Computer and Communications Security, pp. 1252–1254 (2022)

14. Galinkin, E., Pountourakis, E., Carter, J., Mancoridis, S.: Simulation of attacker defender interaction in a noisy security game. In: AAAI-23 Workshop on Artificial Intelligence for Cyber Security (2023)

15. Galinkin, E., Singh, A., Vamshi, A., Hwong, J., Estep, C., Canzanese, R.: The future of cyber attacks and defense is in the cloud. In: Proceedings - IEEE MAL-CON (2019). https://www.researchgate.net/publication/336592029

16. Illés, T., Terlaky, T.: Pivot versus interior point methods: pros and cons. Eur. J. Oper. Res. **140**(2), 170–190 (2002)

17. Khouzani, M.H., Sarkar, S., Altman, E.: Saddle-point strategies in malware attack. IEEE J. Sel. Areas Commun. **30**(1), 31–43 (2012). https://doi.org/10.1109/JSAC.2012.120104

18. Kohgadai, A.: Alert fatigue: 31.9% of it security professionals ignore alerts (2017). https://virtualizationreview.com/articles/2017/02/17/the-problem-of-security-alert-fatigue.aspx

19. Kumar, S., et al.: An emerging threat fileless malware: a survey and research challenges. Cybersecurity **3**(1), 1–12 (2020)

20. Liang, X., Xiao, Y.: Game theory for network security. IEEE Commun. Surv. Tutor. **15**(1), 472–486 (2013). https://doi.org/10.1109/SURV.2012.062612.00056

21. Lowe, R., Wu, Y.I., Tamar, A., Harb, J., Pieter Abbeel, O., Mordatch, I.: Multi-agent actor-critic for mixed cooperative-competitive environments. Adv. Neural Inf. Process. Syst. **30** (2017)

22. Moalla, S., Miele, A., Pascanu, R., Gulcehre, C.: No representation, no trust: connecting representation, collapse, and trust issues in ppo. arXiv preprint arXiv:2405.00662 (2024)
23. Nguyen, T.H., Yadav, A.: The risk of attacker behavioral learning: can attacker fool defender under uncertainty? In: Fang, F., Xu, H., Hayel, Y. (eds.) GameSec 2022, pp. 3–22. Springer, Heidelberg (2022)
24. Pawlick, J., Zhu, Q.: Game Theory for Cyber Deception. Springer, Heidelberg (2021). https://doi.org/10.1007/978-3-030-66065-9
25. Ridley, A.: Machine learning for autonomous cyber defense. The Next Wave: The National Security Agency's Review of Emerging Technologies (2018)
26. Schulman, J., Wolski, F., Dhariwal, P., Radford, A., Klimov, O.: Proximal policy optimization algorithms. arXiv preprint arXiv:1707.06347 (2017)
27. Security, O.: 2022 cloud security alert fatigue report (2022). https://orca.security/lp/sp/2022-cloud-security-alert-fatigue-report-thank-you/
28. Shostack, A.: Threat Modeling. Wiley, Hoboken (2014)
29. Simard, F., Desharnais, J., Laviolette, F.: General cops and robbers games with randomness. Theor. Comput. Sci. **887**, 30–50 (2021)
30. Sokri, A.: Game theory and cyber defense. In: Games in Management Science: Essays in Honor of Georges Zaccour, pp. 335–352 (2020)
31. Thakoor, O., Jabbari, S., Aggarwal, P., Gonzalez, C., Tambe, M., Vayanos, P.: Exploiting bounded rationality in risk-based cyber camouflage games. In: GameSec 2020. LNCS, vol. 12513, pp. 103–124. Springer, Cham (2020). https://doi.org/10.1007/978-3-030-64793-3_6
32. Tomášek, P., Bošanský, B., Nguyen, T.H.: Using one-sided partially observable stochastic games for solving zero-sum security games with sequential attacks. In: GameSec 2020. LNCS, vol. 12513, pp. 385–404. Springer, Cham (2020). https://doi.org/10.1007/978-3-030-64793-3_21
33. TTCP: cage-challenge (2021). https://github.com/cage-challenge
34. Tversky, A., Kahneman, D.: Advances in prospect theory: cumulative representation of uncertainty. J. Risk Uncertain. **5**(4), 297–323 (1992)

Economics

Ransom Roulette: Learning the Games Behind Cyber Extortion

Eckhard Pflügel[1]([✉]) [iD] and Stefan Rass[2,3] [iD]

[1] Faculty of Engineering, Computing and the Environment, Kingston University,
Kingston upon Thames KT1 2EE, UK
e.pfluegel@kingston.ac.uk
[2] LIT Secure and Correct Systems Lab, Johannes Kepler University,
Altenbergerstraße 69, 4040 Linz, Austria
stefan.rass@jku.at
[3] Institute for Artificial Intelligence and Cybersecurity, Alpen-Adria-University
Klagenfurt, Universitätsstrasse 65-67, 9020 Klagenfurt, Austria

Abstract. A ransomware game involves a ransomware attacker $\mathcal{A}$ and a victim $\mathcal{V}$ deciding to cooperate or not. The victim may or may not trust the ransomware attacker to unlock files after paying the ransom to prevent data loss. Simultaneously, the attacker can strategically decide whether or not to unlock the files after receiving payment. This can be modelled as a strategic game, repeated over time. In addition, the attacker may change their mind at any point and stop the game. Likewise, the victim, at any time, might become incapable of playing by being bankrupt, or uninterested by having established recovery and resilience. We develop a novel stochastic game-theoretic model for analysing this scenario and provide equilibria for a single victim and multiple victims. We also study convergence towards equilibria from mutual experience collected by victims and the attacker and compare the equilibrium limits of the model with recommendations from real-life reported experience.

1 Introduction

Ransomware has been an increasingly prolific and impactful cyber attack in recent years. Organisations are facing the difficult decision of whether to give in to ransom payment demands or refuse to cooperate. On the other hand, cyber-criminals weigh the advantages and disadvantages of attempting to convey a reliable reputation [10,11,35], hence increasing the chances of obtaining payments in future ransom attacks by consistently restoring encrypted data after ransom payment [37]. Game theory can help to understand better this strategic decision-making scenario by analysing the motivations underlying the behaviour of the ransom attackers and their victims.

Ransomware attacks may repeat over several users or even a single victim, but eventually will need to stop at some point for several possible reasons. Among them is the adversary having gained its payment and thus lost interest in the victim, or in a worse case, the victim is either unable to pay or bankrupt after

A. Sinha et al. (Eds.): GameSec 2024, LNCS 14908, pp. 67–86, 2025.
https://doi.org/10.1007/978-3-031-74835-6_4

having paid (in case the data is not unlocked afterwards or recoverable). Both possibilities, among others, bear a strategic decision for the players to "stop" the game at some point, and a game theoretic model should thus include such a choice point. On a high level, we do so by letting the process be a random variable X_t that captures the cash flow from the victim to the adversary due to a ransomware attack at time t. The random payment X_t is determined by a strategic interaction in which both players follow their equilibrium strategies. "Stopping" the game then means stopping the respective stochastic process by considering another random variable

$$Z_t := \begin{cases} X_t & \text{if } t \leq T, \\ X_T & \text{if } t > T. \end{cases}$$

This expresses that after one of the players drops out at the (random) time T, the state of both players remains at the outcome of the last round of the game (e.g., the attacker may have won a ransom, the victim could be unable to pay further, or, in a best case, could have recovered from a backup and fixed its vulnerability without having paid anything).

If both players decide to stop purely on retrospective considerations, meaning that the stopping decision is not made anticipating the future, then T is a stopping time (formally, this means that the random variable T only depends on $X_0, \ldots, X_{T-1}$, but is independent of $X_{T+1}, X_{T+2}, \ldots$). Adopting this hypothesis for the game model makes the stopped process a martingale. We can apply the optimal stopping theorem [38, pg. 67] after observing that (i) the expected time to stop is finite, $E(T) < \infty$ (since the adversary *may* chose to go arbitrarily long, but eventually will at some point need to stop), and (ii) the expected gains per round are also finite, meaning $E(|X_{t+1} - X_t| \mid X_0, \ldots, X_{t-1}) < c$ for some constant $c > 0$. Since the game will have continuous payoffs on compact action spaces, the finiteness of payoffs and their differences is assured.

Under these assumptions, the expected gains at time T equal the expected gain in the first round, $E(X_T) = E(X_0)$. This means that, without loss of generality, the analysis of a ransomware attack that may repeat several times until it finishes at a finite but random time T, boils down to considering a single stage game that describes the interaction only in a single instance. The accumulated reward for the attacker upon repetition, by Wald's identity (that holds under the same conditions) then merely come to $E(X_0 + X_1 + \ldots + X_T) = E(T) \cdot E(X_0)$, leaving the average, i.e., equilibrium payoff $E(X_0)$, as the fundamental quantity to study next. Later, towards some generality, we will extend the setting to multiple victims (that may even cooperate by sharing experience about their common adversary).

The contributions of this paper are the following: We devise a flexible two-player, non-zero-sum stochastic stopping game framework for modelling ransomware scenarios informed by attacker, victim, and mixed personality profiles using *birational games*, defined in Sect. 3. To the best of our knowledge, this is the first time such a systematic stochastic game framework has been presented and applied to the ransomware scenario. A stationary equilibrium analysis of the game is provided, and sufficient conditions for pure or mixed Nash equilibria are given for various personality profiles. In particular, the presence of mixed equilibria is discussed. We then focus on the bimatrix stage game and extend it to a multiple-victim scenario, prove that equilibrium solutions can be found through an online learning process based on extending the Fictitious Play (FP) algorithm to $2 \times n$ birational games with a common rank-1 denominator, and provide an illustrative evaluation of this process.

Throughout the paper, we denote the matrix $\mathbf{E}$ (the vector $\mathbf{e}$) consisting of all entries set to one, $\mathbf{e}_i$ denotes the ith unit vector, and $\mathbf{O}$ denotes the zero matrix, with sizes inferred from context. A bimatrix game $\Gamma(\mathbf{A}, \mathbf{B})$ involves two players where the first plays row actions and the second plays column actions. Strategies for the first and second players are denoted by $\mathbf{x}$ and $\mathbf{y}$, respectively, and a strategy profile is represented as $(\mathbf{x}, \mathbf{y})$. A Nash equilibrium (NE) strategy is $(\mathbf{x}^*, \mathbf{y}^*)$. The corresponding game value is denoted by $\mathbf{v} = (v_x, v_y)$. We let players as calligraphic letters like $\mathcal{V}$ (for the "victim"), and let the corresponding latin letter denote the payoff structure of this entity (e.g., $\mathbf{V}$ for the player $\mathcal{V}$). For a matrix $\mathbf{S}$, the symbol $\mathbf{S} > 0$ is to be understood as the inequality holding per element. A similar definition holds for $\mathbf{S} \geq 0$, with $\mathbf{S} \neq \mathbf{O}$ assumed. Matrix pencils are expressions of the form $\mathbf{A} - \lambda\mathbf{B}$. A matrix pencil $\mathbf{A} - \lambda\mathbf{B}$ is called regular if both matrices $\mathbf{A}$ and $\mathbf{B}$ are square of size n and the polynomial $f(\lambda) = \det(\mathbf{A} - \lambda\mathbf{B})$ is non-zero, meaning $f(\lambda) \not\equiv 0$. Finding left (right respectively) generalised eigenvectors of a regular matrix pencil for a finite eigenvalue μ means finding non-zero solutions of $\mathbf{x}^\top(\mathbf{A} - \mu\mathbf{B}) = 0$ (respectively $(\mathbf{A} - \mu\mathbf{B})\mathbf{y} = 0$), where $f(\mu) = 0$.

The remainder of the paper is organised as follows: We relate our work to other results in Sect. 2. Section 3 introduces some definitions and preliminary materials. Section 4 describes the game model for a single stage of a ransom attack, giving the expectation $E(X_0)$ from above, besides the likewise quantity for the other player. We provide equilibrium results (also in the multi-victim case), online learning of best behaviour in this section, and a comparison to official recommendations of security agencies about ransomware. Section 5 compares the model results against real-life reports, and conclusions are drawn in Sect. 6. The appendix provides technical details (proofs) behind the results developed along the main body of the paper.

2   Related Work

Pioneering work on applying game theory to a ransomware scenario involving multiple defending organisations and a ransom attacker was [18]. This paper was motivated by understanding the impact of economic incentives within an organisation on management decisions for investment in backups and willingness to pay the ransom. The game, a multi-stage, multi-defender security game, combines insight from security games and economic considerations and raises further questions: the idea of penalise organisations paying ransoms might be unethical, for example, in a healthcare setting. Another early paper for game-theoretic approaches for ransomware scenarios [8] was inspired by work on game models for kidnapping [15,17,33]. These games are sequential, two-player games with parameters representing various probabilities, such as outcomes of negotiating the ransom fee, the occurrence of deception by the kidnapper, or the likelihood of arrest by the police. The paper is based on the insight that the decision-making processes behind a ransomware attacker and victim scenario are similar to those in the kidnapping games, reflected in the resulting game models. Several crucial issues emerge: negotiating an optimal ransom, the trust in the attacker to release the data upon payment, the idea that the attacker might want to establish some form of "brand", and the challenge of setting up suitable proactive controls. An interesting aspect, the "spillover" effect, relates to the fact that different types of victims are willing to spend different amounts in deterrence, such as backups, hence creating uncertainty for the attacker, which could be seen as an advantage for other subsequent victims. This is a point in common with [18] but approached differently in the two papers.

Modern ransomware attackers increasingly employ diverse hostile strategies, such as threatening to publish the captured data publicly on the internet or selling it off to the black market. This aspect was explored in a series of papers on "Ransomware 2.0" [19–21] through a finite multi-stage game model. An additional preventative measure based on deception was devised and analysed with the model of [21]. Extensive simulations are provided to evaluate the resulting equilibrium payoffs, depending on their decision input parameters. The papers [2–4] embed ransom attacks in the wider network security framework of Advanced Persistent Threats (APTs). While the scope of the developed models is broader, with the vision of a global framework, aiding the response to large-scale ransom attacks orchestrated by entire hostile organisations or nations, the essentials of the model remained the same, centred around the decision-making involved between paying the ransom or not, and the attacker releasing the data after payment, or to deceive by failing to do so. An extended game theoretic analysis of ransomware was developed in [39], where the Attacker-Defender (A-D) game between ransom attacker and victim is complemented by a Defender-Insurer (D-I) game. While the A-D game is similar to previous models, the D-I game models the attacker as a non-strategic third party. Solutions are provided as empirical outcomes due to the complexity of the model. While this approach is innovative, it also has drawbacks due to the restricted interaction level between the two game players. Further refining previous multi-stage ransomware games, the authors in [40] analyse the decision-making in the different stages of an attack based on four subgames: data backup, ransomware development, compromise and data release stages. This framework introduces many parameters, allowing a detailed game customisation for realistic scenarios. The works of [5,14] also divide the attack into different (similiar) stages for an optimal attack/defense orchestration.

In summary, while none of the papers can answer all relevant questions simultaneously, they draw a reasonably comprehensive picture jointly. In our work, we are interested in further investigating the following key aspects:

First, previous models were not all focused on stochastic games. In reality, ransomware attacks may occur repeatedly and certainly will if we consider a generic victim. We are interested in what can be said about the strategic preferences of the two players, their stopping probabilities, and the consequences for the resulting game analysis.

Second, we are interested in a learning process where the user group pools knowledge and experience about security threats and countermeasures (threat intelligence) over time and tackles how a possible collaboration and learning of victims against the attacker affects the attack model. We study a first simple setting in which the user group faces the attacker individually but optimizes a joint loss to model cooperation among the group.

3 Definitions and Preliminaries

Since our model will rely on games with particular rational functions as utilities, we review a few technical results, the proofs of which are given in Appendix A.

Denote $\Gamma(\mathbf{A}, \mathbf{B}, \mathbf{C}, \mathbf{D})$ a general birational game, which is a bimatrix game with rational payoff functions. The payoffs to Player 1 and Player 2 using the strategies $(\mathbf{x}, \mathbf{y})$ are defined as $u_{\mathcal{A}}(\mathbf{x}, \mathbf{y}) = \frac{\mathbf{x}^\top \mathbf{A} \mathbf{y}}{\mathbf{x}^\top \mathbf{C} \mathbf{y}}$, and $u_{\mathcal{B}}(\mathbf{x}, \mathbf{y}) = \frac{\mathbf{x}^\top \mathbf{B} \mathbf{y}}{\mathbf{x}^\top \mathbf{D} \mathbf{y}}$ with $\mathbf{C}, \mathbf{D} > 0$, where the inequality holds per element. Letting $\mathbf{x}, \mathbf{y}$ range over all (discrete) probability distributions, we have $\mathbf{x}^\top \mathbf{C} \mathbf{y} \neq 0$ and $\mathbf{x}^\top \mathbf{D} \mathbf{y} \neq 0$ for all admissible $\mathbf{x}, \mathbf{y}$, and hence the quotients are always well-defined. Hence, $u_{\mathcal{A}}$ and $u_{\mathcal{B}}$ are both continuous functions over a compact strategy set (a closed subset of the Euclidean space), and Glicksberg's theorem [13] assures the existence of an equilibrium.

Definition 1. *A Nash Equilibrium strategy* $(\mathbf{x}^*, \mathbf{y}^*)$ *of a bimatrix game with rational payoff functions satisfies* $v_x = \frac{\mathbf{x}^{*\top} \mathbf{A} \mathbf{y}^*}{\mathbf{x}^{*\top} \mathbf{C} \mathbf{y}^*} \geq \frac{\mathbf{x}^\top \mathbf{A} \mathbf{y}^*}{\mathbf{x}^\top \mathbf{C} \mathbf{y}^*}$ $\forall \mathbf{x}$ *and* $v_y = \frac{\mathbf{x}^{*\top} \mathbf{B} \mathbf{y}^*}{\mathbf{x}^{*\top} \mathbf{D} \mathbf{y}^*} \geq \frac{\mathbf{x}^{*\top} \mathbf{B} \mathbf{y}}{\mathbf{x}^{*\top} \mathbf{D} \mathbf{y}}$ $\forall \mathbf{y}$. *We say that* $(\mathbf{x}^*, \mathbf{y}^*)$ *is a Nash equilibrium and that* $\mathbf{v} = (v_x, v_y)$ *is the corresponding game value profile.*

3.1 Nash Equilibria in Birational Games

The class of birational games was originally defined in [22] as n-player games with rational payoff functions and proven to possess an equilibrium point. For $n = 2$, the authors in [23] introduce the terminology of birational games and investigate mechanism design approaches for completely mixed solutions (similarly, but for the zero-sum game case, [30] give a construction of matrix games with any pre-desired set of Nash equilibria). Our interest in this class of games roots in the possibility of characterizing equilibria by generalized eigenvalues (Proposition 1). As in bimatrix games, pure best responses and equilibrium solutions satisfy the "principle of indifference" in a birational game.

Lemma 1. *If Player 1's mixed strategy* $\mathbf{x}$ *is a best response to the (mixed) strategy* $\mathbf{y}$ *of the other player, then, for each pure strategy* $\mathbf{e}_i$ *such that* $x_i > 0$, *it* *must be the case that* $\mathbf{e}_i$ *is itself a best response. In particular, the payoff* $\mathbf{e}_i \mathbf{A} \mathbf{y}$ *must be the same for all such strategies.*

An analogous fact can be stated for Player 2, for a best response $\mathbf{y}$ to $\mathbf{x}$, and $\mathbf{B}$.

Since $\mathbf{e}_i{}^\top \mathbf{A}$ is the ith row of $\mathbf{A}$, an immediate consequence of Lemma 1 is

$$\frac{\mathbf{e}_i{}^\top \mathbf{A} \mathbf{y}}{\mathbf{e}_i{}^\top \mathbf{C} \mathbf{y}} = v_x \iff \mathbf{e}_i{}^\top (\mathbf{A} - v_x \mathbf{C}) \mathbf{y} = 0.$$

Furthermore, we can combine these equations in vector form as $(\mathbf{A} - v_x \mathbf{C}) \mathbf{y} = 0$.

From this, we obtain the following proposition, which states an alternative definition of equilibrium solutions of a birational game.

Proposition 1. *For the birational game* $\Gamma(\mathbf{A}, \mathbf{B}, \mathbf{C}, \mathbf{D})$, *an equivalent formulation for a Nash Equilibrium strategy* $(\mathbf{x}^*, \mathbf{y}^*)$ *with values* v_x, v_y *is as follows: define* v_y *as the greatest value such that there is* $\mathbf{x}^* \geq 0$ *satisfying* $\mathbf{x}^*(\mathbf{B} - v_y \mathbf{D}) \leq 0$. *Similarly, define* v_x *as the greatest value such that there is* $\mathbf{y}^* \geq 0$ *and* $(\mathbf{A} - v_x \mathbf{C}) \mathbf{y}^* \leq 0$.

This formulation extends the classical von Neumann economic growth model [28] to a non-zero-sum setting. Compared to that of Definition 1, the advantage of this above representation is that it provides a somewhat more convenient definition of equilibrium and potentially an easier equilibrium analysis of the game.

Define a normalised vector as one whose components add up to one. The following theorem uses linear algebra concepts to give a sufficient condition for a Nash equilibrium solution of a birational game, extending Theorem 2 in [29]. Its proof can be done very similarly.

Theorem 1. *Given the birational game* $\Gamma(\mathbf{A}, \mathbf{B}, \mathbf{C}, \mathbf{D})$, *assume the matrix pencils* $\mathbf{A} - \lambda \mathbf{C}$ *and* $\mathbf{B} - \lambda \mathbf{D}$ *are both regular. For each pencil, assume it has a real finite eigenvalue* α *and* β, *respectively. Furthermore, assume that there exists a normalised nonnegative left eigenvector* $\mathbf{x}$ *with* $\mathbf{x}(\mathbf{B} - \beta \mathbf{D}) = 0$ *and a normalised nonnegative right eigenvector* $\mathbf{y}$ *satisfying* $(\mathbf{A} - \alpha \mathbf{C}) \mathbf{y} = 0$. *Then* $(\mathbf{x}, \mathbf{y})$ *is a Nash equilibrium of the birational game, and* (α, β) *are the corresponding game values.*

3.2 Birational Games with Common Rank-1 Denominator

Birational games were previously used in [29] in the context of stochastic games, and this focus continues in this paper. In this section, we consider birational games with a common rank-1 denominator. We will show that if the utility functions have a common denominator matrix $\mathbf{C} > 0$ of rank 1, in which case we abbreviate it as $\Gamma(\mathbf{A}, \mathbf{B}, \mathbf{C})$, then equilibria are computable by solving a conventional bimatrix game. Hence, one can "clear" the denominator and replace the birational game with a bimatrix game for such payoff functions.

Theorem 2. *Consider the* $n \times m$ *birational game* $\Gamma(\mathbf{A}, \mathbf{B}, \mathbf{C})$ *with common denominator matrix* $\mathbf{C} > 0$ *and* $rank(\mathbf{C}) = 1$. *Then there exist real* $p_i, q_j > 0$ $(i = 1, \ldots, m; j = 1, \ldots n)$ *such that the bimatrix game* $\tilde{\Gamma}(\tilde{\mathbf{A}}, \tilde{\mathbf{B}})$ *where* $\tilde{\mathbf{A}} = ((\tilde{a}_{ij}))$ *and* $\tilde{\mathbf{B}} = (\tilde{b}_{ij}))$ *with* $\tilde{a}_{ij} = \frac{a_{ij}}{p_i q_j}$ *and* $\tilde{b}_{ij} = \frac{b_{ij}}{p_i q_j}$ *has the following properties:*

(i) *There is a one-to-one correspondence between the equilibrium solutions of the birational game Γ and those of the bimatrix game $\tilde{\Gamma}$.*

(ii) *Corresponding equilibrium solutions have the same game values.*

4 The Two-Player Ransom Roulette Game

In this section, the two-player ransom roulette game is introduced. We describe the general game model and analyse several instances of games with various aspects, suitable for specific ransomware scenarios.

4.1 Game Definition

The two-player ransom roulette game is a stochastic bimatrix stopping game $\Gamma(\mathbf{V}, \mathbf{A}, \mathbf{S})$, defined by a matrix triple consisting of payoff matrices $\mathbf{A}, \mathbf{B}$ and a stopping matrix $\mathbf{S}$, defined by

$$\mathbf{V} = \begin{pmatrix} -c_p & -c_p - c_\ell \\ 0 & -c_\ell \end{pmatrix}, \quad \mathbf{A} = \begin{pmatrix} b_r - c_d & b_r \\ -c_d & 0 \end{pmatrix} \quad \text{and} \quad \mathbf{S} = \begin{pmatrix} s_{11} & s_{12} \\ s_{21} & s_{22} \end{pmatrix}.$$

This defines the utility functions

$$u_{\mathcal{V}}(\mathbf{x}, \mathbf{y}) := \frac{\mathbf{x}^\top \mathbf{V} \mathbf{y}}{\mathbf{x}^\top \mathbf{S} \mathbf{y}} \quad \text{and} \quad u_{\mathcal{A}}(\mathbf{x}, \mathbf{y}) := \frac{\mathbf{x}^\top \mathbf{A} \mathbf{y}}{\mathbf{x}^\top \mathbf{S} \mathbf{y}}, \tag{1}$$

which shows that Γ is a birational game with common denominator S.

Utilities
c_ℓ is the victim's cost due to data loss.
c_p is the victim's cost due to paying the ransomware attack.
b_r is the attacker's benefit arising from receiving the ransom.
c_d is the attacker's effort to unlock the data.
Stopping Matrix
$s_{ij} \in [0, 1]$ is a stopping probability if strategy profile (i, j) is played.
Assumptions
(A1) All occurring parameters are positive.
(A2) The ransom attack is profitable to the attacker: $b_r > c_d$.
(A3) Paying the ransom costs less than losing access to the data: $c_p < c_\ell$.

Fig. 1. Parameters and their assumptions in the utility functions for the two-player ransom roulette stopping game $\Gamma(\mathbf{V}, \mathbf{A}, \mathbf{S})$.

Figure 1 summarises the different parameters occurring in the matrices $\mathbf{V}$, $\mathbf{A}$ and $\mathbf{S}$ and the assumptions made about them. The generic formulation of the utilities via (1) is flexible, and specific choices for the stopping matrix lead to pertinent cases of interest for this paper. The cases discussed in the sequel are the following: (i) stage game (Sect. 4.2): all of the s_i are equal to one ($\mathbf{S} = \mathbf{E}$), (ii) stopping game (Sect. 4.3): a stopping matrix $\mathbf{S} > 0$ with all strictly positive elements, and in Sect. 5 we will investigate (iii) the online learning of equilibria.

4.2   Stage Game

We put $\mathbf{S} = \mathbf{E}$ to model a single-shot ransomware game $\mathcal{R}^0$, where a ransomware attacker $\mathcal{A}$ and a victim $\mathcal{V}$ need to decide whether to cooperate or not. Before they pay to prevent permanent data loss, the victim must decide whether they can trust the ransomware attacker to unlock the files upon ransom payment. On the other hand, the attacker is weighing up whether they should invest in unlocking the files once payment has been received or whether they keep them encrypted. We can model the situation as a bimatrix game.   By inspecting the

$\mathcal{V} \downarrow \mathcal{A} \rightarrow$	cooperate (unlock)	not cooperate (keep locked)
cooperate (pay)	$-c_p$, $b_r - c_d$	$-c_p - c_\ell$, b_r
not cooperate (not pay)	0 , $-c_d$	$-c_\ell$, 0

Fig. 2. *The ransomware roulette bimatrix stage game* $\mathcal{R}^0$.

players' best responses, Assumptions (A1)–(A3) and the classification in [26, Table 1], we obtain immediately:

Proposition 2. *The stage game* $\mathcal{R}^0 := \Gamma(\mathbf{V}, \mathbf{A}, \mathbf{E})$ *defined as in Fig. 2 has exactly one pure Nash equilibrium (not pay, keep locked). The game is strategically equivalent to a zero-sum game.*

While being a simple game, it nevertheless contains the relevant decision scenarios reported in previous work, and the Proposition is consistent with advice normally issued by cyber security advisory boards such as UK's NCSC [27].

4.3   Stopping Game

Now, we allow both players to drop out at any time (for any reason) from the game, which amounts to using a stopping matrix $\mathbf{S} > 0$ with $\mathbf{S} \neq \mathbf{E}$. Further, we let the choice of stopping be made independently by both players (conversely, we do not assume that they will seek a mutual consensus to stop, but rather decide this for or against the opponent's will). This game may have many equilibrium solutions, both pure and mixed. To identify meaningful and insightful solutions, we will introduce the idea of *personality profiles* reflected in the design of the stopping matrix. Based on the player's specific personality profiles, we propose corresponding stopping matrices and analyse the impact on the equilibrium solutions. Some sufficient conditions for the existence of equilibrium solutions follow this.

A personality profile can help explain the reasons behind a player's design of their stopping probabilities. Repeating the game might alter the overall (stationary) equilibrium compared to that of the stage game. In our ransom roulette game, either of the players might decide on their stopping probabilities depending on how satisfied they are with the (not pay, keep locked) pure NE. Preferences for cooperative or non-cooperative behaviour by one player that are independent of the strategic decisions of the other player yield stopping matrices of a special form. As explained in the sequel, these matrices have the algebraic rank one property.

Attacker Profile. Here, we consider a ransom attacker's preferences independent of the victim's strategic decisions. This leads to a stopping matrix of the form

$$\mathbf{S} = \begin{pmatrix} \alpha_1 & \alpha_2 \\ \alpha_1 & \alpha_2 \end{pmatrix}.$$

One profile can be modelled with stopping probabilities $0 < \alpha_1 < \alpha_2 \le 1$, indicating a higher preference to continue the game when data was unlocked. The attacker might be interested in his "business model" functioning well when returning data to the victims in exchange for the ransom payment. On the other hand, in a scenario where unlocking data happens despite the victim not paying, this preference seems less realistic. Another profile can be modelled with stopping probabilities $0 < \alpha_2 < \alpha_1 \le 1$. This indicates a preference to continue the game when data was not unlocked. This attacker could be described as greedy, or also as risk-taking, as they plan to continue betrayal, ignoring the potential loss of reputation of their specific ransomware as a "brand". But if the ransom was not paid, this profile could also indicate a persevering attacker assuming better future outcomes when they do obtain a ransom.

Victim Profile. For this profile, the counterpart of the previous one, the stopping probabilities of the victim are independent of the attacker's actions. This is expressed by

$$\mathbf{S} = \begin{pmatrix} \beta_1 & \beta_1 \\ \beta_2 & \beta_2 \end{pmatrix}.$$

Several personality traits might be relevant when analysing the victim player. These traits can be grouped into two categories: the informed or cautious victim and the victim acting somewhat unprofessionally. A ransomware victim could act responsively and be aware of guidelines issued by national cyber agencies or citizen advice bureaus, who usually recommend not to pay the ransom. They could also decide not to pay as they mistrust the ransom attacker to unlock their files upon receipt of payment. This scenario can be modelled by $0 < \beta_2 < \beta_1 \le 1$. On the other hand, the victim may be tempted to pay the ransom. This could be rooted in several reasons. They could be emotionally distressed by the prospect of losing their data; they could be impulsive or otherwise emotionally caught up in the experience of being attacked, which we could see as a somewhat unprofessional personality. This leads to $0 < \beta_1 < \beta_2 \le 1$ for the stopping probabilities.

Mixed Rank-1 Profile. In this game, both previous profiles are combined non-cooperatively. The rank-1 condition for $\mathbf{S}$, as introduced in [29], implies a representation as dyadic product with a rank-factorised matrix

$$\mathbf{S} = \begin{pmatrix} \alpha_1\beta_1 & \alpha_2\beta_1 \\ \alpha_1\beta_2 & \alpha_2\beta_2 \end{pmatrix} = \begin{pmatrix} \beta_1 \\ \beta_2 \end{pmatrix} \begin{pmatrix} \alpha_1 & \alpha_2 \end{pmatrix}.$$

We obtain the following equilibrium analysis of these games: for the attacker and victim profile, there is a pure Nash equilibrium which is identical to that of the stage game under certain conditions. However this can be different in the mixed profile.

Theorem 3. *For the ransom roulette stopping game with either attacker, victim or mixed profils and payoffs as in (1), the following holds:*

(i) *For the attacker profile, the game admits the same Nash equilibrium as the stage game: the pure equilibrium (do not pay, keep locked).*

(ii) *For the victim profile, if $\frac{\beta_1}{\beta_2} < 1 + \frac{c_p}{c_\ell}$, there is also the pure NE (do not pay, keep locked). If $\frac{\beta_1}{\beta_2} > 1 + \frac{c_p}{c_\ell}$, there is the pure NE (pay, keep locked).*

(iii) *For the mixed profile, if $\frac{\alpha_1}{\alpha_2} < 1 - \frac{c_d}{b_r}$ and $\frac{\beta_1}{\beta_2} > 1 + \frac{c_p}{c_\ell}$, there is a mixed equilibrium.*

Proof. By Theorem 2, the equilibrium solutions of the stopping game with stopping matrices as specified for the three different profiles can be obtained from those of an associated bimatrix game $\Gamma(\tilde{\mathbf{V}}, \tilde{\mathbf{A}}, \tilde{\mathbf{S}})$, constructed now.

Let us fix $(\mathbf{x}^*, \mathbf{y}^*)$, an equilibrium solution of the birational game satisfying, by Proposition 1, $(\mathbf{V} - v_{\mathbf{x}}\mathbf{S})\mathbf{y}^* \leq 0$ and $\mathbf{x}^*(A - v_{\mathbf{y}}\mathbf{S}) \leq 0$. We will use the rank-factorisation of the stopping matrix to obtain

$$\left(\mathbf{V} - v_{\mathbf{x}}\begin{pmatrix}\beta_1 \\ \beta_2\end{pmatrix}(\alpha_1 \ \alpha_2)\right)\mathbf{y}^* \leq 0 \Longleftrightarrow \left(\tilde{\mathbf{V}} - v_{\mathbf{x}}\mathbf{E}\right)\tilde{\mathbf{y}}^* \leq 0$$

where the transformed variables are

$$\tilde{\mathbf{V}} = \begin{pmatrix}\beta_1^{-1} & 0 \\ 0 & \beta_2^{-1}\end{pmatrix}\mathbf{V}\begin{pmatrix}\alpha_1^{-1} & 0 \\ 0 & \alpha_2^{-1}\end{pmatrix}, \quad \tilde{\mathbf{y}}^* = \begin{pmatrix}\alpha_1 & 0 \\ 0 & \alpha_2\end{pmatrix}\mathbf{y}^*.$$

Similarly, for $\mathbf{x}^*$, we have

$$\mathbf{x}^{*\top}\left(\mathbf{A} - v_{\mathbf{y}}\begin{pmatrix}\beta_1 \\ \beta_2\end{pmatrix}(\alpha_1 \ \alpha_2)\right) \leq 0 \Longleftrightarrow \tilde{\mathbf{x}}^{*\top}\left(\tilde{\mathbf{A}} - v_{\mathbf{y}}\mathbf{E}\right) \leq 0$$

with the transformations

$$\tilde{\mathbf{A}} = \begin{pmatrix}\beta_1^{-1} & 0 \\ 0 & \beta_2^{-1}\end{pmatrix}\mathbf{A}\begin{pmatrix}\alpha_1^{-1} & 0 \\ 0 & \alpha_2^{-1}\end{pmatrix}, \quad \tilde{\mathbf{x}}^* = \mathbf{x}^*\begin{pmatrix}\alpha_1 & 0 \\ 0 & \alpha_2\end{pmatrix}.$$

The computation of an equilibrium in the game with mixed stopping profiles is thus reducible to a solution of the (simpler) stage game. The required solutions are obtained as solutions of the bimatrix game (Fig. 3) $\Gamma(\tilde{\mathbf{V}}, \tilde{\mathbf{A}}, \mathbf{E})$, transformed back.

Inspecting the payoff structure, we can see that crucial conditions for the existence of pure and mixed NEs is the relative ordering of the terms $\delta_1 = (b_r - c_d)/(\alpha_1\beta_1)$, $\delta_2 = b_r/(\alpha_2\beta_1)$, $\delta_3 = -(c_p + c_l)/(\alpha_2\beta_1)$ and $\delta_4 = -c_l/(\alpha_2\beta_2)$. Based on the assumptions in the individual cases, we have for (i) that $\delta_3 < \delta_4$, for (ii) $\delta_1 < \delta_2$ and either $\delta_3 < \delta_4$ or $\delta_3 > \delta_4$ and finally for (iii) that $\delta_1 > \delta_2$ and $\delta_3 > \delta_4$.

$\mathcal{V} \downarrow \mathcal{A} \rightarrow$	cooperate (unlock)	not cooperate (keep locked)
cooperate (pay)	$-\frac{c_p}{\alpha_1\beta_1}$, $\frac{b_r - c_d}{\alpha_1\beta_1}$	$-\frac{c_p + c_\ell}{\alpha_2\beta_1}$, $\frac{b_r}{\alpha_2\beta_1}$
not cooperate (not pay)	0 , $-\frac{c_d}{\alpha_1\beta_2}$	$-\frac{c_\ell}{\alpha_2\beta_2}$, 0

Fig. 3. *Associated bimatrix game for stopping game with mixed profile*

For the mixed profile, with conditions (iii) satisfied, the mixed equilibria can be computed in closed form by computing generalized eigenvalues and eigenvectors, e.g. in a computer algebra system such as Maxima [16][1]. This yields:

Theorem 4. *For the mixed profile, if condition (iii) in Theorem 3 holds, the mixed equilibrium is of the form* $(\mathbf{x}^*, \mathbf{y}^*)$ *where*

$$\mathbf{x}^* = \frac{1}{(\alpha_2 - \alpha_1)b_r} \left(\alpha_2 c_d, \quad -\alpha_2 c_d + (\alpha_2 - \alpha_1)b_r \right)$$

and

$$\mathbf{y}^* = \frac{1}{(\beta_1 - \beta_2)c_\ell} \begin{pmatrix} (\beta_1 - \beta_2)c_\ell - \beta_2 c_p \\ \beta_2 c_p \end{pmatrix}$$

with associated game values

$$v_V = \frac{c_\ell c_p}{\alpha_1(\beta_2 - \beta_1)c_\ell + (\alpha_1 - \alpha_2)\beta_2 c_p}, \quad v_A = \frac{c_d b_r}{\alpha_2(\beta_1 - \beta_2)c_d + (\alpha_2 - \alpha_1)\beta_2 b_r}.$$

4.4   One-to-Many Extended Game: Learning Solutions

Let us now set up the game as one between a single attacker and multiple victims that all interact bilaterally with the attacker and may collude as a team in the sense of cooperative game theory. In each bilateral game, the payoffs for the attacker $\mathcal{A}$ and the i-th victim $\mathcal{V}^{(i)}$ (for $i = 1, 2, \ldots, n$) are given as in Fig. 2 with the additional superscript i.

Where we allow individually different parameters $c_p^{(i)}, b_p^{(i)}, c_d^{(i)}$ and $c_\ell^{(i)}$, constrained only to make the game *non-degenerate* [6], meaning that if either player chooses a pure strategy, then there is a *unique* best response to it. It is a quick matter to check all four cases to verify the game as non-degenerate if $c_d > 0$ and $c_p > 0$ for all players, where we drop the "(i)" annotation here to simplify the notation (it needs to hold for all i anyway):

With the adversary being Player 0, and its victims enumerated as set $V = \{\mathcal{V}_1, \ldots, \mathcal{V}_n\}$, the resulting $(n+1)$-game is of "one-against-all" type, also called a *compound game* [32]. While it directly follows from the classical existence result of Nash equilibria that this game will have an equilibrium, the practical question is whether this equilibrium will also naturally arise between the attacker and its victims. The convergence of FP in the one-against-all setting has been studied in [32], providing the following result as a tool:

---

[1] An implementation is available at https://github.com/epfluegel/sigma.

Table 1. Non-degeneracy of the bilateral games

player and strategy	payoff case 1	payoff case 2	maximum
$\mathcal{V}$ plays "pay"	$b_p - c_d$	b_p	b_p, since $c_d > 0$
$\mathcal{V}$ plays "not pay"	$-c_d$	0	0, since $c_d > 0$
$\mathcal{A}$ plays "unlock"	$-c_p$	0	0, since $c_p > 0$
$\mathcal{A}$ plays "keep locked"	$-c_p - c_\ell$	$-c_\ell$	$-c_\ell$, since $c_p > 0$

Proposition 3 ([32], **Prop. 3**). *Let the compound game have players* $\{0, 1, \ldots, n\}$, *with strategy spaces* $AS_0, AS_1, \ldots, AS_n$, *and payoffs* $u_0 : AS_0 \times \prod_{i=1}^{n} AS_i \rightarrow \mathbb{R}$ *for Player 0, and* $u_i : AS_0 \times AS_i \rightarrow \mathbb{R}$ *for the players* $i = 1, 2, \ldots, n$.

A fictitious play process approaches equilibrium in a compound game Γ_c *if and only if it approaches equilibrium in its reduced game* Γ_r, *which is a two-player game between Player 0 from* Γ_c *and a "collective" Player V (a set of entities) comprising the Players* $1, \ldots, n$ *from* Γ_c, *and with payoffs in* Γ_r *defined as* $v_0(x_0, \mathbf{x}_{-0}) := u_0(x_0, \mathbf{x}_{-0})$ *and* $v_V(x_0, x_1, \ldots, x_n) = \sum_{i=1}^{n} u_i(x_0, x_i)$ *for all* $x_0 \in AS_0, x_i \in AS_i$ *for all* i.

Since the payoff to the attacker is likewise the total of all that it collects from the victim group, the utility function v_0 in the compound game is just the respective sum of the payoff matrices (Fig. 2) over all players. The reduced game is then a $2 \times K$ bimatrix game with $K = 2^n$, whose convergence under fictitious play was studied by Berger [6] and shown to hold under the above non-degeneracy condition[2].

Proposition 3 allows us to reduce the case of many victims to the case of a single "joint" victim whose loss is the total of what the adversary gets by the ransomware attack. Its construction, however, is such that the victim group acts jointly by pooling their losses, i.e., the *victims share their experience and adapt to the benefit of the entire group* (e.g., paying the ransom if the data becomes unlocked, or refusing to pay if experience tells that the data will not be unlocked anyway), such a group's response to the ransomware attacker is a form of fictitious play. This is almost like in cooperative game theory, with the difference only in the fact that the victims will not share their losses subsequently. A form of group rationality still exists since it is in the victim's interest to benefit from the experience of others with this particular attacker.

The strategic choices made by the virtual player (set) V can be such that their decisions to pay or not pay can be coordinated to maximize the total gain nonetheless. This is precisely the coordination mentioned above among the

---

[2] We remark that other authors [25] impose a different condition as "non-degeneracy", synonymously called the "diagonal condition", which is $a_{11} - a_{21} - a_{12} + a_{22} \neq 0$ and $b_{11} - b_{21} - b_{12} + b_{22} \neq 0$ for a bimatrix game $\{(a_{ij}, b_{ij})\}_{i,j=1}^{2}$. Our games do not satisfy this condition, but are non-degenerate in the sense of [6].

victims, and we postpone its discussion until having covered two simpler cases of behaviour first:

1. If the adversary acts in the same way towards all its victims, i.e., always plays the same strategy (lock or unlock) towards $\mathcal{V}_1, \ldots, \mathcal{V}_n$, then the situation is no different to that of a single victim, i.e., 2-player case, and Proposition 2 applies.
2. If the adversary acts individually against each victim, i.e., can per $\mathcal{V}_i$ decide whether or not to unlock, then the compound game becomes a set of identical copies of 2-player games, all of which will converge towards the unique equilibrium that Proposition 2 assures.
3. The attacker acts in the same way towards the entire group (either generally unlocks or generally keeps locked), but the group can orchestrate its response by sharing this experience over time and best respond to it. For example, a victim who has paid once but did not get their data unlocked may publish this experience, which in turn damages the attacker's "reputation" and will make other victims perhaps less willing to choose the "pay" strategy (anticipating that they would not get their data back too). This is the case studied in more detail now.

By construction, the compound game is still non-degenerate since adding up the inequalities from Table 1 will not change where the unique best responses are. Hence, by results of [6], fictitious play will converge to an equilibrium, and the question is which. Implementing the process directly in software is straightforward and readily shows that the one-against-all game (in its reduced form) still has a unique equilibrium in pure strategies, which is "all victims refuse cooperation" and "keep locked" for the attacker. While fictitious play is an impractical method to solve the game (not only for notoriously slow convergence [7] but also for the exponential size of the game), it covers the learning from experience, such as practice has shown that even paying the ransom *does not* mean not to get attacked again in future or having to pay several times even [9]. Hence, our model substantiates the recommendations compiled from practical experience (see Sect. 5).

The existence and form of the equilibrium is provable in the general case by the well-known "graphical method" to solve $2 \times K$ games:

Proposition 4. *Consider a one-against-all game where the adversary attacks $n \geq 1$ victims, all with individual payoff structures as in Fig. 2, but allowed to have individually distinct parameter sets constrained only to satisfy $c_d^{(i)} > 0$ and $c_p^{(i)} > 0$ for $i = 1, 2, \ldots, n$. Let the victim set act cooperatively against the attacker as player 0, by summing up their payments and responding in a coordinated way to minimize their individual payments to the attacker, who also receives the total ransom from all victims.*

Then, this game has a unique Nash equilibrium in pure strategies: for all victims to "not pay" and for the attacker to "keep locked".

Proof. The virtual Player V makes a joint action $\mathbf{a} \in \{\text{pay, not pay}\}^n$, which defines the attacker's payoff in either of its two strategies as:

– if $\mathcal{A}$ plays "unlock", the payoff to the victim group V is

$$v_V(\text{unlock}, \mathbf{a}) = \sum_{i=1}^{n} \begin{cases} -c_p^{(i)}, & \text{if victim } i \text{ pays} \\ 0, & \text{if victim } i \text{ does not pay} \end{cases} \tag{2}$$

and likewise, would the payoffs for the adversary sum up across all victims, defining $v_A(\textit{unlock}, \mathbf{a})$ for the attacker as

$$v_A(\text{unlock}, \mathbf{a}) = \sum_{i=1}^{n} \begin{cases} b_r^{(i)} - c_d^{(i)}, & \text{if victim } i \text{ pays} \\ -c_d^{(i)}, & \text{if victim } i \text{ does not pay} \end{cases} \tag{3}$$

– if $\mathcal{A}$ plays "keep locked", the payoff to the victim group V is

$$v_V(\text{keep locked}, \mathbf{a}) = \sum_{i=1}^{n} \begin{cases} -c_p^{(i)} - c_\ell^{(i)}, & \text{if victim } i \text{ pays} \\ -c_\ell^{(i)}, & \text{if victim } i \text{ does not pay} \end{cases} \tag{4}$$

with a similar summation of the respective payoffs from the bilateral games to yield the revenue for the attacker as

$$v_A(\text{keep locked}, \mathbf{a}) = \sum_{i=1}^{n} \begin{cases} b_r^{(i)}, & \text{if victim } i \text{ pays} \\ 0, & \text{if victim } i \text{ does not pay} \end{cases} \tag{5}$$

Since $c_p > 0$ and $c_\ell > 0$ for each victim, the utility v_V will, in both cases (2) and (4), become larger (maximized) if fewer victims choose to "pay". An arbitrary single column in the $2 \times K$ reduced game is hence given by

$$\begin{array}{c} \mathbf{a} \\ \begin{array}{c} \text{unlock} \\ \text{keep locked} \end{array} \begin{bmatrix} \cdots & v_V(\text{unlock}, \mathbf{a}) & \cdots \\ \cdots & v_V(\text{keep locked}, \mathbf{a}) & \cdots \end{bmatrix} \end{array}$$

and the two values satisfy $v_V(\text{unlock}, \mathbf{a}) > v_V(\text{keep locked}, \mathbf{a})$, since the inequalities added up are $-c_p^{(i)} > -c_p^{(i)} - c_\ell^{(i)}$ or $0 > -c_\ell^{(i)}$ in (2) and (4). Similarly, in (3) and (5) for a fixed victim's strategy $\mathbf{a}$, we sum up inequalities $b_r - c_d < b_r$ or $-c_d < 0$ (because $c_d > 0$), so that the fixed strategy $\mathbf{a}$ has a unique best response since $v_A(\text{keep locked}, \mathbf{a}) > v_A(\text{unlock}, \mathbf{a})$.

Figure 4 displays the two strategies of the attacker as vertical lines, in between each strategy $\mathbf{a}$ represents a straight line that by the previous inequality goes downwards from "unlock" to "lock", and with two lines corresponding to distinct payment profiles $\mathbf{a}', \mathbf{a}''$ differ only in their slopes. The optimal action for the attacker is, for maximizing its payoffs, at the minimum of the two points of the straight line and at the minimum over all lines (two of which are displayed in Fig. 4). Since they all have downward slopes, the optimum for the attacker is a pure strategy. By the non-degeneracy condition, the likewise best reply for the victims is also pure, yielding the claimed Nash equilibrium.

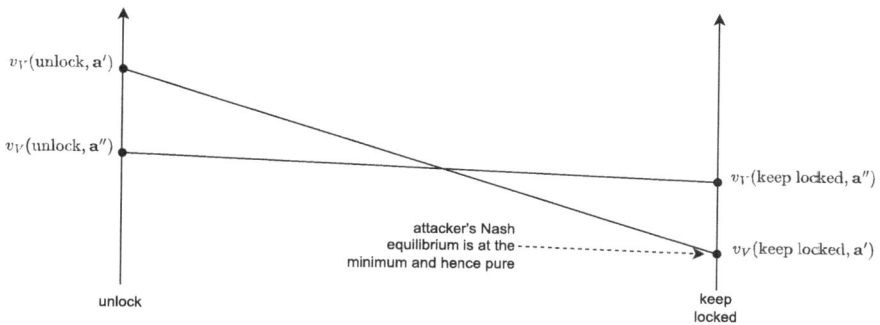

Fig. 4. Graphical method to optimize the attacker's choice among $\mathbf{a}', \mathbf{a}''$

5 Model Validation Against Practical Experience

This section discusses our model's equilibria in light of practical reportings about ransomware cases [36]). We recall that our model generally admits three equilibria: (do not pay, keep locked), which is what security agencies typically recommend (for the victim's behavior), but also (pay, unlock), which is the "best case" for the victim once its data has been encrypted, and finally also (pay, keep locked), which is the worst case that is also practically known to occur. The remaining strategy of (not pay, unlock) is unrealistic, since the attacker would not just revert its attack because the victim refuses to pay; this unrealistic case is not an equilibrium in our game.

Since we may not expect the adversary and its victim to rationally optimize payoff according to a pre-determined equilibrium, we instead look at where their behaviour converges in an iterative learning process (from experience) to best adapt to each other's behaviour. In the simplest instance, the process of taking best replies to the so-far recorded history of past moves of the other player is called fictitious play (FP). Upon convergence, its limit is an equilibrium either in pure or mixed strategies if the process converges in the time-average sense. We implemented the process for the general case of mixed stopping profiles shown in Fig. 3, with the parameters chosen at random under the following constraints: $\alpha_1, \beta_1 \sim \mathcal{U}(0,1)$ with $\alpha_2 = 1 - \alpha_1, \beta_2 = 1 - \beta_1$, and $c_p = 10$ (the victim pays a relatively high ransom), $c_d = 1$ (the attacker's effort to unlock the data is relatively small), $b_r = 0.7 \cdot c_p$ (the attacker's benefit is largely proportional to the payment of the victim, possibly reduced by a fraction to pay a money-mule in between), $c_\ell = 2 \cdot c_p$ (the victim's cost of permanent data loss is much larger than paying the ransom; for otherwise, there would be no point in considering a payment anyway).

We let the process run 1000 times, with 10 000 iterations each, starting from the point $(0,0)$ for player 1, corresponding to not having made any choice to pay or not pay in the past, and letting player 2 start from $(0,1)$, modelling the initial strategy of keeping the data locked. Among the 1000 trials, we observed three kinds of equilibria: two pure equilibria (not pay, keep locked) to which FP converged in 616 cases, (pay, keep locked), which occurred 203 times, and mixed equilibria (in all remaining cases). We have also let the experiments run with further randomization letting $c_p \leftarrow \mathcal{U}[7, 13], c_d \leftarrow \mathcal{U}[0.7, 1.3], b_r \leftarrow \mathcal{U}[0.5, 0.9] \cdot c_p$, and $c_\ell \leftarrow \mathcal{U}[1.3, 2.2] \cdot c_p$, where we slightly abuse the notation in denoting a uniformly random quantity in a defined range by $\mathcal{U}$. Sampling fresh values over each of the 1000 iterations and counting the equilibria found, did not significantly change the results. This indicates that the numeric ranges seem to have only a minor impact on the findings (keeping the magnitudes of the variables in the same mutual relations). We also let the parameter choices be random but satisfying the hypothesis of Theorem 4, finding only mixed equilibria then (as expected).

The situation, where the victim paid, but still could not recover its data has, unfortunately, reported cases in reality. Depending on the source, the number of companies paying the ransom but not getting back their data seems to be low to moderate (between 1% and 12% according to [36, pg.24]). Our model is a bit more pessimistic herein, since it predicts this to occur in about $\approx 20\%$ of the cases (where FP converged to this situation). We may interpret this as adversaries, perhaps not acting "as rational" as we assume here, thankfully to the advantage of the victims. A dark count of unreported cases due to embarrassment, fear of losing customers or reputation, and other means, is possible, but can only be speculated about. The model as such does not account for this additional fraction. However, as statistics indicate [37], the equilibrium of paying but not unlocking, is, in the model, more likely than statistics reports in reality, even if a considerable dark count is assumed. Thus, the model's prediction of this can be regarded as an upper bound approximation.

In the case of online learning, after a certain burn-in period (which can be worst-case exponentially long for FP [7] and occasionally took a few thousand iterations in our experiments), the expected adversarial gain, even after repeating and stopping, is proportional to the expectation $E(X_0)$, which can be taken as the equilibrium payoff to start with. The usually long learning period of an iterative solution of the game substantiates the recommendations made about behaving under a ransomware attack, namely "not pay", and rather invest the effort into a good backup strategy.

6 Conclusion

In this paper, we presented a simple bimatrix game with rational payoff structures designed to capture a set of realistic, i.e., reported, equilibrium cases. Our model covers cases in which both players can drop out at random. This possibility leads to an interesting set of theoretical possibilities that have been practically reported, among them: attackers that unlock the data upon paying the ransom (as victims would hope), attackers that keep the data locked although the victim paid (as is known from practical cases), but also attackers suddenly disappearing from the "market" (e.g., because they were caught) or victims that suddenly disappeared (e.g., because they cannot pay or have sufficiently hardened their systems). On the contrary, the model does not admit unrealistic equilibria like the attacker unlocking without receiving any ransom.

From a theoretical perspective, the game admits analytic solutions despite being nonzero-sum by solving a generalized eigenvalue problem numerically or analytically, but alternatively, converging under online learning of best behaviour. Observe that the summation of payoffs prescribed in prop. 3 will most likely not happen in reality (victim's will not pool their payments to jointly satisfy the attacker), and the summation is only a technical feat. The resulting two-person game (attacker versus "victim group"), however, is like if we would have modelled a cooperative game. The actual collaboration in reality will, most likely, be confined to sharing information towards immunizing itself against the ransomware attack by sharing the vulnerability and letting others patch it accordingly. An instance of this could be groups that are part of already established communities (enterprises, but also ed over online platforms or similar).

The question about whether the equilibrium is meaningful in practice, as already raised in Proposition 2 for $n = 1$, remains—somewhat surprisingly—also in the case of coordinated behaviour among the group of victims. It is, however, consistent with the usual recommendations to not support ransomware as a business model and rather invest in reliable backups rather than savings to pay ransomware in case. Hence, the recommendation for practice to not pay ransom (e.g., [1, 12, 27] to name only a few, although there is no ultimate consensus) is indeed supported by the game-theoretic (economic) considerations made here. As items of future work, it would be interesting to extend our linear algebra approach to allow infinitely repeating strategies. As a first step, one can consider nonnegative stopping matrices $\mathbf{S} \geq 0$. In this case, the results of [34] regarding rational payoffs might not apply due to zero in some entries of $\mathbf{S}$. The framework of birational games will have to be adapted to consider a vanishing denominator in the national payoff functions, which seems problematic.

An open issue is letting the model be dynamic, in the sense of letting the parameters change over time. For example, companies building up savings or insurance against ransomware attacks, or increasing resilience by strengthening their backup and recovery strategies (thus causing payoff discounting eventually, since attacking a more resilient victim requires more resources for the same revenue). The game strategies of either "paying" or "not paying" the ransomware are, currently, consistent with reports by companies [37], but possibilities of negotiating the ransom over several rounds (and thereby changing the payoff structure) may be considered as additional strategies in future work.

Another extension could be an adaptation of the learning algorithm for the one-to-many scenario. Theorem 2 shows that the FP algorithm can be used for any $2 \times n$ nondegenerated stopping game where rank$(\mathbf{S}) = 1$, as the underlying birational game is solvable through a bimatrix game, for which other direct techniques implemented in software exist [24, 31]. However, once the additional parameters α_i and β_j come into play, algebraic non-degeneracy conditions become complicated and inconvenient so that the general convergence of FP is not trivial to establish.

Acknowledgements. This work was partially supported by the LIT Secure and Correct Systems Lab funded by the State of Upper Austria and the Linz Institute of Technology (LIT-2019-7-INC-316).

A   Proofs

Proof (of Lemma 1). Define $v = \frac{\mathbf{x}^\top \mathbf{A} \mathbf{y}}{\mathbf{x}^\top \mathbf{C} \mathbf{y}}$. First, we consider the "shifted" matrix $\tilde{\mathbf{A}} = \mathbf{A} - v\mathbf{C}$ and $\tilde{v} = \frac{\mathbf{x}^\top \tilde{\mathbf{A}} \mathbf{y}}{\mathbf{x}^\top \mathbf{C} \mathbf{y}}$ which implies $\tilde{v} = 0$. Denote the best responses set of a strategy by $\mathcal{BR}(\cdot)$. Since $\mathbf{x} \in \mathcal{BR}(\mathbf{y})$, we have $\frac{\tilde{\mathbf{x}}^\top \tilde{\mathbf{A}} \mathbf{y}}{\mathbf{x}^\top \mathbf{C} \mathbf{y}} \leq 0$ for all strategies $\tilde{\mathbf{x}} \neq \mathbf{x}$. Let us write $\mathbf{x}^\top = (x_1, \ldots, x_i, \ldots, x_n)$ and assume $x_i \neq 0$. Furthermore, denote $\mathbf{e}_i^\top = (\underbrace{0, \ldots, 0}_{i-1}, 1, 0, \ldots, 0)$. It is clear that $\mathbf{e}_i^\top \tilde{\mathbf{A}} \mathbf{y} \leq 0$ because of $\mathbf{C} > 0$.

Now assume $\mathbf{e}_i^\top \tilde{\mathbf{A}} \mathbf{y} < 0$, minimal for all pure strategies. Find $j \neq i$, $x_j \neq 0$ (such j exists since $\mathbf{x}$ is not pure) and define $\hat{\mathbf{x}}^\top = \mathbf{x}^\top - x_i \mathbf{e}_i^\top + x_i \mathbf{e}_j^\top = (x_1, \ldots, 0, \ldots, x_j + x_i, \ldots, x_n)$. This is a mixed strategy, as all components of this vector still add to one. It follows that

$$\hat{\mathbf{x}}^\top \tilde{\mathbf{A}} \mathbf{y} = \mathbf{x}^\top \tilde{\mathbf{A}} \mathbf{y} + x_i \overbrace{(\mathbf{e}_j^\top \tilde{\mathbf{A}} \mathbf{y} - \mathbf{e}_i^\top \tilde{\mathbf{A}} \mathbf{y})}^{>0} > \mathbf{x}^\top \tilde{\mathbf{A}} \mathbf{y}$$

which is a contradiction. Hence we must have $\mathbf{e}_i^\top \tilde{\mathbf{A}} \mathbf{y} = 0$. This shows that $\mathbf{e}_i$ is a best response to $\mathbf{y}$. We now reconsider the matrix $\mathbf{A}$ and obtain $\mathbf{e}_i^\top \mathbf{A} \mathbf{y} = \mathbf{e}_i^\top (\tilde{\mathbf{A}} + v\mathbf{C}) \mathbf{y} = \mathbf{e}_i^\top v\mathbf{C} \mathbf{y}$ hence $\frac{\mathbf{e}_i^\top \mathbf{A} \mathbf{y}}{\mathbf{e}_i^\top \mathbf{C} \mathbf{y}} = v$.

Proof (of Theorem 2). Let us first establish some auxiliary expressions. As $\mathbf{C}$ is of rank 1, we have the rank-factorisation $\mathbf{C} = \mathbf{p}\mathbf{q}^\top$ with positive vectors $\mathbf{p} \in \mathbb{R}^m$, $\mathbf{q} \in \mathbb{R}^n$. To prove the theorem, we fix an equilibrium solution $(\mathbf{x}^*, \mathbf{y}^*)$

$$\mathbf{x}^{*\top}(\mathbf{B} - v_y\mathbf{C}) \leq 0, \quad (\mathbf{A} - v_x\mathbf{C})\mathbf{y}^* \leq 0$$

where v_x and v_y are the corresponding game values. We define the diagonal matrices $\mathbf{P} = \text{diag}(p_1, \ldots, p_m)$, $\mathbf{Q} = \text{diag}(q_1, \ldots, q_n)$ and obtain $\mathbf{x}^{*\top}(\mathbf{B} - v_y\mathbf{C}) \leq 0 \iff \mathbf{x}^{*\top}\mathbf{P}(\mathbf{P}^{-1}\mathbf{B}\mathbf{Q}^{-1} - v_y\mathbf{E}) \leq 0$ and $(\mathbf{A} - v_x\mathbf{C})\mathbf{y}^* \leq 0 \iff (\mathbf{P}^{-1}\mathbf{A}\mathbf{Q}^{-1} - v_x\mathbf{E})\mathbf{Q}\mathbf{y}^* \leq 0$. This shows that with $\tilde{\mathbf{x}}^\top = \mathbf{x}^{*\top}\mathbf{P}$ and $\tilde{\mathbf{y}} = \mathbf{Q}\mathbf{x}^*$, we have that $(\tilde{\mathbf{x}}, \tilde{\mathbf{y}})$ can be normalised to form equilibrium solutions $(\tilde{\mathbf{x}}', \tilde{\mathbf{y}}')$ with the same game values v_x and v_y. As $\mathbf{P}$ and $\mathbf{Q}$ are invertible and $\mathbf{P}^{-1}, \mathbf{Q}^{-1} > 0$, the correspondence is one-to-one.

References

1. Australian Cyber Security Centre. Report and recover from ransomware. Cyber.gov.au (2023)

2. Baksi, R., Upadhyaya, S.: Game theoretic analysis of ransomware: a preliminary study. In: Proceedings of the 8th International Conference on Information Systems Security and Privacy. SCITEPRESS - Science and Technology Publications (2022)

3. Baksi, R.P.: Pay or not pay? A game-theoretical analysis of ransomware interactions considering a defender's deception architecture. In: 2022 52nd Annual IEEE/IFIP International Conference on Dependable Systems and Networks - Supplemental Volume (DSN-S), pp. 53–54 (2022)

4. Baksi, R.P., Upadhyaya, S.: A game theoretic approach to the design of mitigation strategies for generic ransomware. In: Mori, P., Lenzini, G., Furnell, S. (eds.) ICISSP 2021/2022. CCIS, vol. 1851, pp. 104–124. Springer, Cham (2023). https://doi.org/10.1007/978-3-031-37807-2_6

5. Banik, S., Bopardikar, S.D.: Attack-resilient path planning using dynamic games with stopping states. IEEE Trans. Rob. **38**(1), 25–41 (2022)

6. Berger, U.: Fictitious play in $2 \times n$ games. J. Econ. Theory **120**(2), 139–154 (2005)

7. Brandt, F., Fischer, F., Harrenstein, P.: On the rate of convergence of fictitious play. In: Kontogiannis, S., Koutsoupias, E., Spirakis, P.G. (eds.) SAGT 2010. LNCS, vol. 6386, pp. 102–113. Springer, Heidelberg (2010). https://doi.org/10.1007/978-3-642-16170-4_10

8. Cartwright, E., Castro, J.H., Cartwright, A.: To pay or not: game theoretic models of ransomware. J. Cybersecur. **5**(1), tyz009 (2019)

9. Coker, J.: 78% of Organizations Suffer Repeat Ransomware Attacks After Paying (2024)

10. Darknetstats.com Team. Darknet stats | All the Dark web news you need and more (2022). https://www.darknetstats.com/

11. flare.io. Top 5 Dark Web Marketplaces to Monitor - Flare (2023). https://flare.io/learn/resources/blog/dark-web-marketplaces/. Accessed July 2024

12. Freed, A.M.: Three Reasons Why You Should Never Pay Ransomware Attackers (2024)

13. Glicksberg, I.L.: A further generalization of the Kakutani fixed point theorem, with application to Nash equilibrium points. Proc. Am. Math. Soc. **3**(1), 170–174 (1952)

14. Huang, L., Zhu, Q.: Dynamic Bayesian games for adversarial and defensive cyber deception. In: Al-Shaer, E., Wei, J., Hamlen, K.W., Wang, C. (eds.) Autonomous Cyber Deception, pp. 75–97. Springer, Cham (2019). https://doi.org/10.1007/978-3-030-02110-8_5

15. Iqbal, A., Masson, V., Abbott, D.: Kidnapping model: an extension of Selten's game. R. Soc. Open Sci. **4**(12), 171484 (2017)

16. Joyner, D.: Oscas: maxima. ACM Commun. Comput. Algebra **40**(3–4), 108–111 (2006)

17. Lapan, H.E., Sandler, T.: To bargain or not to bargain: that is the question. Am. Econ. Rev. **78**, 16–21 (1988)

18. Laszka, A., Farhang, S., Grossklags, J.: On the economics of ransomware. In: Rass, S., An, B., Kiekintveld, C., Fang, F., Schauer, S. (eds.) GameSec 2017. LNCS, vol. 10575, pp. 394–417. Springer, Cham (2017). https://doi.org/10.1007/978-3-319-68711-7_21

19. Li, Z., Liao, Q.: Ransomware 2.0: to sell, or not to sell a game-theoretical model of data-selling ransomware. In: Proceedings of the 15th International Conference on Availability, Reliability and Security, ARES 2020, pp. 1–9, Article no. 59. Association for Computing Machinery, New York (2020)

20. Li, Z., Liao, Q.: Game theory of data-selling ransomware. JCSANDM 65–96 (2021)

21. Li, Z., Liao, Q.: Preventive portfolio against data-selling ransomware–a game theory of encryption and deception. Comput. Secur. **116**(102644), 102644 (2022)

22. Marchi, E.: Equilibrium points of rational n-person games. J. Math. Anal. Appl. **54**(1), 1–4 (1976)

23. Marchi, E., Ovied, J.A.: Constructing birational games with given equilibrium points. Revista de Ja Union Matematica Argentina **36** (1990)

24. McKelvey, R.D., McLennan, A.M., Turocy, T.L.: Gambit: Software Tools for Game Theory, Version 16.2 (2024). http://www.gambit-project.org. Accessed 5 June 2024

25. Monderer, D., Shapley, L.S.: Fictitious play property for games with identical interests. J. Econ. Theory **68**(1), 258–265 (1996)

26. Moulin, H., Vial, J.-P.: Strategically zero-sum games: the class of games whose completely mixed equilibria cannot be improved upon. Int. J. Game Theory **7**(3), 201–221 (1978)

27. National Cyber Security Center, UK. A guide to ransomware (2024). Accessed 18 June 2024

28. von Neumann, J.: A model of general economic equilibrium. Rev. Econ. Stud. **13**(1), 1–9 (1945)

29. Pfluegel, E.: Shades of grey: Strategic bimatrix stopping games for modelling (Un)Ethical hacking roles. In: Proceedings of Conference on Decision and Game Theory for Security, GameSec (2023)

30. Rass, S., Wiegele, A., König, S.: Security games over lexicographic orders. In: Zhu, Q., Baras, J.S., Poovendran, R., Chen, J. (eds.) GameSec 2020. LNCS, vol. 12513, pp. 422–441. Springer, Cham (2020). https://doi.org/10.1007/978-3-030-64793-3_23

31. Savani, R., von Stengel, B.: Game theory explorer: software for the applied game theorist. Comput. Manag. Sci. **12**(1), 5–33 (2015)

32. Sela, A.: Fictitious play in 'one-against-all' multi-player games. Econom. Theory **14**(3), 635–651 (1999)

33. Selten, R.: A Simple Game Model of Kidnapping. Institut für Mathematische Wirtschaftsforschung an der Universität Bielefeld (1976)

34. Shapley, L.S.: Stochastic games. Proc. Natl. Acad. Sci. U. S. A. **39**(10), 1095–1100 (1953)

35. SOCRadar Cyber Intelligence Inc. Top 10 Dark Web Markets (2024). https://socradar.io/top-10-dark-web-markets/. Accessed July 2024

36. Sophos Ltd. The State of Ransomware. Technical report, Sophos Ltd., 2023. Findings from an independent, vendor-agnostic survey of 3,000 leaders responsible for IT/cybersecurity across 14 countries, conducted in January-March 2023

37. Statista, Inc. Ransomware | Statista (2023). https://www.statista.com/study/43873/ransomware-attacks-worldwide/. Accessed July 2024

38. Stirzaker, D.: Stochastic Processes and Models. Oxford University Press (2005)

39. Yin, T., Sarabi, A., Liu, M.: Deterrence, backup, or insurance: game-theoretic modeling of ransomware. Games **14**, 20 (2023)

40. Zhang, C., Luo, F., Ranzi, G.: Multistage game theoretical approach for ransomware attack and defense. IEEE Trans. Serv. Comput. **16**(4), 2800–2811 (2023)

How Much Should I Double Spend My Bitcoin? Game Theory of Quantum Mining

Zhen Li[1] and Qi Liao[2(✉)]

[1] Department of Economics and Management, Albion College, Albion, USA
zli@albion.edu
[2] Department of Computer Science, Central Michigan University,
Mount Pleasant, USA
liao1q@cmich.edu

Abstract. Quantum computing as an inevitable technology can revolutionize many aspects of our society. One potential impact is on cryptocurrency such as Bitcoin, which relies on proof-of-work mining to secure the underlying blockchain protocol. Miners empowered by quantum computers will have superior computational power to win the competition. The quantum advantage jeopardizes the security and trustworthy of cryptocurrency and the transaction validation process by taking over a majority of the network's computing power, known as a 51% attack. Fraudulent Bitcoin transactions in the form of double spending can happen, and the emerging quantum miner could enable double spending and benefit from it. How much double spending is optimal without causing too much "inflation"? What shall be the optimal strategy of the first quantum miner facing the competition from other quantum miners? What are the implications of having one or multiple quantum miners to the security of the Bitcoin network? We conduct a novel game theoretic and economic analysis to address these questions. Simulation illustrates that quantum miners would have to collude to gain from double spending in a quantum competitive environment. The distribution of cryptocurrency between quantum miners and classical miners and how cost-effective classical miners are can affect the profitability and the sustainability of double spending as well as the collusion of quantum miners. Intensified quantum competition will decrease the chance of collusion and eventually make the Bitcoin network secure again. The critical point of quantum popularity that will eliminate double spending is found.

Keywords: Game Theory · Quantum Computing · Cryptocurrency · Bitcoin · Quantum Mining · Double Spending · Collusion · Cybersecurity · Economics

1 Introduction

Cryptocurrency such as Bitcoin is a decentralized digital currency and payment system based on classical cryptographic technologies which works without a central administrator such as a central bank in traditional currencies. The Bitcoin network operates on the Proof-of-Work (PoW) consensus mechanism to ensure

A. Sinha et al. (Eds.): GameSec 2024, LNCS 14908, pp. 87–106, 2025.
https://doi.org/10.1007/978-3-031-74835-6_5

the integrity of the network, allowing for secure and transparent peer-to-peer transactions without the need for intermediaries.

It is generally believed that Bitcoin is cryptographically protected against malicious modifications. The techniques used in cryptocurrency blockchains make them virtually unhackable if the networks are powerful enough to outpace hackers. However, in theory, Bitcoin can be subject to the so-called "51% attack". A malicious miner or a group of miners who control more than half of the network's mining can launch an attack on the blockchain network. Attackers could use their dominant computing power to alter the blockchain like interrupting the recording of new blocks by preventing other miners from completing blocks. Large miners could freeze any users' funds, erase past transactions, or launch other attacks like reversing transactions to double spend tokens.

With the current status of computation, it is nearly impossible to launch a successful 51% attack on a cryptocurrency like Bitcoin with a large participation rate. A recent report [20] suggests that the current state of security in Bitcoin makes 51% attacks economically unfeasible. However, the situation could change with the recently rapid development of quantum computers. Quantum computing is a cutting-edge computing paradigm that harnesses the principles of quantum mechanics known as quantum bits (qubits) to perform computations. The superposition and entanglement property of qubits as well as quantum gates and quantum algorithms will put the early adopters of quantum computers in an advantageous position also known as "quantum supremacy" where quantum computers can solve the complex problems that classical computers cannot solve.

The emerging technology of quantum computing may impose credible threat on the security of the Bitcoin network. When it comes to Bitcoin mining, miners equipped with quantum computers (i.e., quantum miners) can have incomparable advantage over classical miners in procuring mining rewards and rewriting blockchain history. Although quantum computers are not powerful enough yet [10], and researchers have suggested that 51% attacks on Bitcoin by quantum computers may not be possible until 2028, recent evidence indicates it could happen sooner [13]. With the superior computing power that no one can compete with, the first-moving quantum miner certainly has the potential to benefit from the advantageous computing power such as gaining from double spending.

Double spending can be viewed as digital equivalent of a perfect counterfeit. Intuitively, double spending of Bitcoin benefits the attacker but at a cost of deteriorating Bitcoin value. As the number of tokens increases with the attacker's double fake spending, the value of Bitcoin is eroded partially due to increased currency supply and inflation, and also due to trust in the network being damaged which may eventually destroy Bitcoin. Such dilemma imposes a constraint on the attacker's scale of double spending. What is the optimal double spending scale that is considered "healthy" without destroying Bitcoin? In addition, we believe the first quantum miner's monopolistic superior computing power will not last forever. Once quantum computing is available to one Bitcoin miner, it is only a matter of time until others with quantum computing will join, too. With multiple quantum miners, none would have the 51% computing power to double spend alone. What is the best strategy of the first quantum miner facing emerging quantum competition? How is the situation change with intensifying quantum competition? What are the implications of the popularity of quantum computing on the sustainability and the security of the Bitcoin network?

To address these questions, this study conducts a novel game theoretic analysis on double spending strategies by quantum miners. It explores the appearance and evolution of quantum computing in the Bitcoin network focusing on the quantum miners' incentive to double spend. We first develop an economic model to find the equilibrium Bitcoin price using the supply and demand analysis of the Bitcoin market. We further explore the effects of double spending on the Bitcoin price and the economic well-being of various participants in the Bitcoin market. We develop a game theory model to study the strategic actions by the first quantum miner and other miners from whom more quantum miners emerge. Our work compares the first quantum miner's choices with and without quantum competition. The modeling analysis indicates that the first quantum miner can initially benefit from exercising the superior computing power to double spend. Once facing quantum competition, all quantum miners (including the first quantum miner) have solid financial incentives to collude with no motivation to cheat. Nevertheless, the likelihood of collusion keeps falling with intensified quantum competition. The collusion between quantum miners eventually breaks down, and the Bitcoin network would once again become immune to 51% attacks. We find that there are two critical break points of collusion or the ending points of double spending, one relates to the percentage of Bitcoin in possession of the first quantum miner, and the other relates to the percentage of the Bitcoin mining population that are quantum miners.

We believe this is the first research examining the implications of quantum competition on the Bitcoin network. An important insight is that the threat of quantum computing on Bitcoin security may be limited and short-lived. The first quantum miner and the subsequent quantum miners must walk a fine line to balance the benefit and the cost of double spending and share the profit of double spending. The first quantum miner can benefit from double spending using the superior computing power, but it is extremely difficult, if ever possible, to make double spending profit long-lasting. Collusion is a necessary condition for quantum miners to double spend in a competitive environment. Although quantum miners have the incentive to collude, the profitable and sustainable range of double spending shrinks with spreading quantum computing. In case the first quantum miner holds a large share of Bitcoin in circulation, the emergence of another quantum miner is sufficient to terminate double spending.

2   Background and Related Work

Bitcoin, as a decentralized cryptocurrency, operates by motivating participants to act in a way that benefits the entire network that involves various game situations, e.g., allocating computational power to mining [3], competing for mining rewards [16] and transaction fees [12], etc. Research suggests competition in Bitcoin mining increases energy consumption and may not be socially desirable [14]. Game theory has been applied to the security and trust in the bitcoin networks including 51% attacks and double spending [4,17,25].

Consensus networks like PoW were created to prevent double spending in blockchain-based crypocurrencies [6] but this consensus is only reliable with the assumption that no single miner can hold more than 50% of the network's computational power. Quantum computing promises to have exponential speedup far surpassing classical computers [1] and is expected to impose threats on both the technical and the financial security of Bitcoin [8,13]. Even a single quantum miner with relatively low cartographical computing power can act strategically to manipulate the blockchain network [2].

Double spending is the most straightforward way to monetize the ability of breaching the 50% threshold to launch an attack on blockchain networks [21]. In theory, a double spending attack at any proportion of computing power can be made profitable [9]. It has been suggested that double spending can be prevented by costly mining and delaying settlement [5]. Technical countermeasures include the Proof-of-Stake (PoS) and other algorithms alternative to the PoW algorithm to enhance Bitcoin security [19,24]. Possible solutions and preventive measures are also studied considering the threats a quantum-capable attacker could impose on blockchain networks [10,11,23]. Researchers are taking measures to tackle the quantum challenge. A structured literature review [10] provides insights on weighing up the dangers of quantum computing and the countermeasures.

Quantum computing can also change the way classical games are played. If classic games are played on a quantum computer or played by a quantum computer, the games become quantum games. The emerging quantum computing has had a profound impact on the research domain in the context of multi-agent games [22]. The quantum advantage allows quantum players to have a distinct advantage over classical players to achieve higher payoffs at equilibrium [7]. Economic incentives were analyzed for both quantum and regular miners for optimal double spending [15].

Our research is related to existing literature on the incentive mechanisms of the bitcoin network and the quantum threat on bitcoin security on a novel angle: it focuses on the competition between quantum miners on top of the competition between quantum miners and classical miners. It applies game theory and economic principles to the security of bitcoin networks. To the best of our knowledge, this is the first game theoretic study exploring the threat of quantum computing on bitcoin networks in a quantum competitive environment.

3   An Economic Model of Bitcoin Market

In this section we establish a Bitcoin pricing model to explore the impacts of double spending on bitcoin value. For easy reference, Table 1 provides a list of major variables used in the paper and their brief definitions.

Table 1. Symbols and Definitions

Symbol/Variable	Definition
$\overline{B}$	capped Bitcoin maximum supply
B_0	units of Bitcoin rewarded to classical miners
D	double spending scale by the 1st quantum miner in case of monopoly and by both quantum miners in case of duopoly
D_1	double spending scale by the 1st quantum miner in case of duopoly
D_2	double spending scale by the 2nd quantum miner in case of duopoly
P_B	equilibrium Bitcoin price without double spending
P_D	equilibrium Bitcoin price with double spending
EP_B	expected Bitcoin price without double spending
EP_D	expected Bitcoin price with double spending
P	overall price level of goods and services traded in Bitcoin
Y	quantity of items traded using Bitcoin as medium of exchange
V	velocity of Bitcoin, frequency at which Bitcoin is used to pay
T	units of Bitcoin demanded for transaction purpose
S	units of Bitcoin demanded for speculative purpose
RR	required rate of return on Bitcoin investment
R	expected rate of return on Bitcoin investment
N	classical miner population
C	per-classical-miner operating cost of participation in Bitcoin network

3.1 The Quantity Analysis of Bitcoin as a Medium of Exchange

A medium of exchange is an intermediary instrument within an economy which is used primarily to facilitate transactions. Bitcoin already operates as a medium of exchange and Bitcoin in circulation satisfies the quantity equation

$$P_B TV = PY \tag{1}$$

where P_B is the unit price of Bitcoin, T is the quantity of Bitcoin used as a medium of exchange, V is the velocity of Bitcoin that is a measurement of the rate at which one unit of Bitcoin is being transacted for goods and services in a time period, P is the price level of goods and services traded in Bitcoin, and Y is the units of goods and services traded in Bitcoin. Equation (1) is an identity that holds true by definition, similar to the quantity equation of money defined in economics.

From (1), the transaction demand for Bitcoin is

$$T = \frac{PY}{P_B V} \tag{2}$$

3.2 Supply and Demand Analysis of the Bitcoin Market

The supply and demand analysis is the natural framework to learn insights about price determination. Here we apply the supply and demand analysis to the Bitcoin market to find the equilibrium Bitcoin price. In particular, the supply of Bitcoin comes from block mining which will eventually be fixed at $\overline{B}$, the designed maximum of Bitcoin. The supply of Bitcoin is exogenous to the model. The demand for Bitcoin includes both the transaction demand for payment purpose and the speculative demand for financial investment purpose. The quantity of Bitcoin demanded for transaction purpose is T as in the quantity analysis of Bitcoin. Bitcoin is also demanded for speculative purpose. Let S be the units of Bitcoin demanded for such purpose. The Bitcoin market equilibrium (without double spending) is

$$\overline{B} = \frac{PY}{P_B V} + S \tag{3}$$

where the right-hand-side is the combined demand for Bitcoin consisting of the transaction demand from (2) and the speculative demand.

Solving (3), the equilibrium Bitcoin price is

$$P_B = \frac{PY}{(\overline{B} - S)V} \tag{4}$$

As shown, Bitcoin price is increasing in the speculative demand for Bitcoin and decreasing in the supply of Bitcoin.

The key determining factor of the speculative demand for Bitcoin is the expected rate of return on Bitcoin investment ($R = \frac{EP_B - P_B}{P_B}$), which may or may not be equal or above the required rate of return (RR) holders desire to receive from Bitcoin investment. As in the finance literature, RR is defined as the minimum return an investor will accept for an investment as compensation for a given level of risk. We assume Bitcoin market participants have a common RR to hold Bitcoin for speculative purpose.

Given expected Bitcoin price, if $R < RR$ at the current Bitcoin price, the speculative demand for Bitcoin decreases and the Bitcoin price starts to fall until R rises to RR. If $R > RR$ at the current Bitcoin price, the speculative demand for Bitcoin increases and the Bitcoin price starts to rise until R falls to RR. In the steady state of the Bitcoin market, the rate of return on Bitcoin investment is equal to the required return, and the current Bitcoin price and the expected Bitcoin price have the following relationship:

$$EP_B = (1 + R)P_B \tag{5}$$

where $R = RR$.

In summary, the equilibrium of the Bitcoin market has two-fold meanings:

- The total Bitcoin supply is equal to the total Bitcoin demand including both the transaction demand and the speculative demand for Bitcoin (3).
- The expected rate of return on Bitcoin investment is equal to the required rate of return at the current market price of Bitcoin (5).

The latter implies that in Bitcoin market equilibrium, the market participants have a common expectation to see the Bitcoin price to grow by R each period.

Combining (3) and (5), we solve for the units of Bitcoin demanded for speculative purpose:

$$S = \overline{B} - \frac{PY(1+R)}{EP_BV} \tag{6}$$

In (6), $\overline{B}$, P, Y, R and V are all predetermined. There is a one-to-one correspondence between the expected future price of Bitcoin and the speculative demand for Bitcoin. As EP_B increases, S increases. As $EP_B \to 0$, $S \to 0$.

3.3 The Impact of Increased Bitcoin Supply (Double Spending) on the Bitcoin Market

Suppose the supply of Bitcoin increases from $\overline{B}$ to $\overline{B} + D$. The new Bitcoin market equilibrium satisfies the following two conditions:

$$P_D = \frac{PY}{(\overline{B} + D - S)V} \tag{7}$$

$$EP_D = (1 + R)P_D \tag{8}$$

modified from (3) and (5).

Since the expected rate of return remains at R once the Bitcoin market reaches the new equilibrium, the speculative demand for Bitcoin stays the same as (6). As P, Y and V are all exogenous to the model and S stays unchanged, (7) indicates that an increase in Bitcoin supply apparently decreases the market value of Bitcoin, i.e., $P_D < P_B$. The increase in Bitcoin supply also decreases the expected price of Bitcoin, i.e., $EP_D < EP_B$ comparing (5) and (8).

The increased Bitcoin supply is fully absorbed into the transaction demand for Bitcoin with $P_BT = P_D(T+D)$, according to the quantity analysis of Bitcoin.

The economic impact of an increase in Bitcoin supply implies that the increase in the quantity of Bitcoin waters down the value of Bitcoin. The purchasing power of Bitcoin decreases but the speculative attractiveness of Bitcoin can be conserved so long as speculators receive the same expected rate of return equalling their required rate of return.

How is double spending compared to an authentic increase in Bitcoin supply? Double spending means that the same units of Bitcoin could potentially be spent multiple times. Successful double spending of Bitcoin essentially increases the use of Bitcoin for transaction purpose by the amount of double spending and reaches a total transaction demand for Bitcoin from T to $T + D$ where D is the scale of double spending, which represents both the increased transaction demand for Bitcoin and the increased supply of Bitcoin, keeping the Bitcoin market remain balanced with unchanged speculative demand for Bitcoin.

3.4 Double Spending Can be a Self-destructive Process

Different from increasing the money supply by printing money, the increase in the Bitcoin supply due to double spending is temporary. According to the quantity equation of Bitcoin (1), two scenarios may occur following a successful double spending at constant T, V and P.

Scenario 1: Y is largely unaffected, i.e., the need to use Bitcoin to make payments remains the same. In this case, the Bitcoin price will bounce back to the pre-double-spending level.

Scenario 2: Y decreases, e.g., when double spending makes fewer sellers willing to accept Bitcoin. In this case, the Bitcoin price will stay below the pre-double-spending level.

Scenario 1 is likely to be the case if double-spending does not diminish the need of Bitcoin to make payment. In practice, Bitcoin is often used for underground payments and illegal transactions, for ransomware payments, for governments to evade embargoes, etc. Such needs of Bitcoin is not economic per se and may not be sensitive to the changing market value of Bitcoin. In this case, the value of Bitcoin can self-recover after the temporary damage caused by double spending.

In contrast, the damage of double spending to the market value of Bitcoin is long-lasting in Scenario 2 when the deteriorating value of Bitcoin effectively decreases people's desire or ability to use Bitcoin to buy goods and services. If double spending continues, the Bitcoin price would keep falling and eventually, there could be no need to use Bitcoin to pay and Bitcoin would be worthless and become nonexistent. In other words, double spending can be a self-destructive process that leads to the extinction of Bitcoin, as depicted in Scenario 2.

4   Game Theory of Double Spending By Quantum Miners

As the economic analysis shows, there are both benefits and costs when a quantum miner double spends. We capture the dilemma using a stylized game to study the financial incentive for the first quantum miner to double spend strategically, in absence and with the appearance of subsequent quantum miners. Specifically, we explore the first quantum miner's decision-making in case of "monopoly" (when the first quantum miner is the only quantum miner) and "duopoly" (when there is a subsequent quantum miner).

Suppose initially there are one quantum miner (referred to as the "first quantum miner") and N non-quantum miners (referred to as "classical miners"). Without loss of generality, we assume all the miners are also Bitcoin users and investors in the Bitcoin market. The strategic interaction is between the first-moving quantum miner and classical miners from whom a subsequent quantum miner may emerge. All the parties are money driven.

To focus on the themes, we make the following assumptions to highlight several key features of the Bitcoin protocol and to simplify the situation:

– All miners participate the Bitcoin network with free entry and exit.
– There are no transaction rewards. Miners' welfare is measured by the market value of possessed Bitcoin.

- The total Bitcoin is fixed. Upon acquisition of quantum computing, the first quantum miner wins all mining competition and receives all remaining Bitcoin rewards.
- All classical miners have the same computational power thus their possession of Bitcoin and the mining cost are identical.
- Only quantum miners have the computing power to double spend. Quantum miners have the same computing power.
- Quantity of goods and services traded in Bitcoin is constant but units of Bitcoin needed to buy an item fluctuates with the Bitcoin price.

The unique features of the first quantum miner imply that the miner can act like the monetary authority controlling the supply of Bitcoin by managing double spending. When exercising the superior ability to double spend, the quantum miner has to do the cost-benefit analysis. For classical miners nonetheless, the inferior computing power disables them from winning the mining competition but they reserve the freedom of leaving the Bitcoin network.

The game proceeds as follows: The first quantum miner chooses the scale of double spending, which determines the current "money supply" of Bitcoin and hence the price of Bitcoin. Classical miners choose whether to exit the Bitcoin market. In a quantum competitive environment additionally, the subsequent miner determines whether to counter double spending.

Since all miners are money driven, the welfare effects of their decision-making determine their actions. The first quantum miner's choice of double spending is the key. Although the game is not modeled as a Stackelberg game, the first quantum miner can be viewed as the leader and the game can be solved using backward deduction starting from the classical miners' and the subsequent quantum miner's decision-making.

In the following analysis, we begin with the welfare analysis and the finding of game solutions in absence of quantum competition. We then discuss the situation in a quantum competitive environment.

4.1   Welfare Impact of Double Spending

Double spending by the first quantum miner affects the welfare of all the miners.

Welfare Impact of Double Spending on the First Quantum Miner.
Using the defined variables in Table 1, the units of Bitcoin held by the first quantum miner is $(\overline{B} - B_0)$. Specifically we define D, the double spending scale, as the number of tokens held by the quantum miner the miner uses to double spend once. We ignore the possibility of multiple double spending to make the model traceable and manageable. With this definition, $(\overline{B} - B_0)$ sets the upper bound on the double spending scale of the first quantum miner.

At the moment of double spending, the market value of Bitcoin is P_B so that the quantum miner gains an amount of $P_B D$. As double spending decreases the market value of Bitcoin, the cost of double spending for the quantum miner is

$(P_B - P_D)(\overline{B} - B_0)$. Taking into consideration both the benefit and the cost of double spending, the net welfare gain the first quantum miner receives is

$$\Pi = P_B D - (P_B - P_D)(\overline{B} - B_0) \tag{9}$$

Welfare Impact of Double Spending on Classical Miners. The loss to classical miners come from the decreased value of Bitcoin caused by double spending. For classical miners as a whole, their total loss is

$$(P_B - P_D)B_0 \tag{10}$$

which is equally shouldered by classical miners.

4.2   Finding Profitable and Sustainable Double Spending

The monopolistic quantum miner has the following constraints when making the rational choice of double spending:

- The upper bound of double spending is the monopolistic quantum miner's possession of Bitcoin.
- The quantum miner's net gain is non-negative.
- The Bitcoin network is resilient to double spending "attack" launched by the quantum miner, i.e., classical miners do not exit the Bitcoin network.

The three constraints correspond to the following three math relations:

$$0 \leq D \leq (\overline{B} - B_0) \tag{11}$$

$$P_B D - (P_B - P_D)(\overline{B} - B_0) \geq 0 \tag{12}$$

$$P_D \frac{B_0}{N} \geq C \tag{13}$$

where B_0/N is the holding of Bitcoin by an individual classical miner and C is the per-classical-miner's operating cost that includes the hardware cost, electricity, etc. Classical miners have the financial incentive to support the Bitcoin network as long as the remaining value of Bitcoin exceeds the cost of participating in the network. Although the initial investment in quantum computing is significant, once in operation, the fast quantum computing power largely saves the mining cost. Therefore, for simplicity, the operating cost of the quantum miner is not included. Adding quantum miners' cost function to the model will not change model conclusions. Indeed, it will strengthen the model conclusions by reducing the profit margin of quantum computing.

From (12), double spending is profitable for the first quantum miner at

$$D \geq \frac{(P_B - P_D)(\overline{B} - B_0)}{P_B} \tag{14}$$

Combined with (11), the profitable double-spending satisfies

$$\frac{(P_B - P_D)(\overline{B} - B_0)}{P_B} \leq D \leq (\overline{B} - B_0) \tag{15}$$

Combining (7) and (13), the sustainable double spending falls in the following range to keep classical miners stay in the Bitcoin network:

$$D \leq \frac{PYB_0}{NCV} + S - \overline{B} \tag{16}$$

Combining (15) and (16), we have the final specification of the range of double spending the first quantum miner shall pursue to make double spending both profitable and sustainable:

$$\frac{(P_B - P_D)(\overline{B} - B_0)}{P_B} \leq D \leq min\{(\overline{B} - B_0), \frac{PYB_0}{NCV} + S - \overline{B}\} \tag{17}$$

4.3 The Impact of Quantum Competition

Naturally the first quantum miner can be the monopolistic quantum miner only for a certain time. Eventually subsequent quantum miners will occur. How will quantum competition change various miners' decision-making?

Subsequent Quantum Miner's Choice. Since all quantum miners are assumed to have the same computational power, if there are more than one quantum miner in the Bitcoin network, no individual miner could reach the threshold to launch a 51% attack. With the computational power compatible with the first quantum miner, the second quantum miner needs to choose if to use the power to prevent the first quantum miner from double spending. If yes, the market value of the Bitcoin held by the second quantum miner is $P_B \frac{B_0}{N}$; If not, the second quantum miner's welfare is $P_D \frac{B_0}{N}$. Apparently, the second quantum miner would be better off to prevent the first quantum miner from double spending. In other words, although the second quantum miner does not have the ability to double spend successfully, he/she still benefits from possessing the computational power to protect the Bitcoin network against double spending. Remaining classical miners benefit as well.

The insight learnt is that when there are multiple quantum miners in the Bitcoin network, the network can be resistant to 51% attacks.

The First Quantum Miner's Choice Facing Quantum Competition. Since no individual miner, quantum or classical, would be able to double spend successfully acting alone, the first quantum miner is worse off for sure facing quantum competition. To double spend, the first quantum miner would have to collude with the subsequent quantum miner.

Collusive Quantum Miners. In principle, the two quantum miners can collude to double spend. They jointly choose how much to double spend and share the net gains. Suppose the first quantum miner double spends D_1 and the second quantum miner double spends D_2. They face the following constraints:

$$0 \leq D_1 \leq (\overline{B} - B_0) \tag{18}$$

$$0 \leq D_2 \leq \frac{B_0}{N} \tag{19}$$

$$P_B D_1 - (P_B - P_D)(\overline{B} - B_0) \geq 0 \tag{20}$$

$$P_B D_2 - (P_B - P_D)\frac{B_0}{N} \geq 0 \tag{21}$$

$$P_D \frac{B_0}{N} \geq C \tag{22}$$

Of above, the first two equations limit the feasible range of double spending by each quantum miner, the second two guarantee that double spending is profitable for the quantum miners, and the last serves to keep classical miners from exiting the Bitcoin market. Solving these inequalities, the common ranges that satisfy all of the constraints are

$$\frac{(P_B - P_D)(\overline{B} - B_0)}{P_B} \leq D_1 \leq (\overline{B} - B_0) \tag{23}$$

$$\frac{(P_B - P_D)\frac{B_0}{N}}{P_B} \leq D_2 \leq \frac{B_0}{N} \tag{24}$$

$$D_1 + D_2 \leq \frac{PYB_0}{NCV} + S - \overline{B} \tag{25}$$

There can be various combinations of $\{D_1, D_2\}$ that make double spending profitable and sustainable. We will use simulations to illustrate the sets of solutions and the impacts on the first quantum miner when facing quantum competition.

5   Simulation Analysis And Numerical Examples

In this section, we parameterize the model and illustrate the profitability, feasibility and sustainability of double spending by the first quantum miner and the plausible collusion between quantum miners. Due to lack of transparency in the Bitcoin network regarding Bitcoin ownership and transactions, it is hard to find data sources to assign values to the variables. We look for publicly available data and assign values with the priority of having the relative values meaningful rather than having the values match the real-world data.

5.1   Assigning Values to Variables

Bitcoin was designed from its inception to have a capped supply of 21 million tokens. Bitcoin has a history of fluctuating and ever-increasing price. Starting at a price of zero when it was introduced in 2009, the Bitcoin price reached over $70,000 in May 2024. The price jumps and fluctuations generally reflect investor enthusiasm, demand, and supply. The historical record of Bitcoin shows the market certainly has not yet shown the steady state. The actual data on Bitcoin supply, demand and price may not be a good fit for this simulation purpose.

As for the number of people participating in the Bitcoin market, the exact number of Bitcoin miners is difficult to determine due to the decentralized and anonymous nature of the network. Estimates suggest that there are tens of thousands of active miners worldwide. As of March 2024, there are just over 46 million Bitcoin wallets holding at least $1 of value. Around 40% of Bitcoin ownership falls into identifiable categories, including exchanges, miners, governments, balance sheets of public companies, and dormant supply [18].

We choose an approach to use hypothetical parameter values along with the scaling-down of some realistic data to simulate the effects of double spending. We assume there are initially 1 quantum miner and 100 classical miners. The first quantum miner holds 10% of the total Bitcoin. The total supply of Bitcoin is fixed at $2,000$, of which the first quantum miner holds 200 and each classical miner holds 4.5. In the Bitcoin market equilibrium, 70% Bitcoin is demanded for speculative purpose and 30% is for transaction purpose. That is, the values of the parameters are set as $N = 100$, $\overline{B} = 2,000$, $B_0 = 1,800$, $S = 1,400$, $T = 600$. We also set $P = 1$, $V = 2$ and $Y = 12,000$.

5.2   The Case of No Quantum Competition

At the specified parameters, the initial Bitcoin price is 10 from (4). From (7), The relationship between double spending and the Bitcoin price is

$$P_D = \frac{6,000}{600 + D} \tag{26}$$

In absence of quantum competition, the first quantum miner's choice of profitable and sustainable double spending, from (17), is defined by

$$20(10 - P_D) \leq D \leq min\{200, (\frac{120,000}{C} - 600)\} \tag{27}$$

Replacing P_D in (27) with (26), we can find all the profitable and sustainable scale of double spending the first quantum miner can choose from:

$$20(10 - \frac{6,000}{600 + D}) \leq D \leq min\{200, (\frac{120,000}{C} - 600)\} \tag{28}$$

At $C = 150$, $(\frac{120,000}{C} - 600) = 200$. Such cost can be called the "accommodation cost". If the operating cost of classical miners is no higher than the

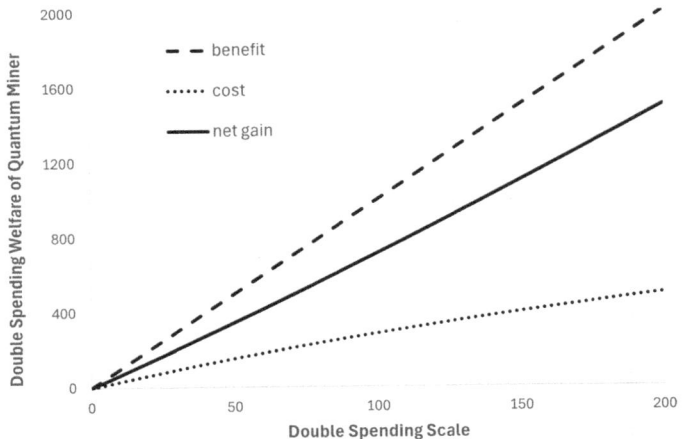

Fig. 1. The welfare effects of double spending (i.e., benefit, cost and net gain) for the monopolistic quantum miner when the miner holds 10% of total Bitcoin. As shown, the net gain of double spending is increasing in the level of double spending. The optimal strategy is to double spend to the upper bound of the profitable and sustainable range of double spending.

accommodation cost, the first quantum miner would be able to double spend all the possessed Bitcoin. Otherwise, the first quantum miner would have to limit the actual double spending at a level below the quantity of possessed Bitcoin. The implication is that the efficiency of classical miners can be beneficial to quantum miners. As cost-effective classical miners are more likely to remain in the Bitcoin network, the quantum miner has more flexibility to double spend.

The first quantum miner's net gain of double spending is

$$\Pi = 10D - 200(10 - \frac{6,000}{600 + D}) \tag{29}$$

which is the difference between the benefit and the cost of double spending.

Figure 1 illustrates how the benefit, the cost and hence the net gain of the first quantum miner changes with the scale of double spending when the first quantum miner holds 10% of total Bitcoin. As shown, both the benefit and the cost increase with the scale of double spending. At the specified parameters, the benefit increases faster than the cost so that the optimal level of double spending is the highest possible double spending that is feasible and sustainable. In other words, the first quantum miner will double spend to the limit of the feasible and the sustainable range.

The ever positive and increasing net gain of double spending at any level of double spending is largely due to the small share of Bitcoin in the possession of the quantum miner whose double spending does not significantly affects Bitcoin supply or Bitcoin price. What if the quantum miner holds a big share of Bitcoin? As an extension of the simulation, we keep other parameters unchanged but assume the first quantum miner holds 60% of total Bitcoin or $1,200$ Bitcoin tokens.

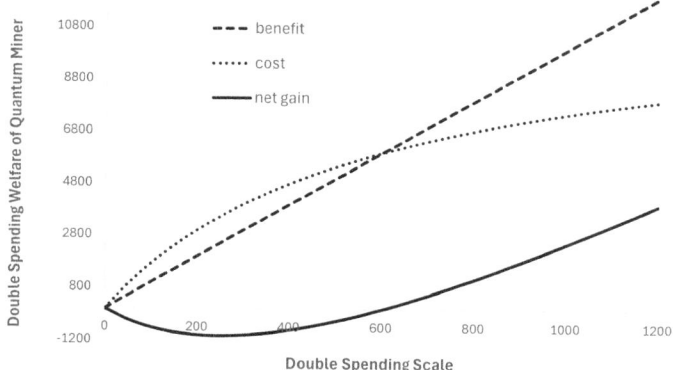

Fig. 2. The welfare effects of double spending (i.e., benefit, cost and net gain) for the monopolistic quantum miner when the miner holds 60% of total Bitcoin. As shown, the net gain of double spending initially falls before it starts rising. When the monopolistic quantum miner holds a large share of total Bitcoin, the miner has to double spend beyond a threshold to make double spending profitable.

Figure 2 illustrates how the benefit, the cost and hence the net gain of the first quantum miner changes with the level of double spending when the first quantum miner holds 60% of total Bitcoin. As shown, the benefit and the cost still increase with the level of double spending, which is true regardless anyway, but the cost is increasing faster than the benefit initially. Therefore when the quantum miner's holding of Bitcoin is a large share of total Bitcoin in circulation, the miner has to double spend beyond a certain threshold to make double spending profitable. In this numerical example, the threshold is $D = 600$, as can be solved from (14).

To generalize, assuming classical miners are sufficiently efficient, i.e., $C \leq 150$, so that the upper bound of double spending by the quantum miner is the Bitcoin held by the quantum miner. The range of profitable and sustainable double spending at various possession of Bitcoin by the quantum miner is illustrated in Fig. 3. Double spending would be profitable and sustainable so long as the quantum miner chooses to double spend within the range. For most part, the width of the range is constant at 600. This is largely because of the model assumptions that lead to a proportional change in the Bitcoin price along with an increase in the Bitcoin supply. If we factor in other considerations such as psychological (e.g., the lost confidence of Bitcoin users when the quantum miner holds more Bitcoin), the range may start narrowing when the Bitcoin holding by the quantum miner reaches a certain level.

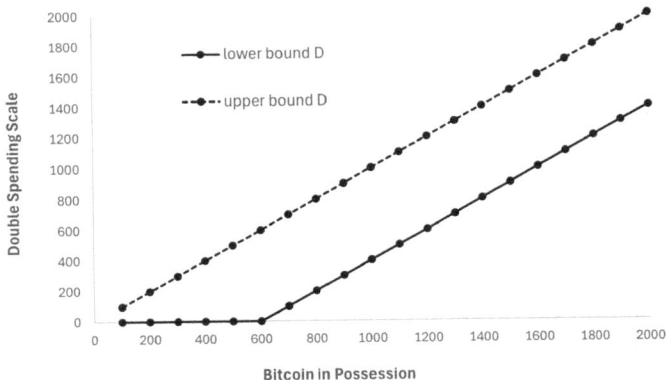

Fig. 3. The range (lower/upper bounds) of the profitable and sustainable scale of double spending for the monopolistic quantum miner at various levels of Bitcoin in possession. The actual double spending by the miner has to fall within such boundary.

5.3 Quantum Mining Collusion in a Competitive Environment

Now we look at the duopolistic competition and collusion between the first quantum miner and a subsequent quantum miner. Jointly, there are three constraints imposed on the two quantum miners' choice of double spending:

$$20(10 - P_D) \leq D_1 \leq 200 \tag{30}$$

$$1.8(10 - P_D) \leq D_2 \leq 18 \tag{31}$$

$$D_1 + D_2 \leq \frac{120,000}{C} - 600 \tag{32}$$

Previous simulations show that the net gain of double spending is increasing in the scale of double spending beyond a threshold (0 or above). An individual quantum miner would want to double spend at the maximum, which would only be possible if $C \leq 147$, in which case $D_1 = 200$ and $D_2 = 18$, and the quantum miners would easily form a coalition. Neither party would have an incentive to deviate. Note the accommodation operating cost of classical miners is smaller at the presence of multiple quantum miners, implying that the prerequisite for the optimal collusion between quantum miners is the improved efficiency of classical miners. The more efficient classical miners are, the more likely for more quantum miners to form an optimal coalition.

Nevertheless, if $C > 147$, not all quantum miners can reach the maximum possible double spending. The quantum miners would have to compromise and each chooses a scale of double spending that is below their upper bound.

Suppose $C = 160$, then $D_1 + D_2 \leq 150$ from (32), i.e., the combined double spending must be no higher than 150. The first quantum miner has to bargain with the subsequent quantum miner to coordinate double spending.

What are the subsequent quantum miner's options? There are three possibilities:

- Do nothing. The welfare effect on the subsequent quantum miner is $-(P_B - P_D)\frac{B_0}{N} = -36$.
- Do not collude but use the quantum power to prevent the first quantum miner from double spending. The welfare effect is 0.
- Collude to share the net gain of double spending with the first quantum miner. The welfare effect is $10D_2 - 36$.

Apparently, the subsequent quantum miner's best strategy is to collude if given an assigned share of double spending $D_2 \geq 3.6$. In this double spending game, both quantum miners have no incentives to cheat. On one hand, the net gain is increasing in the scale of double spending so the parties have no incentives to under spend. On the other hand, since the agreed-upon allocation of double spending satisfied $D_1 + D_2 = 150$. One party's over spending would push classical miners exit the Bitcoin market hence killing the Bitcoin network. Unless the quantum miner is extremely myopic, the quantum miner would limit double spending to make classical miners stay. The numerical example shows that when facing the quantum competition, quantum miners have an incentive to collude, and their coalition is stable.

At $B - B_0 = 200$, the range of profitable and sustainable double spending is $0 \leq D_1 \leq 200$, as shown in Fig. 3. The first quantum miner certainly benefits from collusion that makes double spending possible. Nevertheless, as the number of subsequent quantum miner reaches 42, it would no longer be possible to find any feasible allocation of double spending to enable collusion. There will be no more double spending. $N^* = 42$ is the critical quantum popularity that will effectively terminate double spending. In other words, in this numerical example, when quantum computing reaches about 40% of the mining population, no quantum miners can successfully double spend no matter how collusive and collaborative they are.

In Fig. 4, we illustrate the critical quantum mining penetration rate in relevance to the Bitcoin possession by the first quantum miner at $C = 160$, i.e. $D_2 \geq 0.2\frac{B_0}{100}$, holding $D_1 = 0$ for the purpose of simulating the feasibility of quantum mining collusion. Quantum mining penetration rate is measured by quantum miners as a percentage of the mining population. The critical penetration rate is a break point of double spending beyond which double spending disappears. Figure 4 shows that the distribution of circulating Bitcoin between the first quantum miner and classical miners is essential. At first, at low levels of Bitcoin in possession of the first quantum miner, an increase in the Bitcoin holding by the quantum miner increases the room of quantum mining collusion. The more classical miners hold Bitcoin, the short-lived is double spending. Nevertheless, beyond the turning point of the curve, an increase in the fist quantum miner's holding of Bitcoin decreases the likelihood of collusion and eventually, quantum competition totally disables double spending practice in the Bitcoin network. If the first quantum miner holds a certain amount of circulating Bit-

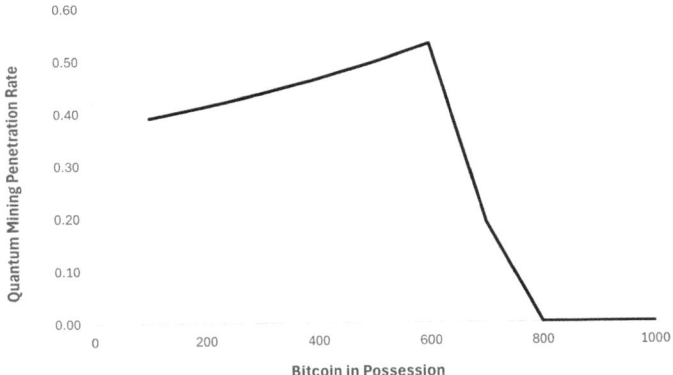

Fig. 4. The critical (maximum) penetration rate of quantum mining to enable collusion among quantum miners. For example, at the turning point 600 Bitcoin possession (30% of total Bitcoins), quantum miners may still collude if quantum mining does not exceed 53% among all mining processes.

coin (around 780 in the simulation), there is no more room to collude with subsequent quantum miners even at $D_1 = 0$.

In other words, collusion between quantum miners is not always feasible. We have to combine Figs. 3 and 4 to find the mutually beneficial shares of double spending between the first quantum miner and the subsequent quantum miners. At $B - B_0 = 800$ for example, the lower bound of the first quantum miner's double spending is 200, which exceeds 150. The first quantum miner will not be able to share double spending with the subsequent quantum miner who will prevent the first quantum miner from double spending. The line in Fig. 4 depicts critical quantum penetration to disable double spending. The intersection of the line and the x-axis is the break point of Bitcoin possession by the first quantum miner to make double spending possible facing quantum competition. Beyond the point, the appearance of just another quantum miner will suffice to terminate double spending practice. Although different parameters will change the numerical values of quantum mining profit, the critical penetration rate, etc., they do not affect the model conclusions.

6   Conclusion and Future Work

The appearance of quantum computing imposes a fundamental threat to the survival of cryptocurrencies such as Bitcoin. Early adopters of quantum computing will have unprecedented advantage over traditional miners and exercise the superior computing power to launch 51% attacks on the Bitcoin network such as profiting from double spending. This paper conducts the economic and game theoretic analysis of the interconnections between emerging quantum computing and cryptocurrency security. The research explores the effects of double spending and quantum computing competition on the welfare of the Bitcoin market participants and the overall security of the Bitcoin network. A stylized game is developed to explore the strategic interactions between Bitcoin miners with a focus on the decision-making by the first quantum miner in absence and with quantum competition from subsequent quantum miners.

The research results suggest that in absence of quantum competition, the first quantum miner, as the money-driven monopolistic quantum miner, shall choose the level of double spending in a sustainable range that is profitable to the monopolistic quantum miner and also provides sufficient financial incentives to encourage the network participation of classical miners. The appearance of subsequent quantum miners makes the first quantum miner worse off. Facing quantum mining competition, quantum miners have to collude to successfully double spend. Simulations illustrate that the key factors determining the profitability and the sustainability of double spending in a quantum competitive environment are the distribution of Bitcoin between the first quantum miner and other miners and the intensity of quantum competition. Most interestingly, the thresholds and critical turning points of collusion among quantum miners were identified in simulations.

Notable findings also indicate the cost effective classical miners are beneficial to quantum miners. The early quantum miners' holding of Bitcoin is a double-edged sword. The increased holding of Bitcoin by the first quantum miner can make double spending more profitable and longer-lived but only up to a certain point. Increased penetration rate of quantum mining and presence of quantum competition will eventually terminate double spending practice and make the Bitcoin network secure again. To that end, we recommend and encourage quantum competition. Future research is necessary to implement quantum security measures against quantum-based double spending practice before its self-healing.

References

1. Arute, F., Arya, K., Babbush, R., et al.: Quantum supremacy using a programmable superconducting processor. Nature **574**, 505–510 (2019)
2. Bailey, B., Sattath, O.: 51% attack via difficulty increase with a small quantum miner. arXiv:2403.08023 (2024)
3. Bertucci, C., Bertucci, L., Lasry, J.M., Lions, P.L.: Mean field game approach to bitcoin mining. arXiv:2004.08167 (2020)
4. Breiki, H.A.: Trust evolution game in blockchain. In: Proceedings of 2022 IEEE/ACS 19th International Conference on Computer Systems and Applications (AICCSA), Abu Dhabi, United Arab Emirates (2022)
5. Chiu, J., Koeppl, T.V.: The economics of cryptocurrency: bitcoin and beyond. Can. J. Econ. **55**(4), 1762–1798 (2022)
6. Chohan, U.W.: The double spending problem and cryptocurrencies. SSRN (2021)
7. Eisert, J., Wilkens, M., Lewenstein, M.: Quantum games and quantum strategies. Phys. Rev. Lett. **83**(15), 3077–3080 (1999)
8. Holmes, S., Chen, L.: Assessment of quantum threat to bitcoin and derived cryptocurrencies. IACR Cryptology ePrint Archive 2021, 967 (2021)
9. Jang, J., Lee, H.N.: Profitable double-spending attacks. Appl. Sci. **10**(23) (2020)

10. Kappert, N., Karger, E., Kureljusic, M.: Quantum computing - the impeding end for the blockchain? In: Proceedings of Pacific Asia Conference on Information Systems (PACIS), Dubai, UAE (2021)
11. Kiktenko, E.O., et al.: Quantum-secured blockchain. Quantum Sci. Technol. **3**(3), 35004 (2018)
12. Kim, D., Ryu, D., Webb, R.I.: Determination of equilibrium transaction fees in the Bitcoin network: a rank-order contest. Int. Rev. Financ. Anal. **86** (2023)
13. Kim, Y., et al.: Evidence for the utility of quantum computing before fault tolerance. Nature **618**, 500–505 (2023)
14. Li, Z., Liao, Q.: Toward socially optimal bitcoin mining. In: Proceedings of 5th IEEE International Conference on Information Science and Control Engineering (ICISCE), Zhengzhou, China (2018)
15. Li, Z., Liao, Q.: Is quantum computing the bitcoin terminator? In: Proceedings of the 30th Americas Conference on Information Systems (AMCIS), Salt Lake City, Utah, pp. 1–10 (2024)
16. Li, Z., Reppen, A.M., Sircar, R.: A mean field games model for cryptocurrency mining. Manag. Sci. **70**(4) (2023)
17. Liu, Z., et al.: A survey on applications of game theory in blockchain. arXiv:1902.10865 (2019)
18. Moore, W.O.: Demystifying bitcoin's ownership landscape. Grayscale (2023)
19. Nguyen, C.T., Hoang, D.T., Nguyen, D.N., Niyato, D., Nguyen, H.T., Dutkiewicz, E.: Proof-of-stake consensus mechanisms for future blockchain networks: fundamentals, applications and opportunities. IEEE Access **7**, 85727–85745 (2019)
20. Nuzzi, L., Waters, K., Andrade, M.: Breaking BFT: quantifying the cost to attack Bitcoin and Ethereum. SSRN (2024)
21. Pinzón, C., Rocha, C.: Double-spend attack models with time advantage for bitcoin. Electron. Notes Theor. Comput. Sci. **329**, 79–103 (2016)
22. Pérez-Antón, R., Sánchez, J.I.L., Corbi, A.: The game theory in quantum computers: a review. Int. J. Interact. Multimed. Artif. Intell. (2023)
23. Stewart, I., Ilie, D., Zamyatin, A., Werner, S., Torshizi, M.F., Knottenbelt, W.J.: Committing to quantum resistance: a slow defence for bitcoin against a fast quantum computing attack. R. Soc. Open Sci. **5**, 180410 (2018)
24. Tas, E.N., Tse, D., Gai, F., Kannan, S., Maddah-Ali, M.A., Yu, F.: Bitcoin-enhanced proof-of-stake security: possibilities and impossibilities. In: Proceedings of 2023 IEEE Symposium on Security and Privacy (SP), San Francisco, CA, USA (2023)
25. Zaghloul, E., Li, T., Mutka, M.W., Ren, J.: Bitcoin and blockchain: security and privacy. IEEE Internet Things J. **7**(10), 10288–10313 (2020)

Equilibrium and Control

Fast Complete Algorithm for Multiplayer Nash Equilibrium

Sam Ganzfried[✉]

Ganzfried Research, Miami Beach, FL, USA
sam.ganzfried@gmail.com
https://www.ganzfriedresearch.com

Abstract. We describe a new complete algorithm for computing Nash equilibrium in multiplayer general-sum games, based on a quadratically-constrained feasibility program formulation. We demonstrate that the algorithm runs significantly faster than the prior fastest complete algorithm on several game classes previously studied and that its runtimes even outperform the best incomplete algorithms. We expect our algorithm to be applicable to important game models in economics, political science, security, and many other fields.

Keywords: Game theory · Equilibrium computation · Multiplayer Nash equilibrium · Optimization

1 Introduction

Nash equilibrium is the central solution concept in game theory. While a Nash equilibrium can be computed in polynomial time for two-player zero-sum games, it is PPAD-hard for two-player general-sum and multiplayer games and widely believed that no efficient algorithms exist [7–9]. Furthermore, even if we were able to compute an equilibrium for these game classes, it would have no performance guarantee. In a two-player zero-sum game, every Nash equilibrium guarantees at least the value of the game in expectation in the worst case. Therefore, if players alternate roles, a Nash equilibrium would guarantee a win or tie in expectation regardless of the strategy used by the opponent. However, for non-zero-sum and multiplayer games, an equilibrium would have no performance guarantee. There can be multiple equilibria with different values, and if the opponents play strategies from a different equilibrium than ours then the resulting strategies may not be in equilibrium.

Despite these computational and conceptual challenges, we must still create agents with strong strategies for these settings, and Nash equilibrium is a compelling starting point. It was shown that an exact Nash equilibrium strategy defeated a variety of agents submitted for a class project in 3-player Kuhn poker [11]. Recently an agent was created for 6-player no-limit Texas hold 'em that defeated strong human players by attempting to approximate Nash equilibrium strategies [6]. The core equilibrium-finding technique used by this agent was

A. Sinha et al. (Eds.): GameSec 2024, LNCS 14908, pp. 109–123, 2025.
https://doi.org/10.1007/978-3-031-74835-6_6

based on the counterfactual regret minimization algorithm, an iterative self-play procedure [26]. It has been demonstrated that counterfactual regret minimization does in fact converge to an ϵ-Nash equilibrium (a strategy profile in which no player can gain more than ϵ by deviating) for small ϵ in three-player Kuhn poker, while it does not converge to equilibrium in the larger game of three-player Leduc hold 'em [1]. These results show that Nash equilibrium strategies (or their approximations) can be successful in practice despite the fact that they do not have a performance guarantee.

Several algorithms have been developed for computing Nash equilibrium in multiplayer games; however, many of them are incomplete, slow, and/or produce solutions with poor approximation quality (i.e., high ϵ). An algorithm is *complete* if it always finds a solution when one exists (at least one Nash equilibrium is guaranteed to exist in all finite games [18]). We present a new algorithm that is complete and runs significantly faster than prior complete algorithms, and even runs faster than the best incomplete algorithms. Our algorithm is based on a novel quadratically-constrained mixed-integer program formulation that can be solved using Gurobi's non-convex quadratic solver [14]. We run experiments on uniform random games with a variety of players and strategy sizes, as well as several games produced from the GAMUT generator [19]. We compare our algorithm against the best prior algorithms, which include several complete methods as well as faster incomplete methods available on the GAMBIT suite [17].

2   Notation

A strategic-form game consists of a finite set of players $N = \{1, \ldots, n\}$, a finite set of pure strategies S_i for each player $i \in N$, and a real-valued utility for each player for each strategy vector (aka *strategy profile*), $u_i : \times_i S_i \to \mathbb{R}$. We will assume that the sets S_i are disjoint, and for simplicity assume that all S_i have the same cardinality. For $s_j \in S_i$ define the *player* function to be $P(s_j) = i$ (which is well-defined under the assumption that the S_i are disjoint). Suppose that $s_{j_k} \in S_{i_k}$ for $k = 1 \ldots n$, and suppose that the $i_k \in N$ are all distinct. Then for $w \in N$ define $\hat{u}_w(s_{j_1}, \ldots, s_{j_n}) = u_w(s_{m_1}, \ldots, s_{m_n})$, where m_q equals the j_k such that $P(j_k) = q$ (and therefore that $s_{m_q} \in S_q$). That is, in the event that the s_{j_k} are not in order of increasing value of the player $P(s_{j_k})$, the $\hat{u}$ function will compute the utility assuming that the vector of strategies is listed in the order of increasing players so that u can be properly applied. For example, suppose that $s_1 \in S_1, s_2 \in S_2, s_3 \in S_3$. Then $\hat{u}_w(s_2, s_3, s_1) = u_w(s_1, s_2, s_3)$, for $w \in N$. This notation will be useful in order to provide more concise representations of our optimization formulations.

A *mixed strategy* σ_i for player i is a probability distribution over pure strategies, where $\sigma_i(s_{i'})$ is the probability that player i plays pure strategy $s_{i'} \in S_i$ under σ_i. Let Σ_i denote the full set of mixed strategies for player i. A strategy profile $\sigma^* = (\sigma_1^*, \ldots, \sigma_n^*)$ is a *Nash equilibrium* if $u_i(\sigma_i^*, \sigma_{-i}^*) \geq u_i(\sigma_i, \sigma_{-i}^*)$ for all $\sigma_i \in \Sigma_i$ for all $i \in N$, where σ_{-i}^* denotes the vector of the components of strategy σ^* for all players excluding player i. For a given candidate strategy profile σ^*, define $\epsilon = \epsilon(\sigma^*) = \max_i \max_{\sigma_i \in \Sigma_i} \left[u_i(\sigma_i, \sigma_{-i}^*) - u_i(\sigma_i^*, \sigma_{-i}^*) \right]$.

3   Algorithm

We first describe a linear mixed-integer feasibility program formulation for computing Nash equilibrium in two-player general-sum games [22]. That work presented four different formulations each using a different objective function and set of constraints, and demonstrated that the first one significantly outperformed the other three. The first formulation was a feasibility program with no objective function, in which the set of Nash equilibria correspond exactly to feasible solutions. We use this as a starting point for our new multiplayer formulations.

3.1   Linear Mixed-Integer Feasibility Formulation for Two-Player Nash Equilibrium

We quote from the original description of the program formulation for two-player Nash equilibrium, and present the formulation below:

> In our first formulation, the feasible solutions are exactly the equilibria of the game. For every pure strategy s_i, there is binary variable b_{s_i}. If this variable is set to 1, the probability placed on the strategy must be 0. If it is set to 0, the strategy is allowed to be in the support, but the regret of the strategy must be 0. The formulation has the following variables other than the b_{s_i}. For each player, there is a variable u_i indicating the highest possible expected utility that that player can obtain given the other player's mixed strategy. For every pure strategy s_i, there is a variable p_{s_i} indicating the probability placed on that strategy, a variable u_{s_i} indicating the expected utility of playing that strategy (given the other player's mixed strategy), and a variable r_{s_i} indicating the regret of playing s_i. The constant U_i indicates the maximum difference between two utilities in the game for player i: $U_i = \max_{s_i^h, s_i^l \in S_i, s_{1-i}^h, s_{1-i}^l \in S_{1-i}} \left[u_i(s_i^h, s_{1-i}^h) - u_i(s_i^l, s_{1-i}^l) \right]$. The formulation follows below [22].

Find $p_{s_i}, u_i, u_{s_i}, r_{s_i}, b_{s_i}$ subject to:

$$\sum_{s_i \in S_i} p_{s_i} = 1 \text{ for all } i \tag{1}$$

$$u_{s_i} = \sum_{s_{1-i} \in S_{1-i}} p_{s_{1-i}} u_i(s_i, s_{1-i}) \text{ for all } i, s_i \in S_i \tag{2}$$

$$u_i \geq u_{s_i} \text{ for all } i, s_i \in S_i \tag{3}$$

$$r_{s_i} = u_i - u_{s_i} \text{ for all } i, s_i \in S_i \tag{4}$$

$$p_{s_i} \leq 1 - b_{s_i} \text{ for all } i, s_i \in S_i \tag{5}$$

$$r_{s_i} \leq U_i b_{s_i} \text{ for all } i, s_i \in S_i \tag{6}$$

$$p_{s_i} \geq 0 \text{ for all } i, s_i \in S_i \tag{7}$$

$$u_i \geq 0 \text{ for all } i \tag{8}$$

$$u_{s_i} \geq 0 \text{ for all } i, s_i \in S_i \tag{9}$$

$$r_{s_i} \geq 0 \text{ for all } i, s_i \in S_i \qquad (10)$$

$$b_{s_i} \text{ binary in } \{0,1\} \text{ for all } i, s_i \in S_i \qquad (11)$$

The first four constraints ensure that the p_{s_i} values constitute a valid probability distribution and define the regret of a strategy. Constraint 5 ensures that b_{s_i} can be set to 1 only when no probability is placed on s_i. On the other hand, Constraint 6 ensures that the regret of a strategy equals 0, unless $b_{s_i} = 1$, in which case the constraint is vacuous because the regret can never exceed U_i. (Technically, Constraint 3 is redundant as it follows from Constraints 4 and 10.) [22]

For clarity, we will rewrite the system with the redundant Constraint 3 removed, as our extensions will be based on this formulation.

Find $p_{s_i}, u_i, u_{s_i}, r_{s_i}, b_{s_i}$ subject to:

$$\sum_{s_i \in S_i} p_{s_i} = 1 \text{ for all } i$$

$$u_{s_i} = \sum_{s_{1-i} \in S_{1-i}} p_{s_{1-i}} u_i(s_i, s_{1-i}) \text{ for all } i, s_i \in S_i$$

$$r_{s_i} = u_i - u_{s_i} \text{ for all } i, s_i \in S_i$$

$$p_{s_i} \leq 1 - b_{s_i} \text{ for all } i, s_i \in S_i$$

$$r_{s_i} \leq U_i b_{s_i} \text{ for all } i, s_i \in S_i$$

$$p_{s_i} \geq 0 \text{ for all } i, s_i \in S_i$$

$$u_i \geq 0 \text{ for all } i$$

$$u_{s_i} \geq 0 \text{ for all } i, s_i \in S_i$$

$$r_{s_i} \geq 0 \text{ for all } i, s_i \in S_i$$

$$b_{s_i} \text{ binary in } \{0,1\} \text{ for all } i, s_i \in S_i$$

3.2   New Formulation for Three-Player Nash Equilibrium

We now describe an extension of the previous two-player formulation to three players. To do this, we introduce new variables, p_{s_i,s_j}, which denote the product of the variables p_{s_i} and p_{s_j}. Note that these new product constraints are now quadratic (while all other constraints remain linear).

Find $p_{s_i}, u_i, u_{s_i}, r_{s_i}, b_{s_i}, p_{s_i,s_j}$ subject to:

$$\sum_{s_i \in S_i} p_{s_i} = 1 \text{ for all } i$$

$$u_{s_i} = \sum_{s_j \in S_2} \sum_{s_k \in S_3} p_{s_j,s_k} u_1(s_i, s_j, s_k) \text{ for all } s_i \in S_1$$

$$u_{s_j} = \sum_{s_i \in S_1} \sum_{s_k \in S_3} p_{s_i,s_k} u_2(s_i, s_j, s_k) \text{ for all } s_j \in S_2$$

$$u_{s_k} = \sum_{s_i \in S_1} \sum_{s_j \in S_2} p_{s_i,s_j} u_3(s_i, s_j, s_k) \text{ for all } s_k \in S_3$$

$$p_{s_i,s_j} = p_{s_i} \cdot p_{s_j} \text{ for all } s_i \in S_1, s_j \in S_2$$

$$p_{s_i,s_j} = p_{s_i} \cdot p_{s_j} \text{ for all } s_i \in S_1, s_j \in S_3$$

$$p_{s_i,s_j} = p_{s_i} \cdot p_{s_j} \text{ for all } s_i \in S_2, s_j \in S_3$$

$$r_{s_i} = u_i - u_{s_i} \text{ for all } i, s_i \in S_i$$

$$p_{s_i} \le 1 - b_{s_i} \text{ for all } i, s_i \in S_i$$

$$r_{s_i} \le U_i b_{s_i} \text{ for all } i, s_i \in S_i$$

$$p_{s_i} \ge 0 \text{ for all } i, s_i \in S_i$$

$$u_i \ge 0 \text{ for all } i$$

$$u_{s_i} \ge 0 \text{ for all } i, s_i \in S_i$$

$$r_{s_i} \ge 0 \text{ for all } i, s_i \in S_i$$

$$b_{s_i} \text{ binary in } \{0,1\} \text{ for all } i, s_i \in S_i$$

We can simplify the presentation by condensing the constraints for u_{s_i} and for the product variables p_{s_i,s_j}, using the notation for $\hat{u}$ defined in Sect. 2.

Find $p_{s_i}, u_i, u_{s_i}, r_{s_i}, b_{s_i}, p_{s_i,s_j}$ subject to:

$$\sum_{s_i \in S_i} p_{s_i} = 1 \text{ for all } i$$

$$u_{s_i} = \sum_{s_j \in S_J} \sum_{s_k \in S_K} p_{s_j,s_k} \hat{u}_{P(s_i)}(s_i, s_j, s_k) \text{ for all } I, J \ne I, K \ne I, J < K, s_i \in S_I$$

$$p_{s_i,s_j} = p_{s_i} \cdot p_{s_j} \text{ for all } I, J \in N, I < J, s_i \in S_I, s_j \in S_J$$

$$r_{s_i} = u_i - u_{s_i} \text{ for all } i, s_i \in S_i$$

$$p_{s_i} \le 1 - b_{s_i} \text{ for all } i, s_i \in S_i$$

$$r_{s_i} \le U_i b_{s_i} \text{ for all } i, s_i \in S_i$$

$$p_{s_i} \ge 0 \text{ for all } i, s_i \in S_i$$

$$u_i \ge 0 \text{ for all } i$$

$$u_{s_i} \ge 0 \text{ for all } i, s_i \in S_i$$

$$r_{s_i} \ge 0 \text{ for all } i, s_i \in S_i$$

$$b_{s_i} \text{ binary in } \{0,1\} \text{ for all } i, s_i \in S_i$$

3.3 New Formulation for Four-Player Nash Equilibrium

We further extend our 3-player formulation to 4 players by introducing new variables p_{s_i,s_j,s_k}. We still retain the p_{s_i,s_j} variables as before, and include additional constraints of the form $p_{s_i,s_j,s_k} = p_{s_i} \cdot p_{s_j,s_k}$. Thus, despite the expected utilities being cubic in the original variables p_{s_i}, we are able to obtain a formulation that only has linear and quadratic constraints.

Find $p_{s_i}, u_i, u_{s_i}, r_{s_i}, b_{s_i}, p_{s_i,s_j}, p_{s_i,s_j,s_k}$ subject to:

$$\sum_{s_i \in S_i} p_{s_i} = 1 \text{ for all } i$$

$$u_{s_i} = \sum_{s_j \in S_2, s_k \in S_3, s_m \in S_4} p_{s_j,s_k,s_m} u_1(s_i, s_j, s_k, s_m) \text{ for all } s_i \in S_1$$

$$u_{s_j} = \sum_{s_i \in S_1, s_k \in S_3, s_m \in S_4} p_{s_i,s_k,s_m} u_2(s_i, s_j, s_k, s_m) \text{ for all } s_j \in S_2$$

$$u_{s_k} = \sum_{s_i \in S_1, s_j \in S_2, s_m \in S_4} p_{s_i,s_j,s_m} u_3(s_i, s_j, s_k, s_m) \text{ for all } s_k \in S_3$$

$$u_{s_m} = \sum_{s_i \in S_1, s_j \in S_2, s_k \in S_3} p_{s_i,s_j,s_k} u_4(s_i, s_j, s_k, s_m) \text{ for all } s_m \in S_4$$

$$p_{s_i,s_j} = p_{s_i} \cdot p_{s_j} \text{ for all } s_i \in S_1, s_j \in S_2$$

$$p_{s_i,s_j} = p_{s_i} \cdot p_{s_j} \text{ for all } s_i \in S_1, s_j \in S_3$$

$$p_{s_i,s_j} = p_{s_i} \cdot p_{s_j} \text{ for all } s_i \in S_1, s_j \in S_4$$

$$p_{s_i,s_j} = p_{s_i} \cdot p_{s_j} \text{ for all } s_i \in S_2, s_j \in S_3$$

$$p_{s_i,s_j} = p_{s_i} \cdot p_{s_j} \text{ for all } s_i \in S_2, s_j \in S_4$$

$$p_{s_i,s_j} = p_{s_i} \cdot p_{s_j} \text{ for all } s_i \in S_3, s_j \in S_4$$

$$p_{s_i,s_j,s_k} = p_{s_i} \cdot p_{s_j,s_k} \text{ for all } s_i \in S_1, s_j \in S_2, s_k \in S_3$$

$$p_{s_i,s_j,s_k} = p_{s_i} \cdot p_{s_j,s_k} \text{ for all } s_i \in S_1, s_j \in S_2, s_k \in S_4$$

$$p_{s_i,s_j,s_k} = p_{s_i} \cdot p_{s_j,s_k} \text{ for all } s_i \in S_1, s_j \in S_3, s_k \in S_4$$

$$p_{s_i,s_j,s_k} = p_{s_i} \cdot p_{s_j,s_k} \text{ for all } s_i \in S_2, s_j \in S_3, s_k \in S_4$$

$$r_{s_i} = u_i - u_{s_i} \text{ for all } i, s_i \in S_i$$

$$p_{s_i} \leq 1 - b_{s_i} \text{ for all } i, s_i \in S_i$$

$$r_{s_i} \leq U_i b_{s_i} \text{ for all } i, s_i \in S_i$$

$$p_{s_i} \geq 0 \text{ for all } i, s_i \in S_i$$

$$u_i \geq 0 \text{ for all } i$$

$$u_{s_i} \geq 0 \text{ for all } i, s_i \in S_i$$

$$r_{s_i} \geq 0 \text{ for all } i, s_i \in S_i$$

$$b_{s_i} \text{ binary in } \{0, 1\} \text{ for all } i, s_i \in S_i$$

As for the 3-player version we can simplify the presentation by condensing constraints and utilizing $\hat{u}$.

Find $p_{s_i}, u_i, u_{s_i}, r_{s_i}, b_{s_i}, p_{s_i,s_j}, p_{s_i,s_j,s_k}$ subject to:

$$\sum_{s_i \in S_i} p_{s_i} = 1 \text{ for all } i$$

$$u_{s_i} = \sum_{s_j \in S_J} \sum_{s_k \in S_K} \sum_{s_m \in S_M} p_{s_j,s_k,s_m} \hat{u}_{P(s_i)}(s_i, s_j, s_k, s_m)$$

$$\text{for all } I, J \neq I, K \neq I, M \neq I, J < K < M, s_i \in S_I$$

$$p_{s_i,s_j} = p_{s_i} \cdot p_{s_j} \text{ for all } I, J \in N, I < J, s_i \in S_I, s_j \in S_J$$

$$p_{s_i,s_j,s_k} = p_{s_i} \cdot p_{s_j,s_k} \text{ for all } I, J, K \in N, I < J < K, s_i \in S_I, s_j \in S_J, s_k \in S_K$$

$$r_{s_i} = u_i - u_{s_i} \text{ for all } i, s_i \in S_i$$

$$p_{s_i} \leq 1 - b_{s_i} \text{ for all } i, s_i \in S_i$$

$$r_{s_i} \leq U_i b_{s_i} \text{ for all } i, s_i \in S_i$$

$$p_{s_i} \geq 0 \text{ for all } i, s_i \in S_i$$

$$u_i \geq 0 \text{ for all } i$$

$$u_{s_i} \geq 0 \text{ for all } i, s_i \in S_i$$

$$r_{s_i} \geq 0 \text{ for all } i, s_i \in S_i$$

$$b_{s_i} \text{ binary in } \{0,1\} \text{ for all } i, s_i \in S_i$$

3.4 Five-Player Nash Equilibrium

We can create a similar extension for 5 players that again only uses linear and quadratic constraints.

Find $p_{s_i}, u_i, u_{s_i}, r_{s_i}, b_{s_i}, p_{s_i,s_j}, p_{s_i,s_j,s_k}, p_{s_i,s_j,s_k,s_m}$ subject to:

$$\sum_{s_i \in S_i} p_{s_i} = 1 \text{ for all } i$$

$$u_{s_i} = \sum_{s_j \in S_J} \sum_{s_k \in S_K} \sum_{s_m \in S_M} \sum_{s_o \in S_O} p_{s_j,s_k,s_m,s_o} \hat{u}_{P(s_i)}(s_i, s_j, s_k, s_m, s_o) \forall I, \{J, K, M, O\} \neq I,$$
$$J < K < M < O, s_i \in S_I$$

$$p_{s_i,s_j} = p_{s_i} \cdot p_{s_j} \text{ for all } I, J \in N, I < J, s_i \in S_I, s_j \in S_J$$

$$p_{s_i,s_j,s_k} = p_{s_i} \cdot p_{s_j,s_k} \text{ for all } I, J, K \in N, I < J < K, s_i \in S_I, s_j \in S_J, s_k \in S_K$$

$$p_{s_i,s_j,s_k,s_m} = p_{s_i} \cdot p_{s_j,s_k,s_m} \text{ for all } I, J, K, M \in N, I < J < K < M, s_i \in S_I, s_j \in S_J, s_k \in S_K, s_m \in S_M$$

$$r_{s_i} = u_i - u_{s_i} \text{ for all } i, s_i \in S_i$$

$$p_{s_i} \leq 1 - b_{s_i} \text{ for all } i, s_i \in S_i$$

$$r_{s_i} \leq U_i b_{s_i} \text{ for all } i, s_i \in S_i$$

$$p_{s_i} \geq 0 \text{ for all } i, s_i \in S_i$$

$$u_i \geq 0 \text{ for all } i$$

$$u_{s_i} \geq 0 \text{ for all } i, s_i \in S_i$$

$$r_{s_i} \geq 0 \text{ for all } i, s_i \in S_i$$

$$b_{s_i} \text{ binary in } \{0,1\} \text{ for all } i, s_i \in S_i$$

3.5 New Formulation for N-Player Nash Equilibrium

One can easily see how our formulation can be generalized to one for n players that has only linear and quadratic constraints. There will be $m^k \binom{n}{k}$ of the $p_{s_{i_1},\ldots,s_{i_k}}$ terms of length k for each $1 \leq k \leq n - 1$, where $m = |S_i|$ is the number of pure strategies for each player. So the total number of the p terms will be $\sum_{k=1}^{n-1} m^k \binom{n}{k}$. From the binomial theorem, we know that $(1+m)^n = \sum_{k=0}^{n} m^k \binom{n}{k}$. So the total number of the p terms is

$$(1+m)^n - m^0 \binom{n}{0} - m^n \binom{n}{n} = (1+m)^n - 1 - m^n < (1+m)^n$$

Note that while this is exponential in the number of players, the size of the game representation is $n \cdot m^n$, since we must specify a payoff for each player for each of m^n pure strategy profiles, which is also exponential in the number of players.

Note that our algorithm does not actually require all of the bilinear p terms; for example, in the 4-player case none of the terms p_{s_i,s_j} for $s_i \in S_1, s_j \in S_2$ are used to form any of the p_{s_i,s_j,s_k} terms. We keep these terms in our formulation only to prevent from further complicating presentation. Removing such extraneous terms would reduce the memory and potentially runtime of the algorithm, though the number of bilinear terms would be still exponential in the number of players. This is not an issue for our experiments since Gurobi removes unused variables automatically during its presolve procedure.

3.6 Computation of Nash Equilibrium from New Quadratic Program Formulation

While we have been able to formulate the problem of computing a Nash equilibrium for $n \geq 3$ players as a quadratically-constrained program (QCP), unfortunately the constraint matrix is not positive semidefinite making the overall program non-convex and more challenging to solve. The best commercial solvers could previously solve convex QCPs but not non-convex QCPs, and the best approach was to approximate products of variables by using piecewise linear approximations [4]; however, this approach introduces a large number of new variables and constraints, leading to large run times, as well as an added layer of approximation error. Recently Gurobi has released an approach that is able to solve non-convex programs with quadratic objective and constraints [14]. The solver allows for both continuous and integral variables, and so can handle mixed-integer quadratically-constrained programs (MIQCPs), which is what we are interested in. The new method addresses non-convex bilinear constraints using an analogue of the simplex algorithm with McCormick envelopes for constructing relaxations with new approaches for cutting planes and spatial branching.

4 Experiments

For our first set of experiments, we generated games with payoffs uniformly random in [0,1] for a variety of number of players n and number of pure strategies m. We used the same parameter values as those used for previous experiments for complete algorithms [3]. For each set of parameter values (n, m), we generated 1,000 random games as the prior work had done (with the exception of the largest game $n = 5, m = 3$ for which we generated 100 games). We set a time limit of 900 s for the random game experiments as the prior work had done.

For all experiments with our algorithm we used version 9.0 of Gurobi's non-convex MIQCP solver, with feasibility tolerance parameter set to 0.0001. For the GAMUT experiments we set the NumericFocus parameter to 2. We used an Intel Core i7-8550U at 1.80 GHz with 16 GB of RAM under 64-bit Windows 10 (8 threads). Prior experiments had been done with similar hardware: Intel Core i7-6500U at 2.50 GHz with 16 GB of RAM under 64-bit Windows 7 [3].

The results from experiments with our MIQCP algorithm on random games are shown in Table 1. For all games other than the largest class ($n = 5, m = 3$) the algorithm had very fast runtimes (in most cases averaging a fraction of a second), with zero runs over the time limit. For the largest class the algorithm hit the time limit in 58% of instances. Analogous results for the best prior complete algorithms are shown in Table 2. Other than for $n = 5, m = 3$, our algorithm outperformed both other algorithms by orders of magnitude in runtime.

Table 1. Results of new MIQCP algorithm for random games.

n	m	Avg. time(s)	Median time(s)	OverTime%
3	2	0.00707	0.0	0
3	3	0.02342	0.02901	0
3	5	0.85763	0.26544	0
4	2	0.02598	0.03124	0
4	3	1.35334	0.40505	0
5	2	0.11873	0.09373	0
5	3	607.68524	900.0	58

Table 2. Results of prior complete algorithms for random games [3].

		Exclusion Method			k-Uniform Search		
n	m	Avg. time(s)	Median time(s)	OverTime%	k	Avg. time(s)	OverTime%
3	2	0.04	0.02	0	2/180	49	1
3	3	26	1.2	1	3/18	191	29
3	5	900	900	100	5	94	33
4	2	99	0.48	8	2/40	23	15
4	3	352	87	30	3/8	85	33
5	2	125	2.7	10	2/8	1.0	30
5	3	520	589	46	3	7.9	36

The Exclusion Method is a complete tree-search-based method that has the best upper bound with respect to the number of players n [3]. The algorithm divides the search space into smaller regions and examines whether an equilibrium can exist in the region. The k-Uniform Search algorithm is based on an improvement to a prior exhaustive complete method [2] where a search is performed over the space of k-uniform strategies for incrementally increasing k. (A *k-uniform strategy* is a strategy where all probabilities are integer multiples of $\frac{1}{k}$.) This approach was used as a benchmark in prior work [3]. Note that these algorithms do not involve the use of a commercial solver such as Gurobi.

We next experimented on several games produced from the GAMUT generator [19]. We used the same games and parameter settings as used in prior work [3]. In particular, we used the variants with 3 players and 3 actions per player. For the congestion game class we used 2 for the number of facilities parameter, and for the covariant game we used $r = -0.5$. All other parameters were generated randomly (as the prior experiments had done). We generated 1,000 games from each class using these distributions.

Results for our new MIQCP algorithm over the GAMUT games are shown in Table 3. We normalized all payoffs to be in [0,1] (by subtracting the smallest payoff from all the payoffs and then dividing all payoffs by the difference between the max and min payoff, or just dividing by the max payoff if the min is nonnegative). Note that linear transformations of the payoffs exactly preserve Nash equilibria, so this normalization would have no effect on the solutions. For some classes several games generated had NaN payoff values, and we ignored these games (we report the number of valid games). We can see that our algorithm ran very quickly for all classes and correctly solved all instances.

Table 3. Results of new MIQCP algorithm for GAMUT games.

Game class	# valid games	Avg. time(s)	# NotSolved
Bertrand oligopoly	970	0.00106	0
Bidirectional LEG	1000	0.00508	0
Collaboration	1000	0.00962	0
Congestion	1000	0.00492	0
Covariant	1000	0.02984	0
Polymatrix	997	0.00803	0
Random graphical	1000	0.01615	0
Random LEG	1000	0.00475	0
Uniform LEG	1000	0.00468	0

Analogous results for the prior best complete algorithms for these same game classes are in Table 4. We can see again that our algorithm typically runs orders of magnitude faster than the others. Note that for these results the NotSolved% column refers to the percentage of runs where the ϵ of the computed strategies exceeded 0.001 (this was the criterion from prior work [3]).

Table 4. Results of prior complete algorithms for GAMUT games [3].

Game class	Exclusion Method		k-Uniform Search	
	Avg. time(s)	NotSolved%	Avg. time(s)	NotSolved%
Bertrand oligopoly	13.7	0	0.01	0
Bidirectional LEG	159	0	0.013	0
Collaboration	2.8	0	0.0009	0
Congestion	29	0	0.027	0
Covariant	95	0	80	16
Polymatrix	172	0	27.2	7
Random graphical	35000	0	0.05	0
Random LEG	880	0	0.02	0
Uniform LEG	793	0	0.02	0

Table 5 shows results for these same game classes using the best algorithms from the GAMBIT software suite [17]. The numbers are the average computation times in seconds and the parentheses show the percentage of instances that were not solved (code got stuck, empty output, or accuracy not within the given $\epsilon = 0.001$). All of these methods are incomplete, and in many cases the NotSolved% was quite large. The runtimes of our algorithm are still about one order of magnitude better than these methods, while also correctly solving all instances.

Table 5. Computation times for GAMBIT algorithms and % of instances not solved [3].

Game class	gnm	ipa	enumpoly	simpdiv	liap	logit
Bertrand oligopoly	0.05 (30)	0.05 (75)	0.04 (50)	0.05	0.24 (99)	0.06
Bidirectional LEG	0.09 (0.3)	0.05 (58)	0.84 (1)	0.06 (0.1)	0.24 (99)	0.06 (0.1)
Collaboration	0.24 (0.1)	0.04	3.3 (50)	0.05	0.34 (99)	0.06 (0.3)
Congestion	0.05 (0.2)	0.05 (85)	0.05 (0.6)	0.05 (0.1)	0.21 (100)	0.05
Covariant	0.13 (3)	0.05 (94)	36	0.67 (2.8)	0.31 (100)	0.05 (1)
Polymatrix	0.06 (1)	0.04 (79)	0.04 (50)	0.07 (0.3)	0.3 (92)	0.05 (0.4)
Random graphical	0.08 (3)	0.04 (96)	6.3 (6)	0.17 (3)	0.31 (99)	0.06 (0.3)
Random LEG	0.05 (1)	0.04 (59)	8.1 (2)	0.05 (0.6)	0.24 (99)	0.06
Uniform LEG	0.07 (0.4)	0.05 (55)	0.04 (17)	0.05	0.23 (99)	0.06

The algorithms are the homotopy method [12] (gnm), its modification using iterated polymatrix approximation [13] (ipa), an algorithm based on solving a polynomial system of equations [20] (enumpoly), the simplicial subdivision method [15] (simpdiv), a function minimization approach (liap), and the quantal response method [16,24] (logit).[1]

Our final comparison is with two recently popular algorithms, counterfactual regret minimization [26] and fictitious play [5,21]. These are iterative self-play procedures that have been proven to converge to Nash equilibrium in two-player zero-sum games, but not for more than two players. However, they can both be run for more than two players, and have been demonstrated to obtain strong empirical performance in certain large extensive-form imperfect-information games. For example, an agent that utilized counterfactual regret minimization (CFR) recently defeated strong humans in 6-player no limit Texas hold 'em [6]. Both CFR and fictitious play (FP) can be extremely effective at quickly approximating equilibrium strategies; however, they can also lead to strategies with extremely high ϵ, even for very small games. So if the goal is to compute an exact Nash equilibrium in multiplayer games, CFR and FP are ineffective. Table 6 shows recent results of CFR and FP for games with uniform random payoffs in [0,1] [10]. We can see that in several cases the average values of ϵ are quite large, and in all cases it exceeds the previously designated benchmark value of 0.001 [3].

Table 6. Results of regret minimization and fictitious play in random games [10].

n	m	# games	# algorithm iterations	Avg. CFR ϵ	Avg. FP ϵ
3	3	100,000	10,000	0.00768	0.00749
3	5	100,000	10,000	0.02312	0.02244
3	10	10,000	10,000	0.05963	0.05574
4	3	100,000	10,000	0.01951	0.01950
4	5	10,000	10,000	0.05121	0.04635
4	10	10,000	10,000	0.08315	0.06661
5	3	10,000	10,000	0.03505	0.03303
5	5	10,000	10,000	0.06631	0.05447
5	10	10,000	1,000	0.06350	0.04341

5   Applicability to Security

While the algorithm applies to general strategic-form games, we briefly highlight how it can be specifically applied to security. Many national security scenarios involve multiple players behaving strategically and are modeled as games. For

---

[1] These experiments were performed using GAMBIT version 15.0 (except 16.0 for simpdiv as it had a bug in 15.0; only simpdiv changed from 15.0 to 16.0, so only that algorithm was rerun with version 16.0) [3].

example, Table 7 depicts a scenario in which a defender (i.e., the police) selects a terminal to defend and an adversary selects a terminal to attack [23]. The players' moves may be modeled as being simultaneous or sequential, and often the game is not zero sum. The numerical values for payoffs are often calculated by domain experts and assumed to be realistic valuations of the scenario (there has also been research done on Bayesian games which model uncertainty over the payoffs). While a full scenario may involve many different participants and actions, in many cases it may be possible to construct a game with a small number of players and strategies that captures critical aspects of the game. It is important to be able to quickly and accurately solve such game models.

Table 7. Example security game. Defender selects row and adversary selects column.

	Terminal 1	Terminal 2
Terminal 1	5, −3	−1, 1
Terminal 2	−5, 5	2, −1

6   Additional Related Research

A preliminary version of this paper appeared on arXiv in February 2020.[2] A subsequent work has generalized our approach to solve a program with a smaller number of bilinear terms [25], using our algorithm as a baseline for comparison.

7   Conclusion

We presented a new complete algorithm for computing Nash equilibrium in multiplayer games based on a mixed-integer quadratically-constrained feasibility program formulation. Our algorithm outperforms the previously best complete algorithms by orders of magnitude for all but the largest game class we considered. Our algorithm even has significantly smaller runtimes than the best prior incomplete methods (which also frequently fail to compute a solution). We also demonstrated that recently popular iterative algorithms have significant approximation error and are unsatisfactory for the goal of computing an exact Nash equilibrium. We ran experiments on a wide variety of game classes, and expect our algorithm to be applicable to important game models in economics, political science, security, and many other fields.

Disclosure of Interests. The author has no competing interests to declare that are relevant to the content of this article. This research received no funding.

---

[2] https://arxiv.org/abs/2002.04734v1.

References

1. Abou Risk, N., Szafron, D.: Using counterfactual regret minimization to create competitive multiplayer poker agents. In: Proceedings of the International Conference on Autonomous Agents and Multi-Agent Systems (AAMAS) (2010)
2. Babichenko, Y., Barman, S., Peretz, R.: Simple approximate equilibria in large games. In: Proceedings of the Fifteenth ACM Conference on Economics and Computation (2014)
3. Berg, K., Sandholm, T.: Exclusion method for finding Nash equilibrium in multiplayer games. In: Proceedings of the AAAI Conference on Artificial Intelligence (AAAI), pp. 383–389 (2017)
4. Bisschop, J.: AIMMS–Optimization Modeling. AIMMS Inc., Bellevue (2006)
5. Brown, G.W.: Iterative solutions of games by fictitious play. In: Koopmans, T.C. (ed.) Activity Analysis of Production and Allocation, pp. 374–376. Wiley, New York (1951)
6. Brown, N., Sandholm, T.: Superhuman AI for multiplayer poker. Science **365**, 885–890 (2019)
7. Chen, X., Deng, X.: 3-Nash is PPAD-complete. Electronic Colloquium on Computational Complexity Report No. 134, 1–12 (2005)
8. Chen, X., Deng, X.: Settling the complexity of 2-player Nash equilibrium. In: Proceedings of the Annual Symposium on Foundations of Computer Science (FOCS) (2006)
9. Daskalakis, C., Goldberg, P., Papadimitriou, C.: The complexity of computing a Nash equilibrium. SIAM J. Comput. **1**(39), 195–259 (2009)
10. Ganzfried, S.: Empirical analysis of fictitious play for Nash equilibrium computation in multiplayer games (2024). arXiv:2001.11165 [cs.GT]
11. Ganzfried, S., Nowak, A., Pinales, J.: Successful Nash equilibrium agent for a 3-player imperfect-information game. Games **9**(33) (2018)
12. Govindan, S., Wilson, R.: A global Newton method to compute Nash equilibria. J. Econ. Theory **110**, 65–86 (2003)
13. Govindan, S., Wilson, R.: Computing Nash equilibria by iterated polymatrix approximation. J. Econ. Dyn. Control **28**, 1229–1241 (2004)
14. Gurobi Optimization, L: Gurobi optimizer reference manual (2019)
15. Laan, G.V.D., Talman, A.J.J., Heyden, L.V.D.: Simplicial variable dimension algorithms for solving the nonlinear complementarity problem on a product of unit simplices using a general labelling. Math. Oper. Res. **12**(3), 377–397 (1987)
16. McKelvey, R., Palfrey, T.: Quantal response equilibria for normal form games. Games Econ. Behav. **10**, 6–38 (1995)
17. McKelvey, R.D., McLennan, A.M., Turocy, T.L.: Gambit: software tools for game theory, version 0.97.1.5 (2004). http://econweb.tamu.edu/gambit
18. Nash, J.: Non-cooperative games. Ph.D. thesis, Princeton University (1950)
19. Nudelman, E., Wortman, J., Leyton-Brown, K., Shoham, Y.: Run the GAMUT: a comprehensive approach to evaluating game-theoretic algorithms. In: Proceedings of the International Conference on Autonomous Agents and Multi-Agent Systems (AAMAS) (2004)
20. Porter, R., Nudelman, E., Shoham, Y.: Simple search methods for finding a Nash equilibrium. Games Econom. Behav. **63**(2), 642–662 (2008)
21. Robinson, J.: An iterative method of solving a game. Ann. Math. **54**, 296–301 (1951)

22. Sandholm, T., Gilpin, A., Conitzer, V.: Mixed-integer programming methods for finding Nash equilibria. In: Proceedings of the National Conference on Artificial Intelligence (2005)
23. Tambe, M.: Security and Game Theory: Algorithms, Deployed Systems, Lessons Learned. Cambridge University Press, New York (2012)
24. Turocy, T.: A dynamic homotopy interpretation of the logistic quantal response equilibrium correspondence. Games Econ. Behav. **51**, 243–263 (2005)
25. Zhang, Y., An, B., Subrahmanian, V.: Computing optimal Nash equilibria in multi-player games. In: Conference on Neural Information Processing Systems (NeurIPS) (2023)
26. Zinkevich, M., Bowling, M., Johanson, M., Piccione, C.: Regret minimization in games with incomplete information. In: Proceedings of the Annual Conference on Neural Information Processing Systems (NIPS) (2007)

Contested Logistics: A Game-Theoretic Approach

Jakub Černý[1(✉)], Chun Kai Ling[1], Darshan Chakrabarti[1], Jingwen Zhang[1], Gabriele Farina[2], Christian Kroer[1], and Garud Iyengar[1]

[1] Columbia University, New York, NY 10027, USA
{jakub.cerny,chunkai.ling,darshan.chakrabarti,jz3093,
christian.kroer,gi10}@columbia.edu
[2] MIT, Cambridge, MA 02139, USA
gfarina@mit.edu

Abstract. We introduce Contested Logistics Games, a variant of logistics problems that account for the presence of an adversary that can disrupt the movement of goods in selected areas. We model this as a large two-player zero-sum one-shot game played on a graph representation of the physical world, with the optimal logistics plans described by the (possibly randomized) Nash equilibria of this game. Our logistics model is fairly sophisticated, and is able to handle multiple modes of transport and goods, accounting for possible storage of goods in warehouses, as well as Leontief utilities based on demand satisfied. We prove computational hardness results related to equilibrium finding and propose a practical double-oracle solver based on solving a series of best-response mixed-integer linear programs. We experiment on both synthetic and real-world maps, demonstrating that our proposed method scales to reasonably large games. We also demonstrate the importance of explicitly modeling the capabilities of the adversary via ablation studies and comparisons with a naive logistics plan based on heuristics.

Keywords: Logistics · Game theory · Equilibrium computation

1 Introduction

Logistics is a multi-million dollar business with applications in numerous real-world domains. In this paper, we study a variant we call Contested Logistics (CL). CL features two players, customarily identified with the names *Blue* and *Red*. Blue is the logistics player, while Red is an interdiction player seeking to reduce Blue's utility. CL captures the strategic interaction between Red and Blue as a two-player zero-sum one-shot game. A solution to the game is identified by the *Nash equilibrium* (NE) solution concept.

Equal contribution between J. Černý and C. K. Ling.

A. Sinha et al. (Eds.): GameSec 2024, LNCS 14908, pp. 124–146, 2025.
https://doi.org/10.1007/978-3-031-74835-6_7

CL is motivated by military considerations, where logistics may be disrupted by an adversary, and robustness considerations, where logistics may be disrupted by acts of God, unforeseen failures, political instability, or other factors. Attacks on supply lines have been extensively documented in real military settings, and are often viewed as more effective than direct kinetic confrontation [30]. Similarly, geopolitical powers such as the US, China, and the EU seek to diversify their supply chains with the intention of being robust against a possible outbreak of hostilities [16]. Likewise, the recent Evergreen Suez canal blockage incident is a painful reminder of the potential risks of having a single-point of failure [28].

While the presence of adversaries in logistics is not new [9], the CL model differs from prior work in that (i) it does not assume a particular behavior of the adversary, instead allowing Red to act in a manner that most hurts Blue, and (ii) we allow for very dramatic attacks by Red, completely destroying routes or segments of railroads, as opposed to relatively tame effects like reducing a route's capacity or introducing small uncertainties in supply or demand.

The inclusion of Red introduces game-theoretic considerations. Since Blue's logistics and Red's interdiction plans are chosen simultaneously, the resultant Nash equilibrium is typically randomized. Additionally, the computation of the equilibrium poses significant challenges. For instance, the number of possible logistics plans is doubly exponential, while the number of interdiction plans grows exponentially with Red's budget. Thus, explicitly specifying the CL problem as a zero-sum bimatrix game is not practical. Our main contributions are as follows:

- We formally propose the framework of Contested Logistics (CL) games, a novel variant of logistics planning that accounts for Red's capabilities. Our min-max formulation *explicitly* models Red actively seeking to thwart Blue, via relatively drastic measures compared to prior work. We show that an optimal strategy exists for both players via von Neumann's minimax theorem.
- We prove that computing a Nash eq., as well as best responses of Red and Blue, are NP-hard problems. Nonetheless, the best responses of Blue (respectively, Red) to a fixed randomized Red (resp., Blue) strategy can be written compactly as a polynomial-size mixed integer linear program (MILP).
- We propose solving CL games via a double oracle method, utilizing our best-response MILPs. We demonstrate scalability via experiments.
- We conduct experiments using *real-world* inspired scenarios, observing the following. (i) Optimal solutions to the CL problem exhibit counter-intuitive behavior, providing insights into what the solution to the CL problem may look like in practice. (ii) A naïve, heuristics-based approach for Blue results in a highly exploitable strategy, suggesting that explicitly accounting for Red's capabilities is important. (iii) The cost of overestimating Red's capabilities (*i.e.*, budget) is relatively low, but conversely, underestimating Red's capabilities leads to a drastic decrease in performance, reaffirming the adage that "it is better to be safe than sorry".

2   Related Work

This paper is related to several fields spanning across disciplines. We concentrate on the fields most pertinent to our game-theoretic model. For traditional (non-adversarial) logistics, refer to the established literature [17,20,33].

Logistics and Routing Models. Logistics in a contested environment, where adversaries actively interfere with supply chain operations, has been explored in various contexts, especially within military logistics [4,24]. Many existing models assume a simplified model of Red, who acts blindly or with limited information and follows a fixed (deterministic or stochastic) behavior [5,22,37]. While bi-level optimization is sometimes incorporated, the solutions typically remain deterministic, limiting their ability to adapt to more dynamic adversaries [6].

Vehicle routing problems involve optimizing routes for vehicles delivering goods or services. The literature on (robust) routing strategies is extensive, but the typical sources of uncertainty in these models are costs, demands, time windows, or customers, rather than adversaries [1,27,32,43]. Models involving adversarial elements face similar challenges as those in the logistics literature. They often assume either simplistic probabilistic models [2,9] or bi-level models with a single vehicle, as seen in ambush avoidance or hazardous materials transport literature [18,29,36]. Alternatively, they provide deterministic solutions, as in routing interdiction problems [8,13,35].

Game-Theoretic Models. Network interdiction games explore optimal arcs in a network for interdiction purposes, initially studied in [45] and applied in cybersecurity, cyberphysical security, or supply-chain attacks [40,41,44,45]. These models typically focus on disrupting traversal paths without accounting for the coordination required among multiple connectors, crucial in logistics scenarios.

Security games have seen practical applications, with defenders choosing distributions over targets and attackers selecting targets to attack [3,23,34,38]. The simplest versions of such games enjoy polynomial-time solvers, even in the general-sum case [14,25]. Many developments have been made to account for large but structured strategy spaces such as defender target schedules [26] and repeated interactions [19]. While efficient in many cases, they often simplify strategies and lack modeling depth for logistics movement and coordination.

Another notable class of games are extensive-form games (EFGs), which are played on game trees where players decide actions at each information set [39]. Notably these were used to generate superhuman poker AIs [10–12]. For CL settings, EFGs could be used to model sequential CL problems, though the action spaces would become potentially prohibitively large. In this paper we focus on single-shot CL problems, which are easier to model and solve, but sequential CL problems are an interesting future direction.

3   Contested Logistics

CL games are played on a directed graph whose nodes correspond to different types of locations—cities, provinces, towns, *et cetera*. There are several types of *packages* (that is, resources) available that may be transported. Some of the nodes are specially designated as *demand, supply,* or *warehouse* nodes. At warehouses, packages may be dropped off and stored. To facilitate transportation of packages, there are several *connectors* (for instance, trucks, trains, or planes) which may be used to transport packages between locations; what a connector can carry, its capacity, and where it can traverse, i.e., edges in the graph, are connector-specific. For example, aircraft cannot carry packages that are too heavy, and while trains have a larger capacity than trucks, they are restricted to traversing only railroads.

Given these specifications, the game proceeds as follows. Red chooses a set of edges to *interdict*, subject to budget constraints. Blue then decides what, where, when, and how packages are sent from supply to demand nodes using the connectors available. Blue aims to satisfy as much demand as possible within a specified time horizon. The game is zero-sum, i.e., Red's goal is to minimize demand satisfied. We adopt a two-stage approach for Blue's logistic plans. In the routing phase, Blue selects where each connector should be routed without committing to any loading. The individual routes can (and often are) correlated across connectors, but are chosen *concurrently* with Red's decision of where to interdict. In the loading phase, Blue observes where Red has chosen to interdict, and uses this information to select a suitable load for connectors, *without changing their routes*. Any connector that was interdicted is forbidden from carrying loads after the point of interdiction, but may still be utilized prior to that. This two-phase approach was introduced by [7], and models situations where unlike routing, loading decisions can be changed easily and on-the-fly. The approach also allows some level of recourse by Blue, while still having a single-shot zero-sum game model, which is preferable from a computational standpoint.

Formally, we represent a CL game as a directed *physical graph* $G = (V, E)$. The nodes in G represent locations in the physical world Blue traverses. The edges E can be interdicted by Red, affecting Blue's ability to enact their logistics.

3.1   Blue's Strategy Space

On the physical graph $G = (V, E)$, Blue has a subset of nodes $W \subseteq V$ designated as warehouses, where they can store packages that are currently not being moved around. We assume there is at most one warehouse in each node. Each warehouse has an initial (possible zero) supply, given by a non-negative function $S : W \times \mathcal{P} \to \mathbb{R}_0^+$, and a demand for packages, given by a function $D : W \times \mathcal{P} \to \mathbb{R}_0^+$.

Moving the packages is done by a set of connectors $\mathcal{C}$. With each connector $c \in \mathcal{C}$ there is an associated subset of edges $E_c \subseteq E$ the connector may use to move across the physical graph, and a function $M : \mathcal{C} \times E \to \mathbb{Z}^+$ determining how many timesteps does it take the connector to cross an edge. We assume this value is infinite for the edges the connector cannot use. In addition, each connector has a designated initial location given by a function $L : \mathcal{C} \to W$, and weight and volume capacities given by functions $W_{\max} : \mathcal{C} \to \mathbb{R}^+$ and $V_{\max} : \mathcal{C} \to \mathbb{R}^+$, respectively. Moreover, Blue has a set of package types $\mathcal{P}$, each with its associated single unit weight $W : \mathcal{P} \to \mathbb{R}^+$, and single unit volume $V : \mathcal{P} \to \mathbb{R}^+$. Finally, all movement happens over a finite number of discrete timesteps $\mathcal{T} = \{0, 1, \ldots, T\}$.

For a given connector $c \in \mathcal{C}$, based on its initial location $L(c)$, movement speed $M(c, e)$, accessible edges E_c, and timesteps $\mathcal{T}$, we unroll the physical graph into individual connector-specific layered directed graphs $\mathcal{G}_c = (\mathcal{V}, \mathcal{E}_c)$, where $\mathcal{V} = (\mathsf{V}_t)_{t \in \mathcal{T}}$ is a series of copies of the physical nodes spread across time. For an edge $e \in \mathcal{E}$, we denote by $\mathcal{V}^-(e)$ the tail node of e and $\mathcal{V}^+(e)$ the head node. The edges between the individual layers are found by a simple breadth-first search from the connector's initial location. We assume that no connector can cross more than a single edge in the physical graph in one timestep. However, note that the edges can jump layers, in case it takes the connector more than one timestep to cross an edge. Note that this unrolling process *does not* create a exponentially sized tree but a compact layered DAG (see Fig. 1).

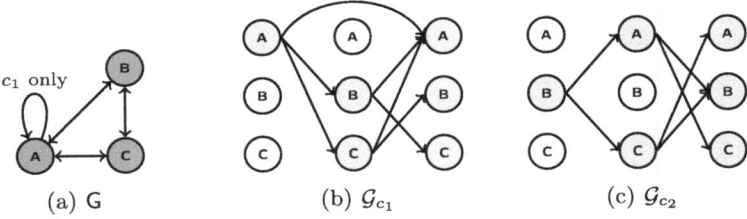

c_1 only		
(a) G	(b) $\mathcal{G}_{c_1}$	(c) $\mathcal{G}_{c_2}$

Fig. 1. Physical graph G and layered graphs $\mathcal{G}_{c_1}, \mathcal{G}_{c_2}$ obtained by unrolling G over 3 steps. Connectors c_1 and c_2 start at A and B, respectively. G has a loop at A for c_1 only, taking 2 steps to cross. All the other edges can be crossed in a single timestep by either connector. Unreachable nodes are in white.

Due to the construction, the layered graph edges in general differ across the connectors, whereas the nodes in the individual layers are the same. Each $v \in \mathcal{V}$ corresponds to some node $\mathsf{v} \in \mathsf{V}$ laying in layer t and we denote this copy of node v as $v = \mathsf{v}_t$. For an edge $e \in \mathcal{E}_c$, we denote the corresponding edge in the physical graph as $\mathsf{E}(e)$. $\mathsf{E}(e)$ is always a singleton. Blue's action space consists of paths in these layered graphs, one per each connector, and can be encoded as solutions to the following feasibility MILP:

$$1 = \sum_{e \in \mathcal{E}_c^-(L(c)_0)} f_c(e) \quad \forall c \in \mathcal{C}$$

$$\sum_{e \in \mathcal{E}_c^-(v_t)} f_c(e) = \sum_{e \in \mathcal{E}_c^+(v_t)} f_c(e) \qquad \forall c \in \mathcal{C}, \ \forall t \in \mathcal{T}, \ \forall v \in \mathsf{V} \qquad \text{(F)}$$

$$f_c(e) \in \{0, 1\} \qquad \forall c \in \mathcal{C}, \ \forall e \in \mathcal{E}_c.$$

We call a feasible tuple of connector paths a *logistics plan* and denote it $\lambda \in \Lambda$, with $\lambda_c = (e_{c,1}, \ldots, e_{c,k})$ being a path of a connector c. For each logistics plan we have (potentially many) associated feasible package flows, described by the following set of constraints R(λ), starting with the initial supply equation

$$S(w,p) = s_{w_0,p} \qquad \forall w \in \mathsf{W}, \ \forall p \in \mathcal{P}, \qquad (\text{R.1})$$

then the flow conservation constraints, distinguishing between physical locations that serve or serve not as warehouses

$$l_{c,p}(e_{c,i}) = l_{c,p}(e_{c,i+1}) \qquad \forall c \in \mathcal{C}, \ \forall p \in \mathcal{P}$$
$$\forall e_{c,i} \in \lambda_c : V^+(e_{c,i}) \notin \mathsf{W} \qquad (\text{R.2})$$

$$s_{w_t,p} + \sum_{c \in \mathcal{C}, e \in \lambda_c : V^+(e) = w_t} l_{c,p}(e) = s_{w_{t+1},p} + \sum_{c \in \mathcal{C}, e \in \lambda_c : V^-(e) = w_t} l_{c,p}(e) \qquad \forall t \in \mathcal{T}, \ \forall p \in \mathcal{P}, \ \forall w \in \mathsf{W}, \qquad (\text{R.3})$$

and the weight and volume limits of each connector

$$W_{max}(c) \geq \sum_{p \in \mathcal{P}} W(p) l_{c,p}(e) \qquad \forall c \in \mathcal{C}, \ \forall e \in \lambda_c \qquad (\text{R.4})$$

$$V_{max}(c) \geq \sum_{p \in \mathcal{P}} V(p) l_{c,p}(e) \qquad \forall c \in \mathcal{C}, \ \forall e \in \lambda_c \qquad (\text{R.5})$$

$$l_{c,p}(e) \geq 0 \qquad \forall c \in \mathcal{C}, \ \forall p \in \mathcal{P}, \ \forall e \in \lambda_c \qquad (\text{R.6})$$

$$s_{w_t,p} \geq 0 \qquad \forall t \in \mathcal{T} \cup \{T+1\}, \ \forall p \in \mathcal{P}, \ \forall w \in \mathsf{W}, \qquad (\text{R.7})$$

where the l variables encode the package flows, while the s variables record the amount of packages stored in warehouses.

3.2   Red's Strategy Space

The strategy space of Red is significantly simpler than Blue's. Our model is similar to the classic network interdiction problems, where Red chooses a subset of edges in the physical graph G to interdict, given a budget $B \geq 0$ and a cost function $C : \mathsf{E} \to \mathbb{R}^+$. Since Red operates on the physical graph instead of any layered graph, we assume an edge is interdicted over the entire game. Red's action space is formed by all feasible solutions of the following MILP:

$$\left\{ y \in \{0,1\}^{|\mathsf{E}|} \mid B \geq \sum_{e \in \mathsf{E}} C(e) y(e) \right\}. \qquad (\text{Y})$$

We call a feasible set of interdicted edges an *interdiction plan* and denote it $\iota \in \mathsf{I}$.

3.3   Utilities

We assume that Blue aims to maximize the (cumulative) Leontief value at each location with demand D at the final timestep T, given a logistics plan λ and feasible package flows l and s. The value is defined as

$$v(\lambda, s, l) = \sum_{w \in \mathsf{W}} P(w) \max \left\{ \min_{p \in \mathcal{P}, D(w,p) > 0} \frac{s_{w_T,p}}{D(w,p)}, U(w) \right\}, \qquad (\text{L})$$

where $P(w), U(w)$ are warehouse-specific payoffs per each unit and maximum numbers of units, respectively, of satisfied demand.

Motivated by the randomized network interdiction problems [7], we make the following two assumptions about the effects of Red's interdiction plan ι on Blue's logistics λ. (i) Whenever a connector attempts to cross an interdicted physical edge, it is destroyed together with its entire package load. Formally, the interdicted logistics plan is hence a "truncated" plan

$$\lambda_c(\iota) = \begin{cases} \lambda_c & \text{if } \forall e \in \lambda_c : \mathsf{E}(e) \notin \iota \\ (e_{c,1}, \ldots, e_{c,j}) & \text{if } \forall e \in (e_{c,1}, \ldots e_{c,j-1}) : \mathsf{E}(e) \notin \iota \text{ and } \mathsf{E}(e_{c,j}) \in \iota. \end{cases}$$

(ii) While the logistics plan (i.e., the connector paths) is fixed, the package flows are *adaptive*, optimizing the Leontief value for the Blue's truncated plan. For a pair (λ, ι), the utility $u(\lambda, \iota)$ can hence be described as the following LP[1]:

$$u(\lambda, \iota) = \max_{s,l} v(\lambda(\iota), s, l) \quad \text{such that } \mathrm{R}(\lambda(\iota)) \text{ are satisfied,} \tag{U}$$

where $\mathrm{R}(\cdot)$ refers to the set of flow constraints (R.1)–(R.7). Note that players cannot alter their strategies once they begin moving, making it, indeed, a one-shot game. We further assume the game is *zero-sum*, i.e., Red minimizes u.

4   Computing Solutions of Contested Logistics

Our goal is to find a Nash equilibrium (NE), possibly mixed, over Blue's logistics plans and Red's interdiction plans. Denote by Δ_b and Δ_r the probability simplices over Λ and I respectively. Then, for some distribution over a player's plans $x_i \in \Delta_i$, $x_i(p_i)$ is the probability that p_i is played by player $i \in \{r, b\}$. The NE problem reduces to solving the bilinear saddle point problem

$$\min_{x_b \in \Delta_b} \max_{x_r \in \Delta_r} \mathbb{E}_{\lambda \sim x_b, \iota \sim x_r} [u(\lambda, \iota)] = \min_{x_b \in \Delta_b} \max_{x_r \in \Delta_r} \sum_{\lambda \in \Lambda} \sum_{\iota \in \mathsf{I}} x_b(\lambda) \cdot x_r(\iota) \cdot u(\lambda, \iota).$$

Since Δ_b and Δ_r are both convex and compact sets, and the objective function is convex-concave, the minimax theorem [31] guarantees the existence of a unique value for the game. Nevertheless, determining the NE in CL games is computationally infeasible, as indicated already by the growth of the number of possible logistics plans that is double exponential in the problem's parameters.

Proposition 1. *It is* NP-*hard in terms of* $|\mathsf{G}|$, $|\mathcal{C}|$, $|\mathcal{P}|$, *and* T *to find a NE for a contested logistics game with Leontief utilities given in Formulation U.*

Proof. We employ a reduction from the 3-SAT problem. Assume we are given a CNF having n variables and k clauses, where each clause has at most 3 literals. We aim to determine the satisfiability of the formula. We construct a CL scenario

---

[1] Note the formulation is indeed an LP because the inner minimization in formulation (L) is easily linearized using an auxiliary variable for each warehouse.

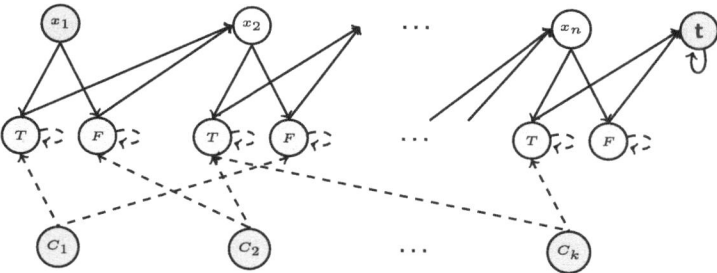

Fig. 2. The physical graph described in Proposition 1, serving as a game for the 3-SAT problem we aim to reduce from. Each node in the top layer, denoted by x_i, corresponds to a variable x_i in the SAT formula, which contains a total of n variables. The nodes in the layer below signify a positive or negative assignment. Each assignment node is connected to the clauses it satisfies. For example, in the depicted graph $C_1 = x_1 \vee \neg x_2$, $C_2 = \neg x_1 \vee x_2$, and $C_n = x_2 \vee x_n$. Edges available to the assignment connector starting from x_1 are solid, edges of the clause connectors starting from C_j are dashed. Every path of the assignment connector of length $2n$ ending in the terminal node t encodes a full assignment.

featuring a single type of package with unit weight and volume, and $k + 1$ connectors: a single assignment connector constrained to weight and volume limits of k, and k clause connectors with limits of 1. The physical graph is depicted in Fig. 2. The top layer consists of a single node per each variable x_i, and a terminal node t. The layer below has two nodes per each x_i, signifying a positive (T) or a negative (F) assignment. The bottom layer contains one node per each clause. Each of the x_i nodes is connected to its assignment nodes. Each clause node has an edge to a corresponding assignment node of every variable included in the clause. Moreover, the assignment nodes of the variable $x_i, i < n$ are connected to the variable node x_{i+1}. The assignment nodes of x_n are connected to t. The first connector starts at node x_1. Other connectors start at their corresponding clause. Moving across each edge takes one time step. The outgoing edges from the assignment nodes are not available to the connectors starting at the clause nodes. The scenario's time horizon is $2n$. There are $2n + k + 2$ warehouses: one at x_1, one at t, and one in every clause and assignment nodes. Only the clause warehouses supply a single unit of the package each. There is only one demand node, t, with demand k and both unit payoff and maximum units set to 1. Red has budget 1, with each edge having a cost of 2, except the loop in t with cost 1. Red's action space is hence trivial. In the equilibrium, the assignment connector collects as many packages from the satisfied clauses as possible. We will show the value of the equilibrium is 1 if and only if the formula is satisfiable.

$\rightarrow$ Suppose there exists a satisfying assignment. Let the satisfying assignment define the path of the assignment connector. For each clause, there exists a literal that the assignment makes true. Let these literals define the paths of the clause connectors. From the definition of the satisfying assignment, the assignment connector's path crosses all the paths of the clause connectors, which enables it to pick up all k packages and bring them to t. The Leontief utility at t is hence $k/k = 1$.

$\leftarrow$ If the value of the equilibrium is 1, then the assignment connector must have picked up all k packages, meeting with all k clause connectors. Due to the construction of the physical graph, the assignment connector can visit only one of the assignment nodes for each variable, effectively encoding a variable assignment. Because the clause nodes are connected with only those assignment nodes that satisfy the clause, meeting with an assignment connector corresponds to satisfying the clause. The path of the assignment connector meeting all k clause connector hence encodes a satisfying assignment.

4.1   Best Response Complexity and Computation

Recall that Blue's and Red's (pure) best responses to fixed strategies x_r and x_b are defined as $\lambda^{\mathrm{BR}} = \arg\max_{\lambda \in \Lambda} u(\lambda, x_r)$ and $\iota^{\mathrm{BR}} = \arg\min_{\iota \in \mathsf{I}} u(x_b, \iota)$, where $u(x_b, \iota) = \mathbb{E}_{\lambda \sim x_b} u(\lambda, \iota)$ and $u(\lambda, x_r) = \mathbb{E}_{\iota \sim x_r} u(\lambda, \iota)$. We note that while best responses are closely related to NE computation, they are generally distinct problems. There are classes of games where computing best responses is difficult but finding a NE is easy, and vice versa [46]. Unfortunately, computing best responses in CL games is also intractable. Indeed, intractability of Blue's best response follows directly from the proof construction of Proposition 1.

Corollary 1. *Let $\tilde{\mathsf{I}} \subseteq \mathsf{I}$ be of size k (possibly smaller than $|\mathsf{I}|$) and $\tilde{x}_r$ be a distribution with support $\tilde{\mathsf{I}}$. Finding Blue's best response against $\tilde{x}_r$ in a CL problem with Leontief utilities is* NP-*hard in terms of $|\mathsf{G}|$, $|\mathcal{C}|$, $|\mathcal{P}|$, T, and k.*

Computing Blue's best response can be done via a polynomially sized MILP. Assume Red plays the interdiction plans $\iota^1, \ldots, \iota^k$ with probabilities $x_r^1, \ldots, x_r^k$. For each ι^i, let us denote the set of Blue's edges in their layered graph that are interdicted by ι^i as $\iota^i_c = \{e \in \mathcal{E}_c : \mathsf{E}(e) \in \iota^i\}$. The best response is formulated as the following max-max BLUEBR formulation (Fig. 3):

$$\max_{f \in F} \max_{l,s,g} \sum_{i \in [k]} \sum_{w \in \mathsf{W}} P(w) x^i_r g^i_w$$

$$S(w,p) = s^i_{w_0,p} \qquad \forall i \in [k],\ \forall w \in \mathsf{W},\ \forall p \in \mathcal{P}$$

$$\sum_{e \in \mathcal{E}^+_c(v_t) \setminus \iota^i_c} l^i_{c,p}(e) = \sum_{e \in \mathcal{E}^-_c(v_t)} l^i_{c,p}(e) \qquad \forall i \in [k],\ \forall c \in \mathcal{C},\ \forall p \in \mathcal{P},$$

$$\forall t \in \mathcal{T} \setminus \{0,T\},\ \forall v \notin \mathsf{W}$$

$$l^i_{c,p}(e) \leq M f_c(e) \qquad \forall i \in [k],\ \forall c \in \mathcal{C},\ \forall p \in \mathcal{P},\ \forall e \in \mathcal{E}_c$$

$$W_{max}(c) \geq \sum_{p \in \mathcal{P}} W(p) l^i_{c,p}(e) \qquad \forall i \in [k],\ \forall c \in \mathcal{C},\ \forall e \in \mathcal{E}_c$$

$$V_{max}(c) \geq \sum_{p \in \mathcal{P}} V(p) l^i_{c,p}(e) \qquad \forall i \in [k],\ \forall c \in \mathcal{C},\ \forall e \in \mathcal{E}_c$$

$$s^i_{w_t,p} + \sum_{c \in \mathcal{C},\, e \in \mathcal{E}^+_c(w_t) \setminus \iota^i_c} l^i_{c,p}(e) = s^i_{w_{t+1},p} + \sum_{c \in \mathcal{C},\, e \in \mathcal{E}^-_c(w_t)} l^i_{c,p}(e) \qquad \forall i \in [k],\ \forall t \in \mathcal{T},\ \forall p \in \mathcal{P},\ \forall w \in \mathsf{W}$$

$$\sum_{\substack{p \in \mathcal{P}, t \in \mathcal{T}, w \in \mathsf{W} \\ e' \in \mathcal{E}^-_c(w_t):e \sqsubset e'}} l^i_{c,p}(e') \leq M \cdot (1 - f_c(e)) \qquad \forall i \in [k],\ \forall c \in \mathcal{C},\ \forall e \in \iota^i_c$$

$$0 \leq g^i_w \leq s^i_{w_{T+1},p}/D(w,p) \qquad \forall i \in [k],\ \forall w \in \mathsf{W},\ \forall p \in \mathcal{P} : D(w,p) > 0$$

$$l^i_{c,p}(e) \geq 0 \qquad \forall i \in [k],\ \forall c \in \mathcal{C},\ \forall p \in \mathcal{P},\ \forall e \in \mathcal{E}_c$$

$$s^i_{w_t,p} \geq 0 \qquad \forall i \in [k],\ \forall t \in \mathcal{T} \cup \{T+1\},$$
$$\forall p \in \mathcal{P},\ \forall w \in \mathsf{W}$$

$$g^i_w \leq U(w) \qquad \forall i \in [k],\ \forall w \in \mathsf{W}.$$

Note that in this MILP, for each $i \in [k]$, we have a different load flow $l^i_{c,p}(e)$. To simulate the truncated logistics plans, any potentially positive load on an interdicted edge is omitted as an *incoming* load from the conservation constraints in the following node. Moreover, we need to make sure that if a connector of a particular logistics plan gets destroyed, its load stays zero for all future time steps, especially if its path is scheduled to cross a warehouse. This is achieved by the second, *load-cancelling* big-M constraint. Here, by $e \sqsubset e'$ we denote for edges $e \neq e' \in \mathcal{E}_c$ that e' is reachable in the layered graph from e.

Proposition 2. *Let $\tilde{\Lambda} \subseteq \Lambda$ be of size k (possibly smaller than $|\Lambda|$) and $\tilde{x}_b$ be a distribution with support $\tilde{\Lambda}$. Finding Red's best response against $\tilde{x}_b$ in a contested logistics problem with Leontief utilities is NP-hard in terms of $|\mathsf{G}|$, b, and k.*

Proof. We reduce the set cover problem with the universe $\mathcal{U} = \{u_1, u_2, \ldots, u_n\}$, a collection of sets $S = \{S_1, S_2, \ldots, S_m\}$, and an integer b to a CL scenario. This scenario features a single package type with unit weight and volume, and a single connector with weight and volume limits of 1. The connector moves across a graph with four layers: the first and last contain only nodes s and t,

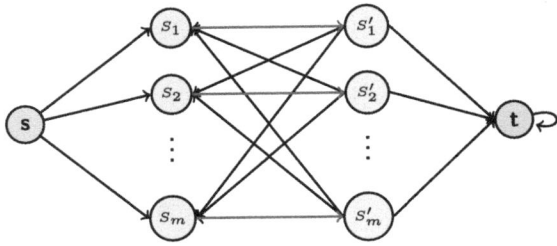

Fig. 3. The physical graph described in Proposition 2, serving as a game for the set cover problem we aim to reduce from. The second and third layers are identical, containing a node for each set S_i. Every u_i corresponds to a path going through the edges S_j, S_j' of all the sets S_j the u_i is contained in. Red can interdict only the forward edges between the second and third layer (depicted in red color), encoding a selection of sets in the cover. (Color figure online)

respectively. The second and third layers are identical, each with one node per set S_j. Node s connects to each S_i in the second layer. The second and third layers are connected by edges between corresponding nodes S_j and S_j'. Each S_j' in the third layer connects to every S_i in the second layer and to t. Node t has a loop to itself. The connector starts at s, each edge takes one time step to cross, and the time horizon is $2n + 1$. There are warehouses at nodes s and t, with a supply of 1 at s and a demand of 1 at t, each with a payoff and maximum of 1. Red has a budget of b and can interdict only the edges between the second and third layers, each costing 1. Blue's mixed strategy is constructed as follows: for each u_i, create $T_i = \{S_j \mid u_i \in S_j\}$, take an arbitrary enumeration $(t_1, \ldots, t_k)$ of T_i, and define a path $P_i = (s, t_1, t_1', \ldots, t_k, t_k', t, \ldots, t)$ with $2n - 2|T_i| + 1$ loops in t at the end, each played with equal probability. Every u_i hence corresponds to a path going through all the sets u_i is contained in, terminated by loops in t. Note that the order in which the sets in T_i are traversed in P_i does not matter. The BR value is 0 if and only if there is a set cover of size at most b.

$\rightarrow$ If the value is 0, then there exists a best response strategy that interdicts all n paths. From the construction, the size of this interdiction plan is at most b, and the selected edges encode a selection of at most b sets from S. Because every path corresponds to one u_i, the selected sets form a set cover.

$\leftarrow$ is analogous.

In practice, we optimize Red's utility using the feasibility formulation (Y). Assume Blue plays the logistic plans $\lambda^1, \ldots, \lambda^k$ with probabilities $x_b^1, \ldots, x_b^k$. The optimal Red's interdicting plan ι, encoded via binary indicators y, can be formulated as the following simple min-max MILP, with the flow constraints (R) for each logistics plan in the support:

$$\min_{y \in Y} \max_{s,l,g} \sum_{i \in [k]} \sum_{w \in \mathsf{W}} P(w) x_b^i g_w^i - \sum_{i \in [k]} \sum_{c \in \mathcal{C}} \sum_{e_{c,j}^i \in \lambda_c^i} \sum_{\substack{e_{c,k}^i \in \lambda_c^i \\ k \geq j}} \sum_{p \in \mathcal{P}} Z y(\mathsf{E}(e_{c,j}^i)) l_{c,p}^i, e_{c,k}^i)$$

$$\mathrm{R}(\lambda^i) \qquad\qquad \forall i \in [k]$$

$$0 \leq g_w^i \leq s_{w_{T+1},p}^i / D(w,p) \qquad \forall i \in [k],\ \forall w \in \mathsf{W},\ \forall p \in \mathcal{P} : D(w,p) > 0$$

$$g_w^i \leq U(w) \qquad\qquad \forall i \in [k],\ \forall w \in \mathsf{W}.$$

Note the penalty term in the objective that plays a similar role to the load cancelling constraint in Blue's BR. Using penalty terms is less numerically stable than the big-M constraints. However, using the same approach as in the BLUEBR would result in bilinear terms in the constraints, that are more cumbersome to linearize, and involve unbounded big-M constants. The constant Z is chosen to make any potential increase in the Leontief utility that Blue might gain by sending a positive load over an interdicted edge undesirable due to the incurred penalty, e.g., $Z = \max_{w \in \mathsf{W}} P(w)$. Since the inner problem is an LP, we can dualize it, which removes the bilinear terms in the objective and gives us the final REDBR integer formulation. Due to space constraints, we have deferred the specific details of this dualization to the extended version of the paper.

4.2   Approximating NE Using Strategy Generation

Despite the exponential size of Blue's strategy space, practical CL scenarios often exhibit equilibria with relatively small supports. This observation leads us to employ the *double oracle* (DO) framework.

The DO algorithm (Algorithm 1) is an iterative, specialized form of concurrent column and row generation. It is frequently used to address large saddle-point problems that have efficient (in practical terms) best-response oracles. The DO algorithm incrementally constructs a subgame – a subset of pure strategies for each player – with the intention of excluding strategies that do not contribute to the equilibrium. At the conclusion of the algorithm, the subgame (ideally a small portion of the entire game) contains a NE that mirrors the NE of the original game. In our context, pure strategies consist of logistic and interdiction plans, and subgames are defined by subsets $\widetilde{\Lambda} \subseteq \Lambda$ and $\widetilde{\mathsf{I}} \subseteq \mathsf{I}$.

The process begins with a small subgame for each player, $\widetilde{\Lambda}$ and $\widetilde{\mathsf{I}}$. In each iteration, it calculates the equilibrium $(\widetilde{x}_b^*, \widetilde{x}_r^*)$ within the current subgame, allowing players to choose distributions of plans only from $\widetilde{\Lambda}$ or $\widetilde{\mathsf{I}}$. For each player i, we determine the best responses λ^{BR} and ι^{BR} against their opponent's sub-game equilibrium strategy $\widetilde{x}_{-i}^*$, using best-response oracles. These best responses introduce new plans into the subgame, and the process repeats.

The DO algorithm terminates when the best-response oracles produce responses that do not enhance any of the player's utility over the subgame value. This indicates that the current subgame equilibrium is also an equilibrium in the full game, and adding more strategies will not yield less exploitable strategies

---

Algorithm 1. Double Oracle for Contested Logistics Games

1: $\widetilde{\Lambda}, \widetilde{\mathsf{I}} \leftarrow \textsc{InitialSubgame}(\Lambda, \mathsf{I})$
2: **repeat**
3:    $\widetilde{x}_b^*, \widetilde{x}_r^* \leftarrow \textsc{NashEquilibrium}(\widetilde{\Lambda}, \widetilde{\mathsf{I}})$
4:    $\lambda^{\mathrm{BR}}, \iota^{\mathrm{BR}} \leftarrow \textsc{BlueBR}(\widetilde{x}_r^*), \textsc{RedBR}(\widetilde{x}_b^*)$
5:    $\widetilde{\Lambda}, \widetilde{\mathsf{I}} \leftarrow \widetilde{\Lambda} \cup \{\lambda^{\mathrm{BR}}\}, \widetilde{\mathsf{I}} \cup \{\iota^{\mathrm{BR}}\}$
6: **until** $\textsc{EquilibriumGap}(\widetilde{x}_b^*, \widetilde{x}_r^*, \lambda^{\mathrm{BR}}, \iota^{\mathrm{BR}}) \leq \epsilon$

---

for either player. In practice, instead of converging to an exact equilibrium, we calculate the equilibrium gap $\nabla = u(\widetilde{x}_b^*, \iota^{\mathrm{BR}}) - u(\lambda^{\mathrm{BR}}, \widetilde{x}_r^*)$ and terminate when $\nabla \leq \epsilon$ for a predetermined threshold $\epsilon > 0$, returning a 2ϵ-approximate-NE.

In practice, the time needed to determine Blue's best response significantly affects the overall runtime. To accelerate the computation, we set a predetermined time limit for solving the MILP, rather than solving it to full completion. This approach yields an approximate best response that is generally close to the optimal solution. Periodically, and before the final termination, we solve Blue's BR MILP to completion to ensure the equilibrium gap is computed accurately.

5   Empirical Evaluation

Now we move to the experiments on contested logistics scenarios. Our goals are (i) to explore qualitatively how optimal strategies behave in real-world scenarios, and (ii) to evaluate the scalability of our proposed double oracle algorithm using synthetically generated maps.

All experiments were conducted on an Intel Xeon Gold 6226 (2.9 Ghz), restricted to 8 threads and equipped with 32GB of RAM. The (MI)LPs were solved with the Gurobi Optimizer version 10.0.3, build v10.0.3rc0 [21], on a Linux 64-bit platform. The double oracle algorithm was implemented in Python 3.7.9, using a tolerance setting of $\epsilon = 10^{-2}$, and 5 s time limit for the MILP solver.

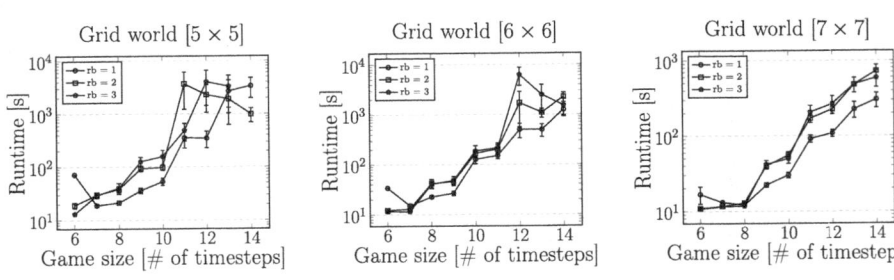

Fig. 4. Computation times of the double oracle algorithm for grid world contested logistics scenarios with *uniform* edge interdiction costs.

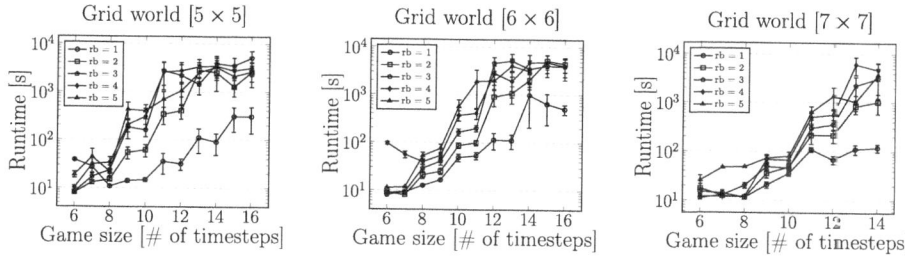

Fig. 5. Computation times of the double oracle algorithm for grid world contested logistics scenarios with *randomly assigned* edge interdiction costs.

5.1   Quantitative Evaluation on a Synthetic Grid World

First, we evaluate the performance of the DO on simple grid world scenarios. In these scenarios, the physical graph consists of an $N \times N$ grid. Blue designates all four corners as warehouses, with an additional warehouse located at the center of the grid. For even values of N, the central warehouse is one of the four central nodes. Additionally, Blue has two trucks, initially positioned at opposing corners. These trucks have sufficient weight and volume limits to transport any available packages, and they can move along any single edge per time step. There are two types of packages, A and B, each with unit weights and volumes. The warehouse at the initial location $(0,0)$ of the first truck holds 4 units of A and 1 unit of B. The warehouse at the location $(N-1, N-1)$ of the other truck holds 1 unit of A and 3 units of B. The central warehouse supplies a single unit of each package. Only two warehouses have positive demands, located in the remaining two corners without the trucks. Both warehouses require 3 A units and 2 B units.

To generate random grid world scenarios, each edge is removed with a probability of 0.1. Each warehouse with a demand is assigned a uniformly random real payoff from the interval $[1, 2]$. Unless the edges have a uniform cost, the cost is selected uniformly from the integer interval $[1, 5]$. For statistical robustness, 20 instances of each game were constructed and solved, with average results reported alongside standard errors. Examples of the initial setup can be seen in the two physical graphs in Fig. 6. In these maps, the starting locations of the two trucks are shown as blue nodes, while the demand nodes are orange. The central warehouse is purple, and each edge is annotated with its interdiction cost.

Figure 4 shows the average runtimes for the DO to solve grid scenarios of sizes 5×5, 6×6, and 7×7, each with uniform edge interdiction costs of 1. Solving the game for Red's budget of 1 (denoted as $rb = 1$) is clearly the easiest, with higher budgets presenting similar levels of difficulty. Notably, the game becomes trivial for a budget of 4, when the trucks can be completely cut off from reaching the demand nodes. In Fig. 5, where interdiction costs are random, the difference between budget 1 and higher budgets becomes even more pronounced.

To illustrate how the game value changes with Blue's horizon and Red's capabilities, we selected two typical scenarios and depicted the generated physical graphs, along with the resulting values as heatmaps, in Fig. 6. In the first map, Red is able to completely cut off the connectors with a budget of 4, resulting in a game value of zero for Blue. In contrast, Red can more efficiently interdict Blue only if they possess a higher budget, and Blue's shorter horizon does not provide enough additional maneuverability to make a difference.

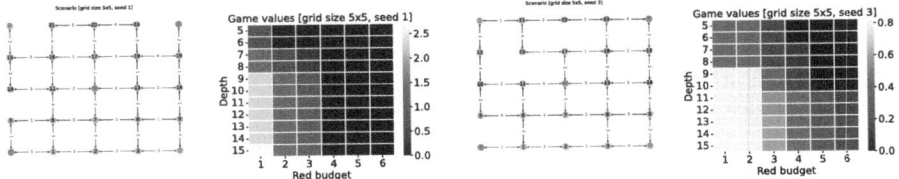

Fig. 6. The physical graphs for two random grid world contested logistics scenarios, and game values as functions of red's budget and blue's horizon. Each grid world has size 5×5. Their corresponding game value heat maps (on the right) have Red's budget on the horizontal axis and time horizon on the vertical axis. Lighter color signifies higher game value. (Color figure online)

5.2   Qualitative Evaluation on Real-World Maps

We also conducted experiments on 2 different maps around the world simulating CL scenarios. These are from (i) the United Kingdom (UK) based on railroads during World War 2, and (ii) Mariupol, a city heavily involved in the ongoing Russo-Ukrainian conflict. The goal of these experiments is not to evaluate the efficiency of our DO method, but rather to showcase (a) how real-world red and blue strategies will look like in practice, (b) the importance of strategic behavior (i.e., randomization) in both Red and Blue, and (c) the relatively low cost that blue pays to be robust to adversarial behavior, and conversely the extremely poor performance when ignoring existence of Red or when using heuristic solutions.

Contested Logistics in the United Kingdom. This scenario is based on the southern region of the United Kingdom. The region is broken into provinces, using data from the World War 2 based video game *Heart of Iron IV* [42]. There are three essentially identical packages: boots, rifles and helmets; each soldier requires 1 unit of each to be equipped (note that we allow for "fractional soldiers"). There are 4 connectors, comprising 2 trains and 2 trucks. Trucks can move between any two adjacent provinces and have a capacity of 5. Trains can only move between provinces connected by railroads, but enjoy a capacity of 20 (for this scenario, weight and size are identical quantities). There are two demand and supply nodes. Each supply node contains 20 of each package. There is unlimited demand for soldiers at each demand node. Red is able to interdict edges between any two adjacent provinces (recall that these are *directed* edges) and has a budget of 2. We set a time horizon of 10 for Blue. The equilibrium

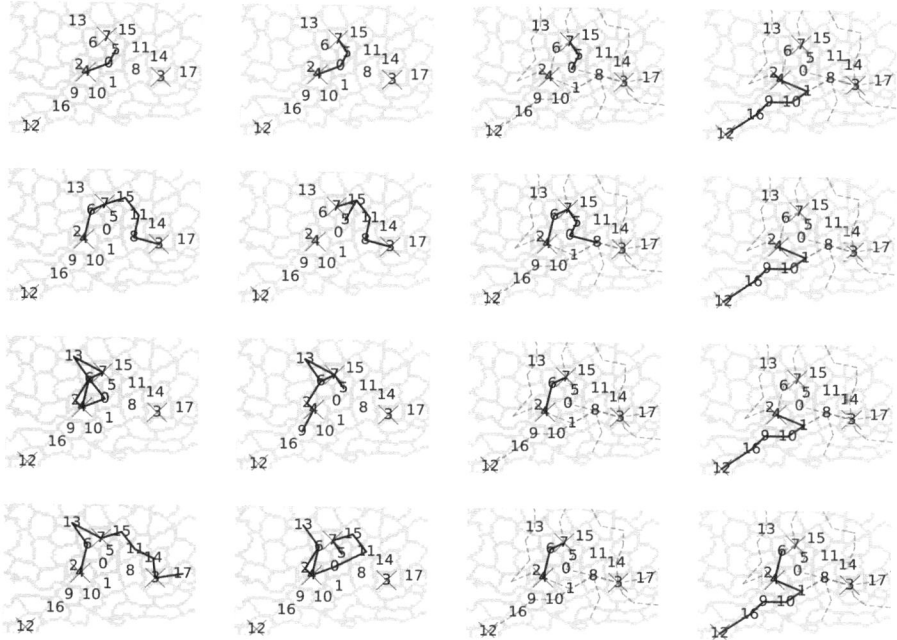

Fig. 7. NE for Blue in the UK scenario. Each row corresponds to a logistics plan played with positive probabilities $4/9, 1/9, 5/21, 13/63$ respectively. Light gray lines demarcate boundaries between provinces, numbers denote province labels: for simplicity we have only included those encountered by some connector logistics plan. Each column shows the movement of a single connector, in the order of Truck 1, Truck 2, Train 1, Train 2, which start at provinces 4, 5, 7, and 1 respectively. Connector paths are denoted by the solid black line. Red crosses at 7 and 12 denote supply nodes, green crosses at 3 and 4 denote demand. Dotted lines denote railroads. (Color figure online)

strategies for Blue and Red are shown in Figs. 7 and 8, which has a Nash value of 9.259. We discuss the most interesting aspects of the NE.

– In all 4 logistics plans, Train 2 behaves essentially deterministically—first, collect supply from 12, then deliver it to the demand at 4. Therefore, Red may interdict anywhere along this path (e.g., edge $16 \rightarrow 12$) and interdict Train 2 *with certainty*. Surprisingly, we find that in interdiction plan 3, Red declines this "freebie", choosing instead to interdict edges $7 \rightarrow 6$ and $7 \rightarrow 5$.
– Second, we observe that Train 1 coordinates with Trucks in a way such as to maximize "throughput". In logistics plan 3 and 4, we observe that Train 1 (which begins at a supply node 7) delivers directly to the demand node at 4 by moving along the left path comprising $7 \rightarrow 6 \rightarrow 2$ and backward. Note that compared to Train 2, the distances between supply and demand is much shorter, so the throughput here is comparatively much higher. Blue also diversifies via logistics plan 1, where Train 1 moves to the right along

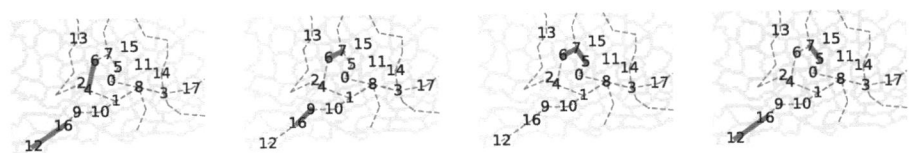

Fig. 8. NE for Red in the UK scenario. Each subfigure corresponds to a single interdiction plan played with probabilities 7/18, 1/9, 7/18, 1/9 respectively. Dotted lines denote railroads and thick red lines edges that are interdicted. (Color figure online)

$7 \rightarrow 5 \rightarrow 0$ instead. It then drops off supplies along the way at province 0, while allowing Trucks 1 and 2 to complete the "last mile delivery" to province 4. This hedges against Red always interdicting the left path $7 \rightarrow 6 \rightarrow 2$. This explain interdiction plan 3: by interdicting $7 \rightarrow 6$ and $6 \rightarrow 4$, Red completely shuts down the joint operation between Train 1 and the Trucks.

- We again observe hedging behavior in Logistics plan 2. Train 1 first takes the right path $7 \rightarrow 5 \rightarrow 0 \rightarrow 8$, drops off its packages (leaving last mile deliveries to Trucks), returns to 7 to pick up fresh supplies, and finally takes the left path $7 \rightarrow 6 \rightarrow 4$ to satisfy the demand at 4. Interestingly, this exposes Train 1 to interdictions both on the left and right. However, if interdiction is on the left (e.g., $7 \rightarrow 6$ via interdiction plan 2), then at least the first batch of supplies would reach demand node 3.
- We point out that because supply and demand nodes are closer at the top of the region, the "throughput", i.e., demand satisfied per unit time is potentially much higher. Because of this, interdicting Train 2 all the time is not necessarily always a good idea, since Train 2 has to take a long trip to province 12 and finally 4 just for a single batch.
- Finally, we remark that Trucks may also operate independently of Train 1. Indeed, if this was not the case, then one would expect Blue to be very brittle. One example of this is seen in Logistics plan 1, Truck 1. Here, Truck 1 moves from province 4 to 7, collects supplies, and transports packages to 3. However, instead of moving directly from 7 to 3, by the path $7 \rightarrow 5 \rightarrow 8 \rightarrow 3$, it takes an detour of $7 \rightarrow 15 \rightarrow 11 \rightarrow 14 \rightarrow 3$. This avoids overlapping with Train 1's right path, which contains the segment $7 \rightarrow 5$.

Contested Logistics in Ukraine. This scenario was constructed based on Ukraine's attack on a key rail bridge connecting the occupied city of Mariupol with Russia on January 7th, 2024. The destruction of this bridge not only disrupts immediate logistical operations but also poses significant long-term challenges to Russia's ability to sustain its military presence in southern Ukraine. Our experiment simulated this scenario using realistic geographical data combined with hypothetical logistics settings to assess the broader impact.

According to the news report [15], the cities this railway passes through include Mariupol, Donetsk, Taganrog, and Rostov-on-Don, so we defined the area of interest as a rectangle containing these cities. We constructed a realistic map within this area using the Open Street Map (OSM) database, which provides global geographical data, including information on roads, railways, and airports. We used the QGIS software to process the OSM data, extracting and visualizing the nodes and edges to construct accurate transportation networks. The resulting physical graph, with 17 nodes, is depicted on the right in Fig. 9.

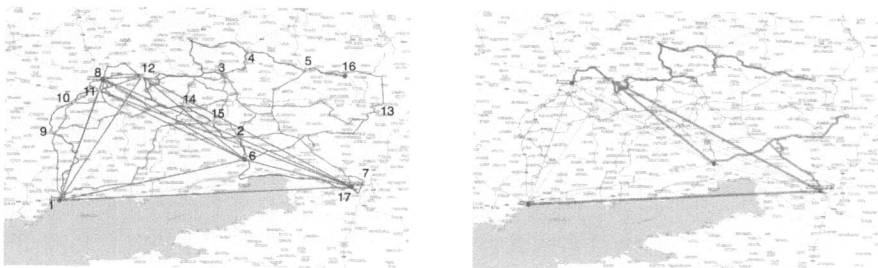

Fig. 9. The physical graph for the Ukrainian scenario. The train edges are depicted in blue, the truck edges in green, and the plane edges in red. On the left, the optimal logistics plan for 5 time steps and no Red. (Color figure online)

Ukraine and Russia are designated as Red and Blue, respectively. Blue employs three types of connectors: trains, trucks, and planes. To identify the train-accessible edges, we extracted nodes marked as "train stations" in the OSM data for the area of interest and selected 17 key stations. These included one station each in Mariupol (node 1), Donetsk (node 8), Taganrog (node 6), and Rostov-on-Don (node 17). These stations served as nodes in the train graph. The truck graph used the same nodes, assuming trucks could travel between any train stations. For the plane graph, we selected nodes tagged as "aerodrome" in the OSM data, representing airports, heliports, and airfields. The plane graph had fewer nodes due to the limited number of airports but included airports in the four major cities. For illustration, each node in the plane graph was considered the same as the closest node in the train and truck graphs, depicted as a single node in Fig. 9. We then defined edges for the connector graphs. For the train graph, we filtered railway paths in QGIS to connect the 17 stations, depicted in blue in Fig. 9. For the truck graph, we selected roads tagged as primary, secondary, or tertiary under "highway" in QGIS and identified the shortest paths connecting the 17 stations, depicted in green in Fig. 9. For the plane graph, we assumed direct flights between airports, defining edges as direct lines between them. We used QGIS to record the distance of each edge, essential for calculating the time for a connector to traverse an edge given its speed.

In the experiments, Blue has one connector of each type: a Train, a Truck, and a Plane, with each time step representing one hour. The Train starts at node 16, moving at 200 km/h, allowing it to traverse any edge in one time step. The Truck starts at node 6, moving at 100 km/h, taking one time step to cross most edges and two time steps for eight specific edges. The Plane also starts at node

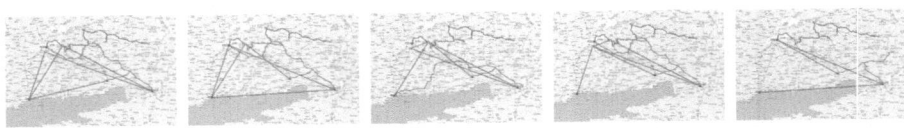

Fig. 10. NE for Blue in the Ukraine scenario. Each subfigure corresponds to a single logistics plan played with probabilities 0.339, 0.337, 0.093, 0.076 and 0.062, respectively. Train, Truck and Plane routes are depicted in blue, green and red. (Color figure online)

Fig. 11. NE for Red in the Ukraine scenario. Each subfigure corresponds to a single interdiction plan played with probabilities 0.462, 0.144, 0.131, 0.131 and 0.131, respectively. (Color figure online)

6, moving at 300 km/h, reaching all destinations in one time step. All connectors have sufficient capacity for transferring available loads.

The railway-connected cities (nodes 1, 6, 8, 17) were considered warehouses. With the conflict pushing from the southeast to the northwest, demand locations were set in the northwest (nodes 1 and 8), and supply locations in the southeast (nodes 6, 7, and 17). Additional supply nodes included 3, 13, and 16, strategically chosen for their proximity to the Russian mainland. Supply nodes had packages of types A and B, with unit weights and volumes. Major supply nodes 6 and 17 had 5 units each of A and B, while nodes 3 and 7 had 3 units of A and 1 of B, node 13 had 2 units of both A and B, and node 16 had 3 units of both. The demand was 11 units of A and 13 units of B at node 1, and 14 units of A and 11 units of B at node 8. The payoff per unit was 1.3 at node 1 and 1.1 at node 8.

Consider Blue's optimal logistics plan for a 5-step horizon, assuming no presence of Red, as shown on the right side of Fig. 9. The Train's route is marked in blue, the Truck's in green, and the Plane's in red. The Plane delivers supplies to node 12, which the Train then transports to node 8. Meanwhile, the Truck collects packages from eastern warehouses and brings them to node 17, where they are loaded onto the Plane and flown to node 1. The value of this plan is 1.5956, but it is highly exploitable. Red can easily reduce the payoff to 0 by interdicting any two critical edges and cutting off deliveries to nodes 1 and 8.

To address this vulnerability, the equilibrium of the corresponding CL game, where Red can interdict any two edges, introduces randomization. Figure 10 depicts Blue's mixed strategy, showing the probabilities of playing each of the five logistics plans. The paths are more randomized, and even the connectors responsible for final deliveries to demand nodes may change. For example, the Truck only follows its original route from the no-Red scenario in the least frequently played plan. More often, it delivers supplies directly to nodes 8 or 1. Similarly, Fig. 11 shows Red's randomized interdiction strategy. As expected, Red consistently targets the Train, which is vulnerable due to movement constraints, and frequently interdicts the route between the region's key cities, which serve as major transport hubs. In other cases, Red attempts to intercept the Plane. The value of this equilibrium is 1.0401, about 65% of the optimal no-Red logistics value, but it is significantly more robust against adversarial actions.

Table 1. The performance of the computed Blue's randomized logistics plans against less or more capable Red in (left) the UK scenario and (right) the Ukraine scenario. Rows correspond to the *expected* budget used during the computation. Columns indicate the *true* Red's budget.

Exp.\True	0	1	2
0		**31.7** 8.33	0.0
1		25.8 **16.7**	6.67
2		23.3 15.9	**9.26**

Exp.\True	0	1	2	3
0	**1.60**	0.40	0.0	0.0
1	1.60	**1.20**	0.78	0.38
2	1.44	1.12	**1.04**	0.64
3	1.32	1.10	0.99	**0.89**

Price of Robustness. It is natural to ask: what if Blue does not know Red's budget? What happens if Blue assumes Red has a high interdiction budget when, in fact, it has none, or vice versa? This leads to a discussion about the *Price of Robustness*, which refers to the amount Blue sacrifices to be robust against Red. We present our findings in Table 1 for both the UK and Mariupol scenarios. It is evident in both cases that underestimating Red's capabilities results in a significant drop in utility. For example, when Blue devises a logistics plan without considering Red (i.e., the first row of each table), its utility drops to zero with just a Red budget of 2. Conversely, adopting a more conservative logistics plan (i.e., assuming Red has a higher budget) leads to a relatively smaller drop in utility. For instance, in the UK scenario, the Price of Robustness is just 31.7-23.3, which is approximately one-quarter of the expected utility. A similar trend is observed in the Ukraine scenario.

Comparisons Against a Non-Game-Theoretic Alternative. We now compare our game-theoretic approach to a simple heuristic that does not explicitly account for Red. Consider the *min-overlap* heuristic, which involves two hyperparameters: k, the minimum target payoff, and # str, the number of logistics plans played with positive probability. The min-overlap heuristic identifies # str logistics plans, each required to achieve a utility of k under the assumption that *Red does not exist*, while minimizing the maximum overlap across edges. Here, overlap on a given physical edge is the total number of connectors using that edge, summed across all # str logistics plans. Blue then randomizes uniformly over these # str logistics plans. The rationale is that by minimizing overlap among "good" logistics plans, no single edge will be excessively used by connectors across the logistics plans. We tested this min-overlap heuristic strategy against a best-responding Red and found that it performs poorly, as shown in

Table 2. For instance, in the UK scenario, none of the instances achieve more than half of the true Nash value (9.259). In the Ukraine scenario, the best-performing instance reached only 69% of the Nash value. This suggests that seemingly reasonable heuristics may actually perform poorly in practice, and that counter-intuitive logistics plans may be necessary for optimal performance.

Table 2. Exploitability of the min-overlap heuristic strategies in (left) the UK scenario and (right) the Ukraine scenario.

$k \setminus \# $ str	3	4	5	6	7
10	1.11	1.67	1.33	1.94	1.67
20	3.89	2.92	3.33	2.50	4.29
30	2.22	3.33	2.33	2.22	3.10

$k \setminus \# $ str	5	10	15	20	25
1.2	0.720	0.410	0.627	0.730	0.641
1.3	0.517	0.496	0.570	0.676	0.577
1.4	0.439	0.588	0.553	0.584	0.648
1.5	0.517	0.496	0.344	0.576	0.637

6 Conclusion

In this paper, we introduced Contested Logistics games, a complex logistics problem that incorporates adversarial disruptions. Our model, formulated as a large two-player zero-sum one-shot game on a graph, identifies optimal logistics plans via a (randomized) Nash equilibrium. We demonstrated the computational complexity of finding these equilibria and proposed a practical double-oracle solver using best-response mixed-integer linear programs. Our experiments, conducted on both synthetic and real-world maps, confirm the scalability of our method for reasonably large games. Additionally, our ablation studies underscore the critical importance of explicitly modeling adversarial capabilities, rather than relying solely on heuristic-based logistics plans.

Acknowledgments. This research was supported by the Office of Naval Research award N00014-23-1-2374. Christian Kroer was additionally supported by the Office of Naval Research award N00014-22-1-2530, and the National Science Foundation awards IIS-2147361 and IIS-2238960.

References

1. Agra, A., Christiansen, M., Figueiredo, R., Hvattum, L.M., Poss, M., Requejo, C.: The robust vehicle routing problem with time windows. Comput. Oper. Res. **40**(3), 856–866 (2013)
2. Alotaibi, K.A., Rosenberger, J.M., Mattingly, S.P., Punugu, R.K., Visoldilokpun, S.: Unmanned aerial vehicle routing in the presence of threats. Comput. Industr. Eng. **115**, 190–205 (2018)
3. An, B., Tambe, M., Sinha, A.: Stackelberg security games (SSG) basics and application overview. Improving Homeland Secur. Decis. **2**, 485 (2017)

4. Ausseil, R., Gedik, R., Bednar, A., Cowan, M.: Identifying sufficient deception in military logistics. Expert Syst. Appl. **141**, 112974 (2020)
5. Barahona, F., et al.: Inventory allocation and transportation scheduling for logistics of network-centric military operations. IBM J. Res. Dev. **51**(3.4), 391–407 (2007)
6. Bell, J.E., Griffis, S.E.: Military applications of location analysis. Appl. Location Anal. 403–433 (2015)
7. Bertsimas, D., Nasrabadi, E., Orlin, J.B.: On the power of randomization in network interdiction. Oper. Res. Lett. **44**(1), 114–120 (2016)
8. Bidgoli, M.M., Kheirkhah, A.: An arc interdiction vehicle routing problem with information asymmetry. Comput. Industr. Eng. **115**, 520–531 (2018)
9. Blom, M., Shekh, S., Gossink, D., Miller, T., Pearce, A.R.: Inventory routing for defense: moving supplies in adversarial and partially observable environments. J. Defense Model. Simul. **17**(1), 55–81 (2020)
10. Bowling, M., Burch, N., Johanson, M., Tammelin, O.: Heads-up limit hold'em poker is solved. Science **347**(6218), 145–149 (2015)
11. Brown, N., Sandholm, T.: Superhuman AI for heads-up no-limit poker: Libratus beats top professionals. Science **359**(6374), 418–424 (2018)
12. Brown, N., Sandholm, T.: Superhuman AI for multiplayer poker. Science **365**(6456), 885–890 (2019)
13. Church, R.L., Scaparra, M.P., Middleton, R.S.: Identifying critical infrastructure: the median and covering facility interdiction problems. Ann. Assoc. Am. Geogr. **94**(3), 491–502 (2004)
14. Conitzer, V., Sandholm, T.: Computing the optimal strategy to commit to. In: Proceedings of the 7th ACM Conference on Electronic Commerce, pp. 82–90 (2006)
15. Cook, E.: Ukraine destroys key rail bridge connecting occupied Mariupol to Russia (2024). https://www.newsweek.com/ukraine-bridge-russia-logistics-mariupol-donetsk-crimea-1858516. Accessed 19 June 2024
16. Cowen, D.: A geography of logistics: market authority and the security of supply chains. Ann. Assoc. Am. Geogr. **100**(3), 600–620 (2010)
17. Daganzo, C.: Logistics Systems Analysis. Springer, Heidelberg (2005). https://doi.org/10.1007/3-540-27516-9
18. Erkut, E., Verter, V.: Modeling of transport risk for hazardous materials. Oper. Res. **46**(5), 625–642 (1998)
19. Fang, F., Stone, P., Tambe, M.: When security games go green: designing defender strategies to prevent poaching and illegal fishing. In: IJCAI, pp. 2589–2595 (2015)
20. Ghiani, G., Laporte, G., Musmanno, R.: Introduction to Logistics Systems Planning and Control. Wiley, Hoboken (2004)
21. Gurobi Optimization, LLC: Gurobi Optimizer Reference Manual (2023). https://www.gurobi.com
22. Hill, R., Pohl, E.: An overview of meta-heuristics and their use in military modeling. Handb. Milit. Industr. Eng. (2009)
23. Jain, M., An, B., Tambe, M.: Security games applied to real-world: research contributions and challenges. In: Jajodia, S., Ghosh, A., Subrahmanian, V., Swarup, V., Wang, C., Wang, X. (eds.) Moving Target Defense II. Advances in Information Security, vol. 100, pp. 15–39. Springer, New York (2013)
24. Jaiswal, N.K.: Military Operations Research: Quantitative Decision Making, vol. 5. Springer, Heidelberg (2012)
25. Kiekintveld, C., Jain, M., Tsai, J., Pita, J., Ordónez, F., Tambe, M.: Computing optimal randomized resource allocations for massive security games (2009)

26. Korzhyk, D., Conitzer, V., Parr, R.: Complexity of computing optimal Stackelberg strategies in security resource allocation games. In: Proceedings of the AAAI Conference on Artificial Intelligence, vol. 24, pp. 805–810 (2010)
27. Lee, C., Lee, K., Park, S.: Robust vehicle routing problem with deadlines and travel time/demand uncertainty. J. Oper. Res. Soc. **63**(9), 1294–1306 (2012)
28. Lee, J.M.Y., Wong, E.Y.C.: Suez canal blockage: an analysis of legal impact, risks and liabilities to the global supply chain. In: MATEC Web of Conferences, vol. 339, p. 01019. EDP Sciences (2021)
29. List, G.F., Mirchandani, P.B., Turnquist, M.A., Zografos, K.G.: Modeling and analysis for hazardous materials transportation: risk analysis, routing/scheduling and facility location. Transp. Sci. **25**(2), 100–114 (1991)
30. McMahon, C.J.: Maritime trade warfare: a strategy for the twenty-first century? Naval War Coll. Rev. **70**(3), 14–38 (2017)
31. v. Neumann, J.: Zur theorie der gesellschaftsspiele. Math. Annalen **100**(1), 295–320 (1928)
32. Ordóñez, F.: Robust vehicle routing. In: Risk and Optimization in an Uncertain World, pp. 153–178. INFORMS (2010)
33. Pfohl, H.C.: Logistics systems. The faculty of ILiM, Poznań (1998)
34. Pita, J., et al.: Armor security for Los Angeles international airport. In: AAAI, pp. 1884–1885 (2008)
35. Sadati, M.E.H., Aksen, D., Aras, N.: The r-interdiction selective multi-depot vehicle routing problem. Int. Trans. Oper. Res. **27**(2), 835–866 (2020)
36. Salani, M., Duyckaerts, G., Swartz, P.G.: Ambush avoidance in vehicle routing for valuable delivery. J. Transp. Secur. **3**, 41–55 (2010)
37. Salmeron, J., Wood, R.K., Morton, D.P.: A stochastic program for optimizing military sealift subject to attack. Milit. Oper. Res. 19–39 (2009)
38. Shieh, E., et al.: Protect: a deployed game theoretic system to protect the ports of the united states. In: Proceedings of the 11th International Conference on Autonomous Agents and Multiagent Systems, vol. 1, pp. 13–20 (2012)
39. Shoham, Y., Leyton-Brown, K.: Multiagent Systems: Algorithmic, Game-Theoretic, and Logical Foundations. Cambridge University Press, Cambridge (2008)
40. Smith, J.C., Lim, C.: Algorithms for network interdiction and fortification games. In: Chinchuluun, A., Pardalos, P.M., Migdalas, A., Pitsoulis, L. (eds.) Pareto Optimality, Game Theory And Equilibria. Springer Optimization and Its Applications, vol. 17, pp. 609–644. Springer, New York (2008). https://doi.org/10.1007/978-0-387-77247-9_24
41. Smith, J.C., Song, Y.: A survey of network interdiction models and algorithms. Eur. J. Oper. Res. **283**(3), 797–811 (2020)
42. Studio, P.D.: Hearts of iron IV (2016). https://www.paradoxinteractive.com/games/hearts-of-iron-iv/about
43. Sungur, I., Ordóñez, F., Dessouky, M.: A robust optimization approach for the capacitated vehicle routing problem with demand uncertainty. IIE Trans. **40**(5), 509–523 (2008)
44. Washburn, A., Wood, K.: Two-person zero-sum games for network interdiction. Oper. Res. **43**(2), 243–251 (1995)
45. Wollmer, R.: Removing arcs from a network. Oper. Res. **12**(6), 934–940 (1964)
46. Xu, H.: The mysteries of security games: equilibrium computation becomes combinatorial algorithm design. In: Proceedings of the 2016 ACM Conference on Economics and Computation, pp. 497–514 (2016)

Cyber Deception

On Countering Ransomware Attacks Using Strategic Deception

Roshan Lal Neupane[1]([✉])[iD], Bishnu Bhusal[1][iD], Kiran Neupane[1][iD]
Preyea Regmi[1], Tam Dinh[1], Lilliana Marrero[1], Sayed M. Saghaian N. E.[1],
Venkata Sriram Siddhardh Nadendla[2][iD], and Prasad Calyam[1][iD]

[1] University of Missouri, Columbia, MO 65211, USA
{neupaner,bhusalb,kngbq,prrgfb,tdbhr,lmmbd8,ssddd,calyamp}@missouri.edu
[2] Missouri University of Science and Technology, Rolla, MO 65409, USA
nadendla@mst.edu

Abstract. Ransomware attacks continue to be a major concern for critical systems that are vital for society e.g., healthcare, finance, and transportation. Traditional cyber defense mechanisms fail to pose dynamic measures to stop ransomware attacks from progressing through various stages in the attack process. To this end, intelligent cyber deception strategies can be effective when they leverage information about attacker strategies and deploy deceptive assets to increase the cost or complexity of a successful exploit or discourage continued attacker efforts. In this paper, we present a novel game theoretic approach that uses deception-based defense strategies at each of the ransomware attack stages for optimization of the decision-making to outsmart attacker advances. Specifically, we propose a multistage ransomware game model that deploys a combination of deception assets i.e., honeytokens, honeypots, honeyfiles, and network honeypots in subgames. Using closed-form backward induction, we evaluated Subgame-Perfect Nash Equilibrium (SPNE). We perform a numerical analysis using real-world data and statistics pertaining to the impact of ransomware attacks in the healthcare sector. Our healthcare case study evaluation results show that the use of deception technologies is favorable to the defender. This work elucidates the profound implications of strategic deception in cybersecurity, demonstrating its capacity to complicate successful exploits and consequently bolster the defense of key societal infrastructures.

Keywords: ransomware · cyber deception · game theory · attacker/defender game

1 Introduction

Deception plays a crucial role in the ever-evolving landscape of ransomware attacks. Deception techniques, such as honey tokens, honeypots, honey files, and network honeypots, are vital tools in combating those attacks [29] so that defenders can gain a competitive edge in the intricate game of ransomware,

© The Author(s), under exclusive license to Springer Nature Switzerland AG 2025
A. Sinha et al. (Eds.): GameSec 2024, LNCS 14908, pp. 149–176, 2025.
https://doi.org/10.1007/978-3-031-74835-6_8

disrupting the attackers' strategies and turning the tables in favor of cybersecurity resilience. This paper presents a novel approach to ransomware defense via modeling the attacker-defender interaction as a multi-stage game and investigates effective techniques to deceive the ransomware attacker at each stage of the attack using tools such as honeytokens, honeypots, honeyfiles, and network honeypots.

Ransomware is a malware type that encrypts target users' data, rendering it inaccessible without a decryption key that the attacker exclusively holds. Typically, victims are directed to pay a ransom to decrypt their data [37]. The Internet Crime Report published by the FBI lists 2385 registered complaints for Ransomware attacks in the year 2022 [3] alone, which has led to economic losses that totalled to more than $34.3 million. These attacks have impacted diverse application domains ranging from healthcare (e.g. emergency departments in San Diego County's healthcare delivery organizations [15]), critical infrastructure (e.g. Colonial Pipeline attack [30]), transportation (e.g. ransomware attacks on Toyota and Kojima), government facilities (e.g. ransomware attacks on the City of Detroit and Washington DC police department), IT (e.g. Acer), and finance (e.g. supply chain attack [13] and Travelex).

To make things worse, ransomware is also offered as a service by some malicious organizations. One such example is REvil [19] (which stands for Ransomware Evil), which is a ransomware-as-a-service (RaaS) platform that has been run by organized criminal groups in Russia. Given the widespread impact of ransomware attacks on diverse application domains, there is an urgent need to investigate advanced defense and impact mitigation techniques to counter these attacks.

In the past, ransomware has been studied as a multi-stage game [42] to thoroughly model the diverse interactions between the attacker and the defender in time. While a detailed account of the past literature on game-theoretic approaches to counter ransomware attacks is presented in Sect. 2.1, there is little work on the design of strategic deception to counter ransomware attacks to the best of our knowledge. Therefore, this paper is the first of its kind to investigate the effectiveness of deception techniques (e.g. honeypots, honeytokens and honeyfiles) against ransomware attacks using multi-stage games. The optimal strategy at each of the stages are computed using backward induction [11] via breaking the game into smaller and manageable sub-games. Such an approach leads to the identification of subgame perfect equilibria where optimal strategies are met in each subgame.

The main contributions of this paper are three-fold. Firstly, the proposed multi-stage game is comprehensive and considers most stages of real-world ransomware attacks (e.g. infection, installation and encryption) and their corresponding defenders' deception assets (e.g. honeytokens, honeypots and honeyfiles) in real-world adversarial environments. In addition, the model also encompasses sub-stages for ransom payment and arrest, aiming to capture attackers and limit defender losses. Secondly, the best-response strategies for both the attacker and the defender are formally evaluated except for the root node. At the root node, the best-response search reduces to a binary quadratic program, which is solved using state-of-the-art integer-programming methods. Thirdly, the SPNE is algorithmically evaluated in numerical experiments, and results are discussed in comparison with state-of-the-art literature.

The remainder of this paper is organized as follows: Sect. 2 presents background of related works and cyber deception techniques. Section 3 models the interaction between a ransomware attacker and a defender. Section 4 presents an equilibrium analysis. Section 5 makes a case for healthcare industry. Section 6 details the numerical results, comparison, and their analysis. Section 7 concludes the paper.

2   Background

In this section, we go over the related literature and background on the deception techniques applicable in mitigating different stages in a ransomware attack.

2.1   Related Works

The related literature is presented briefly in three different themes and gaps are identified in the state-of-the-art to defend against ransomware attacks.

Ransomware Detection and Defense. There have been many approaches to the detection and defense of ransomware attacks. Kolodenker *et al.* in [20] presented a prototype called *Paybreak* that is able to recover files by decrypting them based on insights gained during the process of secure file encryption. A data backup solution is used in [24], called *AMOEBA* which has high ransomware detection accuracy with negligible performance overhead on the backup process. *Ransomwall* [33] is a machine learning approach to defend against ransomware attacks by learning suspicious ransomware behavior processes to initiate a data backup for preserving user data. Patyal *et al.* in [28] proposed a multi-layer architecture defense, with each layer employing different techniques starting from improved policies for enhanced security, recursive folder creation for ransomware detection, process monitoring, to data backup.

These methods target specific stages of a ransomware attack and fall short of considering every stage the attack process for defense. Our novelty lies in considering every stage of the process for the defense against the attack using a game theoretic approach.

Game Theoretic Approaches for Ransomware. There are several forms of game-theoretic models that are applied for the mitigation of ransomware attacks. Authors in [14] treat the problem by presenting finances as the primary motive of the attacker via the models developed by [32] and [21]. Authors in [42] present a multi-stage game that comprehensively models ransomware attack and defense with a fully observable environment set up. To combat ransomware in IoT, authors in [43] present a multi-stage game framework for cyber and economic phases of a ransomware attack. Similarly, there are several consequences discussed in how the stages progress and how the outcome of the previous stage sets the ground for the upcoming stage. Different tangents are discussed in the articles such as [22, 40] where the ransomware attacks are dealt in terms of attacker-defender game, defender-insurer game where the strategies and ransom amounts differ based on the strategy applied by each of the participant in the game.

There are different approaches to defend against ransomware attacks using game theory models showcased in the literature mentioned. Our novelty lies in considering deception techniques as defender strategies within various stages of a ransomware attack and defense process.

Deception-Based Defense Against Ransomware. Authors in [16] pose a solution that uses deception to stop a crypto ransomware attack with minimal spatial or system computation requirement. They deploy a honeyfile that recognizes when an API function is called between software components using a hook and a monitoring file that checks whether the honeyfile has been encrypted or not. Another mitigation technique implemented is called *R-Sentry* [34] that aids how to optimally place honeyfiles based on the file traversal patterns of ransomware variants. Some authors leverage a combination of these tools to come up with a stronger deception-based defense that they claim as an auxiliary ransomware traceable system called *RansomTracer* [38]. Authors in [36] present a stealthy approach to backing up data in order to isolate them from the attacker no matter the level of privilege acquired by them attacker. *RTrap* in [17] is a systematic strategy that utilizes machine learning to create deceptive files, luring attackers or ransomware to access them upon detecting potential access.

As a multi-stage process that involves infection, installation, encryption, data movement or deletion, etc., ransomware attacks need a more robust defense system that considers every stage of the process. Our novelty lies in considering deception for each of the attack stage processes with state-of-the-art deception technologies that we discuss in the next section.

2.2 Cyber Deception Techniques

There are different deception techniques that can be used to deceive attackers accomplished by deliberate placing or positioning of resources that look real and of interest to the attackers. Similar attempts are made by ransomware attackers as well. For safeguarding the system from ransomware attack, we leverage three types of deception techniques. These are:

Honeytokens. Honeytokens are artifacts such as e.g., access tokens, credentials that can be strategically placed in the organizational network (such as e.g., in data stores, code base) for attackers to use [31]. There are various available tools that can generate such honeytokens such as e.g., HoneyGen [12], Canary Tokens [1], SpaceSiren [8]. These tokens are designed such that when they are triggered, they can alert security teams or simply lead the attackers to deception systems such as honeypots.

Honeypots. Honeypots [35] are systems or software applications that are built to monitor hacker activities, or interact with them depending on the level of interactions (low, medium, or high) [25]. A high-interaction honeypot is able to deploy real network services, applications, and operating systems. This can aid in capturing extensive information. In the context of ransomware, attackers can be deceived into infecting and installing malware into the decoy honeypot and subsequently encrypting files that are of no use by containing them in a honeypot. Some examples are: low-interaction (Glastopf [26]), medium-interaction (Kippo [6]), and high-interaction (HIHAT [27]).

Network honeypots can be leveraged for performing protocol inspections to monitor network traces. In the ransomware defense context, we use network honeypots as a strategy to monitor exfiltration of data with the hopes of redirecting the exfiltration attempts to a controlled system and not to the attacker's intended system.

Honeyfiles. Honeyfiles [41], similar to other deception methods are artifacts that can be used as baits to grab an attacker's attention. In the context of the paper, we can leverage honeyfiles portraying them as real files the ransomware attackers might want to encrypt. Encrypting these files can lead to triggering of alarm, or can simply be treated as a fail-safe for the encryption phase of the ransomware attack cycle. To delay the detection of honeyfiles, there are advanced

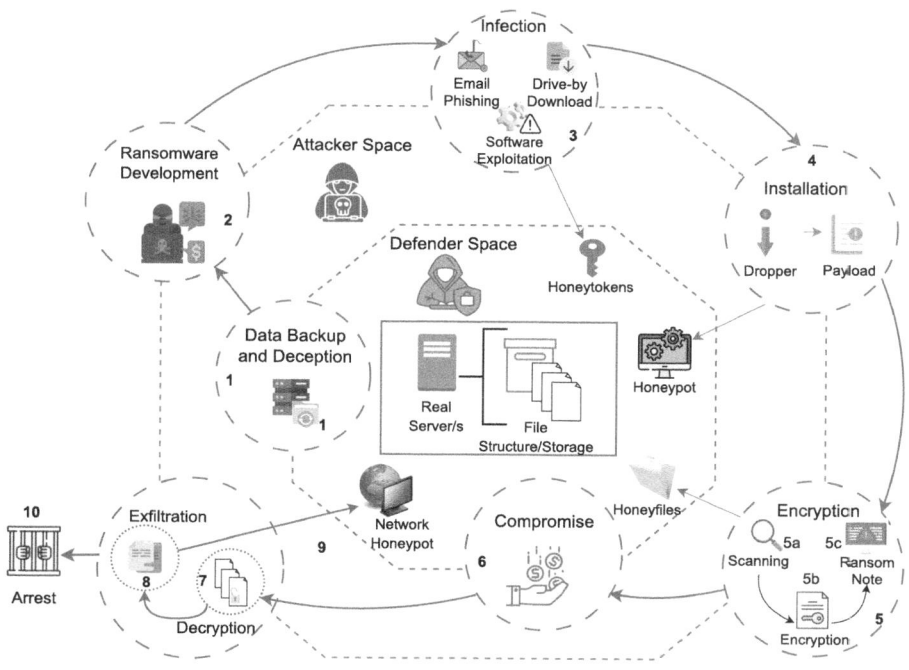

Fig. 1. Attacker and defender interactions in the ransomware game model.

methods such as in [23], where Generative Adversarial Networks (GANs) have been shown to be useful to create effective deception against ransomware using decoy/honeyfiles. RLocker [18] is an example honeyfile-based deception tool.

3   Ransomware Game Model

Consider an adversarial setting with two agents, a ransomware attacker and a defender, and a system-of-interest with N subsystems containing valuable data. Let V_i denote the value of data present in the ith subsystem. The attacker wishes to lock one/more subsystems within a system-of-interest for certain ransom. On the other hand, the defender's goal is to safeguard the entire system from the ransomware threat using three deception techniques, namely *honeytokens*, *honeypots* and *honeyfiles*. This interaction between the attacker and the defender occurs in multiple stages, as illustrated in Fig. 1, and discussed below. For the sake of reader's convenience, a table of notation is also included in Table 1.

Stage 1 - Data Backup and Deception: In this first stage, the defender makes a binary decision b_i whether or not to backup the data on the ith subsystem upon system deployment. Without any loss of generality, let $b_i = 1$ denote the defender's decision to backup data, in which case, the defender incurs a cost B, accounting for cost of data back up and recovery. In other words, the ransomware attack is destined to fail if $b_i = 1$. On the contrary, the attacker may launch a successful ransomware attack if $b_i = 0$. Furthermore, in an attempt to protect the system, the defender has to choose whether or not to deploy a *three-pronged deception technique using honeytokens, honeypots, and honeyfiles*, to prevent the ransomware attacker from gaining access into the ith subsystem. Let $h_i = 1$ denote the binary decision to develop and deploy the aforementioned three-pronged deception strategy, and $h_i = 0$ denote otherwise. If $h_i = 1$, assume that the defender deploys n_{ht} honeytokens, one honeypot and n_{hf} honeyfiles in order to deceive the ransomware attacker. In other words, the defender's decision is a tuple $\left((b_1, h_1), \cdots, (b_i, h_i), \cdots, (b_N, h_N)\right) \in \{0, 1\}^{2N}$. Without any loss of generality, for each subsystem, let B be the cost of data backup, C_{ht} denotes the cost of deploying a single honeytoken, C_{hp} is the cost of deploying the honeypot, and C_{hf} represents the cost of deploying a single honeyfile. For simplicity, we denote the total cost of deception as

$$C_H = n_{ht} \cdot C_{ht} + C_{hp} + n_{hf} \cdot C_{hf}. \tag{1}$$

In addition to the three aforementioned deception strategies, assume that the defender always deploys an additional network honeypot to deceive attackers from data exfiltration [39].

Table 1. Notations used in this paper

Notation	Description
B	Cost of data backup
C_{ht}	Cost of honeytokens deployment
n_{ht}	Number of honeytokens deployed
C_{hp}	Cost of honeypot deployment
C_{hf}	Cost of honeyfiles deployment
n_{hf}	Number of honeyfiles deployed
C_{nh}	Cost of network honeypot deployment
C_H	Total deception cost
C_D	Cost of ransomware development
C_x	Cost of exfiltration
ρ	Probability of successful honeytoken-based deception
τ	Probability of successful honeypot-based deception
γ	Probability of successful honeyfile-based deception
ζ	Probability of successful network honeypot-based deception
V_i	Value of data owned by i^{th} target for the defender
V_i'	Value of data for the attacker after exfiltration
V_p	Value of privacy of data
R_i	Ransom demand proposed by attacker to i^{th} target
b_i	Defender's decision on data backup
d_i	Attacker's decision on ransomware development
c_i	Defender's decision on whether to compromise
e_i	Attacker's decision on whether to decrypt of data
x_i	Attacker's decision on whether to exfiltrate the data
p_0	Natural probability of attacker being arrested when $e_i = 1$, $x_i = 0$
p_1	Natural probability of attacker being arrested when $e_i = 1$, $x_i = 1$
p_2	Natural probability of attacker being arrested when $e_i = 0$, $x_i = 0$
p_3	Natural probability of attacker being arrested when $e_i = 0$, $x_i = 1$
T	Attacker's reputation. $T > 0$ if attacker decrypts data after defender pays, or attacker does not decrypt data when defender does not pay. $T = 0$ for all other cases
F	Loss of attacker for being arrested ($F > 0$)

Stage 2 - Ransomware Development/Delivery: When no data backup is present, the attacker decides whether or not to develop ransomware. Let the decision to develop a ransomware for the ith subsystem be denoted as d_i. If $d_i = 0$, i.e. if the attacker's choice is to not develop ransomware, the game ends. On the other hand, when the attacker chooses to develop ransomware (i.e.

$d_i = 1$), the attacker develops the ransomware attack and incurs a cost C_D for the development of ransomware.

Stage 3 - Infection: Upon the development of ransomware, the attacker uses diverse delivery mechanisms such as email phishing, drive-by download, or software vulnerability exploitation approaches, to infect the desired subsystem. The *honeytokens* lure the attacker into using fake access tokens with independent and identical Bernoulli distribution with probability

$$\rho = 1 - e^{-\frac{C_{ht} * n_{ht}}{C_D}}. \tag{2}$$

The exponential function suggests that the probability decreases exponentially with the product of the cost of honeytokens (C_{ht}), the number of honeytokens (n_{ht}), and the reciprocal of the cost of ransomware development (C_D). All these parameters influence the likelihood of the attacker getting deceived by the usage of honeytokens.

Stage 4 - Malware Installation: Once the attacker has access to some server, the next step in the attack process will be the execution of a dropper. The dropper program leads to running of a successful installation of ransomware payload to the victim's computer. To counter the dropper program at each subsystem, honeypots lure the attacker into installing their malware in a fake server randomly with probability

$$\tau = 1 - e^{-\frac{C_{hp}}{C_D}}. \tag{3}$$

The exponential function suggests that the probability decreases exponentially with the cost of deploying honeypots (C_{hp}), and the reciprocal of the cost of ransomware development (C_D). All these parameters influence the likelihood of the attacker getting deceived by the usage of honeyfiles during the malware installation stage.

Stage 5 - Encryption: Once the attacker gains access to either the original file structure or the honeypot within a given subsystem, the ransomware scans for specific files that are deemed valuable, and locks them using a robust encryption algorithm to restrict user access. However, the honeyfiles deployed by the defender in Stage 3 can steer the attacker away from the actual subsystem, and entices the attacker to encrypt them with probability

$$\gamma = 1 - e^{-\frac{C_{hf} * n_{hf}}{C_D}}. \tag{4}$$

The exponential function suggests that the probability decreases exponentially with the product of the cost of honeyfiles (C_{hf}), the number of honeyfiles (n_{hf}), and the reciprocal of the cost of ransomware development (C_D). All these parameters influence the likelihood of the attacker getting deceived by the usage of honeyfiles during the encryption stage. Upon successful encryption, a note demanding a ransom of R_i for the release of the ith subsystem is sent to the user.

Once the attacker has access to the data, they can engage in exfiltration at any stage of the game, even before administering the ransomware in the file system. It is likely for attackers to perform data exfiltration before administering the ransomware in the file system. For this work, we are discussing a generic ransomware setting, such as the one discussed in [2], where the attacker can release data after the compromise stage regardless of the compromise outcome.

Stage 6 - Compromise: Upon successful lock-down and the receipt of a ransom note, the defender makes a binary decision c_i regarding the payment of ransom. Let $c_i = 1$ denote the decision to pay the ransom, and $c_i = 0$ otherwise. However, if the attacker was successfully deceived (i.e. the attacker encrypted honeyfiles), the defender will not pay the ransom.

Stage 7 - Decryption: If the defender decides to compromise and pay the ransom, the attacker decides whether or not to decrypt the data and release the subsystem back to the defender. Let $e_i = 1$ denote the decision to decrypt the subsystem and give back access to the defender. Otherwise, if $e_i = 0$, the attacker will not decrypt the data and the defender loses the data permanently. Note that if the attacker keeps the promise (i.e. decrypts data upon receiving the ransom, or does not decrypt if the ransom is not paid), the attacker gains a reputation T. Otherwise, the attacker receives a zero reputation.

Stage 8 - Exfiltration: In addition to collecting ransom, assume that the attacker may also exfiltrate data and cause privacy breach. Let $x_i = 1$ denote the decision to exfiltrate the data from the ith subsystem, and $x_i = 0$ otherwise. If the attacker chooses to exfiltrate (i.e. $x_i = 1$), then the attacker incurs a cost of C_x for each subsystem.

Stage 9 - Exfiltration Deception: During exfiltration (i.e. when $x_i = 1$), the attacker moves the data/files to another database through a network. In order to prevent successful exfitration, the network honeypot lures the attacker into moving exfiltrated data through a fake network with probability

$$\zeta = 1 - e^{-\frac{C_{nh}}{C_D}}.$$ (5)

If the data in the ith subsystem is successfully exfiltrated, the attacker obtains a value of V_i'. On the other hand, the defender incurs a cost V_p for the privacy breach.

Stage 10 - Arrest: Depending on the defender's decision to pay ransom c_i and the attacker's decryption and exfiltration decisions (e_i, x_i) respectively, the attacker may get identified, caught and arrested with a different probability according to one of the following three cases: (i) Let p_0 denote the probability of the attacker getting arrested after decrypting the data ($e_i = 1$), while not performing exfiltration ($x_i = 0$), (ii) Let p_1 denote the probability of the attacker getting arrested after decrypting the data ($e_i = 1$) and performing exfiltration ($x_i = 1$), (iii) Let p_2 denote the probability of the attacker getting arrested upon deciding not to decrypt the data ($e_i = 0$) and not performing exfiltration ($x_i = 0$), and (iv) Let p_3 denote the probability of the attacker getting arrested

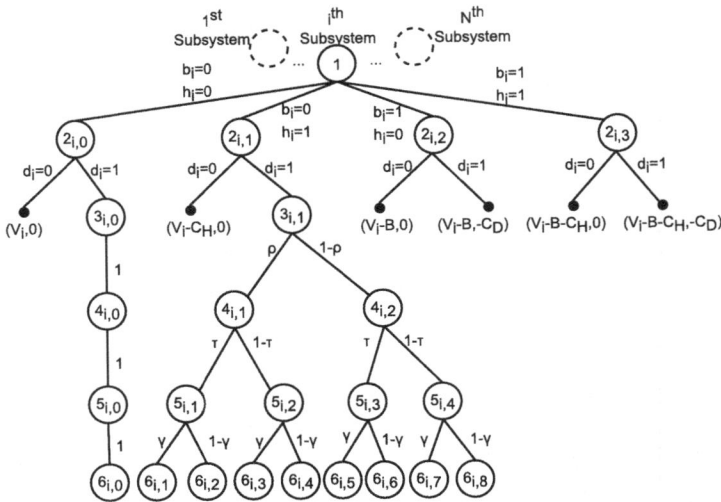

Fig. 2. Subtree of the attacker-defender game, comprising of Stages 1–6.

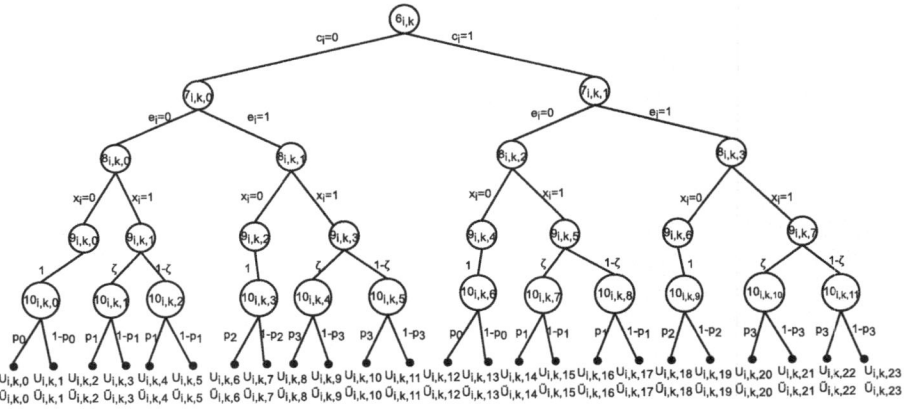

Fig. 3. Subtree of the Attacker-Defender Game, comprising of Stages 6–10.

upon deciding not to decrypt the data ($e_i = 0$), but perform exfiltration ($x_i = 1$). If arrested, the attacker incurs a large cost of F.

Remark: Note that Stages 3, 4, 5, 9, and 10 are chance stages, which introduce uncertainty in the interaction outcome. This uncertainty emerges from the inherent stochasticity present within the interaction, but does not arise due to any agent's decision.

The above multi-stage interaction between the ransomware attacker and the defender is modeled as a complete-information extensive-form game $\Gamma = \{\mathcal{N}, G, \mathcal{U}, \tilde{\mathcal{U}}\}$, where

- $\mathcal{N} = \{D, A\}$ comprises of the two players (D stands for defender and A stands for attacker),
- G represents the decision tree shown in Figs. 2 and 3 that includes the play-order, chance probabilities, and strategies at both attacker and defender, and
- $\mathcal{U}$ and $\tilde{\mathcal{U}}$ denotes the utility functions at the defender and attacker respectively, which are defined in Table 2.

The goal of this paper is to evaluate the subgame-perfect Nash equilibrium (SPNE) for the game Γ. A closed-form equilibrium analysis is presented in the following section using backward induction principles.

Table 2. Utility functions and their payoffs

$U_{i,k,0} = \begin{cases} 0, & \text{if } k = 0 \\ -C_H, & \text{otherwise} \end{cases}$ $\qquad$ $U_{i,k,1} = \begin{cases} 0, & \text{if } k = 0 \\ -C_H, & \text{otherwise} \end{cases}$ $\qquad$ $U_{i,k,2} = \begin{cases} 0, & \text{if } k = 0 \\ -C_H, & \text{otherwise} \end{cases}$

$\tilde{U}_{i,k,0} = T - C_D - F$ $\qquad$ $\tilde{U}_{i,k,1} = T - C_D$ $\qquad$ $\tilde{U}_{i,k,2} = T - C_D - F - C_x$

$U_{i,k,3} = \begin{cases} 0, & \text{if } k = 0 \\ -C_H, & \text{otherwise} \end{cases}$ $\qquad$ $U_{i,k,4} = \begin{cases} -V_p, & \text{if } k = 0 \\ -V_p - C_H, & \text{otherwise} \end{cases}$ $\qquad$ $U_{i,k,5} = \begin{cases} -V_p, & \text{if } k = 0 \\ -V_p - C_H, & \text{otherwise} \end{cases}$

$\tilde{U}_{i,k,3} = T - C_D - C_x$ $\qquad$ $\tilde{U}_{i,k,4} = T - C_D + V'_i - F - C_x$ $\qquad$ $\tilde{U}_{i,k,5} = T - C_D + V'_i - C_x$

$U_{i,k,6} = \begin{cases} V_i, & \text{if } k = 0 \\ V_i - C_H, & \text{otherwise} \end{cases}$ $\qquad$ $U_{i,k,7} = \begin{cases} V_i, & \text{if } k = 0 \\ V_i - C_H, & \text{otherwise} \end{cases}$ $\qquad$ $U_{i,k,8} = \begin{cases} V_i, & \text{if } k = 0 \\ V_i - C_H, & \text{otherwise} \end{cases}$

$\tilde{U}_{i,k,6} = -C_D - F$ $\qquad$ $\tilde{U}_{i,k,7} = -C_D$ $\qquad$ $\tilde{U}_{i,k,8} = -C_D - F - C_x$

$U_{i,k,9} = \begin{cases} V_i, & \text{if } k = 0 \\ V_i - C_H, & \text{otherwise} \end{cases}$ $\qquad$ $U_{i,k,10} = \begin{cases} V_i - V_p, & \text{if } k = 0 \\ V_i - V_p - C_H, & \text{otherwise} \end{cases}$ $\qquad$ $U_{i,k,11} = \begin{cases} V_i - V_p, & \text{if } k = 0 \\ V_i - V_p - C_H, & \text{otherwise} \end{cases}$

$\tilde{U}_{i,k,9} = -C_D - C_x$ $\qquad$ $\tilde{U}_{i,k,10} = -C_D + V'_i - F - C_x$ $\qquad$ $\tilde{U}_{i,k,11} = -C_D + V'_i - C_x$

$U_{i,k,12} = \begin{cases} -R_i, & \text{if } k = 0 \\ -R_i - C_H, & \text{otherwise} \end{cases}$ $\qquad$ $U_{i,k,13} = \begin{cases} -R_i, & \text{if } k = 0 \\ -R_i - C_H, & \text{otherwise} \end{cases}$ $\qquad$ $U_{i,k,14} = \begin{cases} -R_i, & \text{if } k = 0 \\ -R_i - C_H, & \text{otherwise} \end{cases}$

$\tilde{U}_{i,k,12} = R_i - C_D - F$ $\qquad$ $\tilde{U}_{i,k,13} = R_i - C_D$ $\qquad$ $\tilde{U}_{i,k,14} = R_i - C_D - F - C_x$

$U_{i,k,15} = \begin{cases} -R_i, & \text{if } k = 0 \\ -R_i - C_H, & \text{otherwise} \end{cases}$ $\qquad$ $U_{i,k,16} = \begin{cases} -R_i - V_p, & \text{if } k = 0 \\ -R_i - V_p - C_H, & \text{otherwise} \end{cases}$ $\qquad$ $U_{i,k,17} = \begin{cases} -R_i - V_p, & \text{if } k = 0 \\ -R_i - V_p - C_H, & \text{otherwise} \end{cases}$

$\tilde{U}_{i,k,15} = R_i - C_D - C_x$ $\qquad$ $\tilde{U}_{i,k,16} = R_i - C_D + V'_i - F - C_x$ $\qquad$ $\tilde{U}_{i,k,17} = R_i - C_D + V'_i - C_x$

$U_{i,k,18} = \begin{cases} -R_i + V_i, & \text{if } k = 0 \\ V_i - R_i - C_H, & \text{otherwise} \end{cases}$ $\qquad$ $U_{i,k,19} = \begin{cases} V_i - R_i, & \text{if } k = 0 \\ V_i - R_i - C_H, & \text{otherwise} \end{cases}$ $\qquad$ $U_{i,k,20} = \begin{cases} V_i - R_i, & \text{if } k = 0 \\ V_i - R_i - C_H, & \text{otherwise} \end{cases}$

$\tilde{U}_{i,k,18} = R_i + T - C_D - F$ $\qquad$ $\tilde{U}_{i,k,19} = R_i + T - C_D$ $\qquad$ $\tilde{U}_{i,k,20} = R_i + T - C_D - F - C_x$

$U_{i,k,21} = \begin{cases} V_i - R_i, & \text{if } k = 0 \\ V_i - R_i - C_H, & \text{otherwise} \end{cases}$ $\qquad$ $U_{i,k,22} = \begin{cases} V_i - R_i - V_p, & \text{if } k = 0 \\ V_i - R_i - V_p - C_H, & \text{otherwise} \end{cases}$ $\qquad$ $U_{i,k,23} = \begin{cases} V_i - R_i - V_p, & \text{if } k = 0 \\ V_i - R_i - V_p - C_H, & \text{otherwise} \end{cases}$

$\tilde{U}_{i,k,21} = T + R_i - C_D - C_x$ $\qquad$ $\tilde{U}_{i,k,22} = R_i + T - C_D + V'_i - F - C_x$ $\qquad$ $\tilde{U}_{i,k,23} = R_i + T - C_D + V'_i - C_x$

4 Equilibrium Analysis

In this section, SPNE of the game Γ is evaluated in closed-form using backward induction principles. Given the large size of the tree, we present our analysis for every decision stage (i.e. Stages 8, 7, 6, 2 and 1 in the order of backward induction) individually in the following subsections.

4.1 Stage 8: Attacker's Best-Response Exfiltration Strategy

The first decision stage that manifests during the running of backward induction approach is to evaluate the attacker's best-response exfiltration strategy in Stage 8.

Lemma 1. *If the defender compromises ($c_i = 1$) and the attacker opts to decrypt the data ($e_i = 1$), the best response for the attacker on data exfiltration (x_i) is:*

$$x_i^*(8_{i,k,3}) = \begin{cases} 1, & if \; \zeta \geq \zeta^*(8_{i,k,3}) \\ 0, & otherwise \end{cases} \tag{6}$$

where the threshold $\zeta^*(8_{i,k,3})$ is given by

$$\zeta^*(8_{i,k,3}) = \frac{\left(p_2\tilde{U}_{i,k,18} + (1-p_2)\tilde{U}_{i,k,19}\right) - \left(p_3\tilde{U}_{i,k,22} + (1-p_3)\tilde{U}_{i,k,23}\right)}{\left(p_3\tilde{U}_{i,k,20} + (1-p_3)\tilde{U}_{i,k,21}\right) - \left(p_3\tilde{U}_{i,k,22} + (1-p_3)\tilde{U}_{i,k,23}\right)} \tag{7}$$

Proof. In Fig. 3, the node in Stage 8 with a history $c_i = 1$ and $e_i = 1$ is labeled as $8_{i,k,3}$. At this node, the attacker has to pick $x_i \in \{0,1\}$ such that its expected utility is maximized.

The expected utility obtained by the attacker at node $8_{i,k,3}$ for choosing $x_i = 1$ and $x_i = 0$ are respectively given by

$$\tilde{U}(x_i = 1|8_{i,k,3}) = \zeta\left(p_3\tilde{U}_{i,k,20} + (1-p_3)\tilde{U}_{i,k,21}\right) + (1-\zeta)\left(p_3\tilde{U}_{i,k,22} + (1-p_3)\tilde{U}_{i,k,23}\right), \tag{8}$$

$$\text{and } \tilde{U}(x_i = 0|8_{i,k,3}) = p_2\tilde{U}_{i,k,18} + (1-p_2)\tilde{U}_{i,k,19}. \tag{9}$$

Note that $x_i = 1$ is the best response exfiltration strategy if $\tilde{U}(x_i = 1|8_{i,k,3}) \geq \tilde{U}(x_i = 0|8_{i,k,3})$, i.e.,

$$\zeta\left(p_3\tilde{U}_{i,k,20} + (1-p_3)\tilde{U}_{i,k,21}\right) + (1-\zeta)\left(p_3\tilde{U}_{i,k,22} + (1-p_3)\tilde{U}_{i,k,23}\right) > p_2\tilde{U}_{i,k,18} + (1-p_2)\tilde{U}_{i,k,19}. \tag{10}$$

The inclination for data exfiltration stems primarily from the attacker's perception of the exfiltrated data as a strategic asset. This strategic value lies in its potential to provide added leverage for subsequent attacks or negotiations. Additionally, a financial motive is present with the stolen information being seen as valuable on the illicit markets. Moreover, the decision to exfiltrate data may be driven by a lack of trust or opportunistic behavior of the attacker and using it as a means of insurance or an alternative revenue source post-ransom payment. Upon rearranging the terms, the attacker's best response to exfiltrate is to choose $x_i = 1$ if the network honeypot deceives the attacker with probability $\zeta \geq \zeta^*(8_{i,k,3})$, where $\zeta^*(8_{i,k,3})$ is defined in Eq. (7).

Lemma 2. *If the defender compromises and the attacker does not decrypt the data, the optimal strategy for the attacker on data exfiltration (x_i) is:*

$$x_i^*(8_{i,k,2}) = \begin{cases} 1, & if \; \zeta \geq \zeta^*(8_{i,k,2}) \\ 0, & otherwise, \end{cases} \tag{11}$$

where the threshold $\zeta^*(8_{i,k,2})$ is given by

$$\zeta^*(8_{i,k,2}) = \frac{\left(p_0\tilde{U}_{i,k,12} + (1-p_0)\tilde{U}_{i,k,13}\right) - \left(p_1\tilde{U}_{i,k,16} + (1-p_1)\tilde{U}_{i,k,17}\right)}{\left(p_1\tilde{U}_{i,k,14} + (1-p_1)\tilde{U}_{i,k,15}\right) - \left(p_1\tilde{U}_{i,k,16} + (1-p_1)\tilde{U}_{i,k,17}\right)} \tag{12}$$

Proof. In Fig. 3, the node in Stage 8 with a history $c_i = 1$ and $e_i = 0$ is labeled as $8_{i,k,2}$. At this node, the attacker has to pick $x_i \in \{0, 1\}$ such that its expected utility is maximized.

The expected utility obtained by the attacker at node $8_{i,k,2}$ for choosing $x_i = 1$ and $x_i = 0$ are respectively given by

$$\tilde{U}(x_i = 1 | 8_{i,k,2}) = \zeta\left(p_1 \tilde{U}_{i,k,14} + (1 - p_1)\tilde{U}_{i,k,15}\right) + (1 - \zeta)\left(p_1 \tilde{U}_{i,k,16} + (1 - p_1)\tilde{U}_{i,k,17}\right)$$
(13)

$$\text{and } \tilde{U}(x_i = 0 | 8_{i,k,2}) = p_0 \tilde{U}_{i,k,12} + (1 - p_0)\tilde{U}_{i,k,13}.$$
(14)

Note that $x_i = 1$ is the best response exfiltration strategy if $\tilde{U}(x_i = 1 | 8_{i,k,2}) \geq \tilde{U}(x_i = 0 | 8_{i,k,2})$, i.e.

$$\zeta\left(p_1 \tilde{U}_{i,k,14} + (1 - p_1)\tilde{U}_{i,k,15}\right) + (1 - \zeta)\left(p_1 \tilde{U}_{i,k,16} + (1 - p_1)\tilde{U}_{i,k,17}\right) > p_0 \tilde{U}_{i,k,12} + (1 - p_0)\tilde{U}_{i,k,13}. \quad (15)$$

The attacker's intent for exfiltration is similar to what is discussed in Lemma 1. Upon rearranging the terms, the attacker's best response to exfiltrate is to choose $x_i = 1$ if the network honeypot deceives the attacker with probability $\zeta \geq \zeta^*(8_{i,k,2})$, where $\zeta^*(8_{i,k,2})$ is defined in Eq. (12).

Lemma 3. *If the defender does not compromise ($c_i = 0$) and the attacker opts to decrypt the data ($e_i = 1$), the best response for the attacker on data exfiltration (x_i) is:*

$$x_i^*(8_{i,k,1}) = \begin{cases} 1, & \text{if } \zeta \geq \zeta^*(8_{i,k,1}) \\ 0, & \text{otherwise}, \end{cases} \quad (16)$$

where the threshold $\zeta^*(8_{i,k,1})$ is given by

$$\zeta^*(8_{i,k,1}) = \frac{\left(p_2 \tilde{U}_{i,k,6} + (1 - p_2)\tilde{U}_{i,k,7}\right) - \left(p_3 \tilde{U}_{i,k,10} + (1 - p_3)\tilde{U}_{i,k,11}\right)}{\left(p_3 \tilde{U}_{i,k,8} + (1 - p_3)\tilde{U}_{i,k,9}\right) - \left(p_3 \tilde{U}_{i,k,10} + (1 - p_3)\tilde{U}_{i,k,11}\right)} \quad (17)$$

Proof. In Fig. 3, the node in Stage 8 with a history $c_i = 0$ and $e_i = 1$ is labeled as $8_{i,k,1}$. At this node, the attacker has to pick $x_i \in \{0, 1\}$ such that its expected utility is maximized.

The expected utility obtained by the attacker at node $8_{i,k,1}$ for choosing $x_i = 1$ and $x_i = 0$ are respectively given by

$$\tilde{U}(x_i = 1 | 8_{i,k,1}) = \zeta\left(p_3 \tilde{U}_{i,k,8} + (1 - p_3)\tilde{U}_{i,k,9}\right) + (1 - \zeta)\left(p_3 \tilde{U}_{i,k,10} + (1 - p_3)\tilde{U}_{i,k,11}\right), \quad (18)$$

$$\text{and } \tilde{U}(x_i = 0 | 8_{i,k,1}) = p_2 \tilde{U}_{i,k,6} + (1 - p_2)\tilde{U}_{i,k,7}. \quad (19)$$

Note that $x_i = 1$ is the best response exfiltration strategy if $\tilde{U}(x_i = 1 | 8_{i,k,1}) \geq \tilde{U}(x_i = 0 | 8_{i,k,1})$, i.e.

$$\zeta\left(p_3 \tilde{U}_{i,k,8} + (1 - p_3)\tilde{U}_{i,k,9}\right) + (1 - \zeta)\left(p_3 \tilde{U}_{i,k,10} + (1 - p_3)\tilde{U}_{i,k,11}\right) > p_2 \tilde{U}_{i,k,6} + (1 - p_2)\tilde{U}_{i,k,7}. \quad (20)$$

The attacker's intent for exfiltration is similar to what is discussed in Lemma 1. Upon rearranging the terms, the attacker's best response to exfiltrate is to choose $x_i = 1$ if the network honeypot deceives the attacker with probability $\zeta \geq \zeta^*(8_{i,k,1})$, where $\zeta^*(8_{i,k,1})$ is defined in Eq. (17).

Lemma 4. *If the defender does not compromise* $(c_i = 0)$ *and the attacker does not decrypt the data* $(e_i = 0)$, *the best response for the attacker on data exfiltration* (x_i) *is:*

$$x_i^*(8_{i,k,0}) = \begin{cases} 1, & \text{if } \zeta \geq \zeta^*(8_{i,k,0}) \\ 0, & \text{otherwise,} \end{cases} \tag{21}$$

where the threshold $\zeta^*(8_{i,k,0})$ *is given by*

$$\zeta^*(8_{i,k,0}) = \frac{\left(p_0 \tilde{U}_{i,k,0} + (1-p_0)\tilde{U}_{i,k,1}\right) - \left(p_1 \tilde{U}_{i,k,4} + (1-p_1)\tilde{U}_{i,k,5}\right)}{\left(p_1 \tilde{U}_{i,k,2} + (1-p_1)\tilde{U}_{i,k,3}\right) - \left(p_1 \tilde{U}_{i,k,4} + (1-p_1)\tilde{U}_{i,k,5}\right)} \tag{22}$$

Proof. In Fig. 3, the node in Stage 8 with a history $c_i = 0$ and $e_i = 0$ is labeled as $8_{i,k,0}$. At this node, the attacker has to pick $x_i \in \{0, 1\}$ such that its expected utility is maximized.

The expected utility obtained by the attacker at node $8_{i,k,0}$ for choosing $x_i = 1$ and $x_i = 0$ are respectively given by

$$\tilde{U}(x_i = 1 | 8_{i,k,0}) = \zeta \left(p_1 \tilde{U}_{i,k,2} + (1-p_1)\tilde{U}_{i,k,3}\right) \\ + (1-\zeta)\left(p_1 \tilde{U}_{i,k,4} + (1-p_1)\tilde{U}_{i,k,5}\right), \tag{23}$$

$$\text{and } \tilde{U}(x_i = 0 | 8_{i,k,0}) = p_0 \tilde{U}_{i,k,0} + (1-p_0)\tilde{U}_{i,k,1}. \tag{24}$$

Note that $x_i = 1$ is the best response exfiltration strategy if $\tilde{U}(x_i = 1 | 8_{i,k,0}) \geq \tilde{U}(x_i = 0 | 8_{i,k,0})$, i.e.,

$$\zeta \left(p_1 \tilde{U}_{i,k,2} + (1-p_1)\tilde{U}_{i,k,3}\right) + (1-\zeta)\left(p_1 \tilde{U}_{i,k,4} + (1-p_1)\tilde{U}_{i,k,5}\right) \\ > p_0 \tilde{U}_{i,k,0} + (1-p_0)\tilde{U}_{i,k,1}. \tag{25}$$

The attacker's intent for exfiltration is similar to what is discussed in Lemma 1. Upon rearranging the terms, the attacker's best response to exfiltrate is to choose $x_i = 1$ if the network honeypot deceives the attacker with probability $\zeta \geq \zeta^*(8_{i,k,0})$, where $\zeta^*(8_{i,k,0})$ is defined in Eq. (22).

4.2   Stage 7: Attacker's Best-Response Decryption Strategy

Per the attacker's optimal decision on data exfiltration, the attacker's decision on whether to decrypt the data or not is given by the following lemmas.

Lemma 5. *If the defender compromises* $(c_i = 1)$, *the best response for the attacker on data decryption* (e_i) *is:*

$$e_i^* \left(7_{i,k,1} \Big| x_i^*(8_{i,k,3}), x_i^*(8_{i,k,2})\right) = \begin{cases} 1, & \text{if } \lambda(7_{i,k,1}) \geq 0, \\ 0, & \text{otherwise,} \end{cases} \tag{26}$$

where

$$\lambda(7_{i,k,1}) = x_i^*(8_{i,k,3}) \left[\tilde{U}(x_i = 1 | 8_{i,k,3}) - \tilde{U}(x_i = 0 | 8_{i,k,3})\right] - x_i^*(8_{i,k,2})\left[\tilde{U}(x_i = 1 | 8_{i,k,2}) - \tilde{U}(x_i = 0 | 8_{i,k,2})\right] \\ + \tilde{U}(x_i = 0 | 8_{i,k,3}) - \tilde{U}(x_i = 0 | 8_{i,k,2}) \tag{27}$$

Proof. In Fig. 3, the node in Stage 7 with a history $c_i = 1$ is labeled as $7_{i,k,1}$. At this node, the attacker has to pick $e_i \in \{0, 1\}$ such that its expected utility is maximized.

The expected utility obtained by the attacker at node $7_{i,k,1}$ for choosing $e_i = 1$ and $e_i = 0$ are respectively given by

$$\tilde{U}(e_i = 1 | 7_{i,k,1}) = x_i^*(8_{i,k,3}) \cdot \tilde{U}(x_i = 1 | 8_{i,k,3}) + \left(1 - x_i^*(8_{i,k,3})\right) \cdot \tilde{U}(x_i = 0 | 8_{i,k,3}), \quad (28)$$

$$\text{and } \tilde{U}(e_i = 0 | 7_{i,k,1}) = x_i^*(8_{i,k,2}) \cdot \tilde{U}(x_i = 1 | 8_{i,k,2}) + \left(1 - x_i^*(8_{i,k,2})\right) \cdot \tilde{U}(x_i = 0 | 8_{i,k,2}). \quad (29)$$

The attacker's decision to decrypt the data can be attributed to several factors. A pivotal consideration is the establishment of trustworthiness as fulfilling the agreement enhances the attacker's reputation for reliability within the criminal landscape. Additionally, adhering to an implicit criminal code of conduct and seeking to avoid law enforcement attention provide strong motivations for the attacker to proceed with decryption. The strategic move of honoring the agreement not only fosters a perception of dependability but may also encourage future victims to comply with ransom demands.

Hence $e_i = 1$ is the best response decryption strategy if

$$\lambda(7_{i,k,1}) \triangleq \tilde{U}(e_i = 1 | 7_{i,k,1}) - \tilde{U}(e_i = 0 | 7_{i,k,1}) \geq 0.$$

On the contrary, $e_i = 0$ is the best response decryption strategy if $\lambda(7_{i,k,1}) < 0$.

Lemma 6. *If the defender does not compromise ($c_i = 0$), the best response for the attacker on data decryption (e_i) is:*

$$e_i^*\left(7_{i,k,0} \Big| x_i^*(8_{i,k,1}), x_i^*(8_{i,k,0})\right) = \begin{cases} 1, & \text{if } \lambda(7_{i,k,0}) \geq 0, \\ 0, & \text{otherwise,} \end{cases} \quad (30)$$

where $\lambda(7_{i,k,0}) = x_i^*(8_{i,k,1}) \cdot \tilde{U}(x_i = 1 | 8_{i,k,1}) + (1 - x_i^*(8_{i,k,1})) \cdot \tilde{U}(x_i = 0 | 8_{i,k,1}) - \left(x_i^*(8_{i,k,0}) \cdot \tilde{U}(x_i = 1 | 8_{i,k,0}) + (1 - x_i^*(8_{i,k,0})) \cdot \tilde{U}(x_i = 0 | 8_{i,k,0})\right)$

Proof. In Fig. 3, the node in Stage 7 with a history $c_i = 0$ is labeled as $7_{i,k,0}$. At this node, the attacker has to pick $e_i \in \{0, 1\}$ such that its expected utility is maximized.

The expected utility obtained by the attacker at node $7_{i,k,0}$ for choosing $e_i = 1$ and $e_i = 0$ are respectively given by

$$\tilde{U}(e_i = 1 | 7_{i,k,0}) = x_i^*(8_{i,k,1}) \cdot \tilde{U}(x_i = 1 | 8_{i,k,1}) + \left(1 - x_i^*(8_{i,k,1})\right) \cdot \tilde{U}(x_i = 0 | 8_{i,k,1}) \quad (31)$$

and

$$\tilde{U}(e_i = 0 | 7_{i,k,0}) = x_i^*(8_{i,k,0}) \cdot \tilde{U}(x_i = 1 | 8_{i,k,0}) + \left(1 - x_i^*(8_{i,k,0})\right) \cdot \tilde{U}(x_i = 0 | 8_{i,k,0}) \quad (32)$$

The attacker's decision for this lemma is similar to that in Lemma 5. Note that $e_i = 1$ is the best response decryption strategy if

$$\lambda(7_{i,k,0}) \triangleq \tilde{U}(e_i = 1 | 7_{i,k,0}) - \tilde{U}(e_i = 0 | 7_{i,k,0}) \geq 0.$$

On the contrary, $e_i = 0$ is the best response decryption strategy if $\lambda(7_{i,k,0}) < 0$.

4.3   Stage 6: The Defender's Decision-Making on Compromise

Lemma 7. *The defender's decision-making on compromise (c_i) is given by:*

$$c_i^*(6_{i,k}|e_i^*, \boldsymbol{x}_i^*) = \begin{cases} 1, & \text{if } \beta(e_i^*, \boldsymbol{x}_i^*) > 0, \\ 0, & \text{otherwise,} \end{cases} \tag{33}$$

where $\beta(e_i^*, \boldsymbol{x}_i^*)$ is given by

$$\begin{aligned}
\beta(e_i^*, \boldsymbol{x}_i^*) &= e_i^*(7_{i,k,1})\Big[x_i^*(8_{i,k,3})U(9_{i,k,7}) + \big(1 - x_i^*(8_{i,k,3})\big)U(9_{i,k,6})\Big] \\
&+ \Big(1 - e_i^*(7_{i,k,1})\Big)\Big[x_i^*(8_{i,k,2})U(9_{i,k,5}) + \big(1 - x_i^*(8_{i,k,2})\big)U(9_{i,k,4})\Big] \\
&- e_i^*(7_{i,k,0})\Big[x_i^*(8_{i,k,1})U(9_{i,k,3}) + \big(1 - x_i^*(8_{i,k,1})\big)U(9_{i,k,2})\Big] \\
&- \Big(1 - e_i^*(7_{i,k,0})\Big)\Big[x_i^*(8_{i,k,0})U(9_{i,k,1}) + \big(1 - x_i^*(8_{i,k,0})\big)U(9_{i,k,0})\Big]
\end{aligned} \tag{34}$$

Proof. The defender chooses to either compromise ($c_i = 1$), or not pay the ransom ($c_i = 0$) such that the expected utility at node $6_{i,k}$ is maximized.

The defender's expected utility of choosing $c_i = 1$ and $c_i = 0$ at node $6_{i,k}$ is given by

$$\begin{aligned}
U(c_i = 1|6_{i,k}) &= e_i^*(7_{i,k,1})\Big[x_i^*(8_{i,k,3})U(9_{i,k,7}) + \big(1 - x_i^*(8_{i,k,3})\big)U(9_{i,k,6})\Big] \\
&+ \Big(1 - e_i^*(7_{i,k,1})\Big)\Big[x_i^*(8_{i,k,2})U(9_{i,k,5}) + \big(1 - x_i^*(8_{i,k,2})\big)U(9_{i,k,4})\Big]
\end{aligned} \tag{35}$$

$$\text{and} \quad \begin{aligned}
\tilde{U}(c_i = 0|6_{i,k}) &= e_i^*(7_{i,k,0})\Big[x_i^*(8_{i,k,1})U(9_{i,k,3}) + \big(1 - x_i^*(8_{i,k,1})\big)U(9_{i,k,2})\Big] \\
&+ \Big(1 - e_i^*(7_{i,k,0})\Big)\Big[x_i^*(8_{i,k,0})U(9_{i,k,1}) + \big(1 - x_i^*(8_{i,k,0})\big)U(9_{i,k,0})\Big]
\end{aligned} \tag{36}$$

respectively, where

$$\begin{aligned}
U(9_{i,k,7}) &= \zeta\left[p_3 U_{i,k,20} + (1 - p_3)U_{i,k,21}\right] + (1 - \zeta)\left[p_3 U_{i,k,22} + (1 - p_3)U_{i,k,23}\right], \\
U(9_{i,k,6}) &= p_2 U_{i,k,18} + (1 - p_2)U_{i,k,19}, \\
U(9_{i,k,5}) &= \zeta\left[p_1 U_{i,k,14} + (1 - p_1)U_{i,k,15}\right] + (1 - \zeta)\left[p_1 U_{i,k,16} + (1 - p_1)U_{i,k,17}\right], \\
U(9_{i,k,4}) &= p_0 U_{i,k,12} + (1 - p_0)U_{i,k,13}, \\
U(9_{i,k,3}) &= \zeta\left[p_3 U_{i,k,8} + (1 - p_3)U_{i,k,9}\right] + (1 - \zeta)\left[p_3 U_{i,k,10} + (1 - p_3)U_{i,k,11}\right], \\
U(9_{i,k,2}) &= p_2 U_{i,k,6} + (1 - p_2)U_{i,k,7}, \\
U(9_{i,k,1}) &= \zeta\left[p_1 U_{i,k,2} + (1 - p_1)U_{i,k,3}\right] + (1 - \zeta)\left[p_1 U_{i,k,4} + (1 - p_1)U_{i,k,5}\right], \\
U(9_{i,k,0}) &= p_0 U_{i,k,0} + (1 - p_0)U_{i,k,1}.
\end{aligned} \tag{37}$$

Defenders choose to pay a ransom when their data is encrypted due to practical considerations. If the encrypted data is crucial for business operations or contains sensitive information, the cost of downtime and potential damage to reputation becomes a driving factor. The complexity of decryption and the absence of reliable backups can limit options, making payment the quickest way to regain access. The defender will choose $c_i = 1$ if

$$\beta(e_i^*, \boldsymbol{x}_i^*) \triangleq U(c_i = 1|6_{i,k}) - U(c_i = 0|6_{i,k}) \geq 0.$$

Otherwise, the best response strategy of the defender is $c_i = 0$.

4.4   Stage 2: Attacker's Best-Response Ransomware Development Strategy

Lemma 8. *The attacker's best response is to not develop the ransomware, i.e.* $d_i^*(2_{i,3}) = 0$, *when the defender backs up the data (i.e.* $b_i = 1$) *and uses deception (i.e.* $h_i = 1$).

Proof. In Fig. 2, the node in Stage 2 with a history $b_i = 1$ and $h_i = 1$ is labeled as $2_{i,3}$. At this node, the attacker has to pick $d_i \in \{0, 1\}$ such that its expected utility is maximized.

The expected utility obtained by the attacker at node $2_{i,3}$ for choosing $d_i = 1$ and $d_i = 0$ are respectively given by

$$\tilde{U}(d_i = 1|2_{i,3}) = -C_D, \quad \text{and} \quad \tilde{U}(d_i = 0|2_{i,3}) = 0. \tag{38}$$

When the defender has made backups, developing ransomware becomes pointless for the attacker. Backups allow the defender to quickly recover, eliminating the need to pay any ransom. This reduces the attacker's leverage and makes their efforts ineffective. Financial motivation for the attacker also decreases when there's a low chance of getting paid. Instead of gaining, the attacker incurs a loss in the cost of ransomware development. The defender's proactive approach with backups not only safeguards against data loss but also makes ransomware development an impractical and costly endeavor for the attacker.

Since $\tilde{U}(d_i = 0|2_{i,3}) > \tilde{U}(d_i = 1|2_{i,3})$, $d_i = 0$ is the best response ransomware development strategy.

Lemma 9. *Attacker's best response is to not develop the ransomware, i.e.* $d_i^*(2_{i,2}) = 0$, *when the defender backs up (i.e.* $b_i = 1$) *but does not use deception (i.e.* $h_i = 0$).

Proof. In Fig. 2, the node in Stage 2 with a history $b_i = 1$ and $h_i = 0$ is labeled as $2_{i,2}$. At this node, the attacker has to pick $d_i \in \{0, 1\}$ such that its expected utility is maximized.

The expected utility obtained by the attacker at node $2_{i,2}$ for choosing $d_i = 1$ and $d_i = 0$ are respectively given by

$$\tilde{U}(d_i = 1|2_{i,2}) = -C_D \quad \text{and} \quad \tilde{U}(d_i = 0|2_{i,2}) = 0 \tag{39}$$

With the reasons similar to Lemma 8, since $\tilde{U}(d_i = 0|2_{i,2}) > \tilde{U}(d_i = 1|2_{i,2})$, $d_i = 0$ is the best response ransomware development strategy.

Lemma 10. *Attacker's best response when defender does not back up (i.e.,* $b_i = 0$) *but uses deception (i.e.,* $h_i = 1$) *given by* d_i *is:*

$$d_i^*(2_{i,1}) = \begin{cases} 1, & \text{if } \alpha(c_i^*) > 0, \\ 0, & \text{otherwise} \end{cases} \tag{40}$$

where

$$\alpha(\boldsymbol{c}_i^*) = \rho\tau\Big[\gamma\Big\{c_i^*(6_{i,1})\tilde{U}(7_i,1,0) + (1 - c_i^*(6_{i,1}))\tilde{U}(7_i,1,1)\Big\}$$
$$+ (1-\gamma)\Big\{c_i^*(6_{i,2})\tilde{U}(7_i,2,0) + (1 - c_i^*(6_{i,2}))\tilde{U}(7_i,2,1)\Big\}\Big]$$
$$+ \rho(1-\tau)\Big[\gamma\Big\{c_i^*(6_{i,3})\tilde{U}(7_i,3,0) + (1 - c_i^*(6_{i,3}))\tilde{U}(7_i,3,1)\Big\}$$
$$+ (1-\gamma)*\Big\{c_i^*(6_{i,4}) * \tilde{U}(7_i,4,0) + (1 - c_i^*(6_{i,4})) * \tilde{U}(7_i,4,1)\Big\}\Big] \quad (41)$$
$$+ (1-\rho)\tau\Big[\gamma\Big\{c_i^*(6_{i,5})\tilde{U}(7_i,5,0) + (1 - c_i^*(6_{i,5}))\tilde{U}(7_i,5,1)\Big\}$$
$$+ (1-\gamma)\Big\{c_i^*(6_{i,6})\tilde{U}(7_i,6,0) + (1 - c_i^*(6_{i,6}))\tilde{U}(7_i,6,1)\Big\}\Big]$$
$$+ (1-\rho)(1-\tau)\Big[\gamma\Big\{c_i^*(6_{i,7})\tilde{U}(7_i,7,0) + (1 - c_i^*(6_{i,7}))\tilde{U}(7_i,7,1)\Big\}$$
$$+ (1-\gamma)\Big\{c_i^*(6_{i,8})\tilde{U}(7_i,8,0) + (1 - c_i^*(6_{i,8}))\tilde{U}(7_i,8,1)\Big\}\Big]$$

Proof. In Fig. 2, the node in Stage 2 with a history $b_i = 0$ and $h_i = 1$ is labeled as $2_{i,1}$. At this node, the attacker has to pick $d_i \in \{0,1\}$ such that its expected utility is maximized.

The expected utility obtained by the attacker at node $2_{i,1}$ for choosing $d_i = 1$ and $d_i = 0$ are respectively given by

$$\tilde{U}(d_i = 1|2_{i,1}) = \rho\tau\Big[\gamma\Big\{c_i^*(6_{i,1})\tilde{U}(7_i,1,0) + (1 - c_i^*(6_{i,1}))\tilde{U}(7_i,1,1)\Big\}$$
$$+ (1-\gamma)\Big\{c_i^*(6_{i,2})\tilde{U}(7_i,2,0) + (1 - c_i^*(6_{i,2}))\tilde{U}(7_i,2,1)\Big\}\Big]$$
$$+ \rho(1-\tau)\Big[\gamma\Big\{c_i^*(6_{i,3})\tilde{U}(7_i,3,0) + (1 - c_i^*(6_{i,3}))\tilde{U}(7_i,3,1)\Big\}$$
$$+ (1-\gamma)*\Big\{c_i^*(6_{i,4}) * \tilde{U}(7_i,4,0) + (1 - c_i^*(6_{i,4})) * \tilde{U}(7_i,4,1)\Big\}\Big] \quad (42)$$
$$+ (1-\rho)\tau\Big[\gamma\Big\{c_i^*(6_{i,5})\tilde{U}(7_i,5,0) + (1 - c_i^*(6_{i,5}))\tilde{U}(7_i,5,1)\Big\}$$
$$+ (1-\gamma)\Big\{c_i^*(6_{i,6})\tilde{U}(7_i,6,0) + (1 - c_i^*(6_{i,6}))\tilde{U}(7_i,6,1)\Big\}\Big]$$
$$+ (1-\rho)(1-\tau)\Big[\gamma\Big\{c_i^*(6_{i,7})\tilde{U}(7_i,7,0) + (1 - c_i^*(6_{i,7}))\tilde{U}(7_i,7,1)\Big\}$$
$$+ (1-\gamma)\Big\{c_i^*(6_{i,8})\tilde{U}(7_i,8,0) + (1 - c_i^*(6_{i,8}))\tilde{U}(7_i,8,1)\Big\}\Big]$$

$$\text{and } \tilde{U}(d_i = 0|2_{i,1}) = 0. \quad (43)$$

The absence of data backups increases the attacker's leverage as valuable and critical data becomes vulnerable to encryption. This vulnerability persists even if the defender employs deception techniques to lure or mislead the attacker as the potential gains from exploiting the lack of data backups outweighs the risks associated with potential deception. This situation raises the likelihood of the defender paying the ransom to regain access to crucial information and amplifies the attack's impact by causing significant disruption to business operations. Financial motivation and the limited recovery options for the defender further incentivize the attacker to pursue ransomware development as an effective means of achieving their goals. Note that $d_i = 1$ is the best response ransomware development strategy if $\tilde{U}(d_i = 1|2_{i,1}) \geq \tilde{U}(d_i = 0|2_{i,1})$, i.e., $\alpha(\boldsymbol{c}_i^*) > 0$. On the contrary, $d_i = 0$ is the best response decryption strategy if $\alpha(\boldsymbol{c}_i^*) < 0$.

Lemma 11. *Attacker's best response when defender does not back up (i.e. $b_i = 0$) and does not use deception (i.e. $h_i = 0$) given by d_i is:*

$$d_i^*(2_{i,0}) = \begin{cases} 1, & \text{if } \tilde{U}(6_{i,0}) > 0, \\ 0, & \text{otherwise} \end{cases} \quad (44)$$

Proof. In Fig. 2, the node in Stage 2 with a history $b_i = 0$ and $h_i = 1$ is labeled as $2_{i,0}$. At this node, the attacker has to pick $d_i \in \{0, 1\}$ such that its expected utility is maximized.

The expected utility obtained by the attacker at node $2_{i,0}$ for choosing $d_i = 1$ and $d_i = 0$ are respectively given by

$$\tilde{U}(d_i = 1|2_{i,0}) = \tilde{U}(6_{i,0}) \quad \text{and} \quad \tilde{U}(d_i = 0|2_{i,0}) = 0 \tag{45}$$

With reasons similar to Lemma 10, note that $d_i = 1$ is the best response ransomware development strategy if $\tilde{U}(d_i = 1|2_{i,0}) \geq \tilde{U}(d_i = 0|2_{i,0})$, i.e. $\tilde{U}(6_{i,0}) > 0$. On the contrary, $d_i = 0$ is the best response decryption strategy if $\tilde{U}(6_{i,0}) < 0$.

4.5 Stage 1: Defender's Decision-Making on Data Backup and Deception

The defender's decision-making on Stage 1 for the ith subsystem considers the product of the backup decision i.e. b_i and deception decision i.e. h_i making it a bilinear problem. For the ith subsystem, the defender's utility is given by:

$$U_i(1) = \left[(1 - b_i) \cdot (1 - h_i) \cdot U(2_{i,0}) + (1 - b_i) \cdot (h_i) \cdot U(2_{i,1}) + (b_i) \cdot (1 - h_i) \cdot U(2_{i,2}) + b_i \cdot h_i \cdot U(2_{i,3}) \right] \tag{46}$$

Combining the problem across all the N subsystems, the defender wishes to

$$\max_{(b_1, h_1), \cdots, (b_N, h_N)} \sum_{i=1}^{N} \left[(1 - b_i)(1 - h_i)U(2_{i,0}) + (1 - b_i)h_i U(2_{i,1}) + b_i(1 - h_i)U(2_{i,2}) + b_i h_i U(2_{i,3}) \right] \tag{47}$$

In vector notation, let $y = [b_1, h_1, \cdots, b_i, h_i, \cdots, b_N, h_N]^T$ denote the decision variable at node 1. Then, the aforementioned optimization problem can be rewritten as the following mixed-integer linear program

$$\max_{y} y^T \Theta y + \theta^T y + \delta, \tag{48}$$

where

$$\Theta = \begin{bmatrix} \Theta_1 & \cdots & 0 \\ \vdots & \ddots & \vdots \\ 0 & \cdots & \Theta_N \end{bmatrix} \text{ is a block-diagonal matrix with}$$

$$\Theta_i = \begin{bmatrix} 0 & 0 \\ U(2_{i,0}) - U(2_{i,1}) - U(2_{i,2}) + U(2_{i,3}) & 0 \end{bmatrix}, \tag{49}$$

$$\theta = \begin{bmatrix} U(2_{1,2}) - U(2_{1,0}) \\ U(2_{1,1}) - U(2_{1,0}) \\ \vdots \\ U(2_{N,2}) - U(2_{N,0}) \\ U(2_{N,1}) - U(2_{N,0}) \end{bmatrix}, \quad \text{and} \quad \delta = \sum_{i=1}^{N} U(2_{i,0}).$$

Since the above problem is a binary quadratic program, the solution cannot be evaluated in closed-form (a finite number of operations, using a given set of functions and mathematical operations). Instead, the problem has to be computationally solved using a standard integer-programming algorithm to maximize and find the defender's best response for this stage.

5 Ransomware Defense in Healthcare: A Case Study

Ransomware attacks affect the healthcare industry leading to the slowing of critical processes to make them completely inoperable and making important information inaccessible [7]. It is important to analyze our work with respect to the behavior in the real world where ransomware has been highly rampant in the healthcare industry. However, it is difficult to get a well-formed dataset that provides information on different parameters such as ransomware amount demanded, value of data for the victim, cost of ransomware development, compromised amount, value of data privacy (breach of data), etc. To accurately portray this information we had to collect information from a variety of credible sources including news, blogs, and statistics. Our parameter settings for the experiment and numerical analysis thus include information collected from these sources and is depicted in the Table 3. On average the ransomware amount demanded by the cybercriminals in a healthcare sector compromise ranges from $0.25 million to $5 million with a mean of $2.63 million whereas a single attack can cost a healthcare provider about $112 million [10]. The average cost of a healthcare data breach has risen to $10.93 million [5] leading to data privacy compromise. In [9], it is discussed that one healthcare sector invested around $8 million towards cybersecurity. We set the parameters for cyber deception using the honeypot, honeytoken, honeyfiles based on their costs from discussed literature from Sect. 2 whereas the numbers are derived by considering $1 million of the overall cybersecurity investment towards cyber deception. The loss of the attacker after getting caught in fact can be considered in terms of the amount being recovered, and jail time, among others. For the experiment, it is considered to be twice as much of the ransomware amount requested as it is difficult to quantify aspects other than the amount recovered. For cybercrimes such as phishing and ransomware, only 5% of cybercriminals are apprehended for their crimes [4]. This goes to show how difficult it is to apprehend cyber criminals. By using deception techniques, we intend to engage attackers with the targeted systems enough to buy time for cybercriminals to be tracked. The probability of

Table 3. Parameters Settings in the Experiment for Healthcare Industry Ransomware Breach.

Fig.	T	C_D	F	C_x	V_i	V_p	R_i	V_i'	C_{ht}	n_{ht}	C_{hp}	C_{hf}	n_{hf}	C_{nh}	p_0	p_1	p_2	p_3
4	3 m	–	–	1000	112 m	10.93 m	2.63 m	4.38 m	0.05	0.67 m	0.08 m	0.08 m	0.5 m	0.1 m	0.1	0.15	0.18	0.2
5	3 m	–	5.25 m	1000	112 m	10.93 m	2.63 m	4.38 m	0.05	0.67 m	–	0.08 m	0.5 m	0.1 m	0.1	0.15	0.18	0.2
6	3 m	0.1 m	–	–	112 m	10.93 m	2.63 m	4.38 m	0.05	0.67 m	0.08 m	0.08 m	0.5 m	0.1 m	0.1	0.15	0.18	0.2
7	3 m	–	5.25 m	1000	112 m	10.93 m	2.63 m	4.38 m	0.05	0.67 m	–	0.08 m	0.5 m	–	0.1	0.15	0.18	0.2
8	3 m	0.1 m	5.25 m	1000	112 m	10.93 m	2.63 m	–	0.05	0.67 m	–	0.08 m	0.5 m	0.1 m	0.1	0.15	0.18	0.2
9	3 m	0.1 m	5.25 m	1000	112 m	10.93 m	2.63 m	–	0.05	0.67 m	0.08 m	–	0.5 m	0.1 m	0.1	0.15	0.18	0.2

getting apprehended by law enforcers should rise given the deception methods are designed to slow down the attackers and/or stop them from attacking. We define the probability values based on this observation.

6   Numerical Results and Discussion

6.1   Game Experiment Result

The computation experiments are carried out on a single Intel Xeon CPU operating at 2.20 GHz equipped with 12 GB of RAM and a Tesla K80 accelerator. All the required programs for the experiments were developed in Python and executed on this specific configuration. The experiment codebase can be accessed from the GitHub Repository [2].

The observed trend in Fig. 4, where the attacker utility initially increases with the cost of ransomware development C_D and then starts to decrease is attributed to the dynamic interplay between the increasing sophistication of the ransomware and the defender's strategic response. The observed relationship between C_D and attacker utility is further nuanced by the loss of the attacker for being arrested F. A lower value of F encourages a more risk-tolerant approach, contributing to the initial increase in attacker utility, while higher values of F may prompt risk-averse behavior, leading to a subsequent decrease. As C_D rises, the attacker may invest in more advanced ransomware, making it initially more potent and profitable. However, the defender's investment in deception techniques to bolster their cybersecurity defenses creates a threshold beyond which further increases in C_D yield diminishing returns for the attacker.

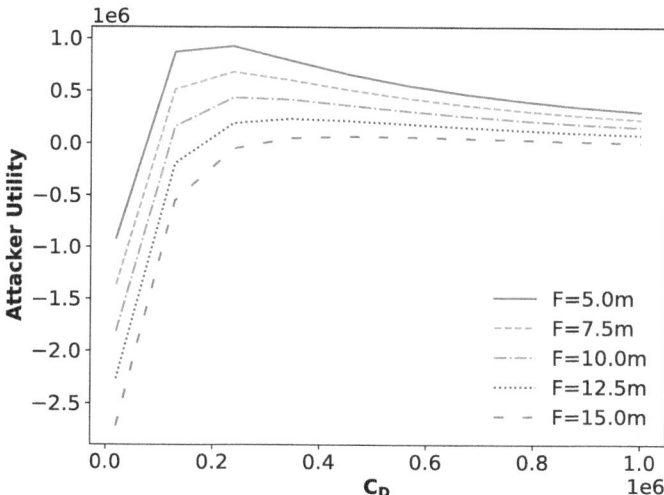

Fig. 4. Impact of attacker loss F and cost of ransomware development C_D on attacker utility.

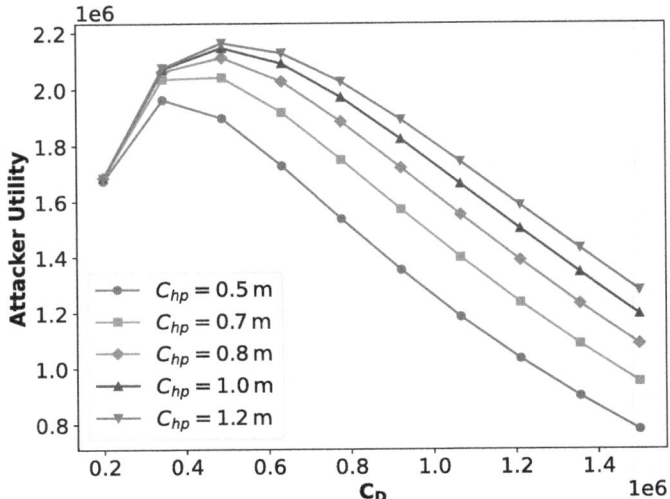

Fig. 5. Impact of cost of honeypot C_{hp} and cost of ransomware development C_D on attacker utility.

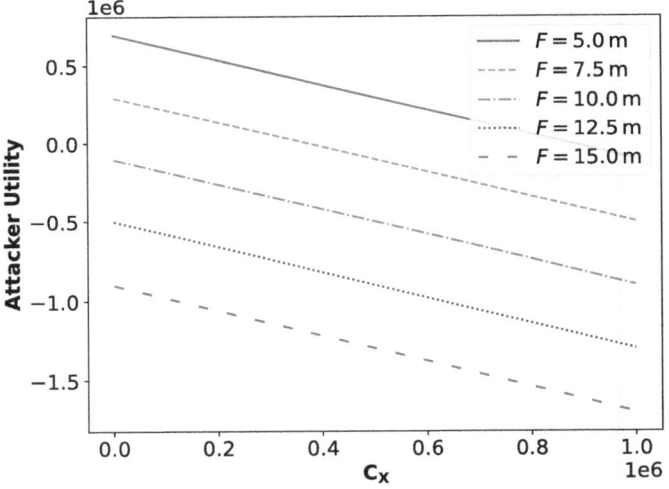

Fig. 6. Impact of cost of exfiltration C_x and attacker loss F on attacker utility.

In Fig. 5, the observed trend in the attacker's utility as C_D increases aligns with the anticipation of deception techniques. Until reaching a threshold, the attacker finds it increasingly cost-effective to develop ransomware. However, beyond this threshold, there is a diminishing return which leads to a linear decline in utility. The effectiveness of this strategy is influenced by C_{hp} with lower values making ransomware attacks more attractive early on, followed by a linear decrease in utility. This suggests that attackers strategically adapt to the evolving security landscape weighing the cost and benefits of different attack methods.

In Fig. 6, the linear decrease in attacker utility as C_x increases indicates a direct and proportional relationship between C_x and F. This trend suggests that the economic burden on the attacker rises linearly with the cost of exfiltration. The observed behavior is indicative of a deterrent effect, wherein higher exfiltration costs discourage attackers due to the linear impact on their overall utility.

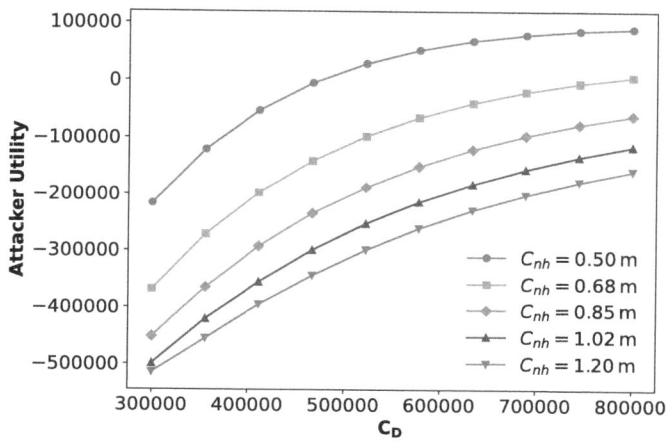

Fig. 7. Impact of cost of n/w honeypot C_{nh} and cost of ransomware development C_D on attacker utility.

In Fig. 7, the observed logarithmic increase in attacker utility with varying C_D for different values of C_{nh} suggests that the impact of increasing countermeasures may have diminishing returns for the attacker. At lower C_{nh}, the attacker finds it more profitable to invest in ransomware development which leads to a sharper increase in utility. However, for higher C_{nh}, the incremental gain in attacker utility diminishes. This reflects a balance between the defender's countermeasures and the attacker's risk tolerance.

The logarithmic curves observed in Fig. 8 and Fig. 9 indicate diminishing returns on defensive investments for different values of V_i. Both figures show that higher values of V_i lead to greater utility for the defender. Notably, the utility is consistently higher for the Cost of Network Honeypot Deployment C_{nh} compared to C_{hp} for equivalent V_i and investment in deception techniques. This implies that network honeypots are more effective in enhancing the defender's utility as they provide a stronger deterrence against attackers in the current game framework. The exponential relationship highlights the importance of optimizing resource allocation in ransomware attacks.

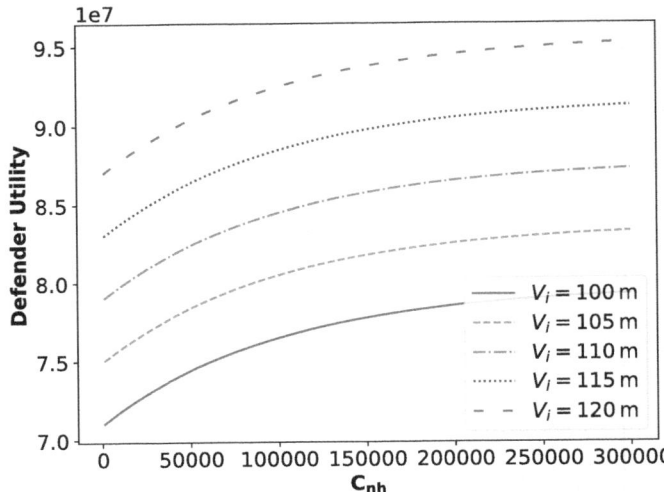

Fig. 8. Impact of cost of n/w honeypot C_{nh} and defender's value of data V_i on defender utility.

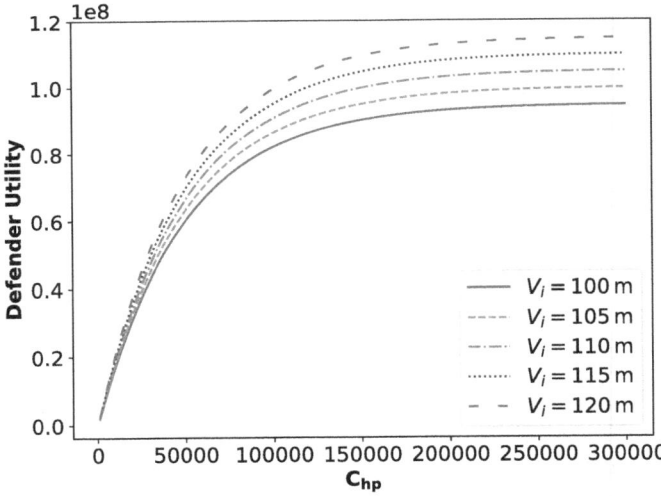

Fig. 9. Impact of cost of honeypot C_{hp} and defender's value of data V_i on defender utility.

Table 4. Parameters settings for comparing the game outcomes with and without the deception.

Fig.	T	C_D	F	C_x	V_i	V_p	R_i	V_i'	C_{ht}	n_{ht}	C_{hp}	C_{hf}	n_{hf}	C_{nh}	p_0	p_1	p_2	p_3
10	1 m	0.1 m	–	10000	112 m	10.93 m	–	4.38 m	0.05	0.67 m	0.08 m	0.08 m	0.5 m	0.08 m	0.06	0.15	0.18	0.2

6.2   Comparison with Ransomware Game Model in the Literature

We compare our numerical results and game performance to the one presented in [42] to show how use of cyber deception achieved by using deception techniques discussed in the paper can be beneficial. The compared paper presents a theoretical approach that uses parameters that are simulated. We considered various common parameters in the two different approaches to show the impact of deception. The parameter settings for the comparison are presented in Table 4. Looking at Fig. 10, a notable trend emerges in the attacker's utility during comparison where A is the utility from the compared paper, while B is from the current game context. The attacker's utility exhibits a slower rate of increase shown by dotted line that is attributed to heightened uncertainties stemming from deceptive elements. This discrepancy in the rate of increase is particularly evident as we plot against R. This observation leads us to conclude that the incorporation of deception techniques serves as an effective measure in shaping the strategic landscape of the adversarial game, offering the defender a valuable tool to influence and mitigate the attacker's utility growth over different scenarios.

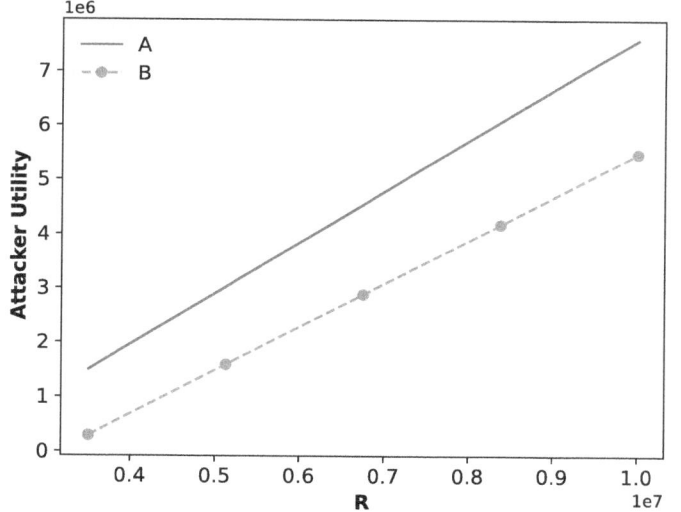

Fig. 10. Comparison of attacker utilities for ransomware amount R in A [42] and B (this work).

7   Conclusion and Future Work

In this paper, we presented a multi-stage ransomware game considering state-of-the-art deception strategies in the form of honey-x deployable to different stages of the ransomware attack. We evaluated Subgame-Perfect Nash Equilibrium (SPNE) for the game in closed form using backward induction principles and standard integer programming. We performed a numerical analysis of the developed game to evaluate the strategies given a realistic game model using real-world data and statistics relating to the healthcare industry. It is seen that the use of deception technologies is favorable to the defender towards thwarting cyber-criminals with higher chances of getting caught. Our findings pave the way for future research and practical applications to strengthen the resilience of critical systems against ransomware threats. This work portrays a complete game as a baseline which can be extended to an exploration of a non-deterministic/incomplete game model for the given problem. Furthermore, it can be extended to experimentation under consideration of more than one subsystem as discussed in the game model.

Acknowledgement. This material is based upon work supported by the National Science Foundation under award number CNS-2243619, and the National Security Agency under award number H98230-21-1-0260. Any opinions, findings, and conclusions or recommendations expressed in this publication are those of the author(s) and do not necessarily reflect the views of the National Science Foundation or the National Security Agency.

References

1. Canarytokens. https://canarytokens.org/generate. Accessed 16 Dec 2023
2. Deception-based Ransomware Defense. https://github.com/bhusalb/gt-ransomware-simulation. Accessed 20 May 2024
3. FBI Internet Crime Report 2022. https://www.ic3.gov/Media/PDF/Annual Report/2022_IC3Report.pdf. Accessed 20 May 2023
4. How Do Hackers Get Caught and Exposed?. https://www.metacompliance.com/blog/phishing-and-ransomware/how-do-hackers-normally-get-caught. Accessed 20 Jan 2024
5. IBM: Average Cost of a Healthcare Data Breach Increases to Almost $11 Million. https://www.hipaajournal.com/2023-cost-healthcare-data-breach/. Accessed 20 Jan 2024
6. Kippo. https://github.com/desaster/kippo. Accessed 16 Dec 2023
7. Ransomware: In the Healthcare Sector. https://www.cisecurity.org/insights/blog/ransomware-in-the-healthcare-sector. Accessed 20 Jan 2024
8. Spacesiren: A honeytoken manager. https://github.com/spacesiren/spacesiren. Accessed 16 Dec 2023
9. The Cost of Cybersecurity in Healthcare. https://www.cdw.com/content/cdw/en/articles/security/the-cost-of-cybersecurity-in-healthcare.html. Accessed 20 Jan 2024
10. The Latest 2023 Ransomware Statistics (2024). https://aag-it.com/the-latest-ransomware-statistics/. Accessed 20 Jan 2024
11. Aumann, R.J.: Backward induction and common knowledge of rationality. Games Econom. Behav. **8**(1), 6–19 (1995)
12. Bercovitch, M., Renford, M., Hasson, L., Shabtai, A., Rokach, L., Elovici, Y.: HoneyGen: an automated honeytokens generator. In: Proceedings of 2011 IEEE

International Conference on Intelligence and Security Informatics, pp. 131–136. IEEE (2011)

13. Cartwright, A., Cartwright, E.: The economics of ransomware attacks on integrated supply chain networks. Digit. Threats: Res. Pract. (2023)

14. Cartwright, E., Hernandez Castro, J., Cartwright, A.: To pay or not: game theoretic models of ransomware. J. Cybersecur. 5(1), tyz009 (2019)

15. Dameff, C., et al.: Ransomware attack associated with disruptions at adjacent emergency departments in the us. JAMA Netw. Open 6(5), e2312270–e2312270 (2023)

16. Feng, Y., Liu, C., Liu, B.: Poster: a new approach to detecting ransomware with deception. In: 38th IEEE symposium on security and privacy (2017)

17. Ganfure, G.O., Wu, C.F., Chang, Y.H., Shih, W.K.: RTrap: trapping and containing ransomware with machine learning. IEEE Trans. Inf. Forensics Secur. 18, 1433–1448 (2023)

18. Gómez-Hernández, J.A., Álvarez-González, L., García-Teodoro, P.: R-locker: thwarting ransomware action through a honeyfile-based approach. Comput. Secur. 73, 389–398 (2018)

19. Keijzer, N.: The new generation of ransomware: an in depth study of Ransomware-as-a-service. Master's thesis, University of Twente (2020)

20. Kolodenker, E., Koch, W., Stringhini, G., Egele, M.: PayBreak: defense against cryptographic ransomware. In: Proceedings of the 2017 ACM on Asia Conference on Computer and Communications Security, pp. 599–611 (2017)

21. Lapan, H.E., Sandler, T.: To bargain or not to bargain: that is the question. Am. Econ. Rev. 78(2), 16–21 (1988)

22. Li, Z., Liao, Q.: Game theory of data-selling ransomware. J. Cyber Secur. Mob. 65–96 (2021)

23. Liu, S., Chen, X.: Mitigating data exfiltration ransomware through advanced decoy file strategies (2023)

24. Min, D., Ko, Y., Walker, R., Lee, J., Kim, Y.: A content-based ransomware detection and backup solid-state drive for ransomware defense. IEEE Trans. Comput. Aided Des. Integr. Circuits Syst. 41(7), 2038–2051 (2021)

25. Mokube, I., Adams, M.: Honeypots: concepts, approaches, and challenges. In: Proceedings of the 45th Annual Southeast Regional Conference, pp. 321–326 (2007)

26. Mphago, B., Bagwasi, O., Phofuetsile, B., Hlomani, H.: Deception in dynamic web application honeypots: case of Glastopf. In: Proceedings of the International Conference on Security and Management (SAM). p. 104. The Steering Committee of The World Congress in Computer Science, Computer ... (2015)

27. Müter, M., Freiling, F., Holz, T., Matthews, J.: A generic toolkit for converting web applications into high-interaction honeypots. Univ. Mannheim 280, 6–1 (2008)

28. Patyal, M., Sampalli, S., Ye, Q., Rahman, M.: Multi-layered defense architecture against ransomware. Int. J. Bus. Cyber Secur. 1(2) (2017)

29. Qin, X., Jiang, F., Cen, M., Doss, R.: Hybrid cyber defense strategies using honey-x: a survey. Comput. Netw. 109776 (2023)

30. Reeder, J.R., Hall, C.T.: Cybersecurity's pearl harbor moment: lessons learned from the colonial pipeline ransomware attack (2021)

31. Săndescu, C., Rughiniş, R., Grigorescu, O.: HUNT: using honeytokens to understand and influence the execution of an attack. eLearn. Softw. Educ. 1 (2017)

32. Selten, R., Selten, R.: A Simple Game Model of Kidnapping. Springer, Heidelberg (1988)

33. Shaukat, S.K., Ribeiro, V.J.: RansomWall: a layered defense system against cryptographic ransomware attacks using machine learning. In: 2018 10th International Conference on Communication Systems & Networks (COMSNETS), pp. 356–363. IEEE (2018)

34. Sheen, S., Asmitha, K., Venkatesan, S.: R-sentry: deception based ransomware detection using file access patterns. Comput. Electr. Eng. **103**, 108346 (2022)

35. Spitzner, L.: Honeypots: Tracking Hackers, vol. 1. Addison-Wesley Reading (2003)

36. Subedi, K.P., Budhathoki, D.R., Chen, B., Dasgupta, D.: RDS3: ransomware defense strategy by using stealthily spare space. In: 2017 IEEE Symposium Series on Computational Intelligence (SSCI), pp. 1–8. IEEE (2017)

37. Tandon, A., Nayyar, A.: A comprehensive survey on ransomware attack: a growing havoc cyberthreat. In: Data Management, Analytics and Innovation: Proceedings of ICDMAI 2018, vol. 2, pp. 403–420 (2019)

38. Wang, Z., Wu, X., Liu, C., Liu, Q., Zhang, J.: RansomTracer: exploiting cyber deception for ransomware tracing. In: 2018 IEEE Third International Conference on Data Science in Cyberspace (DSC), pp. 227–234. IEEE (2018)

39. Wilson, D., Avery, J.: Mitigating data exfiltration in storage-as-a-service clouds. arXiv preprint arXiv:1606.08378 (2016)

40. Yin, T., Sarabi, A., Liu, M.: Deterrence, backup, or insurance: a game-theoretic analysis of ransomware. In: The Annual Workshop on the Economics of Information Security (WEIS) (2021)

41. Yuill, J., Zappe, M., Denning, D., Feer, F.: HoneyFiles: deceptive files for intrusion detection. In: 2004 Proceedings from the Fifth Annual IEEE SMC Information Assurance Workshop, pp. 116–122. IEEE (2004)

42. Zhang, C., Luo, F., Ranzi, G.: Multistage game theoretical approach for ransomware attack and defense. IEEE Trans. Serv. Comput. (2022)

43. Zhao, Y., Ge, Y., Zhu, Q.: Combating ransomware in internet of things: a games-in-games approach for cross-layer cyber defense and security investment. In: Bošanský, B., Gonzalez, C., Rass, S., Sinha, A. (eds.) GameSec 2021. LNCS, vol. 13061, pp. 208–228. Springer, Cham (2021). https://doi.org/10.1007/978-3-030-90370-1_12

A Decentralized Shotgun Approach for Team Deception

Caleb Probine$^{(\boxtimes)}$, Mustafa O. Karabag, and Ufuk Topcu

The University of Texas at Austin, Austin, USA
{cprobine,karabag,utopcu}@utexas.edu

Abstract. Deception is helpful for agents masking their intentions from an observer. We consider a team of agents deceiving their supervisor. The supervisor defines nominal behavior for the agents via reference policies, but the agents share an alternate task that they can only achieve by deviating from these references. As such, the agents use deceptive policies to complete the task while ensuring that their behaviors remain plausible to the supervisor. We propose a setting with centralized deceptive policy synthesis and decentralized execution. We model each agent with a Markov decision process and constrain the agents' deceptive policies so that, with high probability, at least one agent achieves the task. We then provide an algorithm to synthesize deceptive policies that ensure the deviations of all agents are small by minimizing the worst Kullback-Leibler divergence between any agent's deceptive and reference policies. Thanks to decentralization, this algorithm scales linearly with the number of agents and also facilitates the efficient synthesis of reference policies. We then explore a more general version of the deceptive policy synthesis problem. In particular, we consider a supervisor who selects a subset of agents to eliminate based on the agents' behaviors. We give algorithms to synthesize deceptive policies so that, after the supervisor eliminates some agents, the remaining agents complete the task with high probability. We demonstrate the developed methods in a package delivery example.

Keywords: Team deception · Markov decision processes · Centralized planning · decentralized execution

1 Introduction

In interactions with asymmetric information, agents can use deception to create an advantage against an opponent. Examples of applications where deception is useful include human-robot interaction [9] and intrusion or defense of cyber systems [13,15]. We consider a setting where a system manager assigns policies to the system's components so that they complete a task in a distributed manner. For example, one may assign decentralized policies to a team of aerial vehicles to complete a search task [2]. An adversary who gains control of the components, such as an external intruder, may change the components' policies to serve their own goals. However, the system manager may supervise the agents. As such, the

© The Author(s), under exclusive license to Springer Nature Switzerland AG 2025
A. Sinha et al. (Eds.): GameSec 2024, LNCS 14908, pp. 177–197, 2025.
https://doi.org/10.1007/978-3-031-74835-6_9

adversary must choose deceptive policies that deviate from assigned behavior in a plausible manner. Otherwise, the manager will detect the deviation.

We study the synthesis of deceptive policies for the components so that we may understand the weaknesses of these systems and improve their security. To be consistent with [18], we label components as agents and the manager as their supervisor. Figure 1 then shows the setup we consider. The supervisor first assigns reference policies to the agents. The agents then collude to find deceptive policies so that the agents complete a shared alternate task. The agents must choose deceptive policies so that, after the supervisor observes the agents' behavior, they do not detect the agents' deviations and eliminate them.

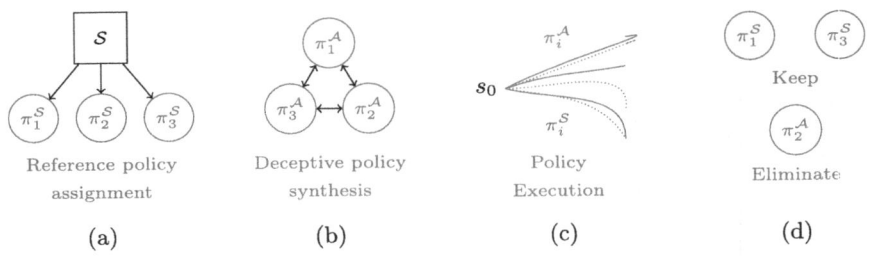

Reference policy assignment (a)   Deceptive policy synthesis (b)   Policy Execution (c)   Keep / Eliminate (d)

Fig. 1. a) Supervisor assigns reference policies. b) Agents decide on deceptive policies. c) Agents execute their policies in the environment. d) Supervisor eliminates a subset of agents based on observed behavior.

We model each agent with a Markov decision process (MDP), and we define success for the team as any agent reaching the goal in their MDP. In particular, certain states in each MDP represent the agents' shared reachability task. The agents' deceptive policies then must satisfy the constraint that, with high probability, at least one agent reaches a target state. For example, in a surveillance task, only one agent must deviate to obtain footage of a secure location.

The agents need centralized synthesis to complete their shared task with high probability, but we limit the agents to decentralized policies to improve the tractability of synthesis and remove the need for communication. The use of decentralized policies is a shotgun approach. Each agent follows a policy independently from the other agents and achieves the task with a small probability, but collectively, the agents achieve the task with high probability.

We use Kullback-Leibler (KL) divergence, as often used in security settings [3,16,22], to measure deviations between agent behavior and the reference policy. In stochastic environments, paths that achieve the agents' task may be feasible under the reference policy, but the likelihood of the paths informs the supervisor's belief about whether an agent is deceptive. The agents can make their paths plausible under the reference policy by ensuring KL divergence is small.

We study two versions of deceptive policy synthesis, which differ in how the agents avoid elimination and whether the agents use decoys. We first formulate deceptive policy synthesis as ensuring all agents' deviations are small.

In particular, we formulate *worst-case deceptive policy synthesis* as minimizing the worst KL divergence among all agents. We then explore settings in which, after the supervisor eliminates some agents, others may complete the task. By choosing policies carefully, one may allocate decoy agents, which the supervisor eliminates. In *elimination-aware deceptive policy synthesis*, we formulate the supervisor's elimination procedure and explore the synthesis of policies such that when the supervisor eliminates decoy agents, the remaining agents succeed.

We give efficient algorithms for each synthesis problem. The shotgun approach we take leads to a non-convex reachability constraint for these problems. However, we give an efficient method to find globally optimal solutions to *worst-case deceptive policy synthesis* via a sequence of convex optimization problems. We also discuss how the supervisor may use this algorithm to increase system security by improving their reference policies. We then explore restrictions to the supervisor's elimination procedure to make *elimination-aware deceptive policy synthesis* more tractable. We solve this problem by extending the algorithm provided for *worst-case deceptive policy synthesis* to allocate decoy agents

1.1   Related Work

We discuss several areas relevant to our work, including team deception, KL divergence in security, deception of observers, and decentralized MDPs.

Team Deception. Various disciplines study application-specific team deception. Examples include the clustering of deceivers in online games [37] or the use of decoy agents to aid a leader in misdirecting a multi-robot team [30]. In contrast to application-specific approaches, we explore the synthesis of deceptive policies for a team of agents represented by MDPs. Existing approaches for team deception include mean-field approaches [7] and reinforcement learning [12]. In contrast, we explore optimization-based approaches in a non-mean-field regime. Furthermore, these works focus on the problem of obscuring a task while we explore the concealment of the policy used to achieve a task. Prior work also explores secure multi-agent planning [14,27,34,38]. These works represent security with opacity-like formulations, where an observer must not be able to determine that the agents have visited some state. Finally, hidden role games are team games where agents are unaware of the team composition. Existing literature explores equilibrium computation [6] and learning-based approaches [1,33,35].

KL Divergence and Security. Most relevant to our setting is the synthesis of deceptive policies in MDPs using KL divergence [18]. Deceptive policy synthesis via KL divergence minimization admits a convex formulation with dimension polynomial in the MDP size. One may also formulate similar KL divergence minimization problems for partially observable agent dynamics [19], continuous dynamics [29], and stochastic games [20]. Our work contrasts [18,19,29] with the addition of multiple supervised agents. One could use the formulation in [18] to explore multi-agent settings, but the resulting implementation would be intractable for many agents and would require communication between agents.

The shotgun approach we use, with decentralized execution, is more tractable and does not need communication. More generally, KL divergence appears in analyzing attack detection [3,16,22]. For example, in the context of input replacement attacks in a linear system, KL divergence relates to an attack's stealthiness [3].

Deception of Observers. Various works explore formulating policies to mask agents' intent from observers in single-agent settings. Quantitative deception literature includes approaches based on minimizing KL divergence, i.e. expected log-likelihood ratio, [18,19,29], as well as constraining the probability of the log-likelihood ratio exceeding a threshold [25]. Meanwhile, in qualitative intention deception, an attacker ensures that observations generated by their behavior are consistent with observations generated by non-deceptive agents [11]. Again, in contrast to [11,25], we consider multiple observed agents. Deceptive path planning also involves an agent masking their intent from an adversary by finding paths that delay an observer's recognition of the agent's goal [10,26]. We consider a distinct problem from deceptive path planning, as in our setting, the agents obscure the decision-making process used to reach a state rather than the state itself. Finally, the likelihood ratio between the paths produced by hidden Markov models defines the form of probabilistic opacity considered in [21] for verification. This work is relevant to our work as we synthesize policies to control the log-likelihood ratio of observations produced by two Markov chains.

Centralized Planning and Decentralized Execution. Our work relates to decentralized execution approaches common in multi-agent learning and planning. For example, multi-agent reinforcement learning may use centralized learning with decentralized execution [24]. In planning, decentralized Markov decision processes (Dec-MDPs) are most relevant to our setting. Solving Dec-MDPs is NEXP-complete [5] in general and NP-complete with independent transitions [4]. However, some classes of Dec-MDPs, such as Dec-MDPs with additive rewards and shared additive resource constraints, have efficient solution methods [28]. Additionally, heuristic methods provide good solutions for chance-constrained problems with additive rewards [36]. We explore a chance-constrained problem where the reward has a maximum structure rather than an additive structure, and we show this maximum structure allows globally optimal policy synthesis.

2   Preliminaries

For n objects a_i indexed by $i = 1, \ldots, n$, the collection is $(a_i)_{i=1}^n$. The set $[n]$ contains the natural numbers $1, \ldots, n$. For probability distributions P_1, P_2 with a support $\mathcal{X}$, the KL divergence is $\mathrm{KL}(P_1 || P_2) = \sum_{x \in \mathcal{X}} P_1(x) \log \left(P_1(x)/P_2(x) \right)$.

Markov Decision Processes. A Markov decision process (MDP) $\mathcal{M}$ is a tuple (S, A, P, s_0) where S and A are state and action spaces, P is a transition function, and s_0 is an initial state. The set of actions available at state s is $A(s)$, and the probability of transitioning from state s to q with action a is $P(s, a, q)$. The set of successor states of s, $\text{Succ}(s)$, contains states q such that there exists an action $a \in A(s)$ with $P(s,a,q) > 0$. For an absorbing state, $\text{Succ}(s) = \{s\}$.

A stationary policy is a map $\pi : S \times A \to [0,1]$ such that $\sum_{a \in A(s)} \pi(s,a) = 1$ for all $s \in S$. For an MDP $\mathcal{M}$, $\Pi(\mathcal{M})$ is the set of stationary policies on $\mathcal{M}$. The Cartesian product of these sets for n MDPs is $\boldsymbol{\Pi}(\mathcal{M}_i) = \Pi(\mathcal{M}_1) \times \ldots \times \Pi(\mathcal{M}_n)$. Note that $\boldsymbol{\Pi}(\mathcal{M}_i)$ contains tuples of stationary policies, rather than policies on the joint state. A path in an MDP with policy π is a state-sequence $\xi = s_0 s_1 \ldots$ such that, for all t, $\sum_{a \in A(s_t)} P(s_t, a, s_{t+1}) \pi(s_t, a) > 0$. If each of n MDPs runs for m_r rounds, the j_{th} path of MDP $\mathcal{M}_i$ is $\xi_{i,j}$. The sequence of paths from $\mathcal{M}_i$ is $\boldsymbol{\xi}_i = (\xi_{i,j})_{j=1}^{m_r}$. A stationary policy π induces a distribution Γ^π on the paths of an MDP, and the KL divergence between policies π_1 and π_2 is $\text{KL}(\Gamma^{\pi_1} \| \Gamma^{\pi_2})$.

For an MDP and stationary policy, the occupancy measure of state-action pair (s,a) is $x_{s,a} = \sum_{t=0}^{\infty} \Pr(s_t = s | s_0) \pi(s,a)$, and is the expected number of visits to (s,a). By an abuse of notation, $x_{s,q} = \sum_{a \in A(s)} x_{s,a} P(s,a,q)$ is the occupancy flow from state s to q. Similarly, $\pi_{s,q} = \sum_{a \in A(s)} P(s,a,q) \pi(s,a)$ is the probability of transitioning from state s to q under policy π.

For a single agent, $\Pr(s_0 \models \Diamond R)$ is the probability of reaching set R with the agent's policy. For a set T of agents, with policies π_i, $\Pr(\exists i \in T : s_0^i \models \Diamond R_i)$ is the probability that at least one agent reaches set R_i in their MDP. We refer to this probability as the disjunctive reachability probability, and we remark that we may compute this probability from the agents' independent failure probabilities using $\Pr(\exists i \in T : s_0^i \models \Diamond R_i) = 1 - \prod_{i=1}^n (1 - \Pr(s_0^i \models \Diamond R_i))$.

3   Problem Formulation

We first discuss the problem setting and then formulate two synthesis problems.

For $i = 1, \ldots, n$, an MDP $\mathcal{M}_i$ governs agent i. The supervisor assigns each agent a stationary policy $\pi_i^{\mathcal{S}}$. The agents have a shared disjunctive reachability task, and they achieve this task if any agent reaches set $R_i^{\mathcal{A}} \subseteq S_i$ in $\mathcal{M}_i$. The agents choose policies $\pi_i^{\mathcal{A}}$ in a centralized manner such that $\Pr(\exists i \in [n] : s_0^i \models \Diamond R_i^{\mathcal{A}}) \geq \nu_{\mathcal{A}}$. We assume s is absorbing for all $s \in \bigcup_{i=1}^n R_i^{\mathcal{A}}$.

Running Example. We give an aerial package delivery example for ease of exposition in Fig. 2. Two agents navigate the state space $S = \{1, 2, 3, 4, *\}$ with actions r (right) and d (down). However, due to weather, the agent may not go in the commanded direction. Additionally, weather may force a landing at state $*$ when taking action r at state 2. A land action is also available, which

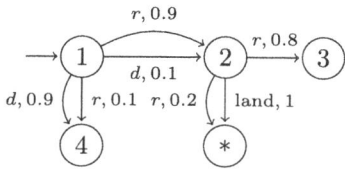

Fig. 2. An MDP for a package delivery example. Circles are states, and arrows are transitions. An arrow labeled $a, P(s,a,q)$, from state s to q, represents an action.

transitions the agent from state 2 to state $*$ with probability 1. Agent i's target is $R_i^{\mathcal{A}} = \{*\}$ for $i \in \{1, 2\}$.

3.1 Worst-Case Deceptive Policy Synthesis

To make the team deceptive, we ensure all agents have low deviation, and we quantify deviation with KL divergence using hypothesis testing arguments as in [18]. The log-likelihood test is the most powerful hypothesis test for a given significance level [8], and we assume the supervisor eliminates an agent i based on this test after observing their path in the state space. Although the paths are infinite, they terminate in some absorbing state, and we take a conservative approach by assuming the supervisor observes this whole path. For a null hypothesis that agent i is not deceptive, i.e. $\pi_i = \pi_i^{\mathcal{S}}$, and an alternative hypothesis that agent i is deceptive, i.e. $\pi_i = \pi_i^{\mathcal{A}}$, the KL divergence between $\pi_i^{\mathcal{A}}$ and $\pi_i^{\mathcal{S}}$ gives the expected log-likelihood ratio. A policy with a lower KL divergence then corresponds to a less detectable agent and a smaller deviation.

We define the optimal deceptive policies as minimizing the maximum KL divergence, thus ensuring that all agents have low deviation. We formulate the agents' problem as finding optimal policies subject to reachability constraints.

Problem 1 (*Worst-Case Deceptive Policy Synthesis*). Given MDP $\mathcal{M}_i$, reference policy $\pi_i^{\mathcal{S}}$, set $R_i^{\mathcal{A}}$ for each agent $i \in [n]$, and threshold $\nu_{\mathcal{A}} \geq 0$, solve

$$\inf_{(\pi_1^{\mathcal{A}},\ldots,\pi_n^{\mathcal{A}})\in\Pi(\mathcal{M}_i)} \max_{i\in[n]} \mathrm{KL}\left(\Gamma^{\pi_i^{\mathcal{A}}}||\Gamma^{\pi_i^{\mathcal{S}}}\right) \tag{1a}$$

$$\text{subject to} \qquad \Pr(\exists i \in [n] : s_0^i \models \Diamond R_i^{\mathcal{A}}) \geq \nu_{\mathcal{A}}. \tag{1b}$$

The shotgun approach we use, with decentralized policies and centralized planning, is beneficial as it leads to a scalable solution and does not need inter-agent communication. One may also consider both centralized policies and planning to make the deceptive team as a whole less detectable. One achieves this approach by using existing deceptive planning methods [18] on a joint MDP, with state and action space formed by products of individual state and action spaces. However, this approach has two issues. First, the approach does not scale, as the joint MDP grows exponentially with n. Also, centralized policies need communication during execution, which may be unavailable. We avoid these issues by using decentralized execution and centralized planning, as commonly used in multi-agent reinforcement learning [24]. Practically, a single party who knows the deceptive agents' identities finds the policies and transmits them to the agents.

Running Example (Continued). Consider reference policies given by $\pi_1^{\mathcal{S}}(1,r)$ $= \pi_1^{\mathcal{S}}(2,r) = \pi_2^{\mathcal{S}}(1,d) = \pi_2^{\mathcal{S}}(2,r) = 1$. Under these policies, $\Pr(s_0^1 \models \Diamond\{*\} \vee s_0^2 \models \Diamond\{*\}) = 0.2$. For $\nu_A = 0.5$, the agents must deviate to satisfy their specification. An example of a feasible deviation is $(\pi_1^{\mathcal{A}})(1,r) = (\pi_1^{\mathcal{A}})(2,\mathrm{land}) = 1$, and $\pi_2^{\mathcal{A}} = \pi_2^{\mathcal{S}}$. The combined probability of success is then 0.9.

3.2 Elimination-Aware Deceptive Policy Synthesis

We explore the synthesis of deceptive policies such that, after a supervisor eliminates some agents, the remaining agents complete the task with high probability.

In some settings, the supervisor eliminates a subset of agents after an observation period, and the agents may want to ensure that the remaining agents still achieve the task with high probability. Alternatively, an agent's success may be contingent on the supervisor not detecting that agent. To explore these settings, we model the supervisor's procedure for eliminating agents, and we introduce a parameter to measure the supervisor's elimination budget. We then define the agents' problem as maximizing the budget for which the remaining agents complete the task with high probability.

A Supervisor Elimination Procedure. For a prior $\Pr(i$ is Deceptive$) = p_{\mathcal{D},i}$, the supervisor computes belief $\theta_i(\boldsymbol{\xi}_i) = \Pr(i$ is Not Deceptive$|\boldsymbol{\xi}_i)$ using

$$\theta_i(\boldsymbol{\xi}_i) = 1 - \frac{p_{\mathcal{D},i}}{p_{\mathcal{D},i} + (1 - p_{\mathcal{D},i})\left(\Pr(\boldsymbol{\xi}_i|i \text{ is Not Deceptive})/\Pr(\boldsymbol{\xi}_i|i \text{ is Deceptive})\right)}. \tag{2}$$

As $\theta_i(\boldsymbol{\xi}_i)$ increases, the supervisor is more sure agent i is not deceptive.

We define the supervisor's procedure for eliminating agents as a subset selection problem with parameters based on $\theta_i(\boldsymbol{\xi}_i)$. The expected utility of agent i to the supervisor is $V_i\theta_i(\boldsymbol{\xi}_i)$, where V_i is a base utility. We then define the supervisor's budget for eliminating agents by an upper bound, C, on the total utility the supervisor may eliminate. Under this constraint, the supervisor maximizes the probability that at least one of the agents eliminated is deceptive, $\Pr(\exists i \in T : i$ is Deceptive$|\boldsymbol{\xi}_i)$. Assuming the supervisor treats the agents as independent, conditioned on paths, $\Pr(\exists i \in T : i$ is Deceptive$|\boldsymbol{\xi}_i) = 1 - \prod_{i \in T} \theta_i(\boldsymbol{\xi}_i)$. Maximizing $\Pr(\exists i \in T : i$ is Deceptive$|\boldsymbol{\xi}_i)$ is then equivalent to maximizing $\sum_{i \in T} - \log(\theta_i(\boldsymbol{\xi}_i))$, and the supervisor's elimination problem is

$$\max_T \quad \sum_{i \in T} - \log(\theta_i(\boldsymbol{\xi}_i)) \quad \text{subject to} \quad \sum_{i \in T} \theta_i(\boldsymbol{\xi}_i)V_i \leq C. \tag{3}$$

We denote the solution of (3) by $T = f(\theta_i(\boldsymbol{\xi}_i), C)$. The supervisor computes T once after observing m_r paths for the agents.

We remark that the independence assumptions affect the form of (3). The conditional independence assumption applies when the supervisor treats the agents' deceptiveness as independent, for example, when the deceptive agents, $1, \ldots, n$, are a subset of a larger agent pool that the supervisor observes.

Deceptive Policy Synthesis with Elimination. We define the agents' problem as synthesizing policies that maximize the value of C, such that the remaining agents, $[n] \setminus f(\theta_i(\boldsymbol{\xi}_i), C)$, complete the task with high probability.

Policies alone do not determine the subset T, as elimination depends on the state sequence produced during execution. As such, we define a belief proxy

$$\hat{\theta}_i(\pi) = 1 - \frac{p_{\mathcal{D},i}}{p_{\mathcal{D},i} + (1 - p_{\mathcal{D},i})e^{-m_r \cdot \text{KL}\left(\Gamma^\pi || \Gamma^{\pi_i^S}\right)}}. \tag{4}$$

Because of the relationship,

$$m_r \cdot \mathrm{KL} \left(\Gamma^\pi || \Gamma^{\pi^S} \right) = \mathbb{E} \left[\log(\Pr(\boldsymbol{\xi}|\pi)) - \log(\Pr(\boldsymbol{\xi}|\pi^S)) \right],$$

the belief proxy has the same form as the expectation $\mathbb{E}[\theta_i(\boldsymbol{\xi}_i)]$, with the expectation operator moved to the exponent in the denominator.

Using this proxy, we formulate the agents' problem as

Problem 2 (*Elimination-Aware Deceptive Policy Synthesis*). Given MDP $\mathcal{M}_i$, reference policy π_i^S, set R_i^A, prior $p_{\mathcal{D},i} \in (0,1)$, and base utility $V_i \geq 0$ for each agent $i \in [n]$, as well as threshold $\nu_A \geq 0$, and number of paths $m_r \in \mathbb{N}$, solve

$$\sup_{(\pi_1^A, \dots, \pi_n^A) \in \Pi(\mathcal{M}_i), C, T} C \tag{5a}$$

$$\text{subject to} \quad T = f(\hat{\theta}_i(\pi_i^A), C), \tag{5b}$$

$$\Pr(\exists i \in [n] \setminus T : s_0^i \models \Diamond R_i^A) \geq \nu_A. \tag{5c}$$

For $V_1 = \dots = V_n$, and fixed policies π_i^A, the supremum of the set of feasible values of C is the smallest amount of utility the supervisor must sacrifice such that the remaining agents no longer satisfy the reachability constraint.

Running Example (Continued). Consider policies formulated for Problem 1 such that constraint (1b) is tight. If $\hat{\theta}_i(\pi_i^A) = y$, and $V_i = 1$, for all $i \in [n]$, then for $C = y$, these policies are no longer feasible, as when the supervisor eliminates either agent, the task is no longer achieved with high probability. Alternatively, each agent may reach $*$ with probability ν_A at the cost of decreasing $\hat{\theta}_i(\pi_i^A)$. If $\hat{\theta}_i(\pi_i^A) = z$ for all $i \in [n]$, then the policies are feasible for any $C < 2z$, as the supervisor must eliminate both agents to violate the reachability constraint.

4   Worst-Case Deceptive Policy Synthesis

We provide a scalable algorithm to solve Problem 1 to global optimality by solving a sequence of convex optimization problems for each agent individually.

We first convert Problem 1 into a formulation based on occupancy measures to facilitate the reachability constraint (1b). This conversion follows a similar process to [18], which we detail in Sect. A.1 of the appendix. The reference policy π_i^S induces a set of transient states, $S_{d,i} \subseteq S_i$, on which π_i^A deviates from π_i^S. The states in $S_i \setminus S_{d,i}$ are closed, and the optimal deceptive policies do not deviate from π_i^S on $S_i \setminus S_{d,i}$. We optimize occupancy measures for $s \in S_{d,i}$, and the elements of vector $\mathbf{x}_i$ are occupancy measures x_{s^i,a^i} for the states $s^i \in S_{d,i}$.

We define the following functions to introduce the new formulation.

$$\mathrm{KL}(\mathbf{x}_i, \pi_i^S) = \sum_{s^i \in S_{d,i}} \sum_{q^i \in \mathrm{Succ}_i(s^i)} x_{s^i,q^i} \log \left(\frac{x_{s^i,q^i}}{\pi_{s^i,q^i}^S \sum_{a^{i'} \in A_i(s^i)} x_{s^i,a^{i'}}} \right). \tag{6}$$

$$F(\mathbf{x}_i, s^i) = \sum_{a^i \in A_i(s^i)} x_{s^i,a^i} - \sum_{q^i \in S_{d,i}} x_{q^i,s^i} - \mathbb{1}_{s_0^i}(s^i). \tag{7}$$

$$\nu(\mathbf{x}_i, R_i) = \sum_{q^i \in R_i} \sum_{s^i \in S_{d,i}} x_{s^i, q^i} + \mathbb{1}_{s_0^i}(q^i). \tag{8}$$

The KL divergence between path distributions is (6), and (6) holds due to the stationarity of the policies [18]. The net occupancy flow at state s^i is (7), and the reachability probability for a set R_i is (8).

We reformulate Problem 1 as the following optimization problem, where the decision variables are the agents' individual occupancy measures.

$$\inf_{(\mathbf{x}_1^{\mathcal{A}}, \ldots, \mathbf{x}_n^{\mathcal{A}})} \quad \max_{i \in [n]} \mathrm{KL}(\mathbf{x}_i^{\mathcal{A}}, \pi_i^{\mathcal{S}}) \tag{9a}$$

$$\text{subject to} \quad F(\mathbf{x}_i^{\mathcal{A}}, s) = 0, \quad \forall s \in S_{d,i}, \forall i \in [n], \tag{9b}$$

$$\prod_{i=1}^{n} (1 - \nu(\mathbf{x}_i^{\mathcal{A}}, R_i^{\mathcal{A}})) \leq 1 - \nu_{\mathcal{A}}, \tag{9c}$$

$$\mathbf{x}_i^{\mathcal{A}} \geq 0, \quad \forall i \in [n]. \tag{9d}$$

Proposition 1 shows the existence of a solution and the equivalence of (9) to Problem 1. We give the proof in Sect. A.1 of the appendix.

Proposition 1. *Problem 1 and the optimization problem (9) share the same optimal value, and there exist policies $(\pi_i^{\mathcal{A}})_{i=1}^n$ that attain the optimal value.*

We remark that (9c) is problematic as it induces non-convexity, and non-convex optimization problems may have sub-optimal local minima. However, Theorem 1 shows that non-convexity is not an issue for Problem 1.

Theorem 1. *Every local minimum of (9) is a global minimum.*

Theorem 1 holds as (9a) is the maximum of a finite set of convex functions, and the disjunctive reachability probability is a coordinate-wise monotone function. In fact, Theorem 1 and the following algorithm hold for any objective that is a maximum of convex functions of individual occupancy measures. For example, one may instead minimize the maximum required battery capacity for a fleet of drones. We prove Theorem 1 in Sect. A.2 of the appendix.

Algorithm 1 uses the maximum structure of (9a) to solve (9) via a series of reachability maximization problems. The reachability maximization problem for agent i, given KL divergence bound K, reference policy $\pi_i^{\mathcal{S}}$, and set $R_i^{\mathcal{A}}$, is

$$\sup_{\mathbf{x}_i^{\mathcal{A}}} \quad \nu(\mathbf{x}_i^{\mathcal{A}}, R_i^{\mathcal{A}}) \tag{10a}$$

$$\text{subject to} \quad \mathrm{KL}(\mathbf{x}_i^{\mathcal{A}}, \pi_i^{\mathcal{S}}) \leq K, \tag{10b}$$

$$F(\mathbf{x}_i^{\mathcal{A}}, s^i) = 0, \quad \forall s^i \in S_{d,i}, \tag{10c}$$

$$\mathbf{x}_i^{\mathcal{A}} \geq 0. \tag{10d}$$

We denote by $\mathrm{REACH}(\pi_i^{\mathcal{S}}, R_i^{\mathcal{A}}, K)$, the optimal value of (10), and we note that (10) is a convex optimization problem due to results in [18]. Algorithm 1 finds the minimum K such that the disjunctive reachability probability exceeds $\nu_{\mathcal{A}}$.

Algorithm 1. Line search applied for deceptive policy synthesis

---

1: **procedure** DECEPTIVESYNTHESIS$((\pi_i^{\mathcal{S}}, R_i^{\mathcal{A}})_{i=1}^n, \nu_{\mathcal{A}}, K_{\max}, \varepsilon)$
2:    $\overline{K} \leftarrow$ BISECTION(REACHEVALUATE$((\pi_i^{\mathcal{S}}, R_i^{\mathcal{A}})_{i=1}^n, \nu_{\mathcal{A}}, \cdot), [0, K_{\max}], \varepsilon)$
3: **end procedure**
4: **procedure** REACHEVALUATE$((\pi_i^{\mathcal{S}}, R_i^{\mathcal{A}})_{i=1}^n, \nu_{\mathcal{A}}, K)$
5:    $\nu \leftarrow 1 - \prod_{i=1}^n (1 - \text{REACH}(\pi_i^{\mathcal{S}}, R_i^{\mathcal{A}}, K))$
6:    **return** $\nu - \nu_{\mathcal{A}}$
7: **end procedure**

Algorithm 1 finds the smallest zero crossing of REACHEVALUATE. BISECTION successively computes intervals $[\underline{K}, \overline{K}]$ containing K^*, which is the smallest K such that REACHEVALUATE$((\pi_i^{\mathcal{S}}, R_i^{\mathcal{A}})_{i=1}^n, \nu_{\mathcal{A}}, K) \geq 0$. We can then use the final value of $\overline{K}$ with REACHEVALUATE to compute feasible policies. Note that BISECTION should not terminate when REACHEVALUATE is zero. Rather, we should continue decreasing $\overline{K}$ to ensure we find K^*.

Algorithm 1 requires $\mathcal{O}(\log_2(K_{\max}/\varepsilon))$ iterations each of which requires solving $\mathcal{O}(n)$ single-agent problems.

We next describe how to find $K_{\max}$, which upper-bounds the optimal value of (9). For each i, construct a new MDP, $\hat{\mathcal{M}}_i$, by removing actions that induce state transitions (s^i, q^i) with zero probability under $\pi_i^{\mathcal{S}}$. For each $\hat{\mathcal{M}}_i$, find policies $\pi_i^{\mathcal{A}}$ that maximize $\nu_i = \Pr(s_0^i \models \Diamond R_i^{\mathcal{A}})$. If $1 - \prod_{i=1}^n (1 - \nu_i) \geq \nu_{\mathcal{A}}$, then the maximum KL divergence among the policies bounds K^*. If the inequality does not hold, the agents must use state transitions with zero probability under $\pi_i^{\mathcal{S}}$.

As REACHEVALUATE is monotonic in K, Algorithm 1 converges to the optimal value of (9) for finite $K_{\max}$. We give a proof in Sect. A.2 of the appendix.

Theorem 2. *The value $\overline{K}$ computed by Algorithm 1 satisfies $\overline{K} < K^* + \varepsilon$, where K^* is the optimal solution of Problem 1.*

4.1 On Reference Policy Synthesis

The supervisor may preempt deceptive policy synthesis by choosing reference policies $\pi_i^{\mathcal{S}}$ that maximize the optimal value of Problem 1. Denoting Problem 1's optimal value by $g((\pi_i^{\mathcal{S}})_{i=1}^n)$, the supervisor's problem is

$$\sup_{(\pi_1^{\mathcal{S}}, \ldots, \pi_n^{\mathcal{S}}) \in \Pi(\mathcal{M}_i)} g((\pi_i^{\mathcal{S}})_{i=1}^n) \tag{11a}$$

$$\text{subject to} \quad \Pr(s_0^i \models \Diamond R_i^{\mathcal{S}}) \geq \nu_{\mathcal{S},i}, \quad \forall i \in [n]. \tag{11b}$$

In (11b), $R_i^{\mathcal{S}} \subseteq S_i$ is a task for each agent, and $\nu_{\mathcal{S},i}$ is a probability threshold.

While solving (11) in the single-agent case is NP-hard [18], [17] uses projected gradient-descent as a heuristic. Extending this approach to multiple agents is non-trivial. The disjunctive reachability constraint underlying g is non-convex, and this non-convexity makes taking projections in the agents' variables difficult.

However, Algorithm 1 facilitates first-order methods for (11). The gradient descent with max-oracle algorithm [23] may solve a $\max - \min$ problem by taking gradient steps in the outer variables and solving the inner problem at each iteration. In (11), the inner problem is deceptive policy synthesis, which we solve with Algorithm 1. Note that we must smooth $\max_i \mathrm{KL}(\mathbf{x}_i^{\mathcal{A}}, \pi_i^{\mathcal{S}})$ for differentiability.

5   Elimination-Aware Deceptive Policy Synthesis

We explore the synthesis of deceptive policies that ensure agents complete the reachability task, even when the supervisor eliminates some agents. We discuss the complexity of the supervisor's subset selection problem, as it appears in this synthesis problem, and we give restrictions that ease policy synthesis. We then extend the methods for *worst-case deceptive policy synthesis*, to solve Problem 2.

5.1   Discussion of Supervisor's Elimination Procedure

The supervisor's elimination procedure appears to lack sufficient structure to facilitate an efficient algorithm for deceptive policy synthesis. A tuple of weights, $(w_i)_{i=1}^n$, and profits, $(p_i)_{i=1}^n$, define a knapsack problem

$$\max_{T \subseteq [n]} \quad \sum_{i \in T} p_i \quad \text{subject to} \quad \sum_{i \in T} w_i \leq C, \tag{12a}$$

and the elimination procedure, (3), is an example with $p_i = -\log(\theta_i(\boldsymbol{\xi}_i))$, and $w_i = \theta_i(\boldsymbol{\xi}_i)V_i$. Proposition 2 indicates that the supervisor's elimination procedure is too general to permit an efficient algorithm for deceptive policy synthesis, as instances of the elimination procedure cover real-valued knapsack problems.

Proposition 2. *Let* $(w_i)_{i=1}^n$ *and* $(p_i)_{i=1}^n$ *be given arbitrary tuples of positive real weights and profits defining a knapsack problem. Then, there exists a tuple,* $(\pi_i^{\mathcal{S}}, \pi_i^{\mathcal{A}}, \mathcal{M}_i, \boldsymbol{\xi}_i, V_i, p_{\mathcal{D},i})_{i=1}^n$, *of reference policies, agent policies, MDPs, state paths, base utilities, and priors, such that* $w_i = \theta_i(\boldsymbol{\xi}_i)V_i$ *and* $p_i = -\log(\theta_i(\boldsymbol{\xi}_i))$.

Proof. Consider an MDP with $S = \{o, a, b\}$, $A = \{1, 2\}$, and $s_0 = o$. States a and b are absorbing, and $P(o, 1, a) = P(o, 2, b) = 1$. For all i, $\mathcal{M}_i = (S, A, P, s_0)$. For all i, fix paths as $\boldsymbol{\xi}_i = (o, a, a, a, \dots)$, and set $p_{\mathcal{D},i} = \kappa \in (0, 1)$. Note that $m_r = 1$. We now design policies $\pi_i^{\mathcal{A}}$ and $\pi_i^{\mathcal{S}}$. Likelihood ratios are given by

$$\frac{\Pr(\boldsymbol{\xi}_i | i \text{ is Not Deceptive})}{\Pr(\boldsymbol{\xi}_i | i \text{ is Deceptive})} = \frac{\pi_i^{\mathcal{S}}(o, 1)}{\pi_i^{\mathcal{A}}(o, 1)}, \tag{13}$$

and we set $\pi_i^{\mathcal{S}}(o,1)/\pi_i^{\mathcal{A}}(o,1) = e^{-p_i}\kappa/((1-e^{-p_i})(1-\kappa))$ so that

$$\theta_i(\boldsymbol{\xi}_i) = 1 - \frac{\kappa}{\kappa + (1 - \kappa)\left(\pi_i^{\mathcal{S}}(o,1)/\pi_i^{\mathcal{A}}(o,1)\right)} = \exp(-p_i). \tag{14}$$

As V_i is free, and $\theta_i(\boldsymbol{\xi}_i) > 0$, we set V_i such that $w_i = \theta_i(\boldsymbol{\xi}_i)V_i$. $\square$

In Problem 2, the function f, which represents the supervisor's procedure for eliminating agents, takes belief proxies $\hat{\theta}$ as input, rather than true beliefs θ. However, we may prove Proposition 2 for $\hat{\theta}$ as well. We simply control $e^{-\text{KL}_i}$ instead of $\pi_i^S(o,1)/\pi_i^A(o,1)$. It is easy to modify the policy pairs to set KL_i to any value in $[0, \infty)$, and $e^{-\text{KL}_i}$ to any value on $(0, 1]$. We then need to choose κ small enough so that $e^{-p_i}\kappa/((1-e^{-p_i})(1-\kappa)) \in (0, 1)$ for all $i \in [n]$.

Problem 2 is also a bi-level knapsack problem, with the agents as the leader and the supervisor as the follower, and the complexity of bi-level knapsack problems [31,32] reinforces the difficulty of Problem 2. For example, if a leader controls weights in a knapsack problem solved by a follower, and the leader gets rewards based on the items selected, the problem of finding the optimal weights is not approximable [31]. While Problem 2 is distinct in form from problems explored in [31,32], the hardness results further suggest the difficulty of Problem 2.

We restrict Problem 2 such that $V_1 = \ldots = V_n = 1$, leading to a simple solution for the supervisor's problem. With this restriction, the supervisor solves

$$\max_T \sum_{i \in T} -\log(\theta_i(\boldsymbol{\xi}_i)) \quad \text{subject to} \quad \sum_{i \in T} \theta_i(\boldsymbol{\xi}_i) \leq C, \tag{15}$$

to find a subset T of agents to eliminate, and we may construct the solution by adding agents to T in increasing order of $\theta_i(\boldsymbol{\xi}_i)$ until we violate the constraint in (15). The interpretation of $V_i = V_j$ is that agents i and j have the same expected utility to the supervisor if i and j are equally believed to be non-deceptive. If $V_i > V_j$, the supervisor may prefer to eliminate agent j even if $\theta_i(\boldsymbol{\xi}_i) < \theta_i(\boldsymbol{\xi}_j)$.

5.2 Synthesis of Optimal Deceptive Policies Under Elimination

We reformulate Problem 2 (*elimination-aware deceptive policy synthesis*) to apply the methods used for Problem 1.

We first replace f, which defines the eliminated agents, with constraints defining the optimal subset T. This replacement yields the optimization problem

$$\max_{(\pi_1^A, \ldots, \pi_n^A) \in \Pi(\mathcal{M}_i), T, C} C \tag{16a}$$

$$\text{subject to} \quad \hat{\theta}_i(\pi_i^A) < \hat{\theta}_j(\pi_j^A), \quad \forall i \in T, \forall j \in [n] \setminus T, \tag{16b}$$

$$\sum_{i \in T} \hat{\theta}_i(\pi_i^A) \leq C, \tag{16c}$$

$$\sum_{i \in T} \hat{\theta}_i(\pi_i^A) + \hat{\theta}_j(\pi_j^A) > C, \quad \forall j \in [n] \setminus T, \tag{16d}$$

$$\Pr(\exists i \in [n] \setminus T : s_0^i \models \Diamond R_i^A) \geq \nu_{\mathcal{A}}. \tag{16e}$$

As $V_1 = \ldots = V_n$, the set T contains the $|T|$ agents with the lowest values of $\hat{\theta}$, and constraint (16b) encodes this fact. Constraint (16c) then enforces the knapsack constraint from (15). Finally, constraint (16d) ensures that T is optimal, as if we add any agent to T, then we violate the constraint in (15). We note that (16b) restricts the set of feasible policies such that the agents in T and $[n] \setminus T$ may not have the same value of $\hat{\theta}$.

We may manipulate $\hat{\theta}$ to force the elimination of certain decoy agents first, and we simplify (16) by considering this interpretation of T as containing decoys. For fixed T and $\pi_i^{\mathcal{A}}$, $C = \sum_{i \in T} \hat{\theta}_i(\pi_i^{\mathcal{A}}) + \min_{i \in [n] \setminus T} \hat{\theta}_i(\pi_i^{\mathcal{A}}) - \delta$ is optimal, where we add $\delta \approx 0$ due to the strict inequality in (16d). This value of C corresponds to the supervisor eliminating all decoy agents $i \in T$ and almost having the budget to eliminate the non-decoy agent with the lowest belief, $\min_{i \in [n] \setminus T} \hat{\theta}_i(\pi_i^{\mathcal{A}})$. The decoys should also have maximum expected utility to the supervisor, subject to the constraint that their expected utility is lower than that of the non-decoy agents. As $V_1 = \ldots = V_n$, we may set $\pi_i^{\mathcal{A}}$ such that $\hat{\theta}_i(\pi_i^{\mathcal{A}}) = \gamma \min_{j \in [n] \setminus T} \hat{\theta}_j(\pi_j^{\mathcal{A}})$ for all $i \in T$. The scalar $\gamma \in (0, 1)$ accounts for the strict inequality in (16b).

Applying these equalities gives the optimization problem

$$\max_{(\pi_1^{\mathcal{A}}, \ldots, \pi_n^{\mathcal{A}}) \in \mathbf{\Pi}(\mathcal{M}_i), T, M} |T|(M \cdot \gamma) + M - \delta \tag{17a}$$

$$\text{subject to} \quad \Pr(\exists i \in [n] \setminus T : s_0^i \models \Diamond R_i^{\mathcal{A}}) \geq \nu_{\mathcal{A}}, \tag{17b}$$

$$\hat{\theta}_i(\pi_i^{\mathcal{A}}) \geq M, \quad \forall i \in [n] \setminus T, \tag{17c}$$

$$\hat{\theta}_i(\pi_i^{\mathcal{A}}) = M \cdot \gamma, \quad \forall i \in T. \tag{17d}$$

To solve (17), we sweep the size of T, and for each $|T| = k$, we optimize the decoy assignment and agent policies to maximize $\min_{i \in [n] \setminus T} \hat{\theta}_i(\pi_i^{\mathcal{A}})$.

For fixed $|T|$, we reformulate (17) by substituting KL divergence for belief proxies so that we may apply a similar line search procedure to Algorithm 1. Assuming $p_{\mathcal{D},1} = \ldots = p_{\mathcal{D},n}$, rearranging the definition of the belief proxy yields

$$\hat{\theta}_i(\pi_i^{\mathcal{A}}) > \hat{\theta}_j(\pi_j^{\mathcal{A}}) \text{ if and only if } \mathrm{KL}\left(\Gamma^{\pi_i^{\mathcal{A}}} || \Gamma^{\pi_i^{\mathcal{S}}}\right) < \mathrm{KL}\left(\Gamma^{\pi_j^{\mathcal{A}}} || \Gamma^{\pi_j^{\mathcal{S}}}\right). \tag{18}$$

As such, we may equivalently minimize the maximum KL divergence among the $n - k$ agents in $[n] \setminus T$, which yields

$$\min_{(\pi_1^{\mathcal{A}}, \ldots, \pi_n^{\mathcal{A}}) \in \mathbf{\Pi}(\mathcal{M}_i), T} \max_{i \in [n] \setminus T} \mathrm{KL}\left(\Gamma^{\pi_i^{\mathcal{A}}} || \Gamma^{\pi_i^{\mathcal{S}}}\right) \tag{19a}$$

$$\text{subject to} \quad \mathrm{KL}\left(\Gamma^{\pi_i^{\mathcal{A}}} || \Gamma^{\pi_i^{\mathcal{S}}}\right) = K \cdot \gamma', \quad \forall i \in T, \tag{19b}$$

$$\Pr(\exists i \in [n] \setminus T : s_0^i \models \Diamond R_i^{\mathcal{A}}) \geq \nu_{\mathcal{A}}, \tag{19c}$$

$$|T| = k. \tag{19d}$$

We replace tolerances γ in $\hat{\theta}_i(\pi_i^{\mathcal{A}})$ with tolerances in KL divergence $\gamma' \in (\bar{\cdot}, \infty)$. Tuning γ' controls how much more decoys deviate compared to non-decoys. We remark that while the non-linear equality constraint (19b) appears difficult to satisfy, we can find the required policy with convex combinations in the policy space between $\pi_i^{\mathcal{S}}$ and a policy π_i with KL divergence greater than $K \cdot \gamma'$.

Algorithm 2 combines a modified version of the line search procedure from Algorithm 1 with a sweep across subset sizes to solve (19). We modify

REACHEVALUATE by computing the disjunctive reachability using the $n - k$ agents that have maximum reachability probability. These $n - k$ agents are non-decoy agents.

Algorithm 2. Elimination-aware deceptive policy synthesis

1: **procedure** DECEPTIVESUBSETSELECTION($(\pi_i^S, R_i^A)_{i=1}^n, \nu_A, K_{\max}, \varepsilon, p, \gamma', m_r$)
2:    **for** $k = 0, \ldots, n - 1$ **do**
3:        $B_k \leftarrow 0$ ▷ Assume initially that k decoys are not feasible
4:        $K, Fail_k \leftarrow$ SUBSETSEARCH($(\pi_i^S, \Diamond R_i^A)_{i=1}^n, \nu_A, K_{\max}, \varepsilon, n - k$)
5:        **if** $\neg Fail_k$ **then**
6:            $M' \leftarrow 1 - \frac{p}{p+(1-p)e^{-m_r K \gamma'}}, M \leftarrow 1 - \frac{p}{p+(1-p)e^{-m_r K}} K, B_k \leftarrow k \cdot M' + M$
7:        **end if**
8:    **end for**
9:    $k^* \leftarrow \arg\max B_k$
10: **end procedure**
11: **procedure** SUBSETSEARCH($(\pi_i^S, R_i^A)_{i=1}^n, \nu_A, K_{\max}, \varepsilon, w$)
12:    $\overline{K} \leftarrow$ BISECTION(REACHEVALUATESUB($(\pi_i^S, R_i^A)_{i=1}^n, \nu_A, \cdot, w$), $[0, K_{\max}]$)
13:    $\nu - \nu_A \leftarrow$ REACHEVALUATESUB($(\pi_i^S, R_i^A)_{i=1}^n, \nu_A, \overline{K}, w$)
14:    **return** $\overline{K}, (\nu - \nu_A < 0)$ ▷ Validate whether the final policy satisfies reach.
15: **end procedure**
16: **procedure** REACHEVALUATESUB($(\pi_i^S, R_i^A)_{i=1}^n, \nu_A, K, w$)
17:    $\nu_i \leftarrow$ REACH(π_i^S, R_i^A, K), $\forall i \in [n]$
18:    $\mathcal{N} \leftarrow$ BESTKELEMENTS($w, \{\nu_i\}$)   ▷ Get indices of w highest ν_i values
19:    $\nu \leftarrow 1 - \prod_{i \in \mathcal{N}} (1 - \nu_i)$
20:    **return** $\nu - \nu_A$
21: **end procedure**

We again give a method to set $K_{\max}$. Compute $K'_{\max}$ using the process given in Sect. 4 for Algorithm 1, and compute B_0 using $K = K'_{\max}$ in Line 6. This B_0 value lower-bounds the optimal value of (17). Then, compute $K_{\max}$ as the value such that, using $K = K_{\max}$ in Line 6, $B_{n-1} = B_0$. For $|T| = n - 1$, if the non-decoy agents have KL divergence above $K_{\max}$, the solution is worse than the solution for $|T| = 0$ with KL divergence of $K'_{\max}$. In fact, for any k, the solution is sub-optimal if the non-decoy agents' KL divergence exceeds $K_{\max}$. The $Fail_k$ flag is set if no solution exists with KL divergence below $K_{\max}$ for $|T| = k$.

We also assume that, for all $i \in [n]$, we may synthesize policies π_i^* with KL divergence value higher than the optimal value of (19), but we can also use Algorithm 2 without this assumption. We need this assumption so that any agent i may be a decoy. Without this assumption, we modify Line 18. If K is above the maximum KL divergence that agent i may attain, then i can not be a decoy, and we include i in $\mathcal{N}$ before adding agents to $\mathcal{N}$ based on their reachability.

6   Numerical Results

We illustrate deceptive policy synthesis in a delivery example, where weather-induced stochasticity provides plausible deniability for deceptive agents. A super-

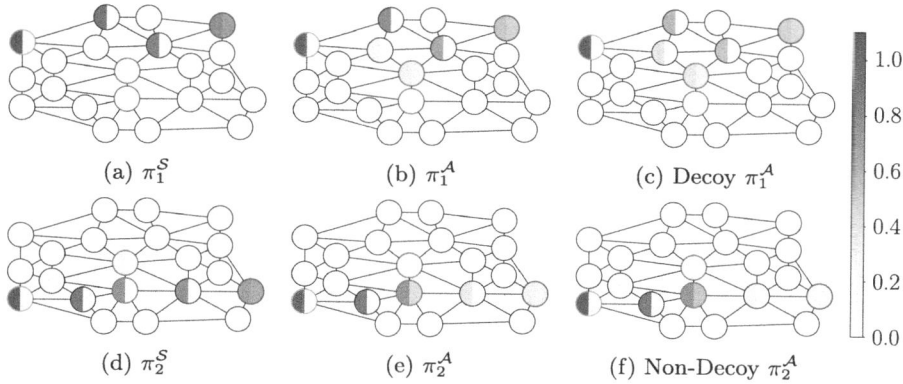

$$\text{(a) } \pi_1^S \qquad \text{(b) } \pi_1^A \qquad \text{(c) Decoy } \pi_1^A$$

$$\text{(d) } \pi_2^S \qquad \text{(e) } \pi_2^A \qquad \text{(f) Non-Decoy } \pi_2^A$$

Fig. 3. Package delivery example policies. The left color of node v is the occupancy measure of state $(v,0)$. The right color of a node v is the occupancy flow into state $(v,1)$, which is equal to $\Pr(s_0^i \models \Diamond\{(v,1)\})$. Nodes with green, red, and orange borders are supervisor target nodes, agent target nodes, and initial states, respectively. (a) and (d) are reference policies. (b) and (e) are deceptive policies for no decoys, and are policies synthesized by Algorithm 1. (c) and (f) show policies synthesized by Algorithm 2 for one decoy agent with $\gamma' = 1.2$.

visor specifies π_i^S for n drones so that each drone delivers a package to some target. However, an external intruder with access to the drones must ensure that, with high probability, at least one drone delivers a package to their location.

We define the drones' MDPs and targets via an undirected graph $G = (V, E)$, where V contains regions, and E contains connections between regions. The state space is $V \times \{0, 1\}$, where a drone in state $(v, 0)$ is in flight in v, and a drone in state $(v, 1)$ has landed in v. Given $N \subseteq V$, the agents' target states, for each $i \in [n]$, are $R_i^A = \{(v, 1) | v \in N\}$. For each $i \in [n]$, the supervisor's target state is $(n_i, 1)$ for some $n_i \in V$. All landed states are absorbing.

The actions available to a drone at state $(v, 0)$ are moving on the graph or landing. If a drone uses action a_u, for node u adjacent to v, the drone will transition to $(u, 0)$ with probability p_{target}. However, due to weather, the drone may transition to $(v, 1)$ with probability p_{land}, or to an adjacent flight node $w \neq u$, with probability $(1-p_{land}-p_{target})/(|\mathrm{adj}(v)|-1)$. The set of nodes adjacent to v is $\mathrm{adj}(v)$. When the drone takes a landing action at state $(v, 0)$, the drone will transition to $(v, 1)$ with probability $p_{target} + p_{land}$ and will transition to an adjacent flight state $(u, 0)$ with probability $(1-p_{target}-p_{land})/|\mathrm{adj}(v)|$.

We specify reference policies such that the agent i moves along the shortest path in the graph G toward the target node n_i.

6.1 Worst-Case Deceptive Policy Synthesis and Reference Policy Synthesis

The first two columns of Fig. 3 show *worst-case deceptive policy synthesis* for $n = 2$ and $\nu_A = 0.6$, and we observe that the relative reachability probabilities

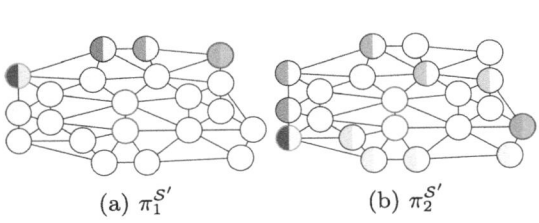

(a) $\pi_1^{S'}$ (b) $\pi_2^{S'}$

Fig. 4. Synthesis of reference policies using gradient-ascent with max oracle with Algorithm 1 used to solve the inner problem.

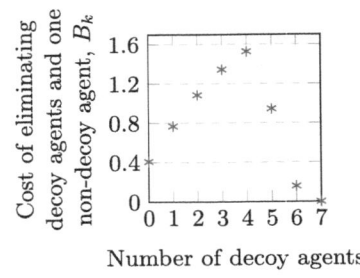

Fig. 5. Values of B_k with $n = 8$.

for the agents match how suited their reference policies are to the task. Under π_2^S, agent 2 already reaches $N \times \{1\}$ with probability 0.09, as opposed to 0.009 for agent 1, and so agent 2 needs to deviate less to achieve higher reachability for the same KL divergence budget. As such, under deceptive policies, agents 1 and 2 reach the target states with probabilities 0.23, and 0.48, respectively.

Figure 4 shows the reference policies we obtain by using Algorithm 1 as a subroutine in the gradient ascent with max-oracle algorithm [23]. As expected, this approach creates reference policies that avoid the agents' target states.

6.2   Elimination-Aware Deceptive Policy Synthesis

Figures 3c and 3f show deceptive policies synthesized with one decoy, and we see that Algorithm 2 allocates agent 1 as the decoy as agent 1 is less capable of completing the task under π_1^S.

We also consider an instance of the package delivery example with $n = 8$ to demonstrate the trade-off between redundancy and detectability that arises when using decoys. In this example, the supervisor assigns π_1^S in Fig. 3 to four agents and π_2^S to the other agents. We show the results in Fig. 5. With no decoys, each agent needs a small reachability probability and has a low KL divergence, but the supervisor only needs to eliminate one agent for the reachability probability to drop below 0.6. Meanwhile, with seven decoys, all agents have large deviations, so the supervisor sacrifices little utility by eliminating all of the agents. A mix of decoy and non-decoy agents maximizes the utility the supervisor must sacrifice so that the remaining agents complete the task with a probability below 0.6.

7   Conclusion

Building secure multi-agent systems requires system designers to consider team deception. We explored the synthesis of deceptive policies for agents who deceive their supervisor by deviating from assigned reference behavior. We formulated the agents' problem as finding decentralized policies that minimize the KL divergence between the agents' behavior and the reference while ensuring that, with high probability, at least one agent reaches a target. While the formulation led to a non-convex optimization problem, we provided a scalable method to synthesize optimal policies. We then demonstrated how a supervisor may use this method to improve the security of reference policies. We also analyzed an extension of the problem where agents synthesize policies to ensure that after the supervisor eliminates some agents, the remaining agents complete the task. This problem is difficult as the agents must reason about the subset selection procedure the supervisor uses to eliminate agents. However, we explored a restriction to make the problem tractable and gave an algorithm for choosing deceptive policies that control the order in which the supervisor eliminates agents.

In this work, we explored disjunctive reachability, and we minimized the maximum deviation among the agents. Future work will explore different couplings of the agents through their objectives and different measures of the team's detectability.

Acknowledgments. This work was supported partially by the Army Research Laboratory (ARL), under grant number W911NF-23-1-0317, partially by the Defence Advanced Research Projects Agency (DARPA), under grant number HR001123S0001, and partially by the Office of Naval Research (ONR), under grant number N000142412432.

Disclosure of Interests. The authors have no competing interests.

A   Appendix

A.1   Sufficiency of Occupancy Measure Formulation

We show the sufficiency of occupancy measure-based formulations for Problem 1, following [18]. We require finiteness of the optimal value of Problem 1 for the following results, but we may check this finiteness by finding $K_{\max}$ with the method we describe in Sect. 4.

We first recall the state-space decomposition from [18]. Let C_i^{cl} be the union of the closed communicating classes of the Markov chain induced by $(\mathcal{M}_i, \pi_i^S)$. With one agent, the agent should follow π_i^S for all $s \in C_i^{cl}$ so that the policy does not have infinite KL divergence [18]. The agent should also follow π_i^S on $R_i^{\mathcal{A}}$. These properties hold for Problem 1 as well, and set $S_{d,i} = S_i \setminus (C_i^{cl} \cup R_i^{\mathcal{A}})$ contains states on which we modify $\pi_i^{\mathcal{A}}$ from π_i^S.

We now restate a result from [18] on the finiteness of occupancy measure. Let Problem 1a be the case of Problem 1 with a single-agent.

Proposition 3 [18]. *If Problem 1a has finite optimal value, with optimal policy $\pi^{\mathcal{A}}$, the state-action occupancy measure $x_{s,a}$ is finite for all $s \in S_d$ and $a \in A(s)$.*

This result extends to Problem 1. Let Problem 1 have finite optimal value, with optimal policies $\pi_i^{\mathcal{A}}$, and define ν_i as $\Pr(s_0^i \models \Diamond R_i^{\mathcal{A}})$ under $\pi_i^{\mathcal{A}}$. Define P1i as the single-agent problem of minimizing the KL divergence of i with probability threshold $\nu'_{\mathcal{A}} = \nu_i$. By construction, $\pi_i^{\mathcal{A}}$ is feasible for P1i, and its KL divergence is finite. Proposition 3 then implies that solution $\pi_i^{\mathcal{A}*}$ to P1i has finite occupancy measure on $S_{d,i}$. As $\pi_i^{\mathcal{A}*}$ is optimal, it also has lower KL divergence than $\pi_i^{\mathcal{A}}$. As such, for each agent $i \in [n]$, we replace $\pi_i^{\mathcal{A}}$ with $\pi_i^{\mathcal{A}*}$, to construct an optimal solution to Problem 1 comprised of policies with finite occupancy measure.

The following result also trivially extends to the problem we explore due to the decentralized approach we take.

Proposition 4 [18]. *For any policy $\pi^{\mathcal{A}}$ that satisfies $\Pr(s_0 \models R^{\mathcal{A}}) \geq \nu_{\mathcal{A}}$, there exists a stationary policy $\pi^{\mathcal{A},St} \in \Pi(\mathcal{M})$ that satisfies $\Pr(s_0 \models R^{\mathcal{A}}) \geq \nu_{\mathcal{A}}$ and*

$$KL\left(\Gamma^{\pi^{\mathcal{A},St}} || \Gamma^{\pi^{S}}\right) \leq KL\left(\Gamma^{\pi^{\mathcal{A}}} || \Gamma^{\pi^{S}}\right). \tag{20}$$

Proof of Proposition 1. This proposition follows from the proof of the equivalence of Problem 1 and (9) in the single-agent case, given in [18].

The extensions of Propositions 3 and 4 to multiple agents justify the restriction to stationary policies with finite occupancy measures for Problem 1.

Regarding the existence of a policy that attains the optimal value of (9), the only comment that needs to be made to extend the proof in [18], is that the objective $\max_{i \in [n]} KL(\mathbf{x}_i, \pi_i^{S})$ remains continuous in $\mathbf{x}_i$. $\square$

A.2   Optimality and Algorithms for Problem 1

Proof of Theorem 1. We show that any strictly sub-optimal point is not a local minimum. Let $(\mathbf{x}_i)_{i=1}^{n}$ be strictly sub-optimal, and let $(\mathbf{x}_i^*)_{i=1}^{n}$ be globally optimal. Let $\nu_i = \nu(\mathbf{x}_i, R_i^{\mathcal{A}})$, $\nu_i^* = \nu(\mathbf{x}_i^*, R_i^{\mathcal{A}})$, and $K_i(\mathbf{x}) = KL(\mathbf{x}, \pi_i^{S})$.

Case 1. Assume constraint (9c) is not tight. Define new occupancy measures through the convex combination $\mathbf{x}_i' = \mathbf{x}_i + \theta(\mathbf{x}_i^* - \mathbf{x}_i)$ for all $i \in [n]$. Constraints (9b) and (9d) define convex sets, and so they will hold for $\mathbf{x}_i'$. The left hand side of (9c) is continuous in $\mathbf{x}$, and constraint (9c) is not tight, so for sufficiently small $\theta > 0$ we have $\prod_{i=1}^{n}(1 - \nu(\mathbf{x}_i', R_i^{\mathcal{A}})) \leq 1 - \nu_{\mathcal{A}}$. Also, as $(\mathbf{x}_i)_{i=1}^{n}$ is strictly sub-optimal, we have that $\max_i K_i(\mathbf{x}_i) > \max_i K_i(\mathbf{x}_i^*)$, and hence $\max_i K_i(\mathbf{x}_i) > \max_i K_i(\mathbf{x}_i')$ for $\theta > 0$. By the above observations, we may generate feasible $(\mathbf{x}_i')_{i=1}^{n}$ arbitrarily close to $(\mathbf{x}_i)_{i=1}^{n}$ with strictly lower objective value, which demonstrates that $(\mathbf{x}_i)_{i=1}^{n}$ cannot be a local minimum.

Case 2. Now, allow constraint (9c) to hold with equality such that $\prod_{i=1}^{n}(1-\nu_i) = 1-\nu_{\mathcal{A}}$. As $(\mathbf{x}_i^*)_{i=1}^{n}$ is feasible we have $\prod_{i=1}^{n}(1-\nu_i) \geq \prod_{i=1}^{n}(1-\nu_i^*)$. If $\nu_i = \nu_i^*$ for all $i \in [n]$, then convex combinations of $(\mathbf{x}_i)_{i=1}^{n}$ and $(\mathbf{x}_i^*)_{i=1}^{n}$ remain feasible, and by the arguments of *Case 1*, $(\mathbf{x}_i)_{i=1}^{n}$ is strictly sub-optimal. If there exists $i \in [n]$ such that $\nu_i \neq \nu_i^*$, then there exists j such that $\nu_j < \nu_j^*$. In this case, we first construct intermediate occupancy measures by defining $\mathbf{x}_j' = \theta\mathbf{x}_j + (1-\theta)\mathbf{x}_j^*$ for some $\theta > 0$, and $\mathbf{x}_i' = \mathbf{x}_i$ for all $i \neq j$. By convexity of KL in the occupancy measure, we then have that $K_j(\mathbf{x}_j') \leq \max(K_j(\mathbf{x}_j), K_j(\mathbf{x}_j^*)) \leq \max_i K_i(\mathbf{x}_i)$ and as such, $\max_i K_i(\mathbf{x}_i') \leq \max_i K_i(\mathbf{x}_i)$. For $\theta > 0$, this construction produces point $\mathbf{x}'$ that satisfies reachability strictly. We can then appeal to *Case 1* to produce point $\mathbf{x}''$ close to $\mathbf{x}'$ with a strictly lower value of the objective function. Point $\mathbf{x}'$ can also be made arbitrarily close to $\mathbf{x}$. As such, we may make point $\mathbf{x}''$, satisfying $\max_i K_i(\mathbf{x}_i'') < \max_i K_i(\mathbf{x}_i') \leq \max_i K_i(\mathbf{x}_i)$, arbitrarily close to $\mathbf{x}$, which implies that $\mathbf{x}$ cannot be a local minimum. $\qquad\square$

Proof of Theorem 2. Let $\nu_\Delta(K) = \text{REACHEVALUATE}((\pi_i^S, R_i^A)_{i=1}^n, \nu_A, K)$. We first note that $K_1 < K_2$ implies $\text{REACH}(\pi_i^S, R_i^A, K_1) \leq \text{REACH}(\pi_i^S, R_i^A, K_2)$ for all $i \in [n]$, which implies ν_Δ is increasing. This inequality holds as the latter REACH problem is a relaxation of the former for all $i \in [n]$.

We now discuss the initial values of $\overline{K}$ and $\underline{K}$, which are $K_{\max}$ and 0 respectively. As $K_{\max}$ is a bound on the optimal value, $\nu_\Delta(K_{\max}) \geq 0$. If $\nu_\Delta(0) \geq 0$, it is optimal to use $\pi_i^A = \pi_i^S$ for all i. As such, we may assume $\nu_\Delta(0) < 0$.

Consider the final values $\overline{K}_t$ and $\underline{K}_t$. At each bisection iteration we compute $K = (\underline{K} + \overline{K})/2$. If $\nu_\Delta(K) < 0$, we then set $\underline{K} = K$, or if $\nu_\Delta(K) \geq 0$, we set $\overline{K} = K$. By the BISECTION definition, and the fact that $\nu_\Delta(0) < 0$, we have $\nu_\Delta(\underline{K}_t) < 0$. Using monotonicity of ν_Δ, we then conclude that there do not exist feasible policies that satisfy $\max_i KL(\mathbf{x}_i, \pi_i^S) < \underline{K}_t$, and so, $K^* \geq \underline{K}_t$. Again, by the BISECTION definition and the fact that $\nu_\Delta(K_{\max}) \geq 0$, we have $\nu_\Delta(\overline{K}_t) \geq 0$ and we may observe that $K^* \leq \overline{K}_t$. At termination, we have $\overline{K}_t \leq \underline{K}_t + \varepsilon$, as ε is the tolerance. We finally conclude $K^* \leq \overline{K}_t \leq \underline{K}_t + \varepsilon \leq K^* + \varepsilon$. $\qquad\square$

References

1. Aitchison, M., Benke, L., Sweetser, P.: Learning to deceive in multi-agent hidden role games. In: Sarkadi, S., Wright, B., Masters, P., McBurney, P. (eds.) DeceptE-CAI/DeceptAI 2020-2021. CCIS, vol. 1296, pp. 55–75. Springer, Cham (2021). https://doi.org/10.1007/978-3-030-91779-1_5
2. Bähnemann, R., Schindler, D., Kamel, M., Siegwart, R., Nieto, J.: A decentralized multi-agent unmanned aerial system to search, pick up, and relocate objects. In: IEEE International Symposium on Safety, Security and Rescue Robotics, pp. 123–128 (2017)
3. Bai, C.Z., Pasqualetti, F., Gupta, V.: Data-injection attacks in stochastic control systems: detectability and performance tradeoffs. Automatica **82**, 251–260 (2017)
4. Becker, R., Zilberstein, S., Lesser, V., Goldman, C.V.: Solving transition independent decentralized Markov decision processes. J. Artif. Intell. Res. **22**, 423–455 (2004)
5. Bernstein, D.S., Givan, R., Immerman, N., Zilberstein, S.: The complexity of decentralized control of Markov decision processes. Math. Oper. Res. **27**(4), 819–840 (2002)
6. Carminati, L., Zhang, B.H., Farina, G., Gatti, N., Sandholm, T.: Hidden-role games: equilibrium concepts and computation. arXiv preprint arXiv:2308.16017 (2023)
7. Chen, S., Savas, Y., Karabag, M.O., Sadler, B.M., Topcu, U.: Deceptive planning for resource allocation. In: American Control Conference (2024)
8. Cover, T.M., Thomas, J.A.: Elements of Information Theory. Wiley, Hoboken (1999)

9. Dragan, A., Holladay, R., Srinivasa, S.: An analysis of deceptive robot motion. In: Robotics: Science and Systems (2014)

10. Fatemi, M.Y., Suttle, W.A., Sadler, B.M.: Deceptive path planning via reinforcement learning with graph neural networks. In: International Conference on Autonomous Agents and Multi-agent Systems pp. 2258–2260 (2024)

11. Fu, J.: On almost-sure intention deception planning that exploits imperfect observers. In: Fang, F., Xu, H., Hayel, Y. (eds.) GameSec 2022. LNCS, vol. 13727, pp. 67–86. Springer, Cham (2022). https://doi.org/10.1007/978-3-031-26369-9_4

12. Ghiya, S., Sycara, K.: Learning complex multi-agent policies in presence of an adversary. In: IROS Workshop on Trends and Advances in Machine Learning and Automated Reasoning for Intelligent Robots and Systems (2020). https://doi.org/10.48550/arXiv.2008.07698

13. Han, X., Kheir, N., Balzarotti, D.: Deception techniques in computer security: a research perspective. ACM Comput. Surv. **51**(4), 80:1–80:36 (2018)

14. He, Z., Yuan, J., Ran, N., Yin, X.: Security-based path planning of multi-robot systems by partially observed Petri nets and integer linear programming. IEEE Control Syst. Lett. **8**, 352–357 (2024)

15. Janczewski, L.J., Colarik, A.M.: Cyber Warfare and Cyber Terrorism. IGI Global (2008)

16. Kanellopoulos, A., Vamvoudakis, K.G.: Bounded rationality in Byzantine sensors under attacks. IEEE Trans. Autom. Control **67**(7), 3606–3613 (2022)

17. Karabag, M.O.: Decision-making for autonomous agents in adversarial or information-scarce settings. Ph.D. thesis, The University of Texas at Austin (2023)

18. Karabag, M.O., Ornik, M., Topcu, U.: Deception in supervisory control. IEEE Trans. Autom. Control **67**(2), 738–753 (2022)

19. Karabag, M.O., Ornik, M., Topcu, U.: Exploiting partial observability for optimal deception. IEEE Trans. Autom. Control **68**(7), 4443–4450 (2023)

20. Karabag, M.O., Ornik, M., Topcu, U.: Identity concealment games: how I learned to stop revealing and love the coincidences. Automatica **161**, 111482 (2024)

21. Keroglou, C., Hadjicostis, C.N.: Probabilistic system opacity in discrete event systems. Discrete Event Dyn. Syst. **28**, 289–314 (2018)

22. Khazraei, A., Pajic, M.: Resiliency of nonlinear control systems to stealthy sensor attacks. In: IEEE Conference on Decision and Control, pp. 7109–7114 (2022)

23. Lin, T., Jin, C., Jordan, M.I.: On gradient descent ascent for nonconvex-concave minimax problems. In: International Conference on Machine Learning, pp. 6083–6093 (2020)

24. Lowe, R., Wu, Y., Tamar, A., Harb, J., Abbeel, P., Mordatch, I.: Multi-agent actor-critic for mixed cooperative-competitive environments. Adv. Neural. Inf. Process. Syst. **30**, 6379–6390 (2017)

25. Ma, H., Shi, C., Han, S., Dorothy, M.R., Fu, J.: Covert planning against imperfect observers. In: International Conference on Autonomous Agents and Multi-agent Systems, pp. 1319–1327 (2024)

26. Masters, P., Sardina, S.: Deceptive path-planning. In: International Joint Conference on Artificial Intelligence, pp. 4368–4375 (2017)

27. Mu, C., Pang, J.: On quantified observability analysis in multiagent systems. In: European Conference on Artificial Intelligence, vol. 372, pp. 1755–1762 (2023)

28. de Nijs, F., Walraven, E., de Weerdt, M.M., Spaan, M.T.J.: Constrained multiagent Markov decision processes: a taxonomy of problems and algorithms. J. Artif. Intell. Res. **70**, 955–1001 (2021)

29. Patil, A., Karabag, M.O., Tanaka, T., Topcu, U.: Simulator-driven deceptive control via path integral approach. In: IEEE Conference on Decision and Control, pp. 271–277 (2023)
30. Pettinati, M.J., Arkin, R.C., Krishnan, A.: Wolves in sheep's clothing: using shill agents to misdirect multi-robot teams. In: Sarkadi, S., Wright, B., Masters, P., McBurney, P. (eds.) DeceptECAI/DeceptAI 2020-2021. CCIS, vol. 1296, pp. 41–54. Springer, Cham (2021). https://doi.org/10.1007/978-3-030-91779-1_4
31. Pferschy, U., Nicosia, G., Pacifici, A.: A Stackelberg knapsack game with weight control. Theoret. Comput. Sci. **799**, 149–159 (2019)
32. Pferschy, U., Nicosia, G., Pacifici, A., Schauer, J.: On the Stackelberg knapsack game. Eur. J. Oper. Res. **291**(1), 18–31 (2021)
33. Serrino, J., Kleiman-Weiner, M., Parkes, D.C., Tenenbaum, J.: Finding friend and foe in multi-agent games. Adv. Neural. Inf. Process. Syst. **32**, 1251–1261 (2019)
34. Shi, W., He, Z., Ma, Z., Ran, N., Yin, X.: Security-preserving multi-robot path planning for Boolean specification tasks using labeled Petri nets. IEEE Control Syst. Lett. **7**, 2017–2022 (2023)
35. Strouse, D., Kleiman-Weiner, M., Tenenbaum, J., Botvinick, M., Schwab, D.: Learning to share and hide intentions using information regularization. Adv. Neural. Inf. Process. Syst. 10249–10259 (2018)
36. Undurti, A., How, J.P.: A decentralized approach to multi-agent planning in the presence of constraints and uncertainty. In: IEEE International Conference on Robotics and Automation, pp. 2534–2539 (2011)
37. Yu, D., Tyshchuk, Y., Ji, H., Wallace, W.: Detecting deceptive groups using conversations and network analysis. In: International Joint Conference on Natural Language Processing, pp. 857–866 (2015)
38. Yu, X., Yin, X., Li, S., Li, Z.: Security-preserving multi-agent coordination for complex temporal logic tasks. Control Engi. Pract. **123**(105130) (2022)

Network and Privacy

Extended Horizons: Multi-hop Awareness in Network Games

Raman Ebrahimi$^{(\boxtimes)}$ and Parinaz Naghizadeh

University of California, San Diego, La Jolla, CA 92093, USA
{raman,parinaz}@ucsd.edu

Abstract. Network/interdependent security games have been extensively used in the literature to gain insights into how firms make optimal security decisions when accounting for spillovers of risks from other firms with whom they have risk interdependencies. We extend these models by proposing *K-hop network (security) games*, in which agents have *extended awareness* of network effects: an agent in a *K*-hop network game accounts for not only its immediate neighbors (those with whom it directly has joint operations or shared infrastructure), but also the spillover of the (security) risks from agents up to *K*-hops away from it. We first establish an equivalence between our proposed *K*-hop network games and a one-hop game played on an appropriately defined adjacency matrix. Then, through analytical results and numerical examples, we illustrate how subtle changes in a network can significantly alter equilibrium behaviors when accounting for multi-hop risk spillovers, emphasizing the dependency of agents' efforts on the nature of their dependencies (complement vs. substitute nature of efforts), agents' different levels *K* of awareness of the network effects, and the reactive vs. passive nature of lower awareness (lower *K*) agents to those with higher awareness (higher *K*). Our findings show that extended awareness of network effects can, in general, benefit agents by allowing them to optimize their security planning and resource allocation, but that decision makers who are less sophisticated and lack this awareness can suffer, and that consequently, overall investment levels in security may deteriorate.

Keywords: Network Games · Interdependent Security Games · Strategic Awareness

1 Introduction

The study of strategic interactions in networked environments has received significant attention in the literature on game theory and its applications to cybersecurity; see [5,13,18] for surveys. In this context, *network (security) games* (also known as *interdependent security games*) are often used to model scenarios where each node represents a strategic decision-maker or firm, and each connection signifies an interdependence in the firms' security state or operations.

© The Author(s), under exclusive license to Springer Nature Switzerland AG 2025
A. Sinha et al. (Eds.): GameSec 2024, LNCS 14908, pp. 201–219, 2025.
https://doi.org/10.1007/978-3-031-74835-6_10

Traditionally, these models are used to gain (qualitative) insight into the strategic security investments of decision-makers who consider how the actions of their immediate (one-hop) neighbors could expose them to spillover security risks (e.g., [7,9,10,17,25,34]). These studies can inform us about the extent of free-riding of agents on each other's effort due to network effects, its impact on equilibrium suboptimality (in terms of social welfare or other notions of cumulative security costs), and potential interventions to alleviate it.

As cyber-physical systems become more complex and interconnected, it is crucial for decision makers to better understand how their interdependence on others should shape their organization's security budgeting and investments, and to do so *beyond their immediate neighbors*. The 2021 Kaseya Attack [21,23] illustrates this clearly. Attackers initially compromised Kaseya's VSA software, then used it to distribute ransomware to Managed Service Providers (MSPs) and their clients. This attack affected over 1,500 organizations, including schools, supermarkets, and a national railway. The disruption to the railway, for example, potentially impacted other businesses reliant on its services, highlighting the far-reaching (multi-hop) effects of one firm's security decisions on other firms in the system. Similarly, the 2021 Colonial Pipeline attack [2] exhibits multi-hop risk dependencies: the ransomware attack led to a shutdown of the pipeline, causing fuel shortages and rising prices. This affected not just consumers but also businesses dependent on fuel, such as airlines and logistics companies. A formal model of network games in which agents are aware of, and best-respond to, the efforts of not only their immediate neighbors, but also of agents multiple hops away, has potential to capture such events, and offer richer insights into strategic behavior and potential security interventions.

Motivated by this, in this paper, we extend the framework of network (security) games considered in prior work (e.g., [3,6,11,16,19,20,32]) to encompass the influence of multi-hop neighbors. These neighbors can be in the same network or can be neighbors in a multiplex network. By incorporating awareness of multi-hop security dependencies, we aim to provide a more comprehensive understanding of how strategic influences propagate through the network and affect agents' decisions to free-ride on others (and potentially underinvest in security which is a public good).

Formally, we propose a model of *K-hop network (security) games*, in which agents have *extended* awareness of network effects: an agent in a K-hop network game considers, or is aware of, the spillover of the (security) efforts of agents up to K-hops away from it when selecting its own effort. We then explore the implications of such extended awareness on agents' strategic security decision making by looking into the Nash equilibria that arise as agents' awareness of the network (the K in the K-hop game) increases. We begin by using illustrative examples to show that these changes are impacted by three factors: (1) the nature of the agents' dependencies (complement vs. substitute nature of efforts), (2) agents' different levels K of awareness of the network effects, and (3) the reactive vs. passive nature of lower awareness (lower K) agents to those with higher awareness (higher K). Accordingly, we provide analytical equilibrium characterizations and comparisons for two settings:

1. *The Nash equilibrium when all agents have K-hop awareness, for general K.* Specifically, for a general K-hop network game, we show that the game is equivalent to a one-hop network game played on a new network interdependency matrix $\hat{G}$, constructed from the original game matrix G, in a way that the links $\hat{g}_{ij}$ between agents i and j account for the spillovers across all paths of length at most K to agent i from agent j.

2. *A mixture of one aware (e.g., $K = 2$) and $N - 1$ unaware (e.g., $K = 1$) agents in games of pure strategic substitutes/complements.* For this case, we show that in a game of strategic substitutes, the agent can free-ride more on others by increasing its awareness compared to other agents. This means that awareness can benefit the aware agent by allowing it to attain the same security outcomes while lowering its effort (and therefore, overall increasing its utility), but that at the same time, it will hurt the other unaware and passive agents, as they will be (incorrectly) assuming that the aware agent is exerting higher effort than it truly is. We also provide a lower bound for the effort of an agent with two-hop awareness in a game of strategic complements, constructed from the agent's efforts in one-hop awareness games.

Finally, we explore the K-hop equilibrium structure and provide numerical experiments for special network structures (e.g., Stars, Directed Acyclic Graphs, and Random Graphs).

To summarize, our main contributions include: (i) proposing a new model to capture extended network awareness in network security games, (ii) showing an equivalence between our proposed K-hop games and a one-hop game played on an appropriately defined adjacency matrix, and (iii) elaborating on the impacts of K-hop awareness on agents' security efforts, as well as on the equilibrium's quality (in terms of agents sum of efforts), both analytically and through numerical experiments. Our findings show that extended awareness of network effects can, in general, benefit agents by allowing them to optimize their security planning and resource allocation, but that decision makers who are less sophisticated and lack this awareness can suffer, and that consequently, overall investment levels in security are highly dependant on network structure and they may improve or deteriorate.

The remainder of this paper is organized as follows. We review the work most closely related to our paper in Sect. 1.1. In Sect. 2, we review the commonly studied model of (one-hop) network security games, and then introduce our proposed model of K-hop network games. We analyze the equilibria of this model in Sect. 3, and illustrate our findings on special network structures and using numerical experiments in Sect. 4. We conclude with directions for future work in Sect. 5.

1.1 Related Work

Game-theoretical studies of security decision making on networks have adopted different modeling choices. We contrast the interdependent/network security game models we consider here, with two other prominent models: network interdiction games, and attack graph models. Network interdiction games focus on the strategic disruption of networks facing adversarial attackers, by identifying and neutralizing critical nodes or links to impede the adversary's operations [26,28,29]. Attack graphs, on the other hand, model the possible pathways an attacker could take to compromise a network, helping defenders understand potential vulnerabilities and prioritize defenses [1,15,24,27,33]. Network security games in general, and our model included, do not consider the potential evolving or stepping-stone nature of attacks, but rather the equilibrium state. That is, unlike network interdiction games and attack graph models, an agent in a network security game model decides on its security investments once, as a best-response to an equilibrium state of the network, before attacks are launched, and does not adjust any links or investments in response to an evolving attack in the graph.

Our work is most closely related to the literature on network games. Some previous works on general network games (not restricted to the security context) include [11,16,19,20,22,31,32,35]. [19] has specifically discussed the existence and uniqueness Nash equilibrium for security decision making using linear influence networks while [20,22] have looked at existence, uniqueness, and stability of one-hop network games where necessary and sufficient conditions for guaranteed uniqueness are introduced. [11] characterizes the price of anarchy in the strategic form game and compares the benefits of improving security technology and improving incentives, and shows that improving technology alone may not offset the price of anarchy. [16] has summarized the modeling assumptions and categorized the equilibrium solutions in interdependent security games, [31,35] explore the bounded rationality of players using quantal response model and prospect theory. Our framework can also be seen as a discussion of boundedly rational agents (those who lack awareness of all network risk spillovers affecting them).

Access to information about other firms' security decisions, and decisions regarding information sharing, can significantly impact firms' security posture, as noted by [4]. Despite the potential benefits, various concerns such as confidentiality often hinder information sharing. To address this, legislation such as the Cybersecurity Information Sharing Act of 2015 [8] and guidance from the National Institute of Standards and Technology (NIST) [12] encourage firms to share intelligence.

In relation to our paper, we suggest that information shared by firms can also be viewed as a means of increasing their network awareness, providing them information about other firms' security behavior and of potential multi-hop risk spillovers (in our terminology, helping them change from passive to reactive agents, even if they do not possess multi-hop awareness). Specifically, we argue that lack of awareness can hurt decision makers when other agents have extended network awareness; mandating or incentivizing information sharing can help alleviate such issues.

2 Model

2.1 One-Hop Model

We consider a network of N interconnected decision-makers; these can include device owners/operators, various divisions within a larger organization, or different sectors of the economy. We specify this network using a graph $\mathcal{G} := \langle \mathcal{V}, G \rangle$ with the N agents as the set of vertices $\mathcal{V}$, and a weighted and directed interdependency matrix G specifying their connections, where $g_{ij} \in \mathbb{R}$ captures the dependence of agent i's security outcomes on agent j's security efforts (as detailed shortly).

Each agent i selects an *effort* $x_i \in \mathbb{R}_{\geq 0}$; this could represent the agent's investment in security (hardware, software, employee training, etc.). This effort impacts not only the agent itself, but also other agents in the network, as captured by the interdependency matrix G. Specifically, when $g_{ij} \geq 0$, we call i and j's relationship a strategic *substitute*; this means that if agent j is better protected, it is less likely that it is compromised and used to launch an attack on agent i, and as a result, i can invest less in security and achieve the same security outcomes. In contrast, $g_{ij} \leq 0$ is a strategic *complement* relation; meaning, if agent j increases its security effort, it is less likely to be attacked, making agent i more likely to be the target of an attack instead, so that i has to invest more in security in order to achieve the same security outcome.

The agent's utility is determined by its own action, as well as the actions of its one-hop neighboring agents. Let $\mathbf{x} \in \mathbb{R}^{N \times 1}$ denote the vector of all agents' actions. Then, agent i's utility is given by:

$$u_i(\mathbf{x}; G) = b_i\left(x_i + \sum_{j=1}^{N} g_{ij} x_j\right) - c_i x_i \ , \tag{1}$$

where $b_i(\cdot) : \mathbb{R} \to \mathbb{R}$ is a twice-differentiable, strictly increasing, and strictly concave *benefit function*, which has as its argument the *aggregate effort* experienced by the agent from its one-hop neighbors in the graph, and $c_i > 0$ is the *unit cost* of effort for agent i.

The (one-hop) network game involving a set of N agents, their efforts $\mathbf{x}$, and their utility functions $u_i(\mathbf{x}; G)$, has been extensively analyzed in previous studies (e.g., [3,6,11,19,20]). These games are known as games of *linear best-replies*, where the Nash equilibrium $\mathbf{x}^*$ is characterized by a set of linear best-response equations:

$$x_i^* = \max\{0, q_i - \sum_{j \in \mathcal{N}_i} g_{ij} x_j^*\}, \tag{2}$$

where q_i satisfies $b_i'(q_i) = c_i$. This condition ensures that the agent's effort is optimal, balancing marginal benefits and costs. The best-response (2) indicates that agent i exerts an effort x_i^* to reach the aggregate effort level q_i, considering the spillover $\sum_j g_{ij} x_j^*$ from its one-hop neighbors' efforts at equilibrium. If the combined effort from neighboring agents already meets or exceeds q_i, agent i will exert no additional effort.

We next propose an extension of this model: K-hop network (security) games, in which agents are more "aware" as they account for the impacts of actions taken by those further away in the network on their security.

2.2 K-Hop Model

We consider the same set of agents on the same network but with an *extended* awareness: an agent in a K-hop network game considers, or is aware of, the spillover of the (security) efforts of other agents up to K-hop away when selecting its effort.

Formally, the utility of an agent i with K-hop awareness is given by:

$$u_i^{(K)}(\mathbf{x}; G) = b_i \Big(x_i + \sum_{k=1}^{K} \sum_{j=1}^{N} g_{ij}^{(k)} x_j \Big) - c_i x_i, \tag{3}$$

where for agents i and j, $g_{ij}^{(k)}$ is the element in the ith row and j^{th} column of the kth power of the adjacency matrix G, and captures the impact of an agent j who is k-hops away on agent i's utility. By summing over the possible k's (from 1 to K), we are considering the impact of all possible effort spillovers from neighbors within k-hops of agent i on its utility.

This model also leads to a network game of linear best-replies. The Nash equilibrium $\mathbf{x}_{(K)}^*$ for agents with K-hop awareness is determined by:

$$x_{i_{(K)}}^* = \max\{0, q_i - \sum_{k=1}^{K} \sum_{j=1}^{N} g_{ij}^{(k)} x_{j_{(K)}}^*\} \tag{4}$$

Note that this model captures the commonly studied network security game model of Sect. 2.1 when $K = 1$. As K increases, the agent has more awareness of other agents further away in the network. As a special case, for $K \to \infty$, we say the agent attains *omni-vision*, as the agent will be accounting for, and best-responds to, the efforts of all other (reachable) agents in the network and all paths through which risk spillovers can propagate and reach it. For this setting, if all agents have omni-vision, agent i's utility (3) at the ∞-hop game's Nash equilibrium is given by:

$$u_i^{(\infty)}(\mathbf{x}_{(\infty)}^*; G) = b_i \Big(\big((I + G + G^2 + G^3 + \ldots) \mathbf{x}_{(\infty)}^* \big)_i \Big) - c_i x_i, \tag{5}$$

Let $S := I + G + G^2 + G^3 + \ldots$. It is easy to see that $S(I - G) = I$, or $S = (I - G)^{-1}$, provided that S converges. It is known that $\lim_{k \to \infty} G^k = 0$ if and only if $\rho(G) < 1$, where $\rho(G)$ is the spectral radius of G; absolute convergence of S is guaranteed under this condition [30, 36]. Using this relation, in our analysis of K-hop games in Sect. 3.1, we will establish a relation between the K-hop game's Nash equilibrium characterization and the matrix $(I - G)^{-1}$.

3   Impacts of Extended Awareness: Nash Equilibria of K-Hop Network Games

In this section, we explore the implications of agents' extended awareness on their strategic security decision making by looking into the Nash equilibria that arise as agents' awareness of the network (the K in the K-hop game) increases.

Warm-Up: No Awareness ($K = 0$) to One-Hop Awareness ($K = 1$). In order to illustrate the impacts of extended awareness, we start with a warm-up case: increasing awareness from $K = 0$ (no awareness; ignoring all network effects) to $K = 1$ (the commonly studied one-hop network security game). The equilibrium of the $K = 0$ game is $\mathbf{x}^* = \mathbf{q}^*$ (i.e., each agent i investing at its respective indifference point q_i). When awareness is upgraded to $K = 1$, the new optimal effort levels depend on whether only some or all agents access a higher awareness. We first consider the case where only one agent (w.l.o.g., agent $i = 1$) can upgrade its awareness from $K = 0$ to $K = 1$: the equilibrium will be $x_1^* = \max\{0, q_1 - \sum_j g_{1j} q_j\}$, and $x_j^* = q_j, \forall j \neq 1$. We can see that the change in agent 1's effort depends on the nature of the game graph. For instance, for games of strategic substitutes (resp. complements) where $g_{ij} \geq 0, \forall j$ (resp. $g_{ij} \leq 0, \forall j$), agent 1 lowers (resp. increases) its efforts and its free riding increases (resp. decreases) as the agent becomes aware of its dependence on other agents. At the other extreme, if all agents can upgrade their awareness from $K = 0$ to $K = 1$, the NE is given by the fixed point of best-responses in (2); again, depending on the substitute/complement effects, the effort of each agent i may increase or decrease compared to the $K = 0$ case.

An Illustrative Example: One-Hop ($K = 1$) to Two-Hop Awareness ($K = 2$). From the above warm-up case, we can see that the impacts of increasing awareness on agents' efforts depend on (1) the strategic or complement nature of their dependencies, and (2) the potential differences in the awareness levels of agents. In the following numerical example, we highlight the same effects when awareness increases from immediate neighbors ($K = 1$) to two-hop away neighbors ($K = 2$), and further show that an additional consideration arises: (3) whether agents with lower awareness are *passive* or *reactive*. In the *passive* case, less aware agents (here, those with 1-hop awareness) best-respond assuming all other agents have lower awareness, too. *Reactive* (but still less aware) agents, on the other hand, best-respond to the observed level of effort of all agents, including the higher-awareness agents. The rationale is that these lower awareness agents assume any higher awareness agents are behaving sub-optimally without attributing a reason to their (perceived) sub-optimal efforts.

Example 1. Consider two network games represented by the adjacency matrices $A = \begin{pmatrix} 0 & 0.3 & 0.2 \\ -0.3 & 0 & 0.5 \\ 0.2 & 0.5 & 0 \end{pmatrix}$ and $B = \begin{pmatrix} 0 & -0.3 & 0.2 \\ -0.3 & 0 & 0.5 \\ 0.2 & 0.5 & 0 \end{pmatrix}$, and with $\mathbf{q} = [1, 1, 1]^T$.
  The only difference between the two networks is in edge g_{12}. As illustrated by Fig. 1 we can see that by changing only this one link in the network, the equilibrium in each scenario (all one-hop aware, only agent 1 two-hop aware and others passive/reactive, and all two-hop aware) changes.

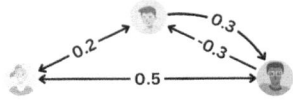

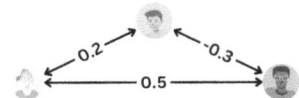

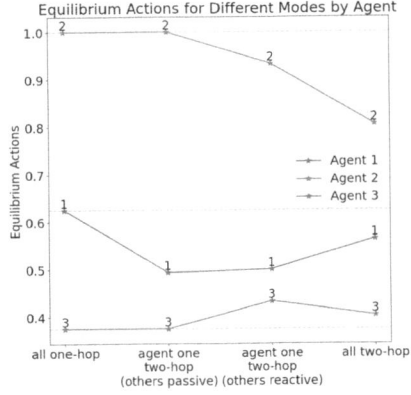

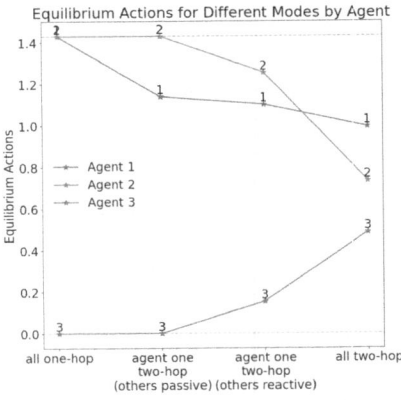

(a) Network A of agents (top) and their actions (bottom)

(b) Network B of agents (top) and their actions (bottom)

Fig. 1. Two different scenarios arise for two largely similar networks as levels of awareness increase.

Focusing on Fig. 1a first, we can see that agent 1 can free-ride more by being two-hop aware. If other agents are unaware themselves but reactive to agent 1's two-hop awareness, they adjust their efforts according to agent 1's lowered investment, agent 2 by decreasing its effort due to the negative link and agent 3 by increasing its own effort due to the positive link. If these agents manage to acquire resources to also become two-hop away, then agent 1 will increase its effort since agents 2 and 3 will also free-ride more by becoming two-hop aware.

Looking at Fig. 1b next, we see a different change in the equilibrium, even though, compared to Fig. 1a, the networks are not very different. Specifically, when other agents become reactive to agent 1's 2-hop awareness, they will have two different reactions: (i) agent 2 will also start free-riding more due to the negative link, (ii) agent 3 tries to make up for this with a higher effort. Lastly, when all agents have two-hop awareness, agents 1 and 2 will free-ride more, and agent 3 will try to make up for this by its own effort.

Motivated by the above examples, we next provide analytical results for two settings: Sect. 3.1 characterizes the equilibrium when all agents have K-hop awareness for general K, while Sect. 3.2 considers a mixture of one aware (e.g., $K = 2$) and $N - 1$ unaware (e.g., $K = 1$) agents in games of pure strategic substitutes/complements, and the impacts of the unaware agents' passive behavior on the ability of the one aware agent to free-ride on them.[1]

3.1 All K-Hop Aware Agents

In this section, we consider games where all agents are aware of their K-hop neighbors (and are reactive). We start with the scenario $K < \infty$, which represents a case in which agents may not have the resources to be aware of all reachable agents and, at best, only take some into account. We also discuss the special case of $K \to \infty$; this case is important as it represents an ideal scenario where agents have unlimited resources and can best-respond to all reachable agents regardless of how distant they are, which we call *omni-vision*. We compare the two cases, and illustrate the differences using an example at the end of the subsection.

Nash Equilibria of K-Hop Network Games. In the following proposition, we identify an equivalence between the Nash equilibria of such K-hop games and that of a one-hop game with a specific adjacency matrix.

Proposition 1. *If $\rho(G) < 1$, then best-response of agents in a K-hop network game is the same as the best-response of agents in a one-hop game on a network with adjacency matrix $\hat{G} = (I - G)^{-1}(I - G^{K+1}) - I$.*

Proof. If $\rho(G) < 1$ we can define $S_K := I + G + G^2 + \ldots + G^K = (I - G)^{-1}(I - G^{K+1})$, we can write agent i's K-hop best-response (4) as:

$$x^*_{i_{(K)}} = \max\{0, q_i - \sum_{j=1}^{N}[S_K - I]_{ij}\, x^*_{j_{(K)}}\}$$

$$= \max\{0, q_i + x^*_{i_{(K)}} - \sum_{j=1}^{N}[(I - G)^{-1}(I - G^{K+1})]_{ij}\, x^*_{j_{(K)}}\} \tag{6}$$

which is equivalent to the best-response (2) of a one-hop game on a network with adjacency matrix $(I - G)^{-1}(I - G^{K+1}) - I$.

In Proposition 1, we are constructing a new network interdependency matrix $\hat{G}$ from the original matrix G in a way that the links $\hat{g}_{ij}$ between agents i and j account for the spillovers across all paths of length at most K to agent i from agent j in the original game.

The following corollary considers the special case of an ∞-hop game where all agents have omni-vision, i.e., they are aware of, and best-respond to, the efforts of all other agents.

Corollary 1. *If $\rho(G) < 1$, then the best-response of agents in a ∞-hop network game is the same as the best-response of agents in a one-hop game on a network with adjacency matrix $\hat{G} = G(I - G)^{-1}$.*

---

[1] We will illustrate similar impacts when $K \geq 2$ and in general games of mixed strategic complements/substitutes through numerical experiments in Sect. 4.

The proof follows from noting that if $\rho(G) < 1$, then $\lim_{K \to \infty} G^{K+1} = 0$, and that the infinite sum $S = I + G + G^2 + \ldots$ can be re-written $S - I = G(I + G + G^2 + \ldots) = GS = G(I - G)^{-1}$.

By reducing a K-hop game to a one-hop game on an appropriately transformed network, analysts can more easily predict and manage the propagation of risks and the strategic interactions between different entities in the network. This reduction allows for the application of existing tools and methodologies designed for one-hop games, which are often more mature and better understood. For example, this approach can be applied to verify the uniqueness of the Nash equilibrium in a K-hop network game which we know the Nash equilibrium of the one-hop network game is unique.

3.2   Mixture of Aware and Unaware Agents

The previous subsection analyzed the K-hop game's Nash equilibrium when all agents can attain K-hop awareness. However, it may not be possible for all agents to attain this awareness. One reason could be limited resources to gather intelligence about other agents' security decisions or the high cost of processing all available information. For instance, higher-level agents in a hierarchical network are expected to have full knowledge of the branches below them, but they may only have limited awareness due to the constraints of the human mind [14].

Motivated by this, we consider a scenario in which only one agent is able to upgrade its awareness (e.g., best-responding to both immediate and 2-hop away neighbors), while others are passive and remain at a lower awareness level (e.g., considering only their immediate neighbors). We discuss the change in the effort of the aware agent, and its ability to free-ride on others given their passive and unaware strategies. We present this analysis for two special network structures: games of strategic substitutes and games of strategic complements, where $g_{ij} \geq 0$ and $g_{ij} \leq 0$, respectively, for all i, j. The former captures networks where a security compromise of one agent negatively impacts others connected to it (due to, e.g., the spread of the attack or disruption of joint operations). The latter is most closely related to networks where attackers are interested in identifying the weakest targets.

We start with the impacts of one agent unilaterally upgrading its awareness in a game of strategic substitutes.[2]

Proposition 2. *Consider a network game of strategic substitutes, where agent i has K-hop awareness, while agents $j \neq i$ have $K' < K$ awareness. Then, agent i's effort will be lower compared to a game where it also had K'-awareness if and only if there is at least one agent l with effort $x^*_{l,(K')} > 0$ is $K' < k \leq K$ hops away from agent i. If no such agent exists, agent i's effort will be the same as the game where it also had K'-awareness.*

---

[2] The results of Proposition 2 also hold for the case of general networks if all paths with distance K have an even number of complement (negative weight) edges.

Proof. When agent i is aware of up to K-hop neighbors in its best-response, while other agents are only aware of others at most $K' < K$ hops away, we can write:

$$x^*_{i_{(k)}} = \max\{0, q_i - \sum_{j=1}^{N}\sum_{l=1}^{K'} g_{ij}^{(l)} x^*_{j_{(K')}} - \sum_{j=1}^{N}\sum_{l=K'+1}^{K} g_{ij}^{(l)} x^*_{j_{(K')}}\} \tag{7}$$

For a game of strategic substitutes, we know $g_{ij}^{(l)} \geq 0$ for all l. Therefore we can conclude that $\sum_{j=1}^{N}\sum_{l=K'+1}^{k} g_{ij}^{(l)} x^*_{j_{(K')}} \geq 0$ and will strictly be positive if at least one agent with positive effort is reachable with $K' < k \leq K$ hops.

Proposition 2 states that if an agent becomes more aware than others in a game of strategic substitutes, it can (weakly) increase its free-riding on others. As a special case, if for the aware agent $x^*_{i_{(K')}} = 0$ at some K', then $x^*_{i_{(K)}} = 0$ for all $K > K'$. This means that awareness can benefit the aware agent by allowing it to attain the same security outcomes while lowering its effort (and therefore, overall increasing its utility), but that at the same time, it will hurt the other unaware and passive agents, as they will be (incorrectly) assuming that the aware agent is exerting higher effort than it truly is.

For *games of strategic complements*, on the other hand, we cannot make a statement as general as Proposition 2, since the sign of all entries of the powers of the adjacency matrix will be alternating, i.e., $g_{ij}^{(2n-1)} \leq 0$, $g_{ij}^{(2n)} \geq 0$ for all i and j. In other words, even though the odd-hop away neighbors maintain a strategic complement relation to agent i's effort, neighbors even number of hops away are turned into *strategic substitutes* from the viewpoint of agent i. That said, we can comment on the efforts at equilibrium when awareness increases from K to $K+1$ hops. Specifically, by defining $\bar{g}_i$ as the impact of agent i's most influential neighbor, i.e., $\bar{g}_i = \{g_{ij} : |g_{ij}| \geq |g_{ik}|, \forall k\}$, we can state the following result.

Proposition 3. *Consider a game of strategic complements where agent i has two-hop awareness while agents $j \neq i$ have one-hop awareness. Then agent i's effort will be lower compared to a game where it also had one-hop awareness, assuming $q_i > 0$, at most by $\bar{g}_i \sum_j \sum_k g_{kj} x^*_j$.*

Proof. Since $q_i > 0$, we can write $x^*_{i_{(1)}} = q_i - \sum_{j=1}^{N} g_{ij} x^*_{j_{(1)}} \geq 0$ and accordingly write $x^*_{i_{(2)}}$ as:

$$x^*_{i_{(2)}} = \max\{0, q_i - \sum_{j=1}^{N}(g_{ij} + \sum_{k=1}^{N} g_{ik}g_{kj}) x^*_{j_{(1)}}\}$$

$$= \max\{0, x^*_{i_{(1)}} - \sum_{j=1}^{N}\sum_{k=1}^{N} g_{ik}g_{kj} x^*_{j_{(1)}}\} \tag{8}$$

Further, since we know $g_{ij} \leq 0$ we can further write $\sum_{k=1}^{N} g_{ik}g_{kj}x_j^* \leq \bar{g}_i \sum_k g_{kj}x_j^*$ where $\bar{g}_i$ is the element with largest absolute value in row i, i.e. most influential neighbor of agent i. Therefore, we can write:

$$x_{i_{(1)}}^* - \bar{g}_i \sum_{j=1}^{N} \sum_{k=1}^{N} g_{kj}x_{j_{(1)}}^* \leq x_{i_{(2)}}^* \leq x_{i_{(1)}}^* \tag{9}$$

The second term on the LHS bound in (9) is non-negative, confirming that for this setting, upgrading the awareness will not make the agents put in more effort.

The term $\sum_{j=1}^{N} \sum_{k=1}^{N} g_{kj}x_j^*$ could be interpreted in the network as the sum of the spillovers of all agents if they all had one-hop awareness. Therefore, the amount that agent i can free-ride by having two-hop awareness, compared to one-hop awareness, is bounded by the sum of spillovers of all agents over the network, weighted by the most influential neighbors of the agents.

We next take advantage of the knowledge of specific network structures and numerical experiments to discuss the more general cases and remove the constraints on edge weights.

4   Special Network Structures

In this section, we examine specific network structures and analyze each, both analytically and numerically. We identify equilibria in synthetic networks where all agents have K-hop awareness with varying K. We employ the sum of efforts as a baseline metric to assess the "quality" of the game. This evaluation is further extended by comparing $\sum_i q_i$ with the outcomes from games incorporating K-hop awareness, represented by $\sum_i x_{i_{(K)}}^*$. Our analysis begins with elementary graph configurations, such as cycles and star graphs, before advancing to a more general case of directed acyclic graphs.

One-Way Cycle: It is relatively easier to understand the changes in the efforts of the agents in cycle graphs. Consider a directed one-way cycle graph with similar connections between agents, meaning that each agent i only has an outgoing link to agent $i + 1$ with weight g. For this case, we have $g_{i,i-1} = 0$. This way, the best-response of agents will come down to:

$$x_{i_{(k)}}^* = \max\{0, q_i - \sum_{l=1}^{k} g^l x_{i+l_{(k)}}^*\} \tag{10}$$

As previously noted, for $g > 0$, it holds that $x_{i_{(k)}}^* \leq x_{i_{(k')}}^*$ for $k > k'$. Conversely, if $g < 0$, oscillations occur due to the alternating sign of the summation term in (10). For $|g| < 1$, these oscillations will converge as the number of considered hops grows, $\lim_{n \to \infty} g^n = 0$. However, if $|g| > 1$, the powers of g will diverge, also with alternating signs. In cases of high awareness levels, an agent may completely free-ride and have, $x^*_{i_{(2k-1)}} = 0$, if aware of an even number of hops and exert significant effort, $x^*_{i_{(2k)}} \gg 0$, when aware of an odd number of hops. This analysis underscores that even in a straightforward case of a one-way cycle with uniform link weights, the increase in agents' awareness can lead to a range of outcomes.

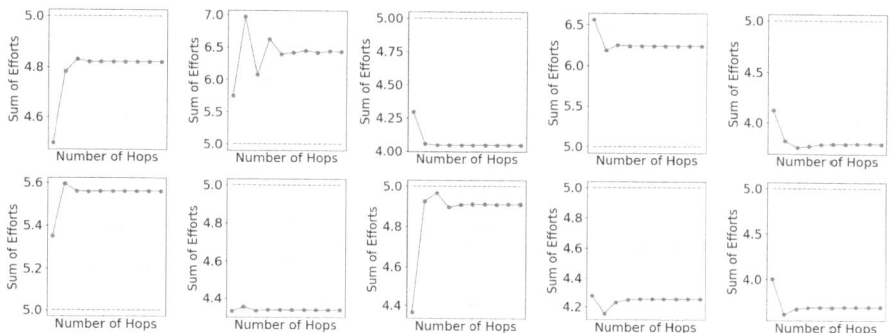

Fig. 2. Game quality comparison for 10 randomly generated one-way cycle networks with 5 K-hop aware agents (K from 1 to 10) with the no awareness case (dashed red line). (Color figure online)

To relax the conditions on the connections in this case, with the aim to comment on the impact of network structure, we work with randomly generated weights within the range $(-1, 1)$ and calculate the equilibrium. In Fig. 2, each data point represents the game quality on a randomly generated network of 5 agents for when agents are aware of K-hops with K going from 1 to 10. We can see that after a few hops the game quality converges, however, we can see that game quality can be either above or below the starting point which is no awareness. This indicates that by considering more hops, the spillovers are becoming less and less important. Also, the jump in game quality after going from one-hop to two-hop is significant.

Star Network: Another simple structure that can be of interest is star networks. Star networks have been studied in various applications, such as the structure of the internet [37]. Consider an undirected star network with the central node labeled as 1, and the remaining nodes are only connected to the central node. This way we have one node with $n - 1$ connections and $n - 1$ nodes with 1 connection, the adjacency matrix of this network will have the form $G = \begin{pmatrix} 0 & g_{1.}^T \\ g_{1.} & \mathbf{0} \end{pmatrix}$ and $G^2 = \begin{pmatrix} \|g_{1.}\|_2^2 & 0 \\ 0 & g_{1.}g_{1.}^T \end{pmatrix}$, where the bottom right block is an $n - 1 \times n - 1$ matrix with i^{th} row being: $[g_{12}g_{1i}, g_{i3}g_{1i}, \ldots, g_{ii}^2, \ldots, g_{1n}g_{1i}]$.

Therefore, the agents' efforts after considering two hops will be as follows:

$$x^*_{1_{(2)}} = \max\{0, q_1 - g_1^T \mathbf{x}^*_{(2)} - \|g_1.\|_2^2 x^*_{1_{(2)}}\} \tag{11}$$

$$x^*_{i_{(2)}} = \max\{0, q_i - g_{1i}(x^*_{1_{(2)}} + \sum_k g_{1k} x^*_{k_{(2)}})\} \tag{12}$$

We can see for the central agent, the rebound of its own effort ($\|g_1.\|_2^2 x^*_{1_{(2)}}$) is allowing it to free-ride more and have a lower effort, while $q_1 - g_1^T \mathbf{x}^*_{(2)}$ is similar to one-hop awareness, with the only difference of accounting for other agents being two-hop aware. The case for non-central agents is rather simple as well. The two-hop spillovers are weighted by the two-hop neighbors' connection to the central agent and then summed with the effort of the only one-hop neighbor of agent i, agent 1. Again, for an easier conclusion, we turn to numerical simulation on synthetic networks with edge weights randomly generated in the range $(-1, 1)$ with 5 agents.

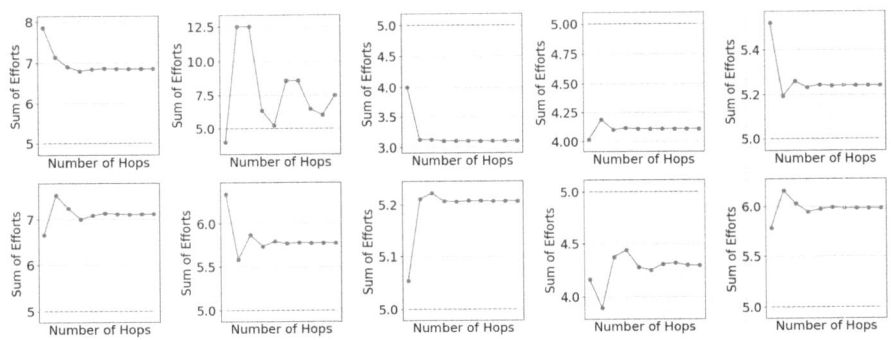

Fig. 3. Game quality comparison for 10 randomly generated star networks with 5 K-hop aware agents (K from 1 to 10) with the no awareness case (dashed red line). (Color figure online)

As seen in Fig. 3, in terms of game quality, this case is very similar to the case of the one-way cycle, even though the effort profiles can be very different.

Directed Acyclic Graph: Hierarchical structures are pervasive across various domains seen in technological systems, such as the Internet, organizational structures, and software architectures. Directed Acyclic Graphs (DAGs) are a specific type of hierarchical network characterized by a directed graph with no cycles, meaning there is a unidirectional flow from one node to another without returning to the starting node.

These types of networks can be represented by upper triangular adjacency matrices with zero diagonals, given that loops are not allowed. Normally, in hierarchical matrices, the higher nodes have the full awareness of the sub-network below them, we can use k-hop model to capture this property of these networks.

For these networks, we can iteratively calculate all equilibrium efforts by starting from the bottom of the hierarchy (agents that have no outgoing links) and moving upwards. This is possible because The kth power of an upper triangular matrix with zero diagonals is an upper triangular matrix with zero diagonal and $k - 1$ zero superdiagonals above.[3]

We can see that for a hierarchical network with n agents, the lowest positioned agent will not be able to take a strategic effort since $G^n = \mathbf{0}$. the following example illustrates how this iterative procedure works:

Example 2. Consider a hierarchical network with the adjacency matrix $G = \begin{pmatrix} 0 & g_{12} & g_{13} \\ 0 & 0 & g_{23} \\ 0 & 0 & 0 \end{pmatrix}$ where we know $G^2 = \begin{pmatrix} 0 & 0 & g_{12}g_{23} \\ 0 & 0 & 0 \\ 0 & 0 & 0 \end{pmatrix}$ and $G^k = 0$ for $k \geq 3$. For the scenario where each agent is aware of two hops, we can write (assuming $q_i > 0$, $\forall i$):

$$x^*_{3_{(2)}} = q_3 \tag{13}$$

$$x^*_{2_{(2)}} = \max\{0, q_2 - g_{23}q_3\} \tag{14}$$

$$x^*_{1_{(2)}} = \max\{0, q_1 - g_{12}x^*_{2_{(2)}} - (g_{13} + g_{12}g_{23})q_3\} \tag{15}$$

As seen in these equations, we can start from the lowest nodes to find the equilibrium for these types of networks. For tree graphs, this model is equivalent to each agent considering the whole branch below them and not being aware of the branches above or parallel. Starting from the lowest nodes, we can find their equilibrium effort independently from other nodes (13), then we move to the nodes in the higher branches (14), and (15) until we know all the efforts in the network.

The numerical experiments for DAGs are more intriguing than previous cases. For these networks, we increased the number of agents to 10 and the range of edge weights to $(-2.5, 2.5)$. With these changes, we see that, as expected, all cases will converge. Even though this is not guaranteed for DAGs, all the random cases have higher game quality than the no awareness scenario. Also, the damping rate fluctuations in Fig. 4 depend on the edge weights; if the edge weights are large, then they can continue on as many hops as there are agents; however, the fluctuations will definitely end since there exists a k for which $G^k = 0$.

---

[3] We can write the elements of the second power of A as $[A^2]_{ij} = \sum_k a_{ik}a_{kj}$. Given $a_{i\cdot} = [0, 0, ..., 0, a_{i,i+1}, ..., a_{in}]$ and $a^T_{\cdot j} = [a_{1j}, ..., a_{j-1,j}, 0, 0, ..., 0]$ we can easily see for $j = i + 1$ we have $[A^2]_{ij} = 0$ since the first i elements of $a_{i\cdot}$ are zero and the last $n - j + 1 = n - i$ elements of $a_{\cdot j}$ are zero, similarly for $j < i + 1$. We can continue this process for higher powers of A and show the results.

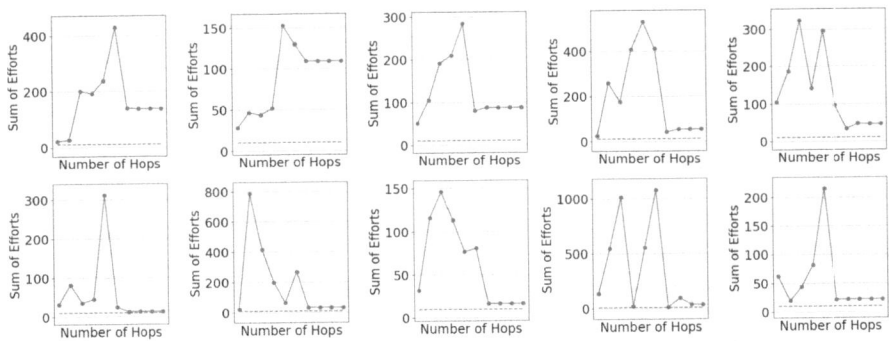

Fig. 4. Game quality comparison for 10 randomly generated DAGs with 10 K-hop aware agents (K from 1 to 10) with the no awareness case (dashed red line). (Color figure online)

5   Conclusion

In this study, we extend the traditional framework of network security games by introducing K-hop network games, where agents possess extended awareness of risk spillovers up to K hops away. Our analysis highlights several key findings:

We demonstrate that agents' strategic security decisions and equilibrium behaviors are significantly influenced by their level of awareness. Increasing awareness results in changes in optimal effort levels, contingent upon the network structure and the nature of dependencies (complements vs. substitutes). In strategic substitutes games, agents with higher awareness can lower their efforts and increase free-riding, particularly if they are aware of agents with positive efforts within their extended network. In strategic complements games, the benefits of increased awareness from one-hop to two-hop are bounded, with efforts potentially decreasing for two-hop awareness but not leading to increased efforts compared to one-hop awareness scenario. Our examination of specific network structures shows varied impacts of increased awareness on agents' efforts. In one-way cycles, we analytically showed that efforts can oscillate with awareness levels, while in star networks, due to two-hop awareness, central agents can free-ride more compared to one-hop awareness. In hierarchical DAGs, agents' efforts are determined iteratively from the lowest to the highest nodes. Our numerical experiments indicate that the overall game quality, measured by the sum of agents' efforts, can both improve and deteriorate with increased awareness. The extent and direction of this change depend on network structure and edge weights.

In conclusion, extended awareness in network security games enables agents to optimize their security investments more effectively, but also exposes potential pitfalls for less aware agents. These insights can inform better policies and resource allocation strategies, emphasizing the necessity for sophisticated awareness in managing K-hop risk dependencies.

Future research can expand on these findings by exploring more complex and dynamic network structures, where agents' awareness levels may change over time. Further studies could also consider the impact of partial or evolving awareness, where agents gradually gain or lose information about their network environment. These extensions would enhance our understanding of strategic interactions in networks and contribute to the development of more robust models for predicting and optimizing agents' efforts in various domains.

Acknowledgments. This work is supported in part by the NSF under award CCF-2416311.

Disclosure of Interests. The authors have no competing interests to declare that are relevant to the content of this article.

References

1. Abdallah, M., Naghizadeh, P., Hota, A.R., Cason, T., Bagchi, S., Sundaram, S.: Behavioral and game-theoretic security investments in interdependent systems modeled by attack graphs. IEEE Trans. Control Netw. Syst. **7**(4), 1585–1596 (2020). https://doi.org/10.1109/TCNS.2020.2988007
2. Beerman, J., Berent, D., Falter, Z., Bhunia, S.: A review of colonial pipeline ransomware attack. In: 2023 IEEE/ACM 23rd International Symposium on Cluster, Cloud and Internet Computing Workshops (CCGridW), pp. 8–15 (2023). https://doi.org/10.1109/CCGridW59191.2023.00017
3. Bramoullé, Y., Kranton, R., D'amours, M.: Strategic interaction and networks. Am. Econ. Rev. **104**(3), 898–930 (2014)
4. Brown, S., Gommers, J., Serrano, O.: From cyber security information sharing to threat management. In: Proceedings of the 2nd ACM Workshop on Information Sharing and Collaborative Security, pp. 43–49 (2015)
5. Do, C.T., et al.: Game theory for cyber security and privacy. ACM Comput. Surv. **50**(2) (2017). https://doi.org/10.1145/3057268
6. Ebrahimi, R., Naghizadeh, P.: United we fall: on the nash equilibria of multiplex and multilayer network games (2024)
7. Ettredge, M.L., Richardson, V.J.: Information transfer among internet firms: the case of hacker attacks. J. Inf. Syst. **17**(2), 71–82 (2003)
8. Fischer, E.A., Liu, E.C., Rollins, J., Theohary, C.A.: The 2013 Cybersecurity Executive Order: Overview and Considerations for Congress. Congressional Research Service Washington (2013)
9. Hinz, O., Nofer, M., Schiereck, D., Trillig, J.: The influence of data theft on the share prices and systematic risk of consumer electronics companies. Inf. Manage. **52**(3), 337–347 (2015)
10. Jeong, C.Y., Lee, S.Y.T., Lim, J.H.: Information security breaches and it security investments: impacts on competitors. Inf. Manage. **56**(5), 681–695 (2019). https://doi.org/10.1016/j.im.2018.11.003, https://www.sciencedirect.com/science/article/pii/S037872061830435X
11. Jiang, L., Anantharam, V., Walrand, J.: How bad are selfish investments in network security? IEEE/ACM Trans. Netw. **19**(2), 549–560 (2011). https://doi.org/10.1109/TNET.2010.2071397

12. Johnson, C., Badger, L., Waltermire, D., Snyder, J., Skorupka, C., et al.: Guide to cyber threat information sharing. NIST Spec. Publ. **800**(150), 35 (2016)
13. Kiennert, C., Ismail, Z., Debar, H., Leneutre, J.: A survey on game-theoretic approaches for intrusion detection and response optimization. ACM Comput. Surv. **51**(5) (2018). https://doi.org/10.1145/3232848
14. Klingberg, T.: Limitations in information processing in the human brain: neuroimaging of dual task performance and working memory tasks. In: Cognition, Emotion and Autonomic Responses: The Integrative Role of the Prefrontal Cortex and Limbic Structures, Progress in Brain Research, vol. 126, pp. 95–102. Elsevier (2000). https://doi.org/10.1016/S0079-6123(00)26009-3, https://www.sciencedirect.com/science/article/pii/S0079612300260093
15. Lallie, H.S., Debattista, K., Bal, J.: A review of attack graph and attack tree visual syntax in cyber security. Comput. Sci. Rev. **35**, 100219 (2020). https://doi.org/10.1016/j.cosrev.2019.100219, https://www.sciencedirect.com/science/article/pii/S1574013719300772
16. Laszka, A., Felegyhazi, M., Buttyán, L.: A survey of interdependent information security games. ACM Comput. Surv. (CSUR) **47**(2), 1–38 (2014)
17. Liang, X., Xiao, Y.: Game theory for network security. IEEE Commun. Surv. Tutor. **15**(1), 472–486 (2013). https://doi.org/10.1109/SURV.2012.062612.00056
18. Manshaei, M.H., Zhu, Q., Alpcan, T., Bacşar, T., Hubaux, J.P.: Game theory meets network security and privacy. ACM Comput. Surv. **45**(3) (2013). https://doi.org/10.1145/2480741.2480742
19. Miura-Ko, R.A., Yolken, B., Mitchell, J., Bambos, N.: Security decision-making among interdependent organizations. In: the 21st IEEE Computer Security Foundations Symposium, pp. 66–80. IEEE (2008)
20. Naghizadeh, P., Liu, M.: Provision of public goods on networks: on existence, uniqueness, and centralities. IEEE Trans. Netw. Sci. Eng. **5**(3), 225–236 (2018)
21. Osborne, C.: Updated Kaseya ransomware attack FAQ: what we know now (2021). https://www.zdnet.com/article/updated-kaseya-ransomware-attack-faq-what-we-know-now/
22. Parise, F., Ozdaglar, A.: A variational inequality framework for network games: existence, uniqueness, convergence and sensitivity analysis. Games Econ. Behav. **114**, 47–82 (2019). https://doi.org/10.1016/j.geb.2018.11.012, https://www.sciencedirect.com/science/article/pii/S0899825618301891
23. Paul, K.: Who's behind the Kaseya ransomware attack–and why is it so dangerous? (2021). https://www.theguardian.com/technology/2021/jul/06/kaseya-ransomware-attack-explained-russia-hackers
24. Qi, Y., et al.: Cybersecurity knowledge graph enabled attack chain detection for cyber-physical systems. Comput. Electr. Eng. **108**, 108660 (2023). https://doi.org/10.1016/j.compeleceng.2023.108660, https://www.sciencedirect.com/science/article/pii/S004579062300085X
25. Roy, S., Ellis, C., Shiva, S., Dasgupta, D., Shandilya, V., Wu, Q.: A survey of game theory as applied to network security. In: 2010 43rd Hawaii International Conference on System Sciences, pp. 1–10 (2010). https://doi.org/10.1109/HICSS.2010.35
26. Sanjab, A., Saad, W., Başar, T.: Prospect theory for enhanced cyber-physical security of drone delivery systems: a network interdiction game. In: 2017 IEEE International Conference on Communications (ICC), pp. 1–6 (2017). https://doi.org/10.1109/ICC.2017.7996862
27. Shandilya, V., Simmons, C.B., Shiva, S.: Use of attack graphs in security systems. J. Comput. Netw. Commun. **2014**(1), 818957 (2014)

28. Smith, J.C., Song, Y.: A survey of network interdiction models and algorithms. Eur. J. Oper. Res. **283**(3), 797–811 (2020). https://doi.org/10.1016/j.ejor.2019.06. 024, https://www.sciencedirect.com/science/article/pii/S0377221719305156

29. Sreekumaran, H., Hota, A.R., Liu, A.L., Uhan, N.A., Sundaram, S.: Multi-agent decentralized network interdiction games. arXiv preprint arXiv:1503.01100 (2015)

30. Stewart, G.W.: Matrix algorithms. Society for Industrial and Applied Mathematics (1998). https://doi.org/10.1137/1.9781611971408, https://epubs.siam.org/doi/abs/10.1137/1.9781611971408

31. Thakoor, O., Jabbari, S., Aggarwal, P., Gonzalez, C., Tambe, M., Vayancs, P.: Exploiting bounded rationality in risk-based cyber camouflage games. In: Zhu, Q., Baras, J.S., Poovendran, R., Chen, J. (eds.) GameSec 2020. LNCS, vol. 12513, pp. 103–124. Springer, Cham (2020). https://doi.org/10.1007/978-3-030-64793-3_6

32. Varian, H.: System reliability and free riding. In: Camp, L.J., Lewis, S. (eds.) Economics of Information Security. Advances in Information Security, vol. 12, pp. 1–15. Springer, Boston (2004). https://doi.org/10.1007/1-4020-8090-5_1

33. Wang, L., Singhal, A., Jajodia, S.: Measuring the overall security of network configurations using attack graphs. In: Barker, S., Ahn, G.-J. (eds.) DBSec 2007. LNCS, vol. 4602, pp. 98–112. Springer, Heidelberg (2007). https://doi.org/10.1007/978-3-540-73538-0_9

34. Wang, T., Wang, Y.Y., Yen, J.C.: It's not my fault: the transfer of information security breach information. J. Database Manage. **30**, 18–37 (2019). https://doi.org/10.4018/JDM.2019070102

35. Yang, R., Kiekintveld, C., Ordonez, F., Tambe, M., John, R.: Improving resource allocation strategy against human adversaries in security games. In: IJCAI Proceedings-International Joint Conference on Artificial Intelligence, vol. 22, p. 458. Barcelona (2011)

36. Young, N.: The rate of convergence of a matrix power series. Linear Algebra Appl. **35**, 261–278 (1981). https://doi.org/10.1016/0024-3795(81)90278-0, https://www.sciencedirect.com/science/article/pii/0024379581902780

37. Zegura, E., Calvert, K., Donahoo, M.: A quantitative comparison of graph-based models for internet topology. IEEE/ACM Trans. Netw. **5**(6), 770–783 (1997). https://doi.org/10.1109/90.650138

FlipDyn in Graphs: Resource Takeover Games in Graphs

Sandeep Banik[1]([✉]) [iD], Shaunak D. Bopardikar[2] [iD], and Naira Hovakimyan[1] [iD]

[1] University of Illinois Urbana-Champaign, Urbana, IL 61801-3633, USA
{baniksan,nhovakim}@illinois.edu
[2] Michigan State University, East Lansing, MI 48823-24, USA
shaunak@egr.msu.edu

Abstract. We present FlipDyn-G, a dynamic game model extending the FlipDyn framework to a graph-based setting, where each node represents a dynamical system. This model captures the interactions between a defender and an adversary who strategically take over nodes in a graph to minimize (resp. maximize) a finite horizon additive cost. At any time, the FlipDyn state is represented as the current node, and each player can transition the FlipDyn state to a node based on the connectivity from the current node. Such transitions are driven by the node dynamics, state, and node-dependent costs. This model results in a hybrid dynamical system where the discrete state (FlipDyn state) governs the continuous state evolution and the corresponding state cost. Our objective is to compute the Nash equilibrium of this finite horizon zero-sum game on a graph. Our contributions are two-fold. First, we model and characterize the FlipDyn-G game for general dynamical systems, along with the corresponding Nash equilibrium (NE) takeover strategies. Second, for scalar linear discrete-time dynamical systems with quadratic costs, we derive the NE takeover strategies and saddle-point values independent of the continuous state of the system. Additionally, for a finite state birth-death Markov chain (represented as a graph) under scalar linear dynamical systems, we derive analytical expressions for the NE takeover strategies and saddle-point values. We illustrate our findings through numerical studies involving epidemic models and linear dynamical systems with adversarial interactions.

Keywords: Game Theory · Graphs · Dynamical Systems

1 Introduction

Cyber-Physical Systems (CPS) are essential for integrating computational elements with physical processes, enabling advanced functionalities in various domains. Examples include smart grids for efficient energy distribution, autonomous vehicles for navigation and safety, and industrial automation systems for enhanced productivity through precise control and sensor feedback [1,2].

© The Author(s), under exclusive license to Springer Nature Switzerland AG 2025
A. Sinha et al. (Eds.): GameSec 2024, LNCS 14908, pp. 220–239, 2025.
https://doi.org/10.1007/978-3-031-74835-6_11

In the context of CPS, each node in a graph can be represented as a dynamical process, such as the generation and consumption of electricity in smart grids, the motion dynamics of autonomous vehicles, or the operational processes in industrial automation. These dynamical processes are interconnected through edges that represent the interactions and dependencies between them. For instance, in a smart grid, nodes may represent dynamic processes of energy generation and consumption at different substations, while edges denote the power flow between these substations [3]. Similarly, in autonomous vehicle networks, nodes could represent the dynamic driving processes of individual vehicles, with edges capturing the communication and coordination required for safe and efficient traffic flow [4–6].

The use of graphs in modeling CPS is crucial for understanding the system's overall behavior and ensuring its robust operation. Graphs facilitate the visualization and analysis of how individual dynamic processes interconnect to form a larger, cohesive system. This interconnection highlights the importance of securing these nodes and their interactions to prevent disruptions that could compromise the entire system [7,8].

Securing CPS critically involves mitigating the risks of stealthy takeovers, where an adversary covertly gains control of system components. The FlipIT game [9] provides a framework for analyzing such scenarios, where both the attacker and defender can stealthily control a static resource without the other party's immediate knowledge. This model captures the continuous and covert nature of security threats in CPS, highlighting the need for persistent vigilance and strategic defense mechanisms.

The FlipIT framework was extended to dynamical systems in FlipDyn [10], where a defender and adversary aim to take over a common resource modeled as a discrete-time dynamical system over a finite horizon. Building on FlipDyn, this paper focuses on resource takeovers in graphs, where each node represents a resource with its own dynamics, and nodes are connected by edges reflecting CPS interactions. Two players, a defender and an adversary, seek to repeatedly take over the graph's resources. This setup captures strategic interactions in a dynamic, interconnected environment, generalizing the FlipDyn framework to multiple states.

Analyzing takeover games involves understanding optimal strategies for both the adversary and defender, considering various graph topologies and CPS characteristics. By leveraging game-theoretic models and topology structures, this paper proposes robust defense mechanisms to enhance CPS resilience against takeover attacks. This approach is crucial for ensuring the continued reliability and safety of essential infrastructures amidst emerging cyber threats.

1.1 Related Works

The seminal FlipIT [9] analyzes a two-player zero-sum game between a defender and an adversary attempting to take over a static resource, such as a computing device, virtual machine, or cloud service [11]. The work of FlipIT was generalized to the games of timing [12], where the actions of each player are dependent on the available exploitable vulnerability, and extended to include time-based exponential discounting [13]. FlipThem [14] expanded the game to multiple resources with AND/OR models. The work in FlipThem was extended to i) a threshold-based version [15], which considered a finite number (threshold) of resources beyond which there exists no incentives to takeover, ii) multiple resource with constraints on the frequency of takeover actions [16], and ii) heterogeneous resource costs and a learning-based method to determine player strategies [17]. Similar extensions include, Cheat-FlipIt model [18], in which the opponent agent may feint to flip the resources first, and then control the resources after a finite delay. Such takeover strategies have also impacted the blockchain system [19], where arbitrage bots in decentralized exchanges engage in priority gas auctions to exploit against ordinary users. Beyond the domain of cybersecurity, the FlipIT model has been introduced in supervisory control and data acquisition (SCADA) to evaluate the impact of cyberattacks with insider assistance. The model of FlipIT has been extensively applied in system security [11]. These works primarily focused on resource takeovers within a static system, lacking consideration for the dynamic evolution of physical systems. In contrast, our work incorporates the dynamics of a physical system in the game of resource takeovers between an adversary and a defender, addressing the need for strategies that account for the continuous and evolving nature of CPS.

A finite-horizon zero-sum stochastic game has been used to analyze probabilistic reachable sets for discrete-time stochastic hybrid systems [20], where both players act simultaneously. Conversely, controllers have been synthesized [21] for intermittent switching between a defender and an adversary in discrete-time systems with multi-dimensional control inputs and constraints [22]. Such takeovers correspond to covert misappropriation of a plant [23], where an attacker controls the plant while remaining hidden from the supervisory system, extending these attacks to load frequency control (LFC) systems [24]. Unlike previous research, our paper provides a feedback signal to infer control and allows taking control of the plant at any instant, balancing operational cost and performance.

The FlipNet model [25] extends FlipIT to a graph, representing a networked system of multiple resources, where each player can take over nodes. Network security in graphs is also viewed as advanced persistent threats (APT), modeled as a zero-sum repeated game with states as compromised edges [26]. Similarly, APTs are modeled as multi-stage zero-sum network hardening games, where the adversary finds the shortest path and the defender allocates resources to block it. Recently, dynamic information flow tracking has been proposed to detect APTs via a multistage game [27]. A similar APT model is explored in Cut-the-Rope [28], where the defender cuts the backdoor access of an adversary, demonstrating efficacy on attack graphs in the robotics domain [29]. FlipIT has also been used to study malware diffusion in epidemic models [30]. This paper addresses FlipIT in a graph-based setting, where the defender and adversary repeatedly aim to take over nodes. Unlike previous works, this zero-sum game is played over a finite horizon with a discrete-time dynamical process on each node and time-varying costs.

Our prior work which extends the `FlipIT` model to incorporate dynamical systems, termed `FlipDyn` [10]. The model of `FlipDyn` was extended to jointly solve the takeover and control policy [31]. In this paper, we extend the `FlipDyn` model to a finite horizon zero-sum game over a graph, where each node represents a dynamical system and the edges correspond to the interaction between these systems. The contributions of this work are two-fold:

1. **Takeover strategies over a graph with discrete-time dynamical system on nodes**: We formulate a two-player zero-sum takeover game involving a defender and an adversary seeking to takeover the nodes of a graph, representing a discrete-time dynamical systems. The costs incurred by each player are contingent on the current node of the graph. Assuming knowledge of the discrete-time dynamics, we establish the Nash equilibrium (NE) takeover strategies and saddle-point values.
2. **State-independent takeover strategies and saddle-point values for scalar/1− dimensional systems**: For a linear discrete-time scalar dynamical system with quadratic takeover and state costs, we determine NE takeover policies independent of the continuous state of both players. Furthermore, for a topology representing a finite state birth-death process, termed *dual deter model*, we derive analytical expression of the NE takeover policies and saddle-point values.

We illustrate our results on an epidemic model with no node dynamics and on an example from finance.

This paper is structured as follows. Section 2 formally defines the `FlipDyn` problem in a graph setting with continuous state and node dependent costs. In Sect. 3, we outline a solution methodology applicable to general discrete-time dynamical systems on nodes. Section 4 presents a solution for takeover policies for linear scalar discrete-time dynamical systems featuring quadratic costs, along with a topology dependent analytical solution and numerical examples in Sect. 5. The paper concludes with a discussion on future directions in Sect. 6.

2   Problem Formulation

Consider a directed multigraph $\mathcal{G} := \{V, E, \phi\}$, where V is the set of nodes with $|V| \in \mathbb{N}^+$, E is the set of edges (paired nodes), and $\phi : E \to \{\{\alpha, \beta\} | \alpha, \beta \in V^2\}$ is the incidence function mapping every edge to an ordered pair of nodes, defining the connectivity of the graph. The term $e_{\alpha,\beta} \in E$ represents the edges connecting the node $\alpha \in V$ with the node $\beta \in V$, such that when $\alpha = \beta$, it represents a self-loop. We consider a single adversary, originating from any node of the graph $\mathcal{G}$. The adversary's goal is to reach nodes within the graph which induces maximum cost, while a defender's mission is to hinder the adversary's advances.

We model the actions of the players and state evolution in discrete-time, with the variable k denoting the current time step, which takes on values from the set $\mathcal{K} := \{1, 2, \ldots, L, L+1\}$. We represent the current node at time k using

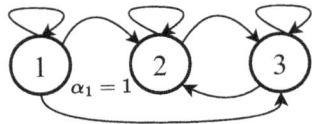

Fig. 1. A directed multigraph consisting of 3 nodes. At time $k = 1$, the `FlipDyn` state is $\alpha_1 = 1$. The actions of both players are $\{1, 2, 3\}$.

a variable $\alpha_k \in V$, referred to as the `FlipDyn` state. The adversary's action is denoted by the variable $\pi_k^{\mathrm{a}} \in \epsilon(\alpha_k)$, where the set $\epsilon(\alpha_k)$ is defined as:

$$\epsilon(\alpha_k) := \{j \in V | e_{\alpha_k, j} \in E\}.$$

Here, $\epsilon(\alpha_k)$ represents the nodes the adversary can potentially target from the current node α_k at time k, with $j = \alpha_k$ indicating the choice to remain idle or stay in the same node. Similarly, the defender's action is denoted by $\pi_k^{\mathrm{d}} \in \epsilon(\alpha_k)$. Notice that the defender's action set is identical to that of the adversary's, to deter or prevent further escalation. The `FlipDyn` state update is based on both the action of the defender and adversary, given by:

$$\alpha_{k+1} = \begin{cases} \pi_k^{\mathrm{d}}, & \text{if } \pi_k^{\mathrm{d}} = \pi_k^{\mathrm{a}}, \\ \pi_k^{\mathrm{d}}, & \text{else if } \pi_k^{\mathrm{d}} \in \{\epsilon(\alpha_k) | \pi_k^{\mathrm{a}} = \alpha_k\}, \\ \pi_k^{\mathrm{a}}, & \text{else if } \pi_k^{\mathrm{a}} \in \{\epsilon(\alpha_k) | \pi_k^{\mathrm{d}} = \alpha_k\}, \\ \alpha_k, & \text{otherwise.} \end{cases} \tag{1}$$

The `FlipDyn` update (1) states that if the actions of both the defender and adversary are identical, then the `FlipDyn` state remains unchanged. However, if the defender opts to choose any node while the adversary remains idle, then the `FlipDyn` state transitions into the chosen node. Similarly, if the defender remains idle while the adversary chooses any node, then the `FlipDyn` transitions to the chosen node. The `FlipDyn` state transition can be compactly written as:

$$\alpha_{k+1} = -\alpha_k \mathbf{1}_{\alpha_k}(\pi_k^{\mathrm{a}}) \mathbf{1}_{\alpha_k}(\pi_k^{\mathrm{d}}) + \mathbf{1}_{\alpha_k}(\pi_k^{\mathrm{a}}) \pi_k^{\mathrm{d}} + \mathbf{1}_{\alpha_k}(\pi_k^{\mathrm{d}}) \pi_k^{\mathrm{a}} + \bar{\mathbf{1}}_{\alpha_k}(\pi_k^{\mathrm{a}}) \bar{\mathbf{1}}_{\alpha_k}(\pi_k^{\mathrm{d}}) \pi_k^{\mathrm{d}}, \tag{2}$$

where $\mathbf{1}_{\alpha_k} : \epsilon(\alpha_k) \to \{0, 1\}$ is the indicator function, which maps to one if $\pi_k^{\mathrm{d}} = \alpha_k$ or $\pi_k^{\mathrm{a}} = \alpha_k$, and maps to zero, otherwise. The term $\bar{\mathbf{1}}_{\alpha_k}$ is the one's complement of $\mathbf{1}_{\alpha_k}$. For illustrative purpose, consider the graph shown in Fig. 1 with the `FlipDyn` state at time $k = 1$ as $\alpha_1 = 1$. The `FlipDyn` state can transition to the node 2, 3 or remain in node 1 based on the update equation (1).

In addition to the described graph environment, there is an underlying dynamical system whose continuous state at time k is indicated by $x_k \in \mathcal{X} \subseteq \mathbb{R}^n$, where $\mathcal{X}$ denotes the Euclidean state space. The state transition is dependent on the node α_{k+1} given by:

$$x_{k+1} = F_k^{\alpha_{k+1}}(x_k), \tag{3}$$

where $F_k^{\alpha_{k+1}} : \mathcal{X} \to \mathcal{X}$ is the transition function for each $k \in \mathcal{K}$ and $\alpha_{k+1} \in V$.

Our objective is to compute a strategy for both the players to transition the FlipDyn state to different nodes of the graph based on the dynamics (2), (3), takeover, and state costs. Given the initial state x_1 and node α_1, we pose the node takeover problem as a zero-sum dynamic game governed by the FlipDyn update (2) and state dynamics (3), over a finite-time L, where the defender aims to minimize an additive cost given by:

$$J(\alpha_1, x_1, \{\pi_{\mathbf{L}}^{\mathrm{a}}\}, \{\pi_{\mathbf{L}}^{\mathrm{d}}\}) = g_{L+1}^{\alpha_{L+1}}(x_{L+1}) + \sum_{t=1}^{L} g_t^{\alpha_t}(x_t) + \bar{\mathbf{1}}_{\alpha_t}(\pi_t^{\mathrm{d}}) d_t^{\pi_t^{\mathrm{d}}}(x_t)$$
$$- \bar{\mathbf{1}}_{\alpha_t}(\pi_t^{\mathrm{a}}) a_t^{\pi_t^{\mathrm{a}}}(x_t), \tag{4}$$

where $g_t^{\alpha_t}(x_t) : \mathcal{X} \to \mathbb{R}$ represents the cost for every FlipDyn state $\alpha_t \in V$, continuous state x_t at time $t \in \mathcal{K}$, with $g_{L+1}^{\alpha_{L+1}}(x_{L+1}) : \mathcal{X} \to \mathbb{R}$ representing the terminal cost for each $\alpha_{L+1} \in V$. The terms $d_t^{\pi_t^{\mathrm{d}}}(x_t) : \mathcal{X} \to \mathbb{R}$ and $a_t^{\pi_t^{\mathrm{a}}}(x_t) : \mathcal{X} \to \mathbb{R}$ represent the instantaneous takeover costs of the defender and adversary, respectively, for each $t \in \mathcal{K}$ and action $\pi_t^{\mathrm{d}}, \pi_t^{\mathrm{a}} \in \epsilon(\alpha_t)$. The defender and adversary actions over the finite-horizon L is given by the notations $\{\pi_{\mathbf{L}}^{\mathrm{a}}\} := \{\pi_1^{\mathrm{a}}, \ldots, \pi_L^{\mathrm{a}}\}$, and $\{\pi_{\mathbf{L}}^{\mathrm{d}}\} := \{\pi_1^{\mathrm{d}}, \ldots, \pi_L^{\mathrm{d}}\}$, respectively. In contrast, the adversary aims to maximize the cost function (4) leading to a zero-sum dynamic game. This formulation characterizes the strategic interaction between the two players in the context of a node takeover problem in a graph environment, termed as FlipDyn-G game.

We seek to find Nash Equilibrium (NE) solutions of the game (4). To guarantee the existence of a pure or mixed NE takeover strategy, we expand the set of player policies to behavioral strategies – probability distributions over the space of discrete actions at each discrete time [32]. Specifically, let

$$\mathbf{y}_k^{\alpha_k} := \{y_{k,j}^{\alpha_k} | j \in \epsilon(\alpha_k)\}, \sum_{j \in \epsilon(\alpha_k)} y_{k,j}^{\alpha_k} = 1, y_{k,j}^{\alpha_k} \geq 0, \text{ and} \tag{5}$$

$$\mathbf{z}_k^{\alpha_k} := \{z_{k,j}^{\alpha_k} | j \in \epsilon(\alpha_k)\}, \sum_{j \in \epsilon(\alpha_k)} z_{k,j}^{\alpha_k} = 1, z_{k,j}^{\alpha_k} \geq 0 \tag{6}$$

be the behavioral strategies for the defender and adversary, respectively, at time instant k for the FlipDyn state α_k. The takeover actions are

$$\pi_k^{\mathrm{d}} \sim \mathbf{y}_k^{\alpha_k}, \quad \pi_k^{\mathrm{a}} \sim \mathbf{z}_k^{\alpha_k},$$

for the defender and adversary at any time k are sampled from the corresponding behavioral strategy. The behavioral strategies are $y_k^{\alpha_k}, z_k^{\alpha_k} \in \Delta_{|\epsilon(\alpha_k)|}$, where $\Delta_{|\epsilon(\alpha_k)|}$ is the probability simplex in $|\epsilon(\alpha_k)|$ dimensions. Over the finite horizon L, let $y_{\mathbf{L}} := \{\mathbf{y}_1^{\alpha_1}, \mathbf{y}_2^{\alpha_2}, \ldots, \mathbf{y}_L^{\alpha_L}\} \in \Delta_{|\epsilon(\alpha_1)|} \times \Delta_{|\epsilon(\alpha_2)|} \times \cdots \times \Delta_{|\epsilon(\alpha_L)|}$ and $z_{\mathbf{L}} := \{\mathbf{z}_1^{\alpha_1}, \mathbf{z}_2^{\alpha_2}, \ldots, \mathbf{z}_L^{\alpha_L}\} \in \Delta_{|\epsilon(\alpha_1)|}^L \times \Delta_{|\epsilon(\alpha_2)|}^L \times \cdots \times \Delta_{|\epsilon(\alpha_L)|}^L$ be the sequence of defender and adversary behavioral strategies. Thus, the expected outcome of the zero-sum game (4) is given by:

$$J_E(x_1, \alpha_1, y_{\mathbf{L}}, z_{\mathbf{L}}) := \mathbb{E}[J(x_1, \alpha_1, \{\pi_L^{\mathrm{a}}\}, \{\pi_L^{\mathrm{d}}\})], \tag{7}$$

where the expectation is computed with respect to the distributions $y_{\mathbf{L}}$ and $z_{\mathbf{L}}$. Specifically, we seek a saddle-point solution $(y_{\mathbf{L}}^*, z_{\mathbf{L}}^*)$ in the space of behavioral strategies such that for any non-zero initial state $x_1 \in \mathcal{X}, \alpha_1 \in V$, we have:

$$J_E(x_1, \alpha_1, y_{\mathbf{L}}^*, z_{\mathbf{L}}) \leq J_E(x_1, \alpha_1, y_{\mathbf{L}}^*, z_{\mathbf{L}}^*) \leq J_E(x_1, \alpha_1, y_{\mathbf{L}}.z_{\mathbf{L}}^*).$$

The FlipDyn game over a graph is completely defined by the expected cost (7) and the space of player takeover strategies subject to the dynamics in (2) and (3). In the next section, we derive the outcome of the FlipDyn game for each node in the graph for general systems.

3   FlipDyn-G for General Problem

3.1   Saddle-Point Value of Any Node

At time instant $k \in \mathcal{K}$, given a FlipDyn state α_k, the saddle-point value comprises the instantaneous state cost and an additive cost-to-go based on the players takeover actions. The cost-to-go is determined via a cost-to-go matrix in each of the FlipDyn state α_k, represented by $\Xi_{k+1}^{\alpha_k} \in \mathbb{R}^{|\epsilon(\alpha_k)| \times |\epsilon(\alpha_k)|}$. Let $V_k^{\alpha_k}(x, \Xi_{k+1}^{\alpha_k})$ be the saddle-point value at time instant k with the continuous state x and cost-to-go matrix, corresponding to the FlipDyn state of α_k. Let us define a set of nodes connected to α_k as, $\{\alpha_k, j_2, j_3, \ldots, j_{m(\alpha_k)}\} \in \epsilon(\alpha_k)$, where $m(\alpha_k) = |\epsilon(\alpha_k)|$. Such a set of nodes will help us define the cost-to-go matrix. The entries of the cost-to-go matrix $\Xi_{k+1}^{\alpha_k}$ corresponding to each pair of takeover actions are:

$$
\begin{array}{c}
\begin{array}{cccc}
\alpha_k & j_2 & \cdots & j_{m(\alpha_k)}
\end{array} \\
\begin{array}{c}
\alpha_k \\
j_2 \\
\cdots \\
j_{m(\alpha_k)}
\end{array}
\underbrace{
\left[
\begin{array}{cccc}
v_{k+1}^{\alpha_k}(\alpha_k, \alpha_k) & \cdots & \cdots & v_{k+1}^{j_{m(\alpha_k)}}(\alpha_k, j_{m(\alpha_k)}) \\
v_{k+1}^{j_2}(j_2, \alpha_k) & v_{k+1}^{j_2}(j_2, j_2) & \cdots & v_{k+1}^{\alpha_k}(j_2, j_{m(\alpha_k)}) \\
\cdots & \cdots & \cdots & \cdots \\
v_{k+1}^{j_{m(\alpha_k)}}(j_{m(\alpha_k)}, \alpha_k) & v_{k+1}^{\alpha_k}(j_{m(\alpha_k)}, j_2) & \cdots & v_{k+1}^{j_{m(\alpha_k)}}(j_{m(\alpha_k)}, j_{m(\alpha_k)})
\end{array}
\right]
}_{\Xi_{k+1}^{\alpha_k}},
\end{array}
\quad (8)
$$

where $v_{k+1}^{\alpha_{k+1}}(\pi_k^{\mathrm{d}}, \pi_k^{\mathrm{a}})$ corresponds to the cost-to-go value of a FlipDyn state $\alpha_{k+1} \in V$, defined as:

$$v_{k+1}^{\alpha_{k+1}}(\pi_k^{\mathrm{d}}, \pi_k^{\mathrm{a}}) := V_{k+1}^{\alpha_{k+1}}(F_k^{\alpha_{k+1}}(x), \Xi_{k+2}^{\alpha_{k+2}}) + \bar{\mathbf{1}}_{\alpha_k}(\pi_k^{\mathrm{d}}) d_k^{\pi_k^{\mathrm{d}}}(x_k) - \bar{\mathbf{1}}_{\alpha_k}(\pi_k^{\mathrm{a}}) a_k^{\pi_k^{\mathrm{a}}}(x_k).$$

The diagonal terms in (8) correspond to the saddle-point value of the FlipDyn states under identical defender and adversary actions. Notice, only under the action of $\pi_k^{\mathrm{d}} = \pi_k^{\mathrm{a}} = \alpha_k$ the takeover costs for both players are zero. The first row of $\Xi_{k+1}^{\alpha_k}$ corresponds to the saddle-point values of FlipDyn states chosen by the adversary, when the defender remains idle. Similarly, the first column corresponds to the saddle-point value of the FlipDyn states chosen by the defender under an idle adversary action. The remaining entries of $\Xi_{k+1}^{\alpha_k}$ correspond to the saddle-point value of the `FlipDyn` state α_k with the corresponding takeover costs. The entries of the cost-to-go matrix are constructed using the `FlipDyn` dynamics (2) and continuous state dynamics (3). Thus, at time k for a given state x and α_k, the saddle-point value satisfies

$$V_k^{\alpha_k}(x, \Xi_{k+1}^{\alpha_k}) = g_k^{\alpha_k}(x) + \text{Val}(\Xi_{k+1}^{\alpha_k}), \tag{9}$$

where $\text{Val}(X_{k+1}^{\alpha_k}) := \min_{y_k^{\alpha_k}} \max_{z_k^{\alpha_k}} {y_k^{\alpha_k}}^{\mathsf{T}} X_{k+1} z_k^{\alpha_k}$, represents the (mixed) saddle-point value of the zero-sum matrix X_{k+1} for the `FlipDyn` state α_k, and $\Xi_{k+1}^{\alpha_k} \in \mathbb{R}^{|\epsilon(\alpha_k)| \times |\epsilon(\alpha_k)|}$ is the cost-to-go zero-sum matrix. The defender's and adversary's action results in either an entry within $\Xi_{k+1}^{\alpha_k}$ (if the matrix has a saddle point in pure strategies) or in the expected sense, resulting in a cost-to-go from state x at time k.

With the saddle-point values established in each of the `FlipDyn` states $\alpha_k \in V$, next, we will characterize the NE takeover strategies and the saddle-point values for the entire time horizon L.

3.2   NE Takeover Strategies of the `FlipDyn-G` game

To characterize the saddle-point value of the game, we restrict the state and takeover costs to a particular domain, stated in the following mild assumption.

Assumption 1. *[Non-negative costs] For any time instant $k \in \mathcal{K}$, the state and takeover costs $g_k^\alpha(x), d_k^\alpha(x), a_k^\alpha(x)$, for all $x \in \mathcal{X}$, and $\alpha \in V$ are non-negative $(\mathbb{R}_{\geq 0})$.*

Assumption 1 enables us to compare the entries of the cost-to-go matrix without changes in the sign of the costs, thereby, characterizing the strategies of the players (pure or mixed strategies). Under Assumption 1, we derive the following result to compute a recursive saddle-point value for the horizon length L and the corresponding NE takeover strategies for both the players in every node of the graph environment.

Lemma 1. *Under Assumption 1, the saddle-point value of the `FlipDyn-G` game (7) at any time $k \in \mathcal{K}$, subject to the `FlipDyn` dynamics (2) and continuous state dynamics (3) is given by:*

$$V_k^{\alpha_k *}(x, \Xi_{k+1}^{\alpha_k}) = g_k^{\alpha_k} + {y_k^{\alpha_k *}}^{\mathsf{T}} \Xi_{k+1}^{\alpha_k} z_k^{\alpha_k *}, \tag{10}$$

where $y_k^{\alpha_k *}$ and $z_k^{\alpha_k *}$ correspond to NE takeover policies obtained upon solving the zero-sum matrix defined by $\Xi_{k+1}^{\alpha_k}$ (cost-constructed backward in time using the saddle-point values at $k+1$) as a linear program [32]. The boundary condition of the saddle-point value recursion (10) at $k = L$ is given by:

$$\Xi_{L+2}^{\alpha_{L+1}} := \mathbf{0}_{m(\alpha_{L+1}) \times m(\alpha_{L+1})}, \forall \alpha_{L+1} \in V. \tag{11}$$

We skip the proof of the Lemma 1 as it involves simple substitutions and the use of recursive optimality. For a finite cardinality of the state space $\mathcal{X}$, FlipDyn states V, and a finite horizon L, Lemma 1 yields an exact (behavioral) saddle-point value of the FlipDyn-G game (7). However, the computational and storage complexities scale undesirably with the cardinality of $\mathcal{X}$, especially in continuous state spaces. For this purpose, in the next section, we will provide a parametric form of the saddle-point value especially in the case of scalar linear dynamics with quadratic costs.

4 FlipDyn-G for scalar LQ Problems

To render a tractable solution for continuous state of the FlipDyn-G game, we restrict ourselves to scalar linear discrete-time dynamical system with quadratic costs (LQ problem). The discrete-time dynamics of a linear system at time instant $k \in \mathcal{K}$ in the FlipDyn state α_{k+1} is given by:

$$x_{k+1} = F_k^{\alpha_{k+1}}(x_k) := f_k^{\alpha_{k+1}} x_k, \tag{12}$$

where $f_k^{\alpha_{k+1}} \in \mathbb{R}$ denotes the state transition scalar coefficient. The stage and takeover costs are assumed to be quadratic for each player and given by:

$$g_k^{\alpha_k}(x) = x^2 \mathbf{g}_k^{\alpha_k}, \quad d_k^{\alpha_k}(x) = x^2 \mathbf{d}_k^{\alpha_k}, \quad a_k^{\alpha_k}(x) = x^2 \mathbf{a}_k^{\alpha_k}, \tag{13}$$

where $\mathbf{g}_k^{\alpha_k} \in \mathbb{R}, \mathbf{a}_k^{\alpha_k} \in \mathbb{R}, \mathbf{d}_k^{\alpha_k} \in \mathbb{R}$ are non-negative ($\mathbb{R}_{\geq 0}$) under Assumption 1.

Under Assumption 1 for scalar dynamical systems of the form (12), we postulate a parametric form for the saddle-point value for each FlipDyn state $\alpha \in V$ of the form:

$$V_k^{\alpha_k}(x, \Xi_{k+1}^{\alpha_k}) \Rightarrow V_k^{\alpha_k}(x) := \mathbf{p}_k^{\alpha_k} x^2, \; \forall \alpha_k \in V, \; k \in \mathcal{K}, \tag{14}$$

where $\mathbf{p}_k^{\alpha_k} \in \mathbb{R}_{\geq 0}$ corresponds to a non-negative coefficient for each of the FlipDyn states. Under the scalar linear dynamical system (12), takeover costs (13) and the parameteric form (14), the cost-to-go matrix $\hat{\Xi}_{k+1}^{\alpha_k}$ can be re-expressed as:

$$
\begin{array}{c}
\begin{array}{cccc}
\alpha_k & j_2 & \cdots & j_{m(\alpha_k)}
\end{array} \\
\begin{array}{c}
\alpha_k \\
j_2 \\
\cdots \\
j_{m(\alpha_k)}
\end{array}
\underbrace{
\left[
\begin{array}{cccc}
\mathbf{v}_{k+1}^{\alpha_k}(\alpha_k, \alpha_k) & \cdots & \cdots & \mathbf{v}_{k+1}^{j_{m(\alpha_k)}}(\alpha_k, j_{m(\alpha_k)}) \\
\mathbf{v}_{k+1}^{j_2}(j_2, \alpha_k) & \mathbf{v}_{k+1}^{j_2}(j_2, j_2) & \cdots & \mathbf{v}_{k+1}^{\alpha_k}(j_2, j_{m(\alpha_k)}) \\
\cdots & & \cdots & \cdots \\
\mathbf{v}_{k+1}^{j_{m(\alpha_k)}}(j_{m(\alpha_k)}, \alpha_k) & \mathbf{v}_{k+1}^{\alpha_k}(j_{m(\alpha_k)}, j_2) & \cdots & \mathbf{v}_{k+1}^{j_{m(\alpha_k)}}(j_{m(\alpha_k)}, j_{m(\alpha_k)})
\end{array}
\right]
}_{\hat{\Xi}_{k+1}^{\alpha_k}},
\end{array}
\tag{15}
$$

where $\mathbf{v}_{k+1}^{\alpha_k}(u, w)$ corresponds to the cost-to-go term of a FlipDyn state independent of the term x^2, defined as:

$$\mathbf{v}_{k+1}^{\alpha_{k+1}}(\pi_k^{\mathrm{d}}, \pi_k^{\mathrm{a}}) := (f_k^{\alpha_{k+1}})^2 \mathbf{p}_{k+1}^{\alpha_{k+1}} + \bar{\mathbf{1}}_{\alpha_k}(\pi_k^{\mathrm{d}}) \mathbf{d}_k^{\pi_k^{\mathrm{d}}} - \bar{\mathbf{1}}_{\alpha_k}(\pi_k^{\mathrm{a}}) \mathbf{a}_k^{\pi_k^{\mathrm{a}}}.$$

Fig. 2. A graph consisting of N nodes .

Notice the cost-to-go entries consists of the system transition coefficients and takeover costs, while factoring out the term x^2. Building on Lemma 1, we present the following result, which provides the NE takeover policies of both players, and outlines the saddle-point value update of $\mathbf{p}_k^{\alpha_k}$ for any FlipDyn state.

Lemma 2. *Under Assumption 1, at any time $k \in \mathcal{K}$, the saddle-point value parameter of the FlipDyn-G game (7) for quadratic state and takeover costs (13), subject to the FlipDyn dynamics (2) and scalar state dynamics (12), is given by:*

$$\mathbf{p}_k^{\alpha_k *} = g_k^{\alpha_k} + y_k^{\alpha_k *^{\mathrm{T}}} \hat{\Xi}_{k+1}^{\alpha_k} z_k^{\alpha_k *}, \tag{16}$$

where $y_k^{\alpha_k *}$ and $z_k^{\alpha_k *}$ correspond to NE takeover policies obtained upon solving the zero-sum matrix $\hat{\Xi}_{k+1}^{\alpha_k}$ as a linear program [32]. The boundary condition of the saddle-point value recursion (10) at $k = L$ is given by:

$$\hat{\Xi}_{L+2}^{\alpha_{L+1}} := \mathbf{0}_{m(\alpha_{L+1}) \times m(\alpha_{L+1})}, \forall \alpha_{L+1} \in V. \tag{17}$$

Substituting the scalar state dynamics (12) along with state and takeover costs (13) yields the NE strategies and saddle-point value parameters (16). We skip the proof of Lemma 2 for brevity. Lemma 2 presents a complete solution for the FlipDyn-G (7) game with NE takeover strategies independent of state of the scalar dynamical system. In the following subsection, we will derive closed-form expressions of the FlipDyn-G game for a special graph structure and show how the structure represents the original FlipDyn game [10].

4.1   Dual Deter FlipDyn-G game

We examine a special case of the graph environment, termed the *dual deter* model, which consists of a start and end node each connecting to only one other node, while the remaining nodes connect to two different nodes. This model can be viewed as a finite state Markov chain birth-death process [33]. We assume the dual deter model has an ordered set of nodes from node 0 to N, resulting in a total of $|V| = N + 1$ nodes, as illustrated in Fig. 2.

A key difference compared to the general graph model lies in the action space of the defender and adversary. At any node $\alpha_k \in \{1, 2, \ldots, N-1\}$, the action space of the adversary is $\pi_k^{\mathrm{a}} := \{\alpha_k, \overline{\alpha}\}$, $\overline{\alpha} \in \{V | \overline{\alpha} > \alpha_k\}$, and of the defender is $\pi_k^{\mathrm{d}} := \{\alpha_k, \underline{\alpha}\}$, $\underline{\alpha} \in \{V | \underline{\alpha} < \alpha_k\}$. The action space of both the defender and adversary in the start and end node $\alpha_k = \{0, N\}$ are given as $\pi_k^{\mathrm{d}} := \{\alpha_k, \tau\}$ and $\pi_k^{\mathrm{a}} := \{\alpha_k, \tau\}$, where τ represents a takeover action in the node α_k, preventing transition to other nodes. Such an action space and model represents the defender deterring an adversary from escalating through the graph. The `FlipDyn` state updates in such a dual deter model as follows:

$$\alpha_{k+1} = \begin{cases} \alpha_k, & \text{if } \pi_k^d = \pi_k^a | \alpha_k = \{0, N\}, \\ 1, & \text{else if } \pi_k^a = \tau | \pi_k^d = 0, \alpha_k = 0, \\ N-1, & \text{else if } \pi_k^a = \tau | \pi_k^d = N, \alpha_k = N, \\ \pi_k^d, & \text{else if } \pi_k^d = \pi_k^a, \\ \underline{\alpha}, & \text{else if } \pi_k^d = \underline{\alpha} | \pi_k^a = \alpha_k, \\ \overline{\alpha}, & \text{else if} \pi_k^a = \overline{\alpha} | \pi_k^d = \alpha_k\}, \\ \alpha_k, & \text{otherwise.} \end{cases} \tag{18}$$

We characterize the NE strategies and saddle-point values of the dual deter model under the assumption of a scalar linear dynamical system (12) and quadratic costs (13) with a parameterized saddle-point value (14). Such an action space leads to a reduced dimension of the cost-to-go matrix independent of the state term x^2 at any node $\alpha_k \in \{1, 2, \ldots, N-1\}$, given by:

$$\begin{array}{cc} & \alpha_k \qquad\qquad \overline{\alpha} \\ \begin{array}{c} \alpha_k \\ \underline{\alpha} \end{array} & \left[\begin{array}{cc} (f_k^{\alpha_k})^2 \mathbf{p}_{k+1}^{\alpha_k} & (f_k^{\overline{\alpha}})^2 \mathbf{p}_{k+1}^{\overline{\alpha}} - \mathbf{a}_k^{\alpha_k} \\ (f_k^{\underline{\alpha}})^2 \mathbf{p}_{k+1}^{\underline{\alpha}} + \mathbf{d}_k^{\alpha_k} & (f_k^{\alpha_k})^2 \mathbf{p}_{k+1}^{\alpha_k} + \mathbf{d}_k^{\alpha_k} - \mathbf{a}_k^{\alpha_k} \end{array} \right]. \end{array} \tag{19}$$

Similarly, the cost-to-go matrix for the start node $\alpha_k = 0$ independent of the state term x^2 is given by:

$$\begin{array}{cc} & 0 \qquad\qquad \tau \\ \begin{array}{c} 0 \\ \tau \end{array} & \left[\begin{array}{cc} (f_k^0)^2 \mathbf{p}_{k+1}^0 & (f_k^1)^2 \mathbf{p}_{k+1}^1 - \mathbf{a}_k^0 \\ (f_k^0)^2 \mathbf{p}_{k+1}^0 + \mathbf{d}_k^0 & (f_k^0)^2 \mathbf{p}_{k+1}^0 + \mathbf{d}_k^0 - \mathbf{a}_k^0 \end{array} \right], \end{array} \tag{20}$$

whereas for the end node $\alpha_k = N$, we have:

$$\begin{array}{cc} & N \qquad\qquad \tau \\ \begin{array}{c} N \\ \tau \end{array} & \left[\begin{array}{cc} (f_k^N)^2 \mathbf{p}_{k+1}^N & (f_k^N)^2 \mathbf{p}_{k+1}^N - \mathbf{a}_k^N \\ (f_k^{N-1})^2 \mathbf{p}_{k+1}^{N-1} + \mathbf{d}_k^N & (f_k^N)^2 \mathbf{p}_{k+1}^N + \mathbf{d}_k^N - \mathbf{a}_k^N \end{array} \right]. \end{array} \tag{21}$$

The transition of the nodes in (19) follows from the `FlipDyn` dynamics (2). Next, we present the NE takeover in both pure and mixed strategies of both the players along with the saddle-point value parameter $\mathbf{p}_k^{\alpha_k}$ for every node in the dual deter model.

Theorem 1. *The unique NE takeover strategies of the* `FlipDyn-G` *game* (7) *at any time $k \in \mathcal{K}$ for quadratic state and takeover costs (13), subject to the* `FlipDyn` *dynamics* (18) *and scalar state dynamics (12) are given by:*

Case i) - $\alpha_k = 0$

$$
y_k^{0*} = \begin{cases} \left[\dfrac{\mathbf{a}_k^0}{\hat{\mathbf{p}}_{k+1}} \quad 1 - \dfrac{\mathbf{a}_k^0}{\hat{\mathbf{p}}_{k+1}}\right]^{\mathrm{T}}, & if \quad \hat{\mathbf{p}}_{k+1} > \mathbf{a}_k^0, \hat{\mathbf{p}}_{k+1} > \mathbf{d}_k^0, \\[4mm] \begin{bmatrix} 1 & 0 \end{bmatrix}^{\mathrm{T}}, & otherwise, \end{cases}
\tag{22}
$$

$$
z_k^{0*} = \begin{cases} \left[1 - \dfrac{\mathbf{d}_k^0}{\hat{\mathbf{p}}_{k+1}} \quad \dfrac{\mathbf{d}_k^0}{\hat{\mathbf{p}}_{k+1}}\right]^{\mathrm{T}}, & if \quad \hat{\mathbf{p}}_{k+1} > \mathbf{a}_k^0, \hat{\mathbf{p}}_{k+1} > \mathbf{d}_k^0, \\[4mm] \begin{bmatrix} 0 & 1 \end{bmatrix}^{\mathrm{T}}, & if \quad \hat{\mathbf{p}}_{k+1} > \mathbf{a}_k^0, \hat{\mathbf{p}}_{k+1} \leq \mathbf{d}_k^0, \\[4mm] \begin{bmatrix} 1 & 0 \end{bmatrix}^{\mathrm{T}}, & otherwise, \end{cases}
\tag{23}
$$

and the saddle-point value parameter satisfies:

$$
\mathbf{p}_k^0 = \begin{cases} \mathbf{g}_k^0 + (f_k^0)^2 \mathbf{p}_{k+1}^0 + \mathbf{d}_k^0 - \dfrac{\mathbf{a}_k^0 \mathbf{d}_k^0}{\hat{\mathbf{p}}_{k+1}}, & if \quad \hat{\mathbf{p}}_{k+1} > \mathbf{a}_k^0, \hat{\mathbf{p}}_{k+1} > \mathbf{d}_k^0, \\[4mm] \mathbf{g}_k^0 + (f_k^1)^2 \mathbf{p}_{k+1}^1 - \mathbf{a}_k^0, & if \quad \hat{\mathbf{p}}_{k+1} > \mathbf{a}_k^0, \hat{\mathbf{p}}_{k+1} \leq \mathbf{d}_k^0, \\[4mm] \mathbf{g}_k^0 + (f_k^0)^2 \mathbf{p}_{k+1}^0, & otherwise, \end{cases}
\tag{24}
$$

where $\hat{\mathbf{p}}_{k+1} := (f_k^1)^2 \mathbf{p}_{k+1}^1 - (f_k^0)^2 \mathbf{p}_{k+1}^0$.

Case ii) - $\alpha_k = \{1, 2, \ldots, N-1\}$

$$
y_k^{\alpha_k *} = \begin{cases} \begin{bmatrix} 1 & 0 \end{bmatrix}^{\mathrm{T}}, & if \quad \tilde{\mathbf{p}}_{k+1}^{\alpha_k} < \mathbf{d}_k^{\alpha_k}, -\check{\mathbf{p}}_{k+1}^{\alpha_k} < \mathbf{d}_k^{\alpha_k}, \\[4mm] \begin{bmatrix} 0 & 1 \end{bmatrix}^{\mathrm{T}}, & else\ if \quad \tilde{\mathbf{p}}_{k+1}^{\alpha_k} > \mathbf{d}_k^{\alpha_k}, -\check{\mathbf{p}}_{k+1}^{\alpha_k} > \mathbf{d}_k^{\alpha_k}, \\[4mm] \left[\dfrac{\tilde{\mathbf{p}}_{k+1}^{\alpha_k} - \mathbf{a}_k^{\alpha_k}}{\tilde{\mathbf{p}}_{k+1}^{\alpha_k} + \check{\mathbf{p}}_{k+1}^{\alpha_k}} \quad \dfrac{\check{\mathbf{p}}_{k+1}^{\alpha_k} + \mathbf{a}_k^{\alpha_k}}{\tilde{\mathbf{p}}_{k+1}^{\alpha_k} + \check{\mathbf{p}}_{k+1}^{\alpha_k}}\right]^{\mathrm{T}}, & otherwise \end{cases}
\tag{25}
$$

$$
z_k^{0*} = \begin{cases} \begin{bmatrix} 1 & 0 \end{bmatrix}^{\mathrm{T}}, & if \quad -\tilde{\mathbf{p}}_{k+1}^{\alpha_k} < \mathbf{a}_k^{\alpha_k}, \check{\mathbf{p}}_{k+1}^{\alpha_k} < \mathbf{a}_k^{\alpha_k}, \\[4mm] \begin{bmatrix} 0 & 1 \end{bmatrix}^{\mathrm{T}}, & if \quad -\tilde{\mathbf{p}}_{k+1}^{\alpha_k} > \mathbf{a}_k^{\alpha_k}, \check{\mathbf{p}}_{k+1}^{\alpha_k} > \mathbf{a}_k^{\alpha_k}, \\[4mm] \left[\dfrac{\tilde{\mathbf{p}}_{k+1}^{\alpha_k} + \mathbf{d}_{k+1}^{\alpha_k}}{\tilde{\mathbf{p}}_{k+1}^{\alpha_k} + \check{\mathbf{p}}_{k+1}^{\alpha_k}} \quad \dfrac{\check{\mathbf{p}}_{k+1}^{\alpha_k} - \mathbf{d}_{k+1}^{\alpha_k}}{\tilde{\mathbf{p}}_{k+1}^{\alpha_k} + \check{\mathbf{p}}_{k+1}^{\alpha_k}}\right]^{\mathrm{T}}, & otherwise, \end{cases}
\tag{26}
$$

and the saddle-point value parameter satisfies:

$$
\mathbf{p}_k^{\alpha_k} = \begin{cases}
\mathbf{g}_k^{\alpha_k} + (f_k^{\alpha_k})^2 \mathbf{p}_{k+1}^{\alpha_K}, & \text{if} & \begin{array}{l} -\tilde{\mathbf{p}}_{k+1}^{\alpha_k} < \mathbf{a}_k^{\alpha_k}, \check{\mathbf{p}}_{k+1}^{\alpha_k} < \mathbf{a}_{k+1}^{\alpha_k}, \\ \check{\mathbf{p}}_{k+1}^{\alpha_k} < \mathbf{d}_{k+1}^{\alpha_k}, \end{array} \\[1.5em]
\mathbf{g}_k^{\alpha_k} + (f_k^{\alpha})^2 \mathbf{p}_{k+1}^{\alpha} + \mathbf{d}_{k+1}^{\alpha_k}, & \text{if} & \begin{array}{l} -\tilde{\mathbf{p}}_{k+1}^{\alpha_k} < \mathbf{a}_k^{\alpha_k}, \check{\mathbf{p}}_{k+1}^{\alpha_k} < \mathbf{a}_{k+1}^{\alpha_k}, \\ \check{\mathbf{p}}_{k+1}^{\alpha_k} > \mathbf{d}_{k+1}^{\alpha_k}, \end{array} \\[1.5em]
\mathbf{g}_k^{\alpha_k} + (f_k^{\overline{\alpha}})^2 \mathbf{p}_{k+1}^{\overline{\alpha}} - \mathbf{a}_{k+1}^{\alpha_k}, & \text{if} & \begin{array}{l} -\tilde{\mathbf{p}}_{k+1}^{\alpha_k} > \mathbf{a}_k^{\alpha_k}, \check{\mathbf{p}}_{k+1}^{\alpha_k} > \mathbf{a}_{k+1}^{\alpha_k}, \\ -\tilde{\mathbf{p}}_{k+1}^{\alpha_k} < \mathbf{d}_{k+1}^{\alpha_k}, \end{array} \\[1.5em]
\mathbf{g}_k^{\alpha_k} + (f_k^{\alpha_k})^2 \mathbf{p}_{k+1}^{\alpha_k} - \mathbf{a}_{k+1}^{\alpha_k} + \mathbf{d}_{k+1}^{\alpha_k}, & \text{if} & \begin{array}{l} -\tilde{\mathbf{p}}_{k+1}^{\alpha_k} > \mathbf{a}_k^{\alpha_k}, \check{\mathbf{p}}_{k+1}^{\alpha_k} > \mathbf{a}_{k+1}^{\alpha_k}, \\ -\tilde{\mathbf{p}}_{k+1}^{\alpha_k} > \mathbf{d}_{k+1}^{\alpha_k}, \end{array} \\[1.5em]
\mathbf{g}_k^0 + \dfrac{(f_k^{\alpha_k})^4 (\mathbf{p}_{k+1}^{\alpha_k})^2 + \mathbf{a}_k^{\alpha_k} \mathbf{d}_k^{\alpha_k}}{\tilde{\mathbf{p}}_{k+1}^{\alpha_k} + \check{\mathbf{p}}_{k+1}^{\alpha_k}} & & \\[1em]
\quad + \dfrac{\tilde{\mathbf{p}}_{k+1}^{\alpha_k} \mathbf{d}_k^{\alpha_k} - \check{\mathbf{p}}_{k+1}^{\alpha_k} \mathbf{a}_k^{\alpha_k}}{\tilde{\mathbf{p}}_{k+1}^{\alpha_k} + \check{\mathbf{p}}_{k+1}^{\alpha_k}} & \text{otherwise}, & \\[1em]
\quad - \dfrac{(f_k^{\alpha})^2 \mathbf{p}_{k+1}^{\alpha} (f_k^{\overline{\alpha}})^2 \mathbf{p}_{k+1}^{\overline{\alpha}}}{\tilde{\mathbf{p}}_{k+1}^{\alpha_k} + \check{\mathbf{p}}_{k+1}^{\alpha_k}}, & &
\end{cases}
\tag{27}
$$

where

$$
\tilde{\mathbf{p}}_{k+1}^{\alpha_k} := (f_k^{\alpha_k})^2 \mathbf{p}_{k+1}^{\alpha_k} - (f_k^{\alpha})^2 \mathbf{p}_{k+1}^{\alpha}, \check{\mathbf{p}}_{k+1}^{\alpha_k} := (f_k^{\alpha_k})^2 \mathbf{p}_{k+1}^{\alpha_k} - (f_k^{\overline{\alpha}})^2 \mathbf{p}_{k+1}^{\overline{\alpha}}.
$$

Case iii) - $\alpha_k = N$

$$
y_k^{N*} = \begin{cases}
\left[1 - \dfrac{\mathbf{a}_k^N}{\bar{\mathbf{p}}_{k+1}} \quad \dfrac{\mathbf{a}_k^N}{\bar{\mathbf{p}}_{k+1}} \right]^{\mathrm{T}}, & \text{if} \quad \bar{\mathbf{p}}_{k+1} > \mathbf{a}_k^N, \bar{\mathbf{p}}_{k+1} > \mathbf{d}_k^N, \\[1.5em]
\left[\quad 0 \quad\quad 1 \quad \right]^{\mathrm{T}}, & \text{if} \quad \bar{\mathbf{p}}_{k+1} \le \mathbf{a}_k^N, \bar{\mathbf{p}}_{k+1} > \mathbf{d}_k^N, \\[1.5em]
\left[\quad 1 \quad\quad 0 \quad \right]^{\mathrm{T}}, & \text{otherwise},
\end{cases}
\tag{28}
$$

$$
z_k^{N*} = \begin{cases}
\left[\dfrac{\mathbf{d}_k^N}{\bar{\mathbf{p}}_{k+1}} \quad 1 - \dfrac{\mathbf{d}_k^N}{\bar{\mathbf{p}}_{k+1}} \right]^{\mathrm{T}}, & \text{if} \quad \hat{\mathbf{p}}_{k+1} > \mathbf{a}_k^N, \hat{\mathbf{p}}_{k+1} > \mathbf{d}_k^N, \\[1.5em]
\left[\quad 1 \quad\quad 0 \quad \right]^{\mathrm{T}}, & \text{otherwise},
\end{cases}
\tag{29}
$$

and the saddle-point value parameter is given by:

$$
\mathbf{p}_k^N = \begin{cases}
\mathbf{g}_k^N + (f_k^N)^2 \mathbf{p}_{k+1}^N - \mathbf{d}_k^N + \dfrac{\mathbf{a}_k^0 \mathbf{d}_k^0}{\hat{\mathbf{p}}_{k+1}}, & \text{if} \quad \hat{\mathbf{p}}_{k+1} > \mathbf{a}_k^N, \hat{\mathbf{p}}_{k+1} > \mathbf{d}_k^N, \\[1.5em]
\mathbf{g}_k^N + (f_k^{N-1})^2 \mathbf{p}_{k+1}^{N-1} + \mathbf{d}_k^N, & \text{if} \quad \hat{\mathbf{p}}_{k+1} > \mathbf{a}_k^N, \hat{\mathbf{p}}_{k+1} \le \mathbf{d}_k^N, \\[1.5em]
\mathbf{g}_k^N + (f_k^N)^2 \mathbf{p}_{k+1}^N, & \text{otherwise},
\end{cases}
\tag{30}
$$

where $\bar{\mathbf{p}}_{k+1} := (f_k^N)^2 \mathbf{p}_{k+1}^N - (f_k^{N-1})^2 \mathbf{p}_{k+1}^{N-1}.$

The boundary condition of the saddle-point value recursion (24), (27), (30) *at* $k = L + 1$ *is given by:*

$$\mathbf{p}_{L+1}^{\alpha_{L+1}} := \mathbf{g}_{L+1}^{\alpha_{L+1}}, \forall \alpha_{L+1} \in V. \tag{31}$$

$\square$

The derivation of the NE takeover policies and saddle-point value parameters in Theorem 1 closely follows the procedure outlined in [31]. Therefore, we omit the proofs for the sake of brevity. Theorem 1 presents a closed-form solution for the FlipDyn-G (7) game with NE takeover strategies independent of state for scalar linear dynamical systems. The dual deter model captures a specific structure of the general FlipDyn-G game. This structure enables us to complete the NE strategies and saddle-point value of the game in closed-form. The following remark indicates when the dual deter model maps to the FlipDyn model [10].

Remark 1. When the dual deter model consists of only two nodes, $\alpha = \{0, 1\}$, the FlipDyn-G game reduces to a FlipDyn [10] model with a full state feedback control, with NE strategy and saddle-point value parameter as described in (22), (23), (24), (28), (29), and (30).

Next, we illustrate the results of Lemma 2 through two numerical examples.

5   Numerical Examples

5.1   Numerical Example I

We evaluate the NE takeover strategy and saddle-point value of the FlipDyn-G game on an epidemic dynamic model, which is a discrete-time linear model capturing the dynamics of infection. This model can be mapped to a graph environment with four nodes: susceptible, infected, recovered, and deceased, termed as the SIRD model. The adversary is assumed to be the source of infection causing transitions between nodes, while a government organization represents the defender preventing transitions that can lead to significant losses. Typically, epidemic models have fixed transition probabilities between nodes; however, in this setup, transitions are governed by NE takeover policies. The SIRD model is shown in Fig. 3a, with four FlipDyn states: susceptible (S), infected (I), recovered (R), and deceased (D). Therefore, the FlipDyn state can take on the value $\alpha_k \in \{S, I, R, D\}$ for all $k \in \mathcal{K}$.

This example presents only a FlipDyn dynamics, as the nodes do not have an underlying continuous state dynamics. In this example, we will consider the costs to be time-invariant, i.e., $\mathbf{g}_k^\alpha = \mathbf{g}^\alpha, \mathbf{d}_k^\alpha = \mathbf{d}^\alpha$, and $\mathbf{a}_k^\alpha = \mathbf{a}^\alpha, \forall k \in \mathcal{K}$ and $\alpha \in \{S,I,R,D\}$. The state costs follow the order given by:

$$\mathbf{g}^D > \mathbf{g}^I > \mathbf{g}^S > \mathbf{g}^R. \tag{32}$$

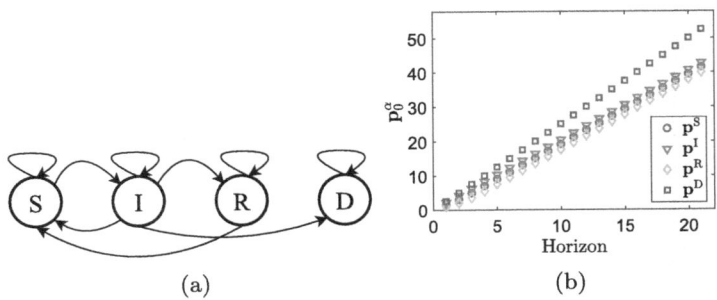

Fig. 3. (a) An epidemic model represented as a graph with four nodes. The `FlipDyn` states of the graph are susceptible (S), Infected (I), Recovered (R), and Deceased (D). (b) Saddle-point parameters for each node $\alpha = \{$S,I,R,D$\}$, over time k, with horizon length $L = 20$.

The state costs (32) imply that the `FlipDyn` state of death ($\alpha = $ D) has the highest cost, while the least is for the recovered ($\alpha = $ R). Similarly, the defender and adversary takeover costs follow the order given by:

$$\mathbf{d}^R > \mathbf{d}^S > \mathbf{d}^I > \mathbf{d}^D, \qquad \mathbf{a}^D > \mathbf{a}^I > \mathbf{a}^S > \mathbf{a}^R. \qquad (33)$$

The costs used in this numerical example are:

$$\mathbf{g}^S = 1.5, \ \mathbf{g}^I = 2.2, \ \mathbf{g}^R = 1.0, \ \mathbf{g}^D = 2.5,$$
$$\mathbf{d}^S = 0.7, \ \mathbf{d}^I = 0.5, \ \mathbf{d}^R = 0.8, \ \mathbf{d}^D = 0.2,$$
$$\mathbf{a}^S = 0.5, \ \mathbf{a}^I = 0.7, \ \mathbf{a}^R = 0.1, \ \mathbf{a}^D = 0.9.$$

We solve for the NE takeover strategies and saddle-point value using Lemma 2. Figure 3b shows the saddle-point value parameters $\mathbf{p}_k^\alpha, \alpha = \{S,I,R,D\}$ for a horizon length of $L = 20$. The saddle-point values corresponding to each of the nodes follow the order described in (32) indicating the cost in transitioning to the state $\alpha = D$ is the highest. We also observe that the value of the node $\alpha = I$ remains close to the other node states $\alpha = \{$R,D$\}$ reflective of the defender policy to prevent transition to $\alpha = D$.

The defender and adversary policies for the state $\alpha = I$ are shown in Figs. 4a and 4b. The state $\alpha = D$ is a sink state, meaning once you transition to it, you cannot transition to other states. We illustrate the policy for the state $\alpha = I$ as it allows both players to transition to any state. The defender's policy involves transitioning only to the susceptible and recovered states, avoiding the death state or remaining in the infected state. In contrast, the adversary has a high probability of transitioning to the death state and a low probability of transitioning to the recovered state, with zero probability of transitioning to the susceptible and infected states.

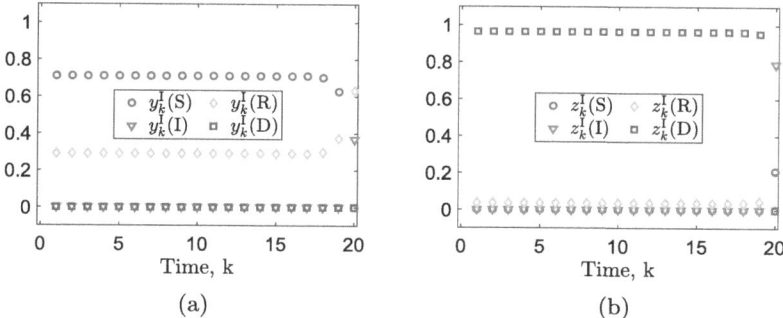

Fig. 4. For the node $\alpha = \mathrm{I}$, the NE policy of the (a) defender and (b) adversary, where $y_k^{\mathrm{I}}(\alpha), z_k^{\mathrm{I}}(\alpha), \alpha = \{\mathrm{S,I,R,D}\}$ corresponds to the probability of selecting the takeover node α, given $\alpha_k = \mathrm{I}$.

5.2   Numerical Example II

We evaluate the NE takeover strategy and saddle-point value of the `FlipDyn-G` game on a stock market Markov chain [34], with node dynamics. This model consists of three nodes: bull market, bear market, and stagnant market. An investor is represented as an adversary attempting to capitalize on the market, while the defender represents the rest of the players in the market. A bull, bear, and stagnant market represent an increase, decrease, and steady market growth, respectively. A graphical representation of this stock market model is shown in Fig. 5a, with three `FlipDyn` states: bull (Bu), bear (Br), and stagnant (St). Therefore, the `FlipDyn` state can take on the value $\alpha_k \in \{\mathrm{Bu, Br, St}\}$ for all $k \in \mathcal{K}$. For this example, we will assume the costs and dynamics are time-invariant, i.e., $\mathbf{g}_k^\alpha = \mathbf{g}^\alpha, \mathbf{d}_k^\alpha = \mathbf{d}^\alpha$, and $\mathbf{a}_k^\alpha = \mathbf{a}^\alpha, f_k^{\alpha_k} = f^{\alpha_k}, \forall k \in \mathcal{K}$ and $\alpha \in \{\mathrm{Bu,Br,St}\}$. The state costs and node dynamics follow the order given by:

$$\mathbf{g}^{\mathrm{Bu}} > \mathbf{g}^{\mathrm{Br}} > \mathbf{g}^{\mathrm{St}}, \qquad f^{\mathrm{Bu}} > f^{\mathrm{Br}} > f^{\mathrm{St}}. \tag{34}$$

The state costs and dynamics (34) indicate the `FlipDyn` state of the bull market ($\alpha = \mathrm{Bu}$) has the highest value with the least being the stagnant market ($\alpha = \mathrm{St}$). Similarly, the defender and adversary takeover costs follow the order:

$$\mathbf{d}^{\mathrm{Bu}} > \mathbf{d}^{\mathrm{St}} > \mathbf{d}^{\mathrm{Br}}, \qquad \mathbf{a}^{\mathrm{Br}} > \mathbf{a}^{\mathrm{St}} > \mathbf{a}^{\mathrm{Bu}}. \tag{35}$$

The dynamics and takeover costs used in this numerical example are:

$$\mathbf{f}^{\mathrm{Bu}} = 1.1, \ \mathbf{f}^{\mathrm{Br}} = 0.95, \ \mathbf{g}^{\mathrm{St}} = 1.0,$$
$$\mathbf{d}^{\mathrm{Bu}} = \mathbf{a}^{\mathrm{Br}} = 0.90, \ \mathbf{d}^{\mathrm{Br}} = \mathbf{a}^{\mathrm{Bu}} = 0.50, \ \mathbf{d}^{\mathrm{St}} = \mathbf{a}^{\mathrm{St}} = 0.75.$$

The `FlipDyn` state costs are time-varying and indicate in Fig. 5b. We solve for the NE takeover strategies and saddle-point value using Lemma 2. Figure 5c shows the saddle-point value parameters $\mathbf{p}_k^\alpha, \alpha = \{\mathrm{Bu,Br,St}\}$ for a horizon length of

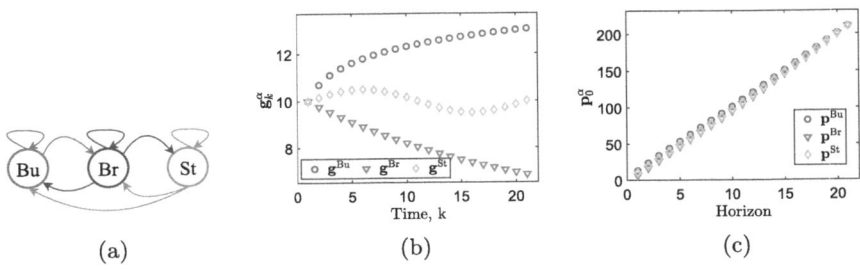

Fig. 5. (a) A stock market Markov chain model represented as a graph with three nodes. The `FlipDyn` states of the graph are Bull (Bu), Bear (Br), and Stagnant (St). (b) The state costs $\mathbf{g}_k^\alpha, \alpha \in \{\mathrm{Bu, Br, St}\}$. (c) Saddle-point parameters for each node $\alpha = \{\mathrm{Bu, Br, St}\}$, over time k, with horizon length $L = 20$.

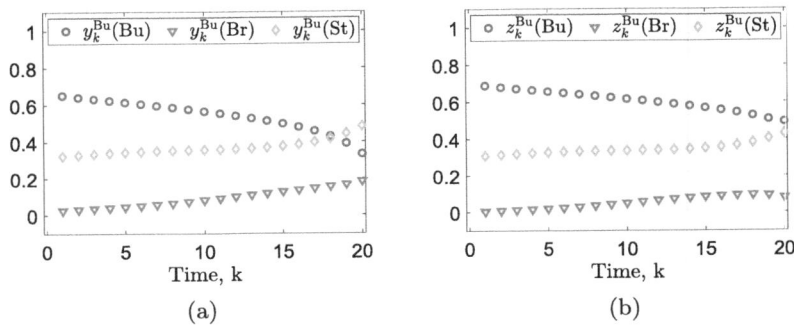

Fig. 6. For the node $\alpha = \mathrm{Br}$, the NE policy of the (c) defender and (d) adversary, where $y_k^{\mathrm{Bu}}(\alpha), z_k^{\mathrm{Bu}}(\alpha), \alpha = \{\mathrm{Bu, Br, St}\}$ corresponds to the probability of selecting the takeover node α, given $\alpha_k = \mathrm{Bu}$.

$L = 20$. At the start of the horizon, the difference between the saddle-point values follows the order (34). However, as the horizon increases, the differences between saddle-point values of the `FlipDyn` states become indistinguishable.

We only illustrate the defender and adversary policy for the state $\alpha = \mathrm{Bu}$ shown in Figs. 6a and 6b, respectively. The policy trends of both players are quite similar, with a high probability of being in the bull market, followed by the stagnant market and bear market. The investor (adversary) indicates a higher probability of being in the bull market and maintains this probability throughout the time horizon. In contrast, the defender exhibits a relatively lower probability of being in the bull state, with the highest probability gradually shifting to transitioning to the stagnant state over time.

This numerical example illustrates the use of the `FlipDyn` model in graphs to determine node takeover strategies for each player. It provides insights into system behavior and stability, which are useful for designing costs that impact takeover policies.

6   Conclusion

In this paper, we have introduced the FlipDyn-G framework, extending the FlipDyn model to a graph-based setting where each node represents a dynamical system. Our model captures the strategic interactions between a defender and an adversary who aim to control node state in a graph to minimize and maximize a finite horizon sum cost, respectively.

Our contributions include modeling and characterizing the FlipDyn-G game for general dynamical systems and deriving the corresponding Nash Equilibrium (NE) takeover strategies. Additionally, for scalar linear discrete-time dynamical systems with quadratic costs, we derived NE takeover strategies and saddle-point values that are independent of the continuous state of the system. For a finite state birth-death Markov chain, we derived analytical expressions for these NE strategies and values. Through numerical studies involving epidemic models and linear dynamical systems with adversarial interactions, we have illustrated the applicability and effectiveness of our proposed methods. The results demonstrate that our approach can robustly determine optimal strategies for both players, enhancing the resilience and security of cyber-physical systems (CPS).

Future work will focus on extending this framework to more complex topologies and multi-agent systems.

Acknowledgments. This research was supported in part by i) the NSF Award CNS-2134076 under the Secure and Trustworthy Cyberspace (SaTC) program, ii) the NSF CAREER Award ECCS-2236537, and iii) AFOSR FA9550-21-1-0411.

Disclosure of Interests. The authors have no competing interests to declare that are relevant to the content of this article.

References

1. Lee, E.A.: Cyber physical systems: design challenges. In: 11th IEEE international Symposium on Object and Component-oriented Real-time Distributed Computing (ISORC). IEEE 2008, pp. 363–369 (2008)
2. Shi, J., Wan, J., Yan, H., Suo, H.: A survey of cyber-physical systems. In: International Conference on Wireless Communications and Signal Processing (WCSP). IEEE 2011, pp. 1–6 (2011)
3. Han, Y., Zhang, K., Li, H., Coelho, E.A.A., Guerrero, J.M.: Mas-based distributed coordinated control and optimization in microgrid and microgrid clusters: a comprehensive overview. IEEE Trans. Power Electron. **33**(8), 6488–6508 (2017)
4. Zheng, Y., Li, S.E., Li, K., Wang, L.-Y.: Stability margin improvement of vehicular platoon considering undirected topology and asymmetric control. IEEE Trans. Control Syst. Technol. **24**(4), 1253–1265 (2015)
5. Zheng, Y., Li, S.E., Wang, J., Cao, D., Li, K.: Stability and scalability of homogeneous vehicular platoon: study on the influence of information flow topologies. IEEE Trans. Intell. Transp. Syst. **17**(1), 14–26 (2015)
6. Li, S.E., et al.: Dynamical modeling and distributed control of connected and automated vehicles: challenges and opportunities. IEEE Intell. Transp. Syst. Mag. **9**(3), 46–58 (2017)

7. Bullo, F., Cortés, J., Martinez, S.: Distributed Control of Robotic Networks: A Mathematical Approach to Motion Coordination Algorithms, vol. 27. Princeton University Press, Princeton (2009)

8. Olfati-Saber, R., Fax, J.A., Murray, R.M.: Consensus and cooperation in networked multi-agent systems. Proc. IEEE **95**(1), 215–233 (2007)

9. Van Dijk, M., Juels, A., Oprea, A., Rivest, R.L.: Flipit: the game of "stealthy takeover". J. Cryptol. **26**, 655–713 (2013)

10. Banik, S., Bopardikar, S.D.: Flipdyn: a game of resource takeovers in dynamical systems. In: 2022 IEEE 61st Conference on Decision and Control (CDC), pp. 2506–2511 (2022)

11. Bowers, K.D., et al.: Defending against the unknown enemy: applying FlipIt to system security. In: Grossklags, J., Walrand, J. (eds.) Decision and Game Theory for Security. GameSec 2012. LNCS, vol. 7638, pp. 248–263. Springer, Berlin, Heidelberg (2012). https://doi.org/10.1007/978-3-642-34266-0_15

12. Johnson, B., Laszka, A., Grossklags, J.: Games of timing for security in dynamic environments. In: Khouzani, M.H.R., Panaousis, E., Theodorakopoulos, G. (eds.) GameSec 2015. LNCS, vol. 9406, pp. 57–73. Springer, Cham (2015). https://doi.org/10.1007/978-3-319-25594-1_4

13. Merlevede, J., Johnson, B., Grossklags, J., Holvoet, T.: Time-dependent strategies in games of timing. In: Alpcan, T., Vorobeychik, Y., Baras, J.S., Dán, G. (eds.) GameSec 2019. LNCS, vol. 11836, pp. 310–330. Springer, Cham (2019). https://doi.org/10.1007/978-3-030-32430-8_19

14. Laszka, A., Horvath, G., Felegyhazi, M., Buttyan, L.: FlipThem: modeling targeted attacks with flipit for multiple resources. In: Poovendran, R., Saad, W. (eds.) Decision and Game Theory for Security. GameSec 2014. LNCS, vol. 8840, pp. 175–194. Springer, Cham (2014). https://doi.org/10.1007/978-3-319-12601-2_10

15. Leslie, D., Sherfield, C., Smart, N.P.: Threshold FlipThem: when the winner does not need to take all. In: Khouzani, M.H.R., Panaousis, E., Theodorakopoulos, G. (eds.) GameSec 2015. LNCS, vol. 9406, pp. 74–92. Springer, Cham (2015). https://doi.org/10.1007/978-3-319-25594-1_5

16. Zhang, M., Zheng, Z., Shroff, N.B.: Defending against stealthy attacks on multiple nodes with limited resources: a game-theoretic analysis. IEEE Trans. Control Netw. Syst. **7**(4), 1665–1677 (2020)

17. Leslie, D., Sherfield, C., Smart, N.P.: Multi-rate threshold flipthem. In: Foley, S.N., Gollmann, D., Snekkenes, E. (eds.) ESORICS 2017. LNCS, vol. 10493, pp. 174–190. Springer, Cham (2017). https://doi.org/10.1007/978-3-319-66399-9_10

18. Yao, Q., Xiong, X., Wang, Y.: Cheat-FlipIt: an approach to modeling and perception of a deceptive opponent. In: Hermanns, H., Sun, J., Bu, L. (eds.) Dependable Software Engineering. Theories, Tools, and Applications. SETTA 2023. LNCS, vol. 14464, pp. 368–384. Springer, Singapore (2024). https://doi.org/10.1007/978-981-99-8664-4_21

19. Daian, P., et al.: Flash boys 2.0: frontrunning in decentralized exchanges, miner extractable value, and consensus instability. In: IEEE Symposium on Security and Privacy (SP). IEEE 2020, pp. 910–927 (2020)

20. Ding, J., Kamgarpour, M., Summers, S., Abate, A., Lygeros, J., Tomlin, C.: A stochastic games framework for verification and control of discrete time stochastic hybrid systems. Automatica **49**(9), 2665–2674 (2013)

21. Kontouras, E., Tzes, A., Dritsas, L.: Adversary control strategies for discrete-time systems. In: European Control Conference (ECC). IEEE 2014, pp. 2508–2513 (2014)

22. Kontouras, E., Tzes, A., Dritsas, L.: Covert attack on a discrete-time system with limited use of the available disruption resources. In: European Control Conference (ECC). IEEE 2015, pp. 812–817 (2015)

23. Smith, R.S.: Covert misappropriation of networked control systems: presenting a feedback structure. IEEE Control Syst. Mag. **35**(1), 82–92 (2015)

24. Mohan, A.M., Meskin, N., Mehrjerdi, H.: Covert attack in load frequency control of power systems. In: 6th IEEE International Energy Conference (ENERGYCon). IEEE 2020, pp. 802–807 (2020)

25. Saha, S., Vullikanti, A., Halappanavar, M.: Flipnet: modeling covert and persistent attacks on networked resources. In: 2017 IEEE 37th International Conference on Distributed Computing Systems (ICDCS). IEEE, 2017, pp. 2444–2451 (2017)

26. Acquaviva, J., Mahon, M., Einfalt, B., LaPorta, T.: Optimal cyber-defense strategies for advanced persistent threats: a game theoretical analysis. In: IEEE 36th Symposium on Reliable Distributed Systems (SRDS). IEEE 2017, pp. 204–213 (2017)

27. Moothedath, S., et al.: A game-theoretic approach for dynamic information flow tracking to detect multistage advanced persistent threats. IEEE Trans. Autom. Control **65**(12), 5248–5263 (2020)

28. Rass, S., König, S., Panaousis, E.: Cut-the-rope: a game of stealthy intrusion. In: Alpcan, T., Vorobeychik, Y., Baras, J.S., Dán, G. (eds.) GameSec 2019. LNCS, vol. 11836, pp. 404–416. Springer, Cham (2019). https://doi.org/10.1007/978-3-030-32430-8_24

29. Rass, S., König, S., Wachter, J., Mayoral-Vilches, V., Panaousis, E.: Game-theoretic apt defense: an experimental study on robotics. Comput. Secur. **132**, 103328 (2023)

30. Miura, H., Kimura, T., Hirata, K.: Modeling of malware diffusion with the flipit game. In: 2020 IEEE International Conference on Consumer Electronics-Taiwan (ICCE-Taiwan). IEEE, 2020, pp. 1–2 (2020)

31. Banik, S., Bopardikar, S.D.: Flipdyn with control: resource takeover games with dynamics, arXiv preprint arXiv:2310.14484, 2023

32. Hespanha, J.P.: Noncooperative Game Theory: An Introduction for Engineers and Computer Scientists. Princeton University Press, Princeton (2017)

33. Li, S.-Q.: Overload control in a finite message storage buffer. IEEE Trans. Commun. **37**(12), 1330–1338 (1989)

34. Peovski, F., Cvetkoska, V., Trpeski, P., Ivanovski, I.: Monitoring stock market returns: a stochastic approach. Croa. Oper. Res. Rev. **13**(1), 65–76 (2022)

Effective Anonymous Messaging: The Role of Altruism

Marcell Frank[1], Balázs Pejó[1,2], and Gergely Biczók[1,2,3](✉)

[1] CrySyS Lab, Department of Networked Systems and Services, Budapest University of Technology and Economics, Budapest, Hungary
marcell.frank@edu.bme.hu, {pejo,biczok}@crysys.hu
[2] BME-HUN-REN Information Systems Research Group, Budapest, Hungary
[3] University of Michigan, Ann Arbor, MI 48109, USA

Abstract. Anonymous messaging and payments have gained momentum recently due to their impact on individuals, society, and the digital landscape. Fuzzy Message Detection (FMD) is a privacy-preserving protocol where an untrusted server performs message filtering for its clients in an anonymous way. To prevent the server from linking the sender and the receiver, the latter can set how much cover traffic they should download along with genuine messages. Clearly, this could cause unwanted messages to appear on the user's end, thereby creating a need to balance one's bandwidth cost with the desired level of unlinkability.

Previous work showed that FMD is not viable with selfish users. In this paper, we model and analyze FMD using the tools of empirical game theory and show that the system needs at least a few altruistic users to operate properly. Utilizing real-world communication datasets, we characterize the emerging equilibria, quantify the impact of different types and levels of altruism, and assess the efficiency of potential outcomes versus socially optimal allocations. Moreover, taking a mechanism design approach, we show how the betweenness centrality (BC) measure can be utilized to achieve the social optimum.

Keywords: Anonymous Messaging · Privacy · Fuzzy Message Detection · Altruism · Game Theory · Best-Response Dynamics

1 Introduction

Anonymous messaging is a critical enabler in the landscape of digital privacy, as it allows individuals to send and receive information without revealing their identities. By doing so, it ensures a degree of confidentiality by providing freedom of expression and freedom of association. Such mechanisms foster trust and autonomy for users seeking advanced confidentiality in their communications and financial transactions. Anonymous messaging is realized by various cryptographic protocols, which offer a shield against surveillance and unauthorized access. One acclaimed cryptographic solution is Fuzzy Message Detection (FMD) [5].

A. Sinha et al. (Eds.): GameSec 2024, LNCS 14908, pp. 240–259, 2025.
https://doi.org/10.1007/978-3-031-74835-6_12

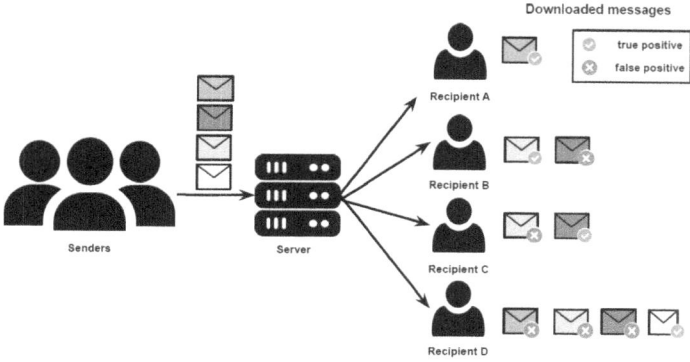

Fig. 1. FMD failure: Recipient D has seemingly maximum protection because it downloads all messages as cover traffic, yet its genuine message (white envelope) is not downloaded by any other participants, so no relationship anonymity is provided.

In a fully relationship-anonymous setup, even intended recipients remain unaware of messages sent to them without decrypting the entire traffic, causing computational inefficiency and wasting bandwidth. Indeed, if messages (transactions) are continuously posted to a public board (e.g., a permissionless blockchain ledger), the user (with limited resources) must scan the entire chain to pick the messages intended for them.

FMD is a relatively new privacy-enhancing cryptographic technique with several desired privacy properties, such as relationship anonymity (i.e., unlinkability). FMD provides a workaround by enabling users to delegate the detection of incoming traffic to an untrusted server in an efficient and privacy-hardened way. It allows users, when online, to download a mixed set of messages in which some are addressed to the user some to others, based on their chosen false-positive detection rate. The cryptographic method ensures that the server cannot distinguish between true and false-positive messages, effectively using the latter as cover traffic. The FMD protocol is illustrated in Fig. 1.

This promising technique has garnered attention for its adaptability in various scenarios; see, e.g., the Niwl anonymous messaging app [27], which planned to implement FMD. Concerning anonymous payments, there have been efforts to incorporate FMD into privacy-preserving cryptocurrencies (such as Penumbra [41]) and into privacy-enhancing overlays (such as Zeth [36]). However, since the initial hype, none of these use cases appear to have come through. (We hope our results can restart the discussions around the real-life viability of FMD.)

Additionally, despite its seemingly attractive properties and fleeting commercial interest, the privacy protection that FMD provides is far from air-tight. Seres et al. showed that statistical attacks can break FMD's guarantees concerning relationship anonymity, recipient unlinkability, and temporal detection ambiguity [39]. In terms of relationship anonymity, they also showed that selfish users had no incentive to maintain non-zero cover traffic, as it is cost-bearing and their own protection level is independent of it; see Fig. 1.

This scenario falls under the tragedy of the commons [15], in the sense that every user benefits from consuming a public good (i.e., privacy) but is not willing to contribute to it (also referred to as free-riding). Many socio-technical systems were shown to exhibit this type of behavior, from peer-to-peer file-sharing [22] through collaborative physical and cybersecurity [25, 26] to pandemic response measures [35]. The economic literature proposes the internalization of externalities and/or appropriate regulatory measures to resolve such situations; however, altruistic behavior also has the potential to alleviate the ineffective equilibrium [4, 14].

We believe that altruistic behavior is especially realistic in privacy-preserving communications, where the actual stakeholders are often members of the same community; it has been shown that individuals in tightly-knit groups (and societies with a strong sense of duty) routinely choose to act for the good of others at a cost to themselves [45]. Interestingly, awareness-raising campaigns (e.g., related to privacy around the introduction of the GDPR or social distancing during the COVID-19 pandemic) try to make people internalize their externalities, changing their mental models [38].

Our Contribution. In this paper, we investigate and quantify the impact of altruism in anonymous messaging networks. Specifically, we seek answers to the following research questions:

RQ1 How do the type of altruism, the number of altruistic players, and the network topology affect the equilibrium outcome?

RQ2 How can a central planner (e.g., messaging app provider) set the false positive rates to achieve social optimum? Is there an easily computable metric that can be an efficient proxy for the optimal false positive rate in a realistic setting?

Our results advance the state of the art in multiple aspects, as we made the following contributions.

- Adhering to the principles of empirical game-theoretic analysis [44], we a) focus on the FMD technology to construct meaningful utility functions, b) use real-world datasets of communication networks and patterns, and c) employ heuristic methods to analyze game outcomes.
- We extend the selfish game in [39] with different notions of altruism, where some nodes care about the welfare of their neighbors (local altruism) or all other nodes (global altruism).
- We show that a) the system reaches a viable, non-trivial equilibrium with only a few altruistic nodes, and b) we characterize emerging equilibria with respect to efficiency and the impact of different types and levels of altruism.
- We find that a central mechanism designer (e.g., the developer/maintainer of a messaging app) could use betweenness centrality as a proxy metric for assigning optimal false positive rates.

The rest of the paper is organized as follows. Section 2 summarizes the relevant background and related work. Section 3 defines the altruistic game model. Section 4 describes our analysis approach. Section 5 presents our findings. Finally, Sect. 6 outlines future work and concludes the paper. Note that an extended version of our paper is available online[1] [11].

2 Background

Here, we establish the preliminaries regarding game theory and the FMD mechanism and give a brief overview of related work.

2.1 Preliminaries

Game Theory. A non-cooperative game model consists of players, strategies, utility functions, and the mechanics of game playing. In this paper, we study one-shot games, where the complexity comes from the large number of players and the underlying network structure.

A Nash Equilibrium (NE) [32] occurs when none of the players can unilaterally deviate from their chosen strategy without incurring lower utility. Notably, such NE always exists if each player can choose from a finite set of actions. In contrast, the Social Optimum (SO) is the set of strategies where the overall utility of all the agents is maximized. The ratio between this and the worst and best NE is called Price of Anarchy (PoA) [23] and Price of Stability (PoS) [2], respectively. These benchmarks express how the overall system performance degrades due to the selfish behavior of its agents.

Relaxations of both NE and SO exist, which are computationally more feasible to obtain. Within the paper, we utilize the ε-Equilibrium concept [37], where agents may gain a limited utility by deviating from their current strategy. Similarly, we define ε-SO, where no user's strategy could be changed in a way that would result in a larger than $\times(1 - \epsilon)$ overall improvement. One way how such equilibria might be found is via the Best Response Mechanism (BRD) [37], where the players are iteratively changing their actions to maximize their payoffs. In particular, if the game is a potential game [31], i.e., the incentive of all players to change their strategy can be expressed using a single function, then the BRD is ensured to converge to an NE.

Finally, altruism refers to a player's willingness to incur personal costs to benefit others, even when it conflicts with their self-interest [40]. It involves acting for the greater good, potentially leading to cooperative behavior that can influence outcomes in strategic interactions [10].

Fuzzy Message Detection. In a sense, Fuzzy Message Detection (FMD) [5] is an extension of asymmetric encryption, where the public keys are replaced with so-called "detection keys". In the classical setup, the users share with the server their public keys, and the server sends back to them the ciphertexts,

---

[1] https://cloud.crysys.hu/s/fmdgt.

which are encrypted with them. In contrast, besides matching with genuine ciphertexts, detection keys would also match other ciphertexts (encrypted with different public keys). This way, the genuine and the cover traffic would be indistinguishable for the server without access to the private key. Consequently, the server may send the same ciphertext to several users, unaware of who was the originally intended recipient. Yet, besides the genuine messages, the clients cannot decrypt other messages, as they do not hold the appropriate private keys. Hence, their sole purpose is to provide cover traffic. As such, FMD prevents the leakage of metadata to some extent by creating ambiguity in the server concerning the destination of each message.

The amount of cover traffic is determined by the false positive detection rate corresponding to each detection key. It determines the probability that a single non-matching ciphertext will be "detected" as matching. Formally, FMD provides Correctness (every message reaches its intended target), Fuzziness (targets receive additional messages proportional to their false positive detection rate), and Detection Ambiguity (only the targets can distinguish between genuine and cover messages). Through this paper, we follow the author's recommendation (regarding the efficiency of implementation) and set all false positive detection rates to be a power of two. We refer to Appendix B of our technical report [11] for further details.

2.2   Related Work

FMD Alternatives. Since the introduction of FMD, a handful of works have attempted to tackle similar problems, such as Private Signaling (PS) [30] or Oblivious Message Retrieval (OMR) [28]. Other related problems were studied within the Private Information Retrieval (PIR) [7] literature. Note that this list is not exhaustive; we merely want to indicate our analysis may also generalize to other systems.

PS provides recipient privacy and key unlinkability, but its constructions rely upon strong environmental constraints, such as trusted hardware and two communicating but non-colluding servers. Although a recent work [19] improved its scalability, trusted hardware is still assumed. OMR provides denial-of-service resistance besides the previously mentioned properties but comes with a heavy computational burden. Although a recent work [29] extended OMR to group messages, the computational burden only increased. Although our analysis is specific to FMD, the game-theoretic framework could be adapted to other anonymous messaging protocols or even generalized further; see Sect. 6 for details.

Free-Riding in Distributed Systems. The free-riding problem, emerging inefficient equilibria, and potential remedies have been studied extensively in distributed systems. One of the most scrutinized domains in this aspect is peer-to-peer systems [9]. In fact, the impact of disincentivized nodes was investigated in multiple real-world systems such as Gnutella [1], Napster [13], and BitTorrent [21]. Another much-researched domain, where the public good to be consumed is physical or cybersecurity, is interdependent security. Starting from the seminal works of Kunreuther and Heal [25] and Varian [42], there has been a line of research on interdependent security games [26]. Furthermore, falling closer to our work, contributor incentives have been taken into account in the design of the Tor anonymous communication network [20]. Specifically, the balance between bandwidth cost and privacy protection was studied in [46].

FMD Analysis. This paper was inspired by Seres et al. [39], which lays the preliminary groundwork for studying anonymous messaging through the lens of game theory. The authors studied FMD from multiple angles and concluded it performs weakly in nearly all privacy aspects. Specifically, they assumed selfish participants and showed that setting the false positive detection rates to zero is an NE, which rendered the entire FMD protocol useless. Their analysis did not consider altruism and assumed homogeneous users with random false positive detection rates.

In this paper, we study the impact of altruistic nodes in the FMD anonymous messaging system, where altruism invokes higher bandwidth costs corresponding to cover traffic. In fact, our results show a phenomenon similar to [42]: the effort induced in equilibrium is highly concentrated at key nodes while others contribute little; yet, the system is functional as opposed to one with only selfish participants [39].

3   Model

In this section, we recap the game-theoretic model of the FMD anonymous messaging system introduced in [39] and extend it with altruism. Following [39], we denote with u the users and the number of their genuine incoming messages with in_u. The total number of messages in the system is M while the false positive detection rate of u is p_u, which implies that the expected number of messages assigned to u by the server is $in_u + p_u \cdot (M - in_u)$.

3.1   The Selfish Game

Seres et al. [39] also defined α_u as the event of a relationship anonymity breach caused by a single message, where the server can link the known sender to recipient u. This event occurs if no other user downloads that particular message providing cover traffic, with a probability of $\alpha_u = \prod_{v \in \mathcal{N}/\{u\}}(1 - p_v)$. Consequently, the probability of a breach from any incoming message is $1 - (1 - \alpha_u)^{in_u}$, i.e., the complement of a single breach happening but for all of the incoming messages.

Using this quantity, they defined the FMD game, where the players are the participants in the FMD protocol, and their strategies are their false positive detection rates (corresponding to the amount of their generated cover traffic). The game focuses on relationship anonymity, i.e., a privacy breach occurs when the server learns that two users are indeed communicating.

Definition 1 (FMD Game). *The FMD Game is a tuple $\langle \mathcal{N}, \Sigma, \mathcal{U} \rangle$, where the set of players is $\mathcal{N} = \{1, \ldots, U\}$, their actions are $\Sigma = \{p_1, \ldots, p_U\}$ where*

$p_u \in \{2^{-1}, 2^{-2}, \dots, 2^{-10}, 0\}$ for $1 \leq u \leq U$, and their utility functions are $\mathcal{U} = \{\varphi_u(p_1, \dots, p_U)\}_{u=1}^{U}$ such that for $1 \leq u \leq U$:

$$\varphi_u(\cdot) = -\underbrace{L \cdot (1 - (1 - \alpha_u)^{in_u})}_{C_u^P} - \underbrace{f \cdot (in_u + p_u \cdot (M - in_u))}_{C_u^{BW}} \tag{1}$$

where L is the cost of a privacy breach, and f is the bandwidth cost of retrieving a single message from the server.

To ease readability, we denote the first privacy-related expression of the equation as C_u^P and the second bandwidth-related part as C_u^{BW}. One would expect a clear trade-off between privacy and bandwidth efficiency; however, Eq. 1 highlights that a larger false-positive rate p_u corresponds only to higher bandwidth (as more messages need to be downloaded from the server), but not (necessarily) to lower privacy loss. Indeed, upon closer inspection, it can be seen that C_u^P is independent of the user's own action p_u. In fact, this renders the entire FMD protocol obsolete, as no rational user would opt-in to utilize any cover traffic.

Theorem 1 (Seres, Pejó, and Burcsi [39]). *The only NE for the FMD Game is where no one utilizes any cover traffic, i.e., $p_u = 0$ for all $1 \leq u \leq U$.*

3.2   The Altruistic Game

As a consequence of this simple theorem, FMD is not viable with only selfish users and no incentive re-design. (Note that the latter could take the form of payments or rewards, similar to peer-to-peer systems [18] or recent federated learning schemes [16]. This direction could be important for future work.)

However, the presence of altruistic users could change the game (both literally and metaphorically). As pointed out in Sect. 1, it is plausible among privacy-conscious individuals in the same community, i.e., users of the same messaging app, to behave altruistically [45]. We consider altruism in the form of extending the utility function to encapsulate the selflessness of the players; they could act in a way that benefits others at a cost to themselves.

Definition 2 (Altruistic player). *A player is altruistic if its utility is directly affected by the welfare of others.*

As opposed to [3], where the entire social welfare is appended to the utility function of the altruistic players, we add only the privacy loss C_u^P of other players as the motivating factor behind altruism (and the community effect) is privacy itself. This third term in the utility function is added through a multiplicative factor referred to as *altruistic constant* a_u, indicating the level of altruism (or selfishness) of the respective user. For a selfish player u, $a_u = 0$. On the other hand, if u is altruistic, this value would be positive, i.e., $a_u > 0$. In a sense, a_u captures a player's willingness to cooperate for the greater good (social welfare). An intuitive expectation is that "enough" altruism would shift the selfish NE towards the SO [3].

The FMD game is played on a communication graph where a weighted directed edge $e(u, v)$ exists if user u sends at least one message to user v. We consider the network topology and the corresponding communication pattern as given: no strategic decisions are made regarding network formation.

In the context of anonymous messaging (and potentially other applications involving an underlying network), altruism itself could have multiple meanings. We consider two kinds of altruism: local (i.e., caring about the welfare of your contacts) and global (i.e., caring about the welfare of the whole society). Although there could be other alternative interpretations, we believe these two have intuitive and inherent significance in our application scenario.

Local Altruism. In the context of FMD, local altruism pertains to cost-bearing actions that improve the welfare of directly connected nodes.

Definition 3 (L-FMD Game). *The L-FMD Game extends the FMD game with the cost of local altruism in the utility function for $1 \leq u \leq U$:*

$$\varphi_u(\cdot) = -C_u^P - C_u^{BW} - a_u \cdot \underbrace{\sum_{v:v \sim u} C_v^P}_{C_u^{LA}} \tag{2}$$

where a_u is the altruistic constant and $v \sim u$ means that user v has a connection with user u, i.e., there is message flow (in any direction) between them. The direction is relaxed as the model regards relationship anonymity (transitive).

Global Altruism. In the context of FMD, global altruism acknowledges other-regarding behavior affecting the welfare of any node in the communication network. Such behavior recognizes the ultimate interdependence of online privacy [6].

Definition 4 (G-FMD Game). *The G-FMD Game extends the FMD game with the cost of global altruism in the utility function for $1 \leq u \leq U$:*

$$\varphi_u(\cdot) = -C_u^{priv} - C_u^{BW} - a_u \cdot \underbrace{\sum_{v \in \mathcal{N}/\{u\}} C_v^P}_{C_u^{GA}} \tag{3}$$

Intuitively, altruistic players may be able to compensate for the lack of cover traffic from selfish nodes by setting their false positive detection rate high, thereby improving the privacy of their immediate neighborhood (local) or the whole society (global).

4   Experiments

As altruistic FMD games do not lend themselves easily to theoretical analysis and we wanted to quantify the effect of various system parameters, we took an empirical approach [44]. Here, we detail i) the real-world communication pattern datasets used, ii) the best-response dynamics (BRD) algorithm implemented, and iii) the importance of choosing the initial candidate strategy distribution for the BRD. Our code, datasets, and results are available online[2].

4.1   Datasets

We simulate FMD game instances on data from real messaging systems[3]. The first is the College Instant Messaging dataset [33], referred to as *message*; it contains the instant messaging network of college students from the University of California, Irvine. The graph consists of $1,899$ nodes (students) and $59,835$ edges (messages) spanning 193 days. The second one is the EU E-mail dataset [34], denoted as *mail*; it contains a collection of emails between members of a large European research institution. The network consists of 986 nodes (researchers) and $332,334$ edges (emails) over 803 days. Note that *mail* represents a much denser communication network compared to *message*.

   While running the BRD algorithm, we realized that we had to ease the computational burden of our experiments. Therefore, we "halved" both graphs: we ordered the nodes by degree and discarded every second node along with any edge connected. The corresponding statistics can be found in Appendix C of our technical report [11]. We conjecture that betweenness centrality captures the "importance" of a node well in this context; we define this measure here for further use.

Definition 5 (Betweenness Centrality (BC) [12]). *The betweenness centrality for each vertex is the number of shortest paths (from the set of all possible shortest paths between all node pairs) that pass through the vertex.*

4.2   Best-Response Dynamics

Applying the BRD to a potential game will always yield an NE; this was also true for the selfish FMD games, revealing a unique all-zero equilibrium [39]. In contrast, the inclusion of altruism modifies the objective function such that it no longer constitutes a potential function. Moreover, the altruism term might add local minima to the objective function; thus, the BRD might stop at multiple different equilibria, depending on the initial state. In this paper, we utilize the ε-BRD [37], which works in a sequential manner where, at each step, a single player changes its strategy, and each time, its chosen strategy value (false-positive detection rate p_u) can be incremented (decremented). To simplify computations, we discretize and bound the value set such that $p_u \in \{0, 2^{-10}, \ldots, 2^{-1}\}$, in accordance with the recommendation of the creators of FMD [5]. For simplicity, we also restricted the possible values for the altruistic constant a_u; in a single experiment, all altruistic actors are characterized by either $a_u = 0.1$ or $a_u = 1$,

[2] https://github.com/m9framar/FMD-GT.
[3] http://snap.stanford.edu/temporal-motifs/data.html.

respectively. We set $\varepsilon = 10^{-5}$ for all experiments. Note that both L-FMD and G-FMD are defined as one-shot games; the BRD algorithm is just a tool to find the ε-NE.

Definition 6 (ε-BRD (Maximum Gain) [37]). *This algorithm is a slight modification of the original BRD, where in one iteration, only a single node (the one corresponding to the highest utility gain) updates its strategy with a single increment/decrement until no player can increase its payoff by at least ε.*

4.3   Initial Strategy Candidates for BRD

We experimented with various initial false positive detection rate settings to ensure the comprehensive exploration of the search space and find all possible ε-NE for both altruism types. We also re-used the same approach to establish the social optimum. We used three different strategies for initial settings.

1. **Thresholding**: players' initial candidate strategy depends on a predetermined value of a node property, either betweenness centrality or degree number. The false positive detection rate is set to either 2^{-1} or 2^{-10} for the nodes above the threshold. Note that a zero threshold still allows for 0 initial false positive detection rates for nodes with 0 property values.
2. **Sorting**: players are assigned an initial candidate strategy based on their relative position in an ordered list according to a node property, either betweenness centrality or degree number. Nodes with the highest values are assigned 2^{-1}, nodes with the lowest values are assigned 2^{-10}, while the initial candidate strategies of in-between nodes are calculated based either on linear (equal cardinality of buckets) or exponential "intrapolation" (size of the buckets follow $[1, 2, 4, \dots]$, where the last bucket consists of the rest of the users).
3. **Random**: similarly to [39], nodes are randomly assigned a possible strategy.

We set the threshold for the normalized betweenness centrality to 0.01 and for degree values to 4. With these values the computational burden for the experiment was still manageable, while they landed themselves on non-trivial results.

The idea behind the uniform initial strategies 2^{-1} and 2^{-10} for *Thresholding* is that ε-BRD could possibly reach the same final strategy distribution, but from the opposite extremum of the search space (a unique equilibrium for the given parameter settings). On the other hand, if they converge to different equilibria, that could form the basis for PoA and PoS calculations. The intuition behind *Sorting* is the "importance" of nodes could be a good proxy for an efficient strategy profile.

5   Results

In this section, we first establish the social optimum of the selfish FMD game (not given in [39]), and then we study altruistic L-FMD/G-FMD games with respect to both equilibrium and social optimum. For all experiments, we set the bandwidth cost of a single message to be $f = 1$ and the privacy loss $L = |E| - \max_u[in_u] + 1$, which yields $L_{\text{college}} = 14797$ and $L_{\text{mail}} = 77947$, respectively. As stated before, we used $\varepsilon = 10^{-5}$ for the ε-BRD and studied the impact of altruism by varying the altruism type (local or global) and the altruism constant: $a_u \in \{0.0, 0.1, 1.0\}$.

5.1 Social Optimum

SO Without Altruism. To facilitate comparability with [39] and to provide an easily understandable baseline, we consider a simple scenario where a Mechanism Designer could only set the false positive rates in a uniform manner (same value for all nodes). Figure 2 shows that the corresponding social welfare is the highest with $p = 2^{-6}$ and $p = 2^{-7}$ for the *message* and *mail* dataset respectively. It can be seen that larger cover traffic is optimal for the sparser graph; this is intuitive as it is easier to infer relationships with fewer nodes and communication flows. Note how applying zero cover traffic (which is the NE without altruism) corresponds to the lowest social welfare.

SO With Altruism. Concerning the altruistic game, the social welfare for the *message* dataset is maximized with the strategy profile shown in Fig. 3. The top row corresponds to global and the bottom to local altruism, with the left column $a_u = 0.1$ and the right column $a_u = 1.0$. It is visible that the more prominent the altruism, the more cover traffic is optimal in the system (from bottom to top and from left to right). Notably, the (local, 0.1) setting yields an SO very close to the homogeneous selfish SO (2^{-6} for all). Also, all nodes contribute in every setting.

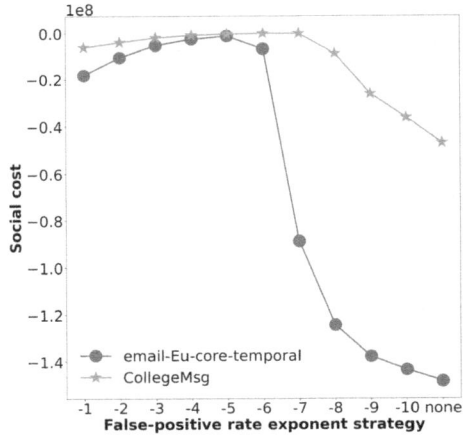

Fig. 2. SO without altruism, uniform false positive rates.

Results are similar for the *mail* dataset with peaks one step lower (not shown); this is in line with the homogeneous selfish SO (2^{-7} for all). Moreover, all initialization strategies yielded near-identical optimal strategy profiles.

5.2   Equilibrium Analysis

Here, we present various ε-equilibria we found; while there are many potential equilibria in these large games, our extensive experiments enabled us to identify the *types* of equilibria that emerge from altruistic FMD games. We discuss these through examples grouped by the BRD initialization strategy used to discover them, allowing us to reflect on the computational aspect organically. Curiously, the *Sorting* initialization scheme resulted in NE that i) were not among the best or worst and ii) did not provide additional insights; hence, we omit them.

Random Initialization. The BRD for the *mail* dataset converges from a random distribution as shown in Fig. 4. The top row corresponds to global and the bottom to local altruism, with the left column $a_u = 0.1$ and the right column $a_u = 1.0$. Similarly to the SO, the resulting NE means more cover traffic when altruism is more prominent, i.e., global vs. local, and a higher altruistic constant $a_u = 1.0$. Local altruism encourages the majority of players not to contribute, while a small subset of nodes (12 or 16, depending on the level of altruism) provides maximum cover traffic. Note that the global altruistic NE is closer to the corresponding SO (see Fig. 3), still with some nodes providing maximum cover traffic but with all nodes contributing.

Thresholding Initialization (Node Degree). Recall that we expected this initialization strategy to reveal extreme equilibria. Figure 5 shows the results for the *message* dataset with global altruism using the node degree of 4 as the separation threshold. The top row corresponds to a high $p_u = 2^{-1}$ and the bottom to a low $p_u = 2^{-10}$ initial setting for non-selfish users, with the left column $a_u = 0.1$ and the right column $a_u = 1.0$. Again, there is a small set of users in NE providing maximum cover traffic (leftmost column in every subfigure), while there are a lot of free-riders (rightmost column). When the BRD is initialized with minimal cover traffic, the NE is extremely polarized (bottom row); while with high initial settings, around half of the population is settled at medium equilibrium values. This result highlights the existence of very different equilibria in the same scenario. Results for the other dataset and local altruism are similar in nature (not shown).

Thresholding Initialization (Betweeness Centrality). Figure 6 displays the results for the *mail* dataset with global altruism using betweenness centrality of 0.01 as the separation threshold. The top row corresponds to global and the bottom to local altruism, with the left column $a_u = 0.1$ and the right column $a_u = 1.0$. From the figure, it is evident that only a few nodes are above the threshold, and even fewer will provide maximum cover traffic in equilibrium. Note that the convergence is the shortest with this initialization method: the BRD algorithm finishes after relatively few steps. Note that the resulting equilibrium is again a polarized one, with a few players shouldering the burden of

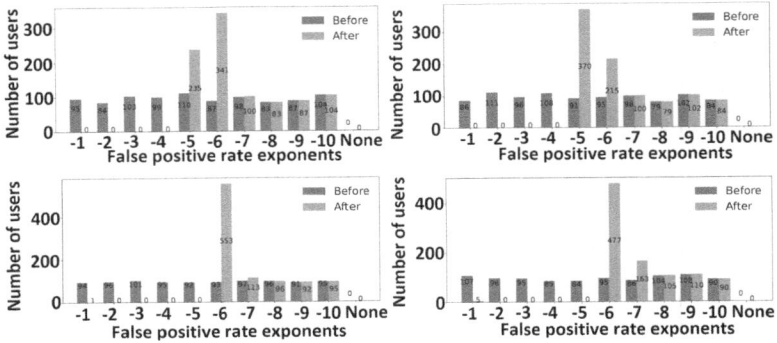

Fig. 3. Strategy profile in SO, *message* dataset, top: global altruism, bottom: local a., left: $a_u = 0.1$, right $a_u = 1.0$.

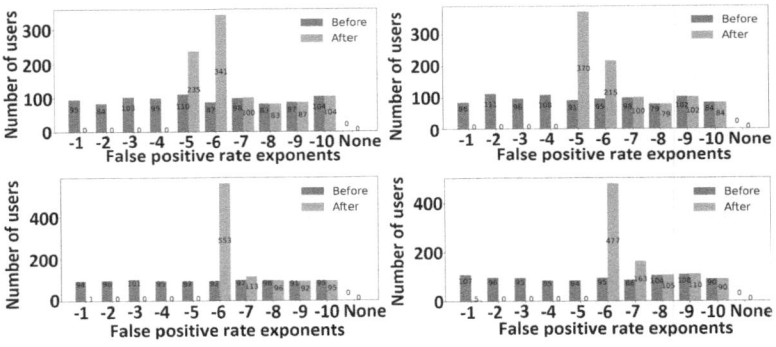

Fig. 4. Strategy profile in ε-NE, random init., *mail* dataset, top: global altruism, bottom: local a., left: $a_u = 0.1$, right $a_u = 1.0$.

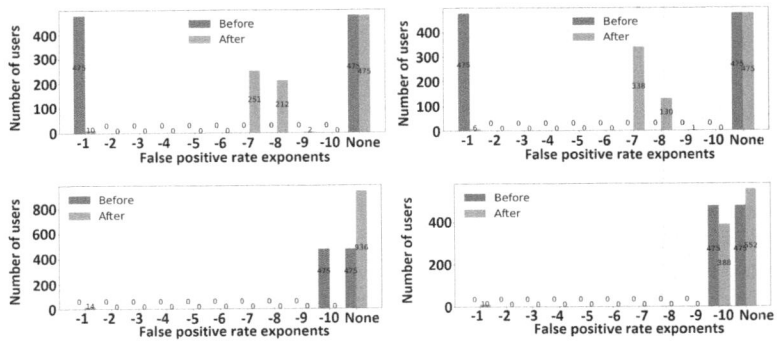

Fig. 5. Strategy profile in ε-NE, threshold init. with node degree of 4, *message* dataset, top: init. $p_0 = 2^{-1}$, bottom: init. $p_0 = 2^{-10}$, left: $a_u = 0.1$, right $a_u = 1.0$.

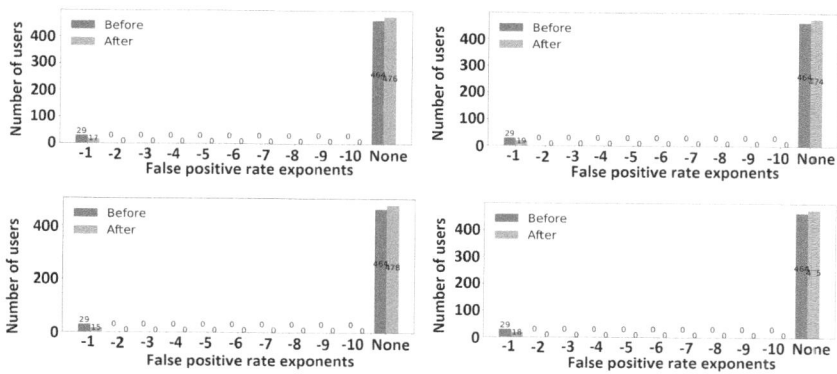

Fig. 6. Strategy profile in ε-NE, threshold init. with betw. centr. of 0.01 and init. $p_0 = 2^{-1}$, *mail* dataset, top: global altruism, bottom: local a., left: $a_u = 0.1$, right $a_u = 1.0$.

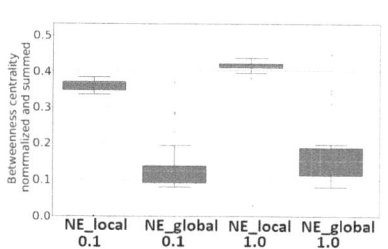

Fig. 7. Aggregated betw. centr. of users with NE strategy $p_u = 2^{-1}$, left: $a_u = 0.1$, right: $a_u = 1.0$.

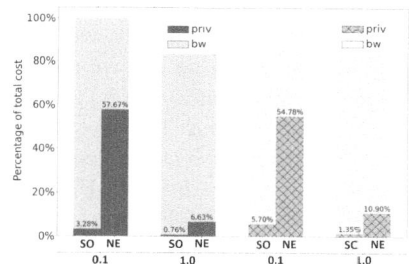

Fig. 8. Composition of overall cost: privacy vs. bandwidth, global altruism, left (blue): *mail*, right (orange): *message*. (Color figure online)

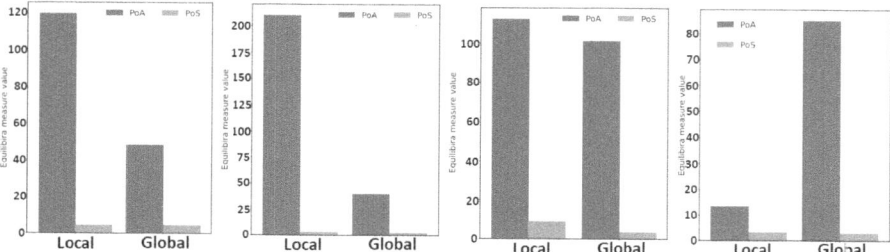

Fig. 9. Equilibrium efficiency: PoA and PoS, local and global altruism, left: *mail*, right: *message*, odd: $a_u = 0.1$, even: $a_u = 1.0$.

Table 1. "Empirical CDF" percentiles of aggregated betw. centr. and costs over users ordered by decreasing cover traffic for SO and best-case NE.

DS	A	Solution	A. model	Priv Cost	BW Cost	BC 10th%	BC 50th%	BC 90th%	Initial setup
Message	0.1	SO	Local	-7694.99	-127389.5	0.8343	1.1985	1.2108	bc, Threshold,all from -10
			Global	-3880.18	-134877.0	0.8343	1.1985	1.2108	bc, Threshold,all from -10
		NE	Local	-427417.87	-82507.0	0.8343	1.1985	1.2108	random 2
			Global	-117871.68	-97305.0	0.8343	1.1985	1.2108	bc, Threshold,all from -10
	1.0	SO	Local	-1948.76	-142394.5	0.8343	1.1985	1.2108	'bc', 'Threshold','all from -10'
			Global	-501.74	-157243.0	0.8343	1.1985	1.2108	'bc', 'Threshold','all from -1'
		NE	Local	-29810.20	-112517.0	0.8343	1.1985	1.2108	random 0
			Global	-14699.95	-120205.5	0.8085	1.1985	1.2108	'degree', 'Threshold','all from -10'
Mail	0.1	SO	Local	-26872.01	-792918.5	0.6891	1.1407	1.2064	'bc', 'Threshold','all from -10'
			Global	-13757.53	-831782.0	0.6329	1.1407	1.2064	'bc', 'Threshold','all from -1'
		NE	Local	-1540593.96	-554842.5	0.6508	1.1407	1.2064	random 5
			Global	-809226.32	-594074.0	0.65	1.1407	1.2064	'bc', 'Threshold','all from -10'
	1.0	SO	Local	-6718.36	-873060.3	0.7233	1.1407	1.2064	'bc', 'Threshold','all from -10'
			Global	-1740.72	-950986.5	0.6802	1.1407	1.2064	'bc', 'Threshold','all from -1'
		NE	Local	-107338.36	-712944.0	0.6809	1.1407	1.2064	random 8
			Global	-53449.33	-753186.0	0.6644	1.1407	1.2064	'bc', 'Threshold','all from -10'

cover traffic. Also, note that we experienced similar behavior when using the same initialization strategy in other experiments.

Motivated by this result, we wanted to characterize how important the small set of nodes *providing maximum equilibrium cover traffic, $p_u = 2^{-1}$* is (we refer to these nodes as *max nodes*). As betweenness centrality is a valid node importance measure when it comes to a communication network [8], we computed the aggregated betweenness centrality of max nodes across all discovered equilibria for the same dataset. Figure 7 shows how these partial aggregates stack up against the network aggregate under both local and global altruism regimes (*mail* dataset, normalized betweenness centrality values, left: $a_u = 0.1$, right $a_u = 1.0$). We can make three observations: i) max nodes (sometimes only 4% of the population) correspond to a large proportion (up to 44%) of betweenness centrality, ii) local altruism results in a stronger concentration of betweenness centrality in max nodes, and iii) stronger altruism (higher a_u) also implies more profound concentration).

We refer the interested reader to Appendix D in our technical report [11] for more results. Interestingly, a large majority of efficient equilibria (i.e., with low social cost) are characterized by such a strong concentration of betweenness centrality. Note that the *Threshold* initialization strategy based on betweenness centrality resulted in equilibria with low social cost and the shortest convergence time.

5.3   Equilibrium Versus Social Optimum

The defining difference between the equilibrium and social optimum strategy profiles is the presence (or absence) of free-riders. Also, SO corresponds to a larger amount of aggregate cover traffic.

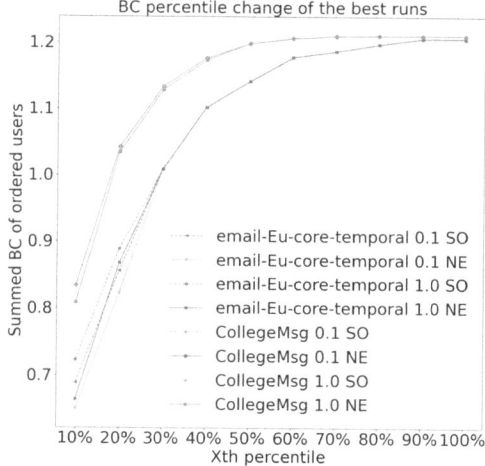

BC percentile change of the best runs

email-Eu-core-temporal 0.1 SO
email-Eu-core-temporal 0.1 NE
email-Eu-core-temporal 1.0 SO
email-Eu-core-temporal 1.0 NE
CollegeMsg 0.1 SO
CollegeMsg 0.1 NE
CollegeMsg 1.0 SO
CollegeMsg 1.0 NE

Fig. 10. "Empirical CDF" of aggregated betw. centr. over users ordered by decreasing cover traffic for SO and best-case NE.

Another somewhat expected result is the change in the composition of overall cost: while in an NE, the privacy cost dominates (e.g., >50% in case of low altruism), at the SO, the bandwidth cost dominates (<90%). This is visualized in Fig. 8 for the global altruism regime; left (blue) and right (orange) denote results for the *mail* and *message* dataset, respectively. It is also clear that stronger altruism, i.e., $a_u = 1.0$, reduces the proportion of the privacy cost. In the case of local altruism, these trends are even more pronounced (see Appendix D in our technical report [11].

Figure 10 combined with Table 1 show the change of concentration of aggregated betweenness centrality in the best NE and at SO over the nodes ordered by their chosen strategies (decreasing order of false positive detection rate/cover traffic). It is clear that already the top 10% of contributors correspond to 60–70% of total betweenness centrality, making it a decisive factor in practical optimal mechanism design. Note that the curves are similar regardless of the dataset, altruism level, or chosen BRD initialization strategy.

Price of Anarchy and Stability. Price of Stability (PoS) and Price of Anarchy (PoA) are valuable for comparing NE and SO as they illustrate the efficiency of strategic decisions: PoS measures the best-case efficiency loss, while PoA assesses the worst-case loss when players act in their self-interest. Figure 9 shows PoA and PoS values for both altruism models, where the worst and best NE were chosen from the equilibrium outcomes of all related experiments. The leftmost (rightmost) two plots correspond to the *mail* (*message*) dataset, where odd (even) plots belong to low (high) a_u values.

Generally speaking, PoA values are quite high, while PoS values are comparably much lower. The impact of different communication networks is also apparent: the PoA is much lower with high but local altruism in the *message* network compared to the *mail* network (fourth plot vs. second plot), while the opposite is true for high global altruism. We leave it to future work, whether this can be attributed to the density difference between the two graphs.

These results imply that in order for the FMD system to achieve near-optimal or optimal operation, a mechanism designer (e.g., the app developer) should either i) be able to set the cover traffic parameters centrally or ii) re-design the system incentives in a way to elicit a favorable equilibrium, similar to the best-case NE in our experiments. With regard to the central optimal design, one should perform a network analysis to determine the participants' betweenness centrality parameter and set the cover traffic parameters accordingly (see Fig. 3).

6   Conclusion

Fuzzy Message Detection has attracted significant academic and some commercial interest since its inception. However, Seres et al. [39] raised some concerns about the privacy guarantees that the Fuzzy Message Detection [5] scheme, gaining popularity and is being integrated into real-world apps, provides. They conjectured that with selfish users, the system is not viable. In contrast, in this paper, we showed that the presence of a few altruistic users may alleviate this situation and yield a viable equilibrium. By means of empirical game-theoretical analysis, utilizing real-world communication datasets, we i) characterized the emerging equilibria, ii) quantified the impact of different types and levels of altruism, and iii) assessed the efficiency of potential outcomes versus socially optimal allocations. Furthermore, taking a mechanism design approach, we showed how the betweenness centrality measure could be utilized to achieve the social optimum.

Practical Considerations. It is not trivial how a messaging app provider can facilitate (near-)optimal operation in a real-life deployment. First of all, the system is dynamic, with nodes and communication patterns changing, even on short timescales. Second, directly computing betweenness centrality is not feasible owing to the inherent properties of the anonymous messaging technology. However, a solution based on secure multi-party computation [24] could be integrated into the messaging logic. Third, the provider could set favorable homogeneous default values (see Fig. 2), which then would be left unchanged with high probability [43].

Limitations and Future Work. We have barely scratched the surface of altruistic anonymous messaging systems. First, we investigated a simple model where players have perfect knowledge and perfect rationality and play a one-shot game. We only provided empirical results, limited the parameter space, and restricted ourselves to two datasets in order to cope with computational constraints. Bounded rationality, imperfect knowledge, and the temporal dynamics of users and communication patterns could call for more sophisticated modeling and simulation studies. Furthermore, concepts from cooperative game theory could be used to integrate rewards into the system.

Second, we decided to focus our analysis on FMD (and its claimed relationship anonymity), a promising technology gaining popularity. While the utility functions studied are FMD-specific, we believe our approach could be generalized to other anonymous messaging/payment protocols, also providing group communication functionality. Even more ambitious and potentially more impactful, we may be able to generalize our empirical game-theoretical analysis to any hiding-in-the-crowd type privacy-preserving mechanism where a user's privacy inherently depends on other users' actions [6,17].

Acknowledgements. Project no. 138903 has been implemented with the support provided by the Ministry of Innovation and Technology from the NRDI Fund, financed under the FK_21 funding scheme.

References

1. Adar, E., Huberman, B.A.: Free riding on gnutella. First monday (2000)
2. Anshelevich, E., Dasgupta, A., Kleinberg, J., Tardos, É., Wexler, T., Roughgarden, T.: The price of stability for network design with fair cost allocation. SIAM J. Comput. **38**(4), 1602–1623 (2008)
3. Apt, K., Schaefer, G.: Selfishness level of strategic games. Ann. Pure Appl. Logic APAL **49** (2011)
4. Barclay, P.: Trustworthiness and competitive altruism can also solve the "tragedy of the commons". Evol. Hum. Behav. **25**(4), 209–220 (2004). https://doi.org/10.1016/j.evolhumbehav.2004.04.002. https://www.sciencedirect.com/science/article/pii/S109051380400025X
5. Beck, G., Len, J., Miers, I., Green, M.: Fuzzy message detection. In: Proceedings of the 2021 ACM SIGSAC Conference on Computer and Communications Security, pp. 1507–1528 (2021)
6. Biczók, G., Chia, P.H.: Interdependent privacy: let me share your data. In: Sadeghi, A.-R. (ed.) FC 2013. LNCS, vol. 7859, pp. 338–353. Springer, Heidelberg (2013). https://doi.org/10.1007/978-3-642-39884-1_29
7. Chor, B., Kushilevitz, E., Goldreich, O., Sudan, M.: Private information retrieval. J. ACM (JACM) **45**(6), 965–981 (1998)
8. Dolev, S., Elovici, Y., Puzis, R.: Routing betweenness centrality. J. ACM **57**(4), 1–27 (2010). https://doi.org/10.1145/1734213.1734219
9. Feldman, M., Papadimitriou, C., Chuang, J., Stoica, I.: Free-riding and whitewashing in peer-to-peer systems. IEEE J. Sel. Areas Commun. **24**(5), 1010–1019 (2006)
10. Fletcher, J.A., Zwick, M.: The evolution of altruism: game theory in multilevel selection and inclusive fitness. J. Theor. Biol. **245**(1), 26–36 (2007)
11. Frank, M., Pejo, B., Biczok, G.: Effective Anonymous Messaging: the Role of Altruism (technical report) (2024). https://cloud.crysys.hu/s/fmdgt
12. Freeman, L.C.: A set of measures of centrality based on betweenness. Sociometry 35–41 (1977)
13. Golle, P., Leyton-Brown, K., Mironov, I.: Incentives for sharing in peer-to-peer networks. In: Proceedings of the 3rd ACM Conference on Electronic Commerce, pp. 264–267 (2001)

14. Greenwood, G.W.: Altruistic punishment can help resolve tragedy of the commons social dilemmas. In: 2016 IEEE Conference on Computational Intelligence and Games (CIG), pp. 1–7 (2016). https://doi.org/10.1109/CIG.2016.7860402

15. Hardin, G.: The tragedy of the commons. Science **162**(3859), 1243–1248 (1968). https://doi.org/10.1126/science.162.3859.1243. https://www.science.org/doi/abs/10.1126/science.162.3859.1243

16. Huang, J., Talbi, R., Zhao, Z., Boucchenak, S., Chen, L.Y., Roos, S.: An exploratory analysis on users' contributions in federated learning. In: 2020 Second IEEE International Conference on Trust, Privacy and Security in Intelligent Systems and Applications (TPS-ISA), pp. 20–29. IEEE (2020)

17. Humbert, M., Trubert, B., Huguenin, K.: A survey on interdependent privacy. ACM Comput. Surv. (CSUR) **52**(6), 1–40 (2019)

18. Ihle, C., Trautwein, D., Schubotz, M., Meuschke, N., Gipp, B.: Incentive mechanisms in peer-to-peer networks — a systematic literature review. ACM Comput. Surv. **55**(14s) (2023). https://doi.org/10.1145/3578581

19. Jakkamsetti, S., Liu, Z., Madathil, V.: Scalable private signaling. Cryptology ePrint Archive (2023)

20. "Johnny" Ngan, T.-W., Dingledine, R., Wallach, D.S.: Building incentives into tor. In: Sion, R. (ed.) FC 2010. LNCS, vol. 6052, pp. 238–256. Springer, Heidelberg (2010). https://doi.org/10.1007/978-3-642-14577-3_19

21. Jun, S., Ahamad, M.: Incentives in bittorrent induce free riding. In: Proceedings of the 2005 ACM SIGCOMM Workshop on Economics of Peer-to-Peer Systems, pp. 116–121 (2005)

22. Karakaya, M., Korpeoglu, I., Ulusoy, O.: Free riding in peer-to-peer networks. IEEE Internet Comput. **13**(2), 92–98 (2009). https://doi.org/10.1109/MIC.2009.33

23. Koutsoupias, E., Papadimitriou, C.H.: Worst-case equilibria. Comput. Sci. Rev. **3**, 65–69 (1999)

24. Kukkala, V.B., Iyengar, S.R.S.: Computing betweenness centrality: an efficient privacy-preserving approach. In: Camenisch, J., Papadimitratos, P. (eds.) CANS 2018. LNCS, vol. 11124, pp. 23–42. Springer, Cham (2018). https://doi.org/10.1007/978-3-030-00434-7_2

25. Kunreuther, H., Heal, G.: Interdependent security. J. Risk Uncertain. **26**, 231–249 (2003)

26. Laszka, A., Felegyhazi, M., Buttyan, L.: A survey of interdependent information security games. ACM Comput. Surv. **47**(2) (2014). https://doi.org/10.1145/2635673

27. Lewis, S.J.: Niwl: a prototype system for open, decentralized, metadata resistant communication using fuzzytags and random ejection mixers (2021). https://git.openprivacy.ca/openprivacy/niwl

28. Liu, Z., Tromer, E.: Oblivious message retrieval. In: Dodis, Y., Shrimpton, T. (eds.) CRYPTO 2022, Part I. LNCS, vol. 13507, pp. 753–783. Springer, Cham (2022). https://doi.org/10.1007/978-3-031-15802-5_26

29. Liu, Z., Tromer, E., Wang, Y.: Group oblivious message retrieval. Cryptology ePrint Archive (2023)

30. Madathil, V., Scafuro, A., Seres, I.A., Shlomovits, O., Varlakov, D.: Private signaling. In: 31st USENIX Security Symposium (USENIX Security 2022), pp. 3309–3326 (2022)

31. Monderer, D., Shapley, L.S.: Potential games. Games Econ. Behav. **14**(1), 124–143 (1996)

32. Nash, J.: Non-cooperative games. Ann. Math. 286–295 (1951)

33. Panzarasa, P., Opsahl, T., Carley, K.: Patterns and dynamics of users' behavior and interaction: network analysis of an online community. JASIST **60**, 911–932 (2009). https://doi.org/10.1002/asi.21015

34. Paranjape, A., Benson, A.R., Leskovec, J.: Motifs in temporal networks. In: Proceedings of the Tenth ACM International Conference on Web Search and Data Mining, WSDM 2017, pp. 601–610. Association for Computing Machinery. New York (2017). https://doi.org/10.1145/3018661.3018731

35. Pejó, B., Biczók, G.: Games in the time of covid-19: promoting mechanism design for pandemic response. ACM Trans. Spatial Algorithms Syst. **8**(3) (2022). https://doi.org/10.1145/3503155

36. Rondelet, A.: Fuzzy message detection in zeth (2021). https://github.com/clearmatics/zeth-specifications/issues/18

37. Roughgarden, T.: Twenty Lectures on Algorithmic Game Theory. Cambridge University Press, Cambridge (2016). https://doi.org/10.1017/CBO9781316779309

38. Schoenherr, J.: Whose privacy, what surveillance? Dimensions of the mental models for privacy and security. IEEE Technol. Soc. Mag. **41**(1), 54–65 (2022). https://doi.org/10.1109/MTS.2022.3147536

39. Seres, I.A., Pejó, B., Burcsi, P.: The effect of false positives: why fuzzy message detection leads to fuzzy privacy guarantees? In: Eyal, I., Garay, J. (eds.) FC 2022. LNCS, vol. 13411, pp. 123–148. Springer, Cham (2022). https://doi.org/10.1007/978-3-031-18283-9_7

40. Simon, H.A.: Altruism and economics. Am. Econ. Rev. **83**(2), 156–161 (1993)

41. de Valence, H.: Determine whether penumbra could integrate fuzzy message detection (2021). https://github.com/penumbra-zone/penumbra/issues/4

42. Varian, H.: System reliability and free riding. In: Camp, L.J., Lewis, S. (eds.) Economics of Information Security, pp. 1–15. Springer, Boston (2004). https://doi.org/10.1007/1-4020-8090-5_1

43. Watson, J., Lipford, H.R., Besmer, A.: Mapping user preference to privacy default settings. ACM Trans. Comput.-Hum. Interact. **22**(6) (2015). https://doi.org/10.1145/2811257

44. Wellman, M.P.: Methods for empirical game-theoretic analysis. In: Proceedings, The Twenty-First National Conference on Artificial Intelligence and the Eighteenth Innovative Applications of Artificial Intelligence Conference, 16–20 July 2006, Boston, Massachusetts, USA, pp. 1552–1556. AAAI Press (2006). http://www.aaai.org/Library/AAAI/2006/aaai06-248.php

45. Yu, S., Kempe, D., Vorobeychik, Y.: Altruism design in networked public goods games. In: Zhou, Z. (ed.) Proceedings of the Thirtieth International Joint Conference on Artificial Intelligence, IJCAI 2021, Virtual Event / Montreal, Canada, 19-27 August 2021, pp. 493–499. ijcai.org (2021). https://doi.org/10.24963/IJCAI.2021/69

46. Zhang, N., Yu, W., Fu, X., Das, S.K.: gPath: a game-theoretic path selection algorithm to protect tor's anonymity. In: Alpcan, T., Buttyán, L., Baras, J.S. (eds.) GameSec 2010. LNCS, vol. 6442, pp. 58–71. Springer, Heidelberg (2010). https://doi.org/10.1007/978-3-642-17197-0_4

Adversarial Machine Learning

Towards a Game-Theoretic Understanding of Explanation-Based Membership Inference Attacks

Kavita Kumari[1(✉)], Murtuza Jadliwala[2], Sumit Kumar Jha[3], and Anindya Maiti[4]

[1] Technical University of Darmstadt, Darmstadt, Germany
kavita.kumari@trust.tu-darmstadt.de
[2] The University of Texas at San Antonio, San Antonio, USA
[3] Florida International University, Miami, USA
[4] University of Oklahoma, Norman, USA

Abstract. Model explanations improve the transparency of black-box machine learning (ML) models and their decisions; however, they can also enable privacy threats like membership inference attacks (MIA). Existing works have only analyzed MIA in a single interaction scenario between an adversary and the target ML model, missing the factors that influence an adversary's capability to launch MIA in repeated interactions. These works also assume the attacker knows the model's structure, which isn't always true, leading to suboptimal thresholds for identifying members. This paper examines explanation-based threshold attacks, where an adversary uses the variance in explanations through repeated interactions to perform MIA. We use a continuous-time stochastic signaling game to model these interactions. Unaware of the system's exact type (honest or malicious), the adversary plays a stopping game to gather explanation variance and compute an optimal threshold for membership determination. We propose a sound mathematical formulation to prove that such an optimal threshold exists, which can be used to launch MIA and identify conditions for a unique Markov perfect equilibrium in this dynamic system. Finally, we evaluate various factors affecting an adversary's ability to conduct MIA in repeated settings through simulations.

1 Introduction

Understanding machine learning (ML) models' decisions is challenging due to their complex, black-box nature. This has led to developing various model explanation techniques [23,32,36]. However, these explanations also expose an attack surface that can be exploited for inferring private model information [34] or launching adversarial attacks [19,38]. One feasible attack is Membership Inference Attacks (MIAs), where adversaries discern the membership status of specific data points in the training set. MIAs are broadly classified into binary classifier-based [35], metric-based [22], and differential comparison-based attacks [18].

This work focuses on metric-based MIAs, particularly those leveraging model explanations. Shokri et al. [34] showed that variance in gradient-based explanations

A. Sinha et al. (Eds.): GameSec 2024, LNCS 14908, pp. 263–283, 2025.
https://doi.org/10.1007/978-3-031-74835-6_13

could indicate membership status when compared to a threshold, although their analysis was limited to a single query instance. This work examines how explanation variance evolves under repeated adversarial queries formulated by a strategic adversary and sent to the system. Our motivation stems from a recognized gap in the existing literature. While many works [27–29,42] have leveraged explanations to design security attacks, none have extensively analyzed the effects of repeated interactions on explanation variance. This understanding is crucial for developing robust defenses against MIAs, which aim to exploit the information in the system's explanations.

Specifically, this work analyzes how explanation variance evolves with repeated queries from a strategic adversary aiming to find the optimal explanation variance threshold. Additionally, while it is straightforward to compute an optimal threshold if the training set membership is known [22], the question arises: how can an explanation-based threshold attack be executed when an adversary lacks knowledge of the model and its training process?

An adversary that iteratively interacts with the target system to compute the explanation variance threshold raises several questions: What is the optimal duration for this interaction? Can the system detect and prevent such malicious interactions? How can the system serve both honest and malicious users effectively? While honest and malicious users may formulate similar queries, the emphasis lies on the malicious user's intention to initiate MIA. Thus, the value of an explanation for an honest end-user is based on its relevance, explaining the model's decision for the query. However, a malicious end-user evaluates an explanation's value based on the information it contains for potential exploitation in launching MIAs. Intuitively, the duration, pattern, and structure of such repeated interactions could impact the degree of private information disclosure by the system. The current understanding of this process is limited, especially when dealing with a strategic adversary that aims to minimize attack costs. At the same time, a system seeks to protect privacy without fully knowing the end-user type.

We aim to bridge this research gap by using game theory to model interactions between an adversary and an ML system in the above context. In particular, we make the following contributions in this paper:

1. We model the interactions between an ML system and an adversary as a *two-player continuous-time signaling game*, where the variance of the generated explanations (by the ML system) evolve according to a *stochastic differential equation (SDE)*.
2. We then characterize the *Markov Perfect Equilibrium (MPE)* of the above stochastic game as a pair of optimal functions $U(\pi)$ and $L(\pi)$, where $U(\pi)$ is the optimal variance path for the explanations generated by the system, $L(\pi)$ is the optimal variance path for the explanations given by the system to an adversary after adding some noise, and π is the belief of the system about the type of the adversary.
3. We evaluate the game for different gradient-based explanation methods, namely, *Integrated Gradients* [41], *Gradient*Input* [37], *LRP* [3] and *Guided Backpropagation* [40]. By means of experiments using benchmark datasets, we demonstrate that the capability of an adversary to launch MIA depends on factors such as the explanation method, input dimensionality, model size, and number of training rounds.

2   Background and Preliminaries

2.1   Gradient Based Explanations

For some input data point $\overrightarrow{x} \in \mathbb{R}^n$ and a classification model F_θ, an explanation method $\mathcal{H}$ simply explains model decisions, i.e., it outputs some justification/explanation of why the model F_θ returned a particular label $y = F_\theta(\overrightarrow{x})$. In this work, we consider feature-based explanations, where the output of the explanation function is an influence (or attribution) vector and where the element $\mathcal{H}_i(\overrightarrow{x})$ of the vector represents the degree to which the ith feature influences the predicted label y of the data point $\overrightarrow{x}$. Specifically, we consider the Gradient method [37], Integrated Gradient (IG) method [41], Layer-wise Relevance Propagation (LRP) [3], and Guided Backpropagation [40]. For more details, please refer to the extended version of the paper [21].

2.2   Membership Inference Attacks

In membership inference attacks (MIA), an adversary with a target dataset $\mathcal{X}_{tgt} \subset \mathcal{R}^n$ aims to identify which data points belong to a target model's training set $\mathcal{X}_{tr}$. The adversary predicts membership by assessing if each point $\overrightarrow{x} \in \mathcal{X}_{tgt}$ is also in $\mathcal{X}_{tr}$. Intuitively, a low model loss typically translates to a prediction vector dominated by the true label, resulting in a high variance, which may indicate model certainty [34] and, thus, the data point (under consideration) as a member of the training dataset. The variance of the feature-based explanation to determine data point membership is as follows:

$$\text{Membership}_{Expl, \tau_E}(\overrightarrow{x}) = \begin{cases} \text{True,} & Var(\mathcal{H}_{GRAD}(\overrightarrow{x})) \leq \tau_E \\ \text{False,} & otherwise \end{cases}$$

where the variance of some vector $\overrightarrow{v} \in \mathbb{R}^n$ is calculated as: $Var(\overrightarrow{v}) = \sum_{i=1}^{n}(v_i - \mu_{\overrightarrow{v}})^2$, where $\mu_{\overrightarrow{v}} = \frac{1}{n}\sum_{i=1}^{n} v_i$.

2.3   Geometric Brownian Motion

A Geometric Brownian Motion (GBM) is a continuous-time stochastic process commonly used to model the evolution of a variable that exhibits random fluctuations over time. A general GBM state process s_t satisfies the stochastic differential equation:

$$ds_t = a(s_t, u(s_t, t), t)s_t dt + b(s_t, u(s_t, t), t)s_t dW_t$$

where, $a(s_t, u(s_t, t), t)$ and $b(s_t, u(s_t, t), t)$ are the drift and volatility parameters of the state process s_t, respectively, W_t is a standard Brownian motion with mean $= 0$ and variance $= t$, and $u(s_t, t)$ is the control. In this paper, an adversary aims to reach a variance threshold to launch explanation-based attacks by repeatedly interacting with the ML model using appropriate queries and historical interaction data. Here, we model the evolving explanation variance EX^v as a GBM due to its ability to capture periodic and random fluctuations in a non-negative continuous-time process.

2.4   Optimal Control and the Stopping Problem

In a two-player game, each agent makes an optimal control decision to either continue or stop interacting with the other agent. Such problems involving optimal control are usually modeled using Bellman's equation and solved with dynamic programming. Let $u_i(s_t, t)$ represent the control of agent i when the system is in state s_t at time t. The value function, denoted by $H_i(s_t, t)$, represents the optimal payoff/reward of the agent i over the interval $t = [0, T]$ can be written as:

$$H_i(s_t, t) = \max_{u_i} \int_0^T f(s_t, u(s_t, t), t) dt$$

Where $f(s_t, u(s_t, t), t)$ is the instantaneous payoff/reward a player can get given the state (s_t) and the control used (u) at time t. the Bellman equation is a *partial differential equation or PDE*, referred to as the *Hamilton Jacobi Bellman (HJB)* equation, and can be written as:

$$rH(s_t, t) = f(s_t, u^*, t) + \frac{\partial H}{\partial t} + \frac{\partial H}{\partial s_t} a(s_t, u^*, t) + \frac{1}{2} \frac{\partial^2 H}{\partial s_t^2} b(s_t, u^*, t)^2$$

Where $u^* = u(s_t, t)$ is the optimal value of the control variable. Using the above equation, we represent the value functions of both the adversary and the system. The optimal control u (for both the adversary and the system) is binary: $u = 1$ means "stop" interacting, and $u = 0$ means "continue" the interaction.

Stopping Problem: A stopping problem models the decision to continue an activity for an instantaneous payoff $f(s_t, u(s_t, t), t)$ or stop for a termination payoff $\lambda(s_t, T)$. It is determined based on the payoff he/she is expected to receive in the next instant. The stopping rule for the state boundary value s_t^* at which an agent decides to stop and get the termination payoff is given by:

$$u(s_t, t) = \begin{cases} \text{stop,} & s_t >= s_t^* \\ \text{continue,} & s_t < s_t^* \end{cases}$$

In other words, when the agent decides to stop, he/she gets:

$$H(s_t, T) = \lambda(s_t, T) \quad \forall s_t \geq s_t^*$$

Value Matching and Smooth Pasting Conditions: Two boundary conditions are required to solve the HJB equation outlined above, First, *value matching condition* tells an agent that if they decide to stop (at that defined boundary), then the termination payoff equals the continuation payoff. It is given by:

$$H(s_t^*, t) = \lambda(s_t^*, t) \quad \forall t$$

Second, the *smooth pasting condition* ensures a smooth transition at the stopping boundary. Intuitively, it helps pin the optimal decision boundary, s_t^* and is given by:

$$H_{s_t}(s_t^*, t) = \lambda_{s_t}(s_t^*, t) \quad \forall t$$

where $H_{s_t}(s_t^*, t)$ is the derivative of $H(s_t^*, t)$ with respect to the state s_t. If one or both conditions are unsatisfied, stopping at the boundary s_t^* can't be optimal. Therefore, an agent should continue and again decide at the next time instant.

3 Game Model

Next, we present an intuitive description of the problem followed by its formal setup as a signaling game. Further, we also characterize the equilibrium concept in this setup.

3.1 Intuition

We consider a platform, the `system`, offering an ML model and feature-based explanations as a black-box service. `End-users` request labels and explanations but cannot download the model. The `system` interacts with two types of users, *honest* and *malicious*, without knowing their type. Honest users seek explanations for their queries, while malicious users exploit explanation variance to conduct MIAs without detection.

The malicious `end-user` or an adversary interacts repeatedly with the `system` to obtain explanations for their formulated queries, leveraging prior variance history modeled with GBM. Explanation-based MIAs rely on explanation variance thresholds [34], making GBM a suitable model for this variance. GBM captures historical data integration and ensures that explanation variance stays positive, reflecting periodic and random fluctuations. Note: Our goal is to establish mathematical proof of an optimal explanation variance threshold that enables an adversary to launch MIAs. Thus, we are not concerned about how an adversary models the query space. The malicious `end-user` strategically decides when to stop interacting with the `system` to achieve their attack objective, modeled as a continuous-time signaling game. If the `system` fails to detect the malicious behavior and considers it honest, this is termed "pooling" or "on-equilibrium path" behavior. Deviations from this behavior are termed "separating" or "off-equilibrium path" behavior. Throughout the game, the malicious `end-user` aims to conduct a threshold-based MIA by leveraging accumulated information (labels + explanations) up to that point.

More specifically, the malicious `end-user` decides whether to continue querying for explanations or to stop and attack the `system` to avoid detection. Conversely, the `system`, upon receiving requests, must decide whether to continue providing explanations and how much noise to add or to block the `end-user` based on an optimal variance path $U(\pi)$. Note: The `system` has imperfect information about the `end-user`'s type. Thus, it determines the explanation's noise level based on its Bayesian prior or belief (π).

Based on this stopping game formulation, we structure the model payoffs for both the `system` and the `end-users` (malicious and honest). Additionally, according to each interaction instance between the system and the end-user, we formulate the noise and the stopping responses. As mentioned before, the added noise/perturbation to the generated explanation is based on the system's belief pertinent to the activity history of the end-user. For an honest end-user, the explanation's value lies in explaining the model's decision, but for a malicious end-user, its value lies in the exploitable information for launching MIAs. In this preliminary effort, we model interactions between a single end-user and the system in a stochastic game-theoretic framework, addressing two key questions: When does a malicious end-user stop and compromise the system? How does the system strategically block malicious end-users while continuing to assist honest ones?

3.2   Setup and Assumptions

We model the above scenario as a two-player, continuous-time, imperfect-information game with repeated play. This framework allows for modeling how a malicious end-user may deviate from pooling behavior (stopping time) at any point and how the system may detect it. Using GBM to model explanation variance involves abrupt transitions, making continuous-time modeling more effective for its evolution. Due to their ability to capture such dynamics effectively, continuous-time frameworks are commonly chosen in literature for problems involving stopping times. The game has two players: Player 1 is the end-user, of privately known type $\Theta \rightarrow \{h, m\}$ (i.e., honest or malicious), who wants to convince Player 2 (i.e., system) that he/she is honest. The game begins with *nature* picking an end-user of a particular type, and we analyze repeated play between this end-user (selected by nature) and the system, which occurs in each continuous-time, $t \in R$. As the system has imperfect information about the type of end-user, it assigns an initial belief $\pi_0 = Pr(\Theta = h)$. We assume both players are *risk neutral*, i.e., indifferent to taking a risk, and each player *discounts* payoffs at a constant rate r. Variance (EX_t^v) computed for an explanation generated by an explanation method of the system follows a GBM, and is given by:

$$dEX_t^v = \mu EX_t^v dt + \sigma EX_t^v dW_t \tag{1}$$

where, μ is the constant *drift* and $\sigma > 0$ is the constant *volatility* of the variance process EX_t^v, and $EX_0^v = ex_0^v > 0$. W_t is a standard Brownian motion with mean = 0 and variance = t. To ensure finite payoffs at each continuous time t, we assume $\mu < r$. The state of the game is represented by the process (EX_t^v, π_t), where π_t is the belief of the system about the type of the end-user at time t.

The system wants to give informative or relevant explanations to the honest end-user, but noisy explanations to the malicious end-user. Hence, depending on the system's belief about the type of the end-user, it will decide how much noise (perturbation) to add to each released explanation, according to the generated variance. Let $U(\pi_t)$ denote the optimal variance path (or functional path) for the system - a non-increasing cut-off function which tells the system the optimal explanation variance computed for an explanation generated by an explanation method and $L(\pi_t)$ denote the optimal explanation variance path for the end-user - an increasing cut-off function which tells the end-user the optimal explanation variance for the explanation given by the `system` at given belief π_t. To simplify the resulting analysis, we assume that the explanations variance computed by the `system` and explanations variance computed by the `end-user` are just different realizations of the explanation variance process EX_t^v. We denote $ex_{s_y,t}^v$ and $ex_{e_u,t}^v$ as the `system`'s and `end-user`'s realization of the process EX_t^v, respectively. Moreover, as the `system` would add some calculated noise to the generated explanation based on its Bayesian belief, we assume that $U(\pi_t) \geq L(\pi_t)$, $\forall \pi_t$. From this point onwards, any reference to an `end-user` implies a malicious `end-user` unless stated otherwise, as we are only interested in modeling the interactions between a malicious `end-user` and the `system`. Next, we outline key model parameters before discussing equilibrium in the proposed game model.

Information Environment: Let $\mathcal{F}_t = \sigma(\{EX_s^v\} : 0 \leq s \leq t)$ be the `end-user`'s information environment, which is the *sigma-algebra* generated by the variance process EX^v. In other words, $\mathcal{F}_t$ represents the information contained in the public history of the explanation variance process. The `system`'s information environment is denoted by $\mathcal{F}_t^+ = \sigma(\{EX_s^v, \phi_s\} : 0 \leq s \leq t)$, where EX_s^v is the variance process representing the history of explanations variance and ϕ_s is the stochastic process representing the historical activity of the `end-user`. If ρ is the time that `end-user` decides to stop, then $\phi_t = \rho$ if $\rho \leq t$ and ∞ otherwise.

Strategies: Next, let us outline the strategy space for both the `end-user` and the `system`.

- `end-user`: We define strategies only for the malicious `end-user` (type m), as they are the ones incentivized to launch explanation-based MIAs. The malicious `end-user` uses a *randomized* strategy: at each time t, they either continue interacting with the `system` or stop querying to attack. Their strategy depends on the history of variance in the explanations provided by the `system`; hence it is a collection of $\mathcal{F}_t$ - adapted stopping times $\{\phi_t\}$ such that $\phi_t = \rho$ if $\rho \leq t$ and ∞ otherwise.
- `system`: We assume the `system` plays a pure stopping time (τ^t) strategy to block a malicious `end-user`. Continuous interaction is a default action to provide model predictions, and their explanations are implicit for the `system`. Its strategy depends on the evolution of the explanation variance process EX^v and the record of the `end-user`'s querying activity. Hence, the strategy space of the `system` is a collection of $\mathcal{F}_t^+$ - adapted stopping times $\{\tau^t\}$.

We use a *path-wise Cumulative Distribution Function (CDF)*, represented as $R_t^{t_0}$, to characterize how fast the computed variance at a given time t is trying to reach the variance threshold (defined later). We compute this CDF from the probability density function ($p_t(ex_{s_y,t}^v)$) of the GBM, given by:

$$p_t(ex_{s_y,t}^v) = \frac{1}{\sqrt{2\pi t}\sigma ex_{s_y,t}^v} \exp\left(-\frac{[ln(ex_{s_y,t}^v) - (\mu - \sigma^2)t]^2}{2\sigma^2 t}\right),$$

where, $ex_{s_y,t}^v \in (0, \infty)$. In other words, the CDF ($R_t^{t_0}$) will give the probability of how close the computed explanation variance is to the explanation variance threshold at time t starting from the explanation variance computed at time t_0, i.e., $ex_{s_y,0}^v$.

Beliefs: Given information $\mathcal{F}_t^+$, the system updates its beliefs at time t from time $t_0 < t$ using *Bayes' rule* shown below. It is defined as the ratio of the probability of the honest end-user sending queries to the system (set to 1) to the total probability of honest end-user and malicious end-user sending queries to the system.

$$
\pi_t = \begin{cases} \frac{1}{1+(1-\pi_{t_0})R_t^{t_0}}, & \text{if } \pi_{t_0} > 0 \quad \text{and} \quad \rho > t. \quad \textbf{(i)} \\ 0, & \text{if } \rho \le t \quad \text{or} \quad \pi_{t_0} = 0. \quad \textbf{(ii)} \end{cases}
$$

Bayes' rule (i) is used when the end-user has not stopped communicating with the system ($\rho \ge t$) and the initial belief of the system about the end-user's type is also not zero. However, if the system has already identified the end-user's type as m or the end-user has already stopped communicating with the system and gets detected by it, then system's belief π_t will be zero, as indicated in (ii).

Table 1. Flow Payoff Coefficients

	Before Detection		After Detection
	Pooling	Separation Starts	Detection and Block (Game Ends)
end-user, type m	P	M_{NS}^m	$-k$
end-user, type h	P	P	P
system	r_e	D_{NS}^Θ	D_B^Θ

Payoffs: Table 1 summarizes the flow payoff coefficients assumed in our game model. The system earns a reward of $D_B^{\Theta=m} = kEX_t^v$ for detecting and blocking the malicious end-user. The end-user's type (malicious) is immediately revealed at this time, thus a cost of $-k$ is incurred by the end-user. In case of an interaction with an honest end-user, the system will always earn a payoff of $r_eEX_t^v$, i.e., $D_{NS}^{\Theta=h} = r_eEX_t^v$ and $D_B^{\Theta=h} = r_eEX_t^v$, while the honest end-user always earns a reward of PEX_t^v in each stage of the game. In case of a malicious end-user who keeps communicating with the system without being detected i.e., pools with the honest end-user, he/she receives a payoff (relevant explanation variance information) of PEX_t^v. Prior to detection, if the malicious end-user stops and is able to compromise the system, then the system will have to pay a lump-sum cost of $D_{NS}^{\Theta=m} = -d'$ and the malicious end-user will earn $M_{NS}^m = (M^m + d')EX_t^v$, where $M^mEX_t^v$ is the gain which relates to the explanation variance information gained from the system, $d'EX_t^v$ is the benefit (can be monetary) achieved after attacking the system. Malicious end-user will also incur cost of deviation d. We make the following assumptions about the payoff coefficients: We assume that $D_B^{\Theta=m} = kEX_t^v > r_eEX_t^v$, as the system will gain more in successfully preventing the attack from the malicious end-user. When the malicious end-user decides to stop and attack the system and is not successful in compromising the system, then $PEX_t^v \ge M^mEX_t^v$ ($d' = 0$) as the system has not yet blocked the malicious end-user and because of the cost of deviation.

3.3 Equilibrium Description

A *Markov Perfect Equilibrium (MPE)* consists of a strategy profile and a state process (EX^v, π) such that the malicious end-user and the system are acting optimally, and π_t is consistent with Bayes' rule whenever possible (in addition to the requirement that strategies be Markovian). A unique MPE occurs when the two types of end-users display *pooling* behavior.

Given this equilibrium concept, our main result is the characterization of querying activity of the malicious end-user and detection (stopping) strategies by the system in a unique equilibrium. We assume that a decision to stop querying (i.e., deviating from honest behavior) is the last action in the game taken by the (malicious) end-user. This decision allows the end-user to either achieve the target of compromising the system and then getting blocked by it or getting blocked without reaching this target at all. In either case, the system's belief about this end-user will jump to $\pi_t = C$. The end-user has no further action, and the game reduces to a straightforward *stopping problem* for the system i.e., the system decides when to stop the game. In that case, the continuation payoffs from that point on can be interpreted as the termination payoffs of the original signaling game.

Next, consider the state of the game before the end-user deviates/reveals and before the system's block action. Since malicious end-user plays a mixed strategy that occurs *on-equilibrium path*, system's belief about the end-user evolves over time. Thus, a unique MPE consists of a state variable process (EX^v_t, π_t) and two cutoff functions, a non-increasing variance function $U(\pi_t)$ for the system and an increasing variance function $L(\pi_t)$ for the end-user, where

- The system immediately blocks the end-user if $ex^v_{s_y,t} \geq U(\pi_t)$, i.e., $\tau = inf\{t >= 0 : ex^v_{s_y,t} \geq U(\pi_t)\}$.
- The malicious end-user keeps querying for explanation (thus, its variance), whenever $ex^v_{e_u,t} < L(\pi_t)$ and mixes between querying and not querying whenever $ex^v_{e_u,t} \geq L(\pi_t)$, so that the curve $\{(L(\pi), \pi) : \pi \in [0, 1]\}$ serves as a *reflecting boundary* for the process $(ex^v_{e_u,t}, \pi_t)$.

We call such a unique MPE equilibrium a (U, L) *equilibrium*. The first condition defines an upper boundary which tells the system that if an explanation variance value $ex^v_{s_y,t}$ at time t (corresponding to a query sent by the end-user) is greater

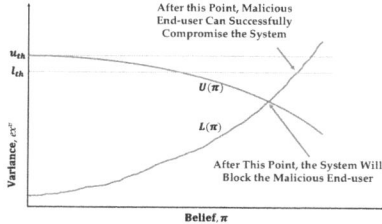

Fig. 1. Illustration of a continuous path analysis of $U(\pi)$ and $L(\pi)$ in Markov Perfect Equilibrium

than or equal to this boundary ($U(\pi_t)$), then the end-user is trying to compromise the system. In this case, the system should block the end-user. The second condition above guides the behavior of the malicious end-user. Function $L(\pi_t)$ represents the upper-bound of the target explanation variance value the malicious end-user wants to achieve given a certain belief π_t at time t. When the explanation variance value corresponding to a query by an end-user is less than this boundary function, i.e., $ex^v_{e_u,t} < L(\pi_t)$, then it is strategically better for the malicious end-user to keep querying (i.e., looks honest from system's perspective). However, if $ex^v_{e_u,t} \geq L(\pi_t)$ then the malicious end-user has an incentive to stop querying. For the malicious end-user, this condition also represents that it is near to the desired (or target) variance threshold value - one more step by the malicious end-user can either lead to success (compromise of the system) or failure (getting blocked by the system before achieving its goal).

To understand the MPE structure, consider the current belief, π_t. If the computed explanation variance is close to the threshold, the system should block the end-user suspicious of moving toward the model's classification boundary. This cutoff for the variance is a non-increasing function of π because, by definition, the end-user is less likely to be honest when the variance value is sufficiently close to the threshold value and π_t is large. Thus, when the threshold value becomes greater than or equal to the optimal function $U(\pi_t)$ at any time t, system will block the end-user. This is intuitively shown in Fig. 1, where u_{th} represents the variance threshold for an explanation generated by the system and l_{th} represents the variance threshold for the explanation after the texttttsystem adds noise based on its belief, which can be given to the end-user. $[0, u_{th}]$ or $[0, l_{th}]$ represents the pooling region where an MPE can occur, if end-user is not blocked by the system.

4   Equilibrium Analysis

Next, we try to analyze conditions under which a unique MPE exists in the game described above, i.e., we try to construct a (U, L) equilibrium by finding conditions under which optimal functions $L(\pi_t)$ and $U(\pi_t)$ exist.

High-Level Idea: As mentioned in Sect. 3, an MPE is defined as a pair of functions $L(\pi_t)$ and $U(\pi_t)$. Thus, we first need to show that these two optimal functions exists. To prove that $L(\pi_t)$ and $U(\pi_t)$ exist, we prove the continuity and differentiability properties of $L(\pi_t)$ (Theorem 1) and $U(\pi_t)$ (Theorem 2) in the belief domain ($\pi_t \in [0, 1]$). As we have assumed that the system plays a pure strategy, we consider that $U(\pi_t)$ (for the system) is optimal, and show that it exists and is continuous. However, computing an optimal $L(\pi_t)$ is non-trivial, as we have assumed that the end-user plays a randomized strategy. Therefore, to compute $L(\pi_t)$, we first construct two bounding functions $L^+(\pi_t)$ (upper) and $L^-(\pi_t)$ (lower) and show that such functions exists (in Lemmas 3 and 4, respectively). To compute these functions we use the boundary conditions (Sect. 2.4) at the decision boundaries, i.e., Pooling, Separating, and Detection and Block (outlined in Table 1) and the value functions defined below. We then show that as π_t increases, $L^+(\pi_t)$ and and $L^-(\pi_t)$ will converge in the range $(0, u_{th})$ (Lemma 1) or $(0, l_{th})$ (Lemma 2) as we have considered that an MPE occurs when both types of end-user pool. Finally, we show that the first intersection point (root) of $L^+(\pi_t)$ and $L^-(\pi_t)$ is a unique MPE, if the end-user is not blocked by the system before that point. At these decision boundaries, both players decide to either continue or stop.

4.1 Value Functions

As mentioned earlier, we are considering an equilibrium that occurs when both types of end-user pool, i.e., $ex^v_{e_u,t}$ is strictly below $L(\pi_t)$. In this pooling scenario, no information becomes available to the system about the type of the end-user; thus, belief (π_t) remains constant. Hence, we write the value functions for both the players conditioned on no deviation by the end-user. As we consider an infinite horizon in our game, there is no known terminal (final) value function. Hence, these value functions are independent w.r.t. $t \in R$, as t singularly has no effect on them. The end-user's value function (F) should solve the following HJB equation representing his/her riskless return:

$$rF(ex^v_{e_u},\pi) = \mu ex^v_{e_u}F'_{ex^v_{e_u}}(ex^v_{e_u},\pi) + \frac{1}{2}\sigma^2(ex^v_{e_u})^2 F''_{ex^v_{e_u}}(ex^v_{e_u},\pi) + \psi ex^v_{e_u}$$

where $F'_{ex^v_{e_u}}$ and $F''_{ex^v_{e_u}}$ are the first and second order partial derivative of the value function $F(ex^v_{e_u},\pi)$ w.r.t. $ex^v_{e_u}$, respectively, and, μ and σ are the drift/mean and the variance/volatility of the variance process EX^v_t, respectively. ψ is the payoff coefficient which depends on the stage payoffs of the end-user, as represented in Table 1. The solution to the above equation can be represented as:

$$F(ex^v_{e_u},\pi) = A_1(\pi)(ex^v_{e_u})^{\beta_1} + A_2(\pi)(ex^v_{e_u})^{\beta_2} + \frac{\psi ex^v_{e_u}}{r-\mu}$$

for some constants $A_1(\pi)$ and $A_2(\pi)$, where $\beta_1 > 1$ and $\beta_2 < 0$ are the roots of the characteristic equation [9]. Similarly, the system's value function $V(ex^v_{s_y},\pi)$ should satisfy the following equation, conditioned on $ex^v_{e_u} < L(\pi)$ and π staying constant:

$$rV(ex^v_{s_y},\pi) = \mu ex^v_{s_y}V'_{ex^v_{s_y}}(ex^v_{s_y},\pi) + \frac{1}{2}\sigma^2(ex^v_{s_y})^2 V''_{ex^v_{s_y}}(ex^v_{s_y},\pi) + \psi ex^v_{s_y}$$

where $V'_{ex^v_{s_y}}$ and $V''_{ex^v_{s_y}}$ are the first and second order partial derivative of the value function $V(ex^v_{s_y},\pi)$ w.r.t. $ex^v_{s_y}$, respectively. As before, ψ is the payoff coefficient which depends on the stage payoffs of the system as shown in Table 1. The solution to the above equation can be represented as:

$$V(ex^v_{s_y},\pi) = B_1(\pi) \times (ex^v_{s_y})^{\beta_1} + B_2(\pi)(ex^v_{s_y})^{\beta_2} + \frac{\psi ex^v_{s_y}}{r-\mu}$$

for some constant $B_1(\pi)$ and $B_2(\pi)$. We will use different boundary conditions to determine $A_1(\pi)$, $A_2(\pi)$, $B_1(\pi)$ and $B_2(\pi)$. Then, we will use these conditions to determine $U(\pi_t)$ and $L(\pi_t)$.

4.2   Analytical Results

We aim to compute the system's threshold u_{th} (Lemma 1) and the end-user's threshold l_{th} (Lemma 2). These thresholds define the region for a potential MPE in the game if the necessary conditions are satisfied. These lemmas help determine if a unique MPE exists. Due to space constraints, we could not add all the proofs here. Thus, please find proofs and other details in the Appendix of the extended paper version [21].

Lemma 1. *There exists a positive upper bound u_{th} on the variance of an explanation generated by an explanation method representing the maximum variance value that can be reached for the query sent by the end-user.*

Lemma 2. *There exists a positive upper bound l_{th} on the variance of an explanation given by the system to the end-user representing maximum variance value needed to be reached by the end-user to compromise the system.*

We aim to characterize the optimal cutoff functions: the system's $U(\pi_t)$ (or $U(\pi)$) and the end-user's $L(\pi_t)$ (or $L(\pi)$). These functions represent the game's MPE and help the system and the end-user to play optimally in each game stage. For example, if the system doesn't have any knowledge of $U(\pi_t)$, then it won't know the range of the variance values being computed for the explanations, which are given to the end-user after adding some noise based on its belief. Hence, an adversary can easily compromise the system. In contrast, $L(\pi_t)$ function knowledge will guide an adversary on how to compromise the system optimally. For that reason, we first prove that $U(\pi_t)$ exists and is non-increasing and continuously differentiable (Theorem 1).

Theorem 1. $U(\pi)$ *is non-increasing and continuously differentiable function in domain* $[0,1]$ *if and only if either* $\beta_2\beta_1 J^{'}(\pi,t)^{\beta_2-1} \leq \beta_1\beta_2 J^{'}(\pi,t)^{\beta_1-1}$ *or* $\beta_2(\beta_1 - 1)J^{'}(\pi,t)^{\beta_2-1} \leq \beta_1(\beta_2 - 1)J^{'}(\pi,t)^{\beta_1-1}$, *where* $J(\pi,t) = \frac{L(\pi)}{U(\pi)}$.

To prove $L(\pi)$ (Theorem 2) exists and is increasing and continuously differentiable, we first characterize an explanation variance path $L^{+}(\pi)$ (Lemmas 3), which represents the maximum variance values that can be computed by the end-user for the given explanations, and a variance path $L^{-}(\pi)$ (Lemma 4), which represents the minimum variance values for the explanations given by the system to the end-user. We write three equations each for $L^{+}(\pi)$ and $L^{-}(z)$ according to the value matching, smooth pasting, and the condition in which the variance of the explanation received is opposite of what end-user expected. Then, we demonstrate that both these functions are increasing and continuously differentiable. The purpose for doing this is to use these lemmas to show that as $\pi \rightarrow 1$, both $L^{+}(\pi)$ and $L^{-}(\pi)$ starts to converge and becomes equal to $L(\pi)$ after some point.

Lemma 3. $L^{+}(\pi)$ *is a well-defined, increasing, continuous and differentiable function in domain* $[0,1]$ *if and only if* $\lambda^{'}(L^{+}(\pi),\pi) > 0$ *and* $P > 0$, *where* $\lambda()$ *is the termination payoff if the end-user decides to deviate and attack the system.*

Lemma 4. $L^{-}(\pi))$ *is a well-defined, increasing, continuous and differentiable function in domain* $[0,1]$ *if and only if either* $(\frac{\partial A_1^{+}(z)}{\partial \pi}L^{-}(\pi)^{\beta_1} + \frac{\partial A_2^{+}(\pi)}{\partial \pi}L^{-}(\pi)^{\beta_2}) < 0$ *or* $(A_1^{+}(\pi)\beta_1 L^{-}(\pi)^{\beta_1-1} + A_2^{+}(\pi)\beta_2 L^{-}(\pi)^{\beta_2-1}) < 0$.

Theorem 2. $L(\pi)$ *is a well-defined, increasing, continuous and differentiable function domain* $[0, 1]$ *if and only if either* $\lambda'(L(\pi), \pi) > 0$ *and* $P > 0$.

Finally, we show that such a point where $L^+(\pi_t)$ and $L^-(\pi_t)$ converge (or intersect) exists, and thus, a unique MPE (Theorem 3) exists in the game.

Theorem 3. *A unique MPE or a point,* $\varsigma = \frac{\lambda(L^+(\pi),\pi) \times (r-\mu)}{P \times L^-(\pi)}$, *exists in the game where the two curves* $L^+(\pi)$ *and* $L^-(\pi)$ *starts to converge, if and only if* $\frac{\beta_2}{\varsigma^{\beta_2+1}} \times$
$\left[L^+(\lambda' - \frac{P}{r-\mu}) - \beta_1(\lambda - \frac{PL^+}{r-\mu}) \right] \geq \frac{\beta_1}{\varsigma^{\beta_1+1}} \left[\beta_2(\lambda - \frac{PL^+}{r-\mu}) - L^+(\lambda' - \frac{P}{r-\mu}) \right]$.

5   Experimental Setup

We use the *Captum* [20] framework to generate four explanation types: *GradientInput*, *Integrated Gradients*, *LRP*, and *Guided Backpropagation*. Next, we use *PyTorch* framework to conduct the training and attack-related experiments. *GradientInput* serves as our baseline to compare the results of the other explanation methods. We assume that when the game ends, both the system and the end-user will have access to their optimal strategies, u_{th} and l_{th}, respectively. Thus, when the game ends, an adversary can use its optimal strategy and optimal threshold to conduct MIA, or a system can use its optimal strategy and optimal threshold to protect against MIA. As a result, we focus on two evaluation objectives in our experiments: (i) *game evolution*, and (ii) *MIA accuracy*. For the game evolution, we simulate and generate the future explanation variances for $t = 100$ stages, according to the expression:

$$EX_t^v = EX_0^v * e^{\left((\mu - \frac{1}{2}\sigma^2) + \sigma W_t\right)} \tag{2}$$

The above equation is the solution to the GBM (Eq. 1) of EX_t^v, derived using the *itô's* calculus [9]. μ and $\sigma > 0$ are computed using the variance generated for the test datapoints for each of the dataset. In our experiments, we take EX_0^v as the last index value of the test data points' generated explanation variance, as we use this initial value to generate future explanations. Using the obtained optimal strategies and thresholds, we compute the attack accuracy in terms of the attacker's success rate in launching the MIA or the accuracy of the system in preventing the MIA.

Table 2. Dataset Configurations.

Datasets	Points	#Features	Type	#Classes
Purchase	197,324	600	Binary	100
Texas	67,330	6,170	Binary	100
CIFAR-100	60,000	3,072	Image	100
CIFAR-10	60,000	3,072	Image	2
Adult	48,842	24	Mixed	2

Datasets. We use five popular benchmark datasets on which we perform our game analysis and attack accuracy evaluations: Purchase and Texas datasets [25], CIFAR-10 and CIFAR-100 [33], and the Adult Census dataset [11]. To ease the comparison, the setup and Neural Network (NN) architectures are aligned with existing work on explanation-based threshold attacks [34]. Table 2 details each dataset's configuration. One can refer to the extended version of the paper for more details [21].

Evaluation Metric. We compute the *True Positive Rate (TPR)* to estimate MIA accuracy after the game ends, with each player having formulated their best response strategy. TPR measures how accurately an attacker infers data point membership. We consider training data points to test against the optimal strategy of the `system`. Since the sample space that we have considered contains only actual training members, there can be only two outcomes: correctly classified and incorrectly classified. The total number of training data points correctly inferred as training points (using u_{th}) are called True Positives (TP), while the number of training members discerned as non-training members are called False Negatives (FN). Thus, $TPR = \frac{TP}{TP+FN}$.

6   Evaluation

This section analyzes our game model to assess two objectives: (i) the equilibrium evolution for optimal strategies and (ii) attack accuracy (TPR) for different factors.

6.1   Impact of Different Attack Information Sources

As detailed in Sect. 5, we initially sample future explanations for each dataset using GBM (Eq. 1). The sampled noise is added to the generated explanations variance based on the computed belief π_t, such that higher belief implies honest user, thus smaller noise added to the explanation variance, and vice-versa.

Then, we compute different functional paths for the `system` and the `end-user` (Sect. 3.3) i.e., we compute $U(\pi_t)$, $L^+(\pi_t)$, $L^-(\pi_t)$ and $L(\pi_t)$ functions. The termination payoff, $\lambda(ex^v_{e_u}, \pi_t)$ (defined in Sect. 2.4), which is used to write the boundary conditions in the computation of $L^+(\pi_t)$, $L^-(\pi_t)$ and $L(\pi_t)$ (Lemma 3 and Lemma 4, and Theorem 2) is assumed to be:

$$\lambda(ex^v_{e_u}, \pi_t) = \frac{0.8 \times ex^v_{e_u} \times log(\pi_t \times 2) + \pi_t \times ex^v_{e_u}}{b}$$

where $ex^v_{e_u}$ is the value of any `end-user`'s functional path (considered for the specific computation) at time t, and b is the model parameter set differently for each explanation method. The parameters for $\lambda(ex^v eu, \pi_t)$ are empirically chosen based on their suitability to each of the four explanation methods. From our numerical simulations, we observe important patterns for each dataset in the baseline setting (*Gradient*Input*) and the other three gradient-based explanation techniques.

Game Evolution in the Baseline Setting: Figure 2 and 3 represent varying game evolution realized for different datasets. Below, we analyze in detail the optimal paths obtained for each dataset.

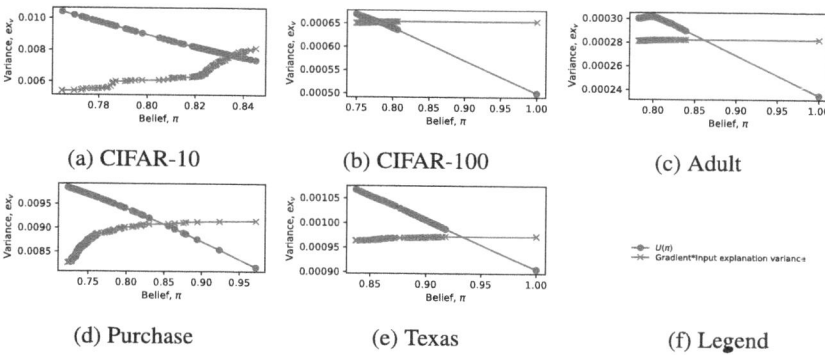

Fig. 2. (a), (b), (c), (d), and (e) represents the optimal functional paths for the `system`.

- From the plots of the optimal functional path $U(\pi_t)$ of the `system` for each of the dataset, as shown in Figs. 2a, 2b, 2c, 2d, and 2e, we can observe that as $\pi_t \rightarrow 1$, $U(\pi_t)$ starts decreasing. This is because, as the `system`'s belief about the type of `end-user` approaches 1, both the variance of the explanation generated by the system and the variance of the noisy explanation given to the `end-user` approach u_{th} and l_{th}, respectively. After a certain point, i.e., when $ex^v_{s_y} > U(\pi_t)$, the `system` will block the `end-user`, which confirms to our intuition.
- From the optimal functional paths $L^+(\pi_t)$, $L^-(\pi_t)$ and $L(\pi_t)$ of the `end-user` for each of the dataset, as shown in Figs. 3a, 3b, 3c, 3d, and 3e, we can observe that as $\pi_t \rightarrow 1$, $L^+(\pi_t)$, $L^-(\pi_t)$ and $L(\pi_t)$ approach the threshold l_{th}. As discussed in Sect. 3.3, as $\pi_t \rightarrow 1$ and the variance of the explanation given to the `end-user` starts to approach the variance threshold, it means a malicious `end-user` is trying to compromise the `system`. Thus, if the `system` doesn't block the `end-user` at the right time (or doesn't have knowledge about optimal $U(\pi)$), then the `end-user` can easily compromise the `system`.
- Earlier we showed that a unique MPE exists when $L^+(\pi_t)$ and $L^-(\pi_t)$ begin to converge as $\pi_t \rightarrow 1$. This is also visible from our results as shown in Fig. 3, where we can observe that as $\pi_t \rightarrow 1$, $L^+(\pi_t)$ and $L^-(\pi_t)$ starts to converge. However, for the CIFAR-10 dataset, one can observe that the curves $L^+(\pi_t)$ and $L^-(\pi_t)$ doesn't converge as $\pi_t \rightarrow 1$. Thus, an MPE doesn't exist in the case of CIFAR-10 dataset. The intuition behind this observation is that the fluctuations (or variance) of the explanation variance computed for the CIFAR-10 is high, making it difficult for them to converge to a single point. Finally, if the `system` doesn't block the `end-user` before the threshold l_{th} or u_{th} is reached, then we say a unique MPE exists in the game.

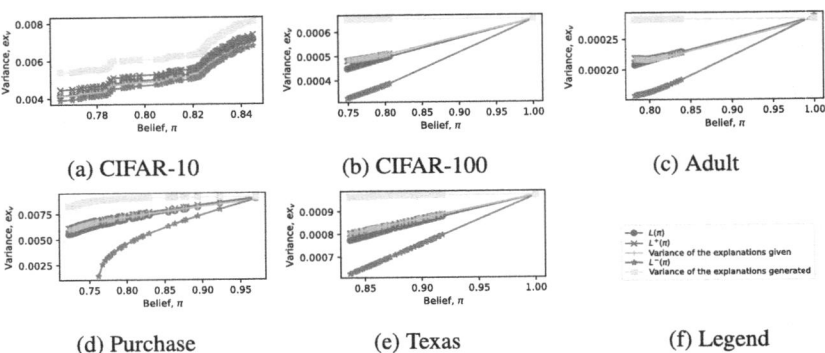

Fig. 3. (a), (b), (c), (d), and (e) represent the optimal functional paths for the `end-user`.

Attack Accuracy in the Baseline Setting: After obtaining the optimal strategies, we use the range of the training data points of each dataset to determine how many data point variances lie below the computed threshold u_{th} to determine their membership. As shown in Fig. 4a, the attack accuracy for all the datasets except CIFAR-10 is more than 50%. This result aligns with the observed game equilibrium analysis. Hence, the fluctuations in explanation variance make it difficult for an adversary to reach the target threshold, in consequence, to launch MIAs. From these obtained results, one can easily observe that the explanations provide a new opportunity or an attack vector to an adversary actively trying to compromise the `system`. In other words, our results are clear indicators that an adversary can repeatedly interact with the `system` to compute the explanation variance threshold and successfully launch membership inference attacks against the `system`.

Results for Other Explanation Techniques: We also analyzed the game for the three other explanation methods considered in this paper. We do not plot the game evolution results in this setting as the plots follow a very similar trend as seen in Fig. ??, i.e., game equilibrium was achieved for all the datasets except for the CIFAR-10. We uses the same setting as the baseline setting (mentioned above) to compute attack accuracy for these three explanation methods. We obtained each dataset's attack accuracy as shown in Fig. 4b. For the Texas and Purchase datasets, 100% accuracy was achieved, i.e., an attacker effectively determines the membership of all the data points used for training the model. However, for the CIFAR-10, the attack accuracy was below 50%, and for the Adult dataset, attack accuracy was above 50% only for the LRP explanation method. The reason is again the high fluctuations in the computed variance for the CIFAR-10 dataset (slightly less for the Adult dataset), thus making it difficult for an adversary to determine the membership of the data points in those datasets. These results clearly indicate that, for different explanation methods, an adversary's capability to launch MIA attacks will vary and may depend on the variance of the explanations.

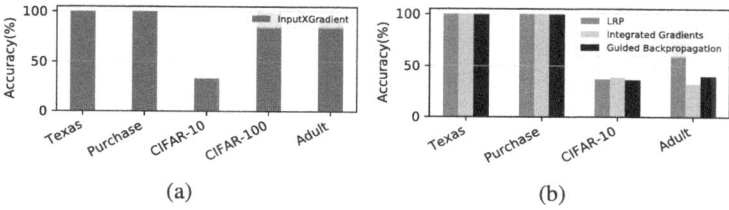

Fig. 4. Accuracy (TPR) for the optimal strategy obtained by the `system` and the `end-user`: a) *Gradient*Input* method and b) Other explanation methods.

6.2 Analysis of Other Relevant Factors

– **Impact of Input dimension.** First, we analyze the impact of input dimension on game evolution using the Sklearn make classification module [30] to generate datasets. We set the number of classes to 2 or 100 and vary the number of features from $t_f \in [10, 100, 1000, 6000]$. We sample 20,000 points for each setting and split them evenly into training and test sets. Second, for each value t_f and for each class, we employ two models to train from this data: model A and model B. Model A is chosen to have fewer layers (or depth) than model B to compare the effect of the complexity of the models on the game evolution and attack accuracy. Model A is a fully connected NN with two hidden layers fifty nodes each, the *tanh* activation function between the layers, and *softmax* as the final activation. The network is trained using *Adagrad* with a learning rate of 0.01 and a learning rate decay of 10^{-7} for 50 epochs. Model B is a five-layer fully connected NN with *tanh* activations. The layer sizes are 2048, 1024, 512, 256 and 100. We use the *Adagrad* optimizer with a learning rate of 0.01 and a learning rate decay of 10^{-7} to train the model for 50 epochs. Next, we demonstrate the effect of these models on our experiment's two main objectives.

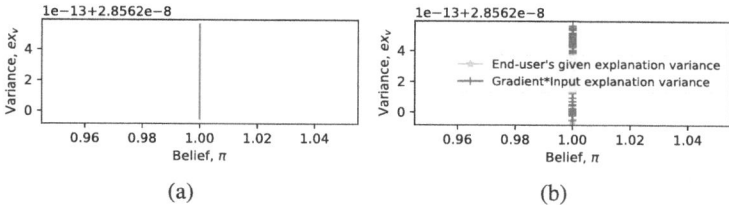

Fig. 5. Explanation variance generated vs. explanation variance given when $\pi_t = 1$.

- **Effect of Model A on Game Evolution and Attack Accuracy.** For $k = 2$ classes, we observe a similar trend in the game evolution, shown in Fig. ?? for each of the features $t_f \in [10, 100, 1000, 6000]$. However, for $k = 100$ classes, we observed that the belief π_t of the `system` about the type of the `end-user` is always set to 1 as shown in Fig. 5a. Consequently, the variance of the explanations generated is equivalent to that of the explanations given (Fig. 5b). Hence, the game didn't evolve as the system explained the same to the end-user. The reason is because of underfitting. Model A lacks sufficient depth (fewer layers) to classify 100 classes accurately, resulting in poor performance. Moreover, the final model's loss was 5.74 for all features, leading to inaccurate predictions and affecting the experimental objectives.

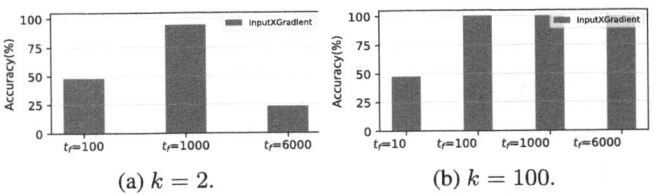

(a) $k = 2$.   (b) $k = 100$.

Fig. 6. MIA accuracy for different features n_f for model B.

- **Effect of Model B on Game Evolution and Attack Accuracy.** Next, we analyze the game results model B, which incurred a training loss of 0.8 across all features. No game evolution was observed for $k = 2$ classes and $n_f = 10$ because we got $\sigma > \mu$ and $\sigma > 1$ for the test data points explanation variance. Consequently, the computed future variance values were zero using Eq. 1. For $t_f \in [100, 1000, 6000]$, we analyzed the game equilibrium and computed the attack accuracy using sampled training data points, depicted in Fig. 6a. For $t_f = 1000$, an attack accuracy greater than 50% was observed; however, for $t_f = 100$ and $t_f = 6000$, an attack accuracy less than 50% was observed. For $k = 100$ classes, we did not observe any equilibrium for any of the features t_f. Based on the final simulated explanation variance index (at $t = 100$), we computed the threshold u_{th} and determined the attack accuracy for each feature (Fig. 6b).

The results for models A and B show that the model choice significantly influences the game evolution and affects an adversary's capability to launch MIA attacks against the system.

- **Impact of Overfitting.** As detailed in [43], overfitting significantly boosts membership inference attack accuracy. To examine its impact, we varied training epochs for Purchase, Texas, and Adult in {30, 50, 60} datasets. Overfitting increased attack accuracy only for the Adult dataset, which remained unchanged for Texas and decreased for Purchase. Hence, the game's evolution and MIA accuracy hinge on multiple factors (experimented above), not just on training epochs. Thus, overfitting alone does not uniformly enhance attack capability, as shown in the aforementioned scenarios.

7 Related Works

Efforts to enhance ML model transparency present privacy risks, as shown in existing works where explanations are exploited for various attacks, such as MIA [34], model reconstruction [24], model inversion [44], and sensitive attribute inference [12] attacks. We focus on MIA, where high explanation variance indicates either exclusion from training data or model uncertainty, enabling potential attacks [34]. Unlike prior work analyzing the single "what if" interaction scenario, our study models repeated interactions between the system and malicious end-user, examining varied settings' impacts on MIA using optimal strategies and thresholds.

Game-theoretic approaches, such as zero-sum games [8, 13], non-zero sum games [10], sequential Bayesian games [14, 45], sequential Stackelberg games [1, 5] and simultaneous games [7] have been used in the research literature to model interactions with ML models, specifically to model adversarial classification. Contrary to these efforts, where an adversary's objective is to target the classification task of an ML model, our research effort focuses on the descriptive task, i.e., explaining the model predictions. Specifically, we use a continuous-time stochastic Signaling Game [2, 4, 26, 39] to model the repeated interactions in a dynamic ML system with explanations to accomplish MIAs. We also make a novel use of GBM [9, 17, 31] to model the explanation variance in order to analyze how an adversary can utilize historical variance information to reach the target variance threshold. To the best of our knowledge, there have been no prior works that utilize a continuous-time game-theoretic formulation to study the privacy leakages (in the form of MIAs) due to model explanations. Similar continuous-time stochastic signaling game models have been used in economic theory to study stock prices [9], dynamic limit pricing [15, 16], and market trading [6]. Our work is one of the first to use modeling concepts from economic theory to study the privacy problem in the ML and model explainability domain.

8 Conclusion

We modeled the strategic interactions between an end-user and a system, where the variance of the explanations generated by the system evolve according to a stochastic differential equation, as a two-player continuous-time signaling game. Our main aim was to study how an adversary computes the optimal variance threshold to launch explanation-based MIAs. Further, our experiments showed that an adversary's ability to launch MIA depends on various factors. A knowledgeable adversary can exploit these factors, particularly the variance in explanations, to effectively conduct MIA.

References

1. Alfeld, S., Zhu, X., Barford, P.: Explicit defense actions against test-set attacks. In: AAAI (2017)
2. Averboukh, Y.: Approximate solutions of continuous-time stochastic games. SIAM J. Control Optim. **54**(5), 2629–2649 (2016)

3. Bach, S., Binder, A., Montavon, G., Klauschen, F., Müller, K.R., Samek, W.: On pixel-wise explanations for non-linear classifier decisions by layer-wise relevance propagation. PloS One **10**(7), e0130140 (2015)
4. Brázdil, T., Forejt, V., Krcal, J., Kretinsky, J., Kucera, A.: Continuous-time stochastic games with time-bounded reachability. In: IARCS Annual Conference on Foundations of Software Technology and Theoretical Computer Science. Schloss Dagstuhl-Leibniz-Zentrum fuer Informatik (2009)
5. Brückner, M., Scheffer, T.: Stackelberg games for adversarial prediction problems. In: ACM KDD (2011)
6. Daley, B., Green, B.: Waiting for news in the market for lemons. Econometrica **80**(4), 1433–1504 (2012)
7. Dalvi, N., Domingos, P., Sanghai, S., Verma, D.: Adversarial classification. In: ACM KDD (2004)
8. Dekel, O., Shamir, O., Xiao, L.: Learning to classify with missing and corrupted features. Mach. Learn. (2010)
9. Dixit, R.K., Pindyck, R.S.: Investment Under Uncertainty. Princeton University Press (2012)
10. Dritsoula, L., Loiseau, P., Musacchio, J.: A game-theoretic analysis of adversarial classification. IEEE Trans. Inf. Forensics Secur. **12**(12), 3094–3109 (2017)
11. Dua, D., Graff, C.: UCI machine learning repository (2017). http://archive.ics.uci.edu/ml
12. Duddu, V., Boutet, A.: Inferring sensitive attributes from model explanations. arXiv preprint arXiv:2208.09967 (2022)
13. Globerson, A., Roweis, S.: Nightmare at test time: robust learning by feature deletion. In: ICML (2006)
14. Großhans, M., Sawade, C., Brückner, M., Scheffer, T.: Bayesian games for adversarial regression problems. In: ICML (2013)
15. Gryglewicz, S.: Signaling in a stochastic environment and dynamic limit pricing. Technical report, mimeo, Tilburg University (2009)
16. Gryglewicz, S., Kolb, A.: Strategic pricing in volatile markets. Kelley School of Business Research Paper (2019)
17. Hu, Y., Øksendal, B.: Optimal time to invest when the price processes are geometric brownian motions. Finance Stochast. **2**(3), 295–310 (1998)
18. Hui, B., Yang, Y., Yuan, H., Burlina, P., Gong, N.Z., Cao, Y.: Practical blind membership inference attack via differential comparisons. arXiv preprint arXiv:2101.01341 (2021)
19. Ignatiev, A., Narodytska, N., Marques-Silva, J.: On relating explanations and adversarial examples. In: NeurIPS (2019)
20. Kokhlikyan, N., et al.: Captum: a unified and generic model interpretability library for pytorch. arXiv preprint arXiv:2009.07896 (2020)
21. Kumari, K., Jadliwala, M., Jha, S.K., Maiti, A.: Towards a game-theoretic understanding of explanation-based membership inference attacks. arXiv preprint arXiv:2404.07139 (2024)
22. Long, Y., Bindschaedler, V., Gunter, C.A.: Towards measuring membership privacy. arXiv preprint arXiv:1712.09136 (2017)
23. Lundberg, S.M., Lee, S.I.: A unified approach to interpreting model predictions. In: NeurIPS (2017)
24. Milli, S., Schmidt, L., Dragan, A.D., Hardt, M.: Model reconstruction from model explanations. In: Proceedings of the Conference on Fairness, Accountability, and Transparency, pp. 1–9 (2019)
25. Nasr, M., Shokri, R., Houmansadr, A.: Machine learning with membership privacy using adversarial regularization. In: CCS (2018)
26. Neyman, A.: Continuous-time stochastic games. Games Econ. Behav. **104**, 92–130 (2017)

27. Nguyen, T., Lai, P., Phan, H., Thai, M.T.: Xrand: differentially private defense against explanation-guided attacks. In: Proceedings of the AAAI Conference on Artificial Intelligence, vol. 37, pp. 11873–11881 (2023)
28. Olatunji, I.E., Rathee, M., Funke, T., Khosla, M.: Private graph extraction via feature explanations. arXiv preprint arXiv:2206.14724 (2022)
29. Patel, N., Shokri, R., Zick, Y.: Model explanations with differential privacy. In: 2022 ACM Conference on Fairness, Accountability, and Transparency (2022)
30. Pedregosa, F., et al.: Scikit-learn: machine learning in Python. J. Mach. Learn. Res. **12**, 2825–2830 (2011)
31. Reddy, K., Clinton, V.: Simulating stock prices using geometric brownian motion: evidence from Australian companies. Australas. Account. Bus. Finance J. **10**(3), 23–47 (2016)
32. Ribeiro, M.T., Singh, S., Guestrin, C.: Why should i trust you? Explaining the predictions of any classifier. In: ACM KDD (2016)
33. Sablayrolles, A., Douze, M., Schmid, C., Ollivier, Y., Jégou, H.: White-box vs black-box: bayes optimal strategies for membership inference. In: ICML (2019)
34. Shokri, R., Strobel, M., Zick, Y.: On the privacy risks of model explanations. In: Proceedings of the 2021 AAAI/ACM Conference on AI, Ethics, and Society, pp. 231–241 (2021)
35. Shokri, R., Stronati, M., Song, C., Shmatikov, V.: Membership inference attacks against machine learning models. In: IEEE S&P (2017)
36. Shrikumar, A., Greenside, P., Kundaje, A.: Learning important features through propagating activation differences. In: ICML (2017)
37. Shrikumar, A., Greenside, P., Shcherbina, A., Kundaje, A.: Not just a black box: learning important features through propagating activation differences. arXiv preprint arXiv:1605.01713 (2016)
38. Slack, D., Hilgard, S., Jia, E., Singh, S., Lakkaraju, H.: Fooling lime and shap: adversarial attacks on post hoc explanation methods. In: Proceedings of the AAAI/ACM Conference on AI, Ethics, and Society, pp. 180–186 (2020)
39. Sobel, J.: Signaling games. In: Complex Social and Behavioral Systems: Game Theory and Agent-Based Models, pp. 251–268 (2020)
40. Springenberg, J.T., Dosovitskiy, A., Brox, T., Riedmiller, M.: Striving for simplicity: the all convolutional net. arXiv preprint arXiv:1412.6806 (2014)
41. Sundararajan, M., Taly, A., Yan, Q.: Axiomatic attribution for deep networks. In: ICML (2017)
42. Yan, A., Huang, T., Ke, L., Liu, X., Chen, Q., Dong, C.: Explanation leaks: explanation-guided model extraction attacks. Inf. Sci. **632**, 269–284 (2023)
43. Yeom, S., Giacomelli, I., Fredrikson, M., Jha, S.: Privacy risk in machine learning: analyzing the connection to overfitting. In: CSF (2018)
44. Zhao, X., Zhang, W., Xiao, X., Lim, B.: Exploiting explanations for model inversion attacks. In: IEEE/CVF ICCV (2021)
45. Zhou, Y., Kantarcioglu, M.: Adversarial learning with Bayesian hierarchical mixtures of experts. In: ICDM (2014)

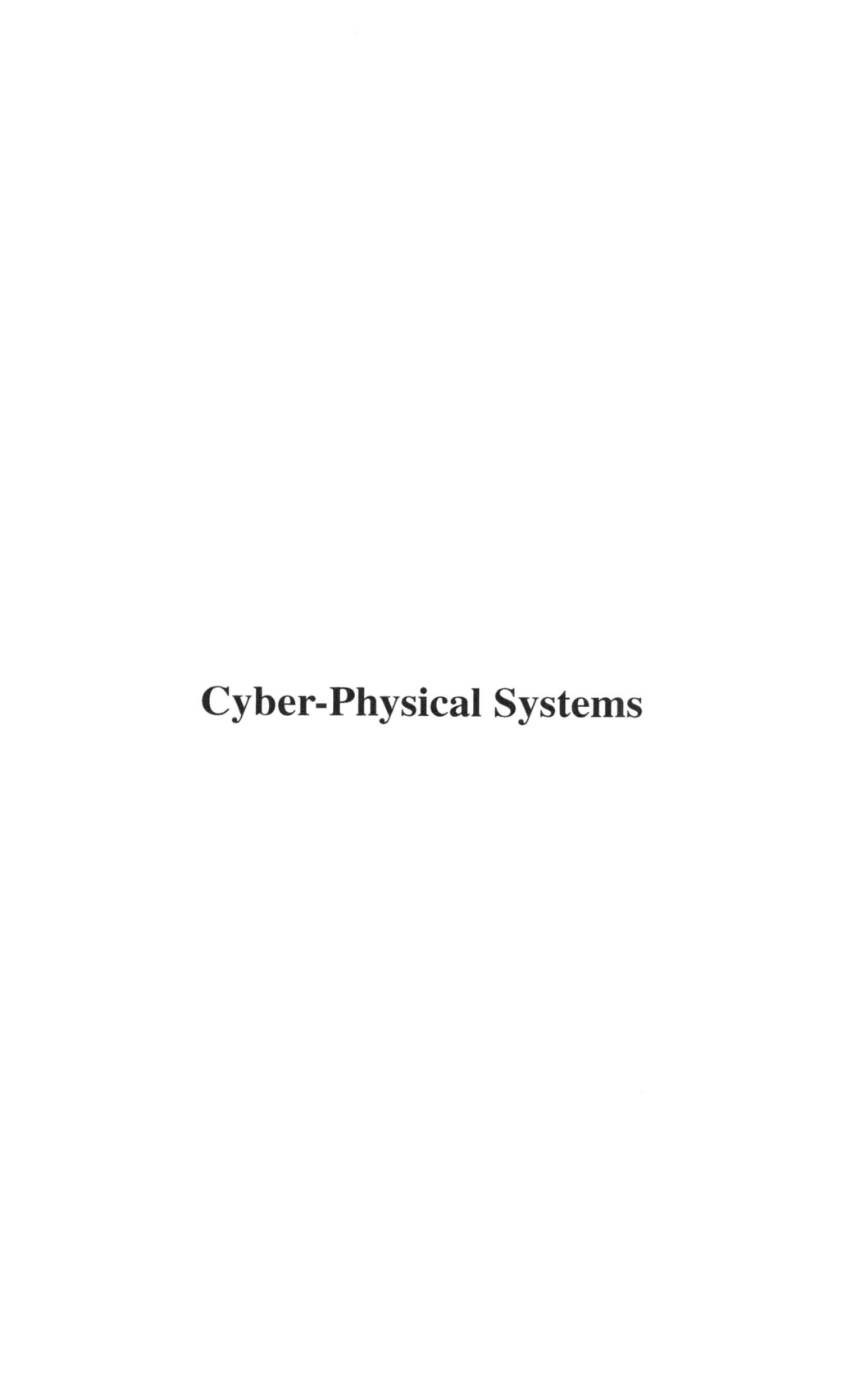

Cyber-Physical Systems

Defending Against APT Attacks in Robots: A Multi-phase Game-Theoretical Approach

Asim Zoulkarni[✉], Sai Sandeep Damera, M. S. Praveen Kumar, and John S. Baras

University of Maryland, College Park, MD 20740, USA
{asimz,sdamera,praveenm,baras}@umd.edu

Abstract. In this work, we propose a two-phase game-theoretic framework to model and defend against Advanced Persistent Threat (APT) attacks in Autonomous Ground Robots (AGRs) running a ROS2-based autonomy stack for safety-critical navigation. In our scenario, the attacker seeks to penetrate the autonomous navigation system and take control over the AGR, causing it to crash into obstacles or fail in its navigation mission, potentially causing catastrophic damage. We use an attack tree abstraction to break the APT attack into two phases and analyze it using appropriate game-theoretical models and solutions to determine the optimal defense strategy for the defenders. For the first phase, we propose a variation of the popular cut-the-rope (CTR) security model by extending it to a probabilistic setting in which applying a spot-check at a given attack tree node does not necessarily result in a "cut" of the "rope". We model this attack tree based on a curated library of real-world exploits in robotic systems and potential security measures that can counter these exploits. We show that this formulation admits a unique mixed Nash Equilibrium (NE) and determines the optimal defense policy for the first phase. Next, we address the scenario in which the defense mechanisms against the APT attack have failed to prevent the attacker from reaching the safety-critical target node in the network and the robotic asset is commandeered. We equip the robot system with a data-driven end-point Anomaly Detection System (ADS) that monitors the robot odometry data and detects anomalous entities being injected into the autonomy stack. We model this phase of the attack using a two-player zero-sum game where the defender needs to select optimal thresholds for the ADS monitor to balance the need for detecting data-poisoning attacks quickly while minimizing the possibility of false alarms and the attacker needs to select the intensity of the attack for the opposing objectives. We use experiments on a Nova Carter AGR running a Nav2-based autonomy stack within a Secure-ROS2 (SROS2) framework to inform the second-phase game-theoretic model and demonstrate the attack and defense mechanisms.

Keywords: Robotics · Security · Game Theory · Advanced Persistent Threats

© The Author(s), under exclusive license to Springer Nature Switzerland AG 2025
A. Sinha et al. (Eds.): GameSec 2024, LNCS 14908, pp. 287–305, 2025.
https://doi.org/10.1007/978-3-031-74835-6_14

1   Introduction

In recent years, the sophistication of cyber-attacks has outpaced traditional security measures designed to protect robotic systems. The notion of achieving absolute security has become an unattainable ideal, as resource limitations always constrain system designers. A more effective approach involves understanding the specific attack tactics and strategies that would-be attackers might employ to compromise a robot's defenses. This requires considering not only the technical aspects of a robot's design but also its operational domain and the potential consequences of a successful attack. For instance, compromising the security of robots operating in safety-critical environments such as robot-assisted surgeries can result in grave casualties.

Game theory offers a powerful framework for designing robust security solutions by modeling and analyzing the strategic interactions between attackers, defenders, and humans. Its key benefits include: (1) capturing the competitive behaviors and constraints of all parties involved; (2) providing algorithms and tools to predict the outcomes of different strategies through equilibrium analysis; (3) incorporating human factors such as bounded rationality, cognitive biases, and risk-sensitivity into the solution concepts; and (4) allowing for a hierarchical modeling of the system at multiple layers of the system and with varying attack scenarios. This enables a comprehensive view of security threats across the system's layers and facilitates the design of integrated, system-wide security solutions. Game theory has been successfully applied to a broad range of cybersecurity applications, offering a valuable toolset for security professionals.

In this work, we construct a multi-phase game-theoretic framework that breaks down a security threat to an autonomous navigation robot into two distinct phases. Each of these phases is modeled using a particular game model. Each of these games is then played from the perspective of the defender (D) and we characterize different kinds of solutions these admit. In modeling the composite multi-phase game, we adapt a hybrid model-based and data-driven approach to security for robotic systems. We extend the `cut-the-rope` game model proposed in [12] by incorporating uncertainty in the ability of a spot-check on a given node on the attack tree to neutralize the APT and force the attacker to re-start the attack vector on a preceding node. The model proposed in [11,12] is chosen to be agnostic to the exact nature of the exploit that the attacker employs on any node in the attack tree. We modify and extend this paradigm by explicitly creating a library of known exploits and defense mechanisms for every node in the attack tree.

Paper Organization: We begin by briefly reviewing the related work in the area of security for networked cyber-physical systems, with a special emphasis on prior work on robotic applications that utilize game-theoretic tools in Sect. 2. We then formalize our problem setting and our proposed methodology in Sect. 4. In Sect. 3, we present the application setting of our case study and discuss the ways in which it motivates and informs our problem formulation and solution methods. Next, we demonstrate the results of our proposed solutions for our use case in Sect. 5. Finally, we conclude this work in Sect. 6 with a discussion on the results of the current work and explore future directions for potential exploration.

2   Related Work

APTs represent complex and sophisticated attacks where adversaries employ multi-stage strategies to infiltrate and compromise systems. In the context of APT defense, game theory has emerged as a robust framework for modeling the interactions between defenders and attackers, where both sides have incomplete information and make strategic decisions. This enables analysis and optimization of the defender's strategy to mitigate the risk of successful APT attacks. A notable approach is the use of differential games, which offer a theoretical foundation for addressing complex multi-agent decision-making problems in robotics. [4] highlights the relevance of differential games in developing effective defense strategies against APTs. Their work suggests that understanding the dynamics between the defender, APT attacker, and potential insiders is crucial for creating a comprehensive defense strategy that can adapt over time, especially given partial information. [15] proposed a framework that integrates machine learning techniques with game-theoretic analysis to enhance the detection of APTs. Meanwhile, [13] developed a game-theoretic framework incorporating several key factors, including the attacker's goals and resources, the defender's detection capabilities, and the dynamics of the attack and response.

The concept of multi-phase frameworks is critical in understanding APTs, as these threats can be divided into distinct temporal phases, each requiring tailored strategies. [16] provided a framework modeling the effective repair strategies against APTs within a differential game context. Their insights reveal that the interplay among the phases is vital for optimizing defense strategies, as actions taken in one phase can significantly impact the outcomes in subsequent phases. This emphasizes the need for robotic systems to have a holistic view of the threat landscape and the ability to adapt their strategies dynamically. In [18] a foundational work on multi-phase and multi-stage game-theoretic modeling of APTs was presented. They demonstrate how game-theoretic frameworks can capture the complex dynamics of APTs, including the attacker's adaptive strategies and the defender's proactive countermeasures across multiple phases and stages. Building on this work, several studies have developed more specific game-theoretic models tailored to different aspects of APTs. [17] proposed a game-theoretic model that considers the attacker's deceptive actions and the defender's responses across multiple stages. Similarly, [5] develop a game-theoretic framework for analyzing the multi-stage, multi-phase movement of APTs in critical infrastructure networks. The anomaly detection problem also naturally admits a game-theoretic treatment due to the competing objectives of the attacker and defender involved. There has been considerable work in recent years to formulate the interactions between a surreptitious attacker injecting malicious data into a network and a machine-learning based tool trained to recognize patterns of data during the nominal operation of the system and flag any out-of-distribution patterns that emerge in the system. In [3], the authors address the challenge of dynamically scheduling the optimal threshold parameter for the anomaly detection application to be sufficiently sensitive so that it quickly detects anomalous data but at the same time, also balances the need to minimize the false positive detection rate. The Stackelberg game is played from the defender's perspective against an adversary with the inner knowledge of the system capable of employing a best-response strategy.

The authors in [2] identify vulnerabilities discovered in current versions of Robot Operating System (ROS2) and Secure ROS2 (SROS2) implementations. The authors mention that the current ROS2 communication protocol design does not account for publisher information, making it difficult to pinpoint the malicious actor after system failures. Additionally, a severe privacy threat originating from owner-specified permission files in the ROS2 system is identified. This vulnerability can cause consequences such as workload termination, robot crashes, and damage to the surroundings, as well as the potential theft of users' private information. [19] presents an introduction to robot system cybersecurity, including the vulnerabilities and potential fixes of ROS. They discuss the application of game theory to model-based security in the context of robotics. [12] presents a novel game-theoretic framework for defending against APTs in robotics. They apply the Cut-The-Rope model to an experimental study of an APT defense game on attack graphs, using a robotic arm with ROS2 as a case study. The framework allows a security officer to establish an optimized defense policy against stealthy intrusions. The framework demonstrates significant value in enhancing the resilience of robotic systems against APTs. In [1] a game-theoretic approach to the security of vehicle platooning is presented, which relies on ROS. They conduct simulations and experiments on a vehicle platoon setup to analyze the vulnerability of components to attacks.

A common theme across these studies is the use of game theory to model the strategic interactions between attackers and defenders in the context of ROS and robotics. The studies often employ dynamic game models to capture the evolving nature of potential attacks and defenses. The methodologies include the design of game-theoretic frameworks, the formulation of attacker and defender utility functions, and the analysis of equilibrium strategies. Some studies also leverage experimental methods, such as attack graphs and simulations, to evaluate the effectiveness of the game-theoretic approaches.

3   Case Study: Autonomous Indoor Navigation Using Nova Carter

Nova Carter[1] is an open-source autonomous robotics development platform aimed towards facilitating the shift from manual forklifts and guided vehicles to complete autonomy. The platform is equipped with a rich sensor suite and

---

[1] https://robotics.segway.com/nova-carter/.

is tightly integrated with NVIDIA Isaac/Omniverse autonomy environment[2] for accelerated and high-fidelity simulation-based development of autonomy. Nova Carter is expected to safely operate alongside humans in highly dynamic and unstructured settings boosting productivity and expedites mass deployment, all while maintaining operational safety in applications such as warehouse management, and logistics.

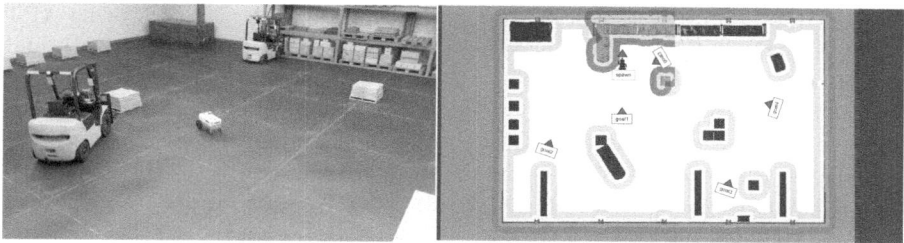

Fig. 1. (left) Isaac Sim warehouse environment for Nova Carter AGR running a navigation stack. (right) Static Map of the warehouse simulation environment with marked goal points.

This makes the Nova Carter platform an appropriate case study for examining its resilience to security attacks and other cyber-related issues. In this work, we consider the scenario of the Nova Carter autonomously navigating an indoor warehouse environment consisting of obstacles of varying size and shape which is shown in Fig. 1. The Nova Carter is commanded to a set of locations multiple times in a different order within the warehouse environment to patrol the space. An example of a security threat in this case study would be, an attack in the computational graph of Nova Carter autonomy stack, and causing it to crash into valuable/dangerous objects in the warehouse while patrolling or causing a glitch in the navigation pipeline to reach one of the locations. We evaluate our work using NVIDIA Isaac Sim, a high-fidelity robotic simulator. The Nova Carter is equipped with a LiDAR, and a fully-operational Nav2-based autonomy stack [7]. Nav2 has been demonstrated to be a highly reliable autonomous navigation robotics package that has seen wide adoption in both academia and industry. We specifically configure the robot to use the NavFn Global Planner and the sampling-based DWB local controller [6,8] to perform the autonomous navigation task. The AGR is assigned the task of autonomously navigating between a set of waypoints that represent specific locations in the warehouse environment shown in Fig. 1. The global planner receives the goal poses that the AGR is expected to navigate and chart a course based on the cost map generated by the sensors to minimize a heuristic cost metric. This *global plan* then serves as the

---

[2] https://developer.nvidia.com/isaac/perceptor.

basis for the local controller which further refines the cost map and drives the robots by generating suitable *command velocities* for the robot to achieve the goal.

4   Problem Formulation

In this section, we describe the two-phase game-theoretic setting for our security problem. In phase I, the security threat actor penetrates the network using APT attacks [18]. Once the APT actor is successful in penetrating the network and reaching the safety-critical node, phase I of the model terminates. The attacker now has the ability to inject malicious data into the autonomy stack. Typically, this is considered a catastrophic failure in terms of maintaining network security because the attacker can easily take over remote control of the AGR and cause it to intentionally crash into an obstacle or make it fail its primary mission of autonomous navigation. However, modern robotic systems are designed with end-point security measures such as data-driven Anomaly Detection Systems (ADS) that constantly monitor the flows of data within the robotic system and raise an alarm when any anomalous flow of data is detected. The robots are then guided into pre-determined safe fallback measures such as terminating autonomous navigation or reaching a certifiably safe state until security operators can review the situation. We consider the scenario in which the APT attacker has some information about the ADS and can strategically inject malicious data to cause damage to the system while remaining undetected by the ADS.

4.1   Two Phases of the Security Attack

We assume that the adversary propagating the APT remains *stealthy* during the penetration phase of the attack. The defender cannot detect the presence or absence of a current or a past attack on any node of the attack tree in this phase. However, the defender does possess a set of defensive mechanisms that have the potential to eliminate the infection from a node. These mechanisms are curated for each node in the attack tree just as the attacker uses a curated set of exploits to attack a given node. This leaves proactive defensive mechanisms as the only viable options for network security. These measures are enacted through a series of "spot-checks" at various locations on the attack tree that seek to "cut" the path of the attack vector, forcing the APT attacker to re-initiate the attack vector at one of the nodes that precede the spot-check node if the spot-check being applied is able to successfully neutralize the exploit.

We use the Robot Vulnerability Scoring System (RVSS) [14] for the evaluation of the RVSS score for the vulnerabilities for each of the nodes in the

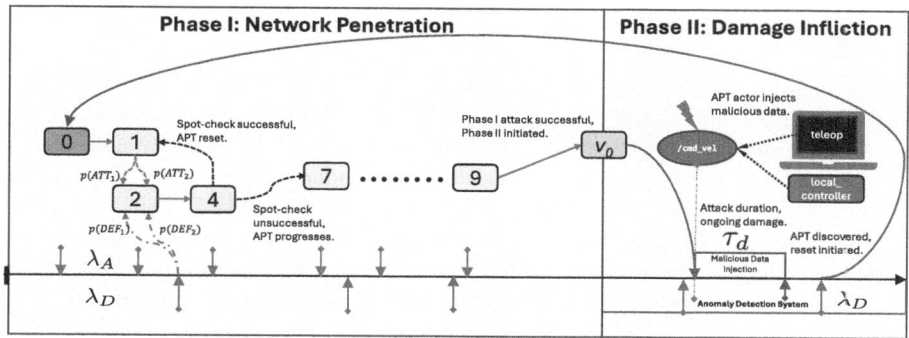

Fig. 2. In the network penetration phase, the adversary traverses the attack tree from the source node towards the sink node v_0, being able to compromise each node in two ways with distinct RVSS-quantified difficulty layers (see Table 1); exploiting the more sophisticated vulnerability has a higher risk of failure, but higher chances of persisting against the reciprocally layered defender's spot-checks. Should the defender's spot-check succeed on a node in the exploited section of an attack vector, the attacker continues from the node preceding the spot-check. The players time their actions based on Poissonian schedules with parameters λ_A, λ_D. Finally, the breaching of the target node v_0 triggers the anomaly detection phase.

attack tree Fig. 3. It provides a scoring system designed to evaluate the security vulnerabilities of robots, as conventional scoring systems like the Common Vulnerability Scoring System (CVSS) are not accurate enough for this purpose.

In the second phase (damage infliction), the attacker actively attempts to sabotage the system by interacting with physical components in the system posing an active safety-critical threat to the system. We relax the *stealthy* assumption on the attacker and assume that while in this phase, the attacker becomes susceptible to detection. We model the scenario in which the sole objective of the attacker is to *"go for the kill"* instead of surreptitiously embedding itself into the host system for other ancillary reasons. The presence of the ADS makes this scenario challenging for the attacker because absolute exploitation could run the risk of near instantaneous detection following which the system can enforce safe fallback policies. On the other hand, every false alarm raised by the ADS application results in an imposed maintenance cost for the operator. Therefore, the ADS application is incentivized against being hyper-vigilant. We model this mutual balancing act between the attacker and the defender in the second phase using a zero-sum game.

4.2   Phase I: Network Penetration

The game in phase I is modeled as a sequential game $(\mathcal{N}, \{\mathcal{A}_i\}_{i \in \mathcal{N}}, \{\mathcal{U}_i\}_{i \in \mathcal{N}})$ with a set of players $\mathcal{N} = \{A, D\}$ with A denoting the attacker, D denoting the defender. Let also $G = (V, E)$ be an attack tree, with the set of nodes $V = \{0, .., 10, v_0\}$, set of edges $E = \{(0, 1), ..., (5, v_0), ..., (10, v_0)\}$, which has an entry point, node 0 for the attacker and a target node v_0 and enables the sequential movements of the attacker, as shown in Fig. 3. The action sets for the two players are described by the sets $\mathcal{A}_A = \bigcup_{u \in V} \{ATT_1^u, ATT_2^u\}$ and $\mathcal{A}_D = \bigcup_{u \in V} \{DEF_1^u, DEF_2^u\}$ for the attacker and defender, respectively; to put this in context, the attacker can move along paths from the source to the sink node of the attack tree by implementing one of the two possible attacks or exploits, while the defender can choose a node from the attack tree to apply one of the two possible spot-checks at each stage. Additionally, the payoffs for the two players U_A and U_D for the attacker and defender respectively, are constructed in such a way to reflect the zero-sum nature of the game and are used to compute the mixed strategy Nash equilibrium where the defender aims to minimize the each player's strategy minimizes the expected payoff given the strategy of the opponent.

At equilibrium, neither player can improve their expected payoff by adapting their strategy, so for a mixed strategy profile $(\mathbf{x}^*, \mathbf{y}^*)$:

$$\forall \mathbf{x} \in \mathcal{S} : U_A(\mathbf{x}^*, \mathbf{y}^*) \geq U_A(\mathbf{x}, \mathbf{y}^*)$$

$$\forall \mathbf{y} \in \mathcal{S} : U_D(\mathbf{x}^*, \mathbf{y}^*) \leq U_D(\mathbf{x}^*, \mathbf{y})$$

further, the defender's objective is to minimize the payoff and the probability the attacker hits the commandeers the cyber-physical system. Equivalently, this means that the optimal strategy for the attacker would be:

$$\mathbf{x}^* \in \arg \max_{x_n \in \mathcal{A}_A} \min_{y \in \mathcal{A}_D} U_A(\mathbf{x}, \mathbf{y})$$

Each node in the attack tree can be compromised using one of two types of exploits, as detailed in Fig. 3. One exploit is easier and more likely to succeed, while the other is more difficult and hence riskier for the attacker. The defender can spot-check each node in two distinct ways: a simpler defense that is likely to succeed if the attacker chooses the easier exploit, and a more robust defense that is more likely to dislodge the attacker if the easier exploit is used, or potentially less effective if the attacker chooses the harder exploit; the likelihood of success for each attack is related to the RVSS value for the respective attack; the likelihood of the spot-check's success is based on the intensity of the defense action, which in turn is informed by the expected attacker's action.

The attacker's payoff reflects the probability of successfully reaching the target node v_0, considering the defender's actions at each stage, while the defender aims at minimizing the attacker's probability of success by appropriately selecting nodes to spot-check. Further, in our probabilistic cut-the-rope [12] framework, there are multiple attack types to achieve the node compromise. Below, we analyze the value function and overall utility function for the attacker and the defender.

$$S_A^n = \sum_{\pi_n \in \mathcal{AS}_1} \sum_{i=1}^{2} y_n(\pi_n, ATT_i) \cdot \Pr(\text{Success at stage } n \mid \pi_n, c_n)$$

with the following quantity representing the probability of success for the attacker considering spot-check type c_n^j by the defender and attack sequence ATT_i over attack segment π_n by the attacker. The probability $\Pr(\text{Success at stage } n \mid \pi_n, c_n)$ depends on the probability that the spot-checks failed over the adversary's traversed attack vector segment and is calculated empirically.

Which represents the weighted probability that the attacker succeeds (i.e., reaches the target node at stage n), considering all possible attack paths (in the attack tree) and types (in the decision tree), given that the defender

$$S_D^n = \sum_{c_n \in \mathcal{AS}_2} \sum_{j=1}^{2} x_n(c_n^j) \cdot S_A^n$$

which represents the sum over the defender's choices of type of spot-check at each stage n. Finally, the total utility for the attacker over all stages is the defender's expected utilities across all stages and with the 0-stage value obtained from the game in the subsequent phase:

$$U_A = S_D^n(0) + \sum_{n=1}^{N} S_D^n$$

Movement Patterns. Similarly with [12], in our probabilistic cut-the-rope framework, both the defender and the attacker operate periodically at time intervals governed by the Poisson distribution with probability mass function (for the random variable X) with parameters λ_A and λ_D for the two players:

$$P(X = k) = \frac{\lambda^k e^{-\lambda}}{k!}$$

Additionally, both the attacker may probabilistically succeed in their actions will have success rate characterized by the ability to succeed in n rounds and fail at round $n - 1$, when the selected m-length path for the attacker is $\pi(m) = [e_i, i \in \{0, .., m\}]$, with $q(e_i)$ denoting the probability of success at node i:

$$f_N(n) = (1 - q(e_{n+1})) \cdot \prod_{k=1}^{n} q(e_k)$$

For the defender, the number of steps the attacker can take before the defender becomes active follows a geometric distribution; this is because the defender's action introduces a pause period affecting the attacker's frequency of movement, with p denoting the probability that the defender becomes active:

$$f_N(n) = p \cdot (1 - p)^n$$

Attack Tree Construction. To construct the attack tree displayed in Fig. 3, we ran experiments on a Nav2-based deployment of the autonomy stack.

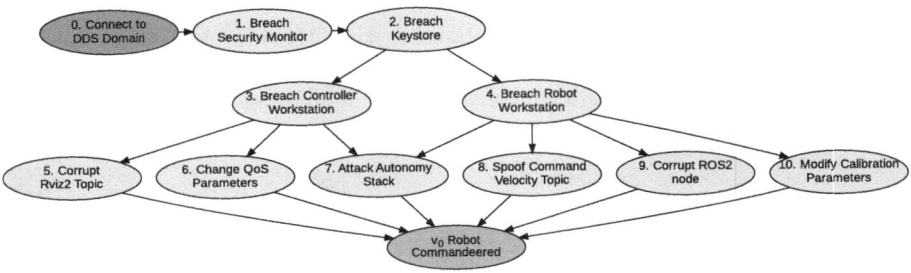

Fig. 3. Attack tree for the Nova Carter cyber-physical system featuring three color-coded phases, with the scope of this work including the network penetration and anomaly detection phase games.

To construct the attack tree that is relevant to our deployment of the Nav2 [9] (ROS2-based implementation) autonomy stack, displayed in Fig. 3, we analyze the potential attack paths targeting various software components of the robotic system (Isaac Sim Nova Carter).

Firstly, the attacker can gain initial access by connecting to the local area network which is composed of the robotic platform or the simulation engine as one machine, and the machine that controls the robot by setting navigation waypoints as another (controller workstation). The attacker may breach this local network (0.) by e.g., exploiting unsecured Wi-Fi connections or otherwise obtaining network authentication credentials. Once connected to the network, the attacker could breach the security monitor (1.) thereby disrupting the normal security operations e.g., by launching denial-of-service attacks to do so.

Next, the attacker can target the keystore (2.), where ROS2 securely stores cryptographic keys and certificates, also known as security artifacts, which along with authentication, encryption and access control policies define the security context that binds a group of ROS2 nodes referred to as security enclaves. We define our enclaves based on the grouping shown in Table 2.

Table 1. RVSS values and defenses for various attack scenarios per node in the attack tree shown in Fig. 3.

Node	Attack	RVSS	Defense
0	Physically access the network by connecting an unauthorized device to the local network	6.0	Implement physical security measures (e.g., access control to network hardware) to prevent unauthorized physical connections
	Exploit vulnerabilities in the network access control to remotely gain access to the local network	7.5	Employ strong network access controls, such as WPA3 encryption, zero-trust and regular device audit
1,3,4	Use compromised credentials obtained through social engineering to gain access to the target machine	7.8	Use endpoint detection and response (EDR) tools and strict administrative access controls
	Exploit a remote code execution vulnerability to gain control over the target machine	8.0	Regularly update and patch OS software
2	Extract the keystore by exploiting open file permissions	7.8	Inspect and apply strict file permissions
	Modify the CA's certificate store to issue fraudulent certificates and compromise the trust chain	9.0	Secure the keystore with hardware security modules (HSMs) and enforce access controls e.g., multi-factor authentication (MFA)
5,6,10	Exploit intra-enclave open topic permissions to inject malicious data	6.0	Implement strict topic permissions and use secure communication channels (e.g., TLS)
	Gain administrative access to the robot workstation and directly use Rviz2 to publish waypoints	7.5	Restrict administrative access and use MFA. Monitor and log all topic communications
7,9	Exploit a software vulnerability in the autonomy stack components	7.8	Use static and dynamic code analysis tools to identify vulnerabilities
	Gain administrative access to the robot workstation and modify the autonomy stack's configuration or code	8.5	Rebuild autonomy stack. Implement integrity checks and monitoring
8, v_0	Use a compromised ROS2 node to send malicious commands to the robot	8.5	Use secure communication channels and monitor command messages for anomalies
	Gain administrative access to the robot's control system and issue commands directly	9.5	Restrict administrative. Implement anomaly detection for control system commands

Following the keystore breach, the attacker could compromise the controller workstation (3.) which manages commands and navigation waypoints for the robot. This would enable waypoint-relevant topic corruption (5.) with attacks targeting the robot's perception and visualization data. Having breached the controller workstation the attacker may also change QoS (the quality of service) parameters (6.) that the ROS2/DDS middleware specifies by modifying relevant parameters to disrupt communication reliability and performance, as well as attack the autonomy stack (7.) by attempting to modify navigation algorithms interfere with sensor data processing or manipulating path planning modules.

Concurrently, the attacker could target the robot workstation (4.), which involves similar methods to the controller workstation compromise but focuses on the machine directly interfacing with the robotic platform. This breach could allow the attacker to interfere with robot directions directly by spoofing the command velocity topics to send false movement commands or infecting legitimate ROS2 nodes (9.), or modifying the calibration of parameters to affect the robot's operational accuracy.

Each of these compromises leads to the final goal of commandeering the robot potentially causing the robot to perform unauthorized tasks or fail to perform the intended task.

RVSS Value Analysis. In the attack tree at Fig. 3, the attacker follows a sequential compromise to the system, starting from gaining unauthorized access to ultimately commandeering the robot. At each node, the attacker can choose between two types of exploits, each with its own RVSS value. The RVSS score categorizes vulnerabilities into five severity ranges: low $(0.1 - 3.9)$, medium $(4.0 - 5.9)$, high $(6.0 - 7.4)$, critical $(7.5 - 8.9)$ and severe $(9.0 - 10.0)$. The thresholds shown in Table 1 were selected based on the lists of previously evaluated vulnerabilities in [10,14]. For example, a score of 6.0 indicates represents high severity level and is assigned to the exploitation of itra-enclave open topic permissions to inject malicious data into the ROS2 system, such as command velocities in the typical `cmd_vel` topic, as an exploit for compromising node 5 in attack tree. On the other hand, a score of 7.5 of critical severity is assigned to an exploit that gives administrative access to the robot workstation and uses tools like Rviz2 to directly publish waypoints.

In the former case, implementing strict topic permissions using rule-based access lists and cryptography helps secure intra-enclave communications by controlling which nodes can publish or subscribe to specific topics. In ROS2, enclaves are logical groupings of nodes that operate within isolated and controlled communication environments, with each enclave being linked with a particular security policy involving access control lists (ACLs) and encryption; an example of Nav2-specific node grouping into enclaves is provided in Table 2.

4.3   Phase II: Anomaly Detection Game

The second phase of the composite game occurs when the threat actor succeeds in propagating the APT vectors through the attack tree and reaches the target

Table 2. Nav2-specific ROS-node partition into security enclaves

Enclave	Nodes
/navigation	`amcl`
	`behavior_server`
	`bt_navigator`
	`bt_navigator_navigate_through_poses_rclcpp_node`
	`bt_navigator_navigate_to_pose_rclcpp_node`
	`controller_server`
	`global_costmap`
	`lifecycle_manager_localization`
	`lifecycle_manager_navigation`
	`local_costmap`
	`map_server`
	`nav2_container`
	`planner_server`
	`smoother_server`
	`waypoint_follower`
	`velocity_smoother`
/sensors	`intel_realsense_r200_depth_driver`
	`pointcloud_to_laserscan`
/monitor	`rviz`
	`rviz_navigation_dialog_action_client`
/teleop	`teleop_twist_keyboard`

node v_0. We now assume that the threat actor has total control over the target node and can maliciously manipulate the target node v_0 with the objective of maximizing the damage to the physical robot while remaining undetected.

In our implementation of the autonomy stack, we equip the robot system with a data-driven Anomaly Detection System (ADS) application that acts as the last line of defense to protect the robot from physical damage resulting from a malicious takeover of the robot system. The ADS application constantly monitors the flow of data within the system and triggers an emergency shutdown procedure in case an anomalous data flow is detected.

The Nova Carter robot is a differential drive robot with the following kinematic model:

$$\begin{bmatrix} \dot{x} \\ \dot{y} \\ \dot{\varphi} \end{bmatrix} = \begin{bmatrix} \cos\varphi & 0 \\ \sin\varphi & 0 \\ 0 & 1 \end{bmatrix} \begin{bmatrix} V \\ \omega \end{bmatrix} \tag{1}$$

where $V \in \mathbb{R}^+$ and $\omega \in \mathbb{R}$ are control variables that represent the linear velocity and angular velocity imparted into the robot. It is in this context that the choice of the attack tree we use to model the penetration phase becomes obvious. The target node in the attack tree, v_0 results in the attacker obtaining direct access to read and write into the ROS2 topic `cmd_vel` that the stack uses to publish the command velocities (V, ω).

In the second phase, the attacker strategically doses the genuine `cmd_vel` with a malicious stream of velocity commands that seek to sabotage the navigation task of the robot. The attacker does not stop the local controller from publishing genuine data and cannot stop the robot from subscribing to it either without enacting a stack configuration change during run-time. ROS2 uses the Data Distribution Service (DDS) as the middleware that handles all inter-node communication. DDS uses a common data bus where all topics are published to and subscribed from. DDS maintains a common memory buffer to store transient messages for each topic. So the rate at which the attacker publishes the malicious data is also important. Our stack is configured with the robot expecting control commands at a frequency of 20 Hz. If the attacker chooses to publish their malicious command velocities at the same rate, in effect the robot will only receive roughly half of these commands. Increasing the malicious topic publish rate too dramatically could result in a buffer overflow and subsequent detection of the attack. We limit the scope of this case study to a pre-determined data injection rate of 20 Hz to match the native rate. The APT attacker implements this poisoning attack using a ROS2 `teleop` node that has gained access privileges to publish to the `cmd_vel` topic. The enclave partition for this node can be seen in Table 2. The attack implementation is described in Fig. 2 and can be visualized using the robot odometry data collected during the attack shown in Fig. 4.

The malicious velocity commands are generated directly by the attacker. We assume that the attacker poisons the velocity commands using a constant amplitude for both V and ω We characterize the *action profiles* of the attacker by parametrizing the attack using an *"aggressiveness"* parameter α. We consider two action profiles for the attacker: *conservative-* with $\alpha_1 : (V, \omega) \mapsto (1.2, 25)$ and *conservative-* with $\alpha_2 : (V, \omega) \mapsto (1.5, 35)$. The units are m/s and rad/s respectively. The greater the value of α, the higher the disruption induced to the AGR's navigation ability. However, the situation becomes more challenging in our case because the autonomy stack is built using a high degree of resilience and quickly adapts to account for the disturbances and overcome minor erratic behavior induced by the malicious commands.

The ADS consists of a neural network that is trained on the AGR pose data that is logged during the nominal operation of the AGR. We train the neural network using five nominal runs of the AGR navigating to 10 different pre-determined waypoints within the warehouse. We use a 3-layer binary neural network 2-class classifier model to build the ADS using cross-entropy training loss, trained using the ADAM optimizer. The ADS then creates a sliding window of the pose data as it is streamed and scores each passing window of pose data in terms of its closeness to the nominal data flow. We set a threshold value μ on the class identifier probability output of the trained model. Lowering this threshold causes the ADS to be hyper-sensitive to minor jitters in the pose data and results in a very high false alarm rate. However, increasing the threshold

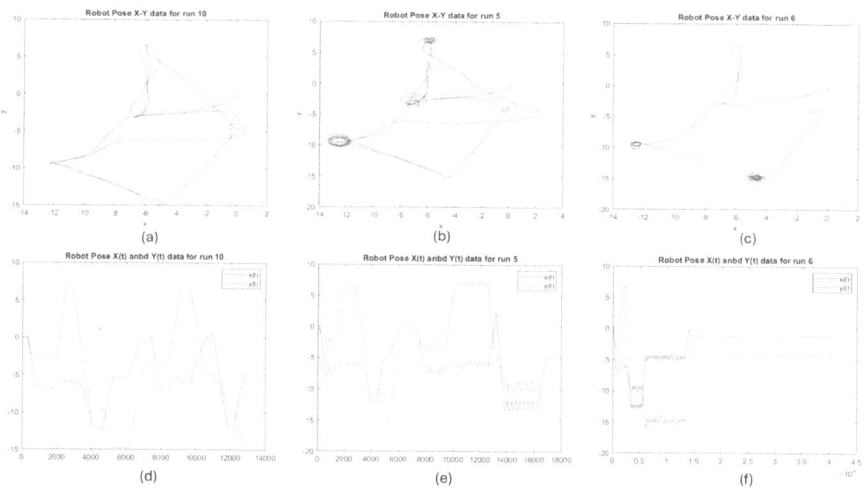

Fig. 4. AGR Data Visualization under various anomalous data injection attack scenarios in Phase-II. (a)–(c) show the trajectory traced by the AGR under thee operational conditions. The first case is under nominal operational conditions while figure (b) shows the case where the attacker takes a conservative approach by choosing a moderate intensity for the attack ($\alpha = \alpha_1$) and continues to disrupt the navigation task for a longer duration. The third case (c) is when an aggressive attacker injects command data with very high intensity ($\alpha = \alpha_2$) seeking to maximize damage while risking faster detection.

lowers the false alarm rate $\mathcal{P}_F$ causing the detection time τ_d to be too long. This results in the attacker remaining in the network for even longer and causing further disruptions. Just as in the case of the attacker, the defender which in this case is the ADS application, also has two action profiles that correspond to conservative ($\mu_1 = 0.9$) and aggressive ($\mu_2 = 0.75$) detection thresholds.

We then formulate the payoff/loss function for the defender/attacker as a scalarized composite objective given by $\mathcal{L}^{AD}(\alpha, \mu)$ shown in the attacker's game described in the equation below:

$$\max_{\alpha,\mu} \mathcal{L}^{AD}(\alpha, \mu) = \mathcal{L}^{AD}_{\mathcal{P}_{fa}}(\mu) + \mathcal{L}^{AD}_{\tau_d}(\alpha) \tag{2}$$

where $\mathcal{L}^{AD}_{fa}(\mu) = \mathcal{P}_{fa}$ is the false alarm rate observed from the ADS implementation during a phase II attack and $\mathcal{L}^{AD}_{\tau_d}(\alpha) = \tau_d$ is the time to detection after the data injection attack is initialized. We note here that there is a fundamental disparity in the units and scales of the two individual loss components. We therefore use the fraction of the time taken to detect the threat out of the expected remaining time during the single waypoint goal navigation sub-task during which the attack was initiated as the detection time metric. We establish the baseline time required for each point-to-point goal as the average time observed during the nominal operation.

5   Results and Discussion

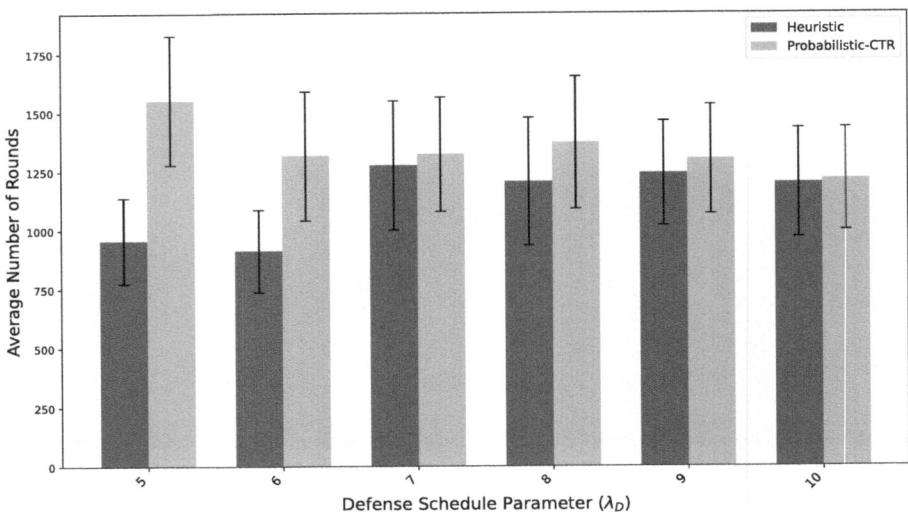

Fig. 5. Evaluation of the number of rounds (vertical axis) the attacker needs on average to breach the final target v_0 under two different strategies and varying schedule parameters; for the above defender schedule parameters λ_D (horizontal axis), the probabilistic CTR method seems to outperform the heuristic approach in defending the system.

For the phase I game, we consider the attack tree framework presented in Sect. 4 and run simulations to evaluate the players' derived strategies against a custom heuristic approach on (i) the attacker's selection of the exploit path or attack vector and the attacker's response to successful spot-checks, and (ii) the defender's selection of node in the attack tree to spot-check and the level of defense enforced at that node.

For the simulation purposes, we consider an attacker whose strategy is informed by the aggregate difficulty of the selected path, as a distribution of normalized exponential sums of the individual exploit difficulty levels of all possible exploits and nodes at which they can take place, the collection of which is used to define the probability mass function (PMF) for the attacker's strategy. The choice of this way of strategy derivation for the attacker is based on the expectation from the attacker to choose the relatively simpler exploit path possible, which at equilibrium will take into account the defender's action of incentivizing the attacker to increase the difficulty level of vulnerabilities exploited to ensure a more likely success. For the defender, the probability of node selection to spot-check takes into account the respective defense intensity level after which, the spot-check probability of success is calculated separately for any node $n \in V$ as follows, along with a value instantiation for our simulation purposes:

$$\text{Pr(on-path spot-check success)} = \begin{pmatrix} \Pr(DEF_1 \mid ATT_1) & \Pr(DEF_2 \mid ATT_1) \\ \Pr(DEF_1 \mid ATT_2) & \Pr(DEF_2 \mid ATT_2) \end{pmatrix} = \begin{pmatrix} 0.5 & 0.8 \\ 0.2 & 0.5 \end{pmatrix}$$

Finally, the attacker and the defender are allowed to issue actions on a Poisson schedule with separate parameters λ_A and λ_D and corresponding frequencies. For evaluation purposes, we set the attack $\lambda_A = 0.1$ and experiment with different values of λ_D. By allowing the game to be played for up to 10^4 rounds, we use the number of rounds the attacker needed to achieve its goal. The attacker uses the strategy prescribed by our probabilistic framework while the defender's strategy is compared against a heuristic approach of random selection of node to spot-check. The results are summarized in bar plots 95% confidence interval in Fig. 5 for 100 experiments of each case, for which we report the average number of rounds. This shows that over varying defense action frequency values, the attacker is consistently delayed more by the probabilistic cut-the-rope prescribed defense strategy.

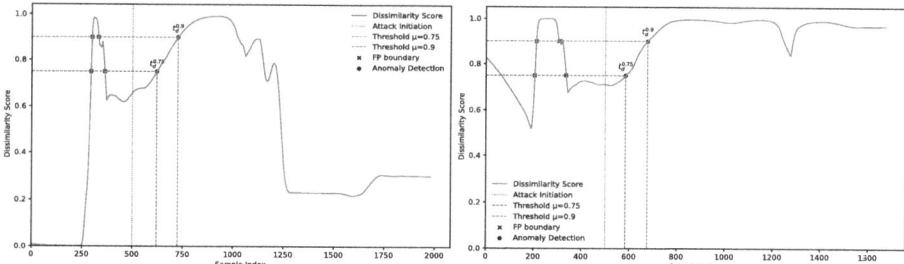

Fig. 6. Plots of the dissimilarity scores for a sample of the pose data while the AGR is under the Phase-II attack by a *conservative* attacker (left, $\alpha = \alpha_1$) and *aggressive* attacker (right, $\alpha = \alpha_2$). The ADS is configured to be either *conservative* (red dotted line, $\mu = 0.9$) or *aggressive* (green dotted line, $\mu = 0.75$). The individual payoff components, τ_d and $\mathcal{P}_{fa}$ were computed four all four cases in $(\mathcal{A}_1 \times \mathcal{A}_2)$. The plots also show the ground truth of the initiation of the data injection attack (violet vertical line at 500 samples). The fraction of samples reported above the threshold before the attack initiation is determined to be the false alarm rate. The detection time is computed as the ratio of the detection time taken after the attack initiation to the attack duration time still left before the attack is deemed successful. (Color figure online)

For the phase II game, we train the ADS neural network on 5 nominal simulation runs of the entire task duration and emulate the attack using an anomalous noise injection node. We now assign specific values to the action profiles of the players $\mathcal{A}_{AD} = \{\text{conservative, aggressive}\}$. For the specific values defined in Sect. 4, we plot the results of the data-injection attack simulation in Fig. 6. The components of the composite pay-off function can be deciphered from the figure.

Combining these using Eq. 2 provides us the payoff matrix for the attacker, $P_A^{AD} = \begin{pmatrix} 0.206 & 0.2125 \\ 0.3346 & 0.3302 \end{pmatrix} = -P_D^{AD}$. From the data-driven payoff matrix, the game admits a pure Nash Equilibrium. We compute the value of the game to be 0.3302 and the optimal strategy for the defender to be $(0, 1)$ and for the attacker to be $(0, 1)$, implying that the aggressive action profiles as defined earlier suit both the players well.

6 Conclusions

For the evaluation of our multi-phase game theoretic approach, we utilize a custom attack tree tailored to our case study involving the Nova Carter Isaac Sim robotic platform and its Nav2-based autonomy stack structure from a software perspective as well as the hardware components involved. Considering each specific component's ways of compromise during the network penetration phase, we provide the framework for a defense strategy aiming to prevent the attacker from taking control of the robot. In the anomaly detection phase, the goal is to identify intrusions and deactivate the robot, as demonstrated using a data-driven Anomaly Detection System. Our approach, which extends the cut-the-rope model to a probabilistic and multi-phase setting, successfully models the attack and defense dynamics, offering a comprehensive strategy to address both phases of the attack. Thus, our work offers a novel perspective on integrating model-based and data-driven approaches to game-theoretic decision-making for security applied to a practical system.

In the future, we would like to further investigate the performance impact on the system when implementing the spot-check measures in phase I and incorporating the incurred cost into the decision-making process. For phase II, we would like to extend the current work to include more advanced means of anomaly detection that rely on multi-modal real-time data monitoring to detect a wider variety of malicious data injection threats.

References

1. Basiri, M.H., Pirani, M., Azad, N.L., Fischmeister, S.: Security of vehicle platooning: a game-theoretic approach. IEEE Access **7**, 185565–185579 (2019)
2. Deng, G., Xu, G., Zhou, Y., Zhang, T., Liu, Y.: On the (in)security of secure ROS2. In: Proceedings of the 2022 ACM SIGSAC Conference on Computer and Communications Security, CCS 2022, pp. 739–753. Association for Computing Machinery, New York (2022). https://doi.org/10.1145/3548606.3560681
3. Ghafouri, A., Laszka, A., Abbas, W., Vorobeychik, Y., Koutsoukos, X.: A game-theoretic approach for selecting optimal time-dependent thresholds for anomaly detection. Auton. Agent. Multi-Agent Syst. **33**, 430–456 (2019)
4. Hu, P., Li, H., Fu, H., Cansever, D., Mohapatra, P.: Dynamic defense strategy against advanced persistent threat with insiders. In: 2015 IEEE Conference on Computer Communications (INFOCOM), pp. 747–755. IEEE (2015)

5. Huang, L., Zhu, Q.: Adaptive strategic cyber defense for advanced persistent threats in critical infrastructure networks. ACM SIGMETRICS Perform. Eval. Rev. **46**(2), 52–56 (2019)
6. Macenski, S., Booker, M., Wallace, J.: Open-source, cost-aware kinematically feasible planning for mobile and surface robotics. Arxiv (2024)
7. Macenski, S., Martín, F., White, R., Clavero, J.G.: The marathon 2: a navigation system. In: 2020 IEEE/RSJ International Conference on Intelligent Robots and Systems (IROS), pp. 2718–2725. IEEE (2020)
8. Macenski, S., Moore, T., Lu, D.V., Merzlyakov, A., Ferguson, M.: From the desks of ROS maintainers: a survey of modern & capable mobile robotics algorithms in the robot operating system 2. Robot. Auton. Syst. **168**, 104493 (2023)
9. Macenski, S., Martin, F., White, R., Ginés Clavero, J.: The marathon 2: a navigation system. In: 2020 IEEE/RSJ International Conference on Intelligent Robots and Systems (IROS) (2020)
10. Moulard, T., Hortala, J., Perez, X., Olalde, G., Erice, B., Olalde, O., Mayoral, D.: ROS 2 robotic systems threat model (2019). https://design.ros2.org/articles/ros2_threat_model.html. Last Modified: 2021-01
11. Rass, S., König, S., Panaousis, E.: Cut-the-rope: a game of stealthy intrusion. In: Alpcan, T., Vorobeychik, Y., Baras, J.S., Dán, G. (eds.) GameSec 2019. LNCS, vol. 11836, pp. 404–416. Springer, Cham (2019). https://doi.org/10.1007/978-3-030-32430-8_24
12. Rass, S., König, S., Wachter, J., Mayoral-Vilches, V., Panaousis, E.: Game-theoretic apt defense: an experimental study on robotics. Comput. Secur. **132**, 103328 (2023)
13. Sahabandu, D.: A game-theoretic framework for detecting advanced persistent threats. Ph.D. thesis, University of Washington (2023)
14. Vilches, V.M., et al.: Towards an open standard for assessing the severity of robot security vulnerabilities, the robot vulnerability scoring system (RVSS) (2021). https://arxiv.org/abs/1807.10357
15. Yan, H., Zhang, Q., Xie, J., Lu, Z., Chen, S., Guo, D.: An intelligent game theory framework for detecting advanced persistent threats. In: 2021 IEEE 27th International Conference on Parallel and Distributed Systems (ICPADS), pp. 450–457. IEEE (2021)
16. Yang, L.X., Li, P., Zhang, Y., Yang, X., Xiang, Y., Zhou, W.: Effective repair strategy against advanced persistent threat: a differential game approach. IEEE Trans. Inf. Forensics Secur. **14**(7), 1713–1728 (2018)
17. Zhang, L., Zhu, T., Hussain, F.K., Ye, D., Zhou, W.: A game-theoretic method for defending against advanced persistent threats in cyber systems. IEEE Trans. Inf. Forensics Secur. **18**, 1349–1364 (2022)
18. Zhu, Q., Rass, S.: On multi-phase and multi-stage game-theoretic modeling of advanced persistent threats. IEEE Access **6**, 13958–13971 (2018). https://doi.org/10.1109/ACCESS.2018.2814481
19. Zhu, Q., Rass, S., Dieber, B., Vilches, V.M.: An introduction to robot system cybersecurity. arXiv preprint arXiv:2103.05789 (2021)

Multimodal Anomaly Detection for Autonomous Cyber-Physical Systems Empowering Real-World Evaluation

Mahshid Noorani[1,2]([✉]), Tharun V. Puthanveettil[2], Asim Zoulkarni[1], Jack Mirenzi[2], Charles D. Grody[2], and John S. Baras[1]

[1] Department of Electrical and Computer Engineering, Institute for Systems Research, The University of Maryland, College Park, MD 20742, USA
{mnoorani,asimz,baras}@umd.edu
[2] Center for Advanced Transportation Technology (CATT) Laboratory, The University of Maryland, College Park, MD 20742, USA
{tvpian,jmirenzi,cdgrody}@umd.edu

Abstract. As autonomous Cyber-Physical Systems (CPS) increasingly operate in critical environments, ensuring their security and reliability becomes paramount. This paper presents a robust anomaly detection framework designed to enhance the resilience of CPS by integrating multiple sensor modalities, including Lidar, Odometry, and Network Traffic. Our approach leverages the strengths of each modality, compensating for potential weaknesses when individual modalities are considered in isolation. A vector-based reconstruction loss function is introduced, significantly improving the detection of subtle anomalies by preserving the contributions of individual features.

Our experimental evaluation, conducted on a custom-built Unmanned Ground Vehicle (UGV) platform, shows that the proposed system achieves an anomaly detection accuracy of up to 98% when using the improved vector-based reconstruction loss, compared to 72% with a standard scalar-based loss. Even when the training data is reduced by 50%, bringing the total training set size down to 92 samples, the system maintains a high accuracy of 97%, demonstrating its robustness under constrained data conditions. These results indicate the effectiveness of our multimodal approach in real-world applications where data availability may be limited. Our work focuses on generalizability and modularity, ensuring adaptability across various CPS platforms and evolving threats, ultimately enhancing the reliability of autonomous systems in real-world scenarios.

Research was sponsored by the Army Research Laboratory and was accomplished under Cooperative Agreement Number **W911NF-23-2-0040**. The views and conclusions contained in this document are those of the authors and should not be interpreted as representing the official policies, either expressed or implied, of the Army Research Laboratory or the U.S. Government. The U.S. Government is authorized to reproduce and distribute reprints for Government purposes notwithstanding any copyright notation herein.

Keywords: Multimodal Anomaly Detection · Cyber-Physical
Systems · Autoencoder-Based Detection

1   Introduction

As autonomous systems proliferate across industries such as cybersecurity and
industrial control systems, the security and reliability of Cyber-Physical Systems
(CPS) have become critical. Compromised CPS can cause substantial physical damage and even loss of life, particularly in high-stakes applications like
autonomous robots and vehicles [14,15]. Consequently, safeguarding CPS is of
paramount importance to prevent catastrophic consequences.

Ensuring the reliability and safety of CPS is a significant challenge, especially
in light of potential anomalies that can disrupt operations [3]. Robust anomaly
detection mechanisms are crucial for maintaining the resilience of CPS, protect-
ing against unexpected events that could compromise system performance and
safety.

Autoencoders are particularly effective in this context due to their ability
to learn intricate patterns in CPS data, making them a strong candidate for
identifying anomalies that deviate from expected system behavior in an unsupervised fashion. While previous research has demonstrated the effectiveness
of autoencoders in detecting anomalies within CPS, their performance can be
inconsistent across different applications, particularly under adversarial conditions. There remains a gap in the literature concerning the enhancement and
fine-tuning of anomaly detection techniques tailored to specific CPS platforms,
particularly for real-world applications and datasets.

1.1   Background and Related Work

Autoencoders have shown promise in detecting anomalies within CPS, achieving high accuracy, recall, and F1 scores while maintaining low false positive
rates. In Cyber-Physical Production Systems, for instance, autoencoders have
been used for dimensionality reduction and anomaly detection, outperforming
state-of-the-art techniques on real-world datasets [10]. Additionally, methods
combining LSTM-Autoencoder for anomaly detection in industrial control systems have demonstrated superior performance over other unsupervised methods,
with a low false negative rate [9].

Recent advances have explored more complex models, such as GRU-based
Gaussian Mixture VAE systems for handling multimodality in time series data,
and Unsupervised Multi-head Attention Autoencoder (UMAA) for improving
performance on real-world CPS datasets [11,13]. The Deep Autoencoding Gaussian Mixture Model (DAGMM) has also been proposed, jointly optimizing a
deep autoencoder and Gaussian Mixture Model for high-dimensional data, significantly improving F1 scores on benchmark datasets [20].

Despite the progress, existing anomaly detection methods face several challenges:

Adaptability to Complex Data: Handling high-dimensional, multimodal data in CPS is challenging due to the system's complexity and heterogeneity. Most research has focused on individual components, overlooking the fusion of multiple sensor modalities, which is crucial for comprehensive system behavior analysis [6, 8].

Generalizability to Real-World Applications: Many methods lack generalizability due to limited testing on real datasets, which reflect the dynamic nature of CPS. Collecting real-world robotic data is logistically complex and resource-intensive, hindering the development of robust anomaly detection systems [7]. Design and evaluation of anomaly detectors based on data collected from robotic simulator environments does not fully capture the complexities and dynamics inherent in real-world scenarios [12]. Simulator data are mainly focused on sensor information neglecting the interconnectedness between network traffic flows and sensor data, thereby impeding comprehensive system behavior analysis. While multimodal approaches are emerging, few studies have successfully integrated network traffic data with multiple sensor modalities, which is essential for a comprehensive understanding of CPS behavior [12, 18].

1.2 Contributions

In this work, we incorporate the best practices for creating unsupervised autoencoder based anomaly detection systems for Cyber-Physical Systems used in previous literature and address some of the limitations of current anomaly detection systems by focusing on several key design questions. Specifically, we propose a robust anomaly detection framework that integrates multiple sensor modalities—namely, Lidar, Odometry, and Network Traffic. This multimodal approach enhances anomaly detection by leveraging the strengths of each modality, compensating for potential weaknesses when individual modalities are considered in isolation. We explore the impact of incorporating these additional modalities into the autoencoder architecture, assessing the system's ability to maintain accuracy and robustness when handling missing or redundant modalities, and evaluating whether modalities with lower detection capabilities affect overall performance.

Furthermore, we introduce a vector-based reconstruction loss function that significantly enhances the ability of our autoencoder to detect subtle anomalies. Unlike traditional scalar-based methods, our vector-based approach preserves the contribution of each individual feature, allowing for more precise anomaly detection, particularly in identifying subtle anomalies across multiple features. This innovation is critical for improving detection accuracy in complex, real-world environments.

To evaluate our approach, we designed and implemented a experimental setup using a custom-built Unmanned Ground Vehicle (UGV) platform. This includes the collection of a real-world dataset under various operational conditions, encompassing both normal and attack scenarios. Additionally, we conducted experiments to assess the robustness of our anomaly detection system under adversarial conditions, including attacks specifically designed to evade detection. Our results demonstrate that the proposed system maintains high accuracy and robustness, even when the available training data is significantly reduced—an important consideration for real-world applications where data may be limited.

Throughout the design process, we emphasized generalizability and a modular architecture, ensuring that the anomaly detection system can be adapted to different CPS platforms and evolving threats. The insights gained from our research contribute to enhancing the reliability and maintenance of autonomous robotic systems in real-world applications.

The remainder of this paper is organized as follows: We explain the detection mechanism in Sect. 2, including the feature engineering for each modality, the spatio-temporal encoding for each modality, and the anomaly detection stage. Then, in Sect. 4, we discuss our experimental set-up including the software and hardware components of the robotic platform as well as the environmental setup for data collection. Section 5 explains the dataset creation and includes insights into the attack implementation mechanism. The experimental results and the conclusion of the paper respectively in Sects. 6 and 7.

2 Detection Model

The proposed detection model consists of three main stages: (1) feature engineering for each modality (Sect. 2.1), (2) learning representations (Sect. 2.2), and (3) anomaly detection (Sect. 2.3). The architecture employs spatiotemporal encoding for each modality, aggregating the encoded features into a unified rep-

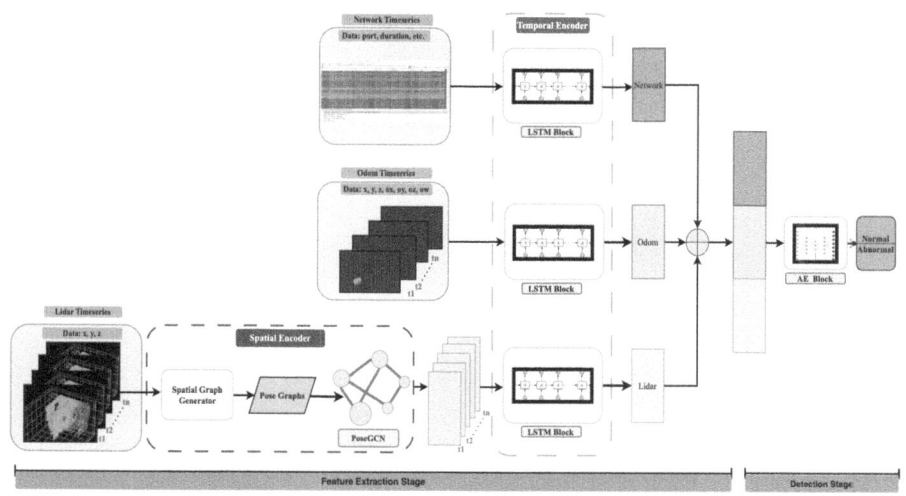

Fig. 1. Our Anomaly Detection System Process Flow

resentation, which serves as input to an Autoencoder (AE) model for anomaly detection (Fig. 1).

2.1   Stage 1: Feature Preparation and Transformation

In the feature preparation stage, spatial and temporal patterns within each modality are encoded to optimize the model's ability to coordinate across the three chosen modalities—network, Lidar, and Odometry—each produced at different rates and indices. By correlating them by time, the model can accurately predict whether the robot's behavior is normal for a specified time interval. This step includes feature encoding, scaling, padding, data sampling, and binning to align the modalities. The raw collected data undergoes preprocessing, feature extraction, and engineering to enable effective data analysis and modeling.

Lidar Data: Lidar data is a time series of 3D spatial positions of points within the point cloud, represented by their x, y, and z coordinates, as shown in Fig. 2. To reduce the computational complexity while preserving essential spatial information, a subset of points is selected based on azimuthal angles (Fig. 3). This subset effectively represents the spatial distribution of objects around the robot, enabling accurate anomaly detection with reduced computational time.

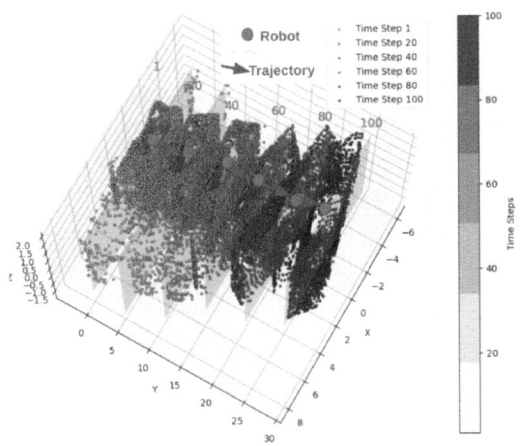

Fig. 2. Lidar Time-series: Progression of the point cloud as observed by the Lidar sensor across 6 sample timesteps: 1, 20, 40, 60, 80, 100.

Odometry Data: The odometry data consists of a time series detailing the registered pose and velocity of the robotic platform. The pose information includes the position (x & y coordinates) and orientation of the robot in quaternion form, while the velocity data includes both linear velocity (m/s) and angular velocity

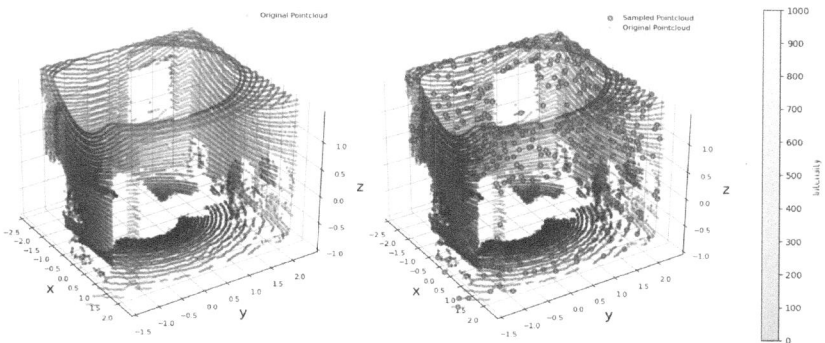

Fig. 3. Azimuthal angle-based sampling of the point cloud data. Original: 26,570 points; Sampled: 5,000 points.

(rad/s). This time series offers insights into how the control algorithms responded and adapted throughout the robot's trajectory during each experiment.

Network Traffic Data: The raw network traffic data is captured in PCAP format, containing details such as source and destination IP addresses, port numbers, timestamps, packet sizes, and protocol types. Inspired by the methodology outlined in [17], we extract 79 features from bidirectional network traffic flows. Our feature space follows the CICFlowMeter format, encompassing a broad spectrum of characteristics including flow duration, packet size, protocol type, and various statistical measures.

2.2   Stage 2: Spatio-Temporal Encoding for Each Modality

In the second stage, the primarily sequential nature of the data necessitates the use of a robust sequential model to encode temporal dependencies. To systematically capture temporal patterns within each modality, we construct an LSTM-based feature extractor [2,4,5,19,21]. This model extracts and retains vital information from the sequential data. Additionally, we introduce a Graph Convolutional Network (GCN) to handle the encoding of spatial patterns within modalities, such as Lidar data. The spatially encoded data is then integrated into the LSTM-based architecture, combining both spatial and temporal encoding.

Upon extracting the essential spatio-temporal features from each modality, these features are aggregated through array concatenation. The concatenated array, which combines features from the three modalities, serves as the input for the AE-based anomaly detection stage.

Let T be the set of time series data, where T_i represents the time series data from sensor i:

$$T = \{T_1, T_2, \ldots, T_n\}$$

where n is the number of sensors. For each T_i, let $LSTM_i$ be the LSTM-based binary classifier trained on T_i. The output of $LSTM_i$, after removing the last layers, is represented as the feature vector $F_i = LSTM_i(T_i)$. The concatenation of all feature vectors into a single 1D vector is denoted as V:

$$V = [F_1, F_2, \ldots, F_n]$$

2.3   Stage 3: Autoencoder-Based Anomaly Detection

AEs are neural networks trained to reconstruct input data, using the error between the original and reconstructed data as the loss function during training:

$$Err(x) = \|x - A(x)\|$$

where x and $A(x)$ are the input and output of the autoencoder, respectively, and $\| \cdot \|$ is typically is a Euclidean norm.

AEs are typically trained with fewer neurons in the hidden layers than in the input and output layers, encouraging the model to learn a compressed representation of the data, effectively performing dimensionality reduction. In anomaly detection, it is common to train the autoencoder on only normal data. During inference, normal data should be reconstructed with low error, while anomalies will exhibit higher error due to following a different distribution. This reconstruction error can be used as an anomaly score; samples with errors above a certain threshold are deemed anomalous.

The AE is trained on the concatenated feature vector V obtained in Stage 2.2 ($V = [F_1, F_2, \ldots, F_n]$) to produce a latent representation Z ($Z = AE(V)$) with high information gain. The network minimizes a reconstruction-based cost function defined as:

Standard Reconstruction Loss (L_{recon}) is the Mean Square Error (MSE) between the input vector and the decoded/reconstructed vector:

$$L_{recon} = \frac{1}{n} \sum_{i=1}^{n} (X_i - \hat{X}_i)^2$$

where n is the number of elements in the input data, X_i is the input data vector (i.e., the concatenated feature vectors from the feature extraction stage), and $\hat{X}_i$ is the predicted or reconstructed vector by the model.

The autoencoder undergoes training with the primary objective of reconstructing the input data while identifying differences between the original input and the reconstructed version, which could indicate anomalies. The model is trained exclusively on normal samples, with its learning progress monitored using a validation set comprising both normal and abnormal samples. Early stopping is implemented with a patience parameter set at 4 epochs, halting training when the validation loss does not decrease for 2 consecutive epochs. The validation loss typically surpasses the training loss due to the inclusion of abnormal samples in the validation set.

Improved Reconstruction Loss: We modify the standard reconstruction loss to a vector-based reconstruction loss that enables the model to detect subtle anomalies that may only affect a subset of features. The vector based approach also preserves the information about which specific features contribute most to the reconstruction error, allowing for more granular and precise anomaly detection. The improved reconstruction loss (imRL) is formulated as follows:

$$\mathbf{r} = \left\| \mathbf{X} - \hat{\mathbf{X}} \right\| = \left(\|X_1 - \hat{X}_1\|, \|X_2 - \hat{X}_2\|, \dots, \|X_n - \hat{X}_n\| \right)$$

$$\mathbf{th} = (th(X_1), th(X_2), \dots, th(X_n))$$

$$th_k = \max_{j=1,\dots,m} \left(\|X_k^j - \hat{X}_k^j\| \right), \quad for \quad k = 1, 2, \dots, \text{n}$$

Here, r represents the improved reconstruction loss, computed as a vector where each element X_i corresponds to an individual feature in the extracted feature vector for a sample. The threshold th_i is determined by the maximum difference observed for the i-th feature across all training samples.

In contrast to the standard approach, where the reconstruction loss is treated as a single scalar value, the improved method considers it as a vector. This approach prevents the undesirable overlap between normal and anomalous data that can occur when all features are summarized into a single value, thereby enhancing the model's ability to detect anomalies.

3   Anomaly Detector Integration in CPS

In achieving a seamless integration of our anomaly detection system into a CPS structure (Fig. 4), and establishing a framework for continuous security monitoring and evaluation, we design and implement the architecture described in Fig. 5. CPSs integrate computation, networking, and physical processes, typically comprising the following components: (a) Physical components, e.g., wheels; (b) Actuators, which receive control commands from control systems and adjust the operational parameters of physical devices; (c) Sensors, responsible for measuring the operational status of devices and transmitting data to the control systems; (d) Control systems, which receive sensor data and issue control commands to actuators based on predefined control logic. The physical component of our CPS is an autonomous robotic platform described in Sect. 4 enabling real-world experimentation and creation of a genuine real-world dataset of normal and abnormal conditions. The Actuators are the 2 motors driving the robot. We also designed a dashboard in which the findings of the anomaly detector is shown and communicated with the operator/observer of the robot.

We build our anomaly detector on top of a (Robot Operating System) ROS-based autonomy stack. ROS is a popular choice in a wide range of robotic applications such as Automated Guided Vehicles (AGVs) and Autonomous Mobile Robots (AMRs) [16], and enables the development and operation of complex robotic systems within CPS environments by facilitating the assembly of a sophisticated system capable of integration with the physical world. This design enables our AD to get real-time input from the sensor suite and to provide live detection information to the robot control system and/or operator.

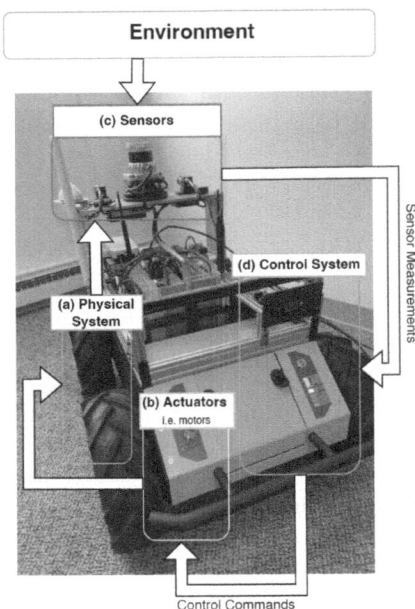

Fig. 4. Our CPS Architecture

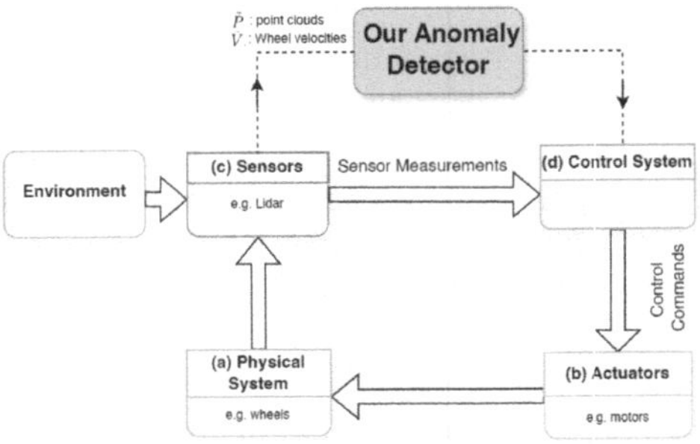

Fig. 5. Our Anomaly Detector Integration into the CPS Architecture

4   Experimental Set-Up

Despite the growing significance of cybersecurity research in autonomous robots, implementing, training, and testing anomaly detection models for real applications remains rare due to the cost, time, and difficulty of having access to authentic real-world datasets and experimental environments. We bridge this critical gap by leveraging a genuine real-world robotic platform as our experimental testbed.

4.1   Robotic Platform: Hardware and Software Components

To support real-world data acquisition and allow for generalization of this work to other autonomous vehicles and CPS, we equipped a Clearpath UGV Husky robot with a diverse sensor suite typical of such systems. This included Lidar, IMU, GPS, RGBD camera, high-resolution cameras, time synchronization, Wi-Fi, Bluetooth, and a 10GB NIC. Weighing approximately 50 kg and reaching speeds up to 1 m/s, the robot is a versatile platform for data collection and experimentation. Two GPU-enabled computing units running ROS Noetic on Ubuntu 20.04 enhance its computational power, enabling efficient decision-making processes for the Autonomous Driving System.

We incorporate the U.S. Army Combat Capabilities Development Command Army Research Laboratory (DEVCOM ARL) autonomy stack [1] into our framework. This endows us with modularity at both the algorithm/node level and the cluster of nodes, establishing a federated world model that facilitates flexible system design concerning data location and communication. It is essential to note that the autonomy stack, entirely proprietary to ARL, stands as a cutting-edge technology, providing a robust foundation for our research endeavors.

The autonomy stack consists of four main components, namely, (1) Perception Pipeline, (2) Simultaneous Localization and Mapping (SLAM), (3) Metric Planning and Execution, and (4) Symbolic Planning and Execution. Where, the perception pipeline makes symbolic observations (i.e. detect objects, estimates location, and image classification) based on sensor data; SLAM estimates robot trajectory from relative pose measurements (pose-graph optimization) using sensor data and perception pipeline products; Metric planning and execution achieves metric goals, such as waypoint navigation, using a metric model of the world; The symbolic planning and execution capability uses a symbolic model of the world to achieve symbolic goals such as going near a particular object.

The autonomy stack is equipped with a Unity-based perceptual and physics simulation engine. The simulator enables Docker-based development and deployment. We build our anomaly detector on top of the autonomy stack. The robots receive sensory inputs to predict control actions. To detect anomalies in the system, a machine learning model is trained and used in parallel to the controller, which identifies if the system input follows a similar pattern to the training set. This set-up allows us to not only capture the sensor reading of the external environment, but also capture the network communications between the sensors and autonomy stack (Fig. 6).

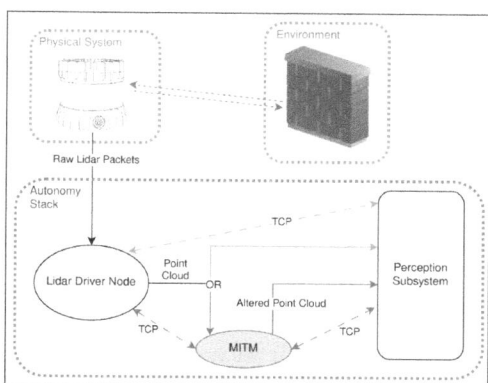

Fig. 6. Lidar attack Architecture

4.2   Experimental Environment

The data collection experiments were conducted in indoor and outdoor settings where obstacles were introduced to provide the desired stochasticity and a challenging environment for the mobility of the vehicle as depicted in Fig. 7a. The indoor setup provides us with a controlled environment where we can ensure the repeatability of the experiments without any foreign objects or weather modifying the parameters of each iteration. The outdoor setup allows us to test robustness and adaptability of our system in a more dynamic and unpredictable scenarios such as including varying terrain and environmental factors such as wind and uneven surfaces. A normal operation of the robot is defined as successful autonomous navigation of the Husky from *start position* to the *goal* pose without collision with obstacles in the course.

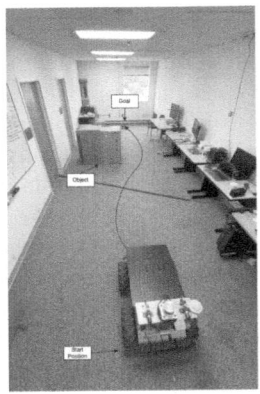
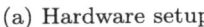

(a) Hardware setup

(b) Husky in the Phoenix Stack simulation environment

Fig. 7. Evaluation Environments

5   Dataset Creation and Attack Design

To assemble our dataset, we collect a diverse array of data during each experimental session. These experiments were conducted both under normal robot operating conditions and attack-induced conditions. In each experiment, data collection encompassed three distinct modalities. The primary modality, Lidar data, held paramount importance as it served as the focal point for all designed attacks. Complementing the Lidar data were two secondary modalities: Odometry data and Network traffic. These secondary modalities were deemed as such because they were not directly targeted; however, they carried significant information, as the infection of the Lidar propagated causal influence onto them. The Transmission Control Protocol/Internet Protocol (TCP/IP) and other data packets being transmitted or received over the husky network are captured using tcpdump packet analyzer program across all active interfaces, while Lidar and Odometry sensor data were collected by recording Robot Operating System (ROS) topics in the form of ROSbags.

5.1   Attack Creation

To test our anomaly detector against different levels of stealth in attacks, we developed and executed a Man-in-the-Middle (MITM) attack on our robotic platform. This attack focused on manipulating point cloud data to trick the robot into detecting a non-existent obstacle. We carefully designed and implemented the MITM attack by intercepting and modifying the point cloud data exchanged between the sensor and the robot's processing unit (Sect. 5.1). Next, we refined our approach by developing a more sophisticated and stealthy version of the MITM attack. This version was specifically designed to evade detection by the Lidar-based detector. We achieved this by minimizing changes to the point cloud data, making the attack more effective and avoiding suspicion (Sect. 5.1).

The ROS framework consists of nodes coordinated by a master node. Initializing a node registers it with the master as a publisher and/or subscriber. When both are registered under the same topic, the master establishes a TCP connection. Our MITM attack targets this process to make our node the only connection between the Ouster Lidar driver (publisher) and the Perception Subsystem (subscriber). Each ROS node functions as an XML/RPC server. Our attack begins by initializing a publisher/subscriber ROS node for the point cloud topic and waits for the valid nodes to initialize. Once the first valid node starts, the master connects it to our attack node. Before the second valid node starts, our attack deregisters the first, so the master only connects the second valid node to our attack node. Finally, our attack deregisters the second node, leaving our attack node as the sole connection. This allows us to manipulate the topic, such as altering the Lidar point cloud.

Attack V1: Man In the Middle Attack (MITM) Implementation. The Attack v1 (Fig. 8b) involves modifying the original point cloud data $P = \{p_1, p_2, \ldots, p_N\}$ to generate a new point cloud including a static obstacle. We select a subset of the original point cloud data $N_{obs} = N/C$ to remove and replace with a fake obstacle $P^* = \{p_1^*, p_2^*, \ldots, p_{N_{obs}}^*\}$. Each point in the raw point cloud P is defined as $p_k = (x_k, y_k, z_k)$. We remove $|N_{obs}|$ points from the original point cloud and replace them by $p_k^* = (x_k^*, y_k^*, z_k^*)$. p_k^* is generated by Eq. 1.

$$x_k^* = R - \hat{y}_k^2 + \epsilon_{x,k}$$
$$y_k^* = \hat{y}_k + \epsilon_{y,k} \qquad\qquad (1)$$
$$z_k^* \sim \mathcal{N}(\mu, \sigma_{z^*}^2)$$

where $\epsilon_{x,k} \sim \mathcal{N}(\mu, .0025^2)$, $\epsilon_{y,k} \sim \mathcal{N}(\mu, .005^2)$, $\hat{y}_1, \hat{y}_2, \ldots, \hat{y}_N \sim$ Uniform $\left(-\frac{w}{2}, \frac{w}{2}\right)$, $\mu = 0$, $\sigma_z^* = 0.125$, $C = 4$, $R = 0.75$, and $w = 1$. This configuration results in the creation of a static 1-meter wide and 0.25-meter tall arc positioned 0.75 m in front of the Lidar sensor that is recalculated once every 60 s.

Attack V2: Hiding the Attack from the Lidar Sensor. Attack v2 (Fig. 8c) creates a dynamic obstacle vs the static obstacle in Attack v1 that allows us to create an obstacle similar to the one described in Attack v1 section but stay closer to a real world scenario in implementation since p_k^* is generated based on the input from the original data points as shown in Eq. 2.

$$x_k^* = R - y_k^2 + \epsilon_k$$
$$y_k^* = y_k \tag{2}$$
$$z_k^* = z_k$$

where $|y_k| < w_y$, $\frac{z_k}{\sqrt{x_k^2 + y_k^2}} < \frac{w_z}{2R}$, $\epsilon_k \sim \mathcal{N}\left(\mu, \sigma_{\epsilon_k}^2\right)$, $\epsilon_k = 0.0125$, $R = .75$, $w_y = 1$, $w_z = .25$.

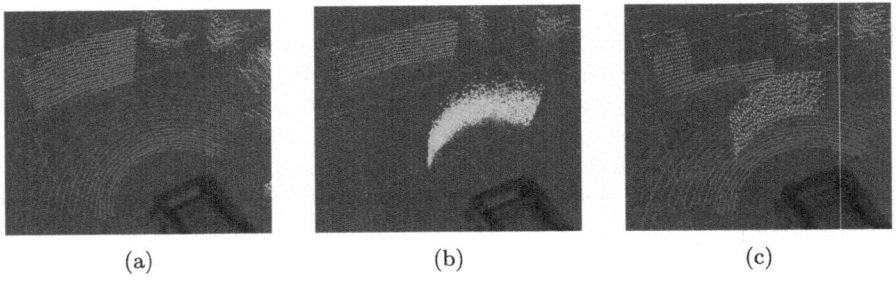

(a)   (b)   (c)

Fig. 8. Comparison of environments: (a) no attack, (b) Attack 1, (c) Attack 2

Both attacks create an extruded parabola surface with some noise in front of the Lidar. We can consider the set S as all of the points in the region of this surface with a thickness of 60 mm. To compare the difference of these two attacks we defined a Stealthiness Score (CS) that corresponds to the difference between the attacked point cloud and the point cloud if the false obstacle was real.

$$CS = \frac{|N_{obs} - n_{obs}| + n_{redundant} + n_{miss}}{N_{tot}} \tag{3}$$

We define N_{obs} as the number of points in the obstacle region ($|S|$) when a true obstacle exists at the described surface. $n_{obs} = |S|$ when the attack is underway, n_{miss} is the number of points removed from the valid point cloud, and $n_{redundant}$ is the number of redundant points (duplicate azimuthal and polar pairings). A point is considered redundant if there is another point in the cloud with the same azimuthal and polar angles, this should not happen under standard applications as it is the equivalent of seeing through an object. The stealthiness scores for each attack are summarized in Table 1.

Table 1. Stealthiness comparison of attacks. A lower Stealthiness Score is indicative of a less detectable attack

Attack	Stealthiness Score
Attack v1	0.4167
Attack v2	0.085

6 Results

6.1 Evaluation Metrics

In evaluating the efficacy of the proposed anomaly detection system, treated as a binary-class classification problem, the key performance metrics employed to assess the model's accuracy, robustness, and generalization capabilities are: **Accuracy** to evaluate the overall performance of the detector, **the Sample-Weighted F1 Score** to mitigates the impact of class imbalances, **Anomaly Recall Rate (ARR)** to quantify the proportion of actual anomaly cases correctly identified, **Normality Precision Rate (NPR)** to quantify the proportion of actual normal cases correctly identified. We consider both ARR and NPR for evaluating the performance of our anomaly detector, to account for differences in the cost of false positives and false negatives.

$$\text{Accuracy} = \frac{\text{Number of Correct Predictions}}{\text{Total Number of Reported Predictions}}$$

$$\text{F1 Score} = 2 \times \frac{TP}{TP + \frac{1}{2}(FP + FN)}$$

$$\text{Sample Weighted F1 Score} = \frac{\sum_i n_i \cdot \text{F1 Score}_i}{\sum_i n_i}$$

where n_i represents the number of samples in class i.

$$\text{ARR} = \frac{\text{Number of Actual Anomaly Cases}}{\text{Total Number of Reported Anomaly Cases}}$$

$$\text{NPR} = \frac{\text{Number of Actual Normal Cases}}{\text{Total Number of Reported Normal Cases}}$$

6.2 Evaluation and Results

Figure 9 illustrates the Principal Component Analysis (PCA)-based visualization showcasing the features extracted from three input modalities: Lidar, Odometry, and Network. Each data point in the plot corresponds to a trial, and its position signifies its location in the feature space for Lidar, Odometry, and Network data respectively. The arrangement of samples in the feature space provides insights into the discriminative capabilities of the extracted features for both attacks.

Table 2 presents the evaluation of the performance of Feature Extractors trained on data from each modality. In the Attack 1 scenario, the arrangement of samples in the Lidar and Network feature spaces suggests that both Lidar and Network features are highly discriminative, effectively distinguishing between normal and abnormal classes. However, the Odometry-based features, while demonstrating a high-level distinction between normal and abnormal classes, exhibit a failure in accurately identifying abnormal instances. In the Attack 2 scenario, the nature of the extracted features in their respective feature spaces remains relatively consistent, with more intermingling between samples belonging to the two categories, particularly in the Lidar feature space. This emphasizes that Attack 2 has notably reduced the distinctiveness of features in abnormal samples, making them more similar to normal samples. Consequently, the identification of abnormal instances becomes more challenging compared to Attack 1. Features associated with the Odometry and Network modalities exhibit minimal alterations in their respective feature spaces during both Attack 1 and Attack 2. This observation is consistent with the understanding that Attack 2 primarily manipulates Lidar data, and the functional impact of both attacks on the autonomy stack remains consistent, albeit with enhanced stealthiness. Consequently, this observation strengthens the rationale behind considering Odometry and Network as secondary modalities in the detection stage, as their features remain relatively unchanged despite the attacks, emphasizing their reliability.

Table 3 compares the performance of our anomaly detection system under the Attack 1 and Attack 2 performed on the real-world robot and a comparison of the effect of combinations of input modalities available at the inference time on the final detection. The data in this table suggests: (i) The combination of Lidar, Odometry, and Network data for training the Anomaly Detector generally leads to higher accuracy, F1 Score, ARR, and NPR compared to using individual modalities or subsets of modalities. (ii) Utilizing all three modalities (Lidar, Odometry, Network) for training results in improved performance in detecting anomalies in autonomous CPS environments. (iii) The presence of feature extraction and anomaly detection stages plays a crucial role in enhancing the Anomaly Detector's performance. (iv) Proper feature extraction from multiple modalities followed by effective anomaly detection contributes to better anomaly detection capabilities in autonomous systems.

The results of our experiments are summarized in Table 3, which presents the anomaly detection accuracy of our system when trained on different combinations of input modalities. Each row corresponds to a different experiment where the anomaly detection system was trained on data from specific modalities, as indicated by the checkmarks on the left side. The columns in the table compare the performance of the system across three distinct conditions:

Standard Reconstruction Loss: The baseline performance using the standard mean square error (MSE) reconstruction loss.

Improved Vector-Based Reconstruction Loss: The performance using our proposed vector-based reconstruction loss (imRL), which offers a more nuanced detection of anomalies by preserving feature-specific reconstruction errors.

Reduced Training Sample Size: The performance when the training set size was reduced by 50%, evaluated with the improved reconstruction loss.

6.3   Standard Reconstruction Loss vs. Improved Vector-Based Reconstruction Loss

The results indicate a significant improvement in detection accuracy when using the vector-based reconstruction loss compared to the standard MSE-based app-roach. This is consistent across all combinations of input modalities. The vector-based loss enhances the system's ability to detect subtle anomalies that may only affect a subset of features, thereby reducing the overlap between normal and anomalous data distributions. For example, when all three modalities (Lidar, Odometry, and Network) are used, the detection accuracy improves from 72% with the standard reconstruction loss to 98% with the improved vector-based loss. This improvement is more pronounced when only two modalities are used, with the accuracy increasing by up to 36% in some cases.

6.4   Impact of Reducing Training Sample Size

When the training sample size is halved, the anomaly detection accuracy nat-urally decreases. However, the system still maintains a relatively high level of performance, particularly when using the vector-based reconstruction loss. For instance, when trained with all three modalities and a reduced dataset, the accuracy only drops by 1%, demonstrating the robustness of the improved loss function even under constrained data conditions. This suggests that the system can effectively generalize from smaller datasets, a critical feature for real-world applications where data availability may be limited.

6.5   Modality-Specific Observations

Lidar Only: Training on Lidar data alone yields the lowest accuracy among all configurations. This outcome is by design, as the attack was specifically crafted to be invisible to the Lidar modality. The purpose of this was to evaluate how effec-tively the other modalities—Odometry and Network—can detect the anomaly when one modality is blind to the attack. Even with the improved vector-based reconstruction loss, the accuracy remains lower compared to configurations that include network data. This result underscores the importance of incorporating multiple modalities for comprehensive anomaly detection, as the system's ability to detect the attack relies on the combined strength of all available data sources.

Odometry and Network: The combination of Odometry and Network data provides better detection accuracy than Lidar alone but is still less effective than using all three modalities. The performance, however, significantly benefits from the vector-based reconstruction loss, which mitigates the shortcomings of excluding Lidar data.

All Modalities: The highest accuracy is consistently achieved when all three modalities are used. This underlines the value of a multimodal approach, where the weaknesses of one modality can be compensated by the strengths of others.

6.6 Summary

The evaluation results clearly demonstrate the effectiveness of our proposed anomaly detection system. The improved vector-based reconstruction loss significantly enhances the system's ability to detect anomalies across various configurations, even when the training data is limited. The findings confirm that utilizing multiple modalities—Lidar, Odometry, and Network—offers superior detection capabilities, making the system robust and adaptable to different scenarios within autonomous Cyber-Physical Systems (CPS). The reduced impact of training sample size on performance further underscores the practicality of our approach in real-world applications, where data constraints are a common challenge.

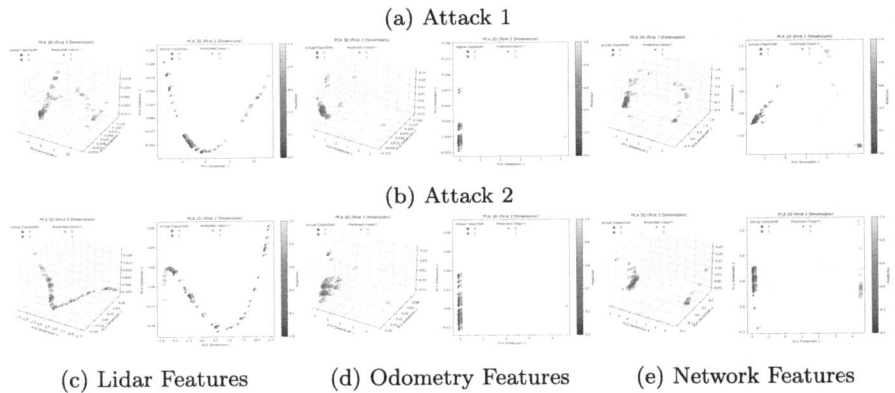

(a) Attack 1

(b) Attack 2

(c) Lidar Features   (d) Odometry Features   (e) Network Features

Fig. 9. Feature space visualization of the Spatiotemporal feature extractor trained on Lidar, Odometry, and Network data.

Table 2. Evaluation of the performance of Feature Extractors trained on the Lidar, Odometry, and Network data based on standard classification metrics.

Attacks	Feature Extraction Stage											
	Lidar				Odometry				Network			
	Accuracy	F1	ARR	NPR	Accuracy	F1	ARR	NPR	Accuracy	F1	ARR	NPR
Attack 1	1.000	1.000	1.000	1.000	0.952	0.951	0.830	1.000	0.940	0.940	0.920	0.957
Attack 2	0.860	0.870	0.600	1.000	0.952	0.951	0.830	1.000	1.000	1.000	1.000	1.000

Table 3. Comparison of results for (1) the standard reconstruction loss, (2) the improved reconstruction loss (imRL), and (3) %50 reduced sample size for the training stage with imRL. Similar improvements were seen in other evaluation metric used in our evaluation such as F1 score, APR, and NPR

Feature Extraction Stage			Anomaly Detection Stage		
Modality			Accuracy		
Lidar	Odom.	Net.	RL	imRL	50% Reduced Sample Size
✓			0.46	0.95	0.90
	✓		0.78	0.84	0.65
		✓	0.66	0.94	0.90
✓	✓		0.75	0.95	0.96
	✓	✓	0.86	0.95	0.94
✓		✓	0.62	0.98	0.97
✓	✓	✓	0.72	0.98	0.97

7 Conclusion and Future Work

In this paper, we presented a robust anomaly detection system, specifically designed for autonomous robotic Cyber-Physical Systems. Leveraging a multimodal approach that integrates a fusion of sensor and network traffic data (Lidar, Odometry, and Network data), our system demonstrates robustness in performance in detecting anomalies, even under sophisticated adversarial attacks designed to evade detection by individual modalities. The introduction of a vector-based reconstruction loss function significantly enhances the system's ability to detect subtle anomalies, thereby improving the overall accuracy and reliability of the detection process.

Our experimental results, conducted on a real-world robotic platform, highlight the system's robustness, particularly when trained with limited data. The performance remains strong even when the training sample size is reduced by 50%, underscoring the practicality and generalizability of our approach in real-world applications. The design and implementation of a Man-in-the-Middle attack, specifically crafted to be invisible to the Lidar modality, further validate the effectiveness of using multiple data sources to compensate for potential vulnerabilities in individual sensors.

The success of our anomaly detector in maintaining high detection accuracy across varying conditions and attack scenarios emphasizes the importance of a holistic, multimodal approach to anomaly detection in autonomous CPS. Moving forward, we plan to integrate our anomaly detection system into real-time decision-making processes within CPS, allowing for continuous learning from live data and enhancing the system's ability to respond to evolving threats. This integration will pave the way for more resilient and secure autonomous systems capable of operating reliably in complex and dynamic environments.

Acknowledgement. We sincerely thank our colleagues at the Army Research Lab for their invaluable help in instrumenting the robotic platform for dataset creation and providing the autonomy stack that enabled the robot's navigation during experiments. We also thank Stephen Raio, Jason Ellis, and Robert Erbacher for insightful discussions that enhanced our understanding of the platform and autonomy stack.

References

1. Sara CRA overview. https://arl.devcom.army.mil/cras/sara-cra/sara-overview/. Accessed 13 Jan 2024
2. Alawneh, L., Mohsen, B., Al-Zinati, M., Shatnawi, A., Al-Ayyoub, M.: A comparison of unidirectional and bidirectional LSTM networks for human activity recognition. In: 2020 IEEE International Conference on Pervasive Computing and Communications Workshops (PerCom Workshops), pp. 1–6 (2020). https://doi.org/10.1109/PerComWorkshops48775.2020.9156264
3. Biró, M., Mashkoor, A., Sametinger, J.: Safe and secure cyber-physical systems. J. Softw. Evol. Process **33**(9), e2340 (2021). https://doi.org/10.1002/smr.2340
4. Bodapati, S., Bandarupally, H., Shaw, R.N., Ghosh, A.: Comparison and analysis of RNN-LSTMs and CNNs for social reviews classification. In: Bansal, J.C., Fung, L.C.C., Simic, M., Ghosh, A. (eds.) Advances in Applications of Data-Driven Computing. AISC, vol. 1319, pp. 49–59. Springer, Singapore (2021). https://doi.org/10.1007/978-981-33-6919-1_4
5. Buestán-Andrade, P.A., Santos, M., Sierra-García, J.E., Pazmiño-Piedra, J.P.: Comparison of LSTM, GRU and transformer neural network architecture for prediction of wind turbine variables. In: García Bringas, P., et al. (eds.) SOCO 2023, pp. 334–343. Springer, Cham (2023). https://doi.org/10.1007/978-3-031-42536-3_32
6. Cai, X., Han, K., Li, Y., Wang, H., Zhang, J., Zhang, Y.: Research on security estimation and control of cyber-physical system. In: 2020 IEEE 39th International Performance Computing and Communications Conference (IPCCC), Austin, TX, USA, pp. 1–5. IEEE (2020). https://doi.org/10.1109/IPCCC50635.2020.9391573
7. Chandola, V., Banerjee, A., Kumar, V.: Anomaly detection: a survey. ACM Comput. Surv. (CSUR) **41**(3), 1–58 (2009). http://ieeexplore.ieee.org/document/5234775/
8. Ding, D., Han, Q.L., Xiang, Y., Ge, X., Zhang, X.M.: A survey on security control and attack detection for industrial cyber-physical systems. Neurocomputing **275**, 1674–1683 (2018). https://doi.org/10.1016/j.neucom.2017.10.009
9. Du, Y., Huang, Y., Wan, G., He, P.: Deep learning-based cyber–physical feature fusion for anomaly detection in industrial control systems. Mathematics (2022). https://api.semanticscholar.org/CorpusID:253788504
10. Eiteneuer, B., Hranisavljevic, N., Niggemann, O.: Dimensionality reduction and anomaly detection for CPPS data using autoencoder. In: 2019 IEEE International Conference on Industrial Technology (ICIT), pp. 1286–1292 (2019). https://api.semanticscholar.org/CorpusID:195831827

11. Guo, Y., Liao, W., Wang, Q., Yu, L., Ji, T., Li, P.: Multidimensional time series anomaly detection: a GRU-based gaussian mixture variational autoencoder approach. In: Asian Conference on Machine Learning (2018). https://api.semanticscholar.org/CorpusID:53639324

12. Hornung, R., Urbanek, H., Klodmann, J., Osendorfer, C., van der Smagt, P.: Model-free robot anomaly detection. In: 2014 IEEE/RSJ International Conference on Intelligent Robots and Systems, pp. 3676–3683 (2014). https://doi.org/10.1109/IROS.2014.6943078

13. Kim, M., Park, S.: Unsupervised multi-head attention autoencoder for multivariate time-series anomaly detection. In: 2024 IEEE International Conference on Big Data and Smart Computing (BigComp), pp. 1–7 (2024). https://api.semanticscholar.org/CorpusID:269091616

14. Kirschgens, L.A., Ugarte, I.Z., Uriarte, E.G., Rosas, A.M., Vilches, V.M.: Robot hazards: from safety to security (2018). https://doi.org/10.48550/ARXIV.1806.06681

15. Langner, R.: Stuxnet: dissecting a cyberwarfare weapon. Secur. Sci. 1–19 (2013)

16. Moshayedi, A.J., Reza, K.S., Khan, A.S., Nawaz, A.: Integrating virtual reality and robotic operation system (ROS) for AGV navigation. EAI Endorsed Trans. AI Robot. **2**(1), e3 (2023). https://doi.org/10.4108/airo.v2i1.3181

17. Noorani, M., Mancoridis, S., Weber, S.: On the detection of malware on virtual assistants based on behavioral anomalies. In: Proceedings of the Malware Conference (MalCon) (2019). https://www.cs.drexel.edu/~mancors/papers/MALWARE19.pdf

18. Park, D., Erickson, Z., Bhattacharjee, T., Kemp, C.C.: Multimodal execution monitoring for anomaly detection during robot manipulation. In: 2016 IEEE International Conference on Robotics and Automation (ICRA), Stockholm, Sweden, pp. 407–414. IEEE (2016). https://doi.org/10.1109/ICRA.2016.7487160

19. Zeyer, A., Bahar, P., Irie, K., Schlüter, R., Ney, H.: A comparison of transformer and LSTM encoder decoder models for ASR. In: 2019 IEEE Automatic Speech Recognition and Understanding Workshop (ASRU), pp. 8–15 (2019). https://doi.org/10.1109/ASRU46091.2019.9004025

20. Zong, B., et al.: Deep autoencoding gaussian mixture model for unsupervised anomaly detection. In: International Conference on Learning Representations (2018). https://api.semanticscholar.org/CorpusID:51805340

21. Zouitni, C., Sabri, M.A., Aarab, A.: A comparison between LSTM and transformers for image captioning. In: Motahhir, S., Bossoufi, B. (eds.) ICDTA 2023, pp. 492–500. Springer, Cham (2023). https://doi.org/10.1007/978-3-031-29860-8_50

Author Index

GPSR Compliance

The European Union's (EU) General Product Safety Regulation (GPSR) is a set of rules that requires consumer products to be safe and our obligations to ensure this.

If you have any concerns about our products, you can contact us on ProductSafety@springernature.com

In case Publisher is established outside the EU, the EU authorized representative is:

Springer Nature Customer Service Center GmbH
Europaplatz 3
69115 Heidelberg, Germany

The manufacturer's authorised representative in the EU is Springer
Nature Customer Service Centre GmbH, Europaplatz 3, 69115 Heidelberg,
Germany. If you have any concerns regarding our products, please
contact ProductSafety@springernature.com

Printed and bound by CPI Group (UK) Ltd, Croydon, CR0 4YY
29/04/2026
02099533-0001